Fodor's

W9-BTN-001

PORTUGAL

9th Edition

Where to Stay and Eat
for All Budgets

Must-See Sights
and Local Secrets

Ratings You Can Trust

Fodor's Travel Publications   New York, Toronto, London, Sydney, Auckland
www.fodors.com

FODOR'S PORTUGAL

Editors: Molly Moker, Alexis Crisman Kelly

Editorial Contributors: Kelly Kealy, Margaret Kelly, Laura M. Kidder

Writers: Alexandre Bezerra, Carrie-Marie Bratley, Brendan de Beer, Lauren Frayer, Matthew Hancock, Josephine Quintero, Alison Roberts, Andrea Smith

Production Editor: Jennifer DePrima
Maps & Illustrations: David Lindroth, *cartographer;* Bob Blake, Rebecca Baer, *map editors;* William Wu, *information graphics*
Design: Fabrizio La Rocca, *creative director;* Guido Caroti, Siobhan O'Hare, *art directors;* Tina Malaney, Chie Ushio, Nora Rosansky, *designers;* Melanie Marin, *senior picture editor*
Cover Photo: (Marvao, Alentejo) SIME/eStock Photo
Production Manager: Angela L. McLean

9th Edition

ISBN 978-0-307-48062-0

ISSN 0071-6510

SPECIAL SALES

This book is available at special discounts for bulk purchases for sales promotions or premiums. Special editions, including personalized covers, excerpts of existing books, and corporate imprints, can be created in large quantities for special needs. For more information, write to Special Markets/Premium Sales, 1745 Broadway, MD 6-2, New York, NY 10019, or e-mail specialmarkets@randomhouse.com.

AN IMPORTANT TIP & AN INVITATION

Although all prices, opening times, and other details in this book are based on information supplied to us at press time, changes occur all the time in the travel world, and Fodor's cannot accept responsibility for facts that become outdated or for inadvertent errors or omissions. So **always confirm information when it matters,** especially if you're making a detour to visit a specific place. Your experiences—positive and negative—matter to us. If we have missed or misstated something, **please write to us.** Share your opinion instantly through our online feedback center at fodors.com/contact-us.

PRINTED IN THE UNITED STATES OF AMERICA

10 9 8 7 6 5 4 3

Eugene Fodor:
The Spy Who Loved Travel

As Fodor's celebrates our 75th anniversary, we are honoring the colorful and adventurous life of Eugene Fodor, who revolutionized guidebook publishing in 1936 with his first book, *On the Continent, The Entertaining Travel Annual.*

Eugene Fodor's life seemed to leap off the pages of a great spy novel. Born in Hungary, he spoke six languages and graduated from the Sorbonne and the London School of Economics. During World War II he joined the Office of Strategic Services, the budding spy agency for the United States. He commanded the team that went behind enemy lines to liberate Prague, and recommended to Generals Eisenhower, Bradley, and Patton that Allied troops move to the capital city. After the war, Fodor worked as a spy in Austria, posing as a U.S. diplomat.

In 1949 Eugene Fodor—with the help of the CIA—established Fodor's Modern Guides. He was passionate about travel and wanted to bring his insider's knowledge of Europe to a new generation of sophisticated Americans who wanted to explore and seek out experiences beyond their borders. Among his innovations were annual updates, consulting local experts, and including cultural and historical perspectives and an emphasis on people—not just sites. As Fodor described it, "The main interest and enjoyment of foreign travel lies not only in 'the sites,' . . . but in contact with people whose customs, habits, and general outlook are different from your own."

Eugene Fodor died in 1991, but his legacy, Fodor's Travel, continues. It is now one of the world's largest and most trusted brands in travel information, covering more than 600 destinations worldwide in guidebooks, on Fodors.com, and in ebooks and iPhone apps. Technology and the accessibility of travel may be changing, but Eugene Fodor's unique storytelling skills and reporting style are behind every word of today's Fodor's guides.

Our editors and writers continue to embrace Eugene Fodor's vision of building personal relationships through travel. We invite you to join the Fodor's community at fodors.com/community and share your experiences with like-minded travelers. Tell us when we're right. Tell us when we're wrong. And share fantastic travel secrets that aren't yet in Fodor's. Together, we will continue to deepen our understanding of our world.

Happy 75th Anniversary, Fodor's! Here's to many more.

Tim Jarrell, Publisher

CONTENTS

MAPS

ABOUT THIS BOOK

Our Ratings

At Fodor's, we spend considerable time choosing the best places in a destination so you don't have to. By default, anything we recommend in this book is worth visiting. But some sights, properties, and experiences are so great that we've recognized them with additional accolades. Orange **Fodor's Choice** stars indicate our top recommendations; black stars highlight places we deem **Highly Recommended**. Disagree with any of our choices? Care to nominate a new place? Visit our feedback center at www.fodors.com/feedback.

Hotels

Hotels have private bath, phone, TV, and air-conditioning, and do not offer meals unless we specify that in the review. We always list facilities but not whether you'll be charged an extra fee to use them.

Restaurants

Unless we state otherwise, restaurants are open for lunch and dinner daily. We mention dress only when there's a specific requirement and reservations only when they're essential or not accepted—it's always best to book ahead.

Credit Cards

We assume that restaurants and hotels accept credit cards. If not, we'll note it in the review.

Budget Well

Hotel and restaurant price categories from ¢ to $$$$ are defined in the opening pages of the respective chapters. For attractions, we always give standard adult admission fees; reductions are usually available for children, students, and senior citizens.

Listings		Hotels & Restaurants	Outdoors
★ Fodor's Choice	✉ E-mail	**Hotels & Restaurants**	**Outdoors**
★ Highly recommended	💺 Admission fee	🏨 Hotel	🏌 Golf
✉ Physical address	⊙ Open/closed times	🛏 Number of rooms	⛺ Camping
✛ Directions or Map coordinates	Ⓜ Metro stations	🍴 Facilities	**Other**
⌖ Mailing address	⊟ No credit cards	🍽 Meal plans	🕭 Family-friendly
☎ Telephone		✕ Restaurant	⇨ See also
🖷 Fax		🍷 Reservations	✉ Branch address
⊕ On the Web		🏛 Dress code	☞ Take note
		✎ Smoking	

Experience Portugal

WORD OF MOUTH

"The thing that's really great about Portugal is that it has all the great stuff you go to Europe for—cute old villages, historic homes, palaces, castles, cathedrals, and museums—BUT nothing is so 'important' that if you find yourself happily lazing away at a cafe and lose the will to execute the afternoon's itinerary, you will not feel guilty later. We were so relaxed in Portugal!"

—spcfa

WHAT'S WHERE

Numbers refer to chapters.

2 Lisbon. One of Europe's smallest capitals, Lisbon encompasses dramatic contrasts. The cobbled streets of Alfama complement Chiado's upmarket cafés and boutiques; out of 18th-century buildings skip designer-clad youths.

3 Lisbon's Environs. At Cascais and Estoril, beachgoing tourists can enjoy seafood or one of Europe's largest casinos. On the stunning coast to the north, wilder seas make for fine windsurfing. South of the Tagus River are sweeping sands on the Setúbal Peninsula.

4 Estremadura and Ribatejo. This region to the north and east of Lisbon boasts several World Heritage Sites, including the headquarters of the Knights Templar, the Convento de Cristo. It also has imposing pine forests and charming seaside resorts, while the Ribatejo is famed for its bull breeding.

5 Évora and the Alentejo. In Évora, medieval walls encircle palatial buildings and a Roman temple: an architectural gem in one of Portugal's poorest regions. Thinly populated, the Alentejo is bracketed by spectacular but windy Atlantic beaches and the striking Guadiana valley.

6 The Algarve. Sheltered by the dramatic Serra de Monchique and Serra de Caldeirão ranges to the north, the Algarve is Portugal's main holiday destination thanks to 3,000 hours of sunshine a year, sweeping beaches, and ample facilities.

7 Coimbra and the Beiras. The central Beiras region contains Portugal's most spectacular mountain range, the Serra da Estrela, ringed by towns that are home to superb Renaissance art. Just inland from the unspoiled sandy coast lies the dynamic city of Coimbra.

8 Porto and the North. The green Minho region is home to *vinho verde,* a distinctive young wine. Porto is a captivating mix of medieval and modern, its center a World Heritage Site. Grapes for the port wine shipped from here come from the Douro Valley—part of ruggedly beautiful Trás-os-Montes.

9 Madeira. Several hundred kilometers off the coast of Morocco lie the subtropical islands of Madeira and Porto Santo. The main island is dominated by spectacular mountains that divide the rugged but lush northern coast from the gentler landscapes around the capital, Funchal.

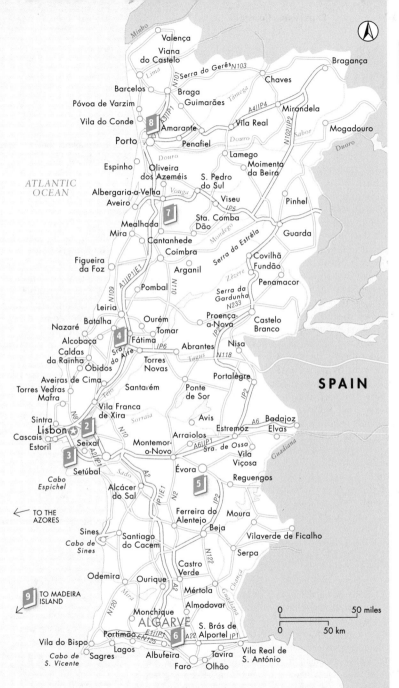

PORTUGAL TODAY

Portugal is one of those countries—a bit like Greece—that harks back to a golden age. From the 14th century onward, its mariners plied far-flung sea routes, bringing back spices, gold, and—let's not forget—slaves. Accession in 1986 to the then European Community brought the Portuguese a new sense of belonging on their own continent. The flood of European development funds has now run its course, though, and the financial crisis seems to be ushering in a period of economic stagnation. Sadly, there are also signs that emigration—a scourge for most of the 20th century—is again on the rise, as even well-qualified youngsters look abroad for opportunities. Still, Portuguese ingenuity is in evidence. Even in sectors hit by globalization, such as textiles, firms are fighting back by specializing and increasing the value added to products. New uses are found for old materials such as cork, with the results sold through design shops. Portuguese wine makers are raising their international profile, applying new methods to a unique roster of native grape varieties. And Portuguese chefs are finally catching up with their Spanish peers in applying new techniques to traditional dishes.

Today's Portugal

. . . is enjoying a renewed tourism boom. Despite fears that the credit crunch and subsequent downturn in Europe and North America would send tourist numbers into a downward spin, tourism recovered in 2010, with hotel occupancy up from the previous year. Lisbon, which has massively expanded its facilities in recent years to attract all groups of visitors, has led the way, with business conferences now a major earner, thanks to mild out-of-season weather, still-affordable facilities, and friendly and competent locals. Porto, too, with a similar combination of picturesque old and trendy new, is emerging as one of Europe's top city break destinations.

. . . is proud of its traditions. Every year, throughout the year, traditional *festas* are held up and down the country on local saints' days or in line with ancient, evidently pagan, traditions. Not for tourists (although you're welcome to join in), festivals are a central part of Portuguese life, and emigrants generally try to ensure that trips home coincide with the local *festa*. Youngsters these days have a renewed interest in their heritage, and are taking an active part in keeping festival traditions

WHAT WE'RE TALKING ABOUT

Futebol (soccer) remains an obsession in Portugal: the three top-selling dailies are dedicated to it. In the early 1960s Lisbon club Benfica lifted an oppressed nation's spirits by twice winning the European Cup; today one footballer above all provides a much-needed lift to wilting national pride. Cristiano Ronaldo, Fifa World Player of the Year in 2009, currently plays in Madrid but is a hero to Portuguese fans for raising the nation's profile. Foreign spectators may boo his frequent on-field petulance, but here he appears in ads for everything from banks to hair gel.

Portugal's art scene is being shaken up by Joana Vasconcelos, who came to international attention with "The Bride"—a chandelier made of thousands of tampons that represented the country at the

live—although they also flock to a growing list of vibrant rock festivals.

. . . is a great value. For all the inflationary impact of rising prosperity and entry into the euro common-currency zone, Portugal is one of Europe's best-value destinations. Especially in rural areas, you can eat delicious traditional food for as little as €6 ($7) for a main dish, a fraction of what you'd pay in a North American city—washed down with invariably drinkable local wine. Portugal is dotted with country houses, grand and simple, that offer comfortable bed-and-breakfast accommodation at affordable prices. And all forms of transport, even in the cities, remain amazingly cheap, with a one-way ride on the Lisbon metro just 90 euro cents ($1) and a taxi in town as little as $5 ($6).

. . . is committed to a major expansion of renewable energy. Portugal has garnered global attention in recent years with a massive program of investment in renewables. From a standing start, it is now fourth in the European Union in terms of capacity relative to population. The EU is committed to getting 20% of energy from renewable sources by 2020, but Portugal has set more ambitious goals. More than half its electricity already comes from wind, solar, or hydro—saving $1.1 billion a year in oil imports. Despite much tighter financial conditions, it is also promoting wave-power projects, and rolling out a nationwide network of charging points for electric cars.

. . . is facing unprecedented economic and political challenges. As the euro zone faces an existential crisis, Portugal is under particular pressure from investors to prove it can service its mountain of debt. Its deficit-cutting efforts—sanctioned by both major parties—have shut off funds for new large-scale public works projects and brought cuts in public-sector salaries and welfare benefits. This austerity drive has been contested not only by established groups such as trade unions but also unprecedented new forces. In March 2011, demonstrations organized via Facebook took place across Portugal, with as many as 200,000 people protesting against being forced into unpaid internships or low-paid temporary employment.

2005 Venice Biennale. In her outdoor installations since, buildings or bridges have been made into artworks with crocheted aprons or colorful stuffed shapes. In 2010, "Marilyn," a scaled-up shoe inspired by Monroe's on-screen heels but made from cooking pans, went for $780,000 at auction. Vasconcelos's Lisbon atelier is deluged with foreign commissions.

Portugal is ahead of the pack in terms of renewable energy; its record on pollution is grimier, with reprimands from European watchdogs stoking public awareness. Air quality on the capital's Avenida da Liberdade is a particular concern. But in early 2011 the city announced plans to ban older, dirtier vehicles downtown, such as aging taxis, delivery vans, and older buses.

QUINTESSENTIAL PORTUGAL

Pastelarias

Only the staunchest dieter will not be tempted by Portugal's deliciously calorific cakes and pastries. The window displays are real cream-cake affairs, invariably wedged between trendy boutiques catering to fashionable beanpoles. Every region has its specialty sweet treat, generally known as *doces conventuais* (convent desserts), which usually originates from the respective local convent. And, yes, they really *are* a touch of heaven. In the Algarve, the Moorish influence is evident in the marzipan and almond biscuits. Farther north in Abrantes the egg pastries known as *bolo de anjo* (angel cake—those nuns again) have a melt-in-the-mouth fluffy topping. If you are seeking true sublimity, however, bite into a warm *pastéis de nata,* straight from the oven. These gorgeous custard tarts are made with flaky light pastry, creamy egg custard, and sprinkled cinnamon.

Feiras

The Portuguese love to party and here (as in neighboring Spain) there are countless annual celebrations and *festas*. Don't miss out when you're traveling around and be sure to check at the local tourist office for upcoming events. For the Portuguese the country's fairs and festivals are far more than holidays from the year's work. They are occasions in which to be immersed with passion and commitment. At saints' days, harvest festivals, pilgrimages, and *feiras* (fairs), you can expect everything from ceremonial pomp and religious processions to wild street parties and quaint traditions. St. John's in Porto (June 23) is a good example of the latter, with everyone hitting each other over the head with plastic hammers or leeks while enjoying a night of drinking, revelry, and dance from dusk to dawn in the city streets.

If you want to get a sense of contemporary Portuguese culture, and indulge in some of its pleasure, start by familiarizing yourself with the rituals of daily life. These are a few highlights—things you can take part in with relative ease.

Bacalhau

Few people understand the bounty of the sea more than the Portuguese. One singularly appetizing delicacy called *bacalhau* (dried, salted cod) appears on the menu at virtually every restaurant, though it is definitely an acquired taste. Shop fronts are chockablock with the stuff: think fossilized white strips of leather and you will be on the right track. There are reputedly 365 ways of preparing this curious delicacy, ranging from roasted with onions and potatoes to fish pie. The Portuguese love affair with seafood encompasses just about everything that swims in the sea, including limpets (normally braised with garlic). Grilled sardines are prevalent as well, but don't expect the tinned variety you might be accustomed to (those can be found in any supermarket). The Portuguese prefer to serve them whole, head and all.

Fado

The dramatic image of a black-shawled fado singer, head thrown back, eyes closed with emotion, has become an emblem of Portugal; the swelling, soulful song with the plaintive *guitarra* (Portuguese guitar) accompaniment seems to embody Portugal's romantic essence. Fado's importance is such that when the great *fadista* Amália Rodrigues died in 1999, the government declared three days of national mourning and awarded her a state funeral. When the singing begins in a fado house, all talking ceases and a reverent silence descends on the tables. A world of immutable sadness appears, populated by many types of people: the lost, the poor and oppressed, the abandoned and rejected. You should not miss an opportunity to witness this unique musical style.

TOP EXPERIENCES

Cafés
Portugal's colonial foothold in Brazil and Africa left its people with a taste for one of the empire's main products, coffee. You're never far from a café or *pastelaria* (pastry shop) in Portugal, where the coffee is always strong and fresh.

Feiras and festas
Whether it's the monthly *feira* in a Minho market town, a summer *festa* in Trás os Montes, or a newly invented winter celebration of cured sausages in the Alentejo, try to plan your itinerary to take in at least one of Portugal's myriad local festivities. These invariably draw crowds of locals, making them great places for getting a true taste of Portugal life.

Port wine tasting
Portugal's most famous drink might be named after the city of Porto, but it's across-the-river Douro, in Vila Nova de Gaia, where the traditionally foreign-owned companies trade this fortified wine. Many of the caves (cellars) here may be visited, with tasting sessions often featuring tips on matching ports not only with different kinds of cheeses but chocolates and other foods, too.

Douro river cruise
The amazing manmade landscapes of the Douro river valley, with its steeply terraced vineyards, collectively form a World Heritage Site. Cruises of varying lengths start from Porto or at Peso da Régua, where the new Museu do Douro now showcases the region's history. Upstream, trips from the town of Miranda, where the "Douro Internacional" forms the border with Spain, afford views of birds of prey nesting high on the river's steep banks.

Hilltop castles
Portugal's interior may suffer from depopulation these days but it has some of the most stunningly situated settlements. From Marvão in the south through Monsanto in the central Beiras to Bragança in the north, these remote fortified towns and villages have often played a surprisingly key role in Portuguese history.

Seafood dinners
Unsurprisingly, Europe's westernmost nation is famed for the quality of its fish and shellfish. You can eat good seafood just about anywhere in Portugal, although obviously a few steps away from the fishing port is the safest bet. And, of course, *bacalhau* (dried, salted cod) doesn't even need to be fresh to be delicious.

Beach bumming
With Portugal squeezed between Spain and the Atlantic, you're spoiled with beautiful beaches. Take your pick from windswept surfing hubs or sheltered coves.

Fado
Locals in Lisbon and Coimbra say you haven't fully experienced their cities unless you've heard fado live. Book a table for dinner and settle in for what many find a deeply moving experience, as male and female singers pour out their feelings about the *fado* (fate) life has in store for them, accompanied by both Spanish and lute-shape Portuguese guitars.

Bar hopping
Lisbon and Porto have firmly established their reputations as nightlife powerhouses. On warm nights it can seem as if everyone in the city is on the street with a beer in his or her hand. But even in smaller towns locals like to party, with the night probably starting—and ending—rather later than you're used to at home.

f you want to get out and experience Portugal like a local, start with the following suggestions.

rink your coffee neat. Milky coffee is all very well in the morning, but ordering t after a meal definitely marks you out s a tourist. The standard local style is eat, or at most with a drop of milk (as a *ingado*), and perhaps with a bag of sugar tirred in. Decaf (*descafeinado*) is now videly available in cafés and restaurants.

Watch the big weekend soccer match. But not n the stadium—in your local bar or café. t any time during the week, one sure-fire vay to get a conversation going is to ask bout how Benfica is doing these days: at east a third of the country's population s said to support the club. To really get n tune with the locals, order an *imperial* small draught beer).

hop till you drop. Consumerism swept a previously poverty-stricken country from he 1980s onward, and it's at the local megamall that you'll find many families on the weekend—though outdoor clothes markets remain popular, too. Larger hopping centers have cinemas, bowling lleys, ice rinks, and sometimes even roller oasters.

Choose your beach by its bar. In summer, the ure of the beach is stronger than the mall. A bar or café is invariably close at hand— s well as the lifeguard it is legally obliged o fund. Especially near cities, the kind of people on a beach is determined by the tyle of the bar that serves it, whether it's or techno music fans or hires out kite-urf equipment.

Patronize likeminded businesses. In a counry with a history of empire and migraion, the name of a business often points o a dramatic life story. Locals know that a hotel named "Pensão Luanda" means

the owner was probably born in colonial Angola (and might never have set foot in Portugal before his and other white and mixed-race families were forced to take refuge here). Similarly, a name like "Café Zurich" is a sure sign the owner had a spell working in Switzerland. Meanwhile, a grocer who migrated to Lisbon from the Beiras region will draw many clients with similar roots, who come to stock up on delicious cheese and sausages from back home.

Nibble local snacks with your beer. A common nibble in drinking dens is a plate of *tremoços* (soaked yellow lupin seeds), which bar staff hand you for free. Break the skin with your teeth and suck out the flesh; they're mild but strangely addictive. In the south of Portugal, locals might order a plateful of *caracóis*—snails cooked in an herby broth—to accompany their afternoon beer. They're smaller (and cheaper) than the ones you might have sampled in France and skewering them with a wooden toothpick can be quite a challenge. A chewier snack is *orelha* (pig's ear), usually flavored with cilantro.

Adjust your hours. Touristy restaurants might start serving dinner at 7 but most Portuguese wouldn't dream of dining at that hour. During the week, 8:30 or 9 would be a more normal time for locals to gather and on Friday or Saturday probably still later. As for going out dancing, don't even bother turning up at a nightclub before 2 am unless you're happy to be the only person on the dance floor.

IF YOU LIKE

Hilltop Villages

The hilltop villages of Portugal are especially beguiling, as they are often made of stone sculpted out of the rock face. Most of them date to Roman times, when they were garrison towns, but they later came in handy during the 17th-century War of Restoration against the Castilians. If you can manage an overnight stay, dusk is the best time of all to visit these castles. Visitors have left and the narrow streets take on a misty otherworldly air.

Marvão. A small population of 1,000 inhabit this dramatic hilltop village in the Alto Alentejo, which is surrounded by the original 17th-century city walls. A castle founded by the Moors in AD 715 still reigns supreme.

Monsaraz. Another jewel in the Alentejo tiara, this tiny village is surrounded by fascinating Neolithic megaliths. Narrow lanes, lopsided cottages, and a handsome castle are here, together with stunning views of the surrounding olive groves which are planted in straight lines along the ancient Roman roads.

Óbidos. Whitewashed houses bordering brilliantly colored bougainvillea make up this pretty medieval village, reputedly a wedding gift from Dom Dinis to his wife (beats a mere ring!). Óbidos has plenty of wining and dining choices and several places to stay.

Azulejos

Somehow, no matter how many catalogs you peruse and stores you tramp through, those tiles you end up decorating your bathroom or kitchen with at home just look so plain compared to Portugal's all-encompassing decorative *azulejos*. These brightly colored tiles are everywhere: houses, shops, monuments, and murals that brighten public spaces all over the country. *Azulejos* probably came to Portugal from Seville in the 15th century, made by Moslem craftsmen. They at first bore geometric designs, but have since gone through many indigenous stylistic revolutions.

Lisbon. The Museu Nacional do Azulejo traces the development of tile making from its Moorish roots. Don't miss the Cervejaria da Trindade, a vaulted beer hall on Rua Nova da Trindade that has stunning azulejos with figurative designs typical of the late 19th century, or the metro stations with their contemplative azulejo designs, including Colégio Militar and Camp Pequeno.

Porto. This is a fabulous city for azulejos, starting at the São Bento train station with its magnificent mural of battle scenes. Churches are literally smothered by tiles here, including the Igreja do Carmo and the Capela das Almas.

Sintra. One of the best places to see the early-16th-century geometric tiles is Sintra's magnificent Palácio Nacional da Pena. Throughout the historic property you'll find beautiful palaces and mansions adorned with azulejos.

Family Pursuits

The Portuguese adore children and welcome them everywhere, including at bars and restaurants where families drink and dine together. If your young ones grow tired of such grown-up pursuits, Portugal also has a healthy dose of sights and activities geared to children of all ages. This is a culture that revolves around family life throughout the day and well into the evening; bedtime is late here, with many children still up at midnight during the summer months.

Algarve. A major holiday destination, the Algarve offers plenty of choice, including

water parks, zoos, boat trips, and horse riding. There are also miniature trains that chug around the various resorts and, of course, the cheapest activities of all: making sandcastles and splashing in the sea.

Churches and Castles. Children will love the fairy-tale quality of Portugal's magnificent churches and castles. Several stand out, including the Knights Templar Convento de Cristo, in Tomar, where kiddies can light a candle and wonder at its other-worldly Da Vinci Code feel. The castles at Sintra and Elvas are other winners.

Dinosaurs. For a real Jurassic Park experience check out the fascinating Parque Natural das Serras de Aire e Candeeiros, near Fátima, where you can follow in the footsteps of the dinosaurs. There are special children's tours available, otherwise just follow the signs.

Beaches

The best-known area for beach holidays is, of course, the Algarve, with its relatively sheltered waters and oodles of tourist facilities. But for unspoiled coastal beauty or the right conditions for water sports, look elsewhere. Even the country's two largest cities have sandy beaches within easy reach, so you can balance sightseeing with sunbathing. If you're going to brave the relatively chilly waters, though, pay heed to the color of the flag flying on the beach: if it's red, stay close to shore.

The Alentejo coast. Some of Portugal's most stunning beaches are in its undeveloped southwest. Here towering cliffs frame broad strands, but local facilities may be limited to a couple of local cafés and a *pensão*. This area and the western Algarve to the south draw water-sports enthusiasts, thanks to strong wind and waves.

Around Porto. South of Porto, the dunes around Espinho are topped by wooden decking that is great for lung-filling walks; to the city's north, Póvoa de Varzim is the gateway to the Costa Verde, named for the deep-green pine forests that line the coast.

Around Lisbon. The seemingly endless strands of the Caparica coast draw many of the capital's residents on warm weekends. Each stretch has its own restaurant or bar, with its specific atmosphere and clientele; in summer some later turn into nightclubs, rocking until dawn. Further south, in the lee of the Serra da Arrábida, sandy beaches are lapped by warmer waters; across the Sado river, are Troía's sweep of sands.

Estremadura. Perhaps the most varied portion of Portugal's long western coast is in this region, around the fishing ports-cum-resorts of Nazaré and Peniche. Excellent and affordable seafood can generally be had just a few steps away from the beach.

FLAVORS OF PORTUGAL

Cuisine is one of the most integral parts of Portuguese culture. From the café culture to innovative restaurants to the markets and roadside stands found in every city, town, and small village, food (and drink) always seems to be on the mind of the Portuguese people.

Style

The heart of traditional Portuguese cuisine is all about simple yet flavorful home-style comfort food to be enjoyed leisurely with family and friends. Historically, the majority of the Portuguese population was poor farmers, and families depended on what they could grow, raise, or hunt. From these ingredients, housewives cooked up whatever could be used, with nothing going to waste. Today, much of this family-style method of cooking and serving remains ingrained into the cuisine, with an emphasis on simple local produce, grains, meats, and fish. However, don't miss out on splurging at some of the fine-dining Portuguese restaurants, especially in Porto, Lisbon, and Algarve, where both local and international chefs have put an interesting twist on simple favorites.

Common Ingredients

Though traditional Portuguese cuisine varies widely throughout each region, there are some general ingredients that you can find used extensively almost everywhere. Onions, garlic, and tomatoes are commonly used as a base, which is found in most stewed and braised fish dishes, such as *caldeirada* (rustic fish stew) and *arroz de marisco* or *tamboril* (shellfish or monkfish stewed with rice). With roasted foods, only roasted garlic and onions tend to be used. *Coentros* (fresh cilantro/coriander) is the favorite seasoning for almost every dish, whether it's stewed or roasted; other common

seasonings include *louro* (bay leaf) and *oregãos* (oregano)—both grown and dried locally—and *pimentão doce* (paprika). Spicy food is not that common, but when the Portuguese want to add some spice, they use *piri-piri*, a small, red chili pepper that's also grown locally and can be found both fresh and ground up.

Regional and Seasonal Products

Central and southern Portugal are filled with acres of beautiful orange trees, and most cafés offer fresh-squeezed, naturally sweet orange juice that is delicious during the winter months. In summer, there's an excellent selection of ripe and juicy melons to choose from, such as your typical *meloa* (cantelope), *melancia* (watermelon), and *melão*, a general term for the other types of green, yellow, and white honeydew–style melons found in Portugal, which are generally the most flavorful. In the fall and early winter up north, wild mushrooms are plentiful. Hunting season is popular, with both local and gourmet restaurants offering fresh game, such as *veado* (venison), *codorniz* (quail), *perdiz*, (partridge), *faisão* (pheasant), and *javali* (wild boar). *Coelho* (rabbit) and *pato* (duck) are generally farm-raised, and available year-round.

Specialties

Simple, comfort food aside, the Portuguese also know how to make some excellent specialty artisanal food products, which you don't want to miss. The most famous are their delicious breads and pastries. Bread-baking originated again from poor farming families having to make their own things, and with the historical abundance of wind mills perched on nearly every hill and mountaintop, flour and corn meal were easy commodities. There are numerous different types

of bread from every region, some notable ones being *broa-de-milho*, a thick corn-bread with a hard outer crust from Tras-os-Montes, and *pão Alentejano*, a chewy and thick "ciabatta-like" bread from Alentejo, which is used in many of their local dishes.

Pastry-making came about as a byproduct from both the wine business and convents, when egg whites were used by winemakers for filtering wines, and by the convents and monasteries for pressing and starching their habits. Thus, there were tons of leftover egg yolks and without wanting them to go to waste, the friars and sisters used them along with sugar and cinnamon imported from the Portuguese colonies to start a business making little egg sweets, which grew rapidly. Nowadays, pastries are so popular, you cannot walk down a street in Portugal without encountering at least a couple of cafés or pastelerias. With all these sweets, it's no surprise then that the Portuguese also have some excellent espresso coffee to enjoy with them; some of the favorite national brands are Delta and Nicola.

If you don't have much of a sweet tooth, try some of Portugal's delicious handmade cheeses *(queijo)* and charcuterie *(enchidos)*, which come in all sorts of flavors and textures. Some of the most internationally famous Portuguese cheeses include *Serra de Estrela* from the mountains in the north and *Azeitão* from the namesake town in the southerly region of Estremadura, both made from sheep's milk, that are pungent in aroma and flavor with an *amanteigado* ("smooth like butter") texture. For a harder and milder cheese, try *Nisa,* made with sheep's milk from the Alentejo, or *Pico,* made with raw cow's milk from the Azores. Charcuterie

produced here has a wide variety of *chouriço* (sausage) and *presunto* (Portuguese-style prosciutto), some favorites being made from the local Iberian black pigs, *chouriço de porco preto*, as well as blood sausage *(morçela)* and a soft sausage generally made from a mixture of pork, poultry, and bread called *alheira*.

Famous Dishes

■ *Açorda Alentejana* (Alentejo), "bread soup" with garlic, olive oil, and cilantro.

■ *Ameijoas à Bulhão Pato* (Estremadura), clams cooked with garlic, white wine, olive oil, and cilantro.

■ *Bacalhau á Bras*, salt cod sautéed with onions, fried potato sticks, egg, and black olives.

■ *Bacalhau com Natas*, salt cod with cream, gratin style.

■ *Bifes de Atum à Madeirense* (Madeira), tuna steaks sautéed with garlic, bay leaf, and parsley.

■ *Bolo de Alfarroba* (Algarve), a sweet cake made from the local Alfarroba tree seed pod.

■ *Chicharros* Recheados (Azores), Azorean stuffed mackerel.

■ *Cozido à Portuguesa*, hearty stew of beef, pork, sausage, cabbage, potatoes, and carrots.

■ *Francesinha* (Porto), sandwich of steak, sausage, and ham covered in melted cheese and spicy tomato sauce.

■ *Leitão à Bairrada* (Bairrada), roasted baby pig (not suckling) with spicy black pepper sauce and oranges.

■ *Polvo à Lagareiro*, roasted octopus with garlic, onions, and potatoes.

■ *Rojões à Minhota* (Minho), fried pieces of pork/pork fat with blood sausage, potatoes, and green olives.

PORTUGUESE WINE

Besides the well-known Port and Madeira, Portugal produces many excellent wines, both high-end and age worthy, as well as honest and straightforward youthful ones that you can buy inexpensively. If you're looking to try something different, Portugal has more than 300 different native grape varieties in use, which makes for an endless procession of delicious experiments. Portuguese wines also come in a wide variety of wine styles, including sparkling, still, rosés, dessert, and fortified wines.

Algarve and Alentejo

Algarve wine is largely red and is quite smooth, fruity, and full-bodied. Among the better producers are Quinta do Barranco Longo and Marques dos Vales Grace.

Alentejo wines and their producers are now among the best in Portugal— Esporão, Cortes de Cima, Malhadinha Nova, Redondo, Borba (with its lovely dark color and slightly metallic astringent flavor), Monsaraz, and Vidigueira. The reds are rich in color and ripe fruits, the whites are pale yellow, citrusy, and fruity. These wines tend to be higher in alcohol than other regions, usually between 13.5% and 14.5%, which go well with the rich Alentejo cuisine.

The Setúbal Peninsula and Moscatel de Setúbal

Wines produced on the Setúbal peninsula are known abroad, mainly through the 150-year efforts of the house of José Maria da Fonseca, based in Azeitão. The Moscatel that Fonseca—together with the small vine growers who make up the local cooperative a few miles east of Azeitão in Palmela—produces is best known as a fortified dessert wine, aged with a mouth-watering taste of honey. If you find some that is 25 years old, you'll see that it has developed a licorice color; enjoy its sweet scent and taste. José Maria da Fonseca produces many other wines besides the Moscatel—fine reds (notably one called Periquita, or "little parrot," made from the native Castelão grape), rosés, of which Lancers is often exported, and some clean, crisp whites, great with the local fresh seafood. Other notable producers on the peninsula include Quinta da Bacalhõa, Casa Ermelinda Freitas, and Pegões.

Bairrada and Dão

South of Porto is the coastal DOC region of Bairrada, producing some notable reds and *sparkling reds*, mainly from the local Baga grape. They have an intense color, with a delicious earthy nose and a smooth taste. They mellow with age and go very well with stronger dishes such as game, roasts, and pungent cheeses. The sparkling reds (*espumante tintos*) are best with a popular local dish, *leitão à Bairrada*—roast baby pig served with a spicy black pepper sauce. Notable Bairrada producers are Luis Pato and Quinta do Encontro.

Much of the wine here is red and matured in oak casks for at least 18 months before being bottled. When mature, the Dão wines have a dark, reddish-brown color, a "complex" nose, and a lasting, velvety taste and go well with roast lamb and pork. Look for Quinta de Cabriz, Casa de Santar, and Vinhos Borges.

Vinho Verde (Minho)

This region to the north of Porto is Portugal's largest demarcated region. The name *vinho verde*, which translates to "green wine" refers not to the wine's color but to its youthful freshness from its particular production methods. Made from a mix of native white grapes, generally Alvarinho and Loureiro, it is gently sparkling due to its high acidity, with a delicate, fruity flavor. Vinho verde goes well with any kind of seafood and can even age well while still maintaining its sprightliness. Vinho verde also comes in full sparkling, both white and rosé and even red, which has an intense red color and flavor, while still being tart and foamy. Notable producers are Aveleda (Quinta da Aveleda, Casal Garcia, Follies), Quinta de Gomariz, Afros, and Soalheiro.

Douro and Port

DOC Douro is home to Port wine and some incredible red and white table wines. Reds are usually made from a blend of the native grape, Touriga Nacional, and are of a deep ruby color, very fruity with a bit of spice and a rounded taste. They go well with richer foods, a variety of meats, casseroles, and stews well flavored with herbs. The whites are dry, have a pale-yellow color with a full nose, pairing well with salads, appetizers, and chicken dishes. Some of the most respected producers of table wines in Douro are a group of five producers called the "Douro Boys"—Quinta do Vallado, Quinta do Vale Dona Maria, Quinta do Vale Meão, Quinta do Crasto, and Nieport.

Port is a fortified wine that can only truly be labeled Port if it's produced in this region under the strict regulations designed for the area. Port can be made from up to 48 different native Portuguese grape varietals and can be divided into two major categories, ruby and tawny. Ruby has its namesake ruby red color, which is restrained to maintain the fruit and strength of a young wine. It is sold in the following categories, in ascending order of quality: Ruby, Reserve, Late Bottled Vintage (LBV), and Vintage, the last two are the finest and good for storing, as they age well in the bottle. Not every

harvest year is declared a vintage, only the most notable ones, and the vintage may only be declared between three and five years after the actual year in question, while LBV may be declared between four and six years after. Tawnys are made from a combination of different wine years that have been aged for different lengths of time in casks or vats. With age, the tawny color slowly develops over time and gets darker and nuttier in flavor. The port is sold as Tawny, Tawny Reserve, and indicated aged Tawnys of 10, 20, 30, and 40 years old. These wines are ready to drink when they are bottled. Another lesser known type of Port is white Port, which is recommended as an aperitif rather than a digestif, and comes in both dry and sweet styles. There has also been another recent addition to the Port world, the rosé Port, made known by the Croft house who first came out with their Croft Pink; it's currently being marketed as another aperitif Port or used to make Port cocktails. Along with Croft, other notable producers include Taylor's, Sandeman, Ramos Pinto, Quevedo, and Nieport.

Madeira

Madeira is a fortified and often blended wine produced on the Madeira Islands. It's produced in four distinct styles with a main grape varietal representing each style. *Boal* and *Malmsey (or Malvasia)* styles are sweet and heavy, and make excellent dessert wines; *Verdelho,* not so sweet, is a nice alternative to Sherry; and *Sercial,* dry and light, makes an excellent aperitif. Producers to look for are Blandy and Leacock.

ECOTOURISM

The word *ecotourism* is believed to have been coined by Mexican environmentalist Héctor Ceballos-Lascuráin in 1983. According to Ceballos-Lascuráin, ecotourism "involves traveling to relatively undisturbed natural areas with the specific object of studying, admiring, and enjoying the scenery and its wild plants and animals." His original definition seemed a bit too general, so in 1993 he amended it with a line that stressed that, "ecotourism is environmentally responsible travel."

Portugal has an astonishing variety of landscapes and habitats for so small a country. This natural wealth was long protected by the tardiness of economic development, but that shelter has now all but melted away.

In the south, cork oaks dot the Alentejo, periodically stripped of their bark for bottle stoppers and other products, in a practice that may be the best way of protecting the region from desertification. In more thickly forested regions, thirsty eucalyptus trees dominate commercial plantations, but traces of primeval forest remain, with evergreen holm-oaks harboring much wildlife. The only full-fledged National Park, Peneda-Gerês in the Minho, is the best example of this. Many areas have in recent years suffered from forest fires, though, so check the situation before traveling, particularly in summer.

In recent years, Portugal's government has earned a reputation as a cheerleader for renewable energy, as it seeks to cut carbon dioxide emissions and oil imports. But much capacity is in the form of hydro dams, which increasingly vocal environmentalists say destroy biodiversity along some of Europe's last major unchained rivers. Indeed, Portugal has a mixed record on nature conservation, having faced European investigations for waving through developments on or near protected land. Still, public awareness about such issues is rising, holding out the hope of stronger protection in the future and boosting the domestic market for ecotourism.

Portugal is an excellent place to see birds, thanks to its location on migration routes between Europe and Africa. Prime sites include the Tagus Estuary Natural Reserve south of the capital, Lisbon, where flamingos are among 250 species recorded. Inland, river trips on the Guadiana in the south and on the Tagus in the north are fine ways to sight eagles and other birds of prey.

In Lisbon, despite the city's hills, a network of cycle paths is being developed, with riverside routes to Belém and out east at the Parque das Nações, which is of most interest to foreign visitors. The latter route offers a chance to see estuary birds without leaving the city. Wheels may be hired downtown at **Bike Iberia** (✉ *Largo do Corpo Santo 5, Baixa* ☎ *21/347–0347* ⊕ *www.bikeiberia.com*) and at the Parque das Nações from **Tejo Bike** (☎ *21/891–9333* ⊕ *www.tejobike.pt*).

Larger fauna in Portugal is limited to roe deer, foxes, and wolves—mainly in the north, although weekend visits to a wolf-breeding project near Mafra, outside Lisbon, **Centro de Recuperação do Lobo Ibérico** (☎ *261/785–037* ⊕ *lobo.fc.ul.pt*) may be booked in advance (€5). Europe's only big cat, the Iberian lynx, has disappeared from the wild in Portugal; moves to breed it in captivity have begun, but the site is not open to the public.

The Web site of the **Institute for the Conservation of Nature and Biodiversity** (☎ *21/350–7900* ⊕ *www.icnb.pt*) has details of

in descending order of protection) the Peneda-Gerês National Park, the 13 Natural Parks, nine Natural Reserves, and six Protected Landscapes.

Accommodations

Places to stay in or near protected areas are listed on the ICNB Web site, but this is no guarantee of ecotourism credentials. A Turismo de Natureza badge was recently created, aimed at certifying minimum standards in terms of environmental impact and contribution to nature conservation. Early successful applicants include **Casa Entre-Palheiros** (⊠ *Rua João Rodrigues Cabrilho 265, Montalegre* ☎ *276/518–125* ⊕ *www.naturbarroso. net*) in Peneda-Gerês; the **Casa do Nevoeiro**, the "house of the mists" (⊠ *Estrada Nacional 114, Pena, Góis* ☎ *239/704–089 or 91/400–9194* ⊕ *www.casadoneveiro. com*), a traditional stone house in a village that forms part of the Aldeias de Xisto (Slate Villages) network; and **Monte do Areeiro** (⊠ *Estrada Nacional 114, São José de Lamarosa, Coruche* ☎ *21/301–5494 or 91/935–9980* ⊕ *www.montedoareeiro. com*), in the horse-breeding heartland of the Ribatejo.

It is worth noting, though, that many traditional rural accommodations have long had a light ecological footprint. The **Central Nacional do Turismo no Espaço Rural** (⊕ *www.center.pt*) lists several private networks on its Web site whose members often organize outdoor activities; it also offers tips and nature itineraries.

Food and Beverages

Much traditional small-scale agriculture in Portugal uses little or no pesticides, but a lack of awareness and labeling schemes mean the sector has not linked up with urban foodies. As a result, stock in urban organic outlets often is imported.

Change is now afoot, in part thanks to enterprising Dutch and other foreign small-holders, but also to Portuguese winemakers, for example, whose organic wines are increasingly widely available. Organic farming association **Agrobio** (☎ *21/364–1354* ⊕ *www.agrobio.pt*) has details of markets, produce stores, and producers nationwide on its (mainly Portuguese) Web site. Portugal's wine promotion agency, **Viniportugal** (☎ *21/364–1354* ⊕ *www.viniportugal.pt*) lists organic producers (*Produtores Vinhos Biológicos*) on the Portuguese pages of its Web site (under Vinha e Vinho). Some vegetarian restaurants, such as Terra in Lisbon, use exclusively organic ingredients.

Tours

Birds & Nature Tours (☎ *91/329–9990* ⊕ *www.birds.pt*) does private tours of the Tagus estuary and other bird sanctuaries, with Lisbon hotel pickups. Prices start at €90 for one person to €210 for four (plus €40 for each extra). Full-day tours start at €140.

Ecoland (☎ *286/611–111* ⊕ *www.ecoland. pt*) specializes in walking tours in natural parks. It organizes activities for kids and has a rural hotel near Mértola, on the Guadiana.

Vertigem Azul (☎ *265/23–000* ⊕ *www. portlandspirit.com*) in Setúbal runs dolphin-watching and bird-watching boat trips (both from €30 per person) on the Sado estuary, plus combined trips including dolphin watching and a jeep trip in the Serra de Arrábida.

GOLFING IN PORTUGAL

Portugal has been attracting golfers from all over Europe since it was discovered that it had the perfect climate for winter golf, particularly on the Algarve's stunning coastline of sandy beaches. It was another Henry, Sir Henry Cotton, winner of three Open Championships and the father of golf on the Algarve, who turned a marshy field near the old fishing village of Portimão into the famous Penina golf course in the mid-1960s, thereby putting Portugal on the world golfing map.

Although Portugal has always rated highly on the international golf map, it has really come into its own this past decade. The hosting of major tournaments, such as the World Cup in 2005 or the Portugal Masters held in the Algarve, has allowed an increasing number of players to discover this once well-kept secret. From the picturesque courses found on the Azores and Madeira islands in the Atlantic to the challenging courses in northern Portugal, no avid golfer will leave Portugal disappointed.

Some of the finest layouts in continental Europe are found in the Algarve, which holds the majority of Portugal's courses and continues to boom as a tourism market. There's also golf on the west coast around Lisbon, and just two courses in the rather remote region of Beiras in the northern center of the country. Four fine 18-hole courses are on the island of Madeira, which this year will include a stunning new course designed by Nick Faldo. Golfers will be able to enjoy views while watching wayward tee-shots fly off the landscaped cliff-tops into the Atlantic Ocean.

Generally, winter weather is perfect for golf, particularly on the southern coast of the Algarve. January can be temperamental with rains, however. The northern courses suffer more in this regard in winter. In summer, high temperatures across the country are made more bearable by cool sea breezes. Motorized golf carts are available at most courses in Portugal, and major courses have caddies available on request. All courses are walkable.

Golf at the most popular courses is expensive, with fees varying with the seasons and ranging from around €60 to €150. Green fees are generally cheaper in the north, but if you shop around online, you can find some discounts for the Algarve. Also calling and speaking to a golf receptionist (most speak English) might allow for additional last-minute bargains, as courses regularly announce promotions whenever bookings appear to have dwindled.

Fodor's Choice Courses

Belas, Lisbon, ⇨ *Chapter 2, Lisbon*

Millennium Course, Vilamoura, ⇨ *Chaper 6, Algarve*

Ocean Course, Vale do Lobo, ⇨ *Chapter 6, Algarve*

Oitavos Quinta da Marinha, Cascais, ⇨ *Chapter 3, Lisbon Environs*

Old Course, Vilamoura, ⇨ *Chapter 6, Algarve*

Penha Longa, Sintra, ⇨ *Chapter 3, Lisbon Environs*

Penina, Portimão, ⇨ *Chapter 6, Algarve*

Quinta da Cima, Tavira, ⇨ *Chapter 6, Algarve*

Royal Course, Vale do Lobo, ⇨ *Chapter 6, Algarve*

Vale da Pinta, Carvoeiro, ⇨ *Chapter 6, Algarve*

ART, ARCHITECTURE, AND AZULEJOS

Portuguese artistic styles were inspired first by the excitement of the newly emerging nation and then by the baroque experimentation that wealth from the colonies made possible.

Painting came into its own in the 15th century with the completion of Nuno Gonçalves's Flemish-inspired polyptych of São Vicente (St. Vincent), which portrayed the princes and knights, monks and fishermen, court figures and ordinary people of imperial Portugal. It's on display in Lisbon's Museu de Arte Antiga. The work of the next great Portuguese painter, the 16th-century Vasco Fernandes (known as Grão Vasco, or the Great Vasco), has an expressive, realistic vigor. His masterpieces are on display in Viseu.

The elaborate decoration that is the hallmark of Manueline architecture is inspiring in its sheer novelty. Structures are supported by twisted stone columns and studded with emblems of seaborne exploration and conquest—particularly under Dom Manuel I (1495–1521)—with representations of anchors, seaweed, and rigging mingling with exotic animals.

Following the discovery of gold in Brazil at the end of the 17th century, churches in particular began to be embellished in a rococo style that employed *talha dourada* (polychrome and gilded carved wood) to stupendous effect. There are superb examples at the churches of São Francisco in Oporto and Santo António in Lagos, and at the Convento de Jesus at Aveiro. For rococo at its most restrained, visit the royal palace at Queluz, near Lisbon.

In the 18th century the sculptor Machado de Castro produced perhaps the greatest equestrian statue of his time, that of Dom José I in Lisbon's Praça do Comércio. Domingos António Sequeira (1768–1837) painted prominent historic and religious subjects. Portrait and landscape painting became popular in the 19th century; works by José Malhoa and Miguel Angelo Lupi can be seen in the Museu de José Malhoa in Caldas da Rainha. The Museu Soares dos Reis in Oporto—named after the 19th-century sculptor of that name (1847–89)—was the country's first national museum. His pupil António Teixeira Lopes (1866–1942) achieved popular success and has a museum named after him in Vila Nova de Gaia, near Oporto.

Of all Portugal's artistic images, its *azulejos* (painted ceramic tiles) are perhaps the best known. It is thought the Moors introduced these tiles to Iberia, and although many are blue, the term azulejo may not come from *azul,* the Portuguese word for that color, but rather from the Arabic *azzulayj,* (little stones). By the 17th century whole panels depicting religious or secular motifs were common, for example at the Fronteira palace on the outskirts of Lisbon.

Tiles in a wide variety of colors adorn many fountains, churches, and palaces. The Paço Real (Royal Palace) in Sintra is one remarkable example of their decorative effect, but there are delightful combinations on the nation's *quintas* or *solares* (country residences) with interesting examples in the Minho region in the north. There are also well-preserved works on display in several museums, including Lisbon's Museu Nacional do Azulejo and Museu de Arte Antiga and Coimbra's Museu Machado de Castro.

GREAT ITINERARIES

CLASSIC PORTUGAL

This classic itinerary hits all the highlights for your first trip to Portugal. You'll start in the Algarve, Portugal's southernmost region of gorgeous beaches, vibrant resorts, and secluded hill villages, and continue north via the country's major towns. Landscapes along the way include the picturesque coast and the arid plains of the south; vibrant Lisbon and its lush environs; and the rivers, valleys, forests, and mountains of the north.

Days 1–2: The Algarve

Faro makes an ideal base for exploring the most attractive resorts and villages in the Algarve. Don't miss lovely riverside Tavira, bustling Lagos, and gorgeous mountain-based Monchique. If you are able, take the train that runs between Lagos and Vila Real; this coastal route is one of the most scenic in Portugal. *Chapter 6, The Algarve.*

Day 3: Évora

On your way north make a half-day diversion to Évora, one of Portugal's most charming and historic cities. Stroll the Cidade Velha (Old Town) maze of narrow streets and lunch on traditional Alentejo regional fare. Before continuing on to Lisbon, consider stopping at one of the area's cromlechs and dolmens—prehistoric stone monuments. ⇨ *Chapter 5, Évora and the Alentejo.*

Days 4–5: Lisbon

Don your walking shoes and range across the seven hills of the Portuguese capital. If your knees can't cope, hop on one of the vintage street trams that snake up and down the hills. You should plan on enjoying at least one meal by the river on a terrace; the views of the city are magnificent. Take in a *fado* show, as well. ⇨ *Chapter 2, Lisbon.*

Day 6: Queluz to Sintra

On the way out of Lisbon take in the rococo palace at Queluz—a treat for architecture buffs. For many visitors to Portugal, though, Sintra is the highlight of the trip, with its roster of palaces, castles, and Romantic gardens together forming a World Heritage Site. The leafy Serra de Sintra range is a lovely place for walks and you could easily spend a day or more here, all told. ⇨ *Chapter 3, Lisbon Environs.*

Day 7: Óbidos to Leiria

After all that trudging, take it easy with a meandering drive through the fertile Estremadura region. You'll pass Mafra, the giant 18th-century palace whose construction was financed by gold from Brazil, and Óbidos, the enchanting walled village once given as a royal wedding present. Move on to the stunning World Heritage Sites of Alcobaça and Batalha. At the journey's end drop by the magnificent medieval castle at the former royal residence of Leiria, one of Portugal's unsung gems. ⇨ *Chapter 4, Estremadura.*

Day 8: Coimbra

Coimbra, a delightful town abuzz with students, boasts heady architecture, a sophisticated shopping scene, and romantic squares and gardens. The place oozes history: Portugal's first king was born and buried here. It's a hilly city so be prepared, but the center is reasonably compact and you should be able to cover all the main sights easily in a day. Don't miss the quirky *elevador*—a combination of funicular, elevator, and walkway—or *fado*, the most characteristic of Portugal's folk music. ⇨ *Chapter 7, Coimbra.*

TIPS

■ Bear in mind that August is the Algarve's hottest and busiest tourist month, so try to plan your trip around this, if possible. Sintra is best avoided on summer weekends, when it gets very crowded; visitors must weigh that against the fact that entry to state institutions is free on Sunday until 2 pm.

■ Drop into the Lisbon Welcome Centre and buy a Lisboa Card; it will prove seriously euro-economizing on travel and admission to museums and monuments.

■ Many monuments close on Monday, though some instead take time out on Tuesday (the palace at Mafra, for instance) or Wednesday (Sintra's National Palace).

Days 9–10: Porto

Portugal's second city and gateway to the north, Porto has a beguiling air of faded grandeur, with its peeling buildings and medieval tangle of river-frontage streets. Start by picking up a map at the tourist office and heading for the atmospheric Ribeira embankment, with its strung-with-washing buildings and superb *tascas* where you can tuck into fresh fish and admire the colorful lights of the impressive port lodges across the water. Some visitors might want to take a half-day boat trip up the River Douro, whose amazing terraced vineyards form another World Heritage Site. ⇨ *Chapter 8, Porto.*

Day 10: Braga

The country's religious nerve center, Braga is an ecclesiastical heavyweight with a massive archbishop's palace at the center. A tiara of impressive religious buildings and sanctuaries encircles the town, including the extravagant Bom Jesus baroque pilgrim church, located 5 km (3 mi) to the east. Braga is a city for strolling. If you have the time, it's an easy day trip from Braga to medieval Guimarães with its lovely town center and magnificent palace of the dukes of Bragança. ⇨ *Chapter 8, The Minho and the Costa Verde.*

Day 11: Viana Do Castelo

A low-key Portuguese resort and the country's folkloric capital, this elegant seaside town has grandiose 16th-century buildings, superb restaurants, and sweeping beaches. Chug across the Rio Lima by ferry to the local strip of sand, stroll around the picturesque town center, and, if your timing permits, visit the bustling Friday market to pick up a few hand-embroidered linens as gifts for the folks back home. ⇨ *Chapter 8, The Minho and the Costa Verde.*

BYWAYS AND BACKWATERS

This meandering tour of the northern rivers, valleys, and mountains steers clear of the hustle-bustle of cities and tourist crowds, allowing you to absorb the local life and culture—Portugal's mellow pleasures. This makes a great add-on to our classic itinerary, or is great for repeat visitors who want to see something new.

Days 1–2: Monção

Now a peaceful spa town on a serene stretch on the Rio Minho, Monção is home to a castle that's the only reminder of more tumultuous times. The local wine, the sprightly *vinho verde*, encourages long lunches and makes the perfect accompaniment to salmon and trout freshly caught from the Minho. The liveliest day to visit is Thursday when the town swings into action with its weekly market. ⇨ *Chapter 8, The Minho and the Costa Verde.*

Day 3: Ponte de Lima

You can do this handsome town justice in a day. Its highlight is the ancient bridge with its 31 arches spanning the River of Oblivion, as it was known. Riverside promenades, mansions, elegant manorhouse accommodations, museums, and churches are included in the attractions; pick up a map at the helpful tourist office. ⇨ *Chapter 8, The Minho and the Costa Verde.*

Day 4: Barcelos

If you like markets, you have come to the right place. Held every Thursday (just follow the shopping baskets), this is celebrated as one of Portugal's biggest and best. Despite the coachloads of visitors, the market is essentially organized by locals for locals and chockablock with ceramics, baskets, toys, fresh produce,

---

TIPS

■ Winter is not the time for this trip. Northern Portugal can be cold and wet from December to February; spring is ideal, however, as much of the countryside is blanketed with a dazzle of wildflowers.

■ The driving conditions are relatively relaxing and easy in this region, mainly because of the lack of Portuguese drivers with their penchant for overtaking on blind corners.

■ One of the most delightful stretches of train track in the country runs from the Douro mainline at Livração to Amarante. There are up to nine trains a day on this narrow-gauge railroad, most with connections to Porto.

agricultural supplies, clothes, shoes, and household equipment. We recommend Barcelos as a day trip, because the market is so well attended that overnight accommodations are scarce. ⇨ *Chapter 8, The Minho and the Costa Verde.*

Day 5: Amarante

If you're looking for love, touching the saintly effigy in the Convento de São Gonçalo is recommended by the locals. Judging by the smooth-as-glass white limestone, there have been plenty of hopefuls. The rest of the day, stroll across the pretty bridge, wander along the riverbanks, or rent a rowboat. ⇨ *Chapter 7, The Coast and the Douro.*

Day 6: Chaves

A few miles from the Spanish border, pretty Chaves once bore the brunt of any attack. Its 14th-century castle is the most prominent feature, but the atmospheric medieval streets, tiled churches, local museums, and thermal springs provide more passive

astimes. While there, rent a paddleboat from the river gardens for the best views of the ancient Roman Ponte Trajano bridge. ⇨ *Chapter 7, Trás-os-Montes.*

Day 7: Bragança

Within the walls of the Cidadela (citadel) is a superbly preserved medieval village. Wander the cobbles and gaze at neighboring Spain from the castle walls, then descend to the modern town. Parking is refreshingly easy in this town, with plenty of places by the bus station and even up in the citadel itself. Just follow the signs. ⇨ *Chapter 7, Trás-os-Montes.*

Days 8–9: The Eastern Beiras

With fertile valleys, medieval villages, castles, and fortresses, this area is atmospheric and rugged with tucked-away villages and towns like Fundão, Castelo Rodrigo, and Almeida. Every castle wall tells a story, while every abandoned house or tower harbors a ghost or two. Note that a car is essential for this part of the route as the bus coverage is patchy and sporadic. ⇨ *Chapter 6, The Eastern Beiras.*

Day 10: Sortelha

It's not quite the land that time forgot, but Sortelha comes as close as anywhere in Portugal. Ancient walls, crumbling houses, cobbled streets, and simple back-to-basic accommodation all contribute to the stuck-in-a-time-warp atmosphere. Again, getting here by public transport is possible but problematic, as several of the bus lines operate only during school-term time. ⇨ *Chapter 6, The Eastern Beiras.*

CASTLES, CROMLECHS, AND CORK

Lisbon residents increasingly see the wide-open spaces of the Alentejo as a refuge from city hustle, and life definitely moves at a slower pace here. Across mile after mile of rolling plains, sheep graze and black pigs root for acorns under cork oaks that are stripped of their bark every few years. The region bears the marks of ancient civilizations, and hilltop fortresses regularly heave into view. There are more fairy-tale castles along the River Tagus, just to the west.

Day 1: Évora

The capital of the Upper Alentejo, the walled town of Évora is steeped in history. Lose yourself in the Cidade Velha, but be sure to see the main square, the Praça do Giraldo, and the impressive Roman temple to Diana. Wine buffs can pick up information on touring the region's wineries at the **Rota dos Vinhos do Alentejo** (✉ *Praça Joaquim António de Aguiar* ☎ *266/746–498* ⊕ *www.vinhosdoalentejo.pt*), which also has tastings. ⇨ *Chapter 4, Évora and the Alentejo.*

Day 2: Arraiolos and Estremoz

Before leaving the Évora area, consider stopping off at a local cromlech or dolmen—prehistoric stone monuments. Then stop off in Arraiolos, famed for its handmade tapestries, before traveling on to Estremoz, the most important of the region's "marble towns" (Portugal is Europe's second biggest producer after Italy). ⇨ *Chapter 4, Évora and the Alentejo.*

Day 3–4: Portalegre

Base yourself in the Portalegre area for a couple of days. Though the charms of the town itself are fairly soon exhausted, many stimulating trips out are possible: to the stunning hilltop villages of Castelo de Vide and Marvão, with its ancient battlements; to the Parque Natural da Serra de São Mamede—a lovely area for walking; or to the former royal stud farm at Alter do Chão. ⇨ *Chapter 4, Évora and the Alentejo.*

Day 5: Abrantes

Head northwest toward the Tagus River, sighting the spectacular castle at Belver on your way. The flower-bedecked village of Sardoal makes for an enjoyable stop on the way to Abrantes—and yet another hilltop castle. ⇨ *Chapter 3, The Ribatejo.*

Day 6: Constância and Almourol

The pretty little town of Constância, on the confluence of the Zêzere and Tagus rivers, is a good base for canoeing and other outdoor pastimes, or just to picnic on the neat riverside parkland. A little farther on, the castle at Almourol on its own island in the Tagus, is perhaps Portugal's most fairytale edifice. ⇨ *Chapter 3, The Ribatejo.*

TIPS

■ High summer is not the time to head inland, where temperatures can be scorching. Spring, by contrast, is delightful, with wildflowers galore. Fall sees many food-related festivals taking place in both the Alentejo and the Ribatejo.

■ The driving conditions are relatively relaxing and easy in this region, with long-distance roads fairly flat and no more than gently curving. As for public transport, the Alentejo is not well served by trains but express and local bus services are reliable.

■ Both the Alentejo and Ribatejo are up-and-coming wine-producing regions, and many vineyards are pleased to welcome visitors. The Portuguese tourist office can provide contact details.

Day 7: Santarém

If you don't need to head straight back to Lisbon to catch a flight, spend at least half a day in the regional capital of Santarém, with its impressive Gothic church and fine views over the plains that you have just traversed. ⇨ *Chapter 3, The Ribatejo.*

SANCTUARY AND SOLITUDE

One of Portugal's best-kept secrets is its southwestern corner, where the protection provided by Natural Park status has limited tourist development. That means facilities are scarce, but beaches are pristine, and the fish and shellfish served at local restaurants is among the freshest and best to be found anywhere in the country. This area also boasts some of the country's best surfing spots.

Day 1: Arrábida and Setúbal

If you're starting out from Lisbon, don't miss the Serra de Arrábida, with its deep-green pine forests. The sheltered beaches on its southern flanks are bathed by warmer waters than those on the west coast of the peninsula. Overnight in the city of Setúbal, which boasts one of Portugal's earliest examples of Gothic architecture. ⇨ *Chapter 2, The Setúbal Peninsula.*

Day 2: Alcácer do Sal

This ancient town is famed for its salt-making tradition, castle, and profusion of storks. The nearby Reserva Natural do Sado offers opportunities for walkers, or you could head for the beach at Comporta, which also has several excellent restaurants. ⇨ *Chapter 4, Évora and the Alentejo.*

Day 3: Santiago de Cacém

This market town is a good base for horse-riding excursions as well as more beach trips. You can also explore the nearby Roman ruins at Miróbriga, or visit the Badoca safari park. ⇨ *Chapter 4, Évora and the Alentejo.*

Day 4: Vila Nova de Milfontes

Just to the south of the port city of Sines, the real wilderness begins: the Parque Natural do Sudoeste Alentejao e Costa Vicentina. Vila Nova de Milfontes is among the few towns along this bit of coast, which has stunning beaches at places such as Zambujeira do Mar. ⇨ *Chapter 4, Évora and the Alentejo.*

Day 5: Vila do Bispo

As you cross the border into the Algarve, smaller local roads continue to lead off the highway to an amazing variety of beaches, such as Arrifana. They lack fancy hotels and restaurants but are popular with water-sports enthusiasts. End your day at Vila do Bispo, a handy local base. ⇨ *Chapter 5, Lagos and the Western Algarve.*

Day 6: Sagres

Even nonsurfers will find plenty to enthuse at Portugal's southwestern corner. The views from the hilltop fort at Sagres and the lighthouse on Cape Saint Vincent are truly spectacular. From here you can head east for a spell at noisier, more sociable resorts such as Albufeira, or head north from there up the motorway to Lisbon. ⇨ *Chapter 5, Lagos and the Western Algarve.*

ON THE CALENDAR

	Religious celebrations, called *festas* (feasts or festivals), *feiras* (fairs), and *romarias* (pilgrimages or processions), are held throughout the year. Some of the leading annual events are listed below. Verify specific dates with the people at the Portuguese tourism office, who can also send you a complete list of events.
January	In many parts of Portugal it is still common to **Cantar as Janeiras**—sing January in. From January 1 to 6 groups of friends go door to door, proclaiming Jesus's birth and wishing their listeners a happy new year. This is often accompanied by traditional instruments. (Originally it was done in the hope householders might hand out Christmas leftovers.)
	The **Feira do Fumeiro**, a celebration of smoked and cured sausages and hams in the village of Montalegre in Trás-os-Montes, draws thousands of visitors every year. A similar event in the same region takes place in February in Vinhais, the self-proclaimed *capital do fumeiro*.
February–March	**Carnaval** *(Carnival)*, the final festival before Lent, is held throughout the country, with processions of masked participants, parades of decorated vehicles, and displays of flowers. Nowadays it is much influenced by the wilder Brazilian celebrations; the most genuinely Portuguese events are generally held in Ovar, Nazaré, Loulé, and Portimão, though there's a big one near Lisbon at Torres Novas.
March	Portugal's biggest wine showcase is **Essência do Vinho**, with thousands flocking to the Palácio da Bolsa, the city's old stock exchange, to sample the products of vineyards around the country. The same venue hosts the Essência do Gourmet food festival in September.
March–April	**Semana Santa** *(Holy Week)* festivities are held in Braga, Ovar, Póvoa de Varzim, and other cities and major towns, with the most important events taking place on Monday, Thursday, and Good Friday. Note that, unlike in Spain, although the Friday is a public holiday, the following Monday is not. Easter also marks the start of the bullfighting season and—outside Lisbon's Campo Pequeno arena at any rate—protests by animal rights groups.
April	Lisbon's biggest gastronomic event, **Peixe em Lisboa**, or Lisbon Fish and Flavors as it's called in English, is organized by the same outfit as Porto's Essência do Vinho. It features top

Portuguese and foreign chefs, who set up food stalls and do cookery demonstrations and talks.

The anniversary of the 1974 revolution (actually a coup) that brought down a dictatorship of four decades is known simply as **25 de Abril**. In Lisbon, official ceremonies mark the day, while nostalgic lefties parade down the Avenida da Liberdade.

May	Legend has it that, in the early 16th century, a peasant who insisted on working on the Day of the Holy Cross saw a perfumed, luminous cross appear on the ground where he was digging. Ever since, Barcelos has held the colorful **Festas das Cruzes** *(of the Crosses)*, with a large fair, concerts, an affecting procession, and a fireworks display on the Rio Cavado. There are smaller celebrations and a fair in Monsanto. During the **Romaria de Fátima**, thousands make the pilgrimage to the town from all over the world to commemorate the first apparition of the Virgin to the shepherd children on May 13, 1917. These are repeated monthly through to October 13, the anniversary of the last vision. The misleadingly named **Estoril Open** tennis tournament, which actually takes place just outside Lisbon at the Estádio Nacional complex, usually draws one or two top international players, and some up-and-coming Iberian stars. Late May sees the start of the music festival season, with the biennial (next in 2012) **Rock in Rio Lisboa** first off the blocks with its family-friendly layout and predominately mainstream fare. Portugal's growing number of rockfests are a great place to see your favorite bands—tickets are cheaper than for events in most of Europe and generally mud-free.
June	Monção celebrates the **Festa do Corpo de Deus** *(Corpus Christi)*, which includes a symbolic battle between good and evil. Amarante hosts the **Festa de São Gonçalo**, when St. Gonçalo is commemorated by the baking of phallus-shape cakes, which are then exchanged between unmarried men and women. Events also include a fair, folk dancing, and traditional singing. The **Festa de Santo António** is the first of June's Festas Populares, and the biggest party of the year in Lisbon. On June 12, trestle tables are set up in the city's traditional neighborhoods (and some modern ones), and grilled sardines and sangria are

served to all and sundry. Throughout the month, there are free concerts and other events around town.

The **Festa de São João** is especially colorful in Porto, where the whole city erupts with bonfires and barbecues and every corner has its own *cascatas* (arrangements with religious motifs). Locals roam the streets, hitting passersby on the head with, among other things, leeks and plastic hammers.

June–July	One of Portugal's longest-running annual cultural events, the **Festival de Sintra** includes classical music and ballet performances by international and Portuguese groups.
July	The **Festa do Colete Encarnado** *(Red Waistcoat)* in Vila Franca de Xira honors the *campinos* (cowboys) who guard the wild bulls in the pastures of the Ribatejo. Streets are cordoned off, and bulls are let loose as would-be bullfighters try their luck at dodging the beasts. The **Festival do Estoril** sees concerts by leading Portuguese and foreign artists in several towns along the Estoril Coast, with a stress on performers from Mediterranean countries.
August	The **Festas da Nossa Senhora da Agonia**, at Viana do Castelo, is just one of myriad summer events in the Minho that feature processions, folk music and dancing, greasy pastries and fireworks. A few weeks later, the Festa da Nossa Senhora dos Remédios in Lamego is a similar party. In the **Festas da Nossa Senhora da Boa Viagem**, at Peniche, locals organize processions on land and sea in honor of the patron saints they hope will keep fishermen safe. The date is also marked at other fishing ports up and down the country, such as Ericeira, near Sintra. **Festival Sudoeste**, Portugal's largest popular music event, held near Zambujeiro on the Alentejo coast on the first weekend of August, has three days of concerts and dance music, with top national and international names. Camping and local transport are included in the ticket. On the first Sunday of August every four years (next in 2011) Tomar hosts the spectacular **Festa dos Tabuleiros** in which young women march through town with trays on their heads piled absurdly high with bread and flowers.
September	The **Romaria de São Gens** *(St. Gens)* brings ceramic vendors from all over the country to Freixo de Cima, west of

	Amarante. The **Festa das Vindimas** *(Grape Harvest)* in Palmela has a symbolic treading of the grapes and a blessing of the harvest, accompanied by a parade of harvesters, wine tastings, the election of the Queen of the Wine, and fireworks.
	In Lisbon, an active film festival season kicks off with **Queer Lisboa,** one of the leading gay and lesbian events of its kind in Europe. The months that follow see showcases and competitive events focusing on genres from documentaries to horror movies.
October	**Feira de Outubro** *(October Fair)* in Vila Franca de Xira, a short distance from Lisbon, has farming and agricultural activities, handicraft displays, bullfights, and a running of the bulls in the streets. The Algarve's **Feira de Outubro** gathers together crafts, goods, and produce from villages throughout the Serra de Monchique. The **Festival Nacional de Gastronomia** *(National Gastronomy Festival)* in Santarém consists of traditional regional dishes, cooking contests, and lectures.
November	The **Festa de São Martinho** on the 11th is celebrated above all by *magustos*—tastings of the first barrels of new wine at which roast chestnuts are usually served. The **Feira Nacional do Cavalo** *(National Horse Fair)* in Golegã coincides with this festival, combining parades of saddle and bullfighting horses with riding competitions, handicrafts exhibitions, and wine tastings.
December	**Festa de São Silvestre** *(St. Sylvester)*, on New Year's Eve, transforms Funchal into a vast fairground, with bands of strolling dancers and singers, thousands of lights, and breathtaking fireworks.
December–January	The remote Trás-os-Montes region unsurprisingly retains some of Portugal's most ancient pagan traditions. The **Festa dos Rapazes** in the villages around Bragança is one example; in the period between Christmas and the Noite dos Reis (the night of January 5) unmarried "Boys" indulge in traditional high jinks, such as dressing up in straw costumes to scare children and girls.

WHEN TO GO

The peak season for visiting Portugal begins in spring and lasts through early autumn. From March to May much of the countryside is at its prettiest; the rolling plains of the Alentejo, for example, are specked with yellow, white, and purple wildflowers. In the Algarve, a similar transformation may come as early as February.

April is often quite rainy (the local saying is *Abril, àguas mil*—a thousand waters), but by May the weather is warming up, fostering outdoor events such as book fairs.

This might be a good time to visit Trás-os-Montes in the far northeast, some parts of which will be baking hot in the high summer. In general, though, it is not unbearably hot in Portugal except in the interior of the Alentejo (where workers nevertheless must harvest cork at this time). Be aware that budget lodgings may not have air-conditioning. Still, along the coast, cool breezes often spring up in the evening, so take an extra layer when out at night.

With locals hitting the beach at every opportunity in July, weekend traffic can be unbearable. In August Lisbon traditionally shuts down (half the city moves to the Algarve for the duration), which makes sightseeing in the capital city less stressful. It is also a great time of year to explore the Minho, where it's cooler and there are festivals going on everywhere. Or head for Portugal's highest mountain range, the Serra de Estrela.

September sees most people back at work; the cultural scene livens up again, but this may also be the best moment to head for rapidly emptying beaches. The Atlantic waters are less chilly now—indeed, they may be at their warmest as late as October. That month may bring rain, but early November is often warm.

Fall is harvest time, of course, and vineyards across the country fill with grape-picking villagers. Though this is the busiest time of the year for winemakers, it is also the most interesting time for you to visit a *quinta.*

Winter in the mountains of the north is cold and usually snowy. Across the rest of the mainland it's generally mild, if rainy. Note, though, that the Portuguese like to pretend winter doesn't exist: cafés often leave their doors open and customers their coats on; homes are generally not well insulated or heated, and budget accommodation might not be, either. For winter sun, head for the Algarve. Locals think foreign tourists are mad for walking around in shorts, but the weather is warm enough.

The exception to all this is Madeira, where it feels like spring every day. Peak season here is Christmas and New Year, when cruise ships gather in Funchal's bay to join the onshore crowds in watching a mammoth fireworks display.

Climate

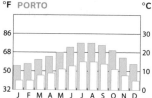

Lisbon

WORD OF MOUTH

"It really has everything—grand palaces and tiny streets. I love the little trams in the higher parts of town—but beware pickpockets!!"

—Charlie_M

"People in Lisbon were soooo friendly. Everyone was so helpful, friendly, pleasant and courteous."

—jan47ete

"Lisbon is the best base from which to explore and also get the feeling that you are really in Portugal not just a tourist town."

—turaj

By Alison Roberts and Alexandre Bezerra

Lisbon bears the mark of an incredible heritage with laid-back pride. Spread over a string of seven hills north of the Rio Tejo (Tagus River) estuary, the city also presents an intriguing variety of faces to those who negotiate its switchback streets.

In the oldest neighborhoods, stepped alleys whose street pattern dates back to Moorish times are lined with pastel-color houses decked with laundry; here and there, *miradouros* (vantage points) afford spectacular river or city views. In the grand 18th-century center, *calçada à portuguesa* (black-and-white mosaic cobblestone) sidewalks border wide boulevards. *Eléctricos* (trams) clank through the streets, and blue-and-white azulejos (painted and glazed ceramic tiles) adorn churches, restaurants, and fountains.

Of course, parts of Lisbon lack charm. Even some downtown areas have lost their classic Portuguese appearance as the city has become more cosmopolitan: shiny office blocks have replaced some 19th- and 20th-century art nouveau buildings. And centenarian trams share the streets with "fast trams" and noisy automobiles.

Some modernization has improved matters, though. In preparing to host the 1998 World Exposition, Lisbon spruced up public buildings, overhauled its subway system, and completed an impressive second bridge across the river. Today the former Expo site is an expansive riverfront development known as Parque das Nações, and the city is a popular port of call for cruises, whose passengers disembark onto a revitalized waterfront. Downtown, all the main squares have been overhauled one by one, after decades of neglect. Often, the newly laid cobblestones cover an underground car park: a blessing in an ancient city not designed to cope with motorized transport.

In its heyday in the 16th century, Lisbon was a pioneer of the first wave of globalization. Now, the empire is striking back, with Brazilians and people from the former Portuguese colonies in Africa enriching the city's ethnic mix. There are also more than a few people from other European countries who are rapidly becoming integrated. (Your blond waiter might be a Ukrainian who is just counting the days until his nursing qualifications from back home are officially recognized.)

But Lisbon's intrinsic, slightly disorganized, one-of-a-kind charm hasn't vanished in the contemporary mix. *Lisboetas* (people from Lisbon) are at ease pulling up café chairs and perusing newspapers against any backdrop, whether it reflects the progress and commerce of today or the riches that once poured in from Asia, South America, and Africa. And quiet courtyards and sweeping viewpoints are never far away.

Despite rising prosperity (and costs) since Portugal entered the European Community in 1986, and the more recent tourism boom, prices for most goods and services are still lower than most other European countries. You can still find affordable places to eat and stay, and with distances between major sights fairly small, taxis are astonishingly cheap. All this means that Lisbon is not only a treasure chest of historical monuments, but also a place where you won't use up all your own hard-earned treasure.

ORIENTATION AND PLANNING

GETTING ORIENTED

Lisbon was built across seven hills on the north bank of the Tagus estuary, whose vast expanse ebbs and flows with the tides from the Atlantic Ocean. Though nowadays, Lisbon sprawls over considerably more than seven hills: the city proper is 85 square kilometers (33 square miles) though the metropolitan area is many times larger. The historic downtown is dominated by a castle perched on the highest of the seven hills. The part of town where business was historically transacted is low-lying area that separates the hillier neighborhoods of Alfama and Chiado. The broad avenues of this modern grid start at the river and run northward.

Alfama. East of the Baixa lies the Alfama, the old Moorish quarter that survived the earthquake. In this part of town are the Sé (the city's cathedral) and, on the hill above, the Castelo de São Jorge (St. George's Castle).

Baixa. The center of Lisbon stretches north from the spacious Praça do Comércio—one of Europe's largest riverside squares—to Praça Dom Pedro IV, universally known by its ancient name of Rossio, a smaller square lined with shops and cafés. The district in between is known as the Baixa (Lower Town), an attractive grid of parallel streets built after the 1755 earthquake and tidal wave.

Chiado and the Bairro Alto. To the west of the Baixa is Chiado, the city's hip shopping district, and Bairro Alto (Upper Neighborhood), an area of intricate 18th-century streets, peeling houses, and Gothic churches.

The Modern City. The modern city begins at Praça dos Restauradores, adjacent to the Rossio. From here the main Avenida da Liberdade stretches northwest to the landmark Praça Marquês de Pombal, dominated by a column and a towering statue of the man himself. This busy traffic roundabout is bordered by the green expanse of the Parque Eduardo VII, named in honor of King Edward VII of Great Britain, who visited Lisbon in 1902.

São Bento. Downhill from the Bairro Alto, this maze of streets harbours cozy restaurants and, on the Rua de São Bento itself, some pricey antique shops.

Lapa. On another hill to the west of São Bento, foreign embassies cluster in the Lapa neighborhood, no doubt providing some of the custom in the posh restaurants and fine hotels found here.

Cais do Sodré and Santos. The riverside district of Cais do Sodré was long a seedy backwater mainly patronized by crews from passing ships, but

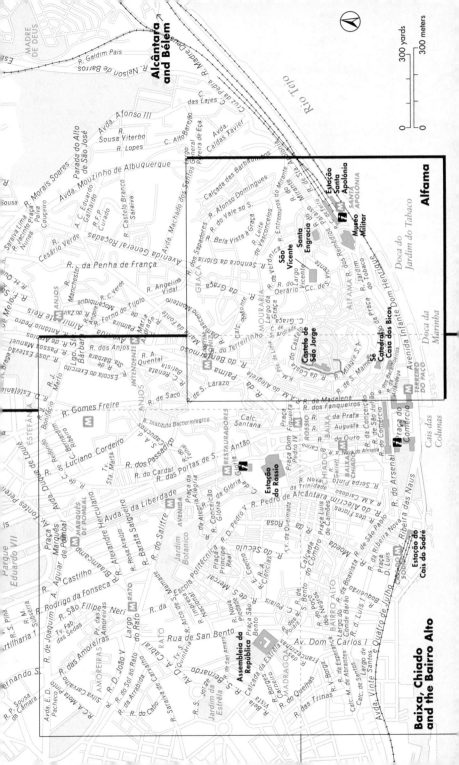

Alcântara and Bélem

MADRE DE DEUS

R. Galdim Pais

R. Nelson de Barros

Rio Tejo

300 yards

300 meters

Alfama

Avda. Afonso III

R. Sousa Viterbo

R. Lopes

C. Altobaréga

C. das Lajes

Cruz da pedra

Avda. Caldas Xavier

Avda. Pereira de Eça

Calçada das Barbadinhos

Estação Santa Apolónia

SANTA APOLÓNIA

R. Afonso Domingues

Museo Militar

R. Morais Soares

Parada do Alto de São José

Praça Jacinto Nunes

R. Nunes

Saraiva Lima

Couceiro

Avda. Mouzinho de Albuquerque

A. C. Eduardo Galhardo

R. P. Curado

Castelo Branco

R. do Vale so S.

R. Bela Vista à Graça

R. Leite de Vasconcelos

Santa Engracia

R. dos Remédios

R. Jardim do Tobaco

Doca do Jardim do Tabaco

Cesário Verde

R. da Penha de França

General Roçadas

Castelo Branco

Saraiva

R. dos Sapadores

Senhora da Glória

R. da verónica

São Vicente

Largo de São Vicente

Cc. de S.

ALFAMA R. dos Remédios

Avenida Infante Dom Henrique

Doca da Marinha

Manchester

R. C. Verde

R. Angelina Vidal

GRAÇA

R. do Oratório

Casa dos Bicos

Moçambique

R. Forno do Tijolo

da Graça

Cc. da Graça

TERREIRO DO PAÇO

Zaire

Maria Andrade

R. Damasceno Monteiro

Calç. do Monte

C. de Santo André

R. Sé

Sé

R. dos Bacalhoeiros

R. de São Mamede

R. da Alfândega

ANJOS

ANTÓNIO Pedro

Almirante Reis

Palmira

Marta

MOURARIA

Largo da Graça

Castelo de São Jorge

Catedral de Sé

R. Miguel S. A.

R. de São João

R. da Madalena

Av. Infante Dom Henrique

R. Braça Manuel

R. José Estevão

R. de Passos Manuel

Escola do Exército

R. Renata

R. C. Renata

Sta. Bárbara

Lgo. de Sta. Bárbara

R. dos Anjos

R. Anselmo Braamcamp

R. Palma

R. do Benformoso

R. do Terreirinho

A. M. W. do Arco

R. da Madalena

R. dos Fanqueiros

R. da Prata

R. Augusta

R. do Ouro

R. Nova do Almada

R. da Conceição

R. do Comércio

Praça do Comércio

Cais das Colunas

INTENDENTE

R. A. Quental

R. de Saco

R. de S. Lázaro

Praça Dom Figueira

Praça Dom Pedro IV

ROSSIO

BAIXA

BAIXA-CHIADO

Garrett

R. Gomes Freire

ESTEFÂNIA

R. J. Marto

R. Bonifácio

Instituto Bacteriológico

Calç. Santana

Antão

Estação do Rossio

R. do Salitre

R. Luciano Cordeiro

R. C. Bernardim Ribeiro

R. L.C. Ribeiro

R. de Regedor

S. A. de Aboim

Tv. Sta. Marta

R. Portas de S.

R. do Cardal

R. das Portas de S.

R. Santa Marta

R. Nova da Trindade

CHIADO

R. Serpa Pinto

A.M. Cardoso

R. Nova do Carmo

Praça Luís de Camões

R. Garrett

R. das Flores

R. de São Paulo

R. Nova da Piedade

R. de São Julião

R. do Arsenal

R. do Ouro

SODRÉ

Ribeira das Naus

Estação do Cais do Sodré

Cais do Sodré

MARQUÊS DE POMBAL

Praça Marquês de Pombal

R. Alexandre Herculano

R. Rosa Araújo

R. Barata Salgueiro

R. do Salitre

AVENIDA

Jardim Botânico

Praça da Alegria

Praça de Alegria

R. D. Pedro V

R. Dom Pedro V

R. da Rosa

R. da Rosa

R. da Atalaia

R. do Século

Praça do Príncipe Real

Calçada da Glória

Praça da Alegria

R. Luz Soriano

R. D. Pedro de Alcântara

Calçada do Combro

R. do Loreto

Moeda

BAIRRO ALTO

R. da Boavista

R. da Boavista

Boqueirão

R. D. Luís I

R. D. Luís

R. Ribeira Nova

Ribeira das Naus

Parque Eduardo VII

Avda. Fontes Pereira

Praça Duque de Saldanha

ESTEFÂNIA

R. Duque de Loulé

Avda. Duque de Loulé

R. de Joaquim

R. A. Aguiar

R. Rodrigo da Fonseca

R. Castilho

R. São Filipe

Neri

MARQUÊS DE POMBAL

RATO

Jardim das Amoreiras

R. das Amoreiras

Pç. das Amoreiras

Tv. Fab. das Sedas

R. de São Marçal

R. da

Largo do Rato

RATO

Escola Politécnica

R. da Escola Politécnica

R. Nacional

R. do Salitre

R. Mercês

Praça São Bento

R. de São Bento

Rua de San Bento

Assembleia da República

Calçada da Estrela

MADRAGOA

Jardim da Estrela

R. da Esperança

R. da Esperança

R. das Trinas

Avda. Vinte Santos

Avda. Quatro de Julho

Avda. Dom Carlos I

R. de São Joaquim

Tv. do Cabral

R. D. João V

R. do Sol ao Rato

R. da Arrábida

R. das Amoreiras

R. do Cabo

Tv. das Amoreiras

R. S. Jorge

Artilharia 1

R. da Mãe d'Água

R. Borges Carneiro

R. Vista

R. V. Borga

Calç. M. de Arroios

Calç. de Sargento de Sousa

R. das Trinas

R. do Quelhas

R. S. Jorge

R. A. Cabral

R. da Quintinha

Praça São Bento

Francisco

R. de São Bernardo

Baixa, Chiado and the Bairro Alto

is now increasingly a place for locals to eat out and go bar hopping. Neighboring Santos is still trendier.

Alcântara and Belém. Two kilometers (1 mi) west of the Baixa, former docks in the Alcântara area have been overhauled and turned into fancy places to drink and dine. More recently, an old warehouse has become one of Lisbon's prime museums. Another three kilometers (2 mi) west along the Rio Tejo is Belém, home to the Mosteiro dos Jerónimos, the famous monastery, as well as a royal palace and several of the city's best museums.

Parque das Nações. Located about five kilometers (3 mi) northeast of Lisbon's center is Parque das Nações, site of the World Expositions in 1998. This revitalized district on the banks of the Rio Tejo includes the spectacular Oceanário de Lisboa, an aquarium built for the Expo.

PLANNING

WHEN TO GO

It's best not to visit at the height of summer, when the city is hot and steamy and lodgings are expensive and crowded. Winters are generally mild and usually accompanied by bright blue skies, and there are plenty of bargains to be had at hotels. For optimum Lisbon weather, visit on either side of summer, in May or late September through October. The city's major festivals are in June; the so-called *santos populares* (popular saints) sees days of riotous celebration dedicated to saints Anthony, John, and Peter.

PLANNING YOUR TIME

You'll want to give yourself a day at least exploring the *bairro* of Alfama, climbing up to the Castelo de São Jorge (Saint's George's castle) for an overview of the city; another in the monumental downtown area, the Baixa, and in the neighboring fancy shopping district of Chiado, and perhaps also in the funkier shops of the Bairro Alto. Another again could be spent in historic Belém, with its many museums and monuments. Note that many are closed Monday, and that churches often close for a couple of hours at lunchtime.

There are other attractions dotted around the modern city, and families will appreciate the child-friendly attractions of the Parque das Nações, the former Expo site. All in all, there's enough to do and see to fill a week—though if you're staying that long you should think about visiting Sintra or other sights in the hinterland.

GETTING HERE AND AROUND

AIR TRAVEL

Lisbon's small, modern airport, sometimes known as Aeroporto de Portela, is 7 km (4½ mi) north of the center, and getting downtown is simple and inexpensive. A special service, Aerobus 91, departs every 20 minutes between 7:45 am and 10:30 pm. Tickets from the driver cost €3.50; these are then valid for all local buses for the rest of the day. It stops near major downtown hotels, at Praça Marquês de Pombal, Avenida da Liberdade, Rossio, Praça do Comércio, and Cais do Sodré train station. There is also the Aeroshuttle 96. It runs between

2

TOP REASONS TO GO

World Treasures. Lisbon's Mosteiro dos Jerónimos and Torre de Belém, both UNESCO World Heritage sites, are grand monuments reflecting Portugal's proud seafaring past.

City Sophistication. The Museu Colecção Berardo and Museu Gulbenkian are just two of the museums that make the city a cultural hub.

Victorian Style. Explore Lisbon on ancient trams that wind through narrow cobbled streets where washing flaps from the windows of pastel-color houses and sardines sizzle on the grill.

Old-Fashioned Hospitality. Even in this modern city, shopkeepers and café owners tend to move at a slower pace, and old-fashioned courteousness prevails.

Buzzing Nightlife. Lisbon has a reputation across Europe as a great place to hit the town, with bars and nightclubs often located in stunning riverside settings.

long-distance rail and bus station Gare do Oriente in one direction and Praça de Espanha in the other; the airport is about midway along the route. Cheaper (€1.50) city bus 44 bound for Cais do Sodré via Rossio departs every 15 to 30 minutes between 5 am and 1:40 am from the main road in front of airport arrivals. For a taxi, you'll pay €10 to €15 to get downtown, plus a €1.80 surcharge per item of luggage in the trunk.

Lisbon Airport Contact **General and flight information** (☎ *21/841–3700* *www.ana.pt*).

BUS TRAVEL

Lisbon's main bus terminal is the Gare do Oriente, adjacent to Parque das Nações, also served by rail and metro. Most international and domestic express buses (mostly run by the Rede Expressos company) operate from the Sete Rios terminal, beside the metro and suburban train stations of the same name.

Express Bus Contact **Rede Expressos** (☎ *21/358–1472* ⊕ *www.rede-expressos.pt*).

CAR TRAVEL

Heading in or out by car, there's rapid access to and from points south and east via the Ponte 25 de Abril bridge across the Rio Tejo (Tagus River), although in rush hour the 17-km-long (11-mi-long) Ponte Vasco da Gama is a better option. To and from Porto, the A1 is the fastest route.

The capital's drivers are notorious and parking is difficult, so your rental car is best left in a lot while in town.

FERRY TRAVEL

Ferries across the Rio Tejo are run by Transtejo, from terminals at Belém, Cais do Sodre, and Terreiro do Paço. They offer unique views of Lisbon, and their top decks are a nice way to catch the sun. The 86-cent (loaded onto a 50-cent electronic card) passenger ticket for the prettiest trip, on the car ferry between Belém and Cacilhas, contrasts favorably with the €15–€20 price of the Transtejo cruises that depart daily at 3 from Terreiro do Paço and 4:30 pm from Cais do Sodré between April and October.

Ferry Contact **Transtejo** (☎ *21/882–4674* ⊕ *www.transtejo.pt*).

PUBLIC TRANSPORT TRAVEL

The best way to see central Lisbon is on foot; most points of interest are within the well-defined older quarters. The city's cobblestone sidewalks make walking tiring, even with comfortable shoes, so at some point you'll want to use the public-transportation system, if only to experience the old trams and *elevadores*: funicular railways and elevators linking high and low parts of the city. Like the buses, they are operated by the public transportation company, Carris.

For all these forms of transport, paying as you board means paying around twice as much (€1.50 a ride for the bus and €2.50 the tram), in cash. It's better to buy a 7 Colinas or Viva Viagem debit card, both of which can also be used on the metro and ferries. Buy them at ticket offices, at Carris kiosks (there's on in Praça de Figueira), and at the foot of the Elevador de Santa Justa.

Lisbon's modern metro system (station entrances are marked with a red "M") is cheap and speedy, though it misses out many sights and gets crowded during rush hour and for big soccer matches. You can purchase single tickets or cards for multiple journeys.

The Lisboa Card, a special pass that allows free travel on all public transportation and entry into 27 museums, monuments, and galleries, is valid for 24 hours (€17), 48 hours (€28.50), or 72 hours (€35). It's sold at the airport (in well-signed kiosks), at the Mosteiro dos Jerónimos, in the Lisbon Welcome Centre, at the tourist office in the Palácio Foz, and major hotels and other places around the city. It comes with a free 72-hour Restaurant Card that gives you discounts to a number of leading restaurants.

Carris operates two tourist trams, tickets for each of which are €18: one rattles through the Old Town, the other takes you out to Belém. It also runs two different hop-on, hop-off routes in open-top buses, starting at Praça do Comércio, and costing €15. One circles downtown and stops at the Belém Tower and the Jerónimos Monastery, the other heads east to the Military Museum, Ceramic Tile Museum, and Parque das Nações. These special trams and buses depart from Praça do Comércio, starting about 10 am. ⚠ **Avoid using public transportation, especially the 28 tram, during rush hours. Pickpockets ply their trade on crowded trains, buses, and trams.**

Carris Contacts **Carris information line** (☎ *21/361–3000* ⊕ *www.carris.pt*). **Carristur** (☎ *96/629–8558* ⊕ *www.carristur.pt*).

Metro **Metropolitano de Lisboa** (☎ *21/361–3054* ⊕ *www.metrolisboa.pt*).

TAXI TRAVEL

Taxis in Lisbon are relatively cheap, and the airport is so close to the city center that many visitors make a beeline for a cab queue outside the terminal. To avoid any hassle over fares you can buy a prepaid voucher (which includes gratuity and luggage charges) from the tourist office booth in the arrivals hall. Expect to pay €10–€20 to most destinations in the city center and around €40 if you're headed for Estoril or Sintra.

Drivers use meters but can take out-of-towners for a ride, literally, by not taking the most direct route. If you book a cab from a hotel or restaurant, have someone speak to the driver so there are no "misunderstandings" about your destination. The meter starts at €2 during the day and €2.50 at night (9 pm to 6 am) and during weekends. You pay what is on the meter. Supplementary charges are added for luggage (€1.60) and if you phone for a cab (€0.80). The meter generally isn't used for journeys outside Lisbon, so you'll have to agree on a fare.

You may hail cruising vehicles, but it's sometimes difficult to get drivers' attention; there are taxi stands at most main squares. Remember that when the green light is on, it means the cab is already occupied. Tips—no more than 10%—for reliable drivers are appreciated.

Taxi Companies Autocoope (☎ 21/793–2756). **Rádio Táxis** (☎ 21/811–9000). **Télétaxi** (☎ 21/811–1100).

TRAIN TRAVEL
International and long-distance trains arrive at Santa Apolónia station, to the east of Lisbon's center, after passing through Gare do Oriente, where commuter trains from south of the river, and fast trains from the Algarve also stop. Services to Sintra use Rossio station, a neo-Manueline building just off Rossio square itself. Trains along the Estoril Coast terminate at the waterfront Cais do Sodré station.

EMERGENCIES
If you need medical attention, many doctors speak English. Ask the staff at your hotel or at the embassy to recommend a reliable one. For general problems or in case of theft, the tourism police have an office open 24 hours. If you need to make a claim against your travel insurance, you must file a report there.

One private clinic with English-speaking staff is Clínica Médica Internacional de Lisboa. Also, you can contact the British Hospital. Public hospitals include Hospital São José, Hospital de São Francisco Xavier, and Hospital Santa Maria.

Emergency Contacts Ambulance (☎ 21/942–1111). **Fire** (☎ 21/342–2222). **General emergencies** (☎ 112). **Police** (☎ 21/765–4242). **Tourism Police** (✉ Palácio Foz, Restauradores ☎ 21/342–1623).

Hospitals British Hospital (✉ Rua Tomás da Fonseca, Edifício B, Torres de Lisboa1600-209 ☎ 21/721–3400 ⊕ bh.gpsaude.pt). **Clínica Médica Internacional de Lisboa** (✉ Av. António Augusto de Aguiar 40 R/C, Marquês de Pombal ☎ 21/351–3310 ⊕ www.cmil.pt). **Hospital Santa Maria** (✉ Av. Prof. Egas Moniz, Campo Grande ☎ 21/780–5111 ⊕ www.hsm.min-saude.pt). **Hospital de São Francisco Xavier** (✉ Estrada do Forte do Alto do Duque, Belém ☎ 21/300–0300 ⊕ www.hsfxavier.min-saude.pt). **Hospital São José** (✉ Rua José António Serrano, Saldanha ☎ 21/884–1000 ⊕ www.chlc.min-saude.pt).

TOUR OPTIONS

Beware of unauthorized guides who approach you outside popular monuments and attractions: they're usually more concerned with "guiding" you to a particular shop or restaurant.

BUS TOURS

Many companies organize half-day tours of Lisbon and its environs and full-day trips to more distant places of interest. Reservations can be made through any travel agency or hotel; some tours will pick you up at your door. A half-day tour of Lisbon will cost from €30. As well as its city tram and bus tours, public transport company Carris also does a half-day tour of Sintra, Cascais, and the stunning coast between them. A full-day trip north to Obidos, perhaps also including Batalha, Alcobaça, Nazaré, and Fátima will be from €60 or €75 including lunch, as will a full day east on the "Roman Route" to Évora and Monsaraz. Several of these companies also organize hop-on, hop-off tours of Lisbon, similar to those Carris offers, with open-top buses departing from the north side of Praça Marquês de Pombal. Cascais-based Guincho Aventours offers not only night tours of Lisbon but has off-road buggies for exploring the countryside outside the city, as well as bicycles for hire.

Operators **Carristur** (☎ 96/629–8558 ⊕ www.carristur.pt). **Cityrama** (✉ Av. Duque d'Avila 116-B, Saldanha ☎ 21/319–1085, 303/394–6920 via Gray Line in U.S. ⊕ www.cityrama.pt). **Cool Tour Lx** (☎ 21/395–1624 ⊕ www.cooltourlx. com). **Dianatours** (☎ 21/799–8540 ⊕ www.dianatours.pt). **Guincho Aventours** (☎ 93/447–9075 ⊕ www.guinchotours.net). **Inside Lisbon** (☎ 96/841–2612 ⊕ www.insidelisbon.com). **Mr. Friend** (☎ 21/895–4083 ⊕ www.mrfriend.pt). **Rota Monumental** (☎ 91/630–6682 ⊕ www.rotamonumental.com).

PRIVATE GUIDES

For names of personal guides, contact Lisbon's main tourist office or AGIC, the Association of Guide Interpreters). They can provide an English-speaking guide for half-day (from €55) or full-day (from €95) tours; the price remains the same for up to 20 people. Get in touch ahead of time as the office is open only Monday and Thursday 1–5. For private walking tours, see also below.

Contact **AGIC** (✉ Rua do Instituto Bacteriológico 8, Palácio Sant'anna, Sala 32, Campo de Santana ☎ 21/885–5500 ⊕ www.agic-portugal.com.

WALKING TOURS

The local tourist office does not organize tours, but several private outfits such as Inside Lisbon and Cool Tour Lx (⇨ see Bus Tours, above) do, from €12 per person. Lisbon Walker does tailor-made walks and also has the widest range of regular theme tours, such as Jewish Lisbon or espionage. For most you don't need to book; just check the schedule and turn up at the meeting point by the tourist office on Praça do Comércio. Lisbon Explorer, by contrast, specializes in prearranged group and individual tours; it has a U.S. contact number.

Contact **Lisbon Explorer** (☎ 96/921-9059, 304/825–3684 from U.S. ⊕ www.lisbonexplorer.com). **Lisbon Walker** (☎ 21/886–1840 or 96/357–5635 ⊕ www.lisbonwalker.com).

VISITOR INFORMATION

The Lisbon branch of Portugal's tourist office—National Tourism Office (Turismo de Portugal)—is open daily 9–8. It's in the Palácio Foz, at the Baixa end of Avenida da Liberdade. A much more rewarding place to get information is the Lisbon Welcome Center, though you may have to wait patiently in a long line. The good news is that the information desk, which is open daily 9–8, is in a small complex with a café, a restaurant, a gallery, and a few shops. There's also a branch at the airport that's open daily 7 am to midnight. For general inquiries, you can try the Linha Verde Turista toll-free number (☎ *808/781–212*).

For information on all the facilities and events at the Parque das Nações, stop at the information desk on Alameda dos Oceanos, in front of the Vasco da Gama shopping center. The desk is open daily 9:30 to 8.

Visitor Info Lisbon Welcome Center (✉ *Praça do Comércio, Baixa* ☎ *21/031–2810, 21/845–0660 airport branch* ⊕ *www.askmelisboa.com*). **Parque das Nações Information** (✉ *Alameda dos Oceanos, Parque das Nações* ☎ *21/891–9333* ⊕ *www.parquedasnacoes.pt*). **Turismo de Portugal (National Tourism Office)** (✉ *Palácio Foz, Praça dos Restauradores, Restauradores* ☎ *21/346–3314* ⊕ *www.visitportugal.com*.

EXPLORING LISBON

Though the Baixa, or downtown, was Lisbon's government and business center for two centuries until the mid-20th century, the most ancient part of the city lies on the slopes of a hill to its east. Most visitors start their exploration there, in Alfama. All but the very fittest ride the antique 28 *eléctrico* (streetcar) most of the way up to Saint George's Castle (or take the 37 bus or a taxi all the way up). The views from its ramparts afford a crash course in the city's topography. You can then wander downhill to absorb the atmosphere (and more views) in the winding streets below. There are several museums and other major sights in this area, so give yourself plenty of time.

Baixa itself is interesting mostly for its imposing architecture and its bustling squares, as well as an unusual cast-iron elevator that affords yet more panoramic views. But a new design museum is what persuades most visitors to linger.

On the slope to the west is the chic Chiado district, traditionally the city's intellectual centre, with theaters, galleries, and literary cafés. A little farther uphill is the Bairro Alto. Originally founded by the Jesuits (whose church is among Lisbon's finest), it was long known for rather sinful pursuits and today is a great place for bar hopping. Both neighborhoods are great places to shop.

Modern Lisbon, meanwhile, begins just north of Baixa. The city's tree-lined central axis, the Avenida da Liberdade, forges up to the Praça Marquês de Pombal roundabout, with a rather formal park beyond. Dotted around the area north of here are major museums and other sights.

A BIT OF HISTORY

It is Lisbon's geographical location, sitting alongside the wide and natural harbor of the Tejo river, that has made it strategically important as a trading seaport throughout the ages. The city was probably founded around 1200 BC by the Phoenicians, who traded from its port and called it *Alis-Ubo*. The Greeks came next, naming it Olisipo. But it wasn't until 205 BC that Lisbon prospered, when the Romans, calling it in their turn *Felicitas Julia*, linked it by road to the great Spanish cities of the Iberian Peninsula. The Visigoths followed in the 5th century and built the earliest fortifications on the site of the Castelo de São Jorge, but it was with the arrival of the Moors in AD 714 that Lisbon, then renamed *Ascbouna*, came into its own. The city flourished as a trading center during the 300 years of Moorish rule, and the Alfama—Lisbon's oldest district—retains its intricate Arab-influenced layout. In 1147 the Christian army, led by Dom Afonso Henriques and with the assistance of northern Crusaders, took the city after a ruthless siege. To give thanks for the end of Moorish rule, Dom Afonso planned a great cathedral, and the building was dedicated three years later. A little more than a century after that, in 1255, the rise of Lisbon was complete when the royal seat of power was transferred here from Coimbra by Afonso III, and Lisbon was declared capital of Portugal.

The next great period—that of *os descobrimentos* (the discoveries)—began with the 15th-century voyages led by the great Portuguese navigators to India, Africa, and Brazil. During this era, Vasco de Gama set sail for the Indies in 1497–99 and Brazil was discovered in 1500. The wealth realized by these expeditions was phenomenal: gold, jewels, ivory, porcelain, and spices helped finance grand buildings and impressive commercial activity. Late-Portuguese Gothic architecture—called Manueline (after the king Dom Manuel I)—assumed a rich, individualistic style, characterized by elaborate sculptural details, often with a maritime motif. Torre de Belém and the Mosteiro dos Jerónimos (Belém's tower and monastery) are supreme examples of this period.

With independence from Spain in 1640 and assumption of the throne by successive dukes of the house of Bragança, Lisbon became ever more prosperous, only to suffer calamity on November 1, 1755, when it was hit by the last of a series of earthquakes. Two-thirds of Lisbon was destroyed, and tremors were felt as far north as Scotland; 40,000 people in Lisbon died, and entire sections of the city were swept away by a tidal wave.

Under the direction of the prime minister, Sebastião José de Carvalho e Melo, later to be named Marquês de Pombal in reward for his efforts, Lisbon was rebuilt quickly and ruthlessly. The medieval quarters were leveled and replaced with broad boulevards; the commercial center, the Baixa, was laid out in a grid; and the great Praça do Comércio, the riverfront square, was planned. Essentially downtown Lisbon has an elegant 18th-century layout that remains as pleasing today as it was intended to be 250 years ago.

West of the Baixa, along the river, former docklands such as Alcântara are now home to stylish restaurants and nightclubs, as well as the odd museum. Farther west is historic Belém, which boasts yet more museums—and some famous pastries. On the city's eastern flank, the Parque das Nações has family-oriented attractions and green spaces.

ALFAMA

The Moors, who imposed their rule on most of the southern Iberian Peninsula during the 8th century, left their mark on much of Lisbon but nowhere so evidently as in the Alfama district. Here narrow, twisting streets and soaring flights of steps wind up to an imposing castle on one of the city's highest hills. This is a grand place to get your bearings and take in supreme views. Because its foundation is dense bedrock, the district—a jumble of whitewashed houses with flower-laden balconies and red-tile roofs—has survived the wear and tear of the ages, including the great 1755 earthquake.

The timeless alleys and squares have a notoriously confusing layout, but the Alfama is relatively compact, and you'll keep circling back to the same buildings and streets. In the Moorish period this area thrived, and in the 15th century—as evidenced by the ancient synagogue on Beco das Barrelas—it was an important Jewish quarter. Although now a somewhat run-down neighborhood, it has a down-to-earth charm—particularly during the June festivals of the Santos Populares—and smart bars and restaurants are slowly moving in.

GETTING HERE AND AROUND The Alfama's streets and alleys are very steep, and its levels are connected by flights of stone steps, which means it's easier to tour the area from the top down. Take a taxi up to the castle or approach it by Tram 28 from Rua Conceição in the Baixa or Bus 37 from Praça da Figueira. The large terrace next to the church of Santa Luzia, just below the castle, gives a fine overview of the Alfama and the river. There are two metro stations on the southern edge of the neighborhood: Terreiro de Paço and Santa Apolónia.

TIMING Allow two to three hours to walk the Alfama, perhaps more on a hot day, when you'll want to rest on the castle grounds or stop for drinks in a café. A visit to the Museu-Escola de Artes Decorativas will occupy at least an hour or two. Note that most museums are closed Monday, and that churches generally close for a couple of hours in the middle of the day.

TOP ATTRACTIONS

Fodor's Choice ★ Castelo de São Jorge. Although St. George's Castle was constructed by the Moors, the site had previously been fortified by Romans and Visigoths. To your left as you pass through the main entrance is a statue of Dom Afonso Henriques, whose forces in 1147 besieged the castle and drove the Moors from Lisbon. The ramparts offer panoramic views of the city's layout as far as the towering Ponte 25 de Abril suspension bridge; be careful of the uneven footing. Remnants of a palace that was a residence of the kings of Portugal until the 16th century house a snack bar, a small museum showcasing archeological finds, and beyond them a cozy, stately restaurant, the Casa do Leão (☎ 21/888–0154). From the

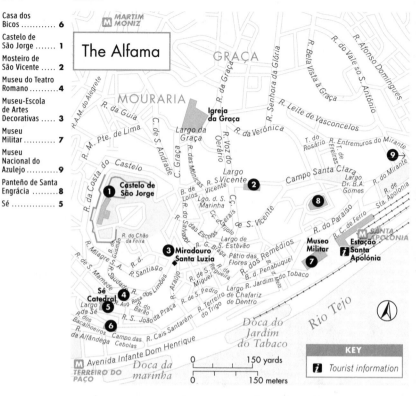

periscópio (periscope) in the Torre de Ulísses, in the castle's keep, you can spy on visitors going about their business below; technical explanations are given in Portuguese, English and Spanish. Beyond the keep, traces of pre-Roman and Moorish houses are visible thanks to recent archeological digs, as well as the remains of a palace founded in the 15th-century. The castle's outer walls encompass a small neighborhood, Castelo, the medieval church of Santa Cruz, restaurants, and souvenir shops. ⊠ *Entrance at Largo do Chão da Feira, Alfama* ☎ *21/880–0620* ⊕ *www.castelodesaojorge.pt* ⊠ *Castle €7* ☉ *Mar.–Oct., daily 9–9; Nov.–Feb., daily 9–6.*

Museu-Escola de Artes Decorativas. The Museum-School of Decorative Arts, in the 17th-century Azurara Palace, has objects that date from the 15th through 19th century. Look for brightly colored Arraiolos—traditional, hand-embroidered Portuguese carpets based on imported Arabic designs—as well as silver work, ceramics, paintings, and jewelry. With so many rich items to preserve, the museum has become a major center for restoration. Crafts such as bookbinding, carving, and cabinetmaking are all undertaken here by highly trained staff; you can view the restoration work by appointment. ⊠ *Largo das Portas do Sol 2, Alfama* ☎ *21/881–4600* ⊠ *€4* ☉ *Wed.–Mon. 10–5.*

Fodor's Choice **Museu Nacional do Azulejo.** To fully understand the craftsmanship
★ that goes into making the ubiquitous azulejos, visit this magnificent
museum at the 16th-century Madre de Deus convent and cloister. Some
of the ceramics exhibited here date from the 1700s. Displays range
from individual glazed tiles to elaborate pictorial panels. The 118-foot
Panorama of Lisbon (1730) is a detailed study of the city and waterfront and is reputedly the country's longest azulejo piece. The richly
furnished convent church contains some sights of its own: of note are
the gilt baroque decoration and lively azulejo works depicting the life
of St. Anthony. There are also a little café-bar and a gift shop that
sells tile reproductions. ⊠ *Rua da Madre de Deus 4 (Bus 104 or 105
from* Ⓜ *Santa Apolónia), Madre de Deus* ☎ *21/810–0340* ⊕ *mnazulejo.
imc-ip.pt* 🎫 *€5* ☉ *Tues. 2–6, Wed.–Sun. 10–6.*

WORTH NOTING

Casa dos Bicos. The House of Spikes, an Italianate dwelling, was built
in 1523 for Bras de Albuquerque, the son of Afonso, who became the
viceroy of India and who conquered Goa and Malacca. It has a striking facade studded with pointed white stones in diamond shapes. The
top two floors were destroyed in the 1755 earthquake, and restoration
did not begin until the early 1980s. Currently closed to the public,
the building is to house the José Saramago Foundation. Set up before
his death in 2010, Saramago is the only Portuguese-language winner
of the Nobel Prize in Literature. ⊠ *Rua dos Bacalhoeiros, Alfama*
Ⓜ *Terreiro do Paço.*

Mosteiro de São Vicente. The Italianate facade of the twin-towered St.
Vincent's Monastery heralds an airy church with a barrel-vault ceiling,
the work of accomplished Italian architect Filippo Terzi (1520–97).
Finally completed in 1704, the church is currently closed for renovation work, but its superbly tiled cloister depicting the fall of Lisbon to
the Moors remains open to visits, as does the former refectory. It now
serves as the pantheon of the Bragança dynasty, who were the first rulers
of an independent Portugal. Only Maria I and Pedro IV are not buried
here. Among the solid tombs and weighty inscriptions lies Catherine
of Bragança, who married Charles II of England in 1661. There's little
to see—save a medieval cistern and a richly decorated entrance hall—
but it's worth the admission fee to climb up to the towers and terrace
for a look over the Alfama, the dome of the nearby Santa Engrácia,
and the river. ⊠ *Largo de São Vicente, Alfama* ☎ *21/882–5652* 🎫 *€4*
☉ *Tues.–Sun. 10–6.*

EN
ROUTE
If you're in Alfama on a Tuesday or Saturday, make sure to take in
the Feira da Ladra flea market, which takes place on Campo de Santa
Clara, from dawn to early afternoon (it runs a bit later on Saturdays).
The quality of the wares on offer varies tremendously, but it's a fun
place for people-watching.

Museu do Teatro Romano. Just uphill from the Sé cathedral, turn left into
Rua da Saudade and ahead of you is one of the few visible traces of
Roman Lisbon: the remains of a small amphitheater that was dedicated
to the emperor Nero. Then step into this free museum (entrances are
opposite the theater on Rua de São Mamede and on the main road

opposite the Sé), which does a good job of describing what is known about the theater using multimedia. ⊠ *Pátio do Aljube 5, Rua Augusto Rosa, Alfama* ☎ *21/882–0320* ⊕ *www.museuteatroromano.pt* ⊙ *Tues.– Sun. 10–1 and 2–6.*

NEED A BREAK?
Hop off Tram 28 at the Miradouro de Santa Luzia, a terrace-garden viewpoint that takes in the Alfama and the river. Here, around the corner at Largo das Portas do Sol and on the roof of a big new car park there are a number of small café-bars with outside seats from which you can watch ships on the Rio Tejo. **Cerca Moura** (⊠ *Largo das Portas do Sol 4, Alfama* ☎ *21/887–4859*) —named after the Moorish walls that surround the district—is the best.

Museu Militar. The spirit of derring-do is palpable in the huge Corinthian-style barracks and arsenal complex of the Military Museum. As you clatter through endless, echoing rooms of weapons, uniforms, and armor, you may be lucky enough to be followed—at a respectful distance—by a guide who, without speaking a word of English, can convey exactly how that bayonet was jabbed or that gruesome flail swung. In this beautifully ornate building there is also a collection of 18th- to 20th-century art. The museum is on the eastern edge of the Alfama, at the foot of the hill and opposite the Santa Apolónia station. It's easy to get here by Bus 9 or Bus 39. ⊠ *Largo de Santa Apolónia, Alfama* ☎ *21/884–2361* ⊠ *€3 (free Fri. 10–noon)* ⊙ *Tues.–Sun. 10–5* Ⓜ *Santa Apolónia.*

Panteão de Santa Engrácia. The large domed edifice immediately behind and below São Vicente is the former church of Santa Engrácia. It took 285 years to build (supposedly because of a curse laid on the works by a Jew wrongly accused of theft in 1630), hence the Portuguese phrase "a job like Santa Engrácia" means one that seems to take forever. Today the building doubles as Portugal's Panteão Nacional (National Pantheon), housing the tombs of Portugal's former presidents as well as cenotaphs dedicated to its most famous explorers and writers. The latest arrival, in 2001, was fado diva Amália Rodrigues, whose tomb is the only one always piled high with flowers from admirers. ⊠ *Campo de Santa Clara, Alfama* ☎ *21/885–4820* ⊠ *€3* ⊙ *Tues.–Sun. 10–5* Ⓜ *Santa Apolónia.*

NEED A BREAK?
For one of Lisbon's loveliest views, take the Tram 28 all the way up to Graça and then walk to the miradouro in front of the local church, the Igreja da Graça, where a kiosk serves snacks and drinks until well past midnight. It's a particularly nice place to watch the sun set over the city.

Sé. Lisbon's austere Romanesque cathedral, Sé (which stands for *Sedes Episcopalis),* was founded in 1150 to commemorate the defeat of the Moors three years earlier; to rub salt in the wound, the conquerors built the sanctuary on the spot where Moorish Lisbon's main mosque once stood. Note the fine rose window, and be sure to visit the 13th-century cloister and the treasure-filled sacristy, which, among other things, contains the relics of the martyr St. Vincent. According to legend, the relics were carried from the Algarve to Lisbon in a ship piloted by ravens; the saint became Lisbon's official patron. ⊠ *Largo da Sé, Alfama*

☎ 21/886–6752 🖂 *Cathedral free, cloister and sacristy €2.50* 🕙 *Cathedral daily 10–7, cloister Mon.– Sat. 10–6, Sun. 2–6; sacristy weekdays 10–1 and 2–5, Sat. 10–5* Ⓜ *Terreiro do Paço.*

**EN
ROUTE** On your way up to the Sé, note the small baroque church on the left: it was built on the birthplace of the man the Catholic Church calls Saint Anthony of Padua, but whom lisboetas just call "Santo António." On his saint's day, June 13, the church hosts mass weddings paid for by the city hall. Most of those present will have been up much of the night, celebrating along with the rest of town the most important of the month's *Santos Populares* festivals. Next door to the saint's church is the Museu Antoniano, with its curious collection of religious and secular items relating to him.

BAIXA

The earthquake of 1755, the massive tidal wave, and subsequent fires killed thousands of people and reduced 18th-century Lisbon to rubble. But within a decade, frantic rebuilding under the direction of the king's minister, the Marquês de Pombal, had given the Baixa, or downtown, a neoclassical look. Full of shops, restaurants, and other commercial enterprises, it today stretches from the riverfront Praça do Comércio to the square known as the Rossio. Pombal intended the various streets to house workshops for certain trades and crafts, something that's still reflected in street names such as Rua dos Sapateiros (Cobblers' Street) and Rua da Prata (Silversmiths' Street). Near the neoclassical arch at the bottom of Rua Augusta you'll find street vendors selling jewelry. Northeast of Rossio, the Rua das Portas de Santo Antão has seafood restaurants, while the area also has three surviving *ginjinha* bars—cubbyholes where local characters throw down shots of cherry brandy. One is in Largo de São Domingos itself, another a few doors up Rua das Portas de Santo Antão, and the third 20 meters (66 feet) east along Rua Barros Queiroz.

**GETTING HERE
AND AROUND** Baixa is Lisbon's downtown, so the area is well served by public transport. Local metro stations include Terreiro do Paço, Baixa-Chiado and Rossio; large numbers of buses also ply the north–south streets of its regular grid, though their stops are all at its northern and southern ends, on Rossio and on or near Praça do Comércio.

TIMING You could walk the Baixa in a half hour, but multiply that by four to allow time to explore the sights and poke into shops. Then add an hour or more for people-watching or lingering in a café, enjoying the Rossio's satisfying chaos.

TOP ATTRACTIONS

Elevador de Santa Justa. Built in 1902 by Raul Mésnier, who studied under Eiffel, the Santa Justa Elevator, inside a Gothic-style tower, is one of Lisbon's more extraordinary structures. After stepping outside the elevator compartment at the upper level, you can either take the walkway leading to the Largo do Carmo, or climb the staircase to the miradouro at the very top of the structure (147½ feet up) for views of the Baixa district and beyond. The elevator return ticket includes

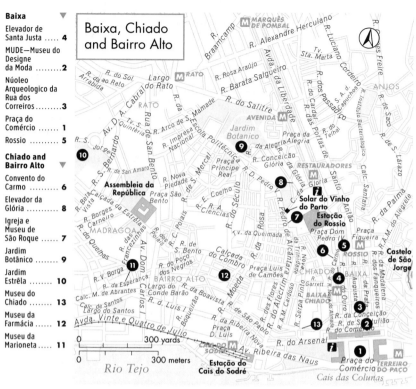

access to the miradouro, as does a Lisboa Card or Aeroshuttle ticket, but if you're using a 7 Colinas swipe card to ride the elevator, you must buy a special €1.50 ticket to climb the last few steps to the miradouro. The same goes for visitors who arrive via the walkway from Largo do Carmo, up in the Bairro Alto. ✉ *Rua Aurea, Baixa* 🖼 *€3 return* ☉ *Daily mid-July–Sept., 7–11, Oct.–mid-July, 7–10* Ⓜ *Baixa-Chiado.*

Praça do Comércio. Known also as the Terreiro do Paço, after the royal palace (the Paço) that once stood here, the Praça do Comércio is lined with 18th-century buildings. Down by the river, steps—once used by occupants of the royal barges that docked here—lead up from the water. On the north side, the Arco Triunfal (Triumphal Arch) was the last structure to be completed in 1873. The equestrian statue in the center is of Dom José I, king at the time of the earthquake and subsequent rebuilding. In 1908, amid unrest that led to the declaration of a republic, King Carlos and his eldest son, Luís Filipe, were assassinated as they rode through the square in a carriage. On the northwest corner the smart **Lisbon Welcome Center** (🖀 *21/031–2810*) has an information desk, craft shops, café, and deli. It's open daily from 9 to 8. The building also houses the **Sala Ogival** (🖀 *21/342–0690* ☉ *Tues.–Sat. 11–7*), a showroom for wine producers' association ViniPortugal, where you can taste Portuguese wines for free. Ⓜ *Terreiro do Paço.*

One of the original buildings on Praça do Comércio houses the **Café Martinho da Arcada** (✉ *Praça do Comércio 3, Baixa* ☎ *21/887–9259*), a literary haunt since 1782, favored by modernist poet Fernando Pessoa. The main rooms contain an expensive restaurant; adjacent to it is a more modest café-bar.

Rossio. Lisbon's main square since the Middle Ages is popularly known as the Rossio, although its official name is Praça Dom Pedro IV (whom the central statue commemorates). Even though it's jammed with traffic, it is a grand space, with ornate French fountains. Public *autos-da-fé* (a Catholic Mass; prayer; a public procession of those found guilty; a reading of their sentences; and most often burning at the stake) of heretics were once carried out here; the site of the Palace of the Inquisition, which oversaw these, is now occupied by the 19th-century Teatro Nacional (National Theater). On nearby Largo de São Domingos, where thousands were burned, is a memorial to Jewish victims of the Inquisition. You'll probably do what the locals do when they come here, though: pick up a newspaper and sit at one of the cafés that line the square, or perhaps have a shoe shiner give your boots a polish—just agree on a price first. Later, if you're daring, pop into the *ginginha* bar here or the other surviving one a few doors up Rua das Portas de Santo Antão—both cubbyholes where unshaven gents and local characters stand around throwing down shots of eye-wateringly strong cherry brandy. Ⓜ *Rossio.*

WORTH NOTING

MUDE—Museu do Design e da Moda. The Portuguese word "mude" is an exhortation to change and that's what this funky design and fashion museum has done to a still rather fussy Baixa. An impressively huge, privately amassed but now city-owned collection of designer gear is displayed here in themed sections in a gutted former bank headquarters. The museum also houses temporary exhibitions on the most varied themes relating to fashion and industrial design. ✉ *Rua Augusta 24, Baixa* ☎ *21/888–6117* ⊕ *www.mude.pt* ✉ *Free* ☉ *Tues.–Thurs. 10–8, Fri. and Sat. 10–10, Sun. 10–8* Ⓜ *Baixa-Chiado or Terreiro do Paço.*

Núcleo Arqueologico da Rua dos Correeiros. If you're in the Baixa on Thursday afternoon or any time on Saturday, make a point of peeping through this amazing window onto the area's past. Underneath a bank headquarters in the middle of the Baixa are Roman remains thought to be of an old fish salting works, back when this area was a river beach. Guided visits underground also offer an insight into how 18th-century builders created foundations on this swampy land for this and other heavy stone buildings put up after the 1755 earthquake. Roman artifacts found during the original archeological dig are on display in the bank's lobby. Opening times periodically change, so try to phone ahead. ✉ *Rua dos Correeiros 9, Baixa* ☎ *21/113–1004* ☉ *Thurs. 3–5, Sat. 10–1 and 10–5* Ⓜ *Baixa-Chiado or Terreiro do Paço.*

CHIADO AND THE BAIRRO ALTO

West of the Baixa is the fashionable shopping district of Chiado. Although a calamitous 1988 fire destroyed much of the area, an ambitious rebuilding program has restored some of the fin de siècle facades. And a chic retail complex, hotel, and metro station on the site of the old Armazéns do Chiado—once Lisbon's largest department store—has given the district a modern focus. Along Rua Garrett and Rua do Carmo are some of Europe's best shoe stores as well as glittering jewelry shops, hip boutiques, and a host of cafés and delis. Chiado's narrow, often-cobbled streets lead to the Bairro Alto and often follow contours of the hills, which can make getting around confusing. Although the settlement of the Bairro Alto dates from the 17th century, most of the buildings are from the 18th and 19th centuries and are an appealing mixture of small churches, warehouses, antiques and art galleries, artisans' shops, and town houses with wrought-iron balconies.

GETTING HERE AND AROUND
Chiado is served by the Baixa-Chiado metro station, with a series of escalators bearing passengers up under Rua Garrett to Largo do Chiado. Tram 28 rumbles through here, on its way between the Baixa and Estrela. Farther uphill, the Bairro Alto can be reached by the Elevador da Glória funicular, which steams up from a standing start on Praça dos Restauradores, at the start of the Avenida da Liberdade, the city's modern central axis. Another approach to the Bairro Alto is from Rato metro station, passing the Jardim Botânico and the Jardim do Príncipe Real on the way.

TIMING
Both Chiado and the Bairro Alto are remarkably compact, and it takes very little time to walk from one end to the other; an hour would cover it. But once you start diving off into the side streets and lingering in the shops, galleries, and bars, you'll find you can happily spend a morning or afternoon here (or an evening, in the case of the late-opening Bairro Alto). Neither the Igreja de São Roque nor the Convento do Carmo will occupy you for more than half an hour, though visitors keen on sacred art may want to spend a bit more time in the Museu de São Roque. Note that on Saturday the Solar do Vinho do Porto doesn't open until 2 pm. If you don't like crowds, avoid the Bairro Alto late at night, especially on weekends, when seemingly the whole of Lisbon comes here to eat, drink, and party.

SAFETY AND PRECAUTIONS
Bairro Alto's streets are filled with the sounds of daily life: children scuffle amid the drying laundry, women carry huge bundles from shop to shop, and old men clog the doorways of barrooms. The neighborhood has always had a reputation as being rather rough-and-ready, and there are still back alleys where it would be unwise to venture after dark. On the whole, however, it's safe to walk around; indeed, the Bairro Alto has more bars, restaurants, fado clubs, and discos than any other district.

TOP ATTRACTIONS

Igreja e Museu de São Roque. Filippo Terzi, the architect who designed São Vicente on the outskirts of the Alfama, was also responsible for this Renaissance church. He was commissioned by Jesuits and completed the church in 1574. Curb your impatience with its plain facade and venture inside. Its eight-sides chapels have statuary and art dating from the early 17th century. The last chapel on the left before the altar is the extraordinary 18th-century Capela de São João Baptista (Chapel of St. John the Baptist): designed and built in Rome, with rare stones and mosaics that resemble oil paintings, the chapel was taken apart, shipped to Lisbon, and reassembled here in 1747. You may find a guide who will escort you around the church and switch on the appropriate lights so the beauty of the chapel is revealed. Adjoining the church, the Museu de São Roque displays a surprisingly engaging collection of clerical vestments and liturgical objects: the capes and drapes are delicately embroidered in gold, and the jewel-encrusted crosses and goblets glitter in their cases. The museum was recently renovated and now has a stylish café with terrace, serving light gourmet meals and snacks; they also do weekend brunches. ⊠ *Largo Trindade Coelho, Bairro Alto* ☏ *21/323–5421* ⊕ *www.museudesaoroque.com* ✉ *Church free; museum €2.50 Mon.–Sat., free Sun.* ☉ *Church Mon. 2–6 pm, Tues., Wed., Fri.– Sun. 9–6, Thurs. 9–9; museum Fri.–Wed. 10–6, Thurs. 2–9* Ⓜ *Baixa-Chiado or Restauradores (then Elevador da Glória).*

WORTH NOTING

Convento do Carmo. The Carmelite Convent—once Lisbon's largest—was all but ruined by the 1755 earthquake. Its sacristy houses the **Museu Arqueológico do Carmo** (Archaeological Museum), a small collection of ceramic tiles, medieval tombs, ancient coins, and other city finds. The lovely square outside—accessible via a walkway from the top of the Elevador da Santa Justa (see below)—is a great place to dawdle over a coffee. ⊠ *Largo do Carmo, Chiado* ☏ *21/347–8629* ✉ *€3.50* ☉ *June– Sept., Mon.–Sat. 10–7; Oct.–May, Mon.–Sat. 10–6.* Ⓜ *Baixa-Chiado or Rossio (then Elevador de Santa Justa).*

Elevador da Glória. One of the finest approaches to the Bairro Alto is via this funicular railway inaugurated in 1888 on the western side of Avenida da Liberdade, near Praça dos Restauradores. It runs up the steep hill and takes only about a minute to reach the São Pedro de Alcântara Miradouro, a viewpoint that looks out over the castle and the Alfama. There are two similar funiculars in central Lisbon, the Elevador da Bica, which steams up from Cais do Sodré to the Bairro Alto, and the Elevador do Lavra, which rises steeply up a hill off the Rua das Portas de Santo Antão, near Praça dos Restauradores. ⊠ *Calçada da Glória, Bairro Alto* ✉ *€3 return* ☉ *Mon.–Thurs. 7 am–midnight, Fri. 7 am– 2 am, Sat 8:30 am–2 am, Sun. 9 am–midnight* Ⓜ *Restauradores.*

Jardim Botânico. Lisbon's main botanical garden was first laid out in 1874. Hidden behind the University's small Museu de História Natural (☏ *21/392–1825* ⊕ *www.mnhn.ul.pt*) about 2 km (1 mi) north of the Bairro Alto, the garden makes a restful stop, with 10 acres of paths, benches, and nearly 15,000 species of subtropical plants. ⊠ *Rua da Escola Politécnica 58, Rato* ☏ *21/396–1893* ⊕ *www.jb.ul.pt* ✉ *Garden €1.50, Natural History Museum €4* ☉ *Garden Apr.–Oct., week-days 9–8, weekends 10–8; Nov.–Mar., weekdays 9–6, weekends 10–6. Museum Tues.–Fri. 10–5, weekends 10–6* Ⓜ *Rato.*

OFF THE
BEATEN
PATH

Jardim da Estrêla. Inside the attractively laid out Estrêla Garden, old men sit at tables playing card games. Watch them a while, stroll the shaded paths, and then pull up a chair in the café for a drink or a snack. Towering over the southwestern side is the 18th-century **Basílica da Estrêla**, which is open daily 8 am–12:30 pm and 3–7:30 pm. This spacious baroque basilica has an unusually restrained interior and offers views of the city from its *zimbório* (dome). The gardens lie on the western edge of the Bairro Alto. You can walk here, although it's more pleasant to catch Tram 28, which runs from Praça Luís de Camões, just west of Largo do Carmo; you'll pass through the São Bento district, dominated by Portugal's grand parliament building, yet another former monastery, on the way. Ⓜ *Rato.*

Museu da Farmácia. The Museum of Pharmacy, within an old palace, covers more than 5,000 years of pharmaceutical history, from prehistoric cures to the fantastic world of fictive potions à la Harry Potter. Ancient objects related to pharmaceutical science and art—from Mesopotamia, Egyptian, Roman, and Incan civilizations—are on display in well-lighted showcases, as are those from Europe. Whole pharmacies have been transported here intact from other parts of Portugal, even a traditional 19th-century Chinese drugstore from Portugal's former territory of Macau. Call ahead to arrange lunch in the very elegant restaurant with excellent food. A very convenient feature of the museum is that it has a private parking lot. ✉ *Rua Marechal Saldanha 1, Chiado* 📞 *21/340–0682* 💶 *€5* 🕐 *Weekdays 10–6 and last Sun. of each month 2–5* Ⓜ *Baixa-Chiado.*

Museu do Chiado. The Chiado's prime art gallery—built on the site of a monastery—specializes in Portuguese art from 1850 to the present day, covering various movements: romanticism, naturalism, surrealism, modernism. The museum also hosts international films and temporary exhibitions of paintings, sculpture, and multimedia installations. ✉ *Rua Serpa Pinto 4, Chiado* 📞 *21/343–2148* 🌐 *www.museudochiado-ipmuseus.pt* 💶 *€4, free Sun. until 2 pm* 🕐 *Tues.–Sun. 10–6* Ⓜ *Baixa-Chiado.*

OFF THE
BEATEN
PATH

Museu da Marioneta. The intricate workmanship that went into the creation of the puppets on display at this museum is remarkable, and it's not just kids' stuff, either: during the Salazar regime, puppet shows were used to mock the pretensions and corruption of the politicians. The collection encompasses both Portuguese and foreign figurines. Those from Santo Aleixo in the Alentejo region (just south of Lisbon) are particularly notable, measuring just over 6 inches high. Puppet shows are often staged in the former chapel at varying times; check the Web site or phone for details. The Museu da Marioneta is in the old fishermen's district of Madragoa, not far from the Museu Nacional de Arte Antiga. ✉ *Convento das Bernardas, Rua da Esperança 146, Madragoa* 📞 *21/394–2810* 🌐 *www.museudamarioneta.pt* 💶 *€3* 🕐 *Tues.–Sun. 10–1 and 2–6 (last entrance 30 min before closing time).*

NEED A
BREAK?

For an Italian-style ice cream with local tradition, drop into **Santini Chiado** (✉ *Rua do Carmo 9, Chiado* 📞 *21/346-8431* 🌐 *www.pasteisdebelem.pt* 🕐 *Open daily 10 am–midnight*), the new Lisbon branch of a family concern

2

founded in 1949 in the nearby resort of Cascais. The *travesseiros* (egg pastries) and *tarte de amêndoa* (almond tart) are also worth trying, as is the self-proclaimed World's Best Chocolate Cake (actually a meringue concoction) supplied by another famous local company.

THE MODERN CITY

The attractions of 19th- to 21st-century Lisbon are as diverse as they are far-flung. Near the large square Praça dos Restauradores, north of Rossio, the southern reaches of the modern city echo some of the Baixa. With its 10 parallel rows of trees, Avenida da Liberdade is an enchanting place in which to linger and an easy-to-find reference point if you get lost in the surrounding backstreets. North of the city's main park, Parque Eduardo VII, the modern city stretches into residential suburbs with only the occasional attraction.

GETTING HERE AND AROUND — Unlike the Baixa, this area cannot be covered easily on foot. You can reach all its sights by metro, in some cases by bus or, if time is short, by taxi.

TIMING — In expansive, modern Lisbon, choosing sights according to your mood and the weather isn't out of line. You really will have to make choices about what to visit if you have just one day—to see everything, allow two or three days. It could take three hours to do justice to the Gulbenkian alone—especially if you have lunch on the premises. The palace and its gardens justify another hour easily; add another for walking (or two if you eschew any travel by taxis or metro), and perhaps another hour for shopping and a coffee break on the Avenida da Liberdade.

TOP ATTRACTIONS

Fodor's Choice ★ — **Museu Calouste Gulbenkian.** On its own lush grounds, the museum of the celebrated Calouste Gulbenkian Foundation, a cultural trust, houses treasures collected by Armenian oil magnate Calouste Gulbenkian (1869–1955) and donated to Portugal in return for tax concessions. The collection is split in two: one part is devoted to Egyptian, Greek, Roman, Islamic, and Asian art and the other to European acquisitions. Both holdings are relatively small, but the quality of the pieces is magnificent, and you should aim to spend at least two hours here. English-language notes are available throughout. Varied and interesting temporary exhibitions are also often staged in the Foundation's main building. In the gardens outside the Fundação Calouste Gulbenkian at **Centro de Arte Moderna**, sculptures hide in every recess. You may want to spend a little time here before following signs to the Modern Art Center—the 20th-century art collection of the Calouste Gulbenkian Foundation, which has at its disposal the finest collection of contemporary and modern Portuguese art, as well as many British works from the same period—a legacy of the foothold the foundation retains in London. There are varied and interesting temporary exhibitions as well as changing displays from this permanent collection. If it's all too much to take in at one time, break up your visit with a stop in the main museum's basement café-restaurant. There's also a large shop that sells posters and postcards. ⊠ *Av. de Berna 45, Praça de Espanha* ☎ *21/782–3000* ⊕ *www. museu.gulbenkian.pt* 🖱 *€4, temporary exhibitions €4–€5, combined ticket €5, combined ticket Museum with Modern Art Center €5, combined ticket for all €7; free Sun.* ☉ *Tues.–Sun. 10–5:45* Ⓜ *São Sebastião or Praça de Espanha.*

DOWN DEEP

Free concerts are given some Sundays at noon in the library atrium, and the foundation also has two concert halls, where there is a full season of classical performances of all kinds. Modestly priced tickets are available at the box office.

OFF THE BEATEN PATH

Palácio dos Marqueses da Fronteira. Built in the late 17th century, the Palace of the Marquises, often called the Palácio Fronteira, remains one of the capital's most beautiful houses, containing splendid reception rooms with 17th- and 18th-century tiles, contemporary furniture, and paintings. Note that visits to this still-family-owned property may be limited to guided tours; phone ahead for information. The grounds harbor a terraced walk, a topiary garden, and statuary and fountains. Some of the city's finest azulejos adorn the fountains and terraces and depict hunting scenes, battles, and religious themes. The palace is tricky to reach by public transport; Bus 70 stops nearby but a taxi might be your best bet. ⊠ *Largo de São Domingo de Benfica 1, São Domingo de Benfica* ☎ *21/778–2023* 🖱 *Palace and gardens €7.50; gardens €3* ☉ *June–Sept., Mon.–Sat. for guided tours (must be booked in advance for groups only) at 10:30, 11, 11:30, and noon; Oct.–May, Mon.–Sat. 11 am and noon* Ⓜ *Jardim Zoológico (then 20-min walk or bus 70).*

WORTH NOTING

Aqueduto das Aguas Livres. Lisbon was formerly provided with clean drinking water by means of the Aqueduct of Free Waters (1729–48), built by Manuel da Maia and stretching for more than 18 km (11 mi) from the water source on the outskirts of the city. It survived the 1755 earthquake. The most imposing section is the 35 arches that stride across the Alcântara river valley beyond the Amoreiras shopping complex: the largest of these is said to be the highest ogival (pointed) arch in the world. There is another more accessible section of 14 arches that soar 200 feet over the pretty neighborhood square of Praça das Amoreiras. The aqueduct is not currently open for visits, but the Praça das Amoreiras is also the site of the associated Mãe d'Agua, an internal reservoir capable of holding more than a million gallons of water. This extraordinary structure is occasionally used for art exhibitions and other cultural displays, giving you the chance to view the vast holding tank, the lavish internal waterfall, and the associated machinery. ☎ *21/810–0215 for exhibition information.*

Avenida da Liberdade. In the Restauradores neighborhood, Liberty Avenue—downtown's spine—was laid out in 1879. What started as an elegant rival to the Champs Élysées has lost some of its allure: many of the late-19th-century mansions and art deco buildings that once graced it have been demolished; others have been turned into soulless office blocks. There are, however, still some high-class hotels on the lower and mid-level sections, mixed in with international fashion outlets. Vehicles roar down both sides. It's still worth a leisurely stroll up the

1½-km (1-mi) length of the avenue, from Praça dos Restauradores to the Parque Eduardo VII, at least once—if only to cool off with a drink in one of the *esplanadas* (garden cafés). There are several amid the plane trees in the middle of the avenue. Halfway up and on the avenue's western side, the few theaters that make up Lisbon's surviving downtown theater district congregate in Parque Mayer. Ⓜ *Avenida.*

Fundação Arpad Szenes—Vieira da Silva. Just to the north of Bairro Alto, the old Amoreiras district with its shaded garden was the site of an 18th-century attempt at industrialization under enlightened autocrat the Marquês de Pombal. Today, a stylishly adapted former royal silk factory is dedicated to Portuguese modernist painter Helena Vieira da Silva (1908–92) and her Hungarian-born husband (1897–1985), both of whom worked mainly in Paris. The museum not only showcases works from its own collection, but often stages interesting exhibitions featuring pieces by Picasso, Chagal, and others from that time. ✉ *Praça das Amoreiras 58, Rato* ☎ *21/388–0044* ⊕ *www.fasvs.pt* 🎫 *€3; free Sun. 10–2* ⏰ *Tues.–Sun. 10–8* Ⓜ *Rato.*

Fundação Medeiros e Almeida. One of central Lisbon's best-kept secrets, this museum displays just part of a staggeringly rich private collection of furniture, porcelain, clocks, paintings, gold, and jewelry. In all, some 2,000 pieces are on show on two floors of the lovely 19th-century mansion where the eponymous collector once lived (a building that had previously been the Vatican's embassy in Portugal). ✉ *Rua Rosa Araújo 41, Avenida da Liberdade* ☎ *21/354–7892* ⊕ *www. fundacaomedeirosealmeida.pt* 🎫 *€5, guided tours €6* ⏰ *Weekdays 1–530, Sat. 10–5:30* Ⓜ *Marquês de Pombal.*

ↂ **Jardim Zoológico.** With a menagerie of 2,000 animals from more than 370 species, the Zoological Garden is a popular spot with kids. Admission is pricey, but covers all attractions except the miniature train. In addition to the usual habitats and enclosures there is a gorilla house, free range–style areas for larger animals such as the newly arrived cheetahs, a children's zoo with miniature houses and small animals, a cable-car ride, and twice-daily animal shows (you have your pick of those that feature parrots, pelicans, dolphins, sea lions, or reptiles). You can pack a picnic lunch or eat at one of the on-site snack bars and restaurants. ✉ *Praça Marechal Humberto Delgado, Sete Rios* ☎ *21/723–2910* ⊕ *www.zoo.pt* 🎫 *Children 3–11 €12.50, adults €17* ⏰ *Daily 10–6* Ⓜ *Jardim Zoológico.*

Praça de Touros de Campo Pequeno. Nothing grabs your attention quite so suddenly as the city's circular, redbrick, Moorish-style bullring, built in 1892. The recently renovated ring holds about 9,000 people who crowd in to watch Portuguese-style bullfights (in which the bull is never killed in the ring), held every Thursday at 10 pm from Easter through September. It's also used as a venue for concerts and other events. Tickets for all are sold from a booth in the new shopping mall under the building, which is open daily 10 am–11 pm. (On show nights only, the little ticket windows on either side of the bullring's main gate are also open.) ✉ *Av. da República* ☎ *21/782–0572 ticket office* ⊕ *www.campopequeno.com* Ⓜ *Campo Pequeno.*

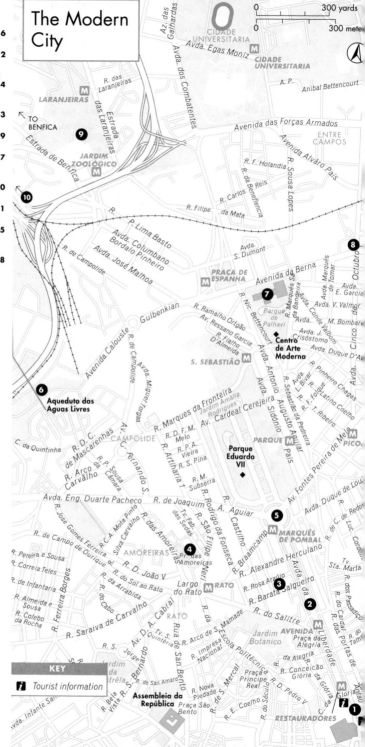

The Modern
City

2

Praça dos Restauradores. This square, which is adjacent to Rossio train station, marks the beginning of modern Lisbon. Here the broad, tree-lined Avenida da Liberdade starts its northwesterly ascent. *Restauradores* means "restoration," and the square commemorates the 1640 uprising against Spanish rule that restored Portuguese independence. An obelisk (raised in 1886) commemorates the event. Note the elegant 18th-century Palácio Foz on the square's west side. Before World War I, it contained a casino; today it houses a national tourist office, the tourist police, and a shop selling reproductions from the country's state museums. The only building to rival the palace is the restored Éden building, just to the south. This art deco masterpiece of Portuguese architect Cassiano Branco now contains the VIP Éden apartment-hotel. Ⓜ *Restauradores.*

Praça Marquês de Pombal. Dominating the center of Marquês de Pombal Square is a statue of the marquis himself, the man responsible for the design of the "new" Lisbon that emerged from the ruins of the 1755 earthquake. On the statue's base are representations of both the earthquake and the tidal wave that engulfed the city; a female figure with outstretched arms signifies the joy at the emergence of the refashioned city. The square is effectively a large roundabout and a useful orientation point, since it stands at the northern end of Avenida da Liberdade with Parque Eduardo VII just behind, and the metro station here is an interchange between two lines. The **Parque Eduardo VII** is worth a visit if you're walking in the area. Established at the beginning of the 20th century in the São Sebastião district, the city's main park was named to honor the British monarch's 1902 visit here during his brief reign. The sloping, formal gardens are used by surprisingly few of Lisbon's residents. There are, however, magnificent views from the avenue at the top of the park, where modernistic towers topped by concrete wheat sheaves stand like sentinels. Just across the road, the landscaped Jardim Amália Rodrigues, inaugurated in 2000 in honor of the fado diva, has a stylish café, the Linha d'Água (☎ *21/381–4327*), with decking by a pretty pool. Ⓜ *Parque or Marquês de Pombal.*

OFF THE BEATEN PATH

For a glimpse into a strange local cult, take the Elevador da Lavra funicular up from the top end of Rua das Porta de Santo Antão and walk north to the Campo dos Mártires de Pátria (known by its original name of Campo de Santana). Just outside the Faculty of Medicinal Sciences, you'll find flowers and inscribed marble tablets heaped at the foot of a statue to 19th-century medic Sousa Martins. The good doctor won such devotion in his lifetime for his work helping the poor and sick that, though he himself was not notably religious, people pray to him to cure illnesses as if he were a Catholic saint.

ALCÂNTARA AND BELÉM

The old port district of Alcântara got a face-lift in the 1990s, and since then it has been a nightlife hub, as well as a great place to relax by the river on warm days. The inauguration in 2008 of the Museu do Oriente marked the advent of one of Lisbon's most enticing tourist attractions.

Farther west, some of Lisbon's grandest monuments and museums are in the district of Belém (the Portuguese word for Bethlehem). It was from here that the country's great explorers set out during the period of the discoveries. The wealth brought back from the New World helped pay for many of the neighborhood's structures, some of which are the best examples of the uniquely Portuguese late-Gothic architecture known as Manueline. The area's historical attractions are complemented by the modern and contemporary art and performances showcased in Lisbon's largest cultural center.

GETTING HERE AND AROUND

Although several buses and Tram 18 will get you here from Lisbon's center, the 30-minute ride on Tram 15 (plied by both antique and modern models) from the Baixa district's Praça do Comércio is very scenic. Tram 15 also passes close by or stops right at several of the important sights. An alternative way to reach Belém is by rail from Cais do Sodré station, but make sure you're on a stopping rather than a fast train. For €6.50, you can also take a 20-minute tour of the area in a horse-drawn carriage run by **Q Tour** (☎ 309/827–096 ⊕ *www.qtour.pt* ۩ *Tues.–Sun. winter 9:30–7, summer 1:30–5:30*) from the eastern side of Praça do Império.

TIMING

Set aside two or three hours for the Museu Nacional de Arte Antiga and another hour or two for the Mosteiro dos Jerónimos. This leaves an hour or two for one of the other museums and monuments—after that, you'll probably want to just flop into a chair at an Alcântara district bar or restaurant. Note that most of Belém's sights are closed Monday. Sunday morning sees free or reduced admission at many attractions.

TOP ATTRACTIONS

Fodor's Choice ★

Mosteiro dos Jerónimos. Conceived and commissioned by Dom Manuel I, who petitioned the Holy See for permission to build it in 1496, Belém's famous Jerónimos Monastery was financed largely by treasures brought back from Africa, Asia, and South America. Construction began in 1502 under the supervision of Diogo de Boitaca.

This UNESCO World Heritage Site is a supreme example of the Manueline style of building (named after King Dom Manuel I), which represented a marked departure from the prevailing Gothic. Much of it is characterized by elaborate sculptural details, often with a maritime motif. João de Castilho was responsible for the southern portal, which forms the main entrance to the church: the figure on the central pillar is Henry the Navigator. Inside, the spacious interior contrasts with the riot of decoration on the six nave columns and complex latticework ceiling. This is the resting place of both explorer Vasco de Gama and national poet Luís de Camões. Don't miss the Gothic- and Renaissance-style double cloister, also designed to stunning effect by Castilho. The Hieronymite community lived in the monastery for more than 400 years until the dissolution of religious orders in 1833. ⊠ *Praça do Império, Belém* ☎ *21/362–0034* ⊕ *www.mosteirojeronimos.pt* ☒ *Church free, cloister €7, €10 combination ticket includes Torre de Belém, €13 includes Torre and Palacio de Ajuda* ☉ *May–Sept., Tues.–Sun. 10–6; Oct.–Apr., Tues.–Sun. 10–5.*

For a real taste of Lisbon, stop at the **Antiga Confeitaria de Belém** (⊠ *Rua de Belém 84-92, Belém* ☎ *21/363-7423* ⊕ *www.pasteisdebelem.pt*), a bakery shop-café that serves delicious, warm custard pastries sprinkled with cinnamon and powdered sugar. Such *pastéis de nata* are sold throughout Lisbon, but those made here, since 1837, are reputed to be the best.

Fodor'sChoice ★ **Museu Nacional de Arte Antiga.** On the route from the center of Lisbon to Belém is the Ancient Art Museum, the only institution in the city to approach the status of the Gulbenkian. Housed in a 17th-century palace once owned by the Counts of Alvor and vastly enlarged in 1940 when it took over the Convent of St. Albert, the museum has a beautifully displayed collection of Portuguese art—mainly from the 15th through 19th century.

The religious works of the Flemish-influenced Portuguese school stand out, especially Nuno Gonçalves' masterpiece, the *St. Vincent Panels.* Painted between 1467 and 1470, the altarpiece has six panels believed to show the patron saint of Lisbon receiving the homage of king, court, and citizens (although there are other theories). Sixty figures have been identified, including Henry the Navigator; the archbishop of Lisbon; and sundry dukes, fishermen, knights, and religious figures. In the top left corner of the two central panels is a figure purported to be Gonçalves himself.

The museum also boasts early Flemish works that influenced the Portuguese, and other European artists are well represented, such as Hieronymous Bosch, Hans Holbein, Brueghel the Younger, and Diego Velázquez. There are also extensive collections of French silver, Portuguese furniture and tapestries, Asian ceramics, and items fashioned from Goan ivory.

Trams 15 and 18 from Praça do Comércio drop you at the foot of a steep flight of steps below the museum. Otherwise, Buses 727 from Praça Marquês de Pombal, 60 from Praça Martim Moniz, and 713 from Praça do Comércio run straight to Rua das Janelas Verdes; coming from Belém, you can pick the 727 up across from the Jerónimos monastery. ⊠ *Rua das Janelas Verdes, Lapa* ☎ *21/391–2800* ⊕ *www.mnarteantiga-ipmuseus.pt* ☒ *€5, free Sun. to 2 pm* ☉ *Tues. 2–6, Wed.–Sun. 10–6.*

Torre de Belém. The openwork balconies and domed turrets of the fanciful Belém Tower make it perhaps the country's purest Manueline structure. It was built between 1514 and 1520 on what was an island in the middle of the Rio Tejo, to defend the port entrance, and dedicated to St. Vincent, the patron saint of Lisbon. Today the chalk-white tower stands near the north bank—evidence of the river's changing course. Cross the wood gangway and walk inside, not so much to see the plain interior but rather to climb the steps to the very top for a bird's-eye view of river and city. However, the best views of the tower are from the nearby Padrão dos Descobrimentos or from the trendy esplanade À Margem

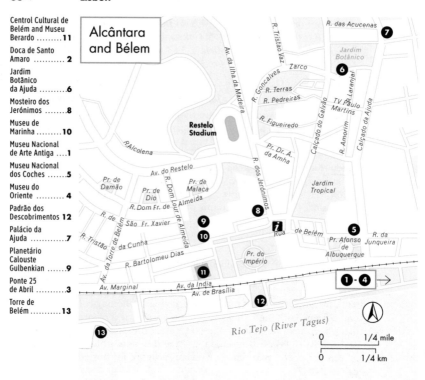

(☎ 91/782 4149) on the Doca do Bom Sucesso, midway between the two. ⊠ *Av. de Brasília, Belém* ☎ *21/362–0034* 🎫 *€5* ⏱ *Oct.–Apr., Tues.–Sun. 10–5; May–Sept., Tues.–Sun. 10–6.30.*

WORTH NOTING

Centro Cultural de Belém and Museu Berardo. Built of pink granite and marble, the modern Belém Cultural Center won few friends when it was constructed in 1991, although all of Lisbon appreciates its cultural offerings. As well as a packed program of classical and popular music, theater and dance in its two auditoriums, and its outdoor events, since 2007 the CCB has also been home to the Museu Berardo, a showcase for one of Europe's most important private collections of modern art. Works from this treasure house—which range from Picasso through Warhol to Portugal's own Paula Rego—are regularly rotated through the galleries and there are also excellent visiting exhibitions. The complex has a restaurant and several cafés. Its roof gardens and terrace bar afford fine views of the Mosteiro dos Jerónimos and the Rio Tejo. ⊠ *Praça do Império, Belém* ☎ *21/361–2400* ⊕ *www.ccb.pt* 🎫 *Museum free* ⏱ *Museum Sun.–Fri. 10–7, Sat. 10–10 (last entry 30 min before closing).*

Doca de Santa Amaro. The docks are alive with music in Alcântara, where late-night bars attract Lisbon's young—and young at heart. Here, in the lee of the huge Ponte 25 de Abril, the old wharves have been made over, and you can walk from here along the landscaped riverfront all the way to Belém (a 30-minute stroll). At Doca de Santo Amaro, invariably known to locals simply as "Docas"—the docks—a line of swanky restaurants and clubs has emerged from the shells of former warehouses. These establishments are often more fashionable than culinary, though, and the constant rumble of cars passing over the bridge combined with occasional low-level airplanes preparing to land may disrupt your dining experience. Either way, the people-watching and potential for late-night mirth are extraordinary. On the terrace in front of the marina, the party goes on until late into the night. During the day, the easiest way to get here is by train from Cais do Sodré station or on Tram 15; at night, take a taxi.

Jardim Botânico da Ajuda. Portugal's oldest botanical garden—laid out in 1768 by the Italian botanist Domenico Vandelli (1735–1816)—is an enjoyable place to spend an hour or so. You can stroll up here from the river at Belém, or take Tram 18 from downtown (it terminates near here). The many species of flora, labeled in Latin, are in several greenhouses covering 4 acres; if you call in advance, you may be able to arrange a guided tour. The larger Jardim Botânico Tropical at the bottom of the hill, whose entrance is just opposite the Mosterio dos Jerónimos, was created later and contains hundreds of species from the Azores, Madeira, and Portugal's former colonies. ⊠ *Calçada da Ajuda, Ajuda* ☎ *21/362–2503* ✉ *Weekdays €2, weekends €1.50* ⊙ *Thurs.–Tues. 10–5.*

Museu de Marinha. In a complex of buildings adjoining the Mosteiro dos Jerónimos is the large, inviting Maritime Museum. Here you get a real grasp of the importance of the seafaring tradition in Portugal through maps and maritime codes, navigational equipment, full-size and model ships, uniforms, and weapons. ⊠ *Praça do Império, Belém* ☎ *21/362–0019* ✉ *€4, free Sun. 10–1* ⊙ *Apr.–Sept., Tues.–Sun. 10–6; Oct.–Mar., Tues.–Sun. 10–5.*

Museu do Oriente. Housed in a former *bacalhau* (salted cod) cold store with impressive bas reliefs on its facade, the Museu do Oriente is one of the most important Lisbon institutions to open in recent years. Funded by the Fundação Oriente (a legacy of colonial Macao and its gaming revenues), this dockside giant seeks both to tell the story of the centuries-long Portuguese presence in Asia and to provide a showcase for Asian cultures. Highlights of the permanent collections include unique maps and charts from the golden age of Portuguese maritime exploration and stunning Chinese and Japanese painted screens. The museum hosts excellent inexpensive concerts in its cozy auditorium, and organizes a plethora of cooking and crafts workshops. Its restaurant serves Asian dishes and has fantastic river views. ⊠ *Av. Brasília, Doca de Alcântara (Norte), Alcântara* ☎ *21/358–5200* ⊕ *www.museudooriente. pt* ✉ *€5, free Fri. 6–10 pm* ⊙ *Tues.–Thurs. and weekends 10–6, Fri. 10–10 (last entry 30 min before closing).*

Museu Nacional dos Coches. In a former royal riding school whose gorgeous painted ceiling makes it worth a visit in itself, the National Coach Museum has a dazzling collection of gloriously painted and gilded baroque horse-drawn carriages. The oldest on display was made for Philip II of Spain in the late 1500s; the most stunning are three conveyances created in Rome for King John V in 1716. The museum, Portugal's most visited, is right next door to the official residence of the President of the Republic, whose Museu da Presidência tells the story of the presidency, profiles the officeholders, and displays gifts they have received on state visits. ⊠ *Praça Afonso de Albuquerque, Belém* ☎ *21/361–0850* ⊕ *www.museudoscoches.pt* 🎫 *€5, free Sun. until 2* ⊙ *Tues.–Sun. 10–6; last entry 5:30.*

Padrão dos Descobrimentos. The white, monolithic Monument of the Discoveries was erected in 1960 to commemorate the 500th anniversary of the death of Prince Henry the Navigator. It was built on what was the departure point for many voyages of discovery, including those of Vasco da Gama for India and—during Spain's occupation of Portugal—of the Spanish Armada for England in 1588. Henry is at the prow of the monument, facing the water; lined up behind him are the Portuguese explorers of Brazil and Asia, as well as other national heroes, including Luís de Camões the poet, who can be recognized by the book in his hand. On the ground adjacent to the monument, an inlaid map shows the extent of the explorations undertaken by the 15th- and 16th-century Portuguese sailors. Walk inside and take the elevator to the top for river views. There are also 15- and 30-minute films about Lisbon's history. ⊠ *Av. de Brasília, Belém* ☎ *21/303–1950* 🎫 *€2.50; 25-min movie €4, combined ticket monument and movie €5, €13 includes Torre de Belém* ⊙ *Oct.–Apr., Tues.–Sun. 10–6; May–Sept., Tues.–Sun. 10–7.*

Palácio da Ajuda. According to legend, in the 16th century a shepherd found an image of the Virgin Mary in a cave close to here. In 1802 construction began on the Ajuda Palace, which was intended as a royal residence; its last regal occupant (Queen Maria) died here in 1911. Today the fussy building is home to a museum of 18th- and 19th-century paintings, furniture, and tapestries—hardly unique in Lisbon and, frankly, hardly an essential sight, although temporary exhibitions keep things interesting. It is also used for official ceremonies and functions by the Presidency of the Republic, and one wing houses the Culture Ministry. It's a 20-minute walk up Calçada da Ajuda from the Museu Nacional dos Coches, but Bus 14 and Tram 18 run this way, too. ⊠ *Largo da Ajuda, Ajuda* ☎ *21/363–7095* 🎫 *€5, €13 combined ticket includes Mosteiro de Jerónimos and Torre de Belém; free Sun. 10–2* ⊙ *Thurs.–Tues. 10–5.*

⟳ **Planetário Calouste Gulbenkian.** Behind the Museu de Marinha, the Calouste Gulbenkian Planetarium presents interesting astronomical shows with various themes several times a week (although the only one with commentary partly in English is the one about the Hubble Space Telescope, at 3 pm on Sunday). Times may change: a bulletin posted in the window announces the current program, or you can get updates from the tourist office. ⊠ *Praça do Império, Belém* ☎ *21/362–0002* ⊕ *planetario.marinha.pt* 🎫 *€4 (€2 under-18s)* ⊙ *Shows Thurs. 4 pm, Sat. 3 and 4 pm., Sun. 11:30 am, 3, and 4 pm.*

Ponte 25 de Abril. Completed in 1966 and originally dedicated to then Portuguese dictator Dr. António de Oliveira Salazar, this bridge earned a name change after the 1974 revolution, which lurched into action on April 25 of that year. Lisbon's first suspension bridge across the Rio

CLOSE UP

Prince Henry the Navigator

The linkage of England and Portugal and the beginning of Portugal's Age of Discovery can be traced back to the 14th century, when England's John of Gaunt gave his daughter, Philippa of Lancaster, in marriage to King João I. The couple's third son, Infante Dom Henrique, is known widely today as Prince Henry the Navigator (1394–1460). By the end of his lifetime, this multidimensional soldier-scientist had conceptualized, funded, and inspired discoveries beyond the borders of the world that Europe knew. No matter how they assess later misuses of exploration and conquest, scholars today generally agree that the prince paved the way for explorers such as Vasco da Gama and Ferdinand Magellan.

Unusual for a royal family in those (or any) times, João and Philippa raised six intelligent, apparently happy children. Alternately contemplative and restlessly athletic, Henry persuaded his father to let the four boys earn their knighthoods in an invasion of Morocco and the capture of its fortress at Ceuta. If the prince had not led his 70 soldier-filled ships to a victory worthy of Steven Spielberg replay, Portugal's Age of Discovery might have been very different.

At least three achievements secured Henry his place in the vanguard of explorers. In the Algarve, where he was governor, he founded a nearly legendary marine navigation school. He also sent ships where none had gone before—especially around Cape Bojador, the "impassable wall" jutting out from West Africa at the end of the European-known Atlantic Ocean. And he required that expeditions chart the seas as they sailed. Charts made of Cape Bojador later led Vasco da Gama to sail around it, then past the Cape of Good Hope and on to India.

Seen through the prism of history, Prince Henry seems a royal contradiction. He earned his knighthood defeating infidels and was eventually named Grand Master of the Order of Christ, the successor to the Knights Templar. But since he lived before the Inquisition began, he may have met some of the Latin-, Greek-, and Hebrew-speaking scholars who came to the royal court. Further, his ships engaged in Africa's lucrative slave trade, but he himself lived simply and, having given away his profits to fund further expeditions, died broke. The navigator-prince was not technically a navigator, and he rarely boarded a ship, but he pointed the way for generations of future explorers—such as yourself. In Lisbon, stop at breezy Belém on the Rio Tejo, where, at the prow of the ship-shaped *Padrão dos Descobrimentos* (Monument to the Discoveries), Prince Henry stands, leading other Portuguese explorers and even King Afonso V.

Tejo, linking the Alcântara and Almada districts, stands 230 feet above the water and stretches almost 2½ km (1½ mi). Reminiscent, for many, of San Francisco's Golden Gate Bridge, it's somewhat smaller but still a spectacular sight from any direction, although most gasps are reserved for the view from the top downward. Overlooking the bridge (which it predates by several years) from a hill on the south bank is the Cristo Rei—Christ the King—statue, it is smaller and stiffer than Rio's more famous Redeemer. The observation deck, from where you can actually look down on the bridge, is open daily.

PARQUE DAS NAÇÕES

To prepare for the World Exposition in 1998, Lisbon's officials wisely kept in mind not only the immediate needs of the event, but also the future needs of the city. The result was the Parque das Nações, or Park of Nations, a revitalized district on the banks of the Rio Tejo, 5 km (3 mi) northeast of Lisbon's center. Before it became the Expo 98 site, empty warehouses and refuse filled the district, which was once a landing area for seaplanes. Today it has apartment buildings, office complexes, hotels, restaurants, bars, the Centro Vasco da Gama mall, and a modern casino, interspersed with landscaped parkland. It's also home to a marina; the Pavilhão Atlântico, a venue for major cultural and sporting events; and the Feira Internacional Lisboa (FIL) convention center.

The centerpiece of the Parque das Nações is the popular Oceanário de Lisboa, an aquarium built for the Expo. Near it is the Pavilhão do Conhecimento: a hands-on science museum that is great fun for kids. The Pavilhão de Portugal, with its stunning concrete canopy, housed the host nation's contribution to the Expo; it was designed by multiple-prize-winning Porto architect Álvaro Siza Vieira, while the soaring Gare do Oriente train station is the work of Spain's Santiago Calatrava. From the cable car that runs through the area, the views are fine. Beyond the Parque das Nações to its north, parkland continues along the river, affording close-up views of the waterbirds that thrive here. You can make the most of all the open space by renting bicycles or inline skates from the Tejo Bike booth near the Vasco da Gama mall (open 10–8 in summer, 11–6 in winter).

Contacts Tejo Bike (☎ 21/891–9333 ⊕ www.tejobike.pt).

GETTING HERE AND AROUND
The Parque das Nações may be on the eastern edge of Lisbon but is easy to reach by public transport. Oriente station here is the terminal for the line that starts at Alameda, an interchange with the green line that runs from Cais do Sodré via Baixa-Chiado and Rossio stations, downtown. (There are plans to extend the red line from Oriente to the airport, too.) Above ground is the elegant Gare do Oriente, designed by Spanish star architect Santiago Calatrava, where fast trains from Porto and the Algarve stop, as well as some express buses. Gare do Oriente is also just a seven-minute trip on a suburban train from Santo Apolónia, downtown, but services are rather irregular.

TIMING
You can spend anywhere from a couple of hours to all day (and all night) sightseeing, shopping, eating, and drinking here. Allot about two hours for the Oceanário de Lisboa and another hour for the Pavilhão do Conhecimento. Although the last metro train departs from Oriente station at 1 am, taxis wait at the Gare de Oriente until all hours.

TOP ATTRACTIONS

Fodor's Choice ★

Oceanário de Lisboa. Europe's largest indoor aquarium wows children and adults alike with a vast salt-water tank featuring an array of fish, including several types of shark. Along the way you pass through habitats representing the North Atlantic, Pacific, and Indian oceans, where puffins and penguins dive into the water, sea otters roll and play, and tropical birds flit past you. You then descend to the bottom of the tank to watch rays float past gracefully and schools of silvery fish darting this way and that. To avoid the crowds, come during the week or early in the day. Note that two adults and one or more children can save quite a bit of money by buying a family ticket (€29). A range of activities is also organized in the Oceanarium outside normal opening hours, such as Saturday morning concerts for under-3s (and parents). ⊠ *Esplanada D. Carlos I (Doca dos Olivais), Parque das Nações* ☎ *21/891–7002* ⊕ *www.oceanario. pt* 🔒 *€12* ⊘ *Apr.–Oct., daily 10–8; Nov.–Mar., daily 10–7; last entry 1 hr before closing* Ⓜ *Oriente.*

DEALS
If you plan to visit several of the park's attractions, consider buying a Cartão Parque das Nações (€17.50). This card—sold at tourist offices, the Parque das Nações information desk, and at the area's various sights—gets you admission to the aquarium and science museum, allows you to ride the excursion train (running between the mall and the aquarium) and the cable car, and gives you discounts on bike and audio-guide rentals, as well as discounts at several restaurants. The card has to be activated at the selling point.

WORTH NOTING

NEED A BREAK?

For pure nectar on a hot day, find one of the many stands or cafés displaying huge bowls of oranges. They have juice machines on which, for about €2, they'll squeeze what seems like a dozen of them for you.

☾ **Pavilhão do Conhecimento.** The white, angular, structure designed by architect Carrilho de Graça for the Expo seems the perfect place to house the Knowledge Pavilion, or Living Science Centre, as it's also known. All of the permanent and temporary exhibits here are related to math, science, and technology; most are also labeled in English (a manual is available for the few that aren't), and all are interactive. A cybercafé with free Internet access, a media library, a gift shop, and a bookstore round out the offerings. The €15 family ticket is particularly good value. ⊠ *Alamada dos Oceanos, Lote 2.10.01, Parque das Nações* ☎ *21/891–9898* ⊕ *www.pavconhecimento.pt/home* 🔒 *€7* ⊘ *Tues.–Fri. 10–6, weekends and holidays 11–7* Ⓜ *Oriente.*

WHERE TO EAT

Meals generally include three courses, a drink, and coffee. Many restaurants have an *ementa turistica* (tourist menu), a set-price meal, most often served at lunchtime. Note that you'll be charged a couple of euros if you eat any of the *couvert* items—typically appetizers such as bread and butter, olives, and the like—that are brought to your table without being ordered.

While in upmarket restaurants all fish will come ready filleted, in other places most grilled fish will not only have bones but come complete with the head and tail, so only a dish described on the menu as *filete* will be bone-free. Traditional rural meat stews also usually contain bits of the animal you may not have eaten before, such as pig's ear (*orelha de porco*) or trotters (*pézinhos*).

Lisbon's restaurants usually serve lunch from noon or 12:30 until 3 and dinner from 7:30 until 11; many establishments are closed Sunday or Monday. Inexpensive restaurants typically don't accept reservations. In the traditional *cervejarias* (beer hall–restaurants), which frequently have huge dining rooms, you'll probably have to wait for a table, but usually not more than 10 minutes. In the Bairro Alto, many of the reasonably priced *tascas* (taverns) are on the small side: if you can't grab a table, you're probably better off moving on to the next place. Throughout Lisbon, dress for meals is usually casual, but exceptions are noted below.

Note that the city tourist board's 72-hour Restaurant Card brings discounts to a number of leading restaurants. The card is free with a discount sightseeing-and-transport Lisboa Card but otherwise costs from €6.15 (for a single person; there are also double and family cards). The cards are available at tourist offices and major hotels.

For fado venues, where prices are generally inflated by the need to pay performers' fees and the food is rarely anything to write home about, see the Nightlife section.

WHAT IT COSTS IN EUROS					
	¢	$	$$	$$$	$$$$
AT DINNER	under €10	€10–€15	€16–€20	€21–€25	over €25

Restaurant prices are per person for a main course at dinner.

THE ALFAMA

$$$
ECLECTIC
✕ **Bica do Sapato.** A favorite among fashionable locals, this riverfront restaurant is known for its stylish interior and furnishings: Knoll, Eero Saarien, and Mies van der Rohe all feature. Choose between the café (all smoking) serving hearty Portuguese fare, the (predominately no-smoking) restaurant offering pricier nouvelle cuisine, or the upstairs sushi bar. Regular mains in the café include duck pie and *bacalhau à bras* (but with fresh cod). The restaurant offers the likes of baked grouper with a bell-pepper crust or roast black pork with truffles; there is at least one vegetarian main dish. Desserts include eggy classics such as *pão-de-rala* (from pumpkin and almonds), served with orange confit. There is also Sunday brunch. ⊠ *Av. Infante D. Henrique, Armazém B, Cais da Pedra, Santa Apolónia* ☎ *21/881–0320* ⊕ *www.bicadosapato.com* ⊟ *AE, DC, MC, V* ☉ *No dinner Sun. No lunch Mon.*

$
PORTUGUESE
✕ **Malmequer Bemmequer.** Sample honest Portuguese fare to the gentle sound of Portuguese folk music at this brightly decorated Alfama favorite. The menu lists classic starters such as *peixinhos da horta* (deep-fried green beans in batter) and *joaquinzinhos* (fried whitebait), while the mains include *arroz de peixe* (fish rice), *bacalhau com natas* (codfish with cream), and *entrecosto com arroz de feijão* (pork ribs with rice and beans). The desserts are more out of the ordinary for Lisbon—the highlight a tasty apfel strudel. ⊠ *Rua de São Miguel 23–25, Alfama*

☎ *21/887–6535* ⊕ *www.malmequer-bemmequer.com* ⊟ *DC, MC, V*
⊙ *Closed Mon. No lunch Tues. Closed wk of Santo António (June 13).*
Closed 2nd half Sept.

¢ ✕**Parreirinha de São Vicente.** In a row of eateries round the corner from
PORTUGUESE the Feira da Ladra flea market, this place is so popular it has taken
over two neighboring house numbers. The food here is well seasoned
and mostly comes in portions large enough for two. The brothers
who run the place are from the northern Beiras region, and many of
the dishes here are meat-rich examples of its traditions, but there is
plenty of seafood on the menu. On Sundays locals pile in for *chocos
à setubalense* (fried battered cuttlefish). As for wine, the house red
and slightly fizzy white come by the glass or jug; there are also pricier
bottles. ⊠ *Calçada de São Vicente 54–58, Alfama* ☎ *21/886–8893*
⊟ *No credit cards.*

$ ✕**Santo António de Alfama.** Up some steps from the Travessa Terreiro
MEDITERRANEAN do Trigo, you'll find this simple but sophisticated restaurant hung with
black-and-white photos of famous artists, including a signed one of pop
singer Nelly Furtado. The mushrooms stuffed with Gorgonzola and
joaquinzinhos fritos (whitebait fried in batter) are tasty starters. Steak,
fish, or duck accompanied by steamed vegetables are the most popular
main dishes, but there are authentic Portuguese flavors such as *morcela
com grelos* (blood sausage and turnip leaves, sautéed with potatoes);
note there's less choice at lunch than at dinner, when the kitchen also
stays open till half past midnight. In summer, good use is made of the
large terrace. ⊠ *Beco de São Miguel 7, Alfama* ☎ *21/888–1328* ⊕ *www.
siteantonio.com* ⊟ *DC, MC, V.*

$ ✕**Solar dos Bicos.** This charming restaurant, with its stone arches and
PORTUGUESE beautiful *azulejos* offers typical Portuguese cuisine at very reasonable
prices. It's right next to the Casa dos Bicos, which you can marvel at
from a large shaded esplanade. Seafood is the main attraction: grilled
sole, grouper, sea bass, bream or squid are all good options, or two diners could split a rich *caldeirada* (fish stew) or *arroz de marisco* (a sort
of wet seafood risotto). There are plenty of no-nonsense meat dishes,
too, such as mixed grill and barbecued pork chops, which come with
fries and salad. Then choose between achingly sweet desserts and fresh
fruit. ⊠ *Rua dos Bacalhoeiros, 8–A, Alfama* ☎ *21/886–9447* ⊕ *www.
solardosbicos.pt* ⊙ *AE, DC, MC, V* ⊙ *Closed Mon. Closed 2 wks late
Dec. or early Jan.*

¢ ✕**Viela d'Alfama.** At this tiny *tasca* near the Feira da Ladra flea market,
PORTUGUESE decorated to look like an "Alfama alley," the day's menu consists of
a paper tablecloth pinned up outside. What's on offer is simple but
tasty: popular local dishes such as *bacalhau à brás* (codfish sautéed
with egg, olives, parsley, and tiny potato fries) or braised pork cutlets
seasoned with garlic. The soundtrack here is provided by Rádio Amália,
as the owner is a fan of the great diva. On fado nights, most Fridays
and Saturdays, they do a great all-in deal: around €25 for nibbles and
a main dish, plus a couple of glasses of wine or beer, dessert, coffee,
and *ginginha* (cherry liqueur). ⊠ *Calçada de São Vicente 26, Alfama*
☎ *21/887–4397* ⌂ *Reservations essential for fado nights* ⊟ *No credit
cards* ⊙ *Closed Wed. and Sun.*

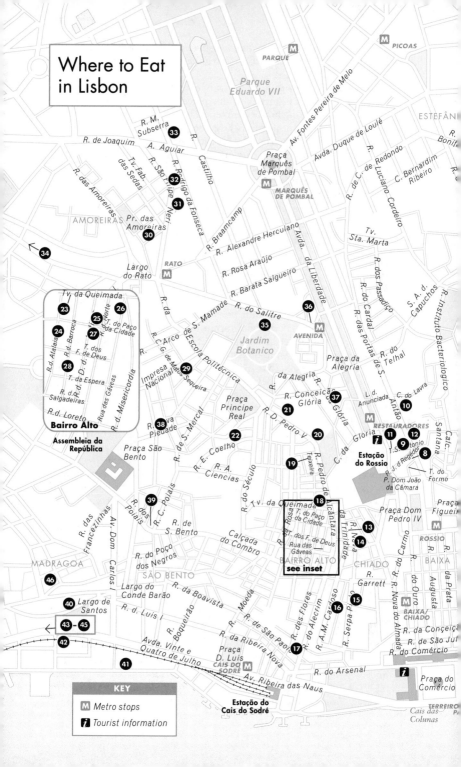

Where to Eat in Lisbon

2

R. Cid. da Horta
R. D.
ánia
R. Pascoal de Melo
R. A. Braga
M ARROIOS
R.F. Sanchez
R.C. Oliveira
R. Morais Soares
R. H. Quionga
R. Saraiva Lima
R. José Estevão
R. Passos Manuel
R. de Arroios
R. António Pedro
Cesário Verde
R. J. Marto
Almirante Reis
R. Angola
R. do Zaire
M ANJOS
R. da Penha de França
Lgo. Sta. Bárbara
R. de Sta. Bárbara
R. dos Anjos
Avenida
Palmira
R. Forno do Tijolo
Moçambique
R.C. Verde
R. Escola do Exercito
R. Castelo Branco Saraiva
General Roçadas
M INTENDENTE
R. Maria Andrade
R. A. Quental
R. C. Renata Batista
R. Angelina Vidal
Avenida
Avda. Machado dos Santos
MARTIM MONIZ
M
R. da Palma
R. do Benformoso
R. do Terreirinho
R. Damasceno Monteiro
R. Maria da Fonte
R. dos Sapadores
R. do Vale so S.
GRAÇA
R. da Graça
R. Senhora da Glória
R. Bela Vista à Graça
Calç. do Monte
Alegrete
R.M. Pte. de Lima
S. C. de Andrade
C. Graça
C. de S. Vicente
MOURARIA
Largo da Graça
R. do Oiteirinho
R. da Verónica
R. Leite de Vasconcelos
R. Entremuros do Mirante
R. da Costa do Castelo
Castelo de São Jorge
Largo Vicente
São Vicente
Santa Engracia
R. do Paraíso
SANTA APOLÓNIA
M
R. de S. Milagre S. A.
ALFAMA
R. dos Remédios
Estação Santa Apolónia
Museu Militar
Sé Catedral
R. S. João da Praça
dos Bacalhoeiros
da Alfândega
Casa dos Bicos
Avenida Infante Dom Henrique
Doca do Jardim do Tabaco
R. Jardim do Tobaco
Rio Tejo
Doca da Marinha

0 ___ 200 yards
0 ___ 200 meters

THE BAIXA

¢   ✕**Bonjardim.** In an alley between Praça dos Restauradores and Rua
PORTUGUESE   Portas de Santo Antão, and known locally as "Rei dos Frangos" ("King
of Chickens"), Bonjardim specializes in superbly cooked spit-roasted
chicken, best eaten with fries and a salad. The restaurant and esplanade are crowded at peak times (8 pm–10 pm), but you shouldn't have
to wait long, and watching the frenzied waiters is entertaining. An
overflow dining room on the opposite side of the alley serves a similar
menu but with more grilled meats and is similarly good value (each
has a different rest day, so one is always open). They also do takeout.
⊠ *Travessa de Santo Antão 11 and 12, Restauradores* ☎ *21/342–4389
or 21/342–7424* ▭ *AE, DC, MC, V.*

$$$$ ✕**Gambrinus.** On a busy street that's full of fish restaurants, Gambrinus
SEAFOOD   stands alone, with more than 70 years of experience in serving the finest
fish and shellfish. In a series of somber, dark-paneled dining rooms, and
even sitting at the bar, you're led through the intricacies of the day's
seafood specials by waiters who know their stuff. Prawns, lobster, and
crab are always available; seasonal choices such as sea bream, sole, and
sea bass are offered grilled or garnished with clam sauce. There are even
a few meat dishes, too, such as stewed partridge with chestnuts, and
English roast beef. ⊠ *Rua das Portas de Santo Antão 23–25, Restauradores* ☎ *21/342–1466* ▭ *AE, MC, V.*

$ ✕**O Churrasco.** With its liveried waiters and airy dining room, O
PORTUGUESE   Churrasco is rather more formal than most eateries nearby. In a street
lined with tourist traps, it also attracts many locals. They come above
all for the grilled meats and fish, but other dishes, such as the paella,
are definitely worth trying. A popular side order is *esparregado*—which
here contains garlic and olive oil and not spinach, as is usual in Portugal, but *nabiças*, or turnip greens, a tasty and vitamin-rich ingredient
in many local dishes. Wine is another house forte (the manager edits
a magazine on the subject). ⊠ *Rua das Portas de Santo Antão 83–85,
Restauradores* ☎ *21/342–3059* ▭ *AE, DC, MC, V.*

$ ✕**Solmar.** Items from the sea figure prominently on the menu and in the
SEAFOOD   restaurant itself: there's a huge mosaic of an underwater scene. Some
have complained that Solmar—which has been bustling about its business for more than 50 years now—is resting on its laurels, but the cooking is more hit than miss. In winter the restaurant entices diners with
wild boar or venison, but the menu also has duck breast cooked in
honey, and various types of steak. Note that this is not the place for
quiet—there are four televisions positioned about the dining main room.
There are cheaper snacks available in the adjacent café, where locals pop
in throughout the day for coffee and cakes. ⊠ *Rua das Portas de Santo
Antão 106–108, Restauradores* ☎ *21/346–0010* ▭ *AE, DC, MC, V.*

CHIADO AND THE BAIRRO ALTO

$$$$
ECLECTIC
✕ **100 Maneiras.** In a cozy, all-white space, Serbian-born Ljubomir Stanisic offers one of Lisbon's most stimulating tasting menus, changing every six weeks. Sit back and enjoy nine creative, often playful starter-size dishes, likely opening with *Estendal do Bairro* (neighborhood clothesline): bacalhau chips hung up like drying linens. Others might include chestnut soup with crab; sea bass in seaweed broth; or a light remake of Brazilian *picanha* (rump steak) and *feijoada* (bean stew). You may request a matching wine-tasting menu. Chef Ljubo also runs lively Bistro 100 Maneiras at nearby Largo de Trindade 9, whose globe-spanning menu includes Serbian dishes. The venues share a phone; when reserving, make clear which you want. ⊠ *Rua do Teixeira 35, Bairro Alto* ☎ *21/099–0475* ⊕ *www.restaurante100maneiras.com* ⌂ *Reservations essential* ▭ *AE, DC, MC, V* ⊘ *No lunch.*

$$$
SEAFOOD
Fodor'sChoice
★
✕ **Aqui Há Peixe.** "There's fish here" is this restaurant's name, and make no mistake: it's one of the most fashionable places in town to eat seafood. Opened in 2009 by the proprietor of a well-known beachside restaurant at Comporta, south of Setúbal, it has a similarly informal vibe. At night it attracts a youngish crowd clearly intent on hitting the Bairro Alto's bars later. Popular dishes here include fish stews and tuna steak sautéed with peppercorns; don't forget to order a light *vinho verde* or a good white wine to wash them down. There are cheaper lunchtime specials, rustled up from whatever was in the market in the morning. ⊠ *Rua da Trindade 18A, Chiado* ☎ *21/343–2154* ⊕ *www.aquihapeixe. pt* ▭ *DC, MC, V* ⊘ *Closed Mon. No lunch weekends.*

$
PORTUGUESE
✕ **Alfaia.** In this traditional restaurant in the former stables of what was once a local nobleman's palace, courteous staff serve up Portuguese classics such as *arroz de galo* (chicken rice), *chocos grelhados* (grilled cuttlefish) and *açorda de gambas* (prawns with garlic and coriander in a sort of breadcrumb stew). As is evident from the dining room decoration, wine is a big deal here; indeed there are 600 for you to choose from. Note that if you just want a drink and a snack, the Alfaia wine bar across the road is an excellent place to stop. ⊠ *Travessa da Queimada 22, Bairro Alto* ☎ *21/346–1232* ⊕ *www.restaurantealfaia.com* ▭ *AE, DC, MC, V* ⊘ *No lunch Sun.*

$
PORTUGUESE
✕ **Bota Alta.** This wood-paneled tavern is one of the Bairro Alto's oldest and most favored eateries—lines form outside by 8 pm. There's little space between the tables, but this only enhances the buzz. Once you've secured a seat, choose from a menu strong on traditional Portuguese dishes—perhaps bacalhau cooked in cream, homemade sausages, steaks in wine sauce, or grilled fish. The house wine comes in ceramic jugs and is very good. ⊠ *Travessa da Queimada 37, Bairro Alto* ☎ *21/342–7959* ▭ *DC, MC, V* ⊘ *Closed Sun. No lunch Sat.*

$
CAFÉ
✕ **Café no Chiado.** At this sophisticated yet friendly downtown café-restaurant, the fare is straightforward but tasty: cheese steak, prawn crêpes, and salads. For dessert, the chocolate mousse is a good bet. The shaded esplanade is a pleasant place to absorb local atmosphere (including the antique trams rumbling past) away from the hustle of Rua Garrett, the area's main shopping drag. The wide selection of Portuguese and international newspapers adds to its laidback attractions. ⊠ *Largo*

do Picadeiro 10–12, Chiado ☎ *21/346–0501* ⊕ *www.cafenochiado.com* 🖃 *MC, V.*

¢   ✕**Casa Faz Frio.** This convivial *adega* (tavern)—complete with wood

PORTUGUESE   beams, stone floors, and bunches of garlic suspended from the ceiling—is starting to look a little faded. But it is now one of just two in Lisbon to boast *gabinetes*—paneled booths traditionally used for trysts but also handy for working lunches—and is as good a place as any to sample rustic food on the cheap. There is a different bacalhau dish every day, and paella is always on the menu; other house specialties include grilled cuttlefish and *secretos*, lean meat from the belly of the *porco preto* pig. ✉ *Rua de Dom Pedro V 96–98, Bairro Alto* ☎ *21/346–1860* 🖃 *No credit cards.*

$ ✕**Cervejaria Trindade.** The colorful wall tiles and vaulted ceiling of this

PORTUGUESE   former monastery hint at its long history, and it's popular with both locals and tourists alike. A homey bar at the entrance will quench your thirst as you wait (you can also just come here for a drink and some *pastéis de bacalhau* (tasty fried cod-and-potato snacks). You might start with *ameijoas Trindade* (clams in a garlic-butter and coriander sauce) before moving on to *bife vazia Trindade* (steak with a choice of three sauces) or *bacalhau á mosteiro de Tibães* (flaked salt cod coated with cornbread crumbs and cilantro). It all tastes great with the house wine. ✉ *Rua Nova da Trindade 20, Bairro Alto* ☎ *21/342–3506* ⊕ *www. cervejariatrindade.pt* 🖃 *AE, DC, MC, V.*

$ ✕**Cocheira Alentejana.** The rustic decor really fits with the traditional

PORTUGUESE   cooking from the rural Alentejo region here, in what is one of the area's coziest, friendliest and best-value restaurants. Dig into regional dishes such as *migas com carne de porco* (pork with breadcrumbs and garlic fried in olive oil), *sopa de cação* (dog fish soup) and *ensopada de borrego* (lamb stew). Dishes may be flavored with locally used herbs such as *poejo* (pennyroyal) as well as the more internationally known cilantro. It's enough to make you resolve to head off for the countryside the very next day. ✉ *Rua Diário de Notícias 74, Bairro Alto* ☎ *21/346–4868* 🖃 *AE, DC, MC, V* ⊗ *Closed Sun. No lunch Sat. Closed mid-June–mid-July.*

$$ ✕**Comida de Santo.** Excellent Brazilian food served in a funky, brightly

BRAZILIAN   painted dining room to a lively Brazilian soundtrack keeps this tiny place buzzing until closing time, at 1 am. Come and enjoy classic dishes, such as fish soups, *feijoada* (black bean stew with sausage, pork and dried beef) or *vatapá* (a spicy shrimp concoction thickened with ground peanuts). Sip a Caipirinha and munch on manioc fries while you wait, and finish your meal with coconut-rich *manjar branco* or *pudim de aipim* (ground manioc, cooked with condensed milk). You can also opt for a tasting menu. Comida de Santo is down a side street off Rua Escola Politécnica; ring the bell for entrance. ✉ *Calçada Engenheiro Miguel Pais 39, Rato* ☎ *21/396–3339* ⚑ *Reservations essential* 🖃 *AE, DC, MC, V.*

$ ✕**Fidalgo.** The local intelligentsia have made this low-key, comfortable

PORTUGUESE   restaurant their refuge, though owner Eugenio Fidalgo has been welcoming every sort of patron for almost four decades now. He'll gladly help you with the Portuguese menu and the excellent, well-priced wine

2

list. Try one of the specialties such as bacalhau or octopus *à lagareiro* (baked in olive oil, with tiny potatoes), or the incredibly succulent *medalhões de javali* (wild boar cutlets). Fidalgo was recently redecorated from top to bottom and is looking better than ever. ⊠ *Rua da Barroca 27, Bairro Alto* ☎ *21/342–2900* ⊕ *www.restaurantefidalgo. com* ⊟ *AE, MC, V* ⊘ *Closed Sun.*

$$$
MEDITERRANEAN
Fodor'sChoice
★

✕ **Largo.** Chef Miguel Castro e Silva was one of Porto's leading culinary lights when he resolved to make his mark in the capital. He has done so in this airy space whose brick arches are offset with modern features, including artfully lit tanks containing jellyfish. Castro e Silva describes his dishes as "Mediterranean revisited": traditional recipes but lighter and with a twist, such as bacalhau cooked at 60°C and served with *migas de poejo e hortelã* (breadcrumbs fried with pennyroyal and mint), and duckling *magret* with truffle risotto and asparagus. There is a two-course lunchtime menu, but two people may also split starters and mains. Largo has a mezzanine for smokers. ⊠ *Rua Serpa Pinto 10A, Chiado* ☎ *21/347–7225* ⊕ *www.largo.pt* ⊟ *AE, DC, MC, V* ⊘ *Closed Sun.*

$$
ARGENTINE

✕ **La Paparrucha.** Lisbon's only Argentine restaurant is known above all for the quality of its meat, but the slick service and great location also help attract well-heeled locals. Tables by the picture windows or on the large wooden deck out back (where you may smoke) afford sweeping views across central Lisbon. On the menu, some starters are meat-free; then it's mainly steaks galore and *parilladas*—mixed grills. For dessert, the *dulce de leite* is a popular milk-based treat. ⊠ *Rua D. Pedro V, 18–20, Bairro Alto* ☎ *21/342–5333* ⊕ *www.lapaparrucha. com* ⊟ *AE, DC, MC, V.*

$$$
MEDITERRANEAN

✕ **Olivier.** Local celebs make regular pilgrimages to Olivier Costa's cozy yet sophisticated main restaurant (he has two others) to revel in his signature starters. It's not a place for experimentation—more high-class comfort food, so come hungry. Many diners go for the *menu de degustação* of nine starters, or a skimpier version with five. These might include salmon and scallop carpaccio, intense tomato soup, linguini with parmesan and black truffles, or *alheira* game sausage in Portuguese cabbage with a quail's egg on top. The wine list is extravagantly large, and the kitchen stays open past midnight. Note that smoking is allowed in the whole dining area. ⊠ *Rua do Alecrim 23, Chiado* ☎ *21/342–2916* ⊕ *www.restaurante-olivier.com* ⊟ *AE, DC, MC, V* ⊘ *No lunch. Closed Sun.*

$$
PORTUGUESE

✕ **Pap' Açorda.** Seen by many as the best restaurant in the Bairro Alto, Pap'açorda is definitely among the hippest. Art and media types scramble to reserve one of the closely packed tables in the minimalist interior. The menu lists cutting-edge versions of Portuguese classics—grilled sea bass; breaded veal cutlets; and *açorda* itself, that bread-based stew, rich in seafood (the luxury version contains lobster) and flavored with garlic and cilantro. For dessert, scrumptious chocolate mousse is spooned with panache from a giant bowl. There's a good wine list (all Portuguese) and a long bar by the door where those unwise enough not to have made a reservation wait for a table. ⊠ *Rua da Atalaia 57, Bairro Alto* ☎ *21/346–4811* ⌂ *Reservations essential* ⊟ *AE, DC, MC, V* ⊘ *Closed Mon.*

$ ✕ **Sinal Vermelho.** At this update of a traditional adega, the split-level
PORTUGUESE   dining room is traditionally tiled, and the food is thoroughly Portuguese. But the prints on the wall are modern, the clientele firmly professional, and the wine list wide ranging. Consider starting with a plate
of clams drenched in oil and garlic and follow it with a fresh seafood
dish such as *polvo salteado* (sautéed octopus). The meat dishes are less
inspiring, although if you feel daring you might try the tripe or the kid-
neys. ✉ *Rua das Gáveas 89, Bairro Alto* ☎ *21/346–1252* ▤ *AE, MC, V*
⊘ *Closed Sun. No lunch Mon. and Sat.*

$$$ ✕ **Tágide.** In a fine old house that looks out over the Baixa and the Rio
PORTUGUESE   Tejo (reserve a table by the window), you can have one of Lisbon's
great food experiences. The dining room lined with 17th-century tiles
is a lovely backdrop for sampling regional Portuguese fare, from both
tasting and seasonal à la carte menus. Try the famous *presunto* (smoked
ham) from Chaves, stuffed squid from the Algarve, or a gourmet take
on the classic *porco à alentejana* (Alentejo-style pork with clams). Other
mains might include duck or wild boar. Vegetarians are well served
with lovely creamy risottos. On arrival at the restaurant, ring the bell
to get in. ✉ *Largo Academia Nacional de Belas Artes 18–20, Chiado*
☎ *21/340–4010* ⊕ *www.restaurantetagide.com* ⌕ *Reservations essen-
tial* ▤ *AE, DC, MC, V* ⊘ *Closed Sun. and Mon.*

$ ✕ **Terra.** It's a buffet feast at Terra, whose dynamic owners are coun-
VEGETARIAN   tering the entrenched local view that vegetarians must suffer for their
ↂ   convictions. The cheaper lunchtime deal includes drink and dessert. At
Fodor's Choice   dinner, dishes are not overly reliant on soya and include adaptations of
★   Portuguese classics: seitan *à bras* instead of *bacalhau*, oyster mushrooms
a Bulhão Pato instead of clams, and so on. A few are not vegan; staff
will point these out. At lunch or dinner, 3- to 11-year-olds eat for little
more than half price. The place is cozy rather than sophisticated, but
the large (no-smoking) back garden is a big plus. ✉ *Rua da Palmeira
15, Bairro Alto* ☎ *707/108–108* ⊕ *www.restauranteterra.pt* ▤ *AE, DC,
MC, V* ⊘ *Closed Mon.*

¢   ✕ **Vá e Volte.** In a few tile-lined dining rooms, staff keep the meals com-
PORTUGUESE   ing with speed and good humor. Fried or grilled fish or meat dishes
such as *escalopes de novilho* (veal cutlets) are served with enough
salad, potatoes, and vegetables to keep the wolf from the door, while
the *arroz de peixe* (fish rice) and *cataplana de peixe* (fish stew) may
be large enough for two. The *arroz doce* (rice pudding) is homemade.
Even if you choose a fine regional wine, the price won't break the bank.
✉ *Rua Diário de Notícias 100, Bairro Alto* ☎ *21/342–7888* ⊕ *www.
restaurantevaevolte.com* ▤ *AE, DC, MC, V.*

THE MODERN CITY

$$$ ✕ **Bocca.** This slick modern newcomer with friendly, sneaker-wearing
MEDITERRANEAN   waiters pulls in bankers at lunchtime, guests from nearby hotels for
ↂ   dinner—and foodies whenever they get the chance. Reliably delicious
Fodor's Choice   mains might include pork cheeks in wine with caramelized apple and
★   blood sausage, or grilled sea bream with clams and quail consommé.
The lunchtime executive menus are good value, or order starters and
split a main dish. If you can, go for the *menus de degustação*, which

surprise and satisfy, with or without expertly matched wines. Half the 240 wines may also be ordered by the glass. On Saturday lunchtimes, there is a gourmet kids' menu. The smoking area has effective ventilation. ☒ *Rua Rodrigo da Fonseca 87D, Rato* ☎ *21/380–8383* ⊕ *www. bocca.pt* ⊟ *AE, DC, MC, V* ☽ *Closed Mon. and Sun.*

$$ ✕**Casa da Comida.** This old gourmands' haven near Jardim das
PORTUGUESE   Amoreiras has been given a culinary makeover by prize-winning chef Bertílio Gomes. Dip rustic breads in gourmet olive oils as you choose from seasonal dishes, before finishing with one of the chef's own ices. There is an executive lunch menu, but we recommend a dinner *menu de degustação* for €35 or €40 (four and five courses respectively). Appetizers such as blood sausage with quince jelly might be followed by *bacalhau a brás* reinvented in layers, and tender *bochechas* (pork cheeks) with cockles. The dining room is cozy and classy, but on warm nights book a table on the candlelit patio. ☒ *Travessa das Amoreiras 1, Amoreiras* ☎ *21/386–0889* ⊕ *www.casadacomida.pt* ⌂ *Reservations essential* ⊟ *AE, DC, MC, V* ☽ *Closed Sun. No lunch Mon. and Sat. No lunch in Aug.*

$ ✕**Casa dos Passarinhos.** This traditional restaurant has been welcoming
PORTUGUESE   diners since 1923 and is today both efficient and friendly. At lunch, workers from the nearby Amoreiras office complex and mall come for house specialties that include *naco na pedra* (stone-cooked steak), *vitela barrosã* (tender veal from the north), grilled fish, and *açorda de gambas* (prawns in a bread-based stew flavored with garlic and cilantro). In the evening, Casa dos Passarinhos draws mainly locals, from its own solidly middle-class Campo de Ourique neighborhood and farther afield. The two dining rooms are decorated in appropriately rustic style. ☒ *Rua Silva Carvalho 195, Amoreiras* ☎ *21/388–2346* ⊟ *AE, DC, MC, V* ☽ *Closed Sun. Closed Aug.*

$$ ✕**Mezzaluna.** Perhaps the most sophisticated of the city's handful
ITALIAN   of Italian restaurants, Mezzaluna serves food that, given the background of owner-chef Michael Guerrieri, might be called Neapolitan-American. Here the freshest of vegetables are combined with fine Italian cheeses in many of the starters and pasta dishes—making the place a boon for vegetarians—and there are always lots of elaborate fish and meat main dishes, too. At lunch the place draws mainly a business crowd from the surrounding banks, and in the evenings prosperous couples. It's a bit of a hike uphill from Marquês de Pombal metro, so take a taxi here or settle for the longer walk downhill from Rato. ☒ *Rua da Artilharia Um 16A, Rato* ☎ *21/387–9944* ⊕ *www. mezzalunalisboa.com* ⌂ *Reservations essential* ⊟ *AE, DC, MC, V* ☽ *Closed Sun. No lunch Sat.*

$ ✕**O Fumeiro.** Two brothers from the Beiras region have been serving
PORTUGUESE   up hearty portions of traditional food in this picturesquely tiled space off Avenida da Liberdade for almost two decades. A plethora of fish stews cooked in traditional oval *cataplanas* is complemented by dishes featuring roast suckling pig, rabbit and hare, or *bacalhau* cooked in so many ways only a few are on the menu. Everything here is cooked from scratch, which means a longish wait if you want off-the-menu dishes such as *chanfana*—kid soaked in red wine and stewed. In theory

O Fumeiro closes at midnight but arrive by 11:30 pm and you will not be turned away hungry. ⊠ *Rua Conceição da Glória 25, Avenida da Liberdade* ☎ *21/347–4203* ▭ *DC, MC, V* ⊘ *No lunch Sat.*

¢   ✕ **Os Tibetanos.** Delicious dishes such as *caril de seitan e cenouras* (wheat gluten and carrot curry), baked *quorn* (made from a relative of mushrooms) and Tibetan *momo* dumplings mean that even carnivores are among those who are most often waiting in line for a table in the dining room or pleasant garden (where you may smoke). Daily specials cost less than €8, while the fixed-price menus are excellent value. Desserts, including a range of fruit tarts and cakes, are equally delicious. Os Tibetanos is part of a Buddhist center; a small shop stocks books and crafts, incense, homeopathic medicines, and other natural products, while yoga and meditation classes take place upstairs. ⊠ *Rua do Salitre 117, Avenida de Liberdade* ☎ *21/314–2038* ⊕ *www.tibetanos.com* ▭ *No credit cards* ⊘ *Closed Sun.*

VEGETARIAN

$$ ✕ **Ribadouro.** Like other Lisbon beer halls, Ribadouro is big on seafood, with aquariums and a counter full of fresh shellfish priced by weight—go easy, since this can be a costly way to eat. Stick to the regular fish and meat dishes such as *gambas ao alhinho*, prawns fried in garlic or *bife do Ribadouro*, steak in a creamy wine and butter sauce, and you should be fine. When crowds spill out of the nearby theaters, you may have to wait for a table; on weekends, try to arrive before 8 pm. A large TV is usually tuned to local soccer games, with the sound down. There is a smoking area. ⊠ *Av. da Liberdade 155, Liberdade* ☎ *21/354–9411* ⊕ *www.cervejariaribadouro.pt* ▭ *AE, DC, MC, V.*

SEAFOOD

$$$$ ✕ **Varanda.** The main restaurant at the Ritz is rare among hotel eateries in staying consistently at the top of its game. Frenchman Pascal Meynard keeps a tight grip on the reins here, overseeing a seasonally changing *menu de degustação* (dinner only) and a wide choice of Portuguese and international dishes. These might include seafood *cataplana*, slow-cooked cod served with celery and garlic fries or, in the colder months, veal mignon with truffles and pine nuts. Expert advice is on hand to help you select wines from the long list. Achingly sweet Portuguese desserts are available, as well as lighter sweets such as berries marinated with herbs. There are children's menus, too. ⊠ *Four Seasons Hotel Ritz Lisbon, Raur Rodrigo de Fonseca 88, Marquês de Pombal* ☎ *21/381–1400* ⊕ *www.fourseasons.com* ⌂ *Reservations essential. Jacket required for dinner* ▭ *AE, DC, MC, V.*

PORTUGUESE/
INTERNATIONAL

SÃO BENTO

$$ ✕ **Cantinho da Paz.** This place is on an alley off the Tram 28 route from Chiado to Estrela, but take a taxi if you're worried about getting lost. It's a joyful mom-and-pop establishment that specializes in the cuisine of Goa—otherwise surprisingly hard to find in Lisbon. The spicy veal *balchão* and ginger-and-cardamom-flavored *xacuti* are particularly rich examples of Goa's unique mix of Portuguese and Indian influences, but there are also tasty seafood dishes. English-speaking staff will guide you through the menu; they may suggest you split a main dish if you're not ravenous. Vegetarians note: you may have been spoiled for choice in Indian restaurants back home, but there are

INDIAN

slim pickings here. The Fernandes family also now runs the swankier restaurant in the Casa de Goa community center on Calçada do Livramento in Lapa (☎ 21/393–0171), which is open daily. ⊠ *Rua da Paz 4, off Rua dos Poiais de São Bento, Bairro Alto* ☎ 21/390–1963 ☰ *No credit cards* ☉ *Closed Sun.*

$ ✕ **Charcutaria Francesa.** Despite the name—inherited from a previous
ECLECTIC   tenant—this cozy out-of-the-way place patronized mainly by thirty-
Fodor'sChoice   and fortysomethings is neither French, nor a delicatessen. Its Portu-
★   guese owners combine ingredients in original ways, such as in bacalhau with *farinheira* (a floury sausage) and duck confit with red berry sauce. The menu changes, but Charcutaria Francesa always offers at least three fish and three meat options, while vegetarians are catered to with risottos or perhaps vegetables roasted with goat's cheese. There's an extensive wine list and scrumptious desserts such as the famed pear and ginger tart. Weekday lunches are buffet only, with three pricing options; on Saturday they do brunch. ⊠ *Rua Manuel Bernardes 5A/B, São Bento* ☎ 21/395–8445 ⊕ *www.charcutaria-francesa.com* ☰ *DC, MC, V* ☉ *Closed Sun.*

LAPA

$$$ ✕ **A Travessa.** Its atmospheric location in a former monastery (also
BELGIAN   home to the Museu da Marioneta) is just one of the trump cards of this Luso-Belgian restaurant. The seasonal menu includes five fish and five meat main dishes, plus any number of delicious starters. On Saturday night it's mainly *moules*, though if you don't like mussels at least one alternative is available. On warm days, they set tables out in the old convent's courtyard. Parking is a puzzle in the narrow streets of this old fishermen's neighborhood, but if you do come by car, call 96/893–9125 and you can leave it for free in the underground car park in Santos where you'll be picked up in the restaurant's liveried camper van. ⊠ *Travessa do Convento das Berardas 12, Madragoa* ☎ 21/390–2034 ⊕ *www.atravessa.com* ⌂ *Reservations essential* ☰ *AE, DC, MC, V* ☉ *Closed Sun. No lunch Mon. and Sat.*

CAIS DO SODRE AND SANTOS

$$ ✕ **Estado Líquido Sushi Lounge.** Scallop carpaccio with salmon, caviar,
JAPANESE   and a spicy sauce, and a house maki featuring salmon, cream cheese, and sesame seeds are among popular dishes at this bustling eatery in the nightlife hub of Santos. Wash it down with hot or cold sake—or a 'Sakerinha', an adaptation of the Brazilian Caipirinha—and perhaps finish with a velvety chocolate mousse. Then write home on a Estado Líquido postcard; staff will mail it for you. The insistent funky soundtrack suits the young crowd here, as do the low tables. For full-size furniture, for lunch, or for sushi with a Californian or Brazilian twist, stable-mate Fusion Sushi is next door. ⊠ *Largo de Santos 5A, Santos* ☎ 21/397–2022 ⊕ *www.estadoliquido.com* ☰ *AE, DC, MC, V* ☉ *No lunch.*

$ ✕ **Portugália.** The largest in a chain of beerhouses, this bright, bustling,
PORTUGUESE   outlet boasts the best site of all: right on the river. As at the original

Portugália (at Avenida Almirante Reis 117), seafood and steak are the staples here, but there are changing daily specials such as bacalhau with prawns, *feijoada* (bean stew), or *alheira* (a garlicky fried sausage). It's all washed down with gallons of the house beer, or wine if you prefer. This is not a great place for vegetarians, though: they'll be limited to an omelet or cheese salad. Access to the restaurant is round the back of Cais do Sodré train station: it's about a 10-minute walk, just before the Meninos do Rio esplanade. ⊠ *Rua da Cintura do Porto de Lisboa, Cais do Sodré* ☎ *21/342–2138* ⊕ *www.portugalia. pt* ⊟ *AE, DC, MC, V.*

$$$$
PORTUGUESE

✕ **Tromba Rija.** This cavernous Lisbon branch of a famous old restaurant near the city of Leiria is a great place to dip into dishes from around the country. You should come hungry as the buffet always has a wide range of starters, such as various regional sausages, as well as a main dish of baked bacalhau. Desserts, fresh fruit, and dried nuts are all included in the price, as is wine or other drinks, plus coffee and a digestif. It's a little pricier on the weekend, when more main dishes are on offer, but that's also a great time for people-watching here, as local families gather for lunch. ⊠ *Rua Cintura do Porto de Lisboa, Edifício 254, Santos* ☎ *21/397–1507* ⊕ *www.trombarija.com* ⊟ *AE, DC, MC, V* ⊗ *No dinner Sun. No lunch Mon.*

ALCÂNTARA AND BELÉM

$
SEAFOOD

✕ **Doca Peixe.** The icy display of the day's catch at the entrance and the small aquarium clue you in to what's served here. In the center of the restaurant a staffer slices well-aged ham or weighs the fish that customers have chosen to have grilled over charcoal (what's available depends on what was in the market at dawn). You might start with a tomato-and-mozzarella salad or prawns seared in cognac, then move on to sea bass with clams, or codfish baked in a cornbread crust served with turnip leaves. Tenderloin steak with an Azeitão cheese sauce is a meaty alternative. ⊠ *Doca de Santo Amaro, Armazém 14, Alcântara* ☎ *21/397–3565* ⊕ *www.docapeixe.com* ⊟ *AE, DC, MC, V* ⊗ *Closed Mon.*

$$
MEDITERRANEAN

✕ **Estufa Real.** Every Sunday starting at noon, a wonderful brunch buffet with lots of salads (€37 per person) is served inside the greenhouse of the Ajuda Botanical Gardens. As you sit surrounded by exotic trees and plants, you will be cordially welcomed with a glass of orange juice or sparkling wine on the house. On other days, the à la carte menu varies according to the season, with Portuguse and international dishes, and each month features a dish flavored by a different herb picked from the on-site greenhouse. ⊠ *Jardim Botânico da Ajuda, Calçada do Galvão, Ajuda* ☎ *21/361–9400* ⊕ *www.estufareal.com* ⊟ *AE, DC, MC, V.*

$$$
BRAZILIAN
Fodor'sChoice
★

✕ **Uai!** The all-in buffet at this airy dockside Brazilian restaurant (take a taxi or walk 10 minutes from the Tram 15 stop) offers one of Lisbon's most impressive culinary voyages. Among the big attractions are rich meat- and bean-based stews from Minas Gerais state, such as black-bean feijoada. But there are also many vegetable-based dishes, featuring pumpkins and other gourds native to the Americas, and coconut desserts from Brazil's African-influenced northeast. Come hungry and take advantage of the restaurant's large list of cachaças—Brazilian rums—to help you digest it all. The lively soundtrack, too, will transport you across the south Atlantic. ⊠ *Doca Rocha Conde d'Óbidos, Armazém 114, Alcântara* ☎ *21/390–0111* ⊕ *www.uai.pt* ▭ *AE, DC, MC, V* ⊘ *Closed Mon. No lunch Tues. and Wed. No dinner Sun.*

PARQUE DAS NAÇÕES

$ ✕ **Senhor Peixe.** "Mr. Fish" knows what he's about: with good reason
SEAFOOD   this is one of the most popular of the fashionable new seafood restaurants that have sprung up in recent years. Fish of various types for grilling over charcoal comes straight from the port of Setúbal; this and the shellfish is sold by weight. Other house specialties in servings for one, two or more people include lobster rice, grouper stew with pasta, and fried cuttlefish. Hardened meat eaters only have steak, but this being Portugal there are lots of desserts and fresh fruit. Senhor Peixe is at the northern end of the former Expo 98 site, beyond the giant Pavilhão Atlântico. ⊠ *Rua da Pimenta, Parque das Nações* ☎ *21/895–5892 www.cidiarte.pt/senhorpeixe* ▭ *AE, DC, MC, V* ⊘ *Closed Mon.*

WHERE TO STAY

Lisbon has an excellent range of accommodation serving just about every market niche, from luxury pads downtown to workaday, business-oriented hotels out at the former Expo site, Parque das Nações. At the bottom end of the market, *pensões* have survived only by drastically upgrading facilities to face new rivals in the form of funky modern hostels that have doubles as well as dorms.

Even in the city's hotels, consider inspecting a room before taking it: street noise can be a problem, and, conversely, quieter rooms at the back don't always have great views (or, indeed, any views). Also, some hotels charge the same rate for each of their rooms, so by checking out a couple you might be able to get a better room for the same price. This is especially true of the older hotels and inns, where no two rooms are exactly alike.

Lisbon is busy year-round, so it's best to secure a room in advance of your trip. Peak periods are Easter and June–September; budget pensões are particularly busy in summer. Despite the high year-round occupancy, substantial discounts—sometimes 30% to 40%—abound from November through February.

WHAT IT COSTS IN EUROS				
	¢	$	$$	$$$	$$$$
FOR TWO PEOPLE	under €80	€80–€140	€141–€200	€201–€260	over €260

Hotel prices are for a standard double room, including tax, in high season (off-season rates may be lower).

THE ALFAMA

$ 🏨 **Albergaria Senhora do Monte.** If you want expansive views of the castle and river, book a room on one of the upper floors of this modern hotel. If it's summer, ask for a balcony or one of the four rooms with large terraces. The top-floor breakfast room, which has huge windows, also doubles as a bar. Staff are a dab hand at cocktails, making this and the adjoining terrace a place for guests to gather for drinks at sunset or a nightcap. Though the hotel is on Lisbon's highest hill, Tram 28 runs nearby. **Pros:** pretty views; helpful staff; off the beaten track. **Cons:** on a steep hill; limited facilities; little local character. ⊠ *Calçada do Monte 39, Alfama* ☎ *21/886–6002* ⊕ *www.senhoradomonte.blogspot. com* 🛏 *24 rooms, 4 suites* ♿ *In-room: a/c, safe, Wi-Fi. In-hotel: room service, bar, laundry service, Wi-Fi hotspot* ⊟ *AE, DC, MC, V* ⦿| *BP.*

$$ 🏨 **Olissippo Castelo.** Just below the castle, this small, elegant hotel pampers guests with luxurious linens, thick carpeting, elegant furnishings, and marble bathrooms. The pricier superior rooms on the second and third floors have lovely terraces where you can breakfast or sip an afternoon drink. Those on the fourth floor have full-length windows, but all guest rooms look out over the city. Families note: children up to age 12 can be accommodated for free in their parents' room. **Pros:** great views; quiet area; free Wi-Fi throughout. **Cons:** on a steep hill; sometimes a wait for breakfast seating; room service to 11 pm only. ⊠ *Rua Costa do Castelo 112–116, Alfama* ☎ *21/882–0190* ⊕ *www. hotelolissippocastelo.com* 🛏 *22 rooms, 2 suites* ♿ *In-room: a/c, safe, refrigerator, Wi-Fi. In-hotel: room service, bar, laundry service, Internet terminal, Wi-Fi hotspot, parking (paid)* ⊟ *AE, DC, MC, V* ⦿| *BP.*

$$$$ 🏨 **Solar do Castelo.** What's better than staying in an 18th-century mansion? How about if it is within the walls of a castle, with Roman ruins below? In this, one of the city's most unusual lodgings, original architectural features have been lovingly restored and archeological finds put on display. Featuring classical furnishings and subtle color schemes, the standard rooms in the original building offer river views; rooms in the newer wing incorporate parts of the castle wall. A sun-drenched courtyard acts as a breakfast area and is home to a family of peacocks. Some guests are amused by their begging for crumbs; others may feel pressured. There's no restaurant, but there are plenty nearby. **Pros:** charm to spare; quiet location; golf cart will fetch you from bus/street-car stop. **Cons:** up a steep cobbled road; some rooms only have showers. ⊠ *Rua das Cozinhas 2, Alfama* ☎ *21/880–6050* ⊕ *www.heritage.pt* 🛏 *14 rooms* ♿ *In-room: a/c, safe, DVD, no TV (some), Wi-Fi. In-hotel: room service, bar, laundry service, Internet terminal, Wi-Fi hotspot, parking (free)* ⊟ *AE, DC, MC, V* ⦿| *EP, BP.*

$$ 🏨 **Solar dos Mouros.** This melon-color town house, owned by an artist, has a great location near the Castelo de São Jorge. The decor, in a contemporary style with bright colors and minimalist furnishings, is a pleasant contrast to the traditional facade. Each room is individually decorated and has a sound system. For the best views, request one on the upper floors overlooking the Rio Tejo: those with castle views are slightly cheaper. The attic room is up a flight of stairs and has low ceilings but a private terrace with great views across the city. The hotel

has a small closed garden. **Pros:** close to the castle; lovely views; funky decor. **Cons:** up a steep hill and with stairs to climb; no Wi-Fi; no bar. ⊠ *Rua do Milagre de Santo Antonio 6, Alfama* ☏ *21/885–4940* ⊕ *www.solardosmouros.com* ⤶ *11 rooms, 1 suite* ⟑ *In-room: a/c, safe, refrigerator, DVD (some), Internet. In-hotel: laundry service, Internet terminal, some pets allowed* ⊟ *AE, DC, MC, V* ⟨◯⟩ *CP.*

THE BAIXA

$$$ ⊡ **Altis Avenida.** In what was once a grime-covered government building, this boutique addition to the Altis group offers glamour and comfort in a central location ideal for most sightseeing. The original modernist facade, with its art deco touches, now gleams, and inside is a mix of vintage and modern styles. Black and cream prevails though the guest rooms but mauve, green, beige, and mocha put in an appearance. Breakfast in the top-floor restaurant, with its views straight up the leafy Avenida da Liberdade, is a great way to start the day. There is a bar here, too. The hotel welcomes small pets for an extra €25 a night. **Pros:** pets welcome; one-hour free Internet use at downstairs terminal. **Cons:** rooms lack private terraces; no exercise facilities. ⊠ *Rua 1° de Dezembro 120, Restauradores* ☏ *21/044–0000* ⊕ *www.altisavenidahotel.com* ⤶ *68 rooms, 2 suites* ⟑ *In-room: a/c, safe, refrigerator, Wi-Fi. In-hotel: restaurant, room service, bar, laundry service, Internet terminal, Wi-Fi hotspot, some pets allowed* ⊟ *AE, DC, MC, V* ⟨◯⟩ *BP, MAP, FAP* ⓜ *Restauradores.*

$$$ ⊡ **Avenida Palace.** Built in 1892, Lisbon's first luxury hotel still costs a pretty penny and mainly attracts older travelers. French architect Lucian Donnat breathed new life into the hotel in the 1990s when refitting it to its original romantic belle epoque style and this was refreshed in 2009. Regal elegance combines with modern comfort here. Classically furnished rooms are completely soundproof, and bathrooms are lined in the finest Portuguese marble. Sumptuously furnished suites, some with Jacuzzis, are decorated in Louis XV, Louis XVI, D. Maria, D. José, and Empire styles. The whole hotel is no smoking except for a small lounge on the first floor. **Pros:** elegant and luxurious; central yet tranquil. **Cons:** some may find it excessively formal; no restaurant or spa; all Internet access paid. ⊠ *Rua 1° de Dezembro 123, Restauradores,* ☏ *21/321–8100* ⊕ *www.hotel-avenida-palace.pt* ⤶ *62 rooms, 20 suites* ⟑ *In-room: a/c, safe, refrigerator, Internet, Wi-Fi. In-hotel: room service, bar, gym, laundry service, Internet terminal, Wi-Fi hotspot, parking (free)* ⊟ *AE, DC, MC, V* ⟨◯⟩ *BP* ⓜ *Restauradores.*

$ ⊡ **Florescente.** Rooms at this inn are on five azulejo-lined floors and Fodor's Choice ★ vary in size; all are bright and cheerful and dotted with naïf paintings. They also have gleaming white-marble bathrooms with touches unusual in this price category, such as hairdryers. Suites with a sleeping alcove are a good choice for budget-conscious families. Florescente now has a restaurant offering Portuguese dishes and a buffet; you're on a street well known for its seafood restaurants, and there are more dining options just steps away in the Baixa. Floresecente is equally well located for sightseeing. **Pros:** friendly staff; great location; free Wi-Fi. **Cons:** can be noisy on show nights at nearby theaters; rooms in front catch

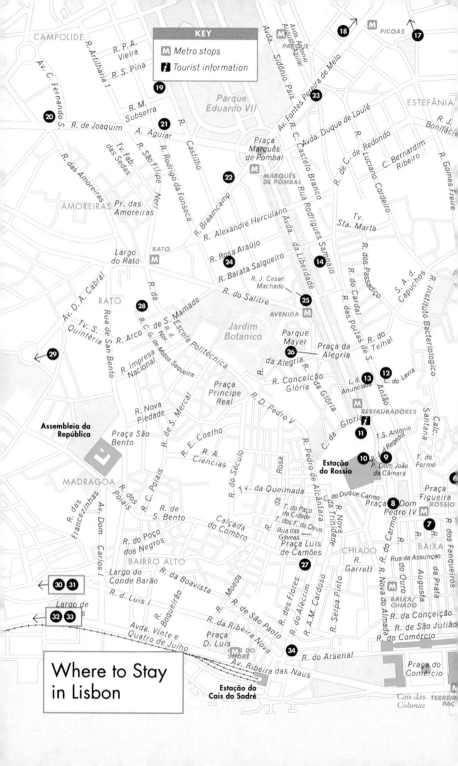

2

M ARROIOS

Cid. da Horta
R. Pascoal de Melo
A. Braga
R. F. Sanchez
R.C. Oliveira
R. H. Quionga
R. Morais Soares
Saraiva Lima
R. Jacinto Nunes
Praça Paiva Couçeiro

15 16

R. José Estêvão
R. Passos Manuel
R. de Arroios
R. Antonio Pedro
M ANJOS
R. Manchester
Cesário Verde
A. C. Eduardo Galhardo

Lgo. Sta. Bárbara
Escola do Exercito
R. de Sta. Bárbara
R. dos Anjos
Avenida
Almirante Reis
Palmira
R. Angola
R. do Zaire
R. Forno do Tijolo
Mozambique
R.-C. Verde
R. da Penha de França
R.F.P. Curado
R. Castelo Branco Saraiva

M INTENDENTE
R. Maria Andrade
R. A. Quental
R. C. Renata Batista
R. Angelina Vidal
R. Maria da Fonte
Avda. Machado dos Santos
R. dos Sapadores

MARTIM MONIZ
M
R. do Benformoso
R. do Terreirinho
R. Damasceno Monteiro
GRAÇA
R. dos Beatas
R. da Graça
R. Sol á Graça
R. J. d. Obidos
Bela Vista á Graça
R. do Vale so S.
R. Senhora da Glória
R. Leite de Vasconcelos
R. da Verónica

MOURARIA
Pte. de Lima
C. de Andrade
S. C. de Graça
Largo da Graça
R. do Oerário
R. Entremuros do Mirante

Largo Vicente
Cc. de S. Vicente
R. do Paraíso

Castelo de São Jorge
R. da Costa do Castelo
R. Milagre S. A.
S. A. Saude
Mamede

Santa Engracia
Estação Santa Apolónia

Sé Catedral
R. S. João da Praça
Casa dos Bicos
Bacalhoeiros
dega

ALFAMA
R. dos Remédios
R. de Ferro
SANTA APOLÓNIA
Museu Militar
R. Jardim do Tobaco

Avenida Infante Dom Henrique
Doca do Jardim do Tabaco
Rio Tejo
Doca da Marinha

1
2
3
4
5
7

0   200 yards
0   200 meters

less sunlight. ☒ *Rua Portas de Santo Antão 99, Baixa* ☎ *21/342–6609* ⊕ *www.residencialflorescente.com* ↘ *68 rooms* ♿ *In-room: a/c, Wi-Fi. In-hotel: restaurant, laundry service, Internet terminal, Wi-Fi hotspot, parking (paid)* ▭ *AE, DC, MC, V* ⦿I *CP* Ⓜ *Restauradores.*

$$$$
Fodor's Choice
★

▦ **International Design Hotel.** Opened in 2009, this four-star hotel facing Rossio square really stands out from the crowd. The violet on the façade continues into reception, with its lounge-music soundtrack. The rooms—designated S, M, L, XL—are decorated in four styles: urban, *tribu* (a sort of 21st-century African), Zen, and pop art. Some have private terraces and views of Rossio and Rua Augusta, a pedestrianized street packed with shops and cafés (which might persuade some not to take the optional hotel breakfast). All rooms have double-glazing. The restaurant features Asian as well as Portuguese cuisine, and there's a wine bar with a view. The hotel is no-smoking. **Pros:** well located for sightseeing; free Wi-Fi; marketed as gay-friendly. **Cons:** decoration over the top for some; not really family-oriented with just three extra beds available. ☒ *Rua daBetesga 13, Baixa* ☎ *21/324–090* ⊕ *www.idesignhotel.com* ↘ *55 rooms, 3 suites* ♿ *In-room: a/c, safe, refrigerator, Wi-Fi. In-hotel: restaurant, room service, bar, laundry service, Internet terminal* ▭ *AE, DC, MC, V* ⦿I *EP, BP* Ⓜ *Rossio.*

$$
▦ **Metrópole.** From its balconied late-19th-century facade to its '20s-style lounge-bar, the Métropole has been known to put a grin on the face of many a guest. Its light- and antique-filled rooms are inviting; some have sofas. The lounge and guest rooms in front overlook the Rossio—with its flower sellers and fountains—the Alfama, and the Castelo de São Jorge; other quarters have views of the Baixa's constantly changing tableaux. What's more, you can also buy bottles of the famous Buçaco wines here. Note that the whole hotel is no-smoking. **Pros:** ultracentral location; small and friendly; Wi-Fi in lobby free. **Cons:** from the street entrance you must climb a few steps to reach elevator and reception; no Wi-Fi in rooms; no parking. ☒ *Praça Dom Pedro IV (Rossio) 30, Baixa* ☎ *21/321–9030* ⊕ *www.almeidahotels.com* ↘ *36 rooms* ♿ *In-room: a/c, safe refrigerator. In-hotel: room service, bar laundry service, Wi-Fi hotspot* ▭ *AE, DC, MC, V* ⦿I *BP* Ⓜ *Rossio.*

$$
▦ **Mundial.** Steps from the Rossio and Restauradores squares, this large property looks uncompromisingly modern, but inside there's lots of good, old-fashioned charm combined with modern facilities. Rooms have simple light-wood furniture, firm mattresses, and well-equipped bathrooms; new carpets were recently laid throughout; guest rooms on the first three floors are earmarked for smokers (some even have their own garden), but some on the upper floors have castle views. Breakfast is served in the first-floor restaurant; lunch and dinner may be taken in the rooftop Varanda de Lisboa, which has views of the Baixa and the castle and where a pianist tinkles away from 8 pm. The bar, downstairs, has a smoking area. **Pros:** central with excellent transport links; friendly staff. **Cons:** ugly building; fills up with tour groups. ☒ *Praça Martim Moniz 2, Baixa* ☎ *21/884–2000* ⊕ *www.hotel-mundial.pt* ↘ *343 rooms, 7 suites* ♿ *In-room: a/c, safe, refrigerator, Wi-Fi. In-hotel: 2 restaurants, bar, laundry service, Internet terminal, Wi-Fi hotspot, parking (free)* ▭ *AE, DC, MC, V* ⦿I *BP, MAP, FAP* Ⓜ *Rossio.*

$ ⊞ **VIP Executive Suítes Éden.** One of downtown's most exciting art deco buildings—the former Eden theater and movie house—was long ago converted into an "aparthotel" aimed above all at families. It is now run by one of Portugal's must dynamic hotel groups. The understated lobby gives little hint at the comfort of the studios and one-bedroom apartments upstairs. Each overlooks a garden and the city and has modern furniture, a tiled bath, and a well-equipped kitchenette. Cribs are available. But the biggest thrill is on the top floor, where a bar (where the optional breakfast is served) opens onto a terrace with castle views; the small pool here gets the sun all day. **Pros:** accommodation well-equipped for longer stays; central location; fabulous views from bar and pool. **Cons:** no restaurant; no gym; Wi-Fi not free. ⊠ *Praça dos Restauradores 24, Baixa* ☎ *21/321–6600* ⊕ *www.viphotels.com* ⊅ *75 studios, 59 apartments* ⚷ *In-room: a/c, safe, kitchen, refrigerator, Wi-Fi. In-hotel: bar, pool, laundry service, Wi-Fi hotspot* ⊟ *AE, DC, MC, V* ❚❓❙ *EP, CP* Ⓜ *Restauradores.*

CHIADO AND THE BAIRRO ALTO

$$$$ ⊞ **Bairro Alto.** Despite its name this member of the Leading Small Hotels of the World is in chic Chiado, with its shops and cafés, but the funky Bairro Alto starts just across the square. Inaugurated in 2005 in a fine 19th-century building, the hotel has stylish guest rooms in muted tones that make it a real home away from home. It is also part of city life: the downstairs bar with its DJ pulls in media types for cocktails, while the river views from the terrace bar make it a still more popular attraction. The Flores restaurant serves Mediterranean cuisine (and Sunday brunch). Parking is in an underground facility out front. **Pros:** less impersonal than many top hotels; great location for sightseeing and nightlife; extra services such as personal shopper. **Cons:** guest rooms and baths less spacious than most upmarket hotels; some complaints about Wi-Fi quality. ⊠ *Praça Luís de Camões 2, Chiado* ☎ *21/340– 8288* ⊕ *www.bairroaltohotel.com* ⊅ *51 rooms, 4 suites* ⚷ *In-room: a/c, safe, refrigerator, DVD, Internet, Wi-Fi. In-hotel: restaurant, room service, 2 bars, gym, laundry service, Internet terminal, Wi-Fi hotspot* ⊟ *AE, DC, MC, V* ❚❓❙ *BP* Ⓜ *Baixa-Chiado.*

$ ⊞ **Casa de São Mamede.** The Casa de São Mamede is a real survivor. One of the first private houses to be built in Lisbon after the 18th-century earthquake was transformed into a relaxed guesthouse endowed with antique, country-style furniture; a tiled dining room; a grand staircase; and stained-glass windows. A thorough renovation in 2009 preserved all the old-world charm. A great deal is available for families: book a superior double room and two children aged up to 12 stay for free. You're just 10 minute on foot from the Bairro Alto or three minutes from the metro. **Pros:** family-friendly; tranquil yet bars and restaurants close by; free Wi-Fi and Internet terminal. **Cons:** no parking; perhaps a little staid for younger travelers. ⊠ *Rua da Escola Politécnica 159, Rato* ☎ *21/396–3166* ⊕ *www.casadesaomamede.com* ⊅ *26 rooms, 1 suite* ⚷ *In-room: a/c, safe, Wi-Fi. In-hotel: room service, laundry service, Internet terminal, Wi-Fi hotspot* ⊟ *DC, MC, V* ❚❓❙ *CP* Ⓜ *Rato.*

THE MODERN CITY

$$$ ⛅ **Altis.** This large, boxy, modern lodging has a broad range of facilities, including an art gallery and a heated indoor lap pool. Its virtue is reliability, which is why it hosts many business travelers. The mezzanine bar-lounge above the lobby is a relaxing spot, and rooms are comfortable, if unexceptional; those on higher floors have fine views of Parque Eduardo VII, as does the top-floor grill and the main bar, each with its own terrace. Next door the new Altis Prime has 50 apartments for longer stays (no pets allowed); they're not outstanding value, but guest may use the main hotel's facilities. **Pros:** great views from upper floors; good free exercise facilities. **Cons:** clear business vocation may be off-putting to leisure travelers; no free Wi-Fi access. ⊠ *Rua Castilho 11, Marquês de Pombal* ☎ *21/310–6000* ⊕ *www.altishotels.com* ⤻ *288 rooms, 12 suites* ⌂ *In-room: a/c, safe, Wi-Fi. In-hotel: 3 restaurants, room service, 2 bars, gym, spa, laundry service, Internet terminal, Wi-Fi hotspot, parking (paid), some pets allowed* ⊟ *AE, DC, MC, V* ⎪◎⎪ *BP, MAP, FAP* Ⓜ *Marquês de Pombal.*

$$ ⛅ **Britânia.** The Britânia is in one of the few 1940s buildings near Avenida da Liberdade to have survived progress unscathed. The onetime town house was the work of architect Cassiano Branco, and it originally housed studio apartments, hence the larger than usual rooms. But it's the art deco touches throughout that really impress—from the original marble panels in the baths to the "porthole" windows in the facade, the columns and candelabra in the lobby, and the murals in the bar. Staff members are really friendly. **Pros:** unique period decoration and furniture; spacious rooms. **Cons:** no restaurant; no exercise facilities. ⊠ *Rua Rodrigues Sampaio 17, Liberdade* ☎ *21/315–5016* ⊕ *www.heritage.pt* ⤻ *32 rooms, 1 suite* ⌂ *In-room: a/c, safe, refrigerator, DVD, Wi-Fi. In-hotel: room service, bar, laundry service, Internet terminal, Wi-Fi hotspot, parking (paid)* ⊟ *AE, DC, MC, V* ⎪◎⎪ *EP, BP* Ⓜ *Avenida.*

$$$$ ⛅ **Dom Pedro Palace.** The classically furnished lobby here hums with comings, goings, and clusters of conversation. It's across from the Amoreiras shopping complex, but the hotel has its own luxury boutiques as well. Rooms and suites have rich fabrics and polished wood furniture, including executive desks and other amenities for the prosperous business travelers who favor the hotel. Vacationers who love to shop also opt to stay here, owing to its location and its weekend rate reductions. The top floors offer amazing views over Lisbon, the river, and the 25 de Abril bridge. The Il Gattopardo serves gourmet Italian cuisine and has a cocktail terrace. The spa is one of Lisbon's most luxurious. **Pros:** great views; across from major mall; ultra-efficient service. **Cons:** no Wi-Fi in rooms; neighborhood often choked with traffic. ⊠ *Av. Eng. Duarte Pacheco 24, Amoreiras* ☎ *21/389–6600* ⊕ *www.dompedro.com* ⤻ *255 rooms, 8 suites* ⌂ *In-room: a/c, safe, Internet (some). In-hotel: 2 restaurants, room service, 2 bar, pools, gym, spa, laundry service, Internet terminal, Wi-Fi hotspot, parking (paid)* ⊟ *AE, DC, MC, V* ⎪◎⎪ *EP.*

$ ⛅ **Evidência Astória Creative.** Now part of the Evidência chain that has been spicing up the midrange market in recent years, the revamped three-star Astória is one of central Lisbon's best-value hotels. The lobby, with its funky decoration, sets the tone. In the very spacious guest rooms, dark browns and white predominate, with natural motifs ad splashes of color. Rooms at the front of the building have small balconies looking onto the Marquês de Pombal roundabout. There are no in-room safes but reception has one. **Pros:** good transport links; free Wi-Fi. **Cons:** no in-hotel parking; restaurant not open for dinner or on weekends. ✉ *Rua Braancamp 10, Marquês de Pombal* ☎ *21/386–1317* ⊕ *www.evidenciaastoria.com* ➡ *51 rooms* ⚘ *In-room: a/c, refrigerator, Wi-Fi. In-hotel: restaurant, bar, laundry service, Internet terminal, Wi-Fi hotspot* ⊟ *AE, DC, MC, V* ⦿| *BP* Ⓜ *Marquês de Pombal.*

$$$ ⊡ **Fontana Park.** A former steelworks was transformed into this aptly described urban refuge by Portuguese architect Francisco Aires Mateus and in-demand interior designer Nini Andrade Silva. Cast-iron pillars—now painted white—dominate the lobby, while Asian art dots public areas. Black and cream predominate in guest rooms whose Zen feel has won awards. Many have sweeping views; all have Philippe Starck chromotherapeutic bathtubs. For breakfast, the buffet includes freshly squeezed juice and eggs cooked on the spot. The Fontana's restaurants use ingredients fresh from the market opposite: one serves Portuguese, the other Japanese cuisine. A DJ livens up the bar most nights. There's a smoking lounge (rooms are no-smoking). **Pros:** great for architecture and design buff; opposite lively market; free espresso from in-room machine. **Cons:** no free Internet access; no exercise facilities. ✉ *Rua Engenheiro Vieira da Silva, Saldanha* ☎ *21/041–0600* ⊕ *www. fontanaparkhotel.com* ➡ *137 rooms, 2 suites* ⚘ *In-room: a/c, safe, refrigerator, Wi-Fi (some). In-hotel: 2 restaurants, room service, bar, laundry service, Internet terminal, Wi-Fi hotspot, parking (paid)* ⊟ *AE, DC, MC, V* ⦿| *BP* Ⓜ *Saldanha.*

$$$$ ⊡ **Four Seasons Ritz Lisbon.** The luxury starts the minute you step into the
Fodor'sChoice marbled reception area and through to the lounge bar, whose terrace
★ overlooks Lisbon's central park. Public areas are filled with tapestries, fine paintings, and antique reproductions, while airy guest rooms have elegant furnishings and balconies looking out to Castelo de São Jorge and the river, or toward Monsanto forest. A superb buffet breakfast is served in the Varanda restaurant, which has a terrace. There are lunch and dinner menus for kids of different ages—also available via room service. The spa is outstanding, while views from the rooftop gym and full-size running track are breathtaking whatever your fitness. **Pros:** smoothly efficient service; stunning views; outstanding exercise facilities and spa. **Cons:** formal decor may intimidate; pricey in-room Internet; free downstairs Wi Fi hotspot limited in size. ✉ *Rua Rodrigo da Fonseca 88, Marquês de Pombal* ☎ *21/381–1471* ⊕ *www.fourseasons.com* ➡ *262 rooms, 20 suites* ⚘ *In-room: a/c, safe, DVD, Internet, Wi-Fi. In-hotel: restaurant, room service, bar, pool, gym, spa, children's programs (ages 6–13), laundry service, Internet terminal, Wi-Fi hotspot, parking (free), some pets allowed* ⊟ *AE, DC, MC, V* ⦿| *BP, MAP, FAP* Ⓜ *Marquês de Pombal.*

$$$ ⊡ **Heritage Avenida da Liberdade.** This style-conscious boutique hotel could hardly be better located for the downtown sights, located as it is just yards from Praça dos Restauradores. Not all its design elements will convince all guests, but there are cute touches, such as the traditional Portuguese paving in the elevator. The optional breakfast is taken in the

lobby, with its outsize armchairs and low tables. There's a small pool with water jets, and a library with computer and a collection of DVDs that guests may view in their rooms. **Pros:** free Internet and Wi-Fi; 24-hour room service. **Cons:** rooms a little boxy; low chairs in lobby not ideal for breakfast. ⊠ *Av. da Liberdade 28, Avenida da Liberdade* ☎ *21/340–4040* ⊕ *www.heritage.pt* ⇱ *41 rooms, 1 suite* ⬦ *In-room: a/c, safe, refrigerator, DVD, Wi-Fi. In-hotel: room service, bar, laundry service, Internet terminal, Wi-Fi hotspot, parking (paid)* ▤ *AE, DC, MC, V* ⍾ *EP, BP* Ⓜ *Restauradores.*

¢　☷ **Lar do Areeiro.** It's hard to beat the value of this modern pension 1 km (½ mi) from the city center, on the main airport route, so reserve ahead. It has both a taxi stand and a metro station at its doorstep that will link you to all the main sights. Neat and spacious guest rooms all have private bathrooms (with shower rather than tub). Breakfast is taken in the café next door, which until 10:30 am is for the exclusive use of hotel guests (and which also has free Wi-Fi). **Pros:** great transport links; refrigerator can be installed in your room on request. **Cons:** hotel located on busy traffic junction; Wi-Fi free only on first two floors. ⊠ *Praça Dr. Francisco Sá Carneiro 4, Areeiro* ☎ *21/849–3150* ⊕ *www.residencialardoareeiro. com* ⇱ *62 rooms* ⬦ *In-room: a/c, safe (some), refrigerator (on request), Wi-Fi. In-hotel: room service, laundry service, Internet terminal, some pets allowed* ▤ *AE, DC, MC, V* ⍾ *CP* Ⓜ *Areeiro.*

$$　☷ **Lutécia.** Five minutes' walk from a metro that whisks you downtown in another 10, this four-star hotel is in a building that also houses a theater and an arthouse cinema. Public and private areas are both stylish and cozy, with colors that include rich browns, creamy whites, and deep reds. Most of the Lutécia's guest rooms have a private terrace, complete with table and chairs. Some guest rooms are set aside for smokers. The In Fusion restaurant has more to offer than most hotel eateries in this price bracket, with Indian, Portuguese, and international cuisine. **Pros:** free Wi-Fi throughout; good transport links. **Cons:** no exercise facilities; guests on lower floors may be disturbed by overground trains at night. ⊠ *Av. Frei Miguel Contreiras, Roma* ☎ *21/841–1300* ⊕ *www.luteciahotel.com* ⇱ *171 rooms, 4 suites* ⬦ *In-room: a/c, safe, refrigerator, Wi-Fi. In-hotel: restaurant, room service, bar, laundry service, Internet terminal, Wi-Fi hotspot, some pets allowed* ▤ *AE, DC, MC, V* ⍾ *BP, MAP, FAP* Ⓜ *Roma.*

$　☷ **Sana Capitol.** This new hotel tucked away in a quiet backstreet near Praça Marquês de Pombal is a sister to the nearby larger Sana Lisboa but offers better value. Facilities are limited, but the location and comfort are exceptional for the price. The Sana Capitol is decorated throughout in light, contemporary colors, with dark-wood furniture and high-tech fittings. There is no gym, but joggers can head for the greensward of Parque Eduardo VII, just 100 yards away. The hotel bar serves light meals. **Pros:** brand new; well located near metro and Lisbon's central park. **Cons:** facilities limited; some taxi drivers may not know street. ⊠ *Rua Eça de Queiroz 24, Marquês de Pombal* ☎ *21/353–6811* ⊕ *www.capitol.sanahotels.com* ⇱ *58 rooms, 1 suite* ⬦ *In-room: a/c, safe, refrigerator, Internet, Wi-Fi. In-hotel: bar, laundry service, Internet terminal, Wi-Fi hotspot, parking (paid)* ▤ *AE, DC, MC, V* ⍾ *BP, MAP, FAP* Ⓜ *Marquês de Pombal.*

$$$$ ⬚ **Sheraton Lisboa Hotel & Spa.** Even those who eschew chain hotels appreciate this Sheraton overlooking modern Lisbon. Its many advantages include a huge reception area with a comfortable bar, a helpful staff, and modestly sized smoking and no-smoking guest rooms with many amenities. Tower rooms have parquet floors, coffeemakers, a club lounge, and private check-in and checkout. Executive rooms have large desks and fax-modem outlets. The top-floor Panorama Bar and Restaurant is perfect for an aperitif or gourmet meal. Exercise in the warm outdoor pool, relax in the huge spa, or consult personal trainers in the gym, which offers an exercise-and-lunch package. The hotel is not far from Parque Eduardo VII and the Gulbenkian. **Pros:** top-notch room amenities; choice of bars and restaurants. **Cons:** pricey Internet and Wi-Fi access; spa and pool not free to guests; need to take transport to reach main sights. ⊠ *Rua Latino Coelho 1, Saldanha* ☎ *21/357–5757* ⊕ *www.sheraton.com* ⤳ *358 rooms, 11 suites* ♿ *In-room: a/c, safe, refrigerator, Internet, Wi-Fi. In-hotel: 2 restaurants, room service, 2 bars, 2 pools, gym, spa, laundry service, Internet terminal, Wi-Fi hotspot, parking (paid)* ⊟ *AE, DC, MC, V* ⑩ *EP, BP* Ⓜ *Picoas.*

$$$$ ⬚ **Sofitel Lisboa.** Right in the middle of the Avenida da Liberdade, the handsome Sofitel has a high-tech edge to its design. Rooms are pleasingly contemporary—decorated in attractive colors and comfortably appointed, with the fluffiest down pillows and spreads. The intimate piano bar, which hosts live jazz Thursdays and Saturdays, makes a good stop after a day's touring, and you can sit by a window in the Cais da Avenida restaurant for sidewalk views of the central artery. The lobby bar, too, is well stocked with newspapers and books. Children aged up to 12 may stay for free in their parents' room here. **Pros:** ultracomfortable rooms. **Cons:** area virtually dead at night; hotel often packed with conference participants; no pool and gym small. ⊠ *Av. da Liberdade 123–125, Avenida daLiberdade* ☎ *21/322–8300* ⊕ *www.sofitel-lisboa.com* ⤳ *167 rooms, 4 suites* ♿ *In-room: a/c, safe, DVD (some), Wi-Fi. In-hotel: restaurant, room service, bar, gym, laundry service, Wi-Fi hotspot, parking (paid), some pets allowed* ⊟ *AE, DC, MC, V* ⑩ *EP, BP, MAP* Ⓜ *Avenida.*

$$$$ ⬚ **Tiara Park Atlantic Lisboa.** Business travelers like the distinctive Park Atlantic (formerly part of the Meridien chain) for its location—right by Parque Eduardo VII—and facilities. There's plenty for vacationers to admire, too, including the split-level atrium with its cozy brasserie and separate conservatory-style bar. All the sleek rooms have smart bathrooms and soundproofing, as well as sound systems; they also have fantastic views over the city and park. There are two floors for smokers. Hotel guests can swim or play tennis or squash at special rates at the Clube VII gym in the park, which also has spa treatments. **Pros:** sophisticated decoration; excellent dining options. **Cons:** all Internet access is paid; no in-house pool or spa. ⊠ *Rua Castilho 149, Marquês de Pombal* ☎ *21/381–8705* ⊕ *www.lemeridien.pt* ⤳ *314 rooms, 17 suites* ♿ *In-room: a/c, safe, refrigerator, Internet, Wi-Fi. In-hotel: restaurant, room service, bar, gym, laundry service, Internet terminal, Wi-Fi hotspot, parking (paid), some pets allowed* ⊟ *AE, DC, MC, V* ⑩ *BP* Ⓜ *Marquês de Pombal.*

$$$$ [🏨] **Tivoli Lisboa.** There's enough marble in the public areas to make you fear for the future supply of the stone, but grandness gives way to comfort in the rooms, which are characterized by stylish, dark-wood, well-equipped bathrooms and a moderate amount of space. Smoking rooms are available. In warmer months the leafy garden with pool offer respite from the bustling city, while the top-floor Sky Bar hosts open-air cinema sessions and DJ nights. It and the adjoining Terraço restaurant present wonderful river and city views. A filling morning buffet is served in the Brasserie Flo, off the lobby, which also serves light gourmet meals. **Pros:** espresso machines in all rooms; metro station out front; garden a real downtown oasis. **Cons:** area has little to offer at night; free Internet access only in business center; public areas often overrun by conferences. ⊠ *Av. da Liberdade 185, Liberdade* ☎ *21/319–8900* ⊕ *www. tivolihotels.com* ⇰ *306 rooms, 48 suites* ⌂ *In-room: a/c, safe, refrigerator, Internet, Wi-Fi. In-hotel: 2 restaurants, room service, 2 bars, pool, gym, laundry service, Internet terminal, Wi-Fi hotspot, parking (paid), some pets allowed* ⊟ *AE, DC, MC, V* ❘◎❘ *BP* Ⓜ *Avenida.*

LAPA

$$$ [🏨] **As Janelas Verdes.** On the same street as the Museu de Arte Antiga, this late-18th-century mansion was once the home of Portuguese novelist Eça de Queirós. Fittings, furnishings, paintings, and tile work throughout are in keeping with the building's historic character. Its guest rooms are individually furnished and tasteful; some have access to the garden via an exterior staircase. On the ivy-covered patio, you can eat breakfast and imagine yourself in a different age. The top-floor library has an ample terrace with bar attached that, like the one downstairs, operates on an honor system. Reservations are vital for stays here. **Pros:** elegant and peaceful; unique literary associations; free Internet and Wi-Fi. **Cons:** just five parking spots; limited facilities; away from the city center. ⊠ *Rua das Janelas Verdes 47, Lapa* ☎ *21/396–8143* ⊕ *www.heritage.pt* ⇰ *29 rooms* ⌂ *In-room: a/c, safe, refrigerator (some), Wi-Fi. In-hotel: room service, 2 bars, laundry service, Internet terminal, Wi-Fi hotspot, parking (paid), some pets allowed* ⊟ *AE, DC, MC, V* ❘◎❘ *EP, BP.*

Fodor's Choice ★

$$$$ [🏨] **Olissippo Lapa Palace.** Housed in an elegant 19th-century manor house, Lapa Palace also boasts the amenities of a luxury resort. The spectacular gardens are dotted with ponds and fountains and have an expansive swimming pool, children's plunge pool, and sundeck. The spa has a heated indoor pool, gym, sauna, and steam bath. Rooms have sun-soaked balconies overlooking the garden; upper floors afford sweeping views of the river. The restaurant offers classic Mediterranean and Portuguese dishes. The bar is a comfortable place for tea (42 varieties) or cocktails, and has piano music most evenings; there's also a smoking lounge. **Pros:** exclusive feel; ultrarelaxing setting; lovely gardens. **Cons:** away from tourist sites; need a taxi to get around. ⊠ *Rua Pau de Bandeira 4, Lapa* ☎ *21/394–9494* ⊕ *www.lapapalace. com* ⇰ *104 rooms, 5 suites* ⌂ *In-room: a/c, safe, refrigerator (some), DVD (some), no TV (some), Internet (some), Wi-Fi (some). In-hotel: restaurant, room service, 2 bars, 2 pools, gym, spa, laundry service,*

Fodor's Choice ★

Internet terminal, Wi-Fi hotspot, parking (free), some pets allowed ⊟ *AE, DC, MC, V* ⏐◎⏐ *BP.*

$$ ▒ **York House.** Although it was a convent in the 17th century, this inn is far from austere. Vine-covered staircases climb to the garden from the street, and a shady courtyard invites you to relax over a meal or a drink. In summer, breakfast may be taken here. Each guest room is unique, though all are spacious and have good-quality reproduction furniture—including four-poster beds—and beautiful rugs, which also adorn the tiled corridors. Although it's a good way west of the center, York House is on tram and bus routes from downtown and near the Museu de Arte Antiga. It has a loyal, predominately British clientele; book well in advance. **Pros:** authentic period charm; handy for one of Lisbon's top museums; anglophone clientele. **Cons:** must climb 32 steps up from street; parking is potluck with just two spots. ⊠ *Rua das Janelas Verdes 32, 1°, Lapa* ☎ *21/396–2435* ⊕ *www. yorkhouselisboa.com* ⤺ *32 rooms* ⌂ *In-room: a/c, safe, refrigerator, Wi-Fi. In-hotel: restaurant, room service, bar, laundry service, Internet terminal, Wi-Fi hotspot, parking (free), some pets allowed* ⊟ *AE, DC, MC, V* ⏐◎⏐ *BP.*

CAIS DO SODRÉ AND SANTOS

$$ ▒ **Lx Boutique.** This design hotel inaugurated in 2010, in what is now one of Lisbon's most happening nightlife areas, is also handy for the sights of Belém and beaches of the Estoril Coast. The place transmits a love of Lisbon: guests are welcomed with an information pack, while rooms are decorated according to themes such as fado music or the poet Fernando Pessoa. Most have city views; those with river views include the Xplendid suite, with its retracting glass roof. There is free Wi-Fi; if you have no laptop, they'll lend you one. The restaurant serves sushi but also afternoon tea and scones. **Pros:** well located for sightseeing; free use of laptop and Wi-Fi; rooms have iPod stations and plasma TVs. **Cons:** rooms rather small; no exercise facilities; just one parking spot. ⊠ *Rua do Alecrim 12, Cais do Sodré* ☎ *21/347–4394* ⊕ *www. lxboutiquehotel.com* ⤺ *44 rooms, 1 suite* ⌂ *In-room: a/c, safe, refrigerator, Wi-Fi. In-hotel: restaurant, room service, bar, laundry service, Internet terminal, Wi-Fi hotspot, parking (paid)* ⊟ *AE, D, DC, MC, V* ⏐◎⏐ *BP* Ⓜ *Cais do Sodré.*

ALCÂNTARA AND BELÉM

$$ ▒ **Altis Belém.** This latest addition to the Altis chain boasts a unique dockside location midway between the Torre de Belém and the Padrão dos Descobrimentos. Appropriately, given the area's history, its decoration draws on themes relating to the golden age of Portuguese maritime exploration, with each wing representing a continent. Prices are kept down by the fact that the hotel's small size isn't ideal for conference business. There are some nice touches in guest rooms, such as espresso machines, and some truly luxurious ones: each suite has a Jacuzzi on its terrace. The Feitoria restaurant offers gourmet tasting menus, while the bar faces onto the river. **Pros:** unique dockside location; convenient for

Belém monuments and museums; free facilities (Wi-Fi, spa, parking). **Cons:** far from downtown sights; must cross rail tracks to reach public transport. ⊠ *Doca do Bom Sucesso, Belém* ☎ *21/040–0200* ⊕ *www. altisbelemhotel.com* 🗘 *45 rooms, 5 suites* ☾ *In-room: a/c, safe, refrigerator, Wi-Fi. In-hotel: 2 restaurants, room service, bar, 2 pools, gym, spa, laundry service, Internet terminal, Wi-Fi hotspot, parking (free)* 🖃 *AE, DC, MC, V* ⍟ *BP, MAP.*

$$$ ⊡ **Jerónimos 8.** Just around the corner from the famous monastery of the same name, Jerónimos 8 harmoniously blends past and present. As one of the first of Lisbon's design hotels it has a look that may no longer be cutting-edge, but remains appealing. Public areas are bright, with blocks of color, guest rooms more restrained. Some have views of the neighboring botanical garden or the monastery. Breakfast includes fresh cream pastries from the famous *pastelaria* nearby. The sun deck is a fine place to relax with a glass of something from the hotel wine bar. And since this is an Almeida hotel, patrons may purchase bottles of the famous Buçaco wines. **Pros:** near top sights; Wi-Fi free; breakfast includes famed local treat. **Cons:** no exercise facilities; a half-hour streetcar or 15-minute taxi ride from downtown. ⊠ *Rua dos Jerónimos 8, Belém* ☎ *21/360–0900* ⊕ *www.jeronimos8.com* 🗘 *61 rooms, 4 suites* ☾ *In-room: a/c safe, refrigerator, no TV (some), Wi-Fi. In-hotel: room service, bar, laundry service, Wi-Fi hotspot, parking (paid)* 🖃 *AE, DC, MC, V* ⍟ *BP.*

PARQUE DAS NAÇÕES

$$ ⊡ **Tivoli Oriente.** This recently renovated five-star hotel is well located for the airport, long-distance trains and sights such as the Oceanarium. Neutral colors in the lobby fit the Tivoli Oriente's vocation as a business hotel, but guest rooms are spacious and comfortable. Those from about the 11th floor up boast stunning river vistas. Superior rooms also have coffee machines. Unusual for pricey Lisbon hotels, Internet access is free throughout. The hotel has a heated indoor pool and Jacuzzi. Guests also have free access to a sauna and steam bath. The Amplo bar—open from 9 am to 1 am daily—has a smokers' section. **Pros:** free spa; free Internet access. **Cons:** far from downtown sights; drivers of large automobiles may find entering hotel car park tricky. ⊠ *Avenida D. João II, Lote 1.14.03, Parque das Nações* ☎ *21/891–5100* ⊕ *www.tivolioriente. com* 🗘 *262 rooms, 17 suites* ☾ *In-room: a/c, safe, refrigerator, Internet, Wi-Fi. In-hotel: restaurant, room service, bar, pool, gym, spa, laundry service, Internet terminal, Wi-Fi hotspot, parking (free)* 🖃 *AE, DC, MC, V* ⍟ *BP, MAP, FAP* Ⓜ *Oriente.*

NIGHTLIFE AND THE ARTS

Lisbon has a thriving arts-and-nightlife scene, and there are listings of concerts, plays, and films in the monthly *Agenda Cultural,* available from the tourist office and in many museums and theaters. Also, the Friday editions of both the *Diário de Notícias* and *O Independente* newspapers have separate magazines with entertainment listings. The weekly magazine *Time Out Lisboa* is still more comprehensive. Although all written in Portuguese, these publication's listings are easy to decipher.

It's best to buy tickets to musical and theatrical performances at the box offices, but you can also get them at several agencies, including the Fnac book, computer, and music store at the Colombo mall, the Valentim Carvalho music store in the Grandes Armazéns do Chiado shopping complex on Rua do Carmo, and the Ticket Line in the Colombo, Vasco da Gama, and Chiado malls. A special ticket office—called ABEP—on Praça dos Restauradores, in front of the Altis Avenida hotel, sells tickets to theater shows and concerts as well as to sporting events such as bullfights and soccer games. You can also buy tickets to most events on the phone or online with Ticketline.

Contacts ABEP (☎ 21/347–5824 ☽ Mon.–Sat. 10–7). **Ticketline** (☎ 707/234–234 ⊕ www.ticketline.sapo.pt).

NIGHTLIFE

Lisbon bars don't get going until after midnight, clubs even later. On weekends, mobs stand shoulder to shoulder in the streets. Many places are dark and silent on Sunday, Monday, Tuesday, and (sometimes) Wednesday. And don't expect to have a quiet drink in a bar: the company is generally young and excitable. ■ TIP→ **Not all bars have signs outside; to find the latest places you might just have to follow the crowds or try a half-open door.**

Some dance clubs charge a cover of €15 (more on weekends), including one drink; if you come early you may get in free. Clubs are open from about 10 or 11 pm (but only start filling up well after midnight) until 4 or 5 am; a few stay open until 8 am.

Plenty of places have live rock, pop, jazz, and Brazilian-music performances. African music is also popular here, with touring groups from Cape Verde and Angola playing regularly alongside homegrown talent.

For a less boisterous evening out, visit a café-bar or a *casa de fado*, where professional or amateur performers sing the city's own style of music.

Lisbon has a well-established gay and lesbian scene, concentrated primarily in and around the Bairro Alto, especially near the Jardim do Príncipe Real on the way to Rato.

FADO

Fado is a haunting music that emerged in Lisbon from hotly disputed roots: African, Brazilian, and Moorish are among the contenders. A single singer—male or female—is accompanied by a Spanish guitar and the 12-stringed Portuguese guitar, a closer relative of the lute. Today most *casas de fado* (fado houses) are in the Bairro Alto or Alfama.

They serve traditional Portuguese food, though it's rarely anything special, and the singing starts at 9 or 10 and may continue until 2 am. Reservations for dinner are essential, but if you want to go along later just to listen in, most establishments will let you do so if you buy drinks, usually around €10 minimum. Whenever you do arrive, fado etiquette is strict on one point: when the singing starts, all chatter must stop. *Silêncio, canta-se fado!*

THE ALFAMA

BARS

Fodor's Choice
★

Bartô. For a drink with a fabulous view in a bohemian setting, drop into Bartô, the bar and esplanade of the Chapitô circus school, just below the castle. ⊠ *Costa do Catelo 1–7, Castelo* ☎ *21/886–7334* ⊕ *www.chapito.org.*

Wine Bar do Castelo. This is a great place to flop down after visiting the castle: it has a good selection of wines to sample, plus authentic Portuguese snacks. ⊠ *Rua Bartolomeu de Gusmão 11–13, Castelo* ☎ *96/292–8956 or 96/402–8175.*

Fodor's Choice
★

Lux. The most stylish club in Lisbon is east of the city center. It's dotted with designer furniture and has two dance floors favored by big-name local and foreign DJs—plus a rooftop terrace with great river views. ⊠ *Av. Infante D. Henrique, Armazém A, Santa Apolónia* ☎ *21/882–0890* ⊕ *www.luxfragil.com* ☽ *Closed Sun.–Wed.*

FADO CLUBS

Fodor's Choice
★

Baiuca. At the family-run Baiuca, the quality of both food and singing varies but a great atmosphere is guaranteed. Nights often end with local amateurs literally lining up outside, raring to perform (you can just drop in after dinner if you order a few drinks). ⊠ *Rua de São Miguel 20, Alfama* ☎ *21/886–7284* ☽ *Fado shows Thurs.–Mon.*

Clube de Fado. Locals like this spot for the guitar playing of both established performers and rising stars. ⊠ *Rua S. João de Praça 92–94, Alfama* ☎ *21/885–2704* ⊕ *www.clube-de-fado.com.*

Mesa dos Frades. A relative newcomer that's all the rage among local fado lovers is housed in a tiny azulejo-lined former chapel. The food here is better than at many places, and they like you to order some, but if you're not going to eat you're also welcome to slip in at the end of the night if you order a couple of drinks. ⊠ *Rua dos Remédios 139A, Alfama* ☎ *91/702–9436* ☽ *Closed Sun.*

Museu do Fado. Prominent fadistas perform most nights in the restaurant attached to the city-run Museu do Fado. As with casas de fado, reservations are essential here. ⊠ *Largo do Chafariz de Dentro 1, Alfama* ☎ *21/882–3470* ⊕ *www.museudofado.egeac.pt* ⊙ *Closed Mon.*

Parreirinha d'Alfama. This little club is owned by fado legend Argentina Santos. She doesn't sing very often herself these days, but the club hires many other highly rated singers. ⊠ *Beco do Espírito Santo 1, Alfama* ☎ *21/886–8209.*

LIVE MUSIC
Onda Jazz. This established jazz venue often hosts performers from Africa and other places around the world. ⊠ *Arco de Jesus 7, Alfama* ☎ *21/888–3242* ⊕ *www.ondajazz.com* ⊙ *Closed Sun. and Mon.*

CHIADO
DANCE CLUB
Silk. On the edge of the Bairro Alto, Silk has a terrace with the best view of any Lisbon club. In theory entry is for members only, but if you are staying at a top-end hotel or dining at a gourmet restaurant, staff will be able to get you on the guest list for a night. ⊠ *Rua da Misericórdia 14, 6th fl., Chiado* ⊕ *www.silk-club.com* ⊙ *Closed Sun. and Mon.*

BAIRRO ALTO
The Bairro Alto, long the center of Lisbon's nightlife, is the best place for barhopping. Most bars here are fairly small, but many have DJs every night and stay open until 2 am or so. A number have a predominately gay clientele but invariably welcome all comers.

BARS
Alfaia. This place has substantial snacks such as *bacalhau à brás* to accompany your wine. ⊠ *Diário de Notícias 125, Bairro Alto* ☎ *21/343–3079.*

Artis. At Artis, you can listen to jazz and blues as you nurse a glass of red or white. ⊠ *Diário de Notícias 95, Bairro Alto* ☎ *21/342–4795* ⊙ *Closed Mon.*

Bairrus Bodega. This is one of several wine bars that have sprung up to meet the growing curiosity of foreign visitors about Portugal's wines. As well as regional cheeses, hams, and sausages, you can sample homemade ginja and other liqueurs—all to an exclusively Portuguese soundtrack. ⊠ *Rua da Barroca 3, Bairro Alto* ☎ *21/346–9060* ⊕ *www. bairrusbodega.com* ⊙ *Closed Sun.*

Bedroom. Young rich kids love the hip-hop and electro soundtrack; it only starts filling up around 11 pm. Dress like a fashion victim if you want to get past the doorman. ⊠ *Rua do Norte 86, Bairro Alto* ⊙ *Closed Sun.–Tues.*

Cinco Lounge. Run by a young British couple, this cocktail bar has a modern vibe. ⊠ *Rua Ruben Leitão 17A, Bairro Alto* ☎ *21/342–4033* ⊕ *www.cincolounge.com* ⊙ *Closed Sun. and Mon.*

Friends Bairro Alto. This is a relaxing place in one of the area's quieter streets. Order a drink and surf the net for free, or browse the books on hand. ⊠ *Rua da Rosa 99, Bairro Alto* ☎ *21/343–2419* ⊙ *Open daily 3 pm–2 am.*

Maria Caxuxa. This unique, DJ-driven venue is often packed with young art and media types. Its toasted sandwiches are perfect for late-night munchies. It has a small smoking room. ⊠ *Rua da Barroca 6–12, Bairro Alto* ☎ *96/503–9094* ☼ *Closed Mon.–Thurs.*

Pavilhão Chinês. For a quiet drink in an intriguing setting, walk uphill to this spot. It's filled to the brim with fascinating junk collected over the years—from old toys to statues—and it has two snooker tables. ⊠ *Rua Dom Pedro V 89, Bairro Alto* ☎ *21/342–4729.*

Solar do Vinho do Porto. The most refined place in Bairro Alto to start off your evening (or perhaps end it) is the relaxed Solar do Vinho do Porto. It's in a formidable old building where you can sink into an armchair and sample ports from a list of several hundred. ⊠ *Rua de São Pedro de Alcântara 45, Bairro Alto* ☎ *21/347–5707* ⊕ *www.ivdp.pt.*

Toca do Cachorrão. It's a friendly cubbyhole of a bar with live Brazilian pop music Thursday through Sunday. Homesick *brazucas (slang for Brazilians)*, locals, and tourists also come for the caipirinhas—and the famous hot dogs. ⊠ *Rua da Atalaia 85, Bairro Alto* ☎ *21/346–8085.*

FADO CLUB

Adega do Ribatejo. For fado at budget prices, consider a meal in here. There's live entertainment nightly, and *fadistas* on the roster might include your cook or waiter. It's a bargain, but it's also one of the less touristy places to see fado. ⊠ *Rua Diário de Notícias 23, Bairro Alto* ☎ *21/346–8343* ☼ *Closed Sun.*

GAY AND LESBIAN CLUBS

As Primas. It's referred to as a lesbian hangout, though everyone drops in to this tasca to hear the '80s music on the jukebox. ⊠ *Rua da Atalaia 154–156, Bairro Alto* ☎ *21/342–5925.*

Finalmente. It has one of the best sound systems in town and attracts a high-camp crowd. ⊠ *Rua da Palmeira 38, Bairro Alto* ☎ *21/347–9923.*

Frágil. Frágil is mainly but not exclusively gay and has a different DJ every night, Thursday through Saturday. ⊠ *Rua da Atalaia 126, Bairro Alto* ☎ *21/346–9578* ⊕ *www.fragil.com.pt.*

Memorial. This lesbian bar can get packed on the weekends. ⊠ *Rua Gustavo de Matos Sequeira 42, Rato* ☎ *21/390–7147.*

Portas Largas. A mostly (but not exclusively) gay crowd spills out into the street from this tiled tavern with barn doors. Sangria and caipirinha are the house drinks. ⊠ *Rua da Atalaia 105, Bairro Alto* ☎ *21/846–1379.*

Purex. This place is known for its '80s music and cocktails. ⊠ *Rua das Salgadeiras 28, Bairro Alto* ☎ *21/342–1942.*

Trumps. The city's longest-serving gay disco (at 30 years and counting) is proudly heterofriendly. ⊠ *Rua Imprensa Nacional 104b, Rato* ☎ *21/395–1135* ⊕ *www.trumps.pt.*

PARQUE DAS NAÇÕES

BAR

Peter Café Sport. If you can't make it to transatlantic yachtie favorite "Peter's bar" on Faial Island in the Azores, you can visit Lisbon's Peter Café Sport. Situated in front of the Garcia da Horta gardens in the former site of the Expo 98 World's Fair, at the eastern edge of town, it's known for its gin and tonics and toasted ham-and-cheese sandwiches. ⊠ *Rua da Pimenta, Parque das Nações* ☎ *21/895–0060* *www.petercafesport.com.*

CASINO

Casino Lisboa. In addition to 22 gaming tables and 1,000 machines, the gleaming black Casino Lisboa has gourmet eateries and a fun rotating bar that often stages free live jazz and blues. There are also paying shows by middle-of-the road performers in a large, comfortable auditorium. ⊠ *Alameda dos Oceanos Lote 1.03.01, Parque das Nações* ☎ *21/892–9000* ⊕ *www.casinolisboa.pt* ⊗ *Sun.– Thurs. 3–3, Fri. and Sat. 4–4.*

ALCÂNTARA AND BELÉM

Along the riverbank, under the bridge in Alcântara, the Doca do Santo Amaro has terrace-bars and restaurants converted from old warehouses. Most dance clubs are in this district and along the Avenida 24 de Julho.

BARS

BBC. Along the river is this slick (no sneakers) waterside restaurant-cum-nightclub. ⊠ *Av. Brasília, Pavilhão Poente, Belém* ☎ *21/362–4232* ⊕ *www.belembarcafe.com* ⊗ *Closed Sun. and Mon.*

Blues Café. If you're looking for an older, more sophisticated crowd (there's even a room set aside for cigar smokers), visit Blues Café, a dockside restaurant and bar with a dance floor. Many elements of the space were inspired by colonial New Orleans. ⊠ *Rua de Cintura do Porto, Armazém H, Alcântara* ☎ *21/395–7085* ⊕ *www.bluescafe.pt* ⊗ *Closed Sun. and Mon.*

Doca de Santo. In the main "Docas" development is this restaurant-bar with a palm-lined esplanade. It's a great place to start the night. ⊠ *Doca de Santo Amaro, Armazém CP, Alcântara* ☎ *21/396–3522* ⊕ *www. grupodocadesanto.com.pt.*

Havana. Get ready for a lively night of salsa here. The right cocktail is a *mojito* (made with crushed mint and rum). ⊠ *Doca de Santo Amaro, Armazém 5, Alcântara* ☎ *21/397–9893* ⊕ *barhavana.pai.pt.*

DANCE CLUBS

Op Art Café. A more down-to-earth place that's ideal for lovers of chillout (most nights), electro (Friday and Saturday), and other dance music is right on the waterfront in Docas. The label "café" is a little misleading: it does serve snacks and drinks during the day, but not so much after 2 am when the action really gets underway. ⊠ *Doca de Santo Amaro, Alcântara* ☎ *21/395–6787* ⊕ *www.opartcafe.com* ⊗ *Closed Mon.*

Twins. Twins attracts an older, well-heeled crowd. ⊠ *Rua de Cascais 57, Alcântara* ☎ *21/361–0310* ⊕ *www.twins.pt* ⊗ *Closed Sun.–Wed.*

GAY AND LESBIAN CLUB

Maria Lisboa. This spot hosts big gay nights, with drag shows on both Friday and Saturday. ⊠ *Rua das Fontainhas 86, Alcântara* ☎ *21/362–2560.*

CAIS DO SODRÉ AND SANTOS

You'll find large designer bars along Avenida 24 de Julho and in the Santos neighborhood, where—because it isn't residential—places can stay open until 5 or 6 am.

BARS

Lounge. This hip joint is where a twenty- and thirtysomething crowd chat—or shout—to the pumping sound of dance music; they also organize the occasional '80s party or other theme event. ✉ *Rua da Moeda 1, Cais do Sodré* ☉ *Closed Mon.*

Fodor's Choice ★ **Meninos do Rio.** Beyond the railway tracks (round the back of Cais do Sodré station whether you're on foot or with wheels) is this riverside bar with a sushi bar attached. It's a terrific hangout in summer; check out the tropical garden. ✉ *Rua Cintura do Porto, Armazém 255, Santos* ☎ *21/324–2910.*

O'Gillin's. Heading down toward Avenida 24 de Julho, the late-night crew stops off at O'Gillin's, Lisbon's only authentic Irish bar, across the road from Cais do Sodré station. It has live music on Monday, Friday, and Saturday. ✉ *Rua das Remolares 8–10, Cais do Sodré* ☎ *21/342–1899* ⊕ *www.irishpub.com.pt.*

Urban Beach. This slick venue right on the river draws a rich, hip crowd. ✉ *Rua da Cintura do Porto, Santos* ☎ *96/131–2721* ⊕ *www.grupo-k.pt* ☉ *Closed Mon.*

DANCE CLUBS

Kapital. Although it's the most high-fashion venue on the Avenida and has a lovely terrace, for some it might also fall under the category of musically unadventurous. ✉ *Av. 24 de Julho 68, Santos* ☎ *21/395–7101* ⊕ *www.grupo-k.pt* ☉ *Closed Sun.–Wed.*

Plateau. Plateau attracts nostalgic Lisboetas longing to dance to classic rock. According to one of the DJs, the Rolling Stones visited here once. ✉ *Rua Escadinhas da Praia 7, Santos* ☎ *21/396–5116.*

LIVE MUSIC

MusicBox. In a seedy but basically safe area, MusicBox regularly provides a stage for local and visiting rock bands, and hosts DJ nights and other live events. Check the Web site for details. ✉ *Rua Nova do Carvalho 24, Cais do Sodré* ☎ *21/347–3188* ⊕ *www.musicbox.com.*

LAPA

FADO CLUB

Fodor's Choice ★ **Senhor Vinho.** It's an institution that attracts some of Portugal's most accomplished fado singers. Since its owner doesn't pay commissions to hotel concierges, as some touristy *casas de fado* do, he'll instead pay €3 of the cost of your taxi if you hand over the receipt. Alternatively, there's a 10% discount coupon on the Web site. ✉ *Rua do Meio à Lapa 18, Lapa* ☎ *21/397–2681* ⊕ *www.srvinho.com* ☉ *Closed Sun. in Aug.*

2

THE MODERN CITY
BARS
Hard Rock Café. Downtown, the famous old art deco Condes cinema is now the Hard Rock Cafe. Lisbon can now send tourists off with a Hard Rock Cafe T-shirt, too. ⊠ *Av. da Liberdade 2, Liberdade* ☎ *21/324–5280* ⊕ *www.hardrock.com.*

LIVE MUSIC
Hot Clube de Portugal. The city's best jazz joint for decades is, for now, in larger premises after a fire gutted its historic basement home. Regardless of the location, its program should continue to include leading local and foreign names. ⊠ *Praça da Alegria 47–49, Liberdade* ☎ *21/361–9740* ⊕ *www.hotclubedeportugal.org.*

THE ARTS

GALLERIES
The city's gallery count has passed 100 and is growing. In addition, the Centro Cultural de Belém has an ever-changing program of art exhibitions, and Lisbon's major art museums and commercial buildings often put on temporary exhibitions alongside their permanent collections. Most galleries are closed Sunday and daily 1–3. All those we list here welcome casual visitors, although eliciting information on prices is a challenge unless gallery owners are convinced you're a serious buyer. ■TIP→ **If you're a collector, most galleries will insure and ship whatever you buy.**

Galeria Arte Periférica. The gallery at the Centro Cultural de Belém is a good source of contemporary art, particularly by younger artists. ⊠ *Centro Cultural de Belém lj. 3, Belém* ☎ *21/361–7100* ⊕ *www. arteperiferica.pt.*

Galeria Cristina Guerra. This gallery shows work by Portuguese heavyweights, including Julião Sarmento. ⊠ *Rua Santo António à Estrela 33, Estrela* ☎ *21/393–9559* ⊕ *www.cristinaguerra.com* ☉ *Closed Sat.–Mon.*

Fodor's Choice **Galeria Filomena Soares.** Housed in a large former warehouse not far
★ from the Museu Nacional do Azulejo, this gallery is owned by (and bears the name of) one of Europe's leading female art dealers. Her roster includes leading local and international artists such as José Pedro Croft and Shirin Neshat. ⊠ *Rua da Manutenção 80, Xabregas* ☎ *21/862–4122* ⊕ *www.gfilomenasoares.com* ☉ *Closed Sun. and Mon.*

Galeria Graça Brandão. The spotlight here is on works from other Portuguese-speaking countries such as Brazil. ⊠ *Rua dos Caetanos 26, Bairro Alto* ☎ *21/346–9183* ⊕ *www.galeriagracabrandao.com* ☉ *Closed Sun. and Mon.*

Galeria Novo Século. If you're looking for contemporary Portuguese art that has yet to catch the eye of critics or collectors, try this gallery. ⊠ *Rua do Século 23A, Bairro Alto* ☎ *21/342–7712.*

Galeria 111. You might spot works of London-based Paula Rego at what is arguably Portugal's best-known gallery. ⊠ *Campo Grande 113-A, Alvalade* ☎ *21/797–7418* ⊕ *www.111.pt.*

Movimento Arte Contemporânea. It was founded in 1993 by Dr. Alvaro Lobato Faria, a Portuguese professor of mathematics, with the aim of fostering cultural exchange between artists in Portugal and Portuguese-speaking countries such as Brazil. Contemporary paintings, sculptures, ceramics, tapestries, and jewelry are on display, 90% of which are by Portuguese contemporary artists and the other 10% by contemporary Portuguese-speaking artists. There's a branch on Avenida Álvares Cabral. ⊠ *Rua do Sol ao Rato 9, Rato* ☎ *21/385–0789* ⊕ *www.movimentoartecontemporanea.com.*

PERFORMING ARTS VENUES

Classical music concerts are staged from about October through June by the Fundação Calouste Gulbenkian. Of particular interest is the Festa da Música de São Roque, held in the church and museum of that name between November and January. The Orquestra Metropolitana de Lisboa performs a regular program at various city venues. Big-name American and British bands, as well as the superstar Brazilian singers so beloved in Portugal, often play in Lisbon's large concert halls and stadiums.

Fodor'sChoice ★ **Centro Cultural de Belém.** The center offers a huge range of reasonably priced concerts featuring national and international artists and musicians. ⊠ *Praça do Império, Belém* ☎ *21/361–2400* ⊕ *www.ccb.pt.*

Coliseu dos Recreios. This circular concert hall is a Lisbon cultural landmark. It hosts international performers and musicals as well as some of the best Portuguese stars. ⊠ *Rua Portas de Santo Antão 96, Restauradores* ☎ *21/324–0580* ⊕ *www.coliseulisboa.com.*

Culturgest. There's a major concert and exhibition program mounted at this auditorium and exhibition center supported by a Portuguese bank. ⊠ *Caixa Geral de Depósitos, Rua Arco do Cego 1, Campo Pequeno* ☎ *21/790–5155* ⊕ *www.culturgest.pt.*

Fodor'sChoice ★ **Fundação Calouste Gulbenkian.** The prime mover behind Lisbon's artistic and cultural scenes not only presents exhibitions and concerts in its buildings but also sponsors events throughout the city. ⊠ *Av. de Berna 45, São Sebastião* ☎ *21/793–5131* ⊕ *www.gulbenkian.pt.*

Pavilhão Atlântico. The country's biggest indoor arena is the main venue for rock concerts. It also hosts large-scale classical concerts, dance performances, and sporting events. ⊠ *Parque das Nações* ☎ *21/891–8409* ⊕ *www.pavilhaoatlantico.pt.*

Praça de Touros. These days this place hosts almost as many rock concerts as bullfights. ⊠ *Av. da República, Campo Pequeno* ☎ *21/782–0575* ⊕ *www.campopequeno.com.*

FILM

You can usually find the latest Hollywood releases playing around town. ■ TIP➔ **Films are generally shown in their original language with Portuguese subtitles.** The exceptions are children's cartoons, which are normally dubbed but often have at least one original-version showing available.

Programs change on Thursday. Ticket prices are around €5 and are even cheaper on Monday; it's best to get to the movie theater early on any day to be assured a seat.

There's a growing number of themed film festivals throughout the year, showcasing everything from horror movies to documentaries.

Cinemateca Portuguesa. Portugal's national film theater screens up to six different films Monday through Saturday, starting at times between 3:30 and 10. This is the place to catch key Portuguese films and art-house reruns. More obscure non-Portuguese movies might have subtitles in English, French, or Spanish rather than Portuguese. ✉ *Rua Barata Salgueiro 39, Marquês de Pombal* ☎ *21/359–6266* ⊕ *www.cinemateca.pt.*

Lusomundo Amoreiras. It's a modern 10-screen facility in the Amoreiras shopping complex. ✉ *Av. Eng. Duarte Pacheco, Amoreiras* ☎ *21/381–0240* ⊕ *www.zonlusomundo.pt.*

Lusomundo Colombo. This multiscreen cinema is in the Columbo mall. ✉ *Av. Lusíada, Benfica* ☎ *21/711–3600* ⊕ *www.zonlusomundo.pt.*

★ Fodor's Choice **Medeia Monumental.** This branch in the Monumental mall and office complex and the sister branch in the Saldanha Residence on the other side of Avenida Fontes Pereira de Melo have eight screens between them. Expect a judicious mixture of arty films and more-commerical releases. ✉ *Av. Fontes Pereira de Melo 51, Saldanha* ☎ *21/314–2223* ⊕ *www.medeiafilmes.pt.*

UCI Cinemas–El Corte Inglés. The latest in modern screen technology and the giant seats for VIPs are among the draws here. Cheap-ticket night is Wednesday. ✉ *Av. António Augusto de Aguiar 31, São Sebastião* ☎ *21/371–1700* ⊕ *www.uciportugal.pt.*

OPERA

Teatro Nacional de São Carlos. Opera season here runs December through June. ✉ *Rua Serpa Pinto 9, Baixa* ☎ *21/325–3000* ⊕ *www.saocarlos.pt.*

THEATER

Chapitô. A good way to hurdle the language barrier is to see a show at this theater, where contemporary clowning and physical theater, often with a mix of languages, is the order of the day. ✉ *Costa do Catelo 1–7, Castelo* ☎ *21/885–5550* ⊕ *www.chapito.org.*

Teatro Nacional de Dona Maria II. Although Lisbon's principal theater stages primarily plays in Portuguese, there are occasional foreign-language productions. Performances are given August–June. ✉ *Praça Dom Pedro IV, Baixa* ☎ *21/325–0835* ⊕ *www.teatro-dmaria.pt.*

SPORTS AND ACTIVITIES

ACTIVITIES

BOATING

Clube Naval. You can arrange to sail at the Clube Naval, which is directly on the river. The office is open Wednesday to Friday 2–5:30 and on weekends 10–1 and 2–6. ⊠ *Av. Brasília, Doca de Belém, Belém* ☎ *21/363–0061.*

GOLF

There are at least nine top-quality golf courses in Lisbon's environs, most of which are concentrated along the Estoril Coast. If you're planning to play golf and don't mind missing out on city-style dining, fado, or nightlife, consider staying at one of the hotels outside Lisbon with golf packages.

Lisboa Sport Clube. There's an 18-hole, par-69 golf course at this club in Queluz, about 20 minutes by car from Lisbon. Greens fees are €45 weekdays and €65 weekends. ⊠ *Casal da Carregueira, Belas* ☎ *21/431–0077* ⊕ *www.lisbonclub.com.*

HEALTH AND FITNESS

Altis. This hotel opens its indoor lap pool to nonguests for about €20 an hour. You also get unlimited use of sauna, steambath, and gym, making it quite the bargain. *Rua Castilho 11, Marquês de Pombal* ☎ *21/310–6000* ⊕ *www.altishotels.com.*

Ateneu Comercial de Lisboa. The 25m top-floor pool here is a cut-price option: €3.50 per hour. It's open 7:30 am to 10 pm weekdays and 9:30 am to 12:30 pm on Saturday. *Rua das Portas do Santo Antão 102, Restauradores* ☎ *21/347–3339.*

Clube VII. A €34 day pass here gives you access to the pool, the gym and tennis courts. A racket may be hired for €5 an hour, and balls are on sale for the same price. *Parque Eduardo VII, Marquês de Pombal* ☎ *808/277–288* ⊕ *www.clubevii.com.*

SPECTATOR SPORTS

BULLFIGHTING

Some people defend Portuguese bullfights because the bull isn't killed in the ring. Nonetheless, any bull injured during the contest is later killed.

First there's a performance by a *cavaleiro* (horseback fighter) whose riding skills are undeniable. Then *forcados* (a team of eight men), dressed in traditional red-and-green costumes, goad the bull into charging them. One man throws himself across the bull's horns (which have been padded) while the other men force the bull down, grabbing hold of whatever they can, including the beast's tail.

Praça de Touros. Portuguese-style bullfights are held on Thursday (and some Sundays) between Easter and October in the ornate bullring at Campo Pequeno. Performances start at 10 pm, and seats cost €15–€45. ⊠ *Praça* *de Touros do Campo Pequeno, Av. da República, Campo Pequeno* ☎ *21/793–2093* ⊕ *www.campopequeno.com* Ⓜ *Campo Pequeno.*

RACQUET SPORTS

Centro de Ténis de Monsanto. The municipal courts are in a lovely leafy setting of the forested park that acts as Lisbon's green lung. They cost from €6.50 (uncovered) to €11.50 (covered) per hour, with lighting €4 an hour extra after dusk; you must bring your own equipment. *Parque Florestal de Monsanto, Estrada do Alvito, Monsanto* ☎ *21/363–8073.*

Lisbon Racket Centre. You can play on one of the nine outdoor tennis courts from €5 per person per hour, plus €4 for lighting if needed. There are also courts for paddleball (€4) and squash (€6). Racket hire is €5; they also sell balls for €3. *Rua Alferes Malheiro, Alvalade* ☎ *21/846–0232* ⊕ *www.lrc.pt.*

SOCCER

Soccer is by far Portugal's most popular sport, and Lisbon has three teams, which play at least weekly during the September–May season. Although you can buy tickets on the day of a game at the stadiums, it's best to get them in advance from the ABEP booth in the Praça dos Restauradores.

Arrive at matches early; there's usually a full program of entertainment first, including children's soccer, marching bands, and fireworks.

■TIP→ **Be wary of pickpockets in soccer stadium crowds.**

Fodor's Choice
★
Estádio da Luz. Benfica, Lisbon's most famous soccer team, plays in the northwest part of the city. Their stadium holds 65,000 spectators, is the biggest in Portugal, and is one of the biggest in Europe. ✉ *Av. Gen. Norton Matos, Benfica* ☎ *707/200–100* ⊕ *www.slbenfica.pt* Ⓜ *Alto dos Moinhos.*

Estádio José de Alvalade Século XXI. Benfica's big local rival, Sporting Clube de Portugal plays at this stadium in the north of city. ✉ *Rua Fernando da Fonseca, Alvalade* ☎ *707/204–444* ⊕ *www.sporting.pt* Ⓜ *Campo Grande.*

SHOPPING

Shopping in Lisbon is less about multinational chains and more about locally owned shops. Instead of the same-old mass produced goods, you'll find ceramics and lace made by Portuguese craftspeople, foodstuffs and wine that impart the nation's flavor, and clothes by established local designers like Ana Salazar, whose collections have remained edgy since the '70s, or José António Tenente, whose classic cocktail dresses have bold twists.

Family-owned stores are still common in Lisbon, especially in the Baixa, where a grid of streets from the Rossio to the Rio Tejo has many small shops selling jewelry, shoes, clothing, and foodstuffs. Trendy Bairro Alto is another district full of little crafts shops with stylish, contemporary ceramics, wooden sculpture, linen, and clothing; some open only in the afternoon and stay open—sometimes with their own resident DJ—until after the restaurants and bars around them have begun filling up.

Bairro Alto is also one of the shopping hubs of Lisbon's flourishing fashion scene. The brightly lighted modern shops of local designers stand in stark contrast to the area's 16th-century layout and dark, narrow streets. The same can't be said of the antiques shops that abound in the Rato and Bairro Alto. Many are on a single long street that changes its name four times as it runs southward from Largo do Rato: Rua Escola Politécnica, Rua Dom Pedro V, Rua da Misericórdia, and Rua do Alecrim. Look on the nearby Rua de São Bento for more stores. There's also a cluster of antiques shops on Rua Augusto Rosa, between the Baixa and Alfama districts.

Chiado, Lisbon's smartest shopping district has a small shopping complex as well as many stores with considerable cachet, particularly on and around Rua Garrett. And Praça de Londres and Avenida de Roma—both in the modern city—form one long run of haute-couture stores and fashion outlets.

Several excellent shops in the Baixa sell chocolates, marzipan, dried and crystallized fruits, pastries and regional cheeses and wines—especially varieties of port, one of Portugal's major exports. Supermarkets also sell local wines, and so do, oddly enough, shops that purvey dried cod, which you'll see stacked outside on the sidewalk or hanging in the window. Rua do Arsenal has several such stores.

The Baixa is also a good place to look for jewelry. What is now called Rua Aurea was once Rua do Ouro (Gold Street), named for the goldsmiths' shops installed on it under Pombal's 18th-century city plan. The trade has flourished here ever since.

LISBON SHOPPING PLANNER

Hours: Most shops are open weekdays 9–1 and 3–7 and Saturday 9–1; malls and supermarkets are often open until 10 and on Sunday.

Money Matters: Credit cards—Visa in particular—are widely accepted.

Discounts and Deals: Apart from designer fashions and high-end antiques, prices are moderate. That said, look into the city tourist board's 24- and 72-hour Shopping Cards, which get you discounts at many leading stores. These are on sale at tourist offices and major hotels.

Shop Like a Local: To learn more about local designers, check out the Web site of Moda Lisboa (⊕ www.modalisboa.pt), the most important fashion showcase in Portugal. It brings together together Portugal's most prominent designers—Ana Salazar, Fátima Lopes, Maria Gambina, José António Tenente, Luís Buchinho, and Manuel Alves, just to mention a few. Their creations are sold in proprietary shops and/or alongside more established labels in other stores.

One-Stop-Souvenir Shopping: Shops at museums such as the Gulbenkian and Museu do Oriente are good for ceramic and jewelry reproductions and other classy souvenirs. Of the state-run institutions the Museu Nacional do Azulejo and Museu Nacional de Arte Antiga are rich hunting grounds. For a selection of what is available nationwide, hit the Loja dos Museus, which is in the same building as the national tourist office.

Buyer Take Note: Although there are shoe shops all over the city, they may have limited selections of large sizes, because the Portuguese tend to have small feet. The better shops, however, can make shoes to order.

DEPARTMENT STORE

Fodor's Choice
★

El Corte Inglés. Lisbon's largest department store, part of a major Spanish chain, sells fashion and household articles and has excellent service—as a visitor you'll be especially appreciative of such offerings as hotel deliveries, interpreter services, and V.A.T. (Value-Added Tax) refunds. Be sure to check out the high-quality supermarket here, a favorite among Lisboetas. ⊠ *Av. António Augusto de Aguiar 31, São Sebastião* ☎ *21/371–1700* ⊕ *www.elcorteingles.pt* Ⓜ *São Sebastião.*

MALLS

Amoreiras. This mall west of Praça Marquês de Pombal has a multitude of shops selling clothes, shoes, food, crystal, ceramics, and jewelry. It also has a hairdresser, restaurants, and seven movie screens; it's open daily 10 am–11 pm. ⊠ *Av Eng. Duarte Pacheco, Amoreiras* ☎ *21/381–0240* ⊕ *www.amoreiras.com.*

Atrium Saldanha. Short distances from some of the hotels in the Liberdade area and in a triangle on the Avenida Fontes Pereira de Melo are three small shopping centers that cater to a selective clientele. Among the highlights is a very good antiques shop, Antiguidades no Atrium. ⊠ *Praça Duque de Saldanha, Saldanha* ☎ *21/317–0850* ⊕ *www.atriumsaldanha.pt/en* Ⓜ *Saldanha.*

Campo Pequeno. Underneath the bullring is this mall with a good range of restaurants, a gourmet supermarket, and a small commercial movie theater with several screens. ⊠ *Av. República, Campo Pequeno* ☎ *21/351–0100* Ⓜ *Campo Pequeno.*

Colombo. One of the largest malls on the Iberian Peninsula has more than 400 stores and restaurants and a multiscreen cinema. The Colégio Militar–Luz metro station has an exit right inside the complex, which is open daily 9 am–midnight. ⊠ *Av. Lusíada, Benfica* ☎ *21/711–3600* ⊕ *www.colombo.pt* Ⓜ *Colégio Militar-Luz.*

Freeport. This huge retail development on the south bank of the Tagus is said to be Europe's largest designer outlet center, with hundreds of big-name labels sold at discount prices. It's a 15-minute drive over the Ponte Vasco da Gama pontoon bridge; Buses 431 and 432 head here directly from Gare do Oriente station. ⊠ *Av. Euro 2004, Alcochete* ☎ *21/234–3500.*

Grandes Armazéns do Chiado. Behind the restored facade of what was once the city's main department store is this stylish complex—designed by acclaimed Portuguese architect Álvaro Siza Vieira. Shops here are open daily 10–10; restaurants in the top-floor food court are open daily 10 am–11 pm. ⊠ *Main entrance on Rua do Carmo, Chiado* ☎ *21/321–0600* ⊕ *www.armazensdochiado.com* Ⓜ *Baixa-Chiado.*

Monumental. This mall is known for its movie theaters and attached bar, which features Belgian beers and hamburgers. Shops here include Pedra Dura, which sells unusual costume jewelry; cheap Internet access is also available in the excellent basement food court. ⊠ *Av. Fontes Pereira de Melo, Saldanha* ☎ *21/351–0500, 21/353–1856 cinemas.*

Saldanha Residence. The selection of shops here is good and includes Hugo Boss and Mandarina Duck. ⊠ *Av. Fontes Pereira de Melo 42-E, Saldanha* ☎ *21/351–0100* ⊕ *www.saldanharesidence.com* Ⓜ *Saldanha.*

Vasco da Gama. Portuguese suburbanites shop or catch a movie at this complex, which is open daily 9 am to midnight. A shopping excursion here teams well with a visit to the Oceanário de Lisboa. ⊠ *Av. D. João II, Parque das Nações* ☎ *21/893–0601* ⊕ *www.centrovascodagama. pt* Ⓜ *Oriente.*

MARKETS

Fodor's Choice
★
Feira da Ladra. One of Lisbon's main shopping attractions is this flea market held on Tuesday morning and all day Saturday. It's fun, but watch your wallet. ⊠ *Campo de Santa Clara, Graça* ☎ *No phone.*

Mercado da Ribeira. The vendors here, opposite the Cais do Sodré station, are entertainment in themselves. The market is open Monday–Saturday 6–2 for fresh produce of all kinds and weekdays 3–7 for florists. Every Sunday the first floor is taken over by the Feira de Coleccionismo (Collectors' Market), open from 9 to 1. ⊠ *Av. 24 de Julho, Cais do Sodré* ☎ *21/346–2966.*

Mercado do Arroios. For food, kitchenwares, and household items head to the covered market at the Arroios metro station. It's open Monday–Saturday 7–2. ⊠ *Rua Ângela Pinto, Praça do Chile* ☎ *21/847–5819.*

Mercado 31 de Janeiro. You'll find a little of everything here, including produce, Monday–Saturday 7–2. It's near the Picoas metro stop and the Sheraton hotel. ⊠ *Rua Eng. Vieira da Silva, Saldanha* ☎ *No phone* Ⓜ *Picoas.*

SPECIALTY STORES BY NEIGHBORHOOD

THE ALFAMA
CERAMICS
Loja dos Descobrimentos. You can often see artists at work in this shop specializing in hand-painted tiles. What's more, they ship worldwide, and you can even order online so there's no need to haul any breakables home in your bags. ⊠ *Rua dos Bacalhoeiros 12–A, Alfama* ☎ *21/886–5563* ⊕ *www.loja-descobrimentos.com.*

CRAFTS AND SOUVENIRS
Fodor's Choice
★
Arte da Terra. Opposite the Sé in the old cathedral stables, Arta da Terra uses old stone mangers as display cases for handiwork, traditional and modern, from around the country. As well as linen, felt hats, wool blankets, embroidery, and toys, you can pick up fado and folk CDs and an amazing range of representations of Santo António, the

What to Wear Home from Lisbon

The upswing in the Portuguese fashion world began in the '70s, when Ana Salazar shook up a national look that was stuck in the '50s. Intellectuals and artists embraced Salazar's asymmetrical shapes, ripped cloth, and cowl-effect drapings, and the international press hailed Salazar as a pioneer of "Made in Portugal" fashion. Her first shop on Rua do Carmo is still a landmark. Minimalist interior decor focuses attention on the clothes, which still use organza, mousseline, crepe, silk, and fishnet to create her trademark asymmetry.

Ana Salazar's former apprentice José António Tenente now has his own line. His cocktail dresses have a classic look and an incredible attention to detail: hand embroidery with sequins, glass, and crystal. He also designs jeans, handbags, and eyeglasses.

Young designer Maria Gambina goes for a more carefree, sporty look. She uses prep school–like polos and sports clothes to create a school-girl look with a touch of devilish flirtation—bustiers and corsets or hook-and-eye fasteners with tied cords.

A show stealer at the Prêt-à-Porter in Paris, Fátima Lopes is one of Portugal's most internationally acclaimed designers. She has taken her fluid cuts, asymmetries, and unusual trimmings (such as her diamond-studded bikini) abroad and has opened shops in Paris. A Barbie doll has been made in her image with long black, shiny hair, accentuated bangs, and daring outfits.

Manuel Alves and José Manuel Gonçalves, a team praised for their skill in using luxurious materials to create very feminine, sophisticated looks, now work out of an atelier in the Bairro Alto.

A new generation of designers is now coming through, led by the likes of Storytailors, whose large atelier and shop in Chiado has been visited by several foreign celebrities.

Perhaps the best time to get familiar with these names in fashion is during winter sales in January and February, and summer sales in July and August. Savings can be as much as 50% (and sometimes up to 70%).

city's favorite son. ⊠ *Rua Augusto Rosa 40, Alfama* ☎ *21/2745975* ⊕ *www.aartedaterra.pt.*

FOOD AND WINE

Fodor's Choice ★ **Conserveira de Lisboa.** There's a feast for the eyes at this shop, whose walls are lined with colorful tins of sardines and other seafood. Staff serve from behind an old wooden counter. ⊠ *Rua dos Bacalhoeiros 34, Alfama* ☎ *21/886–4009* ⊕ *www.conserveiradelisboa.pt.*

THE BAIXA

ANTIQUES

M. Murteira Antiguidades. Several centuries are represented at this shop near the cathedral. It carries furniture, painting, sculpture, and religious art from the 17th and 18th centuries as well as 20th-century artwork. ⊠ *Rua Augusto Rosa 19–21, Baixa* ☎ *21/886–3851* ⊕ *www.murteira-antiguidades.com.*

CLOTHING

Outra Face da Lua. This place is about as unconventional as Lisbon shopping gets. Prepare to be completely engaged by the eclectic mix of vintage clothes, items made using recylced materials, truly unique accessories, music, gadgets, temporary tattoos—you name it, really. Plus there's a tea room and bistro. ⊠ *Rua da Assunção 22, Baixa* ☎ *21/347–1570* ⊕ *www.aoutrafacedalua.com.*

CRAFTS AND SOUVENIRS

Bordados da Madeira. For embroidered goods from Madeira, stop by Bordados da Madeira. ⊠ *Rua 1° de Dezembro 135–139, Baixa* ☎ *21/342–5974.*

Loja dos Museus. In the same building as the national tourism office, this store sells a selection of items for sale in museum shops across Portugal. It's open weekdays 10–7 and almost the same hours on Saturday, when it closes from 1 to 2 for lunch. ⊠ *Palácio Foz, Praça dos Restauradores, Baixa* ☎ *21/343–3008* ⊕ *www.ipmuseus.pt.*

FOOD AND WINE

Manuel Tavares. Just off the Rossio, this shop has cheese, chocolate, vintage ports, and wine. ⊠ *Rua da Betesga 1A, Baixa* ☎ *21/342–4209* ⊕ *www.manueltavares.com.*

Napoleão. The helpful staff here speaks English and can recommend vintages. There's also a branch in Chiado. ⊠ *Rua dos Fanqueiros 70, Baixa* ☎ *21/887–2042* ⊕ *www.napoleao.co.pt.*

JEWELRY

Fodor's Choice
★ **Sarmento.** One of the city's oldest goldsmiths produces characteristic Portuguese gold- and silver-filigree work. ⊠ *Rua Aurea 251, Baixa* ☎ *21/342–6774.*

LEATHER GOODS

Casa da Sibéria. Here you'll find fine leather handbags and luggage. ⊠ *Rua Augusta 254, Baixa* ☎ *21/342–5679.*

Sapataria Bandarra. Not only is this shoe store reliable it also has a good range of sizes. And shoes here are both stylish and practical. ⊠ *Rua de Santa Justa 78, Baixa* ☎ *21/342–1178* ⊕ *www.bandarra.com.*

MUSIC

Discoteca Amália. Come here to shop for soulful fado music. The store also usually has a well-stocked van stationed on Rua do Carmo, blaring out fado. ⊠ *Rua Áurea 272, Baixa* ☎ *21/324–0939.*

CHIADO

ANTIQUES

Antiquália. This shop is packed with furniture, chandeliers, and porcelain. ⊠ *Praça Luís de Camões 37, Chiado* ☎ *21/342–3260.*

CERAMICS

Fábrica Sant'Ana. Founded in the 1700s, this outfit sells wonderful hand-painted ceramics and tiles based on antique patterns. Many think that the pieces sold here are Lisbon's finest. ⊠ *Rua do Alecrim 95, Chiado* ☎ *21/342–2537* ⊕ *www.fabrica-santanna.com.*

Vista Alegre. Portugal's most famous porcelain producer, Vista Alegre, established its factory in 1824. A visit to the flagship store is a must even though you can buy perfect reproductions of their original table services and ornaments at dozens of shops. There are also seven other Vista Alegre–owned stores in the city, including those at the Colombo, Amoreiras, and Vasco da Gama malls. ⊠ *Largo do Chiado 20–23, Chiado* ☎ *21/346–1401* ⊕ *www.vistaalegreatlantis.com.*

CLOTHING

Ana Salazar. Organzas, crepes, silk jerseys, and fishnet—fabrics with great texture—are among the materials designer Ana Salazar uses to create her edgy asymmetrical shapes. Collections lean toward black, charcoal, and other dark neutrals, with an item here or there that lends a splash of color. ⊠ *Rua do Carmo 87, Chiado* ☎ *21/347–2289* ⊕ *www. anasalazar.pt.*

José António Tenente. This designer has some great collections of women's clothing, especially cocktail dresses, featuring classical cuts with a strong graphic presence—hand-embroidered designs, sequins, and crystal applications. ⊠ *Travessa do Carmo 8, Chiado* ☎ *21/342–2560.*

Fodor's Choice ★ **Storytailors.** For some fairy-tale shopping, brows the racks filled with fantastical frocks, capes, and more here. Madonna is whispered to be among the celeb customers to have done so. ⊠ *Calçada do Ferragial 8, Chiado* ☎ *21/343–2306* ⊕ *www.storytailors.pt.*

CRAFTS AND SOUVENIRS

Fodor's Choice ★ **A Vida Portuguesa.** Out of what was once the storeroom of an old perfumery, A Vida Portuguesa, sells vintage Portuguese brands—from toys to toiletries—all of them stylishly packaged. ⊠ *Rua Anchieta 11, Chiado* ☎ *21/346–5073* ⊕ *www.avidaportuguesa.com.*

Fabrica Features. Above a Benetton store, Fabrica Features sells design items made in Portugal and elsewhere and often has art on display. The views from this fourth floor are great, too. ⊠ *Rua Garrett 83, 4th fl., Chiado* ☎ *21/325–6764.*

Nosso Design. The glass objects, ceramics, furniture, lamps, and jewelry here are all contemporary Portuguese designs. ⊠ *Rua Serpa Pinto 12, Chiado* ☎ *21/325–8960.*

FOOD AND WINE

Casa Pereira. This is the place for exotic coffees, teas, and chocolates. ⊠ *Rua Garrett 38, Chiado* ☎ *21/342–6694.*

JEWELRY

António da Silva. This is a great place to shop for antique silver and jewelry. ⊠ *Praça Luís de Camões 40, Chiado* ☎ *21/342–2728.*

Carla Amaro. If you are looking for original contemporary designer jewelry head here. ⊠ *Rua D. Pedro V, 1, Chiado* ☎ *21/347–4043.*

LEATHER GOODS

Luvaria Ulisses. Visit this art nouveau–style shop for gloves in the finest of kid and other leathers, in a variety of colors. ⊠ *Rua do Carmo 87, Chiado* ☎ *21/342–0295* ⊕ *www.luvariaulisses.com.*

MUSIC

Fnac. For chart hits and music from just about everywhere in the world, head to this store inside the Armazéns do Chiado shopping center. It carries books and computer products, too. ⊠ *Armazéns do Chiado, lj. 4.07, Rua do Carmo 2, Chiado* ☎ *21/322–1800.*

Trem Azul. Jazz freaks should make sure to stop by Trem Azul, a music store that also stages experimental concerts and is the home of go-ahead local label Clean Feed Records. ⊠ *Rua do Alecrim 21A, Chiado* ☎ *21/342–3141* ⊕ *www.tremazul.com.*

BAIRRO ALTO

ANTIQUES

J. Andrade Antiguidades. J. Andrade is well known for its unusual objects, paintings, sculptures, and furniture. ⊠ *Rua da Escola Politécnica 39, Bairro Alto* ☎ *21/342–4964* ⊕ *www.jandrade-antiguidades.com.*

Solar. One of Lisbon's best-known antiques shops sells 16th- to 18th-century Portuguese furniture as well as smaller items like paintings and azulejos. ⊠ *Rua Dom Pedro V 68–70, Bairro Alto* ☎ *21/346–5522.*

CLOTHING

A Fábrica do Acessório. For accessories in general, shop here; for hats, head across the street to sister store, A Fábrica dos Chapéus. ⊠ *Rua da Rosa 169, Bairro Alto* ☎ *91/251–4541.*

A Fábrica dos Chapéus. The young proprietor of this funky store sells a huge range of hats and also makes exclusive designs to order. For a broader range of accessories, head across the street to A Fábrica do Acessório ⊠ *Rua da Rosa 130, Bairro Alto* ☎ *91/308–6880* ⊕ *www.afabricadoschapeus.com.*

Eldorado. The draws here are the mix of new and secondhand clothing and the late closing time. You can shop till 11 pm or even midnight (in summer). ⊠ *Rua do Norte 23–25, Bairro Alto* ☎ *21/342–3935.*

Fátima Lopes. One of Portugal's most famous international fashion designers has conquered the limelight with her outrageous, skimpy outfits, including a diamond-studded bikini. ⊠ *Rua da Atalaia 36, Bairro Alto* ☎ *21/324–0546* ⊕ *www.fatima-lopes.com.*

Lena Aires. Stylish, figure-hugging dresses and sweaters made from Portuguese materials are the norm for this designer. ⊠ *Rua da Atalaia 96, Bairro Alto* ☎ *21/346–1815* ⊕ *www.lena-aires.com.*

FOOD AND WINE

Baco Alto. When little local grocery stores have their own Web site, you know something's afoot. Among such Bairro Alto delicatessens is Baco Alto, where you can taste wines and fine foods from around Portugal before buying. ⊠ *Rua do Norte 41, Bairro Alto* ☎ *91/245–6066* ⊕ *www.bacoalto.pt.*

Garrafeira Internacional. This shop selling international wines, as its name suggests, is open 10 am–8 pm every day but Sunday. ⊠ *Rua da Escola Politécnica 15–17, Bairro Alto* ☎ *21/347–6292* ⊕ *www.garrafeirainternacional.com.*

Mercearia da Atalaia. This shop stocks goodies such as wines, cheeses, and cured sausages. ⊠ *Rua da Atalaia 64A, Bairro Alto* ☎ *21/342–1104.*

Perola das Gáveas. Its floor to ceiling shelves are stocked tidily with wines and delicious gourmet olive oils and jams. ⊠ *Rua das Gáveas 44–46, Bairro Alto* ☎ *21/346–1221* ⊕ *www.peroladasgaveas.com.*

Solar do Vinho do Porto. The Solar, which is affiliated with the Instituto dos Vinho do Douro e Porto (Port Wine Institute) has hundreds of varieties to sample and bottles to buy. Sip in elegantly appointed spaces boldly painted in azulejo blue or spring green. ⊠ *Rua de São Pedro de Alcântara 45, Bairro Alto* ☏ *21/347–5707* ⊕ *www.ivp.pt.*

GIFTS AND SOUVENIRS

Bairro Arte. This is one of a number of hip shops in the Bairro Alto that gets going late (noon) but stays open till the wee hours (1 am)—'cause who doesn't sometimes wake up in the middle of the night with the urge browse for nicely milled soaps, colorful messenger bags, Smarties, and replicas of vintage street signs made from tiles? ⊠ *Rua das Salgadeiras 5, Bairro Alto* ☏ *91/057–1594* ⊕ *www.bairroarte.com.*

Jangada Solta. The list of crafts and countries represented is long. Look for ceramics from Portugal and South Africa, statues from India and Nepal, sculptures from Mozambique, and woven bags from Brazil. ⊠ *Rua da Rosa 73–75, Bairro Alto* ☏ *21/346–3228* ⊕ *www.jangadasolta.com.*

País Em Lisboa. This shop has wares from all over Portugal. ⊠ *Rua do Teixeira 25, Bairro Alto* ☏ *21/342–0911.*

LEATHER GOODS

Nouri. Nouri has a good selection of bags, belts, and wallets. ⊠ *Rua da Rosa 137–139, Bairro Alto* ☏ *21/347–6348.*

BELÉM

FOOD AND WINE

Coisas do Arco do Vinho. Within the Centro Cultural de Belém, the Coisas do Arco do Vinho sells prize-winning wines, and the owners, wine connoisseurs, can give you expert advice. ⊠ *Rua Bartolomeu Dias, Lojas 7–8, Belém* ☏ *21/364–2031* ⊕ *www.coisasdoarcodovinho.pt.*

SÃO BENTO

ANTIQUES

Antiguidades Dolls. It not only sells antique dolls but also Portuguese furniture and Indo-Portuguese art. Plan your visit for a weekday, though, as the shop is, oddly enough, closed on weekends. ⊠ *Rua de São Bento 250–254, São Bento* ☏ *21/397–815.*

THE MODERN CITY

CERAMICS

Fodor's Choice ★ **Viúva Lamego.** The prices at Lisbon's largest purveyor of tiles and pottery are competitive. ⊠ *Largo do Intendente 25, Intendente* ☏ *21/885–2408* ⊕ *www.viuvalamego.com.*

CLOTHING

David and Monteiro. This store sells top-quality, mid-range Portuguese and international fashions, such as Tommy Hilfiger and Lacoste. ⊠ *Av. de Roma 9A, Alvalade* ☏ *21/840–4296.*

Piri-Piri. A good place for children's clothing (as well as a wide range of other stores of all kinds) is the prosperous Campo de Ourique neighborhood, at the end of the Tram 28 route. Piri-Piri, for example, sells original, colorful designs for kids ages up to 10. ⊠ *Rua Almeida e Sousa 39A, Campo de Ourique* ☏ *21/396–3207* ⊕ *www.lojapiripiri.com.*

CRAFTS AND SOUVENIRS

Linho Bordado. Along with its competitor Bordados da Madeira, this shop is among the city's best for hand-embroidered goods. ✉ *Centro Comercial Arco Íris, Loja 7, Avenida Júlio Dinis 6–8, Campo Pequeno* ☎ *96/282–7365.*

FOOD AND WINE

Wine O'Clock. The sleek, modern interior and sophisticated lighting make this place seem more like a nightclub than a shop. That said, bottles of wine are sold here, and the stock is diverse. ✉ *Rua Joshua Benoliel 28, Amoreiras* ☎ *21/383–3237* ⊕ *www.wineoclock.pt.*

Lisbon Environs

WORD OF MOUTH

"For day trips close to Lisbon, you could go to Sesimbra. I had great fish at the harbor where the fishing boats dock (a little outside of town) on a picnic table—very informal but great fish. It has a nice old town and there are lots of good fish restaurants there, too. Palmela is nearby and coffee in the pousada/castle is always nice."

—Ireynold1

"I strongly suggest you take a day off to go to Sintra. Magical city. Make sure you go to Palácio da Pena, Castelo dos Mouros, and Quinta da Regaleira. You won't regret it."

—BrunoRibeiro

Updated by
Andrea Smith

The area known as Lisbon Environs—Grande Lisboa
(greater Lisbon) as the Portuguese call it—is a rich combination of historical, architectural, natural, and luxury
sights, all within an hour of Lisbon. Most towns are easily
accessible by public transport, especially if you use the
capital as your base.

Within a 50-km (31-mi) stretch north and south of the Rio Tejo (Tagus
River), you'll find a succession of attractive coastal resorts and important towns—each endowed with unique traditions and characteristics.
You can find impressive palaces in Sintra, luxury entertainment in Cascais and Estoril (such as the well-known Casino Estoril), great beaches
in Guincho and Costa da Caparica, a countryside populated by vines
in the Setúbal peninsula, and some of the best locales to have delicious
fresh seafood in Setúbal and Sesimbra.

Lisbon and its environs have served each other through history. Even
the country's earliest rulers appreciated the importance of one to the
other. It was the Moors who first built a castle northwest of the capital
at Sintra as a defense against Christian forces. The castle at Sintra fell
to the Christians in 1147, a few days after they defeated the Moors
in Lisbon.

Once the Christian Reconquest had been consolidated in Estremadura, there was a less pressing need for defensive measures. The early
Christian kings instead adopted the lush hills and valleys of Sintra as
a summer retreat and designed estates that survive today. Similarly,
Lisbon's 18th- and 19th-century nobility developed small resorts along
the Estoril Coast; the amenities and ocean views are still greatly sought
after. For swimming, modern Lisboetas look a little farther afield—
south across the Rio Tejo to the beaches and resorts of the Costa da
Caparica and the southern Setúbal Peninsula. Whichever direction you
travel and whatever your interests, you'll be delighted with all that's
within a day trip of Lisbon.

ORIENTATION AND PLANNING

GETTING ORIENTED

To the west of Lisbon, the Estoril Coast is a series of small beaches and
rocky coves; the most popular are found around the towns of Estoril
and Cascais. Farther north, the Atlantic makes itself felt in the windswept beaches and capes beyond Guincho and up to the lighthouse at
Cabo da Roca—the westernmost point in Europe. A few miles inland,
the Sintra hills are crisscrossed by winding roads marked by old monastic buildings, estates, gardens, and market villages.

TOP REASONS TO GO

Lovers' destination. Sintra, with its gorgeous palaces, gardens, streets, and landscape sets the mood for an old-fashioned romance for couples of all ages.

Endless beaches. All along the Estoril Coast and from Costa da Caparica to Cabo Espichel and around Arrabida, you'll find an endless number of unique beaches, from the lively ones of Cascais and Caparica, and to the soft and tranquil ones hidden among the cliffs around Guincho, Cabo da Roca, and Cabo Espichel.

Explore the wine region. On the Setúbal Peninsula you can find several well-known wine producers, such as J.M Fonseca, Quinta da Bacalhoa, and João Pires (J.P. Vinhos). It's also the home of Moscatel de Setúbal, a well-appreciated fortified wine. North of the Tejo you can find other historical wine regions, particularly Colares, close to Sintra.

Feast on some of the best seafood. This region is well known for its seafood restaurants, an essential factor of the Portuguese culture. Particularly in Sesimbra and Setúbal, you can find a great variety of such restaurants.

To the south, across the Rio Tejo, the contrast of the Setúbal Peninsula couldn't be more pronounced. The beaches of the Costa da Caparica combine to form a 20-km (12-mi) sweep of sand, backed by the fertile wine-producing countryside where the hilltop town of Palmela looks toward the peaks of the Serra da Arrábida, which overlooks the rugged shoreline.

The Estoril Coast. Just a short, scenic train ride from Lisbon along the Tejo River toward the Atlantic sits the area known as the Portuguese Riviera, with luxury hotels, high-end boutiques, championship golf courses, and high-rolling nightlife.

Sintra and Queluz. Located near the Serra de Sintra Mountain, Queluz and Sintra, a UNESCO World Heritage Site, are studded with magnificent palaces and gardens of rococo and romantic architecture and luxury *quintas*. But take a winding drive along the mountain to the rugged cliffs of Cabo da Roca, Azoia, and Guincho facing the Atlantic, and their natural beauty will surely leave you in awe.

The Setúbal Peninsula. Across the Rio Tejo just south of Lisbon, this peninsula is lined with unique beaches that stretch from lively Costa da Caparica to the mountainous Serra da Arrábida. There's delicious seafood in Cacilhas, further south in Sesimbra, and at the end at the Sado River estuary in Setúbal. Go inland to experience Azeitão's wine-rich farmlands and Palmela's fairy-tale, hilltop castle.

PLANNING

WHEN TO GO

If you're planning to visit in summer, particularly July and August, you *must* reserve a hotel room in advance. If you can, travel to the coastal areas in spring or early fall: the crowds are much thinner, and it could be warm enough for a brisk swim in April and October.

Most of the region's festivals are held in summer. In São Pedro de Sintra, the Festa de São Pedro (St. Peter's Day) celebration is on June 29; there are summer music and arts festivals in Sintra, Cascais, and Queluz; September in Palmela sees the Festa das Vindimas (Grape Harvest Festival); the Feira de Santiago (St. James Fair) takes place in Setúbal at the end of July. Year-round markets include those in São Pedro de Sintra (second and fourth Sunday of every month) and Vila Nogueira de Azeitão (first Sunday of every month).

PLANNING YOUR TIME

With a car you can cover the main sights north and south of the Rio Tejo in two days, although this gives you little time to linger. A week's touring wouldn't be too long to spend, particularly if you plan to soak up the sun at a resort or take an in-depth look at Sintra, whose beautiful surroundings alone can fill two or three days of exploring.

All the main towns and most of the sights are accessible by train or bus from Lisbon, so you can see the entire region on day trips from the capital. This is a particularly good way to explore the resorts on the Estoril Coast and the beaches of the Costa da Caparica, south across the Rio Tejo. The palace at Queluz also makes a good day trip: it's 20 minutes northwest of Lisbon by train. Using the capital as your base, a realistic time frame for visiting the major sights is four days: one each for the Estoril Coast, Queluz and Sintra, Caparica, and Setúbal.

GETTING HERE AND AROUND

BOAT AND FERRY TRAVEL

LisboFerries cross the river to Cacilhas (7 am–9 pm) from Fluvial terminal, adjacent to Praça do Comércio. One-way tickets cost €0.70, and the journey takes about 15 minutes. For information on car ferries from Cais do Sodré, check with the Lisbon tourist office. From Setúbal there's 24-hour ferry service for cars (€4.25) and foot passengers (€1) across to the Tróia Peninsula; the journey takes about 20 minutes. Departures are every 30–60 minutes.

Ferry Info LisboFerries (☎ 21/322–4000 ⊕ www.transtejo.pt).

BUS TRAVEL

Although the best way to reach Sintra and most of the towns on the Estoril Coast is by train from Lisbon, there are some useful bus connections between towns. Tickets are cheap (less than €3.50 for most journeys), and departures are generally every hour (less frequent on weekends); local tourist offices have timetables. Try to arrive 15 minutes before your bus departs.

At Cascais, the bus terminal outside the train station has regular summer service to Guincho (15 minutes) and Sintra (one hour). From the terminal outside the Sintra train station, there are half-hourly departures in summer to the resorts of Praia das Maçãs and Azenhas do Mar (30 minutes) in the west, and north to Mafra in Estremadura (one hour). There's also regular year-round service from Sintra to Cascais and Estoril (one hour). The most useful Sintra service, however, is the circular Stagecoach/Scotturb Bus 434 (daily, every 20–30 minutes, 10:20–5:45; €3.50 ticket valid all day), which connects Sintra station, the town center (the stop is outside the tourist office), Castelo dos Mouros, and the Pena Palace.

Buses to Caparica (45 minutes) depart from Praça de Espanha (Metro: Palhavã) in Lisbon, traveling over the Ponte 25 de Abril. Regular buses to Caparica also leave from the quayside bus terminal at Cacilhas, the suburb immediately across the Rio Tejo from Lisbon, which you can reach by ferry from the Fluvial terminal, adjacent to Praça do Comércio. Bus departures on both routes are as frequent as every 15 minutes in summer, and services run from 7 am until well after midnight, but can be very crowded. There's also a special beach bus (No. 75) that runs to Caparica every 15–30 minutes from the beginning of June to the beginning of September; pick it up in Lisbon at Campo Grande, Saldanha, or Marquês de Pombal metro stations, or outside the Amoreiras shopping center.

Express buses to Setúbal (45 minutes) leave every hour from Lisbon's Praça de Espanha (Metro: Palhavã); a local service also calls at Vila Nogueira de Azeitão (45 minutes) before traveling on to Setúbal (one hour). At Setúbal bus station you can connect with local services north to Palmela (20 minutes) and southwest to Sesimbra (30 minutes). Six buses daily run a 30-minute trip from Sesimbra bus station to the southwestern Cabo Espichel.

Bus Info **Rede Expressos** (✉ *Praça Marechal Humberto Delgado—Estrada das Laranjeiras, Lisbon* ☎ *213/581472* ⊕ *www.rede-expressos.pt*). **TST-Transportes Sul do Tejo** (✉ *Rua Marcos de Portugal—Laranjeiro, Almada* ☎ *212/549325* ⊕ *www.tsuldotejo.pt*).

CAR TRAVEL

Fast highways connect Lisbon with Estoril (A5/IC15) and Setúbal (A2/IP1), and the quality of other roads in the region is generally good. Take care on hilly and coastal roads, though, and if possible, avoid driving out of Lisbon at the start of a weekend or public holiday or back in at the end. Both Rio Tejo bridges—especially the Ponte 25 de Abril but also the dramatic Ponte Vasco da Gama—can be very slow. Parking can be problematic, too, especially in summer along the Estoril Coast. When you do park, *never* leave anything visible in the car, and it's wise to clear out the trunk as well.

Lisbon is the initial point of arrival for almost all the destinations covered here; from the city, it's easy to take public transportation or drive to all the surrounding towns. Driving south from Peniche–Óbidos, you can take the N8/IC1, rather than the main highway, if you prefer to see Sintra before Lisbon. If you're traveling north from the Algarve, you reach the city of Setúbal and its peninsula before arriving in Lisbon.

There are better choices for car rentals in Lisbon, although the tourist offices in Cascais, Estoril, Sintra, and Setúbal can advise you of the local possibilities.

Major Car Rental Agencies **Avis** (✉ *Tamariz Esplanade, Estoril* ☎ *800/201002* ✉ *Av. Luisa Todi 96, Setúbal* ☎ *265/538710*). **Europcar** (✉ *Estrada Marginal, Centro Comércial Cisne, Bloco B, Lojas 4 and 5, Cascais* ☎ *214/864438 or 219/407790*). **Hertz** (✉ *Av. Luisa Todi 277, Setúbal* ☎ *265/535328*).

TAXI TRAVEL

If you don't have your own car, it may pay—at least in time and convenience—to take a taxi to the towns around Lisbon. Cabs are relatively inexpensive, and you can usually agree on a fixed price that will include the round-trip to an attraction (the driver will wait for you to complete your tour). Tourist offices can give you an idea of what fares are reasonable for local trips, although Sintra should cost roughly €30, Queluz should be €20, and Estoril €35 one-way.

Taxi Info **Central taxi lines** (☎ *214/660101 or 214/659500*).

TRAIN TRAVEL

Electric CP commuter trains travel the entire Estoril Coast, with departures every 15–30 minutes from the waterfront Cais do Sodré station in Lisbon, west of the Praça do Comércio. The scenic trip to Estoril takes about 30 minutes, and four more stops along the seashore bring you to Cascais, at the end of the line. A one-way ticket to either costs €1.30; service operates daily 5:30 am–2:30 am. Trains from Lisbon's Rossio station, between Praça dos Restauradores and the Rossio, run every 15 minutes to Queluz (a 20-minute trip) and on to Sintra (40 minutes total). The service operates 6 am–2:40 am, and one-way tickets cost €1.10 to Queluz, €1.30 to Sintra.

Fertagus trains from Lisbon's Sete Rios and Entre Campos stations cross the Rio Tejo via the Ponte 25 de Abril. Passengers on the double-decker railcars benefit from fine views, air-conditioning, and background music during the seven-minute crossing. Taxis at stations across the river can take you on to Cacilhas, Setúbal, and other towns on the Setúbal Peninsula. Trains run between 5:30 am and 2 am. From June through September a narrow-gauge railway runs for 8 km (5 mi) along the Costa da Caparica from the town of Caparica, on the Setúbal Peninsula. It makes 20 stops at beaches along the way, and a one-way ticket to the end of the line costs €2.50.

Train Info **CP-Comboios de Portugal (Portugal Train Line)** (☎ *808/208208* ⊕ *www.cp.pt*). **Fertagus** (☎ *707/127127* ⊕ *www.fertagus.pt*).

RESTAURANTS

Restaurants on the coast stick to seafood and fish, whereas those farther inland may specialize more in grilled meats and codfish. Inexpensive restaurants don't generally take reservations, but it's advisable to reserve for the expensive ones. Dress for meals is usually casual, but people do dress up for dining at the Casino de Estoril or more expensive restaurants, namely those in luxury hotels.

City dwellers make a point of crossing the Rio Tejo to the suburb of Cacilhas for platefuls of *arroz de marisco* (rice with shellfish) or *linguado* (sole). One of Caparica's summer delights is the smell of grilled sardines wafting from restaurants and beachside stalls. Seafood is also the specialty along the Estoril Coast—even the inland villages here and on the Setúbal Peninsula are close enough to the sea to be assured a steady supply of fish.

In Sintra *queijadas* (sweet cheese tarts) are a specialty, and in the Azeitão region of the Setúbal Peninsula locals swear by the *queijo fresco,* a delicious white cheese made either of goat's or sheep's milk. Lisbon's environs also produce good wines. From Colares comes a light, smooth red, a fine accompaniment to a hearty lunch; Palmela, the demarcated wine-growing district of Setúbal, produces distinctive amber-color wines of recognized quality; and the Fonseca winery produces a splendid dessert wine called Moscatel de Setúbal.

HOTELS

Outside Lisbon, you can stay in *pousadas,* inns that are members of the Turismo de Habitação organization. These are often in converted historic buildings, and they generally have superior facilities and restaurants. The three in this region are at Queluz, Setúbal, and Palmela. Since they typically have few rooms, availability is limited. Regardless of where you stay, in summer it's essential that you book in advance. Out of season, many places discount their prices substantially.

WHAT IT COSTS IN EUROS					
	¢	$	$$	$$$	$$$$
Restaurants	under €10	€10–€15	€16–€20	€21–€25	Over €25
Hotels	under €80	€80–€140	€141–€200	€201–€260	Over €260

Restaurant prices are per person for a main course at dinner. Hotel prices are for a standard double room, including tax, in high season (off-season rates may be lower).

SHOPPING

There are shopping opportunities galore outside of Lisbon, from clothes sold in smart Cascais and Estoril boutiques to the ceramics and woven and leather goods at roadside stalls and at weekly village markets. Quality and prices vary greatly, so shop around before buying. While bargaining isn't commonplace, a firm command of Portuguese may allow you to negotiate a small discount at markets and roadside stalls.

EMERGENCIES

In all the towns, a notice on the door of every *farmácia* (drugstore) indicates the name and address of the nearest all-night pharmacy.

Emergency Info General emergencies (☎ 112). **Police** (☎ 214/839100 or 214/839101 in Cascais, 214/646700 or 214/646706 in Estoril, 265/522022 in Setúbal, 219/198630 in Sintra ⊕ www.psp.pt).

VISITOR AND TOUR INFORMATION

The main Lisbon office of Turismo de Portugal, the Portuguese national tourist board, is in between the Campo Pequeno and Entrecampos metro stations. It has information on the city's environs. Local tourist offices are usually open June–September, daily 9–1 and 2–6, sometimes later in the tourist-resort areas. Hours are greatly reduced after peak season, and most offices are closed Sunday.

Most travel agents and large hotels in Lisbon or its environs can reserve you a place on a guided tour. Cityrama has half-day trips to Queluz, Sintra, and Estoril and a tour of the area's royal palaces (each €51); nine-hour tours of Sintra and Cascais (€76 including lunch); and even an evening visit to Estoril's famous casino (€71.50 including dinner).

Gray Line Tours has day trips into Lisbon and the Arrábida Mountain range and to local crafts centers for around €71.

For guided tours of the Sintra area, ask at the tourist information center, which has current schedules and can sell tickets. Half-day tours typically encompass visits to all the principal sights and a wine tasting in Colares.

National Visitor Info Turismo de Portugal (Portugal Tourism) (✉ *Rua Ivone Silva, Lote 6, Lisbon* ☎ *211/205050 or 211/140200* ⊕ *www.visitportugal.com*).

Tour Info Cityrama (✉ *Av. Duque D'Avila 116B, Saldanha, Lisbon* ☎ *213/191090* ⊕ *www.cityrama.pt*). **Gray Line Tours** (✉ *Av. João XXI 78 E, Campo Pequeno, Lisbon* ☎ *213/191090* ⊕ *www.grayline.com*).

THE ESTORIL COAST

The Estoril Coast extends for 32 km (20 mi) west of Lisbon, taking in the major towns of Estoril and Cascais as well as smaller settlements that are part suburb, part beach town. It's a favored residential area, thanks to its proximity to (and milder winters than) the capital as well as its coastal charms. Some fancifully refer to the region as the Portuguese Riviera, and certainly the casino at Estoril and the luxurious seaside villas and hotels lend the area cachet.

In summer, count on crowds. And not only are the towns and beaches crowded, but the ocean—sparkling from a distance—suffers from a long-standing pollution problem. The quality of the water varies greatly from beach to beach, and although ongoing work is slowly rectifying the situation, you should avoid swimming in an area unless the water has been declared safe. Look for a blue Council of Europe flag, which signals clean water and beach; consult local tourist offices if you're unsure.

GETTING HERE AND AROUND

Unless you intend to tour the wider region, it's better to travel by train from Lisbon rather than drive. This section has been arranged accordingly, with coverage of Estoril first, followed by Cascais, which marks the end of the train line; from here, it's a short walk to the Boca do Inferno and a brief bus ride to the magnificent beach at Guincho. If you drive, leave Lisbon via the Avenida/Estrada Marginal (follow signs for Cascais and Estoril) and take the scenic coastal route (the N6), or the faster Auto-Estrada da Oeste (A5/IC15).

TIMING

The best time to visit the Estoril Coast is in the spring (late March–May) and fall (late September–late October) when it usually gets warm enough to go to the beaches, which are a lot less crowded. During the summer months, especially late July and all of August, the Estoril Coast is packed with tourists and locals, both on the beaches and in the cities. Avoid driving on Avenida/Estrada Marginal to or from Cascais and Estoril during the afternoon on summer weekends, as the traffic is horrendous from beachgoers.

SAFETY AND PRECAUTIONS

In the summer, pickpocketers like to wander through the crowded streets, beaches, and public transportation to take advantage of the unaware tourists so be careful with your belongings when out and about.

ESTORIL

26 km (16 mi) west of Lisbon.

In the 19th century, Estoril was preferred by the European aristocracy, who wintered here in the comfort and seclusion of mansions and gardens. Although the town has elegant hotels, restaurants, and sports facilities, reminders of its genteel history are now few. It presents its best face right in the center, where today's jet set descends on the casino, at the top of the formal gardens of the Parque do Estoril.

Across the busy main road, on the beachfront Tamariz esplanade, are alfresco restaurants and an open-air seawater swimming pool. The best and longest local beach is at Monte Estoril, which adjoins Estoril's beach; here you'll find restrooms and beach chairs for rent, as well as plenty of shops and snack bars.

Estoril is also very much a sporting place, with major sailing events, windsurfing, tennis, horse shows, and motoring events at the old Formula 1 racetrack.

GETTING HERE AND AROUND

The best way to get here is through the CP urban train (Linha de Cascais) (⇨ *see CP info under Train Travel, above*) departing from the Cais do Sodré station in Lisbon that runs directly to Estoril, or get off at the previous station, São João do Estoril, and walk 2 km (1 mi) along the seafront promenade path; it's a fine route with excellent views. The drive by car will take 25 minutes from Lisbon, either by the A2 highway or the scenic Avenida Marginal running along the coast. Avoid driving on Marginal to or from Estoril during the afternoon on summer weekends, as the traffic is horrendous from beachgoers.

ESSENTIALS

Visitor Info Estoril Tourism (✉ *Av. Clotilde, Edifício Centro de Congressos 3° A* ☎ *214/647576* ⊕ *www.estoril-portugal.com).*

EXPLORING

Estoril Casino. In addition to gambling salons, the casino is one of the largest in Europe and has a nightclub, bars, and restaurants. Tour groups often make an evening of it here, with dinner and a floor show, but it's a pricey night out. Most visitors, however, are content to feed one of the 1,200 slot machines in the main complex and then check out the other entertainment options: art exhibits, movies, nightly cabaret performances, and concerts and ballets (in summer). To enter the gaming rooms you must pay €4 (slots are free) and show your passport to prove that you're at least 21. Reservations are essential for the restaurant and floor show. For €37.50 you can see the show and have one drink on the house; €50 buys you entrance to the show and dinner. ✉ *Parque do Estoril* ☎ *214/667700* ⊕ *www.casino-estoril.pt* ☉ *Daily 3–3; floor show nightly at 11.*

GREAT ITINERARIES

IF YOU HAVE 2 DAYS

Start in Lisbon and drive to **Estoril,** where you can soak up the atmosphere in the gardens and on the seafront promenade. From here, it's only a short distance to **Cascais**—the perfect place for an alfresco lunch. Afterward, explore the little cove beaches, and the **Boca do Inferno.** The next day, it's less than an hour's ride north to **Sintra,** where before lunch you'll have time to see its palace and climb to the **Castelo dos Mouros.** After lunch, return to Lisbon, stopping in **Queluz** to see the Palácio Nacional. For dinner, you might cross the Rio Tejo from Lisbon to **Cacilhas** for seafood.

IF YOU HAVE 4 DAYS

From Lisbon, head for **Queluz** and its Palácio Nacional. In the afternoon, make the short drive to **Sintra,** where you can spend the rest of the day seeing the sights in and around the town. Consider having dinner in the adjacent village of **São Pedro de Sintra.** Head out early the next day to the extraordinary **Palácio Nacional de Pena.** To contrast this haughty palace with a more humble sight, travel west to the **Convento dos Capuchos** before continuing to the headland of **Cabo da Roca.** Wind south to the wonderful beach at **Guincho** to catch the late afternoon sun and have a bite to eat. Stick to the coastal road as it heads east toward **Cascais,** where you can spend the night.

On the third day, drive back into Lisbon through **Estoril.** Cross the Rio Tejo via the mighty Ponte 25 de Abril, and detour for lunch at either **Cacilhas** or **Costa da Caparica.**

It's then only an hour's drive to the region's two attractive pousadas, one at **Palmela,** the other 10 km (6 mi) down the road in **Setúbal.** On the fourth morning drive through the **Serra da Arrábida,** stopping for lunch at an esplanade restaurant in **Sesimbra.** From here, you can return to Lisbon in around 90 minutes.

IF YOU HAVE 7 DAYS

Seven days exploring this region will allow the luxury of two nights in **Sintra,** providing time to see all the surrounding sights with ease. On the third day, drive straight to **Cabo da Roca** and then south to **Guincho,** if you fancy a half day at the beach, before following the coast around to **Cascais.** Two nights spent here will allow you to really get to know the town and travel to and from **Estoril.**

From Cascais, return to Lisbon and aim for lunch at either **Cacilhas** or **Costa da Caparica.** Spend the night at the pousada in **Palmela** or the one in **Setúbal.** On the final day, plan to have lunch in **Vila Nogueira de Azeitão** and continue on a drive through the **Serra da Arrábida.** If you spend the night in the fishing port and resort town of **Sesimbra,** you'll have time to visit the windswept **Cabo Espichel** before driving back to Lisbon.

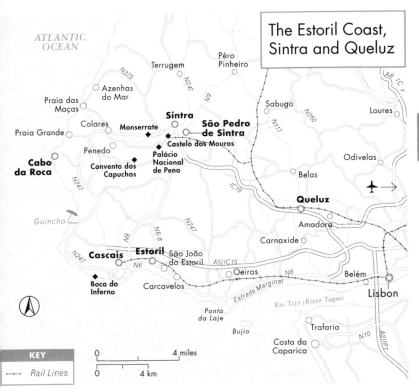

ATLANTIC
OCEAN

The Estoril Coast,
Sintra and Queluz

3

KEY

↦ *Rail Lines*

0   4 miles

0   4 km

Museu Exílio. Inaugurated in 1942 and located above the post office, this museum has a collection of memorabilia relating to Portugal's mid-20th-century history. It consists mostly of black-and-white photos with captions in Portuguese, focusing on Estoril's community of aristocratic exiles who fled here from northern Europe during World War II. There's also an exhibit devoted to the Nazi persecution of the Jews. ⊠ *Av. Aida* ☎ *214/825022* 🖾 *Free* ⊘ *Mon.–Sat. 10–6.*

WHERE TO EAT

$$$

PORTUGUESE

✕ **A Choupana.** Just east of town, this restaurant has views of Cascais Bay from its picture windows. It's a reliable establishment, where you can ask the English-speaking staff about the daily specials. Fresh seafood is the mainstay—try the *cataplana,* a tangy, typically Portuguese dish of clams and pork. Live music usually accompanies dinner, and in summer there's dancing nightly until 2. ⊠ *Estrada Marginal* ☎ *214/664123* 🖃 *AE, DC, MC, V* ⊘ *Closed Mon.*

$$

ECLECTIC

✕ **Cimas.** You're in for a good meal in these baronial surroundings of burnished wood, heavy drapes, and oak beams that have played host to royalty, high-ranking politicians, and other celebrities. The menu is an international hybrid: choose from game in season, fresh fish, chicken curry, even Indonesian *saté* (skewered, charcoal-broiled meats served with a peanut sauce). ⊠ *Av. Marginal* ☎ *214/681254* 🖃 *AE, DC, MC, V* ⊘ *Closed Sun.*

$ ✕ **La Villa.** Whatever you do, book a table by a window at this seaside
ECLECTIC   restaurant. Although the building is a Victorian landmark, it houses
an elegant modern restaurant with the area's most interesting seafood
dishes. Appetizers include fresh cod with cilantro marinated in gazpacho
and soft-shell crab filled with broccoli purée. For an entrée you might
try monkfish braised with pepper mustard over a baby onion and green
pepper confit. Or go international with oysters, sushi, and sashimi.
⊠ *Praia do Tamariz* ☎ *214/680033* ▤ *AE, DC, MC, V* ⊗ *Closed Mon.*

WHERE TO STAY

$$ ⬚ **Amazonia Hotel.** This four-star boutique aparthotel sits on a hill just far
enough off the main drag so that it's hidden from the noise and crowds
but still convenient walking distance to all the attractions. Choose from
a regular room, a studio, or a one-bedroom apartment, which all come
equipped with crisp white linens and either look down to a pretty little
pool shaded by palm trees or the top floors looking up and out to the
ocean horizon. Almost all rooms have a balcony and are quite spacious.
The small restaurant ($$) serves inexpensive Portuguese and international
cuisine all day. **Pros:** near enough to downtown but still a great place to
relax and get away from the mess; private and tranquil; beautiful views
of the ocean from top floor rooms. **Cons:** breakfast not included in room
price; can get tiring walking up hill to get to hotel; Internet is not free.
⊠ *Rua Engenheiro Álvaro Pedro de Sousa 175, Cascais* ☎ *214/680424*
⊕ *www.amazoniahoteis.com/estoril* ⤵ *28 rooms* ⚙ *In-room: a/c, safe
(some), kitchen (some), refrigerator (some), Wi-Fi (some). In-hotel: restaurant, room service, bar, pool, children's programs (ages 2–12), laundry
service, Wi-Fi hotspot, parking (free)* ▤ *AE, MC, V* ⑩*EP.*

$$ ⬚ **Estoril Eden Apartamentos Suites Hotel.** Looking for a good base with
☾   the kids? The comfortable studios and suites in this modern apartment
hotel are reasonably sized and equipped with cable TV, fold-out beds,
and a basic kitchenette. All rooms have balconies and are soundproof
as well. Ask for one of the front rooms, which have coastal views. Chil-
dren might enjoy the free summer-entertainment program and the good
sports facilities; parents can keep an eye on things from the poolside café.
The ocean is just a few minutes' walk away via an underpass that starts
behind the Monte Estoril train station. **Pros: great ocean views; conve-
nient location right in front of beach; very pleasant staff. Cons:** outside
of city; have to take train or walk a long way to get here; furniture is
a bit dated and run-down; breakfast lacking in selection. ⊠ *Av. Sabóia*
☎ *21/466–7600 or 800/604–4274* ⊕ *www.hotelestorileden.pt* ⤵ *162
units* ⚙ *In-room: a/c, safe (some), kitchen (some), refrigerator (some),
Wi-Fi (some). In-hotel: restaurant, room service, bar, golf course, pools,
gym, beachfront, children's program (ages 2–12), laundry facilities, laun-
dry service, Wi-Fi hotspot, parking (paid)* ▤ *AE, DC, MC, V* ⑩*BP.*

$ ⬚ **Hotel Inglaterra.** Displaying the splendor of an early-20th-century
Portuguese colonial mansion, the hilltop Hotel Inglaterra—completely
renovated in 2004—offers classy ambience. Although the interior decor
is contemporary, the minimalist black wooden furniture, combined with
exotic wooden cupboards and China-red embellishments, lends an
Asian flavor. Most guest rooms have king-size beds, and the bathrooms
covered in white azulejos match the rooms in their spaciousness. Some

of the rooms have a private balcony overlooking either the Cascais Bay or the Sintra hills. If it weren't for the contemporary bathing suits by the pool, you could imagine you were in the Hollywood of the 1920s. **Pros:** convenient central location; walking distance to beach; very friendly and helpful staff. **Cons:** many rooms and bathrooms are very small; no parking; Internet isn't free. ⊠ *Rua do Porto 1* 🕾 *214/684461* ⊕ *www. hotelinglaterra.com* ↯ *55 rooms* ⌂ *In-room: a/c, safe (some), Internet (some). In-hotel: restaurant, room service, bar, golf course, pool, gym, spa, diving, bicycles, children's programs (ages 2–12), laundry service, Internet terminal* ⊟ *AE, DC, MC, V* |◯| *BP.*

$$

Fodor's Choice
★

🏨 **Palácio Estoril Hotel & Golf.** Exiled European courts waited out World War II in this luxurious 1930s hotel. Several of the well-appointed, Regency-style guest rooms have balconies, and public areas are adorned with monumental columns and chandeliers. A comfortable bar has views over the outdoor pool to the town's central park. A charming afternoon tea service is offered in the lounge daily. The Thai spa, run by Banyan Tree, is known for their signature "rain mist massage," and the spa's Sandalwood Café offers Thai cuisine and light spa fare. There's no more-elegant spot in town to dine than the Four Seasons Grill ($$$–$$$$; reservations and a smart outfit are essential). Golfers who stay here can tee up at the Clube de Golfe do Estoril at reduced rates. **Pros:** impeccable old-world service and helpful staff; excellent restaurant food; beautiful hotel. **Cons:** Internet isn't free; service prices expensive. ⊠ *Rua do Parque, Parque do Estoril* 🕾 *214/680000* ⊕ *www. palacioestorilhotel.com* ↯ *129 rooms, 32 suites* ⌂ *In-room: a/c, safe (some), Internet (some). In-hotel: 3 restaurants, room service, bars, golf courses, pool, gym, spa, children's programs (ages 2–16), laundry service, Internet terminal, parking (free)* ⊟ *AE, DC, MC, V* |◯| *BP.*

NIGHTLIFE

At night, the casino is a big draw, and most other barhopping takes place within the hotels. Most places are open 10 pm–3 am.

Bauhaus (⊠ *Av. Sabóia, 3- Monte do Estoril* 🕾 *214680965* ⊕ *www. discoteca-bauhaus.com* 🕙 *Fri. and Sat. 12 am–6 am*), next to the Estoril Eden hotel, attracts a lively clientele.

Forte Velho (⊠ *Estrada Marginal* 🕾 *214/681337* 🕙 *Nightly 11 pm–4 am*), a medieval fort on the edge of town, has been converted into a dance club where the young and the restless head at night.

OUTDOOR ACTIVITIES

GOLF

The superb golf courses near Lisbon attract players from far and wide. Most are the creations of renowned designers, and the climate means that you can play year-round. Many hotels offer golf privileges to guests; some places even have their own courses. Package deals abound. For more information about most major golf courses in this area, check the Estoril Golf Coast Web site (*www.estorilgolfcoast.com/en*).

The Clube de Golfe do Estoril (⊠ *Av. da República* 🕾 *214/680176* ⊕ *www. clubegolfestoril.com* ⌂ *Reservations essential* ⚑ *18 holes. 5,313 m. Par 69* ⛳ *€57 per round* ☞ *Facilities: driving range, putting green, golf carts, hand-pulled carts, rental clubs, pro shop, restaurant, 2 bars,* *changing rooms, swimming pool*) has an immaculate 18-hole championship course as well as a 9-hole course. Guests of the Hotel Palácio receive special rates and privileges. Note that on weekends only members can play here.

The **Estoril Sol** (✉ *Quinta do Outeiro, EN9, north toward Sintra, then farther up turn left and follow signs to Lagoa Azul, Linhó Sintra* ☎ *219/240331* ⊕ *www.portugalgolfe.com* ⚓ *Reservations essential* ⚑ *18 holes. 3,609 m. Par 62* ⚐ *€26 per round* ☞ *Facilities: driving range (limited), putting green, hand-pulled carts, rental clubs, pro shop, restaurant, bar*), on the Estoril–Sintra road, 7 km (4½ mi) north of Estoril, has scenic 9- and 18-hole courses on the fringes of the Serra de Sintra.

SHOPPING

Each July and August, the **Feira do Artesanato** (✉ *Av. Amaral Estoril, Estoril* ☎ *214/678210* ☉ *Weekdays 6 pm–midnight, weekends 5 pm–midnight*) has an open-air crafts fair near the casino. Stall vendors sell local art, crafts, and food every evening.

The **Galeria do Casino Estoril** (✉ *Casino Estoril, Largo José Teodoro dos Santos* ☎ *214/667700 ask for art gallery* ⊕ *www.casino-estoril.pt* ☉ *Daily 1:30–1*) holds three big art exhibitions during the year: in spring, talented young artists from Portuguese art schools are featured; naive art is the theme in summer; in October, Portuguese and international artists grab the spotlight. During the year there are also eight individual exhibitions. All the works—paintings, bronzes, ceramics, drawings, and sculptures, including marble pieces by Portugal's most famous sculptor, João Cutileiro—are for sale. Just off the main gallery is the Boutique de Arte, which sells smaller pieces by the same artists exhibited.

The **Mercado de Carcavelos,** (✉ *Rua do Mercado, Parede, Cascais* ☉ *Tues.–Sun. 8 am–1 pm*) in the nearby town of Carcavelos, 7 km (4½ mi) southeast of Estoril, has a busy market that sells food, clothes, and crafts; you can reach it by local train.

CASCAIS AND BOCA DO INFERNO

Fodor's Choice
★

3 km (2 mi) west of Estoril.

Once a mere fishing village, the town of Cascais—with three small, sandy bays—is now a heavily developed resort packed with shops, restaurants, and hotels. Despite the masses of people, though, Cascais has retained some of its small-town character. This is most visible around the harbor, with its fishing boats and yachts, and in the old streets and squares off Largo 5 de Outubro, where you'll find lace shops, cafés, and restaurants. The beaches are attractive, too, although bear in mind the pollution problems here: unless signs indicate otherwise, stay out of the sea.

GETTING HERE AND AROUND

The best way to get here is through the CP urban train departing from Cais do Sodré (Linha de Cascais) in Lisbon that arrives close to the Cascais downtown. To visit the surrounding area of Cascais, there's an urban bus line (SCOTTurb) that will take you also to Sintra, Estoril, and Oeiras. The drive by car will take 25 minutes from Lisbon, either by the A2 highway or the more scenic Avenida Marginal, which runs along the coast and will provide an easier way to travel to the Cascais outer interest points such as Boca do Inferno. Avoid driving on Marginal to or from Estoril during the afternoon on summer weekends, as the traffic is horrendous from beachgoers.

ESSENTIALS

Bus SCOTTurb (⊠ *R. de S. Francisco, n° 660, Adroana, Alcabideche* ☎ *214/699125* ⊕ *www.scotturb.com*).

Bus Station Cascais bus terminal (⊠ *On lower level of Cascais Villa* ☎ *214/836357*).

Emergencies Cascais hospital (⊠ *Av. Ultramar and Rua Padre J.M. Loureiro* ☎ *214/653000*).

Taxis Cascais and Estoril Taxis (☎ *214/659500 or 214/660101*).

Visitor Info Cascais (⊠ *Rua Visconde da Luz 14* ☎ *214/868204* ⊕ *www.cm-cascais.pt*).

EXPLORING

Boca do Inferno *(Mouth of Hell)*. The most visited attraction in the area around Cascais is the forbiddingly named Boca do Inferno, one of several natural grottoes in the rugged coastline, and just 2 km (1 mi) west of Cascais. It's best to visit at high tide or in stormy weather, when the waves are thrust high onto the surrounding cliffs. You can walk along the fenced paths to the viewing platforms above the grotto and peer down into the abyss. A path leads down to secluded spots on the rocks below, where fishermen cast their lines. Afterward, shop for lace, leather items, and other handicrafts at roadside stalls, and stop in one of the nearby cafés.

Museu do Mar *(Sea Museum)*. For an understanding of development in Cascais, visit the modern, single-story museum. Here, the town's former role as a fishing village is traced through model boats and fishing gear, period clothing, analysis of local fish, paintings, and old photographs. ⊠ *Rua Júlio Pereira de Melho* ☎ *214/861377* 🎫 *Free* ⊙ *Tues.–Sun. 10–5*.

Museu dos Condes Castro Guimarães *(Counts of Castro Guimarães Museum)*. One of Cascais's 19th-century town houses serves as the museum's home with displays of 18th- and 19th-century paintings, ceramics, and furniture, as well as artifacts from nearby archaeological excavations. ⊠ *Av. Rei Humberto II de Itália* ☎ *214/825407* 🎫 *Free* ⊙ *Tues.–Fri. 10–5, weekends 10–1 and 2–5*.

🔄 **Parque do Marechal Carmona.** The most relaxing spot in Cascais, apart from the beach, is this municipal park, which has a shallow lake, a café, a small zoo, and tables and chairs under the trees for picnickers. ⊠ *Av. da Republica* ⊙ *June–Sept., daily 8:30–7:45; Oct.–May, daily 8:30–5:45*.

NEED A BREAK?

Santini Cascais (⊠ *Av. Valbom 28F, Cascais* ☎ *214/833709* ⊕ *www.santini.pt* ⊙ *Tues.–Thurs. 11–11, Fri. and Sat. 11–midnight, Sun. 11–8*), in the heart of old-town Cascais is by far the most well-known ice-cream parlor in Portugal and has what people consider to be the best (Italian-style) gelato in the world. In 1949, Italian immigrant Attilio Santini opened up his shop, serving hand-crafted gelato made from 100% natural fresh ingredients, which is still practiced today. His business rapidly grew in popularity and throughout the years has been visited by various great social and political figures, and even European royalty (the king and queen of Spain dined here). Santinis currently produces 31 different flavors in both ice cream and fruit sherbet. Try some of the classics like chocolate, strawberry, pistachio, and hazel-nut or the newer, more creative ones such as caramelized red berries and raspberry-lemon. A seasonal favorite is their blood-orange sherbet, made from imported Sicilian blood oranges. Visit the original shop in Cascais or try the recent editions in São João de Estoril and downtown Lisbon.

WHERE TO EAT

$
SEAFOOD

✕**Beira Mar.** One of several well-established and unpretentious restaurants behind the fish market, the Beira Mar has a comfortable, tiled interior. An impressive display of the day's catch shows you the best of the seafood, although, as ever, you can end up paying top dollar for dinner if you're not careful, because it's all sold by weight. Make sure you know the price first, or stick to the dishes with fixed prices—rice with clams or steaks cut from swordfish or tuna are always worth trying. ⊠ *Rua das Flores 6* ☎ *214/827380* ⊕ *www.beiramarcascais.com* ⊟ *AE, DC, MC, V* ⊘ *Closed Tues.*

¢
FAST FOOD

✕**Dom Manolo.** The surroundings aren't sophisticated in this Spanish-owned grill-restaurant, but for down-to-earth fare it's a good choice. The waiters charge back and forth delivering excellent spit-roasted chicken (*frango* in Portuguese) to a largely local clientele. Whatever your main dish, order potatoes or fries on the side; avoid the poor, overpriced salads and factory-made desserts. ⊠ *Av. Marginal 13* ☎ *214/831126* ⊟ *No credit cards* ⊘ *Closed Jan.*

¢
PORTUGUESE

✕**O Pereira.** Popular it may be, but this restaurant remains simple, with paper tablecloths and no decorations. The menu includes very cheap—and very good—dishes from every region in Portugal. The owner's cooking attracts many customers, so get there early: 12:30 for lunch and 7:30 for dinner. Don't expect much other than really good food. ⊠ *Rua Visconde da Luz 43* ☎ *214/831215* ⊟ *No credit cards* ⊘ *Closed Thurs.*

$
SEAFOOD

✕**O Pescador.** Fresh seafood fills the menu at this folksy restaurant, a favorite since 1964, where a cluttered ceiling and maritime-related artifacts distract the eye. Sole is a specialty, and this is also a good place to try *bacalhau* (dried salt cod); it's often baked here, either with cream or with port wine and onions. ⊠ *Rua das Flores 10* ☎ *214/832054* ⊕ *www.restaurantepescador.com* ⊟ *AE, DC, MC.*

$
PIZZA

✕**Pizza Itália.** There are plenty of other pizza joints in Cascais, but Pizza Itália is probably the best of the bunch. In its indoor dining rooms or on its sunny terrace you can choose from a range of authentic pies and pastas. ⊠ *Rua do Poço Novo 1* ☎ *214/830151* ⊟ *MC, V* ⊘ *Closed Wed. No lunch Thurs.*

WHERE TO STAY

$ ⊡ **Casa da Pérgola.** Set back from the road amid gardens, this intimate town house has been in the hands of the same family for more than 100 years. The painted-and-tiled facade sets a refined, solidly 19th-century tone that's continued inside by the heavy drapes, impressive stairway, period furniture, and art. In cooler weather you eat breakfast in the dining room surrounded by cabinets of old porcelain; on warmer days you can enjoy the day's first meal in the garden. ■TIP→ **Book well in advance to secure a room here. Pros: beautiful house; intriguing historical ambience; excellent central location. Cons:** old-fashioned style not for everyone; books up very quickly; difficult parking. ⊠ *Av. de Valbom 13* ☎ *21/484–0040* ⊕ *www.pergolahouse.com* ⋈ *6 rooms* ⅄ *In-room: a/c, safe (some), Wi-Fi (some). In-hotel: laundry service, Wi-Fi hotspot, parking (paid)* ⊟ *DC, MC, V* ☉ *Closed Dec.–Feb.* |○| *BP.*

$$$ ⊡ **Estalagem Villa Albatroz.** If Portugal's 18th-century writer Maria Amália de Carvalho could return today to her house on the harbor at Cascais Bay, she would surely check in and open up her laptop. Each light-filled room is individually furnished; some have balconies or fireplaces, and all have sea views. In the bathroom, the hair dryer, the phone, and the view of the greatly changed marina might surprise Dona Maria, but the huge tubs wouldn't. **Pros:** good central location; friendly staff; excellent breakfast that's included. **Cons:** not nearly up to standard for a supposedly five-star hotel; a bit overpriced. ⊠ *Rua Fernandes Tomas 1* ☎ *21/486–3410* ⊕ *www.albatrozhotels.com* ⋈ *11 rooms* ⅄ *In-room: a/c, safe (some), kitchen, Internet (some). In-hotel: restaurant, room service, bar, golf course, diving, laundry service, Wi-Fi hotspot, parking (free)* ⊟ *AE, DC, MC, V* ☉ *Closed Nov.–Mar.*

$$$$ ⊡ **Hotel Albatroz.** On a rocky outcrop above the crashing waves, this
Fodor's Choice gorgeous hotel was once the summer residence of the dukes of Loulé.
★ Although expanded and modernized, its character has been retained, particularly in the fabric-lined corridors and the cozy terrace bar. The guest rooms combine elegance (old prints and floral drapes) with comfort (good beds and spacious bathrooms); it's worth paying extra for a sea view. The small pool and the terrace overlook the ocean. A fine buffet breakfast is served in the Albatroz restaurant ($$–$$$; reservations and dressy-casual attire are essential), where fish dishes are the specialty. The hotel also rents three adjoining small villas. **Pros:** fantastic seaside and central location; superior views; wonderful ambience and stylish decor. **Cons:** pool is pretty small; adjacent beach is small and gets crowded quickly. ⊠ *Rua Frederico Arouca 100* ☎ *21/484–7380* ⊕ *www.albatrozhotels. com* ⋈ *37 rooms, 3 suites, 3 villas* ⅄ *In-room: a/c, safe (some), Wi-Fi (some). In-hotel: restaurant, room service, bar, golf courses, tennis courts, pool, gym, beachfront, water sports, bicycles, laundry service, Internet terminal, Wi-Fi hotspot, parking (free)* ⊟ *AE, DC, MC, V.*

$$$ ⊡ **Hotel Cascais Miragem.** Perfectly integrated into the landscape, the
☾ newest and most luxurious of the hotels is built in steps up the side of
Fodor's Choice the hill above the sea. Each floor has different designer furniture and a
★ different color scheme in which reds, oranges, and yellows predominate. View the sailboats on the sea from one of the many panoramic windows or from your balcony overlooking the bay. The infinity-edged pool has

been spectacularly designed to give the illusion of extending into the sea. The hotel offers special services for children, including in-room toys and DVD cartoons, plus a children's pool. A minivan provides a shuttle into town and to golf courses. **Pros:** near train station and city center; excellent complimentary breakfast; excellent service. **Cons:** style of the rooms looks very commercial; the noise from the main road below can be annoying at times; paid parking. ⊠ *Av. Marginal 8554* ☎ *21/006–0600* ⊕ *www.cascaismiragem.com* ↩ *180 rooms, 20 suites* ⚹ *In-room: a/c, safe (some), Internet (some). In-hotel: 2 restaurants, room service, 2 bars, pool, gym, spa, beachfront, children's programs (ages 4–12), laundry service, Wi-Fi hotspot, parking (paid)* ▭ *AE, DC, MC, V* ⟨○⟩ *BP.*

$$ 🏨 **Penha Longa Resort.** Hidden among the rolling green hills and valleys
Fodor'sChoice   in the Sintra-Cascais nature reserve, which is halfway between either
★   city, is this five-star dream resort, which is operated by the Ritz-Carlton Hotel Company. All rooms have balconies with breathtaking views of either the surrounding forest or landscaped resort and come equipped with a Nespresso coffee machine, iPod plug-in, and a welcome amenity of little Portuguese pastries or something of your preference. All double beds are extra-large and super soft and luxurious. Along with both indoor and outdoor pools and two championship golf courses, the resort's bright and refreshing Six Senses Spa boasts a private Asian garden with thermal-regulated wading pools and platforms for practicing Tai Chi and yoga. Aside from light dining at the hotel's indoor and outdoor bars, choose a different cuisine each day from the resort's three restaurants: the traditional Portuguese Assa Massa ($$$$); Midori ($$$$), voted the best Japanese restaurant in the Lisbon area; and Arola, the newest from prestigious chef Sergi Arola ($$$$) serving a selection of signature tapas, sweets, and cocktails in a stylish and trendy setting with a DJ spinning every night. With all that Penha Longa has to offer, you'll never want to leave. **Pros:** spacious rooms and gorgeous views; extra-large beds that are comfortable; excellent selection of delicious food. **Cons:** everything in the resort is pricey; Wi-Fi not free. ⊠ *Estrada da Lagoa Azul, Sintra-Cascais* ☎ *219/249011* ⊕ *www.penhalonga.com* ↩ *194 rooms, 27 suites* ⚹ *In-room: a/c, Internet (some). In-hotel: 3 restaurants, room service, 2 bars, golf courses, pools, gym, spa, bicycles, children's programs (ages 1–15), laundry service, Internet terminal, Wi-Fi hotspot, parking (free), some pets allowed* ▭ *AE, D, DC, MC, V* ⟨○⟩ *BP.*

NIGHTLIFE AND THE ARTS

Cascais has plenty of bars on and around the central pedestrian street, Rua Frederico Arouca, and in Largo Luís de Camões. The marina is also a lively place to barhop, with a wide choice of places that stay open until around 2 am.

Chequers (⊠ *Largo Luís de Camões 7* ☎ *214/830926* ⊙ *9:30 pm–2 am*) blasts rock music into the square nightly in summer.

You can hear fado, the mournful Portuguese folk music, at **Forte D. Rodrigo** (⊠ *Rua de Birre 961* ☎ *214/871373*).

On hot summer nights, customers of the English-style pub **John Bull** (✉ *Largo Luís de Camões 8* ☎ *214/833319* ◔ *10 pm–2 am*) spill out into the square.

Nuts Club (✉ *Av. Rei Humberto II de Itália* ☎ *214/844109* ⊕ *www. nuts-club.com* ◔ *11 pm–6 am*), a popular disco close to the marina, has seven bars, two dance floors, and nice sea views from a terrace. Nothing much happens before midnight, but the action doesn't finish until 6 am.

OUTDOOR ACTIVITIES

FISHING

Marlin Boat Tours (✉ *Marina de Cascais* ☎ *919/275509 www.marlinboattours. com*) organizes deep-sea fishing tours for €250 for a half-day and €450 for a full-day, which includes a Portuguese picnic lunch and drinks.

GOLF

Fodor's Choice ★ **Oitavas Quinta da Marinha.** American architect Arthur Hills built this fine golf course among pine woods and reforested dunes in an area of great natural beauty. The course lies within the Sintra-Cascais Natural Park, and Hills made the most of three distinct landscape forms: umbrella pine forest, dunes, and the open coastal transition area. Every hole has a view of the Atlantic Ocean and the Sintra Hills. This was the first course in Europe to be recognized as a Golf Certified Signature Sanctuary, which is awarded by American Audubon International. A handicap certificate is required to play here. It was voted 88th in the Top 100 golf courses in the world by Golf Magazine in 2009. ✉ *25 Quinta da Marinha, Cascais* ☎ *21/486–0600* ⊕ *www.quinta-da-marinha.pt* ⚑ *18 holes. 6,303 m. Par 71* ⛳ *€90 weekdays, 150 weekends per round* ☞ *Facilities: driving range, putting green, chipping area, golf carts, hand-pulled carts, electric trolleys, rental clubs, pro shop, golf academy/ lessons, restaurant, bar.*

WATER SPORTS

You can rent surfing equipment from **Equinócio** (✉ *Varandas de Cascais, Rua Mário Viegas, Lote 1, Loja 3, Alvide, Alcabideche* ☎ *214/835354* ⊕ *www.equinocio.pt*).

Behind the train station, the dive shop **Exclusive Divers** (✉ *Praia da Duquesa* ☎ *214/868099* ⊕ *www.exclusive-divers.net*) offers scuba diving courses on the beach. Call a day in advance. A 2½-hour course costs €60. Their services also include specialized dive trips.

Call ahead and you can have lessons in kite surfing, windsurfing, and surfing from **Guincho Wind Factory** (✉ *Villa Internacional, Aldeia de Juzo* ☎ *214/841930 or 966/301378* ⊕ *www.guinchowindfactory.com*). You can either meet at the shop in Aldeia de Juzo, 1 km (½ mi) from Guincho beach, or arrange to meet right on the beach. Lessons are €25 for one hour, €80 for five hours (over the course of one or two days) or €160 for 10 hours (over a minimum of two days).

SHOPPING

Cascais is the best shopping area on the Estoril Coast, with pedestrian streets lined with stores and small market stalls. For smart fashions, gifts, and handmade jewelry, browse around Rua Frederico Arouca. Markets are held north of town at Rua Mercado (off Avenida 25 de

Abril) on Wednesday and Saturday; you'll find fruit, vegetables, cheese, bread, and flowers. On the first and third Sunday of each month, a large market is held at the Praça de Touros (Bull Ring) on Avenida Pedro Álvares, west of the center.

Casa da Guia (✉ *Av. Nossa Senhora do Cabo Nº 101, Cascais* ☎ *214/843215, 214/842005, or 214/818207* ⊕ *www.casadaguia.com* ☾ *Tues.–Sun. 10–8*) is a pretty outdoor shopping center that sits on the former summer residence of the Counts of Alcáçovas, which is on a cliff right on the ocean at the far end of Cascais after Boca do Inferno. The shops are all high-end brand name boutiques, and there are several restaurants, bars, bakeries, and delis with large outdoor terraces scattered throughout the property.

Cascais Villa (✉ *Av. Dom Pedro I* ☎ *214/828250* ⊕ *www.cascaisvilla.com*) is on the Marginal (coastal road) into Cascais from Lisbon. The shopping center has cinemas and shops carrying internationally known brands.

In **Ceramicarte** (✉ *Largo da Assunção 3–4* ☎ *214/840170* ⊕ *www. ceramicarte.pt*) Fátima and Luís Soares present their carefully executed, modern ceramic designs alongside more traditional jugs and plates. There's also a small selection of tapestries and artworks. The store is near the church.

In the Cascais shopping mall on the road between Cascais and Sintra, the bookstore/computer/record shop **Fnac** (✉ *N9, Alcabideche* ☎ *214/699000* ⊕ *www.fnac.pt*) sells English-language books as well as tickets to cultural events.

Manueis (✉ *Frederico Arouca 91* ☎ *214/833452*) sells tablecloths, bedspreads, and other fine linens.

For typical Portuguese handmade jewelry such as filigree, go to **Torres** (✉ *Frederico Arouca 13* ☎ *214/830977* ⊕ *www.torres.pt*), which has its own designers and trademark brand.

For fine Portuguese porcelain visit **Vista Alegre Atlantis** (✉ *Av. 25 de Abril 64* ☎ *21/483–8942*).

GUINCHO

9 km (5½ mi) north of Boca do Inferno.

There's a wide beach at Guincho, where Atlantic waves pound onto the sand even on the calmest of days, providing perfect conditions for windsurfing (the annual world championships are often held here in summer). The undertow here is notorious; even the best swimmers should take heed. But the cool winds during the summer are a refreshing break from the stuffier, crowded beaches on the Cascais line and with the picturesque backdrop of the Serra da Sintra mountains, this is the perfect place to watch the sunset. Whether you surf or not, savor some fresh fish served at one of the restaurant terraces overlooking the beach.

GETTING HERE AND AROUND

You can get to Guincho by bus both from Cascais and Sintra (405 and 415 lines). SCOTTurb buses leave Cascais's train station every two hours (7:45 am–5:45 pm, journey time 25 minutes). Driving will take

5–10 minutes from Cascais, 20 minutes from Sintra, and 35 minutes from Lisbon (on the highway).

ESSENTIALS

Bus Info SCOTTurb (✉ *R. de S. Francisco, N° 660, Adroana, Alcabideche* ☎ *214/699125* ⊕ *www.scotturb.com*).

WHERE TO EAT AND STAY

$$$
PORTUGUESE

✕ **João Padeiro.** "John the Baker," undoubtedly the most eclectic restaurant you are likely to find in this area, was named after the owner who opened a small restaurant in Cascais 40 years ago that catered to local fishermen. The place became so famous that it attracted Portuguese royalty. In 2001, John opened this establishment in what was once an indoor swimming pool—though he did keep the outdoor pool— in an isolated part of the Guincho beach. Now, under an elaborate wooden ceiling and surrounded by modern art and a wall of photographs showing guests of the old place, you can enjoy fabulous seafood dishes, including the famous Cascais Dover Sole. ✉ *Estrada do Guincho* ☎ *214/857141* ▤ *AE, DC, MC, V* ⊗ *No dinner Sun. and during important football (soccer) matches.*

$

▨ **Estalagem Muchaxo.** This inn is nestled in the rocks over Guincho beach. Although most of the rooms have ocean views, there are some at the back overlooking the nearby hills; the beach itself is just steps away. Much of the building is rustic, with stone floors, petrified wood tables and chairs, and maritime bric-a-brac, but the ever-present soft aroma of smoked wood from the fireplace is pleasant. In the lounge during the afternoon, you can enjoy some lively piano music played by one of the owner's longtime friends. You can often find the owner and his piano-playing friend around the hotel; they are delightful storytellers regaling guests with tales of the famous people who have stayed and dined here over the years. In the well-known restaurant ($$), fish specialties such as *caldeirada* (fish stew) are the order of the day. Meals are a little overpriced, but the service is friendly and what you're ultimately paying for is the unrivaled view through picture windows. **Pros:** prime beachfront location with views of the ocean and mountains; the old-fashioned rustic decor and petrified wood furniture; friendly staff. **Cons:** rooms are plain and a bit run-down; parking is difficult during beach season; a bit overpriced. ✉ *Praia do Guincho* ☎ *21/487-0221* ⊕ *www.muchaxo.com* ⤸ *60 rooms* ♿ *In-room: a/c (some), safe (some), Wi-Fi (some). In-hotel: restaurant, room service, bar, pool, beachfront, bicycles, laundry service, parking (free), some pets allowed* ▤ *AE, DC, MC, V* ⧖| *CP.*

$$$
Fodor'sChoice
★

▨ **Fortaleza do Guincho.** Perched on the cliffs looking out to the ocean in Guincho lies this historical military fort turned hotel. It may look cold and stiff from the outside, but on entry you'll be surprised to find a charming old-world palace that is a mix of royalty and fantasy. Each of the magnificent arch-stone-ceiling rooms is decorated in exquisitely designed 17th-century reproduction furniture and rich, colorful linens; all bathrooms are equipped with a whirlpool bathtub. A winding stone staircase leads up to the second-floor suites, which have an enclosed balcony with incredible views of the ocean. The bar and lounge also look out to the ocean and Guincho beach, and there's an outside deck for lounging and sunbathing. The hotel's renowned one-star Michelin restaurant ($$$$) is one of the best for gourmet dining, with lush, colorful carpeting and vibrant blue chairs that almost glow in the light. The restaurant offers nouvelle French cuisine with a Portuguese flair, both à la carte and special tasting menus created by three-star Michelin chef Antoine Westermann and executive chef Vincent Farges. You'll really feel like you've eaten and slept like a king after staying here. **Pros:** beautifully designed hotel; gorgeous location and views; excellent service and food. **Cons:** standard rooms are quite small with a small window; bathtubs are not that large; no pool. ⊠ *Estrada do Guincho, Cascais* ☎ *214/870491* ⊕ *www.guinchotel.pt* ⤣ *27 rooms, 3 suites* ⌂ *In-room: a/c, safe (some), Wi-Fi (some). In-hotel: restaurant, room service, bar, beachfront, laundry service, Wi-Fi hotspot, parking (free)* ▭ *AE, D, DC, MC, V* ¡◎¡ *BP.*

SINTRA AND QUELUZ

The lush woods and valleys on the northern slopes of the Serra de Sintra (Sintra Mountains) have been inhabited since prehistoric times, although the Moors were the first to build a castle on the peaks. Later Sintra became the summer residence of Portuguese kings and aristocrats, and its late medieval palace is the greatest expression of royal wealth and power of the time. In the 18th and 19th century, English travelers, poets, and writers—including an enthusiastic Lord Byron—were drawn by the region's beauty. The poet Robert Southey described Sintra as "the most blessed spot on the whole inhabitable globe." Its historic importance has been recognized by UNESCO, which designated it a World Heritage site in 1995.

GETTING HERE AND AROUND

Sintra is a good base for exploring the countryside. Driving is the easiest way to cover the area, but you could also take a guided tour (arranged through the tourist office) or see the sights by taxi. The nearest attractions are within walking distance or are accessible by bus or horse-drawn carriages. Trains will bring you to Sintra but not any farther.

The best public transportation to Sintra is by train. The urban train, Linha de Sintra, departs from several Lisbon stations on a regular basis; it takes about 10–15 minutes to get to Queluz from Lisbon and about 30–40 minutes to get to Sintra (including switching trains in Cacém) from Lisbon. Sintra can also be reached by bus (SCOTTurb) from Cascais and Estoril. By car, the drive takes 25 minutes from Lisbon and 15 from Cascais or Estoril. Avoid driving during rush hour on weekdays between 5:30 and 7:30 pm; otherwise it may take twice as long. ⇨ *For more info about bus and train travel, see Bus Travel and Train Travel, above.*

SAFETY AND PRECAUTIONS

Keep a good eye on your belongings if traveling on the Linha de Sintra train: the crowd traveling to and from the poorer neighborhoods in between can get a little suspicious at times.

SINTRA

30 km (18 mi) northwest of Lisbon; 13 km (8 mi) north of Estoril.

It was the Moors who first built a castle northwest of the capital at Sintra as a defense against Christian forces, which, under Dom Afonso Henriques, moved steadily southward after the victory at Ourique in 1139. The castle fell to the Christians in 1147, a few days after Lisbon. Sintra's lush hills and valleys later became the summer residence of Portuguese kings and aristocrats, its late medieval palace the greatest expression of royal wealth and power of the time. In the 18th and 19th centuries English travelers, poets, and writers—including an enthusiastic Lord Byron—were drawn by the area's beauty. The poet Robert Southey described Sintra as "the most blessed spot on the whole inhabitable globe." Its historic importance in the Romantic movement in 1995 brought it UNESCO recognition as a World Heritage Site.

Sintra's main attractions are within walking distance or accessible by bus or horse-drawn carriages. There are several marked walks in the surrounding countryside (ideal for escaping the summer crowds), which is crisscrossed by minor roads and marked by old monastic buildings, estates, gardens, and market villages. But it is most easily covered by car, particularly if you want to range as far north as Mafra, with its giant palace-convent. You could also take a guided tour (arranged through the tourist office) or see sights by taxi.

To the west, the Atlantic makes itself felt in windswept beaches and capes, including Cabo da Roca—the westernmost point in Europe, topped by a lighthouse. In the other direction, the town of Queluz, halfway betweeen Lisbon and Sintra, is dominated by its magnificent Baroque palace, in gardens dotted with statuary.

GETTING HERE AND AROUND

Sintra is 30 km (18 mi) northwest of Lisbon. Trains from Lisbon's Rossio station, between Praça dos Restauradores and Rossio square, run every 15 minutes to Queluz (a 20-minute trip to Queluz-Belas station; turn left outside and follow the signs for the 1-km [½-mi] walk to the palace) and on to Sintra (40 minutes total). The service operates 6 am–2:40 am, and one-way tickets cost €1.20 to Queluz-Belas, €1.90 to Sintra. ⇨ *For more info about train travel, see Essentials, below.*

Buses are a good way to explore the Sintra area, including Cabo da Roca. Tickets are cheap (less than €3.50 for most journeys), more so if bought in advance. Regional operator SCOTTurb (F*see SCOTTurb info under Bus Travel, above*) has one-day passes and also a combined pass that includes train travel to and from Lisbon. From outside Sintra train station there are half-hourly departures in summer to the resorts of Praia das Maçãs (also reached by antique tram) and Azenhas do Mar (30 minutes) in the west, and north to Mafra (one hour). There's also regular year-round service to Cascais and Estoril (one hour).

By car, Queluz is 20 minutes from Lisbon, signposted off route N249/IC19, making this a good half-day option, or a fine stop on the way to or from Sintra (40 minutes from Lisbon).

In Sintra itself, for those who don't want climb the steep hills, you can take SCOTTurb's Bus 434 (ticket €3.50), which you can hop on and off so long as you don't backtrack. It stops at the two national palaces and the Moorish castle.

VISITOR AND TOUR INFO

The local tourist office, the Turismo, has full information on opening hours and prices, on walking trails in the countryside, and on tour companies. The Turismo also houses an art gallery, the Galeria do Museu Municipal, specializing in works associated with Sintra.

Sintratur offers old-fashioned horse-and-carriage rides in and around the town. A short tour costs €30 for up to four people; longer trips run between €60 and €100 and go as far afield as Pena Palace and Monserrate.

ESSENTIALS

Emergencies **Hospital Professor Doutor Fernando Fonseca, EPE** (✉ *IC 19-Venteira* ☎ *214/348200*).

Tour Info **Sintratur** (✉ *Rua João de Deus 82* ☎ *219/241238* ⊕ *www.sintratur.com*).

Train Info **Rail information line** (☎ *808/208208* ⊕ *www.cp.pt*).

Visitor Info **Turismo** (✉ *Praça da República 23* ☎ *219/236932 or 210/991882* ✉ *Free* ☉ *Tues.–Fri. 9–noon and 2–6, weekends 2:30–7* ✉ *Sintra train station* ☎ *219/241623*).

EXPLORING

There are various ways to get to Palácio Nacional de Pena, Castelo dos Mouros, and Convento dos Capuchos. You can take a local bus or a horse-drawn carriage, sign up for a tour, or make the long but pleasant walk up from the center of Sintra (about 1½ hours). It's possible to drive, but there's limited parking once you get there. However you choose to arrive, note that the walk back down to Sintra is delightful: the route is through shaded woods with viewpoints under the cork trees.

Castelo dos Mouros (Moorish Castle). The battlemented ruins of this 9th-century castle still give a fine impression of the fortress that finally fell to Christian forces led by Dom Afonso Henriques in 1147. It's visible from various points in Sintra itself, but for a closer look follow the steps that lead up to the ruins from the back of the town center (40 minutes going up, 25 minutes coming down), or catch the SCOTTurb's Bus 434 or rent a horse-drawn carriage in town. Panoramic views from the serrated walls explain why the Moors chose the site. ✉ *Estrada da Pena* ☎ *219/237300* ⊕ *www.parquesdesintra.pt* ✉ *€5, guided tours* ☉ *Apr.–mid-Sept., daily 9:30–8; mid-Sept.–Mar., daily 10–6. Last admission 1 hr before closing.*

Convento dos Capuchos. The main entrance to this extraordinarily austere convent, 13 km (8 mi) southwest of Sintra, sets the tone for the severity of the ascetic living conditions—its simple tile roof and wooden beams lined with cork attempt to keep in what little warmth there might be. From 1560 until 1834, when it was abandoned, seven monks—never any more, never any less—inhabited the bare, cork-lined cells and prayed in the tiny chapel hewn out of the rock. Impure thoughts meant a spell in the Penitents' Cell, an excruciatingly small space. Guides for the 45-minute tour bring the history of the place to life with zest and humor. No vehicles are allowed close to the convent, so the peace is disturbed only by birdsong. ⊠ *Convento dos Capuchos* ☎ *219/237300* ⊕ *www. parquesdesintra.pt* ✉ *€5, guided tour €10* ☉ *Apr.–mid-Sept., daily 9:30–8; mid-Sept.–Mar., daily 10–6. Last admission 1 hr before closing.*

> **TOURS**
>
> On Friday, Saturday, and Sunday, a scenic **streetcar** ride originates next to the contemporary art museum on Avenida Heliodoro Salgado (first ride leaves at 9:30 am). The 45-minute trip takes you through the countryside and down the mountain to the Praia das Maçãs on the sea. Seafood restaurants line the beach at the last stop. It costs €1 one-way.

Fodor's Choice ★ **Palácio da Pena.** This Disney-like castle is a glorious conglomeration of turrets and domes awash in pastels. In 1503 the Monastery of Nossa Senhora da Pena was constructed here, but fell into ruins after religious orders were expelled from Portugal in 1832. Seven years later the ruins were purchased by Maria II's consort, Ferdinand of Saxe-Coburg. Inspired by the Bavarian castles of his homeland, Ferdinand commissioned a German architect, Baron Eschwege, to build the castle of his fantasies, in styles that range from Arabian to Victorian. Work was finished in 1885 when he was Fernando II. The surrounding park is filled with trees and flowers from every corner of the Portuguese empire. Portugal's last monarchs used the Pena Palace as a summer home, the last of whom—Queen Amália—went into exile in England after the Republic was proclaimed on October 5, 1910. Inside is a rich, sometimes vulgar, and often bizarre collection of Victorian and Edwardian furniture, ornaments, and paintings. Placards explain each room. A minitrain takes you from the park gate up to the palace. A path beyond an enormous statue (thought to be Baron Eschwege, cast as a medieval knight) on a nearby crag leads to the **Cruz Alta,** a 16th-century stone cross 1,782 feet above sea level, with stupendous views. ⊠ *Estrada da Pena* ☎ *21/910–5340, 21/923–7300 advance booking* ⊕ *www.parquesdesintra.pt* ✉ *Park €5; combined ticket for park and palace €9 mid-Sept.-Mar., €12 Apr.–mid-Sept. Minitrain €2* ☉ *Mid-Sept.–Mar., daily 10–6 (last admission 5); Apr.–mid-Sept., daily 9:45–7 (last admission 6:15).*

NEED A BREAK? | Sintra is known for its local pastry, *queijadas* (cottage-cheese cakes), and one baker with two outlets on the same street is their most renowned purveyor. **Piriquita dois** (⊠ *Rua das Padarias 18* ☎ *219/231595* ☉ *Closed Tues.*), the larger of the two, has fine views from its terrace.

Fodor's Choice ★ **Palácio Nacional de Sintra** *(Sintra Palace).* The conical twin white chimneys of the Palácio Nacional de Sintra are the town's most recognizable landmarks. There has probably been a palace here since Moorish times, although the current structure, also known as the Paço Real, dates from the late 14th century. It is the only surviving royal palace in Portugal from the Middle Ages, and displays a fetching combination of Moorish, Gothic, and Manueline architecture. Bilingual descriptions in each room let you enjoy them at your own pace. The chapel has Mozarabic (Moorish-influenced) azulejos from the 15th and 16th centuries. The ceiling of the Sala das Armas is painted with the coats of arms of 72 noble families, and the grand Sala dos Cisnes has a remarkable ceiling of painted swans. The Sala das Pegas (magpies) figures in a well-known tale about Dom João I (1385–1433) and his dalliance with a lady-in-waiting. The king had the room

painted with as many magpies as there were chattering court ladies, thus satirizing the gossips as loose-tongued birds. ⊠ *Largo Rainha D. Amélia* ☎ *21/910–6840* ⊕ *pnsintra.imc-ip.pt* 🖼 *€7, free Sun. until 2* ⊙ *Daily 9:30–5:30 (last admission 5), closed Christmas Day, New Year's Day, Easter Sun., and May 1.*

Fodor'sChoice   **Parque de Monserrate.** This estate, 4 km (2½ mi) west of Sintra, was
★   laid out by Scottish gardeners in the mid-19th century at the behest of a wealthy Englishman, Sir Francis Cook. The centerpiece is the Moorish-style, three-dome **Palácio de Monserrate**. The original palace was built by the Portuguese viceroy of India, and was later home to Gothic novelist William Beckford. A regular ticket allows you to visit the park and part of the palace, and there are guided 1½-hour tours available at various times throughout the day. The gardens, with their streams, waterfalls, and Etruscan tombs, are famed for their array of tree and plant species, though labels are lacking. ⊠ *Estrada da Monserrate* ☎ *219/237300* ⊕ *www.parquesdesintra.pt* 🖼 *€5, guided tours of palace and garden €10* ⊙ *Apr.–mid-Sept., daily 10–1 and 2–7; mid-Sept.–Mar., daily 10:30–1 and 2–5. Last admission 30 min before closing.*

Fodor'sChoice   **Quinta da Regaleira.** Among Sintra's many privately owned mansions
★   is the intriguing Quinta da Regaleira, a five-minute walk along the main road past the tourist office. Built in the early 20th century for a Brazilian mining magnate with a vivid imagination and a keen interest in freemasonry and the Knights Templar (who made their 11th-century headquarters on this site), the estate includes gardens where almost everything—statues, water features, grottoes, lookout towers—is linked to freemasonry or the Knights Templar. Spookiest of all is the 100-foot-deep Poço do Iniciático (Initiation Well)—an inverted underground "tower." The house has an uninspired exhibit on freemasonry, a café, and a restaurant. ⊠ *Rua Barbosa do Bocage 5* ☎ *219/106650* ⊕ *www.regaleira.pt* 🖼 *€5, guided tours (call ahead for tours in English) €10* ⊙ *Apr.–Sept., 10–8 (last admission 7); Nov. and Dec., 10–5:30 (last admission 5); Oct., Feb., and Mar., 10–6:30 (last admission 6).*

FESTIVAL DE SINTRA

Festival de Sintra (✉ *Praça Dr. Francisco Sá Carneiro* ☎ *219/107110* ⊕ *www. festivaldesintra.pt*), the Sintra music and dance festival, takes place during June and July at the Centro Cultural Olga Cadaval as well as in the many palaces and gardens around Sintra and Queluz: Palácio Nacional de Sintra, Pena Palace, Quinta da Regaleira, Quinta da Piedade, Palácio de Seteais, and Queluz Palace. The Gulbenkian Symphony Orchestra and the Gulbenkian Ballet company as well as other international groups perform at the Olga Cadaval Cultural Center. The gardens of the Seteais Palace are well known for their open-air ballet and classical music performances. Tickets can be reserved and bought at the Olga de Cadaval Cultural Centre or at any Fnac store (there is one in the Cascais Shopping mall) as well as at the Lisbon Welcome Center. Programs are sometimes distributed at the arrivals area at the Lisbon airport.

WHERE TO EAT

¢ ✕**Alcobaça.** The friendly owner bustles around to make sure guests are well served in this simple restaurant on a town-center side street. Try the excellent grilled fish, arroz de marisco, or tasty fresh clams *bulhão pato* (in garlic sauce). ✉ *Rua das Padarias 7–11* ☎ *219/231651* ▭ *MC, V.*

PORTUGUESE

$ ✕**Curral dos Caprinos.** On the site of a former sheep corral, this rustic restaurant has clay pots, smoked hams, onions, and dried corn cobs hanging from its ceiling, while the walls are lined in cork. The most spectacular meat dish is the *cabrito à moda de Oleiros*, a whole lamb roasted over laurel branches. ■TIP➜ **Order in advance for the lamb.** ✉ *Rua 28 de Setembro 13, Cabriz* ☎ *219/233113* ▭ *AE, DC, MC, V.*

PORTUGUESE

$ ✕**Neptuno.** Praia das Maçãs is a popular place to go for seafood restaurants on the beach. One of the favorites is Neptuno, a glassed-in restaurant practically on the sand. Hanging on the walls are photos of boats, big catches, and the sea—one photo shows the sea coming right up to the restaurant. Try the *peixe a bulhão pato* (fish with garlic, olive oil, and coriander) and *arroz de marisco* (seafood rice). ✉ *Praia das Maçãs* ☎ *219/291222* ▭ *AE, DC, MC, V* ☺ *Closed Wed. No dinner Tues.*

SEAFOOD

$ ✕**Páteo do Garrett.** Arches divide three rooms where long tables are covered in yellow tablecloths that match the chair cushions and curtains. Named after the restaurant, bacalhau *à garrette* (cooked with onions, garlic, peppers, and olive oil and garnished with coriander and boiled egg) is a good choice. Join the guests on the terrace who pose for pictures with views of the twin chimneys of the Paço Real, the church tower, and the distant beach. ✉ *Rua Maria Eugénia Navarro* ☎ *219/243380* ▭ *AE, DC, MC, V* ☺ *Closed Wed. and second half Jan.*

PORTUGUESE

$ ✕**Tacho Real.** Locals climb a steep hill to this restaurant for traditional dishes cooked with panache, such as bacalhau *à brás* (with eggs, onions, and sliced potato), steaks, and game in season. The dessert cart allows you to choose from a selection of house-made cakes and tarts. On

PORTUGUESE

warm days the small terrace is delightful, and there is live guitar music welcoming you at the door. ✉ *Rua do Ferraria 4* ☎ *219/235277* ▭ *AE, DC, MC, V* ☯ *Closed Wed.*

WHERE TO STAY

$
Fodor's Choice
★

☐ **Casa Miradouro.** The Belgian owners of this candy-stripe 1890s house at the edge of Sintra have a keen eye for style and comfort. Rooms have grand views, wrought-iron bedsteads, and polished tile floors. The downstairs breakfast room opens onto a terrace. **Pros:** all rooms have views; in-room double-glaze windows and heating an unusual winter bonus in this category; special week and five-night deals in winter. **Cons:** requires very early booking; no phone or TV in rooms. ✉ *Rua Sotto Mayor 55* ☎ *21/923–5900* ⊕ *www.casa-miradouro.com* ⤴ *6 rooms* ☖ *In-room: no a/c, no phone, no TV, Wi-Fi (free). In-hotel: bar* ▭ *DC, MC, V* ☯ *Closed 2 wks in Jan.* ☉❘ *BP.*

$$$
Fodor's Choice
★

☐ **Hotel Palácio de Seteais.** Built in the 18th century as a home for the Dutch consul to Portugal, this hotel is surrounded by pristine grounds 1 km (½ mi) or so from the center of Sintra. You enter under an arch that joins the building's two wings. In them, public rooms have period furnishings, delicate frescoes, and Arraiolos carpets, and guest rooms are individually styled, some with hand-painted wallpapers. The restaurant ($$$; reservations essential; dressy attire requested) serves set, four-course, Continental meals. In summer, having coffee or tea on the terrace is a delight. **Pros:** unique ambience of staying in a palace; beautiful location and views; excellent room amenities. **Cons:** very expensive; no spa or gym. ✉ *Rua Barbosa do Bocage 8* ☎ *21/923–3200* ⊕ *www. tivolihotels.com* ⤴ *30 rooms, 1 suite* ☖ *In-room: a/c, safe (some), Internet (some). In-hotel: restaurant, room service, bar, golf course, tennis court, pool, bicycles, laundry service, Wi-Fi hotspot, parking (free)* ▭ *AE, DC, MC, V* ☉❘ *BP.*

$$
Fodor's Choice
★

☐ **Lawrence's Hotel.** When this 18th-century inn, the oldest on the peninsula, reopened in 1999, the U.S. secretary of state and the Netherlands' Queen Beatrix were among the first guests. The intimate rooms—with wood and terra-cotta predominating—are bathed in light from French windows, and deluxe touches abound. Staff can arrange anything from jeep tours to babysitting. In the old-world restaurant ($$$; reservations recommended) specialties are served on Portugal's Vista Alegre porcelain. **Pros:** rich in historical associations; cozy refuge from at times chilly local climate; charming rear terrace. **Cons:** no pool, gym, or garden; some rooms little bigger than their bathrooms. ✉ *Rua Consiglieri Pedroso 38–40* ☎ *21/910–5500* ⊕ *www.lawrenceshotel.com* ⤴ *11 rooms, 5 suites* ☖ *In-room: a/c, safe, Wi-Fi (free). In-hotel: restaurant, bar, laundry service, Wi-Fi hotspot (free)* ▭ *AE, DC, MC, V* ☉❘ *BP.*

$$
Fodor's Choice
★

☐ **Quinta das Sequóias.** This 19th-century manor house on 40 wooded acres underwent inspired renovations to transform it into a hotel. One of the bathrooms was cleverly built around monolithic boulders, and a tower was chosen as a place for a guest room as well as a flower-filled, ground-floor sitting area. Antique touches proliferate: here an old parasol, there a period jewelry box. Buffet breakfasts (and light dinners on request) are served in a large, galleried dining room. The gardens include a pool, a Jacuzzi, and a terrace. ■TIP→**Note there's a two-night minimum stay in peak season. Pros:** beautiful location with great views; gorgeous rooms; very romantic setting. **Cons:** very few rooms so books up quickly; difficult to find. ⌧ *Estrada de Monserrate Ap. 1004, 2 km (1 mi) from Sintra center, past Palácio de Seteais (Box 4), Sintra* ☎ *219/243821 or 219/230342* ⊕ *www.quintadasequoias.com* ⌨*5 rooms* ⚓ *In-room: a/c, no phone (some), no TV (some) Wi-Fi (some). In-hotel: pool, bicycles, laundry service, Wi-Fi hotspot, parking (free)* ⊟ *AE, DC, MC, V* ⊙ *Closed Nov.–Feb.* |O|*BP.*

OUTDOOR ACTIVITIES

The **Centro Hípico da Costa do Estoril** (⌧ *Estrada da Charneca 186, Cascais* ☎ *214/872064* ⊕ *www.centrohipicocostaestoril.com* ⊙ *Tues.–Sun. 9–1 and 3–7*) offers horseback rides in the Sintra hills and elsewhere.

The **Grupo Ecológico de Cascais-GEC** (☎ *21/487–2646, 96/754–9492, or 91/965–1882* ⊕ *www.gec.pt* ⊙ *Weekdays 2–7*) leads walks through the Sintra-Cascais Natural Park.

From the town of Sintra itself, there are five walks through the hills and past the palaces. Information and maps are available at the **tourist office** (⌧ *Praça da República 23* ☎ *21/923–1157 or 21/924–1700* ⊙ *June–Sept., daily 9–8; Oct.–May, daily 9–5*).

GOLF

Penha Longa. With magnificent ocean views, the Sintra Hills, and Estoril and Cascais in the foreground, architect Robert Trent Jones Jr. had a wonderful setting in which to create one of Portugal's most memorable courses. The Atlantic Course has great sweeping changes in elevation and often tight fairways that put a premium on driving accuracy. With the elevation often come strong breezes that add another dimension to what is in any case a demanding layout. Lower-handicap players will savor the challenge, but there is plenty of enjoyment here for all abilities. A handicap certificate is required. ⌧ *Estrada do Lagoa Azul, Linhó, Sintra* ☎ *21/924–9031* ⊕ *www.penhalonga.com* ⚓ *Reservations essential* ⚲ *18 holes. 6,290 m. Par 72. Slope 124* ⛳*€90 weekdays, €120 weekends per round* ☞ *Facilities: driving range, putting green, chipping area, golf carts, hand-pulled carts, electric trolleys, rental clubs, pro shop, golf academy/lessons, restaurant, bar.*

SHOPPING

Sintra is a noted center for antiques, curios, and ceramics, although you'll need to choose carefully: prices are on the high side, and there's a fair amount of poor-quality goods. Keep an eye out for special in-store displays of hand-painted ceramics, many of them reproductions of 15th- to 18th-century designs, signed by the artists. Most stores in the historical center are open by 9 or 10 am, close for lunch (1–2 pm) and reopen until 7 pm.

Almoraviva (⌧ *Rua Visconde de Monserrate 12–14* ☎ *219/240539* ⊙ *Closed Wed.*) has handicrafts from all over Portugal, including embroidery from Madeira and the Azores, Vista Alegre porcelain, crystal from the north, Arraiolos rugs—you name it. **Casa Alegria** (⌧ *Escandinhas Felix Nunes 5* ☎ *219/234726.*) sells hand-painted tiles. They can also reproduce pictures or drawings you supply them. Vintage port wines are on sale in **Loja de Vinho** (✉ *Praça da República 3* ☎ *219/244410* ⊕ *www.screstauracao.com*), whose owners can recommend vintages. **Sr. Henrique Teixeira** (✉ *Rua Onsiglieri Pedroso 2* ☎ *219/231043*) sells antiques: 17th- and 18th-century tiles, sculptures, and bronze pieces. For hand-embroidered linen tablecloths, bedspreads, towels, and sheets, visit **Violeta** (✉ *Rua das Padarias 19* ☎ *21/923–4095*).

The small town of **Pêro Pinheiro** is known for its marble, and several shops here sell stacks of cachepots, plaques, and other garden objects. The town is on route N9, 9 km (5½ mi) northeast of Sintra.

SÃO PEDRO DE SINTRA

2 km (1 mi) southeast of Sintra.

This little hillside village is most famous for its fair, the Feira de São Pedro, held every second and fourth Sunday of the month in the vast Praça Dom Fernando II (also called the Largo da Feira), where stalls are set up under the plane trees. Dating from the time of the Christian Reconquest, the fair is one of Portugal's best, with livestock and agricultural displays as well as local crafts, antiques, and food for sale. Even on nonfair days, it's worth coming to São Pedro to see the village church in its own enclosed little square. There are also several good restaurants in São Pedro, which makes it a good lunch stop.

GETTING HERE AND AROUND
São Pedro de Sintra is easily reached by bus through the SCOTTurb buses, taking around 10 minutes. Driving will take 5 minutes from the Sintra center.

ESSENTIALS
Bus Info **SCOTTurb** (☎ *214/699125* ⊕ *www.scotturb.com*).

EXPLORING
Parque da Liberdade. These gardens, off the road between Sintra train station and the National Palace, are a short cut to São Pedro, but you can also catch a local bus from outside Sintra station. (✉ *Volta do Duche, Sintra* ☎ *219/238811* 🎫 *Free* 🕙 *June–Sept., weekdays 10–7, weekends 10–8; Oct.–May, daily 10–6*).

WHERE TO EAT
$ ✗ **Adega do Saloio.** Families fill this popular rustic restaurant on weekends, drawn by the juicy steaks being cooked over the open fire as you walk in. The dining room is festooned with garlands of onions and garlic. House wine is served in brown clay jugs, and little plates of smoked ham, cheese, and black olives decorate the tables to whet the appetite. It's fun just watching the waiters bustling about with skewers of grilled meat and fish. The *espetada à madeira* (beef and laurel leaves on a skewer) that drips its juices as it's hung in front of you on the table is quite a spectacle. ✉ *Rua Álvaro Reis 49, Chão de Meninos* ☎ *219/231422* 🍽 *AE, DC, MC, V.*

PORTUGUESE

$ ✗ **Cantinho de São Pedro.** Imaginative Portuguese cuisine with a French twist is served at this busy, rustic restaurant in a small courtyard of artisans' workshops, just off the main square. Locals consider the

PORTUGUESE

food well worth the wait for a table. Try the trout with almonds and cream, or look for the fresh shellfish on the list of *pratos do dia* (dishes of the day). ⊠ *Praça Dom Fernando II 18* ☎ *219/230267* ⊕ *www. cantinhosaopedro.com* ▤ *AE, DC, MC, V.*

SHOPPING

The **Lojas do Picadeiro** (⊠ *Praça Dom Fernando II*) is a row of artisans' workshops that sell wooden toys, furniture, and art; a couple of taverns help restore flagging spirits.

EN ROUTE

Past Monserrate the road leads west for 3 km (2 mi) to the small village of **Colares,** associated with the locally produced red wine. The town, its winding streets alive with colorful flowers and trees, is also known for its parish church, which is adorned with ceramic tiles, and its main square is bordered by 18th-century houses.

For terrific views of the sea and surrounding mountains, take the winding road that climbs up to the village of **Penedo,** less than 2 km (1 mi) away from Colares.

AZOIA AND CABO DA ROCA

Fodor's Choice

★ *15 km (9 mi) west of Sintra; 20 km (12 mi) northwest of Cascais.*

GETTING HERE AND AROUND

The SCOTTurb 403 line will take you to Cabo da Roca from both Cascais or Sintra with regular departures from outside either town's train station. The journey takes about 30–40 minutes.

The drive will take 20 minutes from both Sintra and Cascais and 40 minutes from Lisbon.

ESSENTIALS

Bus Info SCOTT-urb (☎ *214/699125* ⊕ *www.scotturb.com*).

EXPLORING

Cabo da Roca. Between enchanting, culturally rich Sintra and the beach resort of Cascais you'll discover a totally different face of Lisbon's environs in this protected natural park. The windswept Cabo da Roca and its lighthouse mark continental Europe's westernmost point and are the main reason that most people make the journey. As with many such places, stalls purvey shell souvenirs and other gimmicks; an information desk and gift shop sells a certificate that verifies your visit. Even without the certificate, though, the memory of this desolate granite cape will linger. The cliffs tumble to a frothing sea below, and on the cape a simple cross bears an inscription by Portuguese national poet Luís de Camões.

WHERE TO EAT

$ ✕ **A Casa de Luis.** This typical restaurant in the heart of Azoia is fashioned right out of the family house of the owner, Joaquim Luis Da Silva. The walls and ceiling are decorated with hanging *presuntos* (cured ham) and old-fashioned knickknacks. All diners start the meal with several little *entradas* of the hanging cured ham, local cheeses, olives, and fresh bread. The restaurant serves excellent grilled fish and

PORTUGUESE

Fodor's Choice

★

meats with personalized tableside service by Senhor Luis himself. The *polvo á lagareiro* (grilled octopus with garlic) and the *robalo grelhado* (grilled seabass) for two are absolutely delicious. For meat, try the *espetada mista de carne* (mixed grilled meat skewers). ⊠ *Cabo da Roca, Rua Corredouras 2, Azoia, Colares* ☎ *219/292721* ▤ *AE, D, DC, MC, V* ☉ *Closed Wed.*

¢   ✕ **Moinho Dom Quixote.** On the outskirts of Azoia, this bar and patio is
CAFÉ built out of an old-fashioned windmill on a cliff overlooking the ocean with the mountain as the backdrop. The inside bar and lounge are decorated in a colorful Mexican theme with hanging lanterns, a fireplace, and tables and chairs made from petrified wood. The outdoor seating area has a staggered patio down the cliff with either café tables and chairs or stone benches and tables blended throughout a beautiful garden of pines and flowering cacti and shrubs. Enjoy a *café com natas* in the winter or one of their Mexican inspired frozen cocktails in the summer with some absolutely fabulous views. ⊠ *Rua do Campo da Bola-Azoia, Colares* ☎ *219/292523* ⊕ *www.moinhodquixote.com* ▤ *No credit cards* ☉ *Daily noon–2 am.*

OFF THE
BEATEN
PATH
The Atlantic Coast. North of Cabo da Roca, the natural parkland extends through the villages of Praia Grande, Praia das Maças, and Azenhas do Mar. The first two have good beaches, and all have seafood restaurants. On the way down, there is a pretty open market with fresh fruit and vegetable stands along the side of a fork in the road, a nice place to shop with the locals.

QUELUZ

15 km (9 mi) east of Sintra; 15 km (9 mi) northwest of Lisbon.

Halfway between Lisbon and Sintra is the town of Queluz, dominated entirely by its magnificent palace and gardens, located in the plaza of the town's center. Across from the palace stand the rebuilt Royal Guard's quarters, which has been turned into a lovely pousada. Unlike its metropolitan surroundings, the rest of the town's buildings still mimic the 18th-century style of the palace, which gives you the unique feeling that you're stepping back in time once you cross the bridge into the area.

GETTING HERE AND AROUND

Queluz is just off route N249/IC19, and the drive from Lisbon takes about 20 minutes, making this a good half-day option or a fine stop on the way to or from Sintra. It's also easy to take the train: get off at the Queluz-Belas stop, turn left outside the station, and follow the signs for the 1-km (½-mi) walk to the palace.

ESSENTIALS

Visitor Info Queluz (⊠ *Largo do Palácio* ☎ *214/343860*).

EXPLORING

Fodor'sChoice **Palácio Nacional de Queluz** *(Queluz National Palace).* This palace was
★   inspired, in part, by the palace at Versailles. The salmon-pink rococo edifice was ordered as a royal summer residence by Dom Pedro III in 1747. Architect Mateus Vicente de Oliveira took five years to make

the place habitable; Frenchman Jean-Baptiste Robillon spent 40 more executing a detailed Baroque plan that also comprised imported trees and statues, and azulejo-lined canals and fountains. You can tour the apartments and elegant staterooms, including the frescoed Music Salon, the Hall of Ambassadors, and the mirrored Throne Room with its crystal chandeliers and gilt trim. Some are now used for concerts and state visits, while the old kitchens have been converted into an ordinary café and a fancy restaurant with an imposing open fireplace and a vast oak table. ⊠ *Largo do Palácio* ☎ *214/343860* ⊕ *pnqueluz.imc-ip. pt* ⊠ *€7, free Sun. until 2* ☉ *Palace: Wed.–Mon. 9–5 (last admission 4:30). Palace Gardens: May–Sept., Wed.–Mon. 9–6 (last admission 5:30), Oct.–Apr., Wed.–Mon. 9–5 (last admission 4:30). Closed Tues., Christmas, and New Year's Day, Easter Sun., and May 1.*

WHERE TO STAY

$ ⚐ **Pousada de Dona Maria I.** The Royal Guard quarters beneath the clock tower opposite the palace have undergone a stunning transformation: marble hallways lined with prints of old Portugal give way to crisp, high-ceilinged rooms furnished with exacting 18th-century reproductions. Only breakfast is served in the pousada itself, but the cooking hits the mark across the road in the old palace kitchens, now the Restaurante de Cozinha Velha ($$$; reservations essential), with its imposing open fireplace and a vast oak table. The Portuguese specialties on the ever-changing menu are occasionally tempered by a French touch. **Pros:** excellent restaurant and service; great location; ambience, ambience, ambience. **Cons:** Wi-Fi access isn't free; not a suitable place for children; lacking in activities. ⊠ *Rte. IC19* ☎ *214/356158* ⊕ *www. pousadas.pt* ↝ *24 rooms, 2 suites* ⚅ *In-room: a/c, safe (some), Wi-Fi (some). In-hotel: restaurant, room service, bar, laundry service, Wi-Fi hotspot, parking (free)* ⊟ *AE, DC, MC, V* ⎮◎⎮ *BP.*

SPORTS AND THE OUTDOORS

Belas. Architect Rocky Roquemore built this tough but interesting layout in rolling countryside close to Lisbon and the Castle of Queluz with its famous gardens. Perhaps not the easiest golf course to walk—a golf cart is a must during the heat of summer—it is a serious test and will be better appreciated by lower-handicap players. The handicap limit here is 28 for men and 36 for women. ⊠ *Estrada Nacional, Belas* ☎ *21/962–6640* ⊕ *www.belasgolf.com* ⚐ *Reservations essential* ⛳ *18 holes. 6,380 m. Par 72* ⚑ *€78 weekdays, €90 weekends per round* ☞ *Facilities: driving range, putting green, chipping area, golf carts, hand-pulled carts, pro shop, golf academy/lessons, restaurant, bar.*

THE SETÚBAL PENINSULA

The Setúbal Peninsula, south of the Rio Tejo, is popular for its beaches in Costa da Caparica, Sesimbra, Arrábida, Tróia, and everywhere in between, which provide the cleanest ocean swimming closest to Lisbon. Other highlights include the delicious local seafood, pastries, and regional wines; the historic castles of Palmela and Sesimbra and the fort in Setúbal; and the scenic mountain range—the Serra da Arrábida—that separates the port from the peninsula's southernmost beaches and fishing villages.

GETTING HERE AND AROUND

If you're intent on eating seafood at Cacilhas, spending the day at a beach, or simply touring the town of Setúbal, traveling by public transportation from Lisbon via bus (TST) or train (Fertagus) is easiest. If you want to see most of the sights covered in this section, however—and particularly if you want to tour the southern coastal and mountainous region—you should rent a car. Apart from the ferry ride to Cacilhas, connections between the Setúbal Peninsula and Lisbon are via the capital's two bridges. Returning on the impressive suspension bridge, the Ponte 25 de Abril, you're guaranteed terrific views of Lisbon.

■TIP→ Avoid crossing the Ponte 25 de Abril when coming from Lisbon during evening rush hour as well as early afternoon on weekends in summer because the traffic can be horrendous. When returning to Lisbon via the bridge, avoid crossing early evening on Sunday and late-afternoon-early evening in summer.

SAFETY AND PRECAUTIONS

The city of Almada, where Cacilhas is located, is not the best place to be after dark, so take the ferry directly there and stay in the immediate area. Be careful in Costa da Caparica and Setúbal at night as well, during the busy summer tourist season.

ESSENTIALS

Bus Info Rede Expressos (⊠ *Praça Marechal Humberto Delgado–Estrada das Laranjeiras, Lisbon* ☎ *213/581472* ⊕ *www.rede-expressos.pt*). **TST-Transportes Sul do Tejo (Main Bus Line)** (⊠ *Rua Marcos de Portugal–Laranjeiro, Almada* ☎ *212/549325* ⊕ *www.tsuldotejo.pt*).

Visitor Info Almada (⊕ *www.m-almada.pt*).

CACILHAS

6 km (4 mi) south of Lisbon.

Although a town in its own right, Cacilhas appears little more than a suburb of Lisbon, albeit one with the bonus of several reliable seafood restaurants along its main street, Rua do Ginjal. The town is immediately across the Rio Tejo from the capital; at night, and especially on weekends, it's a popular destination. Waiters armed with menus linger outside their doors—these are not tourist traps and you can get a good, reasonably priced meal here—ready to assist passersby who can't decide where to eat; once inside, you're tempted with the best of the day's catch.

GETTING HERE AND AROUND

The ferries run frequently from Terminal Fluvial (Transtejois), adjacent to Praça do Comércio, and from Cais do Sodré. One-way tickets cost €0.75, and the journey takes about 15 minutes. There are many bus lines that depart from Lisbon and several locations in the Setúbal Peninsula, including, Almada, Costa da Caparica, and Setúbal (TST). The drive will take 20 minutes from Lisbon, 5 minutes from Almada, and 15 minutes from Costa da Caparica.

ESSENTIALS

Bus Station **Cacilhas bus terminal** (✉ *Largo Alfredo Diniz 12* ☎ *212/750064*).

Ferry Info **Terminal Fluvial** (✉ *Largo Alfredo Dinis* ☎ *212/729741*).

Visitor Info **Almada Tourism Office** (✉ *Largo dos Bombeiros Voluntários* ☎ *212/739340*).

EXPLORING

Cristo Rei. This huge, white statue of Christ, built in 1959—was modeled on the famous statue of Christ the Redeemer in Rio de Janeiro. The figure stands proudly above Cacilhas, its outstretched arms seemingly embracing the city of Lisbon across the water. Take the elevator to the platform beneath the statue's feet for panoramic city views. If your schedule is tight, though, opt for the vista from Lisbon's Torre Vasco da Gama. Buses from Cacilhas dockside can take you directly to the Cristo Rei statue every 20 to 30 minutes, daily 8 am–9 pm. If you're driving, cross the Ponte 25 de Abril and follow the signs. ☎ *212/751000* ⊕ *www.cristorei.pt* ☞ *€4* ☉ *Daily 9:30–6*.

WHERE TO EAT

$ ✕**Atira-te ao Rio.** From Cais do Sodré in Lisbon, this Brazilian restaurant
BRAZILIAN is just a boat ride across the Tagus River and a five-minute walk along the riverfront (the eatery's name means "jump into the river"). The many outdoor tables afford a splendid view of Lisbon and a romantic summer evening. On Saturday you can listen to live Brazilian music and fill up with the all-you-can-eat *feijoada* (black bean stew with different kinds of meats served with slightly toasted cassava flour, hot sliced cabbage, and slices of orange). Other dishes are grilled fish and lasagna de bacalhau (codfish lasagna). The choice cocktail with kick is the *caipirinha* (cachaça—a spirit distilled from sugarcane—and crushed limes with crushed ice and sugar). ✉ *Cais do Ginjal 69–70* ☎ *212/751380* ⊕ *www.atirateaorio.pt* ☐ *DC, MC, V* ☉ *Closed Mon.*

$$ ✕**Marisqueira Vale do Rio.** Set back a bit from the docks in Cacilha's
SEAFOOD restaurant plaza is another great Portuguese seafood place, decorated with beautiful traditional blue-and-white-tiled murals on the walls. The restaurant specializes of course in mistos de Marisco (mixed shellfish platters)—choose from a variety of crab, shrimp, prawns, mussels, lobster, and many others. A good starter is the *ameijoas á bulhão pato* (small local clams) cooked with fresh garlic, butter, cilantro, parsley), which are great to slurp up right from the shell (Portuguese style) with a squeeze of lemon and the juice mopped up with some crunchy toasted fresh bread. The restaurant is part of a group with two other restaurants in the area, try the Farol Restaurant, which is

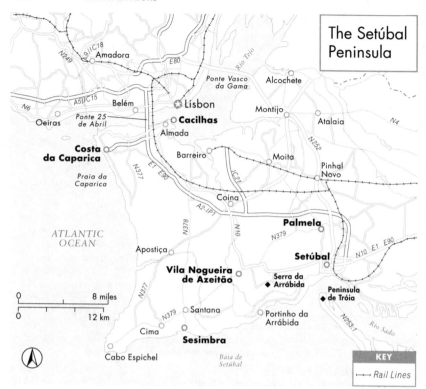

the one closest to Vale do Rio. ⊠ *Largo Alfredo Dinis 13, Cacilhas, Almada* 🖀 *212/723160* ⊕ *www.restaurantefarol.com* ▤ *AE, DC, MC, V* ☯ *Closed Mon.*

COSTA DA CAPARICA

14 km (8½ mi) southwest of Lisbon; 8 km (5 mi) west of Cacilhas.

GETTING HERE AND AROUND

Costa da Caparica is served by several bus lines from TST that will get you to and from Lisbon (158, 159, 161, and 190), Almada (124, 127, and 135), and Cacilhas (106, 124, 125, 126, and 127). The drive from Lisbon takes 25 minutes. Take the minor N377, a slower, more scenic route than the main IC20 route (off the A2/IP1).

From June through September, a small narrow-gauge train departs from Caparica and travels along an 8-km (5-mi) coastal route, making stops along the way; a one-way ticket to the end of the line costs €2.50.

TIMING

To get the most out of your beach experience along this coast, you may be able to avoid the worst of the heavy traffic coming from Lisbon by heading here early in the morning and leaving earlier in the afternoon or early morning if you stay overnight.

ESSENTIALS

Visitor Info Caparica (⊠ *Av. da República 182825-017* ☎ *21/294–7000* ⊕ *www.costadacaparica.com.pt*).

EXPLORING

Costa da Caparica. When Lisbon's inhabitants want to go to the beach, their preferred spot is the Costa da Caparica, a 20-km (12-mi) stretch of sand on the northwestern coast of the Setúbal Peninsula. The coastal strip centers on the lively resort of Caparica itself, at the northern end of the beach, less than an hour from the capital. Formerly a fishing village, it's now packed in summer with Portuguese tourists who come to enjoy the relatively unpolluted waters, eat grilled sardines, and stroll the seafront promenade. You may be able to avoid the crowds by heading south toward the less accessible dunes and coves at the end of the peninsula. Each beach is different: the areas nearest Caparica are family oriented, whereas the more southerly resorts tend to attract a younger crowd (there are some nudist beaches as well).

WHERE TO EAT AND STAY

$ ╳**Borda D' Água.** Either drive to Praia da Morena or catch the small
BRAZILIAN train at Caparica and hop off in front of this Brazilian restaurant—a glassed-in wooden cabana built in the sand dunes. The owner's wife has done a wonderful job decorating with colorful pillows, hammocks, and weathered wooden tables. The menu features *picanha* (Brazilian grilled beef with an outer layer of fat) and feijoada, but they also have a selection of fresh fish to choose from. ⊠ *Praia da Morena, Costa da Caparica* ☎ *212/975213* ⊕ *www.bordadagua.com.pt* ▭ *AE, DC, MC, V* ⊗ *Closed Dec. 1–Jan. 14.*

$$ ╳**O Capote.** An outdoor terrace, red-tile roof, and rustic wooden tables
SEAFOOD and chairs beckon passersby to this seafood restaurant. The fresh fish is sold by the kilo (2.2 pounds) and can be prepared either boiled or grilled. The meal *massa no caldo* is unique to the Caparica area: first you are served fish steamed with tomatoes, onions, and potatoes in a copper pot. When you are finished, the pot is taken back to the kitchen, where noodles, parsley, and mint are added to the leftover juice. The pot returns to your table holding a delicious soup. ⊠ *Rua dos Pescadores 40B, Almada2825* ☎ *212901274* ▭ *AE, DC, MC, V* ⊗ *Closed Oct. and Wed.*

$ 🏨**Mélia Aldeia dos Capuchos.** Opened in June of 2007, this four-star resort
Ⓒ is just above Costa de Caparica beach in the historic village of Aldeia dos Capuchos. As you enter, the sky-high glassed-in lobby looks straight out to the ocean and the hotel's two heated outdoor pools and 9-hole golf course below. There's also a large heated indoor pool and gym, complete with an aerobics room, which offers a variety of classes including spinning, step, Pilates, and yoga. The resort's spacious spa boasts a strength-training therapy room along with the classic treatments and includes a sauna, Jacuzzi, steam room, and ice fountain. Beachgoers to Caparica can hop on the hotel's shuttle for round trips back and forth from the city. Rooms are decorated in earth-tone "spa chic" and are divided into half regular hotel rooms and half studio, one- and two-bedroom apartments, all with balconies and many with sea views. The restaurant Terrace Restaurant Al-Madan ($$$) serves both regional Portuguese and

Mediterranean a la carte cuisine as well as themed buffets. **Pros:** location away from crowds; excellent fitness center; great value for money. **Cons:** rooms aren't very soundproof; furniture is a bit cramped in smaller rooms. ⊠ *Largo Aldeia dos Capuchos, Caparica* ☎ *212/909000* ⊕ *www. meliacapuchos.com* ⇦ *180 rooms* ⚙ *In-room: a/c, safe (some), kitchen (some), refrigerator (some), Wi-Fi (some). In-hotel: restaurant, room service, bars, golf course, pools, gym, spa, children's programs (ages 2–10), laundry service, Wi-Fi hotspot, parking (free), some pets allowed* ▭ *AE, D, DC, MC, V* ⍩ *BP, MAP, FAP.*

PALMELA

38 km (24 mi) southeast of Lisbon.

The small town of Palmela lies in the center of a prosperous wine-growing area, and every September the community holds a good-natured Festa das Vindimas (Grape Harvest Festival) that draws inhabitants from their whitewashed houses onto the cobbled streets. The village is dominated by the remains of a 12th-century castle that was captured from the Moors and enlarged by successive kings. In the 15th century the monastery and church of Sant'Iago were built within the castle walls. The structures were damaged in the 1755 earthquake and lay abandoned for many years. After extensive restoration, a pousada was opened in the monastic buildings. From this height, on a clear day, you can see Lisbon.

GETTING HERE AND AROUND

Public transportation to Palmela includes bus lines (TST) that will take you to and from Lisbon (565), Setúbal (413, 767, and 789), and Azeitão (767), as well as the urban line train (Fertagus) between Lisbon and Setúbal. Driving will take 10 minutes from Setúbal or Azeitão and 30 minutes from Lisbon.

ESSENTIALS

Bus Station **Palmela bus station** (⊠ *Largo do Chafariz D. Maria I* ☎ *212/350078*).

Visitor Info **Palmela** (⊠ *Largo do Município* ☎ *212/332122*).

NEED A BREAK? O Gaiteiro (⊠ *Quinta da Fonte Seca-Barris, Palmela* ☎ *212/350109* ⊙ *Daily 9:30–2 am*), a *Casa de Chá* (teahouse), is in the valley of Serra de Louro down the road from Palmela. It is one of the most picturesque places around to relax with a drink. There are two distinctly different cafés on the property: a winter one on the lower end among the pines with cozy seating and a summer one perched on a small cliff with glassed in walls and a balcony with outdoor seating that overlooks a swimming pool—you can swim in the summer—and faces rolling hills of vineyards and forest-land. The summer café serves one of the best *café com natas* in the area, which is a tall snifter filled with half coffee and half sweet whipped cream dusted with cinnamon on top—if you get this you won't need dessert. However, having one of their ice-cream sundaes in the warmer months is the preferred choice.

WHERE TO STAY

$$ 🏨 **Pousada de Palmela.** On a hill at the eastern end of the Arrábida range,
Fodor's Choice this building was originally a medieval fortress and later a monastery. In
★ 1979 it was converted into a luxury pousada, and the designers made
inspired use of the flagstone corridors and old cloister (now a lounge).
Most rooms have views of the valley and the sea; bathrooms are well
equipped, and beds are comfortable. There's little trace of monastic ascet-
icism in the monks' former refectory, now a dependable restaurant ($$$)
that serves traditional Portuguese food and a good range of wines. **Pros:**
great location in a castle and right in the city center; incredible views;
unique ambience. **Cons:** bathrooms can smell sometimes due to the old-
fashioned piping below; no pool. ⊠ *Castelo de Palmela* ☎ *21/235–1226*
⊕ *www.pousadas.pt* ⇔ *28 rooms* ⚒ *In-room: a/c, safe (some), Internet
(some). In-hotel: restaurant, room service, bar, laundry service, Internet
terminal, Wi-Fi hotspot, parking (free)* ▭ *AE, D, DC, MC, V* ⑩ *BP.*

SHOPPING

Just down the road from Palmela is **Espaço Fortuna** (⊠ *Quinta do Anjo,
Estrada Nacional 379, Palmela* ☎ *12/871068* ⊕ *www.espacofortuna.
com* ⊗ *Tues.–Sun. 10–7*), a wonderful little "quinta" in the country that
has a shop selling Portuguese hand-painted ceramics and azulejos along
with a small selection of gourmet food and wine. On the top floor is
the Cheiro a Lume café with an outdoor terrace, which is a great place
to take a break after shopping to enjoy some coffee with a choice of
local sweets and pastries from Palmela. The café also has a restaurant
down below, serving gourmet regional cuisine Tuesday through Sunday; lunches only.

SETÚBAL

10 km (6 mi) south of Palmela; 50 km (31 mi) southeast of Lisbon.

Many travelers use Setúbal as a spot to spend the night before driving
on to the Algarve, since the Fort de São Filipe has been converted into a
pretty pousada with an exceptional view looking out to the sea. Even if
you decide to go on, you may want to dine here, as the inexpensive selections of fresh fish and seafood are some of the best around, including the
local dish *choco frito* (fried cuttlefish, similar to a large, thick and meaty
fried squid), which is what the city is best known for. At the mouth of
the Rio Sado, Setúbal is the country's third-largest port and one of its
oldest cities. A significant industrial town in Roman times, it became one
again during Portugal's Age of Discovery and took off during the 19th
century. Its center remains an attractive blend of medieval and modern,
and the handsome Igreja de Jesus in itself makes the city worth a stop.

Better still, spend half a day in the city, strolling cobbled pedestrian
streets that open into pretty squares with cafés. The tourist office is built
atop Roman ruins discovered during (and saved from) a construction
project. Inside, you'll be standing above and peering down through the
glass floor into a 5th-century fish-processing room. Near the port, an
agreeable clutter of boats and warehouses is fronted by gardens, where
you can stock up for a picnic at a huge indoor fish-and-produce market
(open Tuesday–Sunday 7–2).

GETTING HERE AND AROUND

Setúbal can be reached by bus from most of the locations in the Setúbal Peninsula and Lisbon. It's also the last stop of the Fertagus urban train, which has an hourly departure to and from Lisbon. The drive from Lisbon takes 35 minutes, and it's 10 minutes from either Palmela or Azeitão. If you're heading directly for Setúbal, take the northern route across the Rio Tejo via the Ponte Vasco da Gama, from which the fast A12 highway cuts south and avoids the bottleneck over the Ponte 25 de Abril.

ESSENTIALS

Bus Station **Setúbal bus station** (✉ Av. 5 de Outubro 44 ☎ 265/525051).

Emergencies **Setúbal hospital** (✉ Rua Camilo Castelo Branco ☎ 265/549000).

Visitor Info **Setúbal** (✉ Paços do Concelho 2900 ☎ 265/541500).

EXPLORING

Convento de Arrábida. From Portinho da Arrábida, the lower, coastal road hugs the shore nearly all the way to Setúbal; the upper road leads to this ramshackle, white-walled, 16th-century monastery built into the hills of the Serra da Arrábida. The views from here are glorious, but you'll have to contact the tourist office in Setúbal in advance to arrange a visit.

Igreja de Jesus *(Church of Jesus).* This 15th-century Church of Jesus, perhaps Portugal's earliest example of Manueline architecture, was built with local marble and later tiled with simple but affecting 17th-century azulejos. The architect was Diogo de Boitaca, whose work here predates his contribution to Lisbon's Mosteiro dos Jerónimos (Jerónimos Monastery). Six extraordinary twisted pillars support the vault; climb the narrow stairs to the balcony for a closer look. These details would soon become the very hallmark of Manueline style. Outside, you can still admire the original, although badly worn, main doorway and deplore the addition of a concrete expanse that makes the church square look like a roller-skating rink.

The church's original monastic buildings and Gothic cloister—on Rua Balneário Paula Borba—house the **Museu de Setúbal,** a museum with a fascinating collection of 15th- and 16th-century Portuguese paintings, several by the so-called Master of Setúbal. Other attractions include azulejos, local archaeological finds, and a coin collection. ✉ *Praça Miguel Bombarda* ☎ 265/537890 💳 €1 *suggested donation to church* ☉ *Tues.–Sat. 9–1 and 2–5.*

Portinho da Arrábida. The main road through the Parque Natural da Arrábida is the N10, which you can leave at Vila Nogueira de Azeitão to travel south toward the small fishing village of Portinho da Arrábida, at the foot of the mountain range. The village is a popular destination for Lisboetas, who appreciate the good local beaches. In summer, when the number of visitors makes parking nearly impossible, leave your car above the village and make the steep walk down to the water, where you'll find several modest seafood restaurants that overlook the port.

Serra da Arrábida. Occupying the entire southern coast of the Setúbal Peninsula is the Parque Natural da Arrábida, dominated by the Serra da Arrábida, a 5,000-foot-high mountain range whose wild crags fall steeply to the sea. There's profuse plant life at these heights, particularly in spring, when the rocks are carpeted with wildflowers. The park is distinguished by a rich geological heritage and numerous species of mammals, birds, butterflies, and other insects.

WHERE TO EAT AND STAY

$ ✕ **El Toro.** This pretty little Spanish hacienda is right next to the bull-
SPANISH fighting ring and is run by Spanish immigrant Alfonso Vasquez and his Portuguese wife, Zélia Marques. The food is regional Spanish, mixed with local Portuguese ingredients made by Zélia herself in their open kitchen. The kitchen overlooks a beautiful enclosed outdoor terrace that's draped in flowering vines and hanging bird cages. The inside dining room is just as nice to look at with bright-gold-painted walls dotted with colorful framed paintings. Try the *pontillitas* (fried baby squid) to start, followed by the *parrillada* (mixed grill of meat, chicken, and chorizo)—a half portion is big enough to feed two people. Save some room at the end to indulge in one of the couple's homemade flavored liquors served up in chilled shot glasses. The alfarroba (the sweet seed pod of the carob tree) is one of the best. ⊠ *Rua António José Batista 111–115, Setúbal* ☎ *265/524995* ⊟ *AE, MC, V* ⊘ *Closed Wed.*

¢ ✕ **Rebarca.** On the *Choco Frito* restaurant row at the east end of the
SEAFOOD main drag on Avenida Luisa Todi, this is one of many typical, casual restaurants in the city that serve up inexpensive but delicious fresh grilled fish and, of course, choco frito. Some of the grilled fish favorites are the *dourada* (gilt-head bream), *robalo* (sea bass), and *peixe espada* (literally means swordfish but actually scabbard fish). Enjoy a light seafood lunch with a carafe of the local house white wine, which always has a refreshingly light effervescence to it. ⊠ *Av. Luisa Todi 70, Setúbal* ☎ *265/221309* ⊟ *AE, MC, V* ⊘ *Closed Tues.*

$ ✕ **Rio Azul.** This *marisqueira* (seafood restaurant) is hidden on a side
SEAFOOD street off Avenida Luisa Todi, on the way to the castle and west of the harbor. Although it's signposted from the main road, it's a little tricky to find. As you'd expect, the dishes to go for are the fresh fish grilled to perfection and the arroz de marisco. ⊠ *Rua Placido Stichini 1* ☎ *265/522828* ⊟ *AE, DC, MC, V* ⊘ *Closed Sun.*

$$ ▦ **Pousada de São Filipe.** From the ramparts of this 16th-century fort-cum-pousada, the views of the town and the Rio Sado are fantastic. The approach to the main entrance takes you up a tunneled flight of stairs and past an 18th-century chapel decorated with azulejos depicting the life of São Filipe. The traditional guest rooms have carved headboards, tile floors, rugs, and white walls. The interior is also awash with azulejo tiling, especially in the bar. The restaurant ($$$) is strong on Portuguese cuisine, with such dishes as fish broth, stewed broad beans with cuttlefish, roast veal with Moscatel wine, and orange tart. ■TIP➔ **To get the most for your money, book a room with a sea view so the fresh breezes can provide natural a/c in the warmer months. Pros:** beautiful location at the top of a cliff overlooking the sea; excellent views of the town and the river; unique ambience. **Cons:** very expensive; inside temperatures can get very cold or warm in the dead of winter and summer; reservation usually needs to be confirmed twice due to poor

Internet connection in reception. ⊠ *Castelo de São Filipe, Estrada de São Filipe* ☎ *265/550070* ⊕ *www.pousadas.pt* ⤴ *16 rooms* ♿ *In-room: no a/c, safe (some), Wi-Fi (some). In-hotel: restaurant, room service, bar, laundry service, parking (free)* ▤ *AE, DC, MC, V* ⦿ *BP.*

PENINSULA DE TRÓIA

20 min from Setúbal by boat.

GETTING HERE AND AROUND

Car and passenger ferries to the peninsula run every 30 to 60 minutes (24 hours a day) from Setúbal's port and cost about €2.50 (passenger ferry) and €11 (car ferry) per person.

ESSENTIALS

Ferry Info Atlantic Ferries (⊠ *Doca do Comércio* ☎ *265/235101* ⊕ *www.atlanticferries.pt).*

Visitor Info Tróia Resort (⊠ *Tróia—Carvalhal* ☎ *265/105500* ⊕ *www.troiaresort.net).*

EXPLORING

Peninsula de Tróia. Across the estuary from Setúbal is the Peninsula de Tróia, a long spit of land blessed with fine beaches and clean water. Troia has been a popular summer vacation place since the 1970s, though its popularity decreased in the late 1990s and early 2000s. Nowadays, the recent Troia Resort has introduced several modifications to the area with the rehabilitation of the golf course, construction of a marina, conference center, and a casino, as well as architectural changes. Being a beach destination as well as a peninsula, it allows you to choose between the Sado estuary beaches or the Atlantic side beaches. The area has managed to retain a little of its history, though: the peninsula is the site of the Roman town of Cetobriga, destroyed by a tidal wave in the 5th century. You can visit its scant ruins, opposite the marina.

WHERE TO STAY

$$　⌂ **Aqualuz Suite Hotel Apartamentos Tróia Mar.** Facing the beach and Serra
☉　da Arrábida, Aqualuz is a three-tower complex that offers studio, and one- and two-bedroom apartments with all the amenities of a four-star resort. All apartments are equipped with a kitchenette, large balcony, and either a pullout trundle bed or bunk beds for children (up to 12 years old), which makes it great for families who are seeking to spend an extended summer holiday. ■TIP→ **One bedroom apartments also have a unique feature where the bedroom has a glassed-in "wall" and door (with curtains) looking to the living room and balcony so parents can still keep an eye on their children while relaxing in bed.** The hotel has both indoor and outdoor pools, one each for adults and children, along with a spa, tennis courts, and special rates to the Troia golf course. **Pros:** a couple minute's walk from beach; excellent views of the beach and mountains; ideal for families. **Cons:** gets very crowded in summer; paid parking. ⊠ *Tróia—Carvalhal, Tróia* ☎ *265/499000* ⊕ *www.aqualuz.com* ⤴ *79 apartments* ♿ *In-room: a/c, safe (some), kitchen (some), refrigerator (some), Internet (some). In-hotel: restaurant, room service, bars, golf course, tennis courts,*

pools, gym, spa, beachfront, bicycles, children's programs (ages 2–12), laundry service, Wi-Fi hotspot, parking (paid) ▤ *AE, MC, V* ⦿ *BP.*

$$ ▣ **Tróia Design Hotel.** Designed by some of the world's leading architects and designers, this luxury hotel is a true work of art. From the innovative architecture of the balconies overlooking the marina to the casino and show center with a capacity of 900, this hotel has stopped at nothing to provide the latest and greatest from the design world. There are two rooftop pools—an infinity pool and a children's pool—that have incredible views of nearby Serra da Arrábida. All rooms have balconies, and you can choose from an array of one-, two-, and three-bedroom apartment suites and studios, some with their own Jacuzzi tub on the balcony. The B&G Restaurant ($$$) showcases international cuisine using local products and regional wines with an emphasis on fresh fish. **Pros:** on the beach, next to the shops and ferry boat marina; incredible views of the mountains; spacious rooms. **Cons:** pricey; staff a little inexperienced; unlike the rooftop pools, the indoor pool is small and plain and you have to pay to use the sauna, Jacuzzi, and steam rooms. ✉ *Marina de Tróia–Carvalhal, Grândola* ☎ *265/498000* ⊕ *www. troiadesignhotel.com* ⤳ *61 rooms, 144 suites* ⚲ *In-room: a/c, safe (some), kitchen (some), refrigerator (some), Wi-Fi (some). In-hotel: 2 restaurants, room service, 3 bars, golf course, 3 pools, gym, spa, beachfront, bicycles, children's programs (ages 3–12), laundry facilities, laundry service, Internet terminal, parking (free)* ▤ *AE, DC, MC, V* ⦿ *BP.*

OUTDOOR ACTIVITIES

Troia. What Robert Trent Jones had in mind when he laid out Troia back in 1981 is sometimes hard to figure out. Built on a peninsula close to the sea, there are hints of traditional links golf here, but some might say a little too much so. Without a doubt, it is a strategic layout requiring a great deal of thought and first-class shot making, but it might create too much of a test for the average player to find totally enjoyable. A lot of sand, maritime pines, and flora make for a very beautiful setting. The course is accessible by ferry from Setúbal, which is a much shorter journey than by road around the Sado Estuary. A handicap certificate is required. ✉ *Complexo Turistico de Troia, Carvalhal* ☎ *265/494112* ⊕ *www.troiagolf.com* ⚲ *Reservations essential* ⚐ *18 holes. 6,320 m. Par 72* ⚑ *€60.50 weekdays, €72.50 weekends per round* ⚐ *Facilities: driving range, putting green, chipping area, golf carts, hand-pulled carts, pro shop, restaurant, bar.*

VILA NOGUEIRA DE AZEITÃO

14 km (8½ mi) west of Setúbal.

The region around the small town of Vila Nogueira de Azeitão, on the western side of the Serra da Arrábida, retains a disproportionately large number of fine manor houses and palaces. In earlier times, many of the country's noblemen maintained country estates here, deep in the heart of a wealthy wine-making region. Wines made here by the José Maria da Fonseca Company are some of the most popular in the country (and one of Portugal's major exports); the best known is the fortified dessert wine called Moscatel de Setúbal.

GETTING HERE AND AROUND

Azeitão can be reached by the TST buses, from Lisbon (754, 755), Setúbal (230, 754, 755, 767, 783), Palmela (767) and Sesimbra (208, 230). Driving from Palmela or Setúbal takes about 10–15 minutes. From Lisbon it will be about a 30-minute drive.

ESSENTIALS

Visitor Info Azeitão **Tourism Office** (⊠ *Rua José Augusto Coelho, 27Vila Nogueira de Azeitão* ☎ *212/180729*).

EXPLORING

José Maria da Fonseca Company. For a close look at the wine business, seek out the original headquarters of the José Maria da Fonseca Company; their Manor House and cellars stand on the main road through town. The intriguing tours talk about the long history of the winery and allow you to see all stages of production, including a peek into their dark and mysterious prized Moscatel cellars, where 200-plus year-old bottles are still aging gracefully. The tour takes around 20 to 40 minutes, depending on the size of the group, and at the end you are brought to their wine shop, where selected tastings can be done as well as purchasing. ⊠ *Rua José Augusto Coelho 11–13* ☎ *212/198940* ⊕ *www.jmf.pt* ⊠ *Free* ☉ *Daily tours 10–noon and 2:30–5:30.*

NEED A BREAK?

Aside from great cheese and wine, one cannot miss the local sweet treat, Tortas de Azeitão, which are little rolled tortes filled with an egg and cinnamon custard. Fábrica de Tortas Azeitonense (⊠ *Estrada Nacional N10, Km 17, Setúbal* ☎ *212/190418* ⊕ *www.tortasdeazeitao.com* ☉ *Daily 9–7*) started making this regional pastry along with other varieties of egg-custard pastries in 1995 and have become the best-known producers of the tortas and other pastries in the area. Their main factory and café shop is on the main road in town (Estrada Nacional N10), just before the roundabout headed toward Coina, on the right. Stop in after lunch to savor some delicious tortas with a Portuguese *café* and then buy a box of them to take with you to enjoy later.

Praça da República. Although it's not open to the public, the 16th-century Palácio de Tavora (Tavora Palace), on the central Praça da República, has an interesting history. In the 18th century, the Marquês de Pombal accused the Duke of Aveiro, who owned the palace, of collaborating in the assassination plot against the king, Dom José. Subsequently the duke was executed by the marquês, and the Tavora coat of arms was erased from the Sala das Armas in Sintra's National Palace.

Quinta da Bacalhoa. The pride and joy of this late-16th-century L-shape mansion is its box-hedged garden and striking azulejo-lined paths. You can't tour the villa, which is a private house, but the garden is open to the public and contains a pavilion with three pyramidal towers—the so-called Casa do Fresco, which houses the country's oldest azulejo panel. Dating from 1565, it depicts the story of Susannah and the Elders. Scattered elsewhere are Moorish-influenced panels, fragrant groves of fruit trees, and enough restful spots to while away an afternoon.

TO MARKET

Vila Nogueira de Azeitão's agricultural traditions are trumpeted on the first Sunday of every month, when a **country market** is held in the center of town. Apart from the locally produced wine, you can buy *queijo fresco* (fresh sheep's milk cheese) and the renowned local Queijo de Azeitão, a handmade D.O.P. (Designated Product of Origin) certified cheese also made from sheep's milk and cured for a period of 20–40 days. This short curing process gives the cheese a very soft and creamy *amanteigado* texture, which literally means "smooth like butter" and therefore should be served as if it was. The cheese is sold in small rounds of various sizes; the top rind can be easily sliced off to spoon out sheep's milk spread on a big hunk of excellent fresh bread from one of the market's bakery stalls. ■ TIP→ **You can buy everything you need here to make the perfect picnic lunch.**

■ TIP→ **For a one-hour guided tour and tasting, reservations must be made a week in advance.** ⊠ *4 km (2½ mi) east of Vila Nogueira de Azeitão on N1* ☎ *212/198060* 🖾 *Weekdays €4 (Fri. until 12:30), weekends €8* ⊙ *Mon.–Thurs. 9–6, Fri. 9–12:30 (minimum 2 people) and 2–6, Sat. 9–6 (minimum 6 people)* ⊙ *Closed Sun. and holidays.*

SHOPPING

The **Azulejos de Azeitão** (⊠ *Rua dos Trabalhadores da Empresa Setubalense 15, Setúbal* ☎ *212/180013* ⊕ *www.azulejosdeazeitao.com* ⊙ *Tues.–Sun. 10–6*) is a great place to stop if you've been dying to get your hands on some of those lovely decorative Portuguese tiles seen throughout the country. The company uses traditional European methods to sketch, fabricate, hand-paint, and glaze each and every one of the tiles sold in the shop. Reproduction Portuguese styles and murals range from the 16th to 19th century, along with Spanish, Islamic, Hispano-Moorish, French, Italian, English, and Dutch from similar periods. Choose from their premade selection or design your own to be made and framed. They ship to the U.S. if you don't want to risk breaking your tiles on the trip back. To get to the store from Azeitão, follow N10 to the split with N379 and bear right staying on N10; the turnoff is the second left.

SESIMBRA

40 km (25 mi) south of Lisbon; 30 km (18 mi) southwest of Setúbal.

Sesimbra, a lively fishing village surrounded by mountains and isolated bays and coves, owes its popularity to its proximity to the capital. And, despite high-rise apartments that now mar the approaches to the town, its few surviving narrow, central streets reflect a traditional past. Moreover, the long beach is lovely, if a little crowded in summer, and perfectly fine for swimming. The waterfront is guarded by a 17th-century fortress and overlooked by outdoor restaurants serving fresh-fish meals. A short walk along the coast to the west takes you to the main port, littered with nets, anchors, and coils of rope and packed with fishing boats—which unload their catches at entertaining auctions. You can also take a 40-minute walk to the hilltop remains of a Moorish castle northwest of town.

GETTING HERE AND AROUND

Sesimbra can be reached by the TST buses from several locations in the Setúbal Peninsula, including Setúbal (230), Azeitão (208), and Cacilhas (203). The 207 line will take you to and from Lisbon. The driving time from Lisbon and Setúbal is 35 minutes. Coming from Azeitão will take 20 minutes.

ESSENTIALS

Bus Station **Sesimbra bus station** (✉ Av. da Liberdade ☎ 212/233071).

Visitor Info **Sesimbra Tourist Office** (✉ Largo da Marinha 26-27, off Av. dos Naufragios ☎ 212/288540 ⊕ visit.sesimbra.pt).

EXPLORING

Cabo Espichel (Espichel Cape). This salt-encrusted headland with a number of 18th-century pilgrim rest houses and a forsaken church is the southwestern point of the Setúbal Peninsula. It's a rugged and lonely place, where the cliffs rise hundreds of feet out of the stormy Atlantic. To the north, unsullied beaches extend as far as Caparica, with only local roads and footpaths connecting them. There are six buses a day here from Sesimbra.

Castelo de Sesimbra. Sitting high above the city is the Castelo de Sesimbra, which was conquered in 1165 by Dom Afonso Henriques but fell back into the hands of the Moors until 1200 when under the reign of Dom Sancho I. The castle lost importance and fell into disrepair during the next several hundred years until Dom João IV ordered that it be adapted for the use of artillery in 1648. Classified as a National Monument, after the great earthquake of 1755 reconstruction was done to restore it to its previous glory. Follow the signs on the road that splits off right before arriving in Sesmbra and it will take you straight up to the castle. Aside from the incredible views of the ocean and the city of Sesimbra below, there is a small photo museum in the front tower and a café with an outdoor patio, where you can enjoy an afternoon coffee or a *bagaço* (a clear Portuguese liquor) as the sun goes down.

WHERE TO EAT AND STAY

$
PORTUGUESE
✕**Café Filipe.** Set in a line of sidewalk restaurants overlooking the waterfront, the Filipe is always busy with diners digging into the terrific grilled fish—cooked outside on a charcoal grill—or arroz de marisco. There's no nicer spot for lunch, but you may have to wait in line for a table. It's worth it. ✉ Av. 25 de Abril ☎ 212/231653 ⊕ www.restaurantefilipe.com ▤ MC, V.

$$
SEAFOOD
Fodor'sChoice
★
✕**Praia Mar.** Though not right on the ocean, this is by far the best restaurant in the area for seafood lovers. The menu is extensive and offers a wide variety of mixed shellfish or grilled fish platters to share, in every size and price range so diners can easily enjoy the local catch. Try a mixed platter with some of the regional favorites, such as *sapateira recheada* (whole stuffed stone crab), *santola* (spider crab), *lagosta* (spiny lobster), and langostines, which look a bit like crawfish but are

much bigger and taste more like lobster. The shellfish comes broken down into smaller pieces, which you can easily crack open with the little hammer and board provided for you to indulge in some finger-licking goodness. ■TIP➔ **The restaurant doesn't take reservations, so come early to avoid the crowds that line up for a table very quickly.** ⊠ *R. Latino Coelho 2, Sesimbra* ☎ *212/234176* ⊕ *www.praiamar.com* ☐ *AE, MC, V* ⊗ *Closed during Oct.*

¢ 🏠 **Casa da Terrina.** This cute little 19th-century Portuguese country house turned bed-and-breakfast is in the little village of Quintola de Santana, a five-minute drive up the hill from Sesimbra beach. The five rooms have rustic-style furniture with en suite bathroom; a couple rooms have balconies and two have double beds. The owners are wonderful hosts and make a fabulous homemade breakfast that can be enjoyed on the pretty outdoor terrace when it's warm. The rest of the property is a maze of beautifully landscaped gardens filled with flowers that lead to the hidden outdoor pool complete with a wooden patio and lounge rockers. If you want to explore the surrounding countryside, the owners are happy to provide you with information on what to see and where to dine. **Pros:** friendly staff; beautiful location; great breakfast. **Cons:** minimal amenities; only two rooms have a double bed. ⊠ *Estrada Quintola de Santana, Quintola de Santana* ☎ *212/680264* ⊕ *www.casadaterrina.com* ⇨ *5 rooms* ⚏ *In-room: no a/c, no phone (some), no TV (some). In-hotel: pool, Wi-Fi hotspot, parking (free), no kids under 12* ☐ *No credit cards* ⊗ *Closed late Oct. through end of Mar.* ⌡◎⌠ *BP.*

$ 🏠 **Quinta do Miguel.** In the small village of Aldeia do Meco, just 12.3

Fodor'sChoice
★

km (7 mi) northwest of Sesimbra, is this secret gem. Perfect for a romantic getaway, this private, gated farm is filled with lush green gardens with native pines mixed with palm trees and groves of orange and olive trees. The family's two friendly dogs and cat roam about the farm along with ducks and a prancing peacock. There are five stylish apartment rooms, including a loft and two villas that open out to terraces facing the garden. The Quinta's owners really emphasize privacy and relaxation, so guests are registered inside their accommodations and given a personal tour of the property. There's a patio with a stone-roofed barbecue and Jacuzzi tub, which the owner recommends using on a clear night for star gazing. Guests are welcome to handpick vegetables and herbs from the Quinta's biological (different from organic in that they use "natural fertilizers") garden to use for meals in the apartment, a salad for a picnic lunch on the beach, or even some fresh mint for a happy-hour mojito. If you don't feel like cooking, you can request the services of a local chef to cook for you inside or outside the apartment or dine at one of the fabulous local restaurants in the nearby village of Alfarim. Breakfast is extra but can be prepared fresh, in-room on request. **Pros:** minutes from the beach but hidden among the pretty forest; private and peaceful; nice staff. **Cons:** breakfast not included; bit difficult to find; not good if you don't want to be around animals. ⊠ *Rua Do Casalinho, Aldeia do Meco* ☎ *212/684607* ⊕ *www.quintadomiguel.com* ⇨ *5 apartments, 1 loft, 2 villas* ⚏ *In-room: a/c (some), kitchen (some), refrigerator* *(some), DVD (some), Wi-Fi (some). In-hotel: room service, water sports, bicycles, laundry facilities, Internet terminal, Wi-Fi hotspot, parking (free)* ⊟ *No credit cards* ⊺◎⊺ *EP.*

$$ ⊡ **Sana Park Sesimbra.** This modern hotel is right across from the beach. Gold curtains and bedspreads in the white rooms contrast well with the deep blue of the sea outside the windows. You can have breakfast at the little round table and chairs on your room's private terrace. On the sixth floor, yellow-and-white deck chairs around the wedge-shape heated pool are a nice place to take in the sun while viewing the sea. **Pros:** location right on main drag; excellent views of the beach; nice outdoor pool. **Cons:** paid parking in a small space; Wi-Fi isn't free; can get very noisy from outside. ⊠ *Av. 25 de Abril* ☏ *212/289000* ⊕ *www. sanahotels.com* ⇝ *100 rooms, 3 suites* ⟐ *In-room: a/c, safe (some). In-hotel: restaurant, room service, bar, pools, gym, beachfront, laundry service, Wi-Fi hotspot, parking (paid)* ⊟ *AE, DC, MC, V.*

$ ⊡ **Sesimbra Hotel & Spa.** This hotel sits on a cliff just above the beachfront's main drag and is the only hotel in the area with a spa. All rooms have a balcony with a sea view and are quite large with soft carpeting and decorated in a mix of spa-styled sea blues, tans, and greens, and the walls patterned with various regional marine birds from the area. The sea theme continues throughout the hotel with the hallways carpeted in authentic reproductions of the sea maps that local fishermen use, and walls in the summer bar are covered with an incredible handmade "enchantment under the sea" mosaic. The spa specializes in hot-stone massages and has free access to the indoor and outdoor infinity pool, whose waterfall cascades down in front of the windows of the *marisqueira* restaurant Aquarius ($$$). **Pros:** great beachfront location; beautiful views of the ocean and surrounding hills; large rooms. **Cons:** Wi-Fi isn't free; poor variety at breakfast, and restaurants closed for lunch and dinner during the winter (November–March); indoor pool very cold. ⊠ *Praça da Califórnia, Sesimbra* ☏ *212/289800* ⊕ *www.sesimbrahotelspa.com* ⇝ *92 rooms, 8 suites* ⟐ *In-room: a/c, safe (some), Internet (some). In-hotel: 2 restaurants, room service, bars, pools, gym, spa, beachfront, diving, water sports, bicycles, children's programs (ages 2–12), laundry service, Internet terminal, Wi-Fi hotspot, parking (free)* ⊟ *AE, MC, V* ⊺◎⊺ *BP.*

OUTDOOR ACTIVITIES

Sesimbra, a deep-sea fishing center, is renowned for the huge swordfish that are landed in the area.

The **Clube Naval de Sesimbra** (⊠ *Via Mar Sol* ☏ *212/233451*) offers coastal fishing trips most Saturdays.

Estremadura and the Ribatejo

WORD OF MOUTH

"We spent our summer holiday in Ericeira this year. There is a coastal walk that links all the beaches and the town centre is largely pedestrian-friendly. The beaches are beautiful. Seafood lovers: watch out for the word Marisqueira [Portuguese seafood restaurant] and you can't go wrong."

—ter2000

"If you like beaches you should go to Peniche and/ or Nazaré. Be sure to check out the following: Mosteiro de Alcobaça (in Alcobaça); Mosteiro da Batalha (in Batalha); the Medieval Castles in Leiria, Ourém, and Tomar; and the Convent of the Order of Christ in Tomar (World Heritage Site)."

—BrunoRibeiro

Updated by
Andrea Smith

Estremadura and Ribatejo are the two (former) provinces north and northeast of Lisbon. Estremadura is called the Oeste (West) region, characterized by a mix of maritime activities with green rural valleys where the old traditions and feelings combine harmoniously with modernity. Ribatejo, on the banks of the Tejo River, is a land of agriculture and livestock, known as the heart of Portuguese bullfighting and a bastion of the famous Lusitano horse.

Water shapes the character of these two provinces. Estremadura stretches itself out along the coast, extending north from Lisbon to include the one-time royal residence of Leiria, 119 km (74 mi) from the capital. Closely tied to the sea, the narrow province is known for its fine beaches, coastal pine forests, and picturesque fishing villages. Some of these have evolved, for better or worse, into popular resorts. Fruits and vegetables grow in fertile coastal valleys, and livestock contentedly graze in rich pastures, but Estremadura hasn't always been so peaceful. During the Wars of Reconquest, which raged from the 8th through the 13th century, it was the scene of a series of bloody encounters between Christians and Moors. The province's name means "farthest from the Douro River," an indication of how far south of the Douro River the Christians had advanced against the Moors. In the aftermath of the wars, Portuguese sovereignty was secured with the defeat of the Spanish at Aljubarrota in 1385 and the turning back of Napoléon's forces in 1810 at Torres Vedras. The bloodshed left behind masterpieces of religious architecture—such as those at Alcobaça and Batalha—that commemorate Portuguese triumphs.

Over the centuries Romans, Visigoths, Moors, and Christians built and rebuilt various castles and fortifications to protect the strategic Tejo. You'll see fine examples along the river at Belver, Abrantes, and Almourol. Tomar, spanning the banks of the Rio Nabão (a tributary of the Tejo), is dominated by the hilltop Convento de Cristo (Convent of Christ), built in the 12th century by the Knights Templar. In the brush-covered hills at the province's western edge lies Fátima, one of Christendom's most important pilgrimage sites. As it flows south approaching Lisbon, the Tejo expands, often overflowing its banks during the winter rains, and the landscape changes to one of rich meadows and pastures and broad, alluvial plains, where grains grow in abundance.

The Ribatejo region developed along both sides of the Rio Tejo (Tagus River), and it is this waterway, born in the mountains of Spain, that has shaped and sustained the province. In the north, inhabitants tend groves of olive and fig trees in a peaceful landscape that has changed little since Roman times. Ribatejans are said to be more reserved than their fellow Portuguese—that is, until they step into the arena to test their mettle against a ton or so of charging bull. This is bullfighting country, the heartland of one of Portugal's richest and most colorful traditions. On

TOP REASONS TO GO

Soak up the pleasures of the Atlantic Coast. Forty unique beaches dot Estremadura's 60-mi coastline, allowing for a variety of choices including relaxing in the sun and sand, catching the waves, or watching the sunset.

Experience the Middle Ages. Cities like Mafra, Tomar, Alcobaça Batalha, and Leiria boast medieval monasteries and castles, and royal palaces that provide an incredible view of times past.

Savoring the freshest seafood. The fishing towns of Ericeira, Peniche, and Nazaré are some of the best places in the country for seafood lovers.

Admire Portugal's beautiful countryside. The landscape along the Tejo and Zêzere rivers is a perfect venue to experience the culture of the Portuguese countryside.

Horseback riding with famous horses. The Ribatejo is home to the famous breed of Lusitan horses, used in dressage and bullfighting.

the vast plains along the east bank of the Tejo, you'll encounter men on horseback carrying long wooden prods and often wearing the traditional waistcoats and stocking caps of their trade. These are *campinos,* the Portuguese "cowboys," who tend the herds of bulls and horses bred and trained for arenas throughout the country.

ORIENTATION AND PLANNING

GETTING ORIENTED

The sea is never far from sight in coast-hugging Estremadura, especially in fishing towns like Nazaré and Peniche. The same holds true for the lively town of Ericeira, where surfing also reigns supreme with its big waves. Coastal valleys witnessed many bloody battles between rival groups, including the Moors, but from them came extraordinary monasteries, such as the ones in Batalha and Alcobaça, built to celebrate Portuguese victories.

The Rio Tejo flows through the Ribatejo, where vast plains spread out from the riverbanks. The region is dotted with monuments and fortifications that emulate the country's religious history, from the impressive Convento do Cristo of the Knights Templar in Tomar, a World Heritage site, to the most famous pilgrimage site, the sanctuary in Fátima.

Estremadura. North of Lisbon, this area, which borders the Atlantic, is a coastal paradise of endless beaches, spectacular cliffs, and pastoral coastal valleys. You'll experience delicious seafood and some of the most beautiful monasteries and picturesque castles in Portugal.

Ribatejo. To the east of Lisbon, the Tejo river valley—its namesake—is filled with lush farmland, vineyards, cork forests and is rich in old-world tradition and country hospitality. This is the home of the country's finest bullfighters and equestrians.

PLANNING

WHEN TO GO

To avoid the busloads of visitors who inundate major monuments and attractions during July and August, visit the popular ones such as Óbidos and Mafra in the early morning. ■TIP→ **Most religious and historical monuments have free admission on Sunday and national holidays until 2 pm.** This also helps to beat the oppressive summer heat, particularly inland. The best time of year for touring is in early spring and from mid-September until late October. The climate during this period is pleasant, and attractions and restaurants aren't crowded. If throngs of people don't bother you, time your visit to Fátima to coincide with May 13, when between 500,000 and 1 million pilgrims overwhelm this otherwise sleepy country town. Less spectacular pilgrimages take place year-round.

GETTING HERE AND AROUND

AIR TRAVEL

Estremadura and the Ribatejo are served by Lisbon's Aeroporto de Portela, 7 km (4½ mi) north of the city.

No trains run directly between the Airport and Estremadura and the Ribatejo, but you can catch one at Lisbon's Campo Grande or suburban Cacém stations. If you are landing in Lisbon and traveling directly to this area, your best bet is to rent a car.

Airport Contacts Aeroporto Portela (☎ 218/413500 or 218/413700 ⊕ www.ana-aeroportos.pt).

BUS TRAVEL

There are few, if any, places in this region that aren't served by at least one bus daily. Express coaches run by several regional lines travel regularly between Lisbon and the larger towns such as Santarém, Leiria, and Abrantes. If you have the time and patience, bus travel is an inexpensive way to get around. It's best to do your booking through a travel agent. If you know some Portuguese, you can also get a schedule and fee information by calling the bus stations.

Bus Contacts Boa Viagem (Ribatejo) (☎ 217/582212 Campo Grande station in Lisbon ⊕ www.boa-viagem.pt). **Mafrense (Estremadura)** (☎ 217/587212 Campo Grande station in Lisbon ⊕ www.mafrense.pt). **Rede Expressos** (☎ 707/223344 ⊕ www.rede-expressos.pt). **Ribatejana (Ribatejo)** (☎ 217/582212 Campo Grande station in Lisbon ⊕ www.ribatejana.pt).

CAR TRAVEL

It's easy to reach Estremadura and the Ribatejo from Lisbon, because both provinces begin as extensions of the city's northern suburbs. There are two principal access roads from the capital: the A1 (also called E80 and IP1), which is the Lisbon–Porto toll road, provides the best inland access; the A8 (also called IC1) is the fastest route to the coast. From Porto there's easy access via the A1 tollway.

The roads are generally good, and traffic is light, except for weekend congestion along the coast. There are no confusing big cities in which to get lost, although parking can be a problem in some of the towns. Hotels don't usually charge for parking. Drive with extreme caution.

Affable as they are on foot, the Portuguese are among Europe's most aggressive drivers.

There are major car-rental agencies in Leiria and Nazaré, as well as in Lisbon.

Car Rental Contacts Avis (☎ 262/562190 in Nazaré). **Hertz** (☎ 244/826781 in Leiria, 800/238238 toll-free).

TRAIN TRAVEL

Travel by train within central Portugal isn't for people in a hurry. Service to many of the more remote destinations is infrequent—and in some cases nonexistent. Even major attractions such as Nazaré and Mafra have no direct rail links. Nevertheless, trains will take you to most of the strategic bases for touring the towns in this chapter.

The Lisbon–Porto line (Santa Apolónia station) provides reasonably frequent service to Vila Franca de Xira, Santarém, Torres Novas, Tomar, and Fátima. Towns in the western part of the region, such as Torres Vedras, Caldas da Rainha, Óbidos, and Leiria, are served on another line from Lisbon's Rossio station.

Train Contacts CP (☎ 707/201280 or 808/208208 ⊕ www.cp.pt).

RESTAURANTS

Between mid-June and mid-September, reservations are advised at upscale restaurants. Most moderate or inexpensive establishments, however, don't accept reservations. They also have informal dining rooms, where sharing a table with other diners is common. Dress is casual at all but the most luxurious places.

In Estremadura restaurants, the emphasis is on fish, including the ubiquitous *bacalhau* (dried salt cod) and *caldeirada* (a hearty fish stew). The seaside resorts of Ericeira, Nazaré, and Peniche are famous for lobster. In Santarém and other spots along the Rio Tejo, an *açorda* (bread soup) made with *savel,* a river fish also known as shad, is popular, as are *enguias* (eels) prepared in a variety of ways. Pork is a key component in Ribatejo dishes, and roast lamb and kid are widely enjoyed. Perhaps the result of a sweets-making tradition developed by nuns in the region's once-numerous convents, dessert menus abound with colorful-sounding—although often cloyingly sweet and eggy—dishes such as *queijinhos do céu* (little cheeses from heaven). The straw-color white wines from the Ribatejo district of Bucelas are among the country's finest.

HOTELS

Estremadura has plenty of good-quality lodgings, especially along the coast. In summer, you'll need reservations. Most establishments offer substantial off-season discounts. *Estalagem* is the term for inn. The best accommodations in the Ribatejo are the government-run inns called *pousadas.* The pousadas are small, some with as few as six rooms, so reserving well in advance is essential. There are also a number of high-quality, government-approved private guesthouses. Look for signs reading "Turismo Rural" or "Turismo de Habitação."

WHAT IT COSTS IN EUROS				
¢	$	$$	$$$	$$$$
Restaurants	under €10	€10–€15	€16–€20	€21–€25	over €25
Hotels	under €80	€80–€140	€141–€200	€201–€260	over €260

Restaurant prices are per person for a main course at dinner. Hotel prices are for a standard double room, including tax, in high season (off-season rates may be lower).

EMERGENCIES

All sizable towns have at least one pharmacy open weekends, holidays, and after normal store hours. Local newspapers usually keep a schedule, and notices are posted on the door of every pharmacy.

Emergency Contacts Caldas da Rainha Hospital Distrital (⌂ *Rua Diário de Notícias* ☎ *262/830300*). **General emergencies** (☎ *112*). **Leiria Hospital Distrital** (⌂ *Rua das Olhalvas Pousos* ☎ *244/817000*). **Santarém Hospital Distrital de Santarém** (⌂ *Av. Bernardo Santareno-Apartado 115* ☎ *243/300200*).

TOUR OPTIONS

ORIENTATION TOURS

Few regularly scheduled sightseeing tours originate within the region, but many of the major attractions are covered by a wide selection of one-day tours from Lisbon. For information contact Cityrama.

Contact Cityrama (⌂ *Av. Praia da Vitória 12-B, Saldanha, Lisbon* ☎ *213/191090* ⊕ *www.cityrama.pt*).

BOAT TOURS

Boat trips along the Rio Zêzere depart at noon in summer from a dock at the Estalagem Lago Azul, upstream from the Castelo de Bode dam. The four-hour cruises cost €36.41, including a buffet lunch with wine, but they take place only when there are enough passengers; this is most likely to happen on weekends and national holidays. For reservations and information, contact Hotel dos Templários in Tomar.

Contacts Estalagem Lago Azul (⌂ *Hwy. N348, Ferreira do Zêzere, Castanheira* ☎ *249/361445*). **Hotel dos Templários** (⌂ *Largo Candido dos Reis 1, Tomar* ☎ *249/310100* ⊕ *www.hoteldostemplarios.pt*).

ESTREMADURA

The narrow province surrounding Lisbon and extending north along the coast for approximately 160 km (100 mi) is known as Estremadura, referring to the extreme southern border of the land the Portuguese reconquered from the Moors. This is primarily a rural region characterized by coastal fishing villages and small farming communities that produce mostly fruit and olives. A tour through the region includes visits to towns with some of Portugal's most outstanding architectural treasures, including Mafra, Alcobaça, Óbidos, Tomar, and Batalha.

GREAT ITINERARIES

Three days will give you a sense of the region, five days will allow you to include a visit to the shrine at Fátima and the Convent of Christ, and a full week will give you enough time to cover the major attractions as well as explore the countryside. With additional days you can easily extend your itinerary to include Évora and the Alentejo or head north to Coimbra and the Beiras. It's best to explore these regions by car, unless you have a great deal of time and patience: trains don't serve many of the most interesting towns, and bus travel is slow.

IF YOU HAVE 3 DAYS

Start with a visit to the imposing monastery and palace at **Mafra,** then head for the coast, with a stop at the resort and fishing village of **Ericeira.** Continue north along the shore to **Peniche,** with its imposing fortress. Head inland to spend the night in the enchanting walled city of **Óbidos.** The next morning continue north, stopping at ceramics shops in **Caldas da Rainha.** En route to **Nazaré,** tour the church and cloister at **Alcobaça.** On your third day head inland to the soaring, multispired monastery church in **Batalha.** Return to Lisbon along N1/IC2 with a stop in **Vila Franca de Xira** (after joining the A1 toll road at Aveiras da Cima) to visit the

bullfighting museum. Alternatively, you could take N356 east from Batalha and then A1 down to Vila Franca from the Fátima junction, which will take slightly longer but is handy if you want to visit Fátima en route.

IF YOU HAVE 5 DAYS

Follow the three-day itinerary to **Batalha,** and then continue north to **Leiria** and its hilltop castle. Take N113 east to the A1 and drive down to **Fátima,** one of Christendom's most renowned destinations. The next morning, continue east on N113 to **Tomar,** an attractive town dominated by its hilltop convent. Later in the day, follow N110 south and then take N358-2, a scenic road that follows the Rio Zêzere, to its union with the Rio Tejo. Just west of their confluence, on an island in the Tejo, is the **Castelo de Almourol,** one of Portugal's finest. From here, follow N118 southwest along the Tejo, stopping in **Alpiarça** to visit the Casa dos Patudos, a large country house containing the art collection of its former owner, and in **Almeirim** to see the winery at the Quinta da Alorna. Spend the night in **Santarém,** an important farming and livestock center with many fine sights. The next day return to Lisbon with a drive along the Tejo on N118 through the region of marshy plains known as the Lezíria.

4

ERICEIRA

11 km (7 mi) northwest of Mafra.

Ericeira, an old fishing town tucked into the rocky coast, is a popular seaside resort. Its core fans out from the sheer cliff, beneath which boats are hauled up onto a small, sheltered beach. The growth of summer tourism has caused a proliferation of bars, pubs, discos, pizzerias, and the like in the increasingly gentrified but still-attractive town center. But along the waterfront are a number of traditional seafood restaurants that are popular with both locals and visitors. Either

Estremadura and the Ribatejo

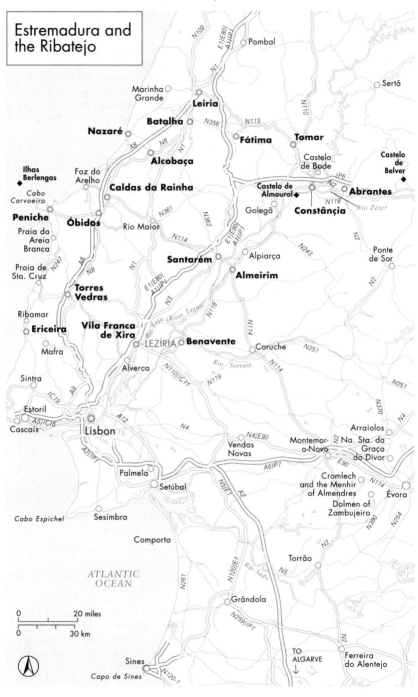

end of the town has good sand for sunbathing, but the south end is preferred by surfers.

Perched atop the cliffs, the town's historic center is a beautiful place to walk around and explore, as it has completely maintained the traditional Portuguese coastal architecture that was popular in the 17th and 18th centuries when the fishing village really thrived. The buildings are all sand-blasted white and framed with deep, sea blues. The main fishing port in the center is also where the Portuguese royal family departed to exile in 1910 after the Republic was declared, not to return for a couple generations.

GETTING HERE AND AROUND

There are several daily bus lines between Ericeira, Mafra, and Lisbon run by Mafrense. Driving from Lisbon is close to 45 minutes and getting to Ericeira from Mafra takes 15 minutes.

ESSENTIALS

Bus Info Mafrense (☏ *217/587212* ⊕ *www.mafrense.pt*).

Visitor Info Ericeira Tourism Office (✉ *Rua Eduardo Burnay 46* ☏ *261/863122*).

WHERE TO EAT

$ ✕ **Mar à Vista.** This revived Portuguese fisherman's tavern has a genuine
SEAFOOD feel—fishing nets and baskets hang from walls, and the loud service adds to its character. Seafood is the only option, and most diners come for the *arroz de marisco* (shellfish and rice stew) or grilled fish. You'll have to go elsewhere for coffee afterward. ✉ *Rua Santo António 16* ☏ *261/862928* ⚓ *Reservations essential* ⊟ *No credit cards* ⊗ *Closed Wed.*

$ ✕ **O Barco.** This quiet family-run restaurant resides on the harbor at the
PORTUGUESE bottom of the town. Except for its big glass window with a view of the sea, the setting and decor are very simple, but people come for its excellent food. Try the *feijoada de polvo* (bean stew with octopus) or *pato à portuguesa com arroz* (Portuguese style duck with rice). ✉ *Capitão João Lopes, Ericeira* ☏ *261/862759* ⊟ *AE, DC, MC, V* ⊗ *Closed Thurs.*

$ ✕ **Ribas.** This is your typical Portuguese *marisqueira* (seafood restau-
SEAFOOD rant), large and noisy with family-style seating and the hammering and cracking of crab shells. Overlooking the harbor with indoor and outdoor tables, beautiful murals of Ericeira's harbor, and a huge display of fresh shellfish greet you upon arrival. If you're a seafood lover, this is the place to go. Crabs and lobsters can be ordered individually, priced by the kilo or piled upon a large *mariscada* (mixed seafood platter) with clams, mussels, shrimp, and other native mollusks. The dish is served with warm, toasted bread and can be shared between two or more people. The heaps of empty shells piled on plates are testimony to the feasts that have taken place. ✉ *Rua Mendes Leal 32, Ericeira* ☏ ⊟ *AE, DC, MC, V* ⊗ *Closed Wed.*

$$ ✕ **Viveiros do Atlântico.** Live seafood crawling around in a vivarium
SEAFOOD shaped like a blue-and-white fisherman's boat at the entrance gives you an idea of what to find on the menu. Pick out the fish or shellfish of your choice to be prepared especially for you, such as a *sapateira recheada* (stuffed crab) brought to the table in its shell. Try the *cataplanas* (mixed seafood served in a copper steamer). The restaurant

has fantastic views—some stretch all the way to Peninha de Sintra—and there are only a few places from which you can't see the ocean. ⊠ *Estrada Nacional 247, Ribamar* ☏ *261/860300* ⊟ *AE, DC, MC, V* ⊙ *Closed for 12 days in Mar. and 18 days in Nov. for vacation.*

WHERE TO STAY

¢   🖼 **Hotel Pedro O Pescador.** If you prefer your hotels on the small side, then you'll like this intimate, pastel blue, family-run place near the beach. Cheerful rooms surround a central courtyard and have hardwood floors, floral print fabrics, and Alentejo furniture. Be sure to visit the lively bar. **Pros:** hotel right on the main drag; minutes from beach. **Cons:** difficult parking; the hotel is on a pedestrian path, and no cars can pull up to it; not good for couples (mostly separated twin beds). ⊠ *Rua Dr. Eduardo Burnay 22* ☏ *261/869121* ⊕ *www.hotelpedropescador. com* ⇨ *25 rooms* ⚭ *In-room: a/c, no phone (some), Wi-Fi (some). In-hotel: room service, bar, laundry service, Wi-Fi hotspot, parking (free)* ⊟ *AE, DC, MC, V* |◎| *CP.*

$$ 🖼 **Hotel Vila Galé.** This luxurious hotel with its white facade and green
ⵛ   tile roof overlooks the Atlantic from the center of Ericeira. It has been aesthetically modernized, retaining traditional Portuguese features: clay-potted geraniums hang outside room windows, the floors are of red tiles, and *azulejos* (glazed tiles) decorate the walls. Bedrooms have yellow-and-green fabrics and are equipped with every modern amenity; half have ocean views with beautiful stone terraces. There are three ocean-side swimming pools, including one salt water and one children's, and a small children's playground next to the pools. In summer the bar opens its prow-shape terrace overlooking the sea. You feel like you are sailing away on a cruise ship. **Pros:** great beach location; great for either couples or families; plenty of amenities. **Cons:** the spa was built under the outdoor patio so you have to go down the patio stairs to the only entrance, which is not covered; can get crowded with families and groups in summer. ⊠ *Largo dos Navegantes* ☏ *261/869900* ⊕ *www.vilagale.pt* ⇨ *202 rooms* ⚭ *In-room: a/c, safe, Internet (some). In-hotel: restaurant, bar, pools, gym, spa, beachfront, laundry service, public Internet, Wi-Fi hotspot, parking (free), children's programs (ages 2–12)* ⊟ *AE, DC, MC, V* |◎| *CP.*

**EN
ROUTE**   The town of Mafra is one of the oldest in Portugal, with evidence of prehistoric settlements and remains of Roman and later Moorish occupation. Over the centuries the crown, church, and nobility have contested the ownership of the **Mosteiro Palácio Nacional de Mafra** (*Monastery and Royal Palace*), which is 8 km (5 mi) southeast of Ericeira. In the 17th, 18th, and 19th centuries the monastery was a favorite residence for nobility. In 1711, after nearly three years of a childless union with his Hapsburg queen, Mariana, a despairing King João V vowed that should the queen bear him an heir, he would build a monastery dedicated to St. Anthony. In December of that same year, a girl—later to become queen of Spain—was born; João's eventual heir, José I, was born three years later. True to his word, King João V built an enormous monastery, which still looms above the small farming community of Mafra. The original project—entrusted to the Italian-trained German architect Friedrich Ludwig—was to be a modest facility that could house

13 friars. What emerged in 1750 after 18 years of construction was a rectangular complex containing a monastery large enough for hundreds of monks as well as an imposing basilica and a grandiose palace that has been compared to El Escorial outside Madrid, Spain. The numbers involved in the construction are mind-boggling: at times 50,000 workers toiled. There are 4,500 doors and windows, 300 cells, 880 halls and rooms, and 154 stairways. Perimeter walls that total some 19 km (12 mi) surround the park.

The one-hour guided tours are enlightening; those conducted by English-speaking docents take place at 11 am and 2:30 pm. The highlight is the magnificent baroque library: the barrel-vaulted, two-tiered hall holds some 40,000 volumes of mostly 16th-, 17th-, and 18th-century works and a number of ancient maps. The basilica contains 11 chapels and was patterned after St. Peter's in the Vatican. The balcony of the connecting corridor overlooks the high altar and was a favorite meeting place for Dom João and Mariana, who had separate bedrooms. When you're in the gilded throne room, notice the life-size renditions of the seven virtues, as well as the impressive figure of Hercules, by Domingos Sequeira. On display in the games room is an early version of a pinball machine. Note the hard-planked beds in the monastery infirmary; the monks used no mattresses. You'll be fortunate if you arrive on a Sunday afternoon between 4 and 5, when the sonorous tones of the 92-bell carillon ring out. ⊠ *Terreiro de D. João V* ☎ *261/817550* 🖃 *€4, including tour* ☾ *Mon. and Wed.–Sun. 10–5:30 (last tour at 4:30).*

TORRES VEDRAS

20 km (12 mi) northeast of Ericeira.

A bustling commercial center crowned with the ruins of a medieval castle, Torres Vedras is best known for its extensive fortifications—a system of trenches and fortresses erected by the Duke of Wellington in 1810 as part of a secret plan for the defense of Lisbon. It was here, at the Lines of Torres Vedras, that the surprised French army under Napoléon's Marshal Masséna was routed. You can see reconstructed remnants of the fortifications on a hill above town and throughout the area. The surrounding hills and countryside make for a picturesque drive to one of the several beaches on the coast 20–30 minutes away.

GETTING HERE AND AROUND

Torres Vedras can be reached by bus (Mafrense and Rede Expressos) from Lisbon or train (regional train line between Sintra and Figueira da Foz). Driving from Lisbon takes 30 minutes, from Mafra 20 minutes. ⇨ *For more info about bus and train travel, see Bus Travel and Train Travel, above.*

ESSENTIALS

Visitor Info Torres Vedras Tourism (⊠ *Rua 9 de Abril* ☎ *261/310483*).

EXPLORING

Castelo. Perched on top of a hill on the outer part of the city is the medieval castelo. Built in the 12th century, it has been reinforced and reconstructed several times throughout the centuries, with the last repairs done in the 1980s. The cement recovered from the cisterns and various coins are on display in the Municipal Museum attest to the presence of the Roman occupation here. The castle exhibits both Gothic and Manueline styles in its outside walls, and a medieval cemetery once existed where the church of Santa Maria stands. While exploring the towers, don't miss out on the incredible views of the city and surrounding valley and hills. ⌨ *Free* ☉ *Tues.–Sun. 10–1 and 2–6. Closed during Carnaval, Easter Sun., May 1, Christmas Day, and New Year's Day.*

Museu Municipal de Leonel Trindade (Municipal Museum). In the Convento de Graça in the 25th of April Plaza, this museum has exhibits about the city's historical fortifications, as well as interesting archeological finds around the area. ✉ *Praça 25 de Abril, Convento da Graça, Torres Vedras* ☎ *261/310484* ⌨ *€0.75* ☉ *Tues.–Sun. 10–1 and 2–6. Closed during Carnaval, Easter Sun., May 1, Christmas, and New Year's Day.*

WHERE TO EAT AND STAY

$ ✕ **Trás de Orelha.** The restaurant's name is also the Portuguese expression for "it's really good," and indeed this restaurant lives up to its name. Located five minutes outside of Torres Vedras in Catefica, the restaurant is built out of an old wine cellar but has the elements and style of a rustic hunting and fishing lodge, complete with mounted deer heads and antlers on the walls. So it's no surprise then that some of the best dishes are wild game selections, such as the *javali* (wild boar) with sweet potatoes and sautéed cabbage sprouts or *lebre com feijão branco* (wild hare with white beans). For fish, try their *linguado com arroz de ameijoas* (sole with clam rice). ✉ *Rua da Paz 9, Catefica, Torres Vedras* ☎ *261/326018* ⊕ *www.trasdorelha.com* ⊟ *AE, DC, MC, V* ☉ *Closed Sun.*

PORTUGUESE

$$$$ ⊡ **Areias Do Seixo Charm Hotel & Residences.** Opened in April 2010, this small, five-star hotel was built with complete respect and focus on the natural resources and surroundings among the pine trees and dunes in front of Santa Cruz beach. The room decorations are inspired by African, Indian, and romantic country styles and include rich colors, natural stone, and luxurious fabrics. All rooms have a rain shower, fireplace, and wooden patio with views of the ocean and dunes; some even have a large indoor or outdoor Jacuzzi. For guests who want the ultimate in luxury, the hotel also has a three-bedroom penthouse complete with living room, kitchen, deck terraces, a barbecue area, and a Jacuzzi, as well as two three-bedroom villas with the same amenities but with their own private, outdoor swimming pool instead. For all guests, there is a heated, outdoor pool, and the restaurant ($$) serves up creations made from the hotel's biological (any method of farming or gardening that uses natural, biological processes and methods) garden; you can buy the produce for yourself at the restaurant's grocery store. Don't miss out on the hotel's range of "experiences," from biological farming, fishing for mussels at the beach, or a biological cooking class and lunch. The hotel is in *Póvoa De Penafirme*, 25–30 minutes by car from Torres Vedras or Ericeira. **Pros:** amazing accommodations; great location; perfect for couples. **Cons:** very expensive; not recommended for kids, unless they stay in the penthouse or villas; food can be a little plain. ✉ *Praceta Do Atlântico–Mexilhoeira, Póvoa De*

Fodor'sChoice
★

Penafirme, A-Dos-Cunhados (Torres Vedras) ☎ *261/936340* ⊕ *www. areiasdoseixo.com* ⤳ *10 rooms, penthouse, 2 villas* ⚭ *In-room: a/c, no phone (some), safe (some), kitchen (some), refrigerator (some), DVD (some), no TV (some), Internet (some), Wi-Fi (some). In-hotel: restaurant, room service, bar, golf course, pool, gym, spa, beachfront, water sports, bicycles, laundry service, Wi-Fi hotspot, parking (free), no kids under10* ☐ *AE, D, DC, MC, V.* ⍩ *BP.*

$ ⌘ **Hotel Golf Mar.** The idyllic location—on a rise overlooking an abso-
☺ lutely breathtaking view of the ocean, pounding waves, and the nearby cliffs, rolling hills, and lush green valley—is by far the best thing about this place. The large hotel is plain and a little worn down in some areas but makes up for it with a wide variety of amenities in excellent condition, such as a large indoor pool and solarium, recently remodeled outdoor pool with an ocean view, and spa, fitness center, Jacuzzi, sauna and steam room. Outside are tennis courts, golf, and an equestrian center with lessons offered. And there is always the beach, one of the few in the region that doesn't get too crowded in the summer. The hotel can also arrange for several water sports such as kite surfing and parasailing. A huge renovation project is in the works, but until it gets under way your best bet is to book a comfortable superior room, which has a/c, for a little extra. The hotel is near the town of Lourinhã, 16 km (10 mi) northwest of Torres Vedras. **Pros:** excellent location; panoramic views; plenty of amenities. **Cons:** a bit run-down; only superior rooms and suites have a/c; Wi-Fi isn't free. ✉ *Praia do Porto Novo* ☎ *261/980800* ⊕ *www.hotelgolfmar.com* ⤳ *252 rooms, 9 suites* ⚭ *In-room: a/c (some), safe, Wi-Fi. In-hotel: restaurant, room service, bars, golf course, tennis courts, pools, spa, beachfront, diving, water sports, bicycles, children's programs (ages 3–12), laundry service, Wi-Fi hotspot, parking (free)* ☐ *AE, DC, MC, V* ⍩ *BP, FAP, MAP.*

¢ ⌘ **Hotel Império Jardim.** This bright, cheerfully appointed hotel is a good deal. It has several on-site eateries and shops, including a café that has a well-known cake shop and an enoteca wine bar and restaurant complete with a wine shop selling some of the oldest and rarest Ports and Madeiras around. It's right in the center of town as well, located in the pretty April 25th Plaza. Rooms are large with simple, modern furnishings; 20 rooms have balconies with some beautiful views of the castle. **Pros:** right in city center; great food and beverage options; 20-minute drive to beaches. **Cons:** can get noisy from outside city activity; parking facility on next block. ✉ *Praça 25 de Abril 17* ☎ *261/314232* ⊕ *www.hotel-imperio.com* ⤳ *47 rooms* ⚭ *In-room: a/c, safe, Wi-Fi In-hotel: restaurant, room service, bar, laundry service, Wi-Fi hotspot, parking (free)* ☐ *AE, MC, V* ⍩ *BP.*

SPORTS AND THE OUTDOORS

The therapeutic properties of the waters at the **Termas do Vimeiro** (✉ *Praia do Porto Novo* ☎ *261/984484* ⊕ *www.termasvimeiro.com* ⊙ *Closed Oct. 16–May 28*) are good for respiratory, digestive, circulatory, and skin problems. Treatments last a minimum of eight days, and you have to make an initial appointment with a doctor.

The 9-hole **Clube do Golfe do Vimeiro** (✉ *Praia do Porto Novo* ☎ *261/980800* ⊕ *www.hotelgolfmar.com* ⛳ *Reservations essential* 🏌 *9 holes. 2,400 m. Par 34* 🏷 *€20–€25 per round* ☞ *Facilities: driving range, putting green,* *hand-pulled carts, rental clubs, tennis courts, restaurant, bar*), designed by Frank Pennink, is on the beach and is part of the Hotel Golf Mar. Guests of the hotel golf for free; both guests and nonguests must reserve greens in advance.

PENICHE

32 km (20 mi) northwest of Torres Vedras.

In the lee of a rocky peninsula, Peniche is a major fishing-and-canning port that's also a popular summer resort known for its fine trimmed bilro lace. There are several beaches to choose from in the area as well as the beaches and fishing of the Berlengas Islands, available to visit in the summer months. Besides it being a major fishing port, locals and tourists know that this is one of the best places around to enjoy delicious fresh fish and seafood, especially sardines.

> ### GREAT DRIVES
>
> For the most scenic drive to Peniche, return to the coast and follow N247 north for 43 km (27 mi) to Cabo Carvoeiro. About 3 km (2 mi) north of Torres Vedras is the archaeological site Castro do Zambujal, the remains of an Iron Age settlement of people who worked the copper mines that once existed here. Farther on, the jagged coast is interrupted by fine beaches at Ribamar, Santa Cruz, and Areia Branca.

GETTING HERE AND AROUND

Peniche can be reached by bus (Rede Expressos) from Lisbon. Driving from Lisbon takes 50 minutes and 15 minutes from Óbidos. ⇨ *For more info about Rede Expressos, see Bus Travel, above.*

ESSENTIALS

Visitor Info Peniche (✉ *Rua Alex. Herculano* ☎ *262/789571* ⊕ *www.cm-peniche.pt*).

EXPLORING

Fortaleza Museu *(Fort Museum)*. The busy harbor is watched over by a sprawling 16th-century fort. At one time the fort's dungeons were full of French troops captured by the Duke of Wellington's forces. During Portugal's dictatorship, which ended in 1974, it was a prison for opponents of the regime. With the restoration of democracy, it became a museum covering all of its eras. You can tour the former cells and take in a small archaeological exhibit. There are also some beautiful views of the ocean from its towers. For a good view of the fortress and the harbor, drive out to Cabo Carvoeiro; the narrow road winds around the peninsula, along the rugged shore, and past the lighthouse and bizarre rock formations. ⊞ *€1.30* ⊙ *Tues.–Sun. 10:30–12:30 and 2–6; closes at 5 in winter.*

Igreja de São Leonardo *(Church of St. Leonard)*. The most interesting of the area's several churches is the 13th-century Igreja de São Leonardo with its primitive Gothic and Manueline elements along with the ceiling depicting scenes from the Old Testament. The church is in the village of Atouguia da Baleia. ☎ *262/759142 town council office* ⊙ *Apr.–Oct., daily 9–12:30 and 2–5:30.*

Ilhas Berlengas (Berlenga Islands). The harbor at Peniche is the jumping-off point for excursions to the Ilhas Berlengas. These six islets are part of a nature reserve and a favorite place for fishermen and divers. It is also a nesting place and migratory route for many birds and marine life. Berlenga, the largest of the group, is the site of a pretty lighthouse and the Forte de São João Baptista, a 17th-century fortress built to defend the area from pirates. There are trails around the island, including through caves. You can visit the islands only by boat from May to September; the largest boat company, Viamar, operates round-trips on the Cabo Avelar Pessoa daily during the summer. The sea is often rough, so don't be alarmed by the rows of buckets under your seats. You can even stay at Berlenga overnight; the island has a campground as well as a bar and restaurant. ☎ *262/785646 Viamar ⊕ www.viamar-berlenga. com* 🖃*€18 round-trip ⊗ May 15–June 30 and Sept. 1–15, departs 10 am and returns 4:30 pm, July and Aug., departs 9:30 and 11:30 am, returns 4:30 and 6:30 pm.*

4

WHERE TO EAT AND STAY

$$$
SEAFOOD
✕ **Corteçais.** This modern restaurant is built into a cliff overlooking the sea, a favorable location to cast your line into the water and fish while you eat. *Festival de Mariscos,* a tray of seven different kinds of seafood, including lobster, oysters, and spider crabs, is served on a bed of natural seaweed and is a real feast. ⊠ *Porto de Areia-Sol* ☎ *262/787262* ⊕ *www.doscorticais.com* ▭ *DC, MC, V* ⊗ *Closed Wed., except in Aug.*

$
SEAFOOD
✕ **Katekero II.** On Peniche's restaurant row, this is your typical Portuguese seafood restaurant, serving inexpensive grilled fish such as *robalo* (seabass), *carapaus* (mackerel), and of course, roasted sardines. Traditional specialties include *caldeirada* (fish stew), *arroz de tamboril* or *marisco* (monkfish or seafood with rice), and *mariscadas* (mixed seafood platters). The restaurant has a glassed in dining patio with views of the fishing port. ⊠ *Av. Mar 68, Peniche* ☎ *262/787107* ⊕ *www. feriaskatekero.com* ▭ *V* ⊗ *Closed Tues.*

$$
SEAFOOD
✕ **Nau dos Corvos.** On the Cabo Carvoeiro cliffs with a dramatic view of the sea and the lighthouse, this restaurant specializes in traditionally prepared seafood dishes. Be sure to try the *arroz de tamboril com gambas* (rice casserole with monkfish and prawns). ⊠ *Cabo Carvoeiro* ☎ *262/783168* ⊕ *www.naudoscorvos.com* ▭ *AE, DC, MC, V* ⊗ *Closed Mon.*

$
☪
🛏 **Hotel Atlântico Golfe.** Even if you're not a golfer, the views from your balcony (all rooms have them) over the links and the long beach will appeal. The hotel is on a sandy stretch famed for the health-giving properties of its waters, which are attributed to the local rock. The hydrotherapy center at the hotel uses tap water for its treatments, but there are thermal baths 2 km (1 mi) away. The hotel is outside the center of the city in nearby Praia da Consolação. **Pros:** beachfront location; great views of the golf course and beach; lots of activities. **Cons:** staff not very professional; Wi-Fi access is not free; hotel a bit dated. ⊠ *Praia da Consolação* ☎ *262/757700* ⊕ *www.atlanticogolfehotel.com* ▭*96 rooms* ⚐ *In-room: a/c, safe, dial-up. In-hotel: restaurant, bar, golf course, tennis court, pools, gym, spa, bicycles, children's programs (ages 2–12), beachfront, diving, water sports, laundry service, Wi-Fi hotspot, some pets allowed, parking (free)* ▭ *AE, DC, MC, V* ⦿ *BP.*

¢ 🏨 **Hotel Soleil Peniche.** The nice thing about this modern hotel is that only a street and sand dunes separate it from the Cova da Alfarroba beach in the middle of Peniche Bay. Shaped like an L, the hotel has rooms with terraces overlooking the swimming pool or with views of the ocean. For additional comfort ask for a room with a king-size bed. There is also a golf course about 2 mi away, at which you can make a reservation through the hotel's concierge. **Pros:** near the beach; nice views; large rooms. **Cons:** far from city's shops and restaurants; next to a busy road; Wi-Fi isn't free. ⊠ *Estrada do Baleal* ☎ *262/780400* ⊕ *www.soleilhotels.com* ⊙ *Closed New Year's Day through 1st half of Jan.* 🛏 *102 rooms* ⚅ *In-room: a/c, safe, Internet. In-hotel: restaurant, bar, pools, laundry service, Wi-Fi hotspot, parking (free)* ⊟ *AE, DC, MC, V.*

> ### WATER SPORTS
>
> The clear waters and bizarre rock formations along Estremadura's coast make it a favorite with anglers, snorkelers, and scuba divers. A wet suit is recommended for diving and snorkeling, as the chilly waters don't invite you to linger long, even in summer. The area's most commonly caught fish are sea bass, bream, and red mullet. The placid waters of the Rio Zêzere (Zêzere River) provide excellent conditions for waterskiing.

SPORTS AND THE OUTDOORS

Peniche Sportagua (⊠ *Av. Monsenhor Manuel Bastos* ☎ *262/789125* ⊕ *www.sportagua.com* 🎟 *€11 for adults, €9 for children, free under 5 years* ⊙ *Mid-July–mid-Sept., daily 10–7*) is a large water-park complex with slides and separate adults' and children's swimming pools. The park also has a restaurant and snack bar.

FISHING

The most commonly caught fish are sea bass, bream, and red mullet. A fishing license isn't required. The charter-boat company **Nautipesca** (⊠ *Rua das Ancoras 31, Peniche* ☎ *262/789648, 936/222658, or 917/588358*) ⊕ *www.nautipesca.com.pt* offers deep-sea fishing excursions. Boats leave when conditions permit and when a minimum of 10 people are interested in heading out. Per-person rates are €30 on weekdays, €35 on weekends.

SCUBA DIVING

The clear (and somewhat chilly) waters and bizarre rock formations off the Ilhas Berlengas are popular with scuba divers and snorkelers. **Haliotis** (⊠ *Hotel Praia Norte, Av. Monsenhor Bastos* ☎ *262/781160* ⊕ *www.haliotis.pt*) offers diving and snorkeling trips and dolphin watches around the Berlengas Islands.

ÓBIDOS

Fodor'sChoice
★

20 km (12 mi) east of Peniche.

Once a strategic seaport, Óbidos is now high and dry—and 10 km (6 mi) inland—owing to the silting of its harbor. On the approach to town, you can see bastions and crenellated walls standing like sentinels over the now-peaceful valley of the Ria Arnoia. It's hard to imagine fishing boats and trading vessels docking in places that are today filled by cottages and cultivated fields.

As you enter town through the massive, arched gates, it seems as if you've been transported into medieval Portugal. The narrow Rua Direita, lined with boutiques and white, flower-bedecked houses, runs from the gates to the foot of the castle: you may want to shop for ceramics and clothing on this street. The rest of the town is crisscrossed by a labyrinth of stone footpaths, tiny squares, and decaying stairways. Each nook and cranny offers its own reward. Cars aren't permitted inside the walls except to unload luggage at hotels. Parking is provided outside town.

Óbidos has a long association with prominent Portuguese women. Young Queen Isabel was so enchanted with Óbidos—which she visited with her husband, Dom Dinis, shortly after their marriage in 1282—that the king gave it to her as a gift, along with Abrantes and Porto de Mós; the town remained the property of the queens of Portugal until 1834. Queen Leonor (the wife of João II) came here in the 15th century to recuperate after the death of her young son; the town pillory bears her coat of arms. Famous primitive painter and daughter of an Óbidos artist, Josefa de Óbidos lived in the Capelaria mansion just outside town during the 17th century. She is buried in the São Pedro Church in Óbidos.

GETTING HERE AND AROUND
Obidos can be reached by bus (Rede Expressos) from Lisbon. The regional train line between Sintra and Figueira da Foz stops in Óbidos as well. Driving from Lisbon takes 40 minutes, and coming from Peniche takes 15 minutes. ⇨ For Rede Expressos info, see Bus Travel, above.

ESSENTIALS
Visitor Info Óbidos (✉ *Largo de São Pedro-Outside town walls, at entrance to parking lot* ☎ *262/955560* ⊕ *www.obidos.pt*).

EXPLORING
Castelo. The walls of the fine medieval *castle* enclose the entire town, and it's great fun to walk their circumference, viewing the town and countryside from their heights. Extensively restored after suffering severe damage in the 1755 earthquake, the multitower complex has both Arabic and Manueline elements. Since 1952 parts of the castle have been a pousada.

Igreja de Santa Maria (*St. Mary's Church*). The 17th-century artist Josefa de Óbidos came as a small child and lived here until her death in 1684. You can see some of her work in the azulejo-lined church, which was a Visigoth temple in the 8th century. The church is in a square off Rua Direita. ☎ *No phone* ◷ *Apr.–Sept., daily 9:30–12:30; Oct.–Mar., daily 2:30–7.*

WHERE TO EAT
$$
PORTUGUESE
Fodor's Choice
★

⨯ **A Ilustre Casa de Ramiro.** Portuguese architect José Fernando Teixeira reworked this old building outside the castle walls into a rustic-chic restaurant with Moorish motifs. The main culinary feature is the open grill, where authentic regional dishes are prepared. Try the *arroz de pato* (rice with duck), a favorite dish among the Portuguese, who often serve it at their own dinner parties. ✉ *Rua Porta do Vale, Obidos* ☎ *262/959194* ▤ *AE, DC, MC, V* ◷ *Closed Thurs.*

CLOSE UP   Óbidos's Fun Festivals

Every July, the 10-day market **Mercado Medieval** (☎ 262/959231 tourism office ⊕ www.mercadomedievalobidos.pt) enlivens the town. Each day there is a parade of people in medieval costumes around the city walls. You can rent costumes and take part, too. To buy some of the typical products of the region—ceramics, cheeses, hams, and flowers—exchange your money for medieval coins and symbolic torreos. Battles and court scenes are dramatized daily, and music animates the market all day up to midnight. As for a meal, consider a hunk of the wild boar being roasted over spits.

☾ From mid-December through New Year's, the **Óbidos Vila Natal** (☎ 262/959231 tourism office ⊕www.obidosvilanatal.pt) is the perfect miniature winter wonderland for children. The Christmas Village is constructed in the picturesque villa below the castle with everything covered in a light dusting of "snow." There's ice-skating, the Carousel de Natal, puppet shows, Christmas musicals, sing-a-longs with Disney characters, and, of course, Santa Claus. There are also several organized games for all ages as well as a Christmas market selling traditional Portuguese Christmas sweets and other artisanal crafts. For the parents who might want to enjoy a little of adult fun, there is the Bar de Gelo (ice bar), which is open on weekends and holidays to "chill out" and enjoy a drink.

Sometime in the first part of the year, Óbidos hosts the two-week **Festival de Chocolate** (☎ 262/959231 tourism office ⊕www.festivalchocolate.cm-obidos.pt). Like a real-life Willy Wonka chocolate factory but even bigger, this outdoor chocolate feast attracts more than 200,000 people every year. There are tons of activities to choose from, including chocolate workshops and demonstrations, cake design, chocolatherapy (think spa), body painting, and an annual chocolate sculpture contest done by locally known chefs with a new theme each year. Along with the many stands selling all kinds of delicious chocolate goodies, many local restaurants offer a chocolate-theme menu to indulge in. To avoid the famously long ticket lines, which can go on for miles, your best chance is to buy your ticket online ahead of time. Even if you don't want to wait in line, there are always a couple of smart sellers who set up chocolate stands outside the entrance so people can at least buy some sweets to take home.

$ ✕**Alcaide.** From the upstairs dining room and terrace of this rustic
PORTUGUESE   tavern, you can enjoy a lovely view of rooftops with the countryside beyond. The Alcaide is often jammed with hungry sightseers, especially from May through October; this isn't a quiet hideaway. The food, however, is always carefully prepared, and the service is attentive. Try the bacalhau *à casa* (with chestnuts and roasted apples). ⊠ *Rua Direita, Obidos* ☎ *262/959220* ⊕ *www.restaurantealcaide.com* ▤ *AE, DC, MC, V* ☉ *Closed Wed.*

GINJA CHERRY LIQUOR

One cannot visit Óbidos without trying their delicious cherry liquor, Ginja. Also known as Ginjinha de Óbidos, it's made from the Ginja cherry, whose origin is difficult to establish but is supposedly derived from the banks of the Caspian River and was gradually dispersed among the Mediterranean countries via trade routes. Thanks to the particular microclimate around the area of Óbidos, Portugal actually has the best wild Ginja cherry in Europe. As for the drink, it is thought to have originally started in the 17th century by a local friar who took a part of the large quantities of the fruit in the region and refined them into the liquor that is known today.

The liquor has a deep, dark red color with an intense flavor and aroma perfumed by the fermented cherries.

It's produced and sold in two distinct varieties, the liquor on its own or the liquor with actual Ginja cherries inside, sometimes flavored with vanilla or cinnamon. You can find numerous little shops and cafés in the walled village selling Ginja as well as offering tastings. The best thing the locals recommend to have with Ginja is chocolate, which they have cutely crafted into little chocolate cups to serve the liquor in. Or, you can enjoy it with a big slice of one of the shops' house-made chocolate cakes. The chocolate cups are also sold in packs of 6 and 12 to enjoy the Ginja experience at home.

The two Ginja producers in Óbidos are **FRUTÓBIDOS** (⊕ *www. frutobidos.pt*) and **OPPIDUM** (⊕ *www.ginjadeobidos.com*).

WHERE TO STAY

$ 🏨 **Casa d'Óbidos.** Standing in the midst of extensive lawns, gardens, and orchards is this white manor house dating from the 19th century. There are views of the castle from its swimming pool and from all over the property. It is elegantly decorated with selected antiques and traditional Portuguese tiling by local craftsmen. There are six rooms in the main house, plus four spacious apartmentlike accommodations in the 18th-century two-story cottage and a renovated wine cellar. If you're looking for a real bed-and-breakfast, they really put the emphasis back in breakfast, as they are known to have the best breakfast around; everything is fresh and homemade, with a wide selection of breads, cakes, pastries, jams, marmalades, and honey crafted on-site. Along with the usual cereals, yogurts, tea, and coffee, they also do fresh boiled eggs and omelets to order, as well as bacon and hot chocolate—now that's the way to start your day exploring Óbidos **Pros:** excellent breakfast; peaceful atmosphere; great views of the city and castle. **Cons:** outside the city; a little difficult to find; no elevator. ⊠ *Quinta de S. José* ☎ *262/950924* ⊕ *www.casadobidos. com* ⇆ *6 rooms, 4 apartments* ♿ *In-room: no a/c, no TV. In-hotel: tennis court, pool, Internet terminal, bicycles, parking (free)* ▭ *MC, V* ⎮◯⎮ *BP.*

$$ 🏨 **Casa das Senhoras Rainhas.** True to its namesake, this charming hotel just inside the castle walls pays a beautiful tribute to Óbidos's many queens. All the rooms are named after the queens; three have balconies, and three have ground terraces and are all decorated in a modern yet elegant style with soft rose, orange, beige, and light blue colors that give

them just a hint of feminine touch. Guests are greeted in their room with a basket of fruit, water, a welcome drink of Ginjinha, and a little home-made chocolate and cherry "Queen's Cake." There's also the choice of having a continental breakfast served in the room for no extra charge. The restaurant ($$$) looks out to the garden and has outdoor seating in the warmer months, serving a gourmet fusion of Portuguese and French cuisine. Try the *Travesseiros Regis* (seafood ravioli in cream with sautéed seaweed) or the Eucalyptus ice cream for dessert. **Pros:** great location just inside the castle walls; great service; excellent food. **Cons:** parking is difficult; a bit pricey; no elevator. ⊠ *Padre Nunes Tavares 6, Óbidos* ☎ *262/955360* ⊕ *www.senhorasrainhas.com/pt* ⤴ *10 rooms, 1 superior* ⟁ *In-room: a/c, safe (some). In-hotel: restaurant, room service, bar, laundry service, Wi-Fi hotspot* ▭ *AE, D, DC, MC, V* ⦿⊣ *BP.*

$$$ 🔳 **Pousada do Castelo.** Except for the electric lights and the relatively
Fodor's Choice   modern plumbing, the style of the Middle Ages prevails in this pousada,
★   which occupies parts of the castle that Dom Dinis gave to his young bride, Isabel, in 1282. Room 2, in one of the massive stone towers, is especially evocative of ancient times; other rooms are individually furnished with 16th- and 17th-century reproductions. The restaurant's ($$$$) food and service are worthy of royalty; there's a curtained alcove where you can dine in privacy and still enjoy a view of the castle walls and valley below. Try the foie gras with green salad and Portuguese Apple "Bravo Esmolfe." **Pros:** great location in the city center; incredible views of the castle and valley; fine service. **Cons:** no elevator; must walk up a steep hill from parking to enter; pricey. ⊠ *Paço Real* ☎ *262/955080* ⊕ *www.pousadas.pt* ⤴ *9 rooms, 3 suites* ⟁ *In-room: a/c. In-hotel: restaurant, bar, no elevator, laundry service, Wi-Fi hotspot, parking (free)* ▭ *AE, DC, MC, V* ⦿⊣ *BP.*

$$$ 🔳 **Praia d'el Rey Marriott Golf and Beach Resort.** The pride and joy of the
☾   western region is this five-star luxury resort hotel 16 km (10 mi) west of the walled city Óbidos. You have easy access to the Praia d'el Rey beach and special rates at the Praia d'el Rey Golf and Country Club's 18-hole seaside golf course and its tennis courts. There is even a soccer field and plenty of water sports to chose from. The Clube Aventura provides a team of qualified supervisors that offer a place for children to stay and do fun activities, games, computers, and outdoor sports and field trips while the parents can have a relaxing holiday. Morning comforts in the rooms include coffeemakers and bathrobes. The luxurious indoor pool is surrounded by white columns reminiscent of a Roman bath. The Atlantic Grill ($$$) and the Romy restaurant ($$$) specialize in Mediterranean and nouvelle cuisine. Live jazz on Friday and Saturday night takes place in the Atlantic Bar. **Pros:** great location; ocean views; plenty of amenities and activities. **Cons:** food and drink are very expensive; far from any city; can get crowded in summer. ⊠ *Av. D. Inês de Castro N°1, Vale de Janelas* ☎ *262/905100* ⊕ *www.praia-del-rey.com/pt* ⤴ *179 rooms* ⟁ *In-room: safe, Wi-Fi. In-hotel: 2 restaurants, 2 bars, 7 tennis courts, pools, gym, spa, beachfront, diving, water sports, bicycles, children's programs (ages 2–16), laundry service, Internet terminal* ▭ *AE, DC, MC, V* ⦿⊣ *FAP, MAP.*

SPORTS AND THE OUTDOORS

There are three pleasant walks to take in Óbidos. It's a 1-km (½-mi) trek from the city gate through farmlands, a grove of poplar trees, and along the Arnoia River to the Eburobritium Roman ruins (established 1 BC to AD 5), where you can see ancient baths and a forum. Another walk is through the free Lagoa de Óbidos Observatory, which has aquatic birds and birds of prey. There's also a park behind the walls of the town. Maps and brochures are available at the **tourist office** (☎ 262/959231) in the parking lot at the gate into the city wall.

GOLF

Golden Eagle. Golden Eagle—has fast gained the reputation as one of the finest golf courses in Portugal. This creation of American architect Rocky Roquemore is set in tranquil countryside and features rolling fairways, plenty of water, and stiff bunker protection around the greens. From the back tees it is a fine test for the better player, but it is much easier from the regular tees, which reduce the overall length by close to 545 yards. Women will also find much to like here. Handicap restrictions are 28 for men and 36 for women. ⊠ *Apartado 219, Rio Maior* ☎ *243/908148* ⊕ *www.camin.pt* ⚲ *18 holes. 6,049 m. Par 72. Slope 126* ⊠ *€75 weekdays, €90 weekends per round* ✆ *Facilities: driving range, putting green, chipping area, golf carts, hand-pulled carts, pro shop, restaurant, bar.*

Fodor's Choice
★
Praia d'El Rey. Less than an hour's drive from Lisbon's international airport, Praia d'El Rey Golf & Country Club is an excellent beachfront resort with one of the most picturesque golf courses in Europe. Bold, deep bunkers, undulating greens, and natural sand-border areas are the hallmarks of this Cabell Robinson design. The architect was at great pains to make the course friendly to women players by creating sensible women's tees that are placed far enough forward. The handicap limit here is 28 for men and women. ⊠ *Óbidos* ☎ *262/905005* ⊕ *www. praia-del-rey.com* ⚲ *18 holes. 6,501 m. Par 73* ⊠ *€100 weekdays, €125 weekends per round* ✆ *Facilities: driving range, health club, 2 putting greens, chipping area, golf carts, hand-pulled carts, rental clubs, pro shop, restaurant, swimming pool, bar.*

CALDAS DA RAINHA

5 km (3 mi) north of Óbidos.

Caldas da Rainha (Queen's Baths), the hub of a large farming area, is best known for its sulfur baths. In 1484 Queen Leonor, en route to Batalha, noticed people bathing in a malodorous pool. Having heard of the healing properties of the sulfurous water, the queen interrupted her journey for a soak and became convinced of the water's beneficial effects. She had a hospital built on the site and was reputedly so enthusiastic that she sold her jewels to help finance the project. There's a bronze statue of Leonor in front of the hospital, which continues to treat patients today for rheumatism and respiratory diseases.

GETTING HERE AND AROUND

Caldas da Rainha can be reached by bus (Rede Expressos) from Lisbon. The CP regional train line between Sintra and Figueira da Foz stops in Caldas da Rainha as well. Driving from Lisbon takes 50 minutes and coming from Óbidos takes 10 minutes. ⇨ *For Rede Expressos info, see Bus Travel, above. For CP info, see Train Travel, above.*

ESSENTIALS

Visitor Info Caldas da Rainha (✉ *Rua Engº Duarte Pacheco* ☎ *262/839700*).

EXPLORING

Museu de Cerâmica *(Ceramics Museum).* This museum is in the house of the noted 19th-century artisan Rafael Bordalo Pinheiro, who was also a well-known painter, cartoonist, and caricaturist. Some of his most famous ceramic figurines, done in gaudy colors, are the fat peasant "Zé Povinho," "Ama das Caldas" (the Caldas da Rainha wet nurse), the civil guard, and John Bull. Other amusing figures include a pig's head on a platter and leaping frogs. The collection contains ceramic works from all over the region, as well as works by Bordalo Pinheiro himself. There are a gift and book shop and a cafeteria here as well. ✉ *Rua Dr. Ilídio Amado, Apartado 97* ☎ *262/840280* ⊕ *www.ipmuseus.pt* ☏ *€2, free Sun. and public holidays until 2 pm* ☉ *Tues.–Sun. 10–12:30 and 2–5. Closed Mon., New Year's Day, Easter Sun., May 1, and Christmas Day.*

Museu Malhoa. The expansive wooded park surrounding the spa contains a museum with works mostly by local painter José Malhoa (1854–1933). ✉ *Parque D. Carlos I* ☎ *262/831984* ⊕ *mjm.imc-ip.pt* ☏ *€3, free Sun. and public holidays until 2 pm* ☉ *Tues.–Sun. 10–12:30 and 2–5. Closed Mon., New Year's Day, Easter Sun., May 1, and Christmas Day.*

WHERE TO EAT

$

PORTUGUESE

✕ **A Lareira.** Portuguese for "fireplace," this elegant romantic restaurant is nestled in the pinewoods between Caldas da Rainha and the Foz do Orelho beach; it's a favorite with locals for special occasions. Try their prizewinning *folhado de caranguejo* (crab with flaky pastry), the salmon fillet with caviar sauce, or, for the more daring, the *ensopado de enguia* (stewed eel). Note that weekend meal prices are more expensive than the weekly set menu option. ✉ *Rua da Lareira 35, Alto do Nobre, Nadadouro* ☎ *262/823432* ⊕ *www.restaurantealareira.com* ▭ *DC, MC, V* ☉ *Closed Tues.*

$$

ITALIAN

✕ **Sabores d'Itália.** This widely acclaimed restaurant is the place to go for genuine Italian food in Portugal. Everything—the pasta, bread, ice cream—is homemade by the owner Norberto Marcelino and his wife. Salmon carpaccio with truffles, lobster with moscatel sauce, green lasagna with monkfish and shrimp, tagliatelle with foie gras, and risotto with champagne and truffles are among the mouthwatering dishes on the menu. You can wash everything down with a bottle of Chianti or a good Portuguese wine from the extensive wine list. ✉ *Praça 5 de Outubro 40* ☎ *262/845600* ⊕ *www.saboresditalia.com* ▭ *AE, MC, V* ⊘ *Closed Mon.*

$ ✕ **São Rafael.** Many of the artisan Bordalo Pinheiro's ceramic pieces are
ECLECTIC displayed in glass showcases that line the wall of this restaurant adjoining the Bordalo Pinheiro Factory Museum. The windows are hung with the famous Alcobaça "Chita" cloth stamped in blue and burgundy floral motifs. While dining you can entertain yourself by looking at all the different ceramic figures. The menu includes traditional Portuguese cuisine and international dishes served on Bordalo Pinheiro plates and blue table mats. ✉ *Rua Rafael Bordalo Pinheiro 53* ☎ *262/839383* ▭ *MC, V.*

WHERE TO STAY

$ ⌂ **Quinta da Foz.** An important heir of King D. Felipe I built this large
FodorsChoice manor house in the 16th century, and 20-some generations later it is
★ still owned and operated by the original family. The property is surrounded by lawns at the edge of the Óbidos Lagoon, some 15 minutes' walk from the beach. The family also has stables and a corral housing their prize *Lusitano* stallions, which are available for horseback riding lessons and excursions. Explore Caldas da Rainha, which is 9 km (5½ mi) away, or the other area towns from this quiet base. The sitting room has beautiful arched stone walls and columns, and the bedrooms are large and comfortably furnished with a couple having French doors opening to the back terrace. There are two cottages on the grounds, which are available for stays of a minimum of three nights. Ask the family to give you a tour of their on-site chapel, which is also original to the manor house and has an interesting history including an inscription in old-world Portuguese on the floor dated 1592. **Pros:** intriguing historical atmosphere; near the beach; quiet and peaceful. **Cons:** few modern amenities; far from the city; a little difficult to find. ✉ *Largo do Arraial, Foz do Arelho* ☎ *262/979369 or 917/557786* ⊕ *www.quinta-dafoz.com* ⇌ *5 rooms, 2 cottages* ⌂ *In-room: no a/c, no phone, no TV (some). In-hotel: Wi-Fi hotspot* ▭ *No credit cards* ⊙ *BP.*

SHOPPING

Caldas da Rainha is famous for its cabbage-leaf and vegetable-shape ceramic pieces produced in several of the town's factories and workshops, which you can visit if you reserve ahead of time. **Fábrica Rafael Bordalo Pinheiro** (✉ *Rua Rafael Bordalo Pinheiro 53* ☎ *262/880568* ⊕ *www.bordallopinheiro.pt*), a factory named after the artist who made the Caldas da Rainha–style ceramics famous, is worth touring. **SECLA** (✉ *Rua São João de Deus, Apartado 37* ☎ *262/842151* ⊕ *www.secla. pt*) is one of the area's leading ceramics workshops. Its shop is open Monday to Saturday from 9:30 to 7.

SPORTS AND THE OUTDOORS

Escola de Vela da Lagoa (✉ *Lagoa de Óbidos, 2½ km (1½ mi) after traffic circle at Foz* ☎ *262/978592* ⊕ *www.escoladeveladalagoa.com* ⊙ *June–Oct., daily 10–dusk. Call ahead rest of yr*) is the large wooden clubhouse with a sailing school on the north banks of the Óbidos lagoon near Foz de Arelho. Rentals are by the hour: small sailboat

€20, Windsurfer €14, canoe €8, and catamaran €20–€30. They also run a kite-surfing course costing €130 for six hours of private tuition. Its snack bar serves hamburgers, salads, fresh fruit juices, and milk shakes.

🛈 **Kiro Karting** (✉ *Quinta do Falcão, Bombarral* ☎ *262/609330* ⊕ *www. kiro-karting.com* 🕙 *Daily 10–1 and 2–7*), a well-run go-kart track, is a three-minute drive from the Lisbon–Leiria A8 N11 turnoff. It also has a children's track for ages above six (or for those who can reach the pedals). Prices vary depending on the car, but the average is €18 per person for 15 minutes. Call ahead, because sometimes the track is rented for private races.

The **Lagoa de Óbidos** (✉ *Rua dos Reivais 40* ☎ *262/978592*), at Foz do Arelho, is a lagoon that's popular with windsurfers. You can rent equipment from the Escola de Vela da Lagoa, near the beach: the cost for just the rig is €14 per hour; rental and lessons cost about €60 for two hours. You can also rent Catamaran sailing boats by the hour for €20.

NAZARÉ

24 km (15 mi) northwest of Caldas da Rainha.

Not so long ago you could mingle on the beach with black-stocking-capped fishermen and even help as the oxen hauled boats in from the crashing surf. But Nazaré is no longer a village and has long ceased to be quaint. The boats now motor comfortably into a safe, modern harbor, and the oxen have been put to pasture. The beachfront boulevard is lined with restaurants, bars, and souvenir shops, and in summer the broad, sandy beach is covered with a multicolor quilt of tents and awnings.

You can still catch an interesting piece of culture that has survived: the many *sete saias Nazarenas* or "seven skirts Nazarean women," who can be see all around the town, dressed in colorful miss-matching attire and of course wearing seven skirts. These women also sell crafts and souvenirs as well as little dried, salted fish (a local tradition) that they dry on wire racks along the boardwalk. They also have shops selling their particular style of clothing if you're adventurous enough to try them. It's said that the seven skirts represent in religious terms, the seven virtues, the seven days of the week, the seven colors of the rainbow, the seven waves of the sea, and other biblical, magical attributes.

GETTING HERE AND AROUND

Nazaré can be reached by bus (Rede Expressos) from Lisbon. Driving from Lisbon takes one hour, and the drive from Alcobaça will take you close to 15 minutes. ■ TIP→ For the most interesting route to Nazaré, head west from Caldas along the lagoon to the beach town of Foz do Arelho, then take the coast road 26 km (16 mi) north.

ESSENTIALS

Visitor Info Nazaré Tourism Office (✉ *Av. Manuel Remígio-Centro Cultural da Nazaré* ☎ *262/561944* ⊕ *www.cm-nazare.pt*).

EXPLORING

Sitio. To find what's left of the Nazaré once hailed by many as "the most picturesque fishing village in Portugal," come in the spring or early fall and either climb the precipitous trail or take the scenic funicular to the top of the 361-foot cliff called Sitio. Clustered at the cliff's edge overlooking the beach is a small community of fishermen who live in tiny cottages and seem unaffected by all that's happening below.

WHERE TO EAT AND STAY

$$ ✕ **A Celeste.** Owner Celeste personally greets guests at the entrance to
SEAFOOD her well-known seafood restaurant on the Atlantic seafront. She recommends *espadarte à celeste* (swordfish with cream-and-mushroom sauce) and squid or monkfish on the spit. This coast is famous for its caldeirada (a Portuguese version of bouillabaisse with nine kinds of seafood and fish). Try Celeste's. The most spectacular dish is the *cataplana de marisco* for two (a variety of steamed seafood that's served with a flourish). ⊠ *Av. República 54* ☎ *262/551695* ▭ *AE, DC, MC, V.*

¢ ⊞ **Adega Oceano.** Balconies overlook the beach at this white, pleasantly appointed hotel. The marisqueira restaurant ($), which has an outdoor seating area, serves fresh fish, seafood, and typical Portuguese cuisine, including noteworthy caldeiradas. ■ TIP➔ **Hotel guests receive a 10% discount in the restaurant. Pros:** perfect location right on beach; location on the main drag lends to great accessibility; great beachfront restaurant; inexpensive. **Cons:** gets booked up super early in summer; very noisy at times; rooms without sea views are no good. ⊠ *Av. da República 51, Nazaré* ☎ *262/561161* ⊕ *www.adegaoceano.com* ↪ *32 rooms* ⟳ *In-room: a/c. In-hotel: restaurant, bar, Wi-Fi hotspot, beachfront* ▭ *AE, DC, MC, V* ⦿ *BP.*

$ ⊞ **Hotel Mar Bravo.** This stylish boutique hotel is right on the beach, just steps from both the sea and the center of town. All rooms have a water view and almost all have balconies. The classy restaurant ($$$) serves regional and international dishes; the seafood is always fresh, with lobster plucked straight from the tank at the entrance. **Pros:** beautiful views; great in-house restaurant right on the beach; romantic setting. **Cons:** Wi-Fi isn't free; can get noisy from outside traffic; difficult parking. ⊠ *Praça Sousa Oliveira 71, Nazaré* ☎ *262/569160* ⊕ *www.marbravo. com* ↪ *16 rooms* ⟳ *In-room: a/c, Wi-Fi (some). In-hotel: restaurant, bar, beachfront* ▭ *AE, DC, MC, V* ⊙ *Closed Christmas weekend* ⦿ *CP.*

$ ⊞ **Hotel Miramar.** The sea and town views from this inn are fantastic: it's
☿ about 1 km (½ mi) *above* Nazaré, in the village of Pederneira. The inn's smooth white facade is contrasted by its terra-cotta-tile roof, turquoise-blue swimming pool, Jacuzzi, and emerald-green lawns. A sauna and steam room are also available for guests. The carpeted rooms were recently renovated with 95% of them having sea views and most with balconies. The one- and two-bedroom apartments have sitting areas and refrigerators. **Pros:** incredible views; great amenities; away from the city crowds. **Cons:** far from beach; gym facilities located outside in separate building. ⊠ *Rua Abel da Silva, Pederneira* ☎ *262/550000* ⊕ *www.hotelmiramar.com* ↪ *40 rooms* ⟳ *In-room: a/c, safe (some), refrigerator (some), Wi-Fi (some). In-hotel: restaurant, room service, bar, pool, gym, children's programs (ages 2–12), laundry service, Wi-Fi hotspot, parking (free)* ▭ *AE, DC, MC, V* ⦿ *CP.*

4

$$ ⬚ **Hotel Praia.** This design hotel is from the same company as Hotel Mar Bravo and offers a lot more amenities for vacationers. Along with being only minutes away from the beach, the hotel has a rooftop, glass-covered "indoor" pool and Jacuzzi that practically give an infinity view of the ocean and surrounding city. The outdoor rooftop terrace next to the pool is also a great place to sunbathe or watch the sunset; you can also get food and cocktails on the terrace. The hotel's soundproof rooms are modern and decorated in bright oranges, while the duplex apartments are bathed in sea blues. Almost all the rooms have a balcony and 75% have an indirect sea view. **Pros:** great ocean view from the pool and rooftop terrace; short walk from beach; soundproof rooms. **Cons:** paid parking (but cool underground garage); Internet is free only in public areas; restaurant is pricey. ⊠ *Av. Vieira Guimarães N° 39, Nazaré* ☎ *262/569200* ⊕ *www.hotelpraia.com/hp/* ➘ *80 rooms, 4 junior suites, 4 duplex apartments* ⭣ *In-room: a/c, safe (some), kitchen (some), refrigerator (some), Internet (some). In-hotel: restaurant, room service, bar, pool, gym, laundry service, Wi-Fi hotspot, parking (paid), some pets allowed* ▤ *AE, D, DC, MC, V* ⎟⊙⎟ *BP.*

SHOPPING

The many shops and stands along the beachfront promenade have a good selection of traditional fishermen's sweaters as well as a wide array of caps and plaid shirts (the best are made of wool rather than acrylic blends). You'll find several shops that sell handcrafted ceramics and tiles in Sitio. It pays to shop around: prices vary widely, and bargaining is the order of the day.

ALCOBAÇA

10 km (6 mi) southeast of Nazaré; 20 km (12 mi) northeast of Caldas da Rainha.

Alcobaça is a town that still shows its old-world roots in its downtown architecture—pretty red-tile roofs and French chateau turrets. The town is in a picturesque valley between the towns of Nazaré and Batalha, and is known for its crystal. It's also the site of a museum devoted to wine making, but the town really is best known for its impressive church and monastery that date back to the 12th century.

GETTING HERE AND AROUND

Alcobaça can be reached by bus (Rede Expressos) from Lisbon. Driving from Lisbon takes one hour, while the drive from Nazaré will take you close to 15 minutes. ⇨ *For Rede Expressos info, see Bus Travel, above.*

ESSENTIALS

Visitor Info Alcobaça (⊠ *Praça 25 de Abril* ☎ *262/582377* ⊕ *alcobaca.no.sapo.pt*).

EXPLORING

Fodor'sChoice ★ **Mosteiro de Alcobaça.** Like the monastery at Mafra, the Mosteiro de Alcobaça was built as the result of a kingly vow, this time in gratitude for a battle won. In 1147, faced with stiff Muslim resistance during the battle for Santarém, Portugal's first king, Afonso Henriques, promised to build a monastery dedicated to St. Bernard and the Cistercian Order. The Portuguese were victorious, Santarém was captured from the Moors, and shortly thereafter a site was selected. Construction began in 1153 and was concluded in 1178. The church, the largest in Portugal, is awe inspiring. The unadorned, 350-foot-long structure of massive granite blocks and cross-ribbed vaulting is a masterpiece of understatement: there's good use of clean, flowing lines, with none of the clutter of the later rococo and Manueline architecture. At opposite ends of the transept, placed foot-to-foot some 30 paces apart, are the delicately carved tombs of King Pedro I and Inês de Castro.

> **BEACHES**
>
> Starting with Ericeira and extending north to São Pedro de Moel by Marinha Grande, there are a number of pleasant sandy beaches at convenient intervals along the coast. Some of the more popular stretches—with the customary range of facilities, hotels, and restaurants—are in Nazaré, Peniche, and Foz do Arelho. All beaches in Portugal are public.

The graceful twin-tiered cloister at Alcobaça was added in the 14th and 16th centuries. The Kings Hall, just to the left of the main entrance, is lined with a series of 18th-century azulejos illustrating the construction of the monastery. ⊠ *Praça 25 de Abril* ☎ *262/505128* ☜ *€6* ☉ *Apr.–Sept., daily 9–7, cloisters 9–6:30; Oct.–Mar., daily 9–5, cloisters 9–4:30. Closed New Year's Day, Easter weekend, May 1, and Christmas Day.*

Museu Nacional do Vinho *(National Wine Museum).* While in Alcobaça, you may want to visit the interesting Museu Nacional do Vinho to see wine-making implements and presses. The museum is in an old winery, on N8 heading north and just off the edge of town. ⊠ *Rua de Leiria* ☎ *262/582222* ☜ *€1.50* ☉ *Tues.–Fri. 9–12:30 and 2–5:30; additional hrs. May–Sept. weekends 10–12:30 and 2–6.*

WHERE TO EAT AND STAY

$

PORTUGUESE

✕ **Trindade.** The intimate dining room of this unpretentious restaurant is lined with old photos of local scenes that reveal some of Alcobaça's history. Try the specialties, *açorda de marisco* (with shellfish) or *Frango na Púcara* (chicken), and for dessert, the homemade pastry. ⊠ *Praça D. Afonso Henriques 22* ☎ *262/582397* ▤ *AE, DC, MC, V* ☉ *Closed Wed.*

¢

🏠 **Casa da Padeira.** This family-run guesthouse 5 km (3 mi) outside Alcobaça is named after a baker who fought the Spaniards with a wooden shovel—and pushed them into her oven—during the Battle of Aljubarrota in 1385. You're free to wander the well-tended gardens and mingle with the family. The large guest rooms are furnished with period reproductions. Homemade bread, fresh from the oven, is the highlight of breakfast; dinner is available on request. **Pros:** picturesque location; away from noise; playground for children; barbeque facilities. **Cons:** no a/c in guest rooms; far from monastery; no elevator. ⊠ *Hwy. N8, 19, Aljubarrota* ☎ *262/505240* ⊕ *www.casadapadeira.com* ⇆ *10 rooms, 1 suite* ⌂ *In-room: no a/c. In-hotel: bar, pool, laundry service, Wi-Fi hotspot, parking (free), some pets allowed* ▤ *No credit cards* ⦿ *BP.*

$

🏠 **Challet Fonte Nova.** This charming B&B, 200 meters' walking distance from the monastery, was the estate of Brazilian nobility until it was renovated and converted in 1993. The Challet appears to take its name from the outside facade's architecture that is reminiscent of an

Pedro and Inês

The story of Pedro and Inês, one of the most bizarre love stories in Portuguese history, was immortalized by Luís de Camões in the epic poem *Os Lusiads*.

Pedro, son of King Afonso IV and heir to the throne, fell in love with the beautiful young Galician Inês de Castro, a lady-in-waiting to Pedro's Castilian wife, Constança. Fearful of the influence of Inês's family on his heir, the king banished her from the court. Upon the death of Constança, Pedro and Inês secretly married, and she lived in Coimbra, in a house later known as the Quinta das Lagrimas (the House of Tears); two sons were born of this union. King Afonso, ever wary of foreign influence on Pedro, had Inês murdered. Subsequently, Pedro took the throne and had Inês's murderers pursued: two of the three were captured and executed, their hearts wrenched from their bodies. Pedro publicly proclaimed that he had been married to Inês and arranged an elaborate and macabre funeral for his wife. Before the procession, Inês's body, in royal garb, was enthroned beside him, and the courtiers were forced to kiss her lifeless hand. She was then placed in the tomb in Alcobaça that Pedro had designed, which lay, according to his wishes, opposite his own—so that on Judgment Day the lovers would ascend to heaven facing each other.

Austrian chalet. Inside, it has 10 individually decorated rooms—four are in the new wing—in the classical period style. A small spa was also added when the new wing was built in 2008, and massages and hydro-massages are available. At the back of the chalet is a trellised garden and walkway with benches scattered along the path, perfect for sitting and relaxing with a book or cozying up with your sweetheart. **Pros:** great location; romantic setting; superb service. **Cons:** no pool; no restaurant. ⊠ *Rua da Fonte Nova N° 8, Alcobaça* ☎ *262/598300* ⊕ *www.challetfontenova.pt* ↪ *10 rooms, 2 junior suites* ⚹ *In-room: a/c, Wi-Fi (some). In-hotel: bar, spa, laundry service, Wi-Fi hotspot, parking (free)* ⊟ *AE, D, DC, MC, V* ⦿ *BP.*

¢ ⟳ 🔲 **Hotel Rural Quinta Do Pinheiro.** This country manor house turned hotel is about 15 minutes outside of Alcobaça, on the way to Nazaré. It's the perfect place to stay for visiting both areas or to just get away from the city. The rooms are all decorated differently in a modern yet simple style. Several open to the outside pavilion, which has a shared common area for small groups or families. The Quinta sits right in front of a picturesque lake, overlooking the hills in the background, and there is a handful of rooms with a shared terrace that face this view. There are horse stables next door, which are available for horseback riding lessons and excursions by reservation. The hotel also offers several outdoor activities and sports, including soccer, tennis, children's games, and a petting zoo. The restaurant ($$$) is in the old wine cellars with a wine press still sitting on display and serves traditional and gourmet Portuguese cuisine. **Pros:** great outdoor activities; beautiful location; perfect for kids. **Cons:** no pool; a little tricky to find. ⊠ *Valado dos Frades, Valado dos Frades (Maiorga)* ☎ *262/590530* ⊕ *www.*

quintapinheiro-nazare.com 🛏 *26 rooms* ♿ *In-room: a/c, refrigerator (some), Wi-Fi (some). In-hotel: restaurant, tennis courts, bicycles, children's programs (ages 2–16), laundry service, parking (free), some pets allowed* ▤ *AE, D, DC, MC, V* ¶◎¶ *BP.*

¢ 🔆 **Hotel Santa Maria.** Gardens surround this hotel, which the monastery faces. Some rooms have balconies; all rooms are simply furnished, comfortable, and, according to the manager, "good for the soul." There's no restaurant, but the wood-panel bar is agreeable. **Pros:** great downtown location; soundproof rooms; rental cars available. **Cons:** shabby rooms in need of refurbishing; hotel overall a bit run-down. ✉ *Rua Dr. Francisco Zagalo 20–22* ☎ *262/590160* ⊕ *www.hotelsantamaria.com.pt* 🛏 *73 rooms* ♿ *In-room: a/c, safe. In-hotel: room service, bar, laundry services, Wi-Fi hotspot, parking (free)* ▤ *AE, DC, MC, V* ¶◎¶ *CP.*

SHOPPING

Casa Lisboa (✉ *Praça 25 de Abril* ☎ *No phone*), across from the monastery, has a good selection of fine lead crystal.

The Atlantis outlet shop **Cristal Atlantis** (✉ *Zona Industrial de Casal da Areia* ☎ *262/540200* ☉ *Mon.–Sat. 10–7, Sun. and holidays 2–7*) sells both its first-rate crystal and its seconds. If you don't want to pay high prices for their normal wares, look through the second-choice pieces. Groups of more than five can visit the factory and the museum for €2.60 per person. Factory visits are conducted Tuesday–Friday at 10:30, 11:30, 2:30, 3:30, and 5 (English-speaking guides are available). Closed during August and December.

Fábrica Spal (✉ *Ponte da Torre, Valado dos Frades* ☎ *262/580498*), the Spal outlet shop for seconds, is a great place to buy porcelain. The defects are minimal, and they'll box and ship for you.

BATALHA

18 km (11 mi) northeast of Alcobaça.

Batalha, which means "battle" in Portuguese, is the site of another of the country's religious structures that memorialize a battle victory. The monastery, classified as a UNESCO World Heritage Site, is surrounded by the small city center, with several other smaller, historical monuments scattered around the area.

Batalha is right into the Estremadurean countryside, with rolling hills, mountains, old windmills, pastures, and farming villages that create a fairy tale–like view from higher points of the city. It's a great area to drive around and explore.

GETTING HERE AND AROUND

Batalha is served by the Rede Expressos buses from Lisbon to Leiria as well as other vicinities in between. Coming to Batalha from Lisbon is a 1 hour 10 minute drive, and a 15-minute drive if coming from Leiria.

ESSENTIALS

Visitor Info Batalha (✉ *Rua Infante D. Fernando* ☎ *244/769110* ⊕ *www.cm-batalha.pt/en*).

EXPLORING

The Battle of Aljubarrota Interpretation Center (*CIBA*). On N8, 5 km (3 mi) south of Batalha's monastery, the interpretation center is a project of the Battle of Aljubarrota Foundation, which is remodeling almost all of the former **Museu Militar** and aims to preserve and enhance the history surrounding the S. Jorge military field. The main focus of the exhibition area of course is on the Battle of Aljubarrota, but it also documents conflicts with Spain from the early Middle Ages through the early 15th century. ⊠ *Campo Militar de São Jorge* ☎ *244/480060* ⊕ *www.fundacao-aljubarrota.pt* ▨ *€7* ⊘ *May–Sept., Tues.–Sun. 10–7; Oct.–Apr., Tues.–Sun., 10–5:30. Closed Mon., Christmas Day, New Year's Day, and May 1.*

Santa Maria da Vitória (*St. Mary of Victory*). The church monastery was built to commemorate a decisive Portuguese victory over the Spanish on August 14, 1385, in the Battle of Aljubarrota. In this engagement the Portuguese king, João de Avis, who had been crowned only seven days earlier, took on and routed a superior Spanish force. In so doing he maintained independence for Portugal, which was to last until 1580, when the crown finally passed into Spanish hands. The heroic statue of the mounted figure in the forecourt is that of Nuno Álvares Pereira, who, along with João de Avis, led the Portuguese army at Aljubarrota.

The monastery, a masterly combination of Gothic and Manueline styles, was built between 1388 and 1533. Some 15 architects were involved in the project, but the principal architect was Afonso Domingues, whose portrait, carved in stone, graces the wall in the chapter house. In the great hall lie the remains of two unknown Portuguese soldiers who died in World War I: one in France, the other in Africa. Entombed in the center of the Founder's Chapel, beneath the star-shaped, vaulted ceiling, is João de Avis, lying hand in hand with his English queen, Philippa of Lancaster. The tombs along the south and west walls are those of the couple's children, including Henry the Navigator. Perhaps the finest parts of the entire project are the Unfinished Chapels, seven chapels radiating off an octagonal rotunda, started by Dom Duarte in 1435 and left roofless owing to lack of funds. Note the intricately filigreed detail of the main doorway. ▨ *€6, free Sun. and holidays until 2 pm* ⊘ *Apr.–Sept., daily 9–6; Oct.–Mar., daily 9–5.*

WHERE TO STAY

¢ ⛉ **Casa do Outeiro.** This cheerful little pension in one of the quietest areas of Batalha offers a superb view of the historic monastery and valley below. Rooms are individually decorated with touches of vibrant colors and have terraces. A selection of welcome drinks is offered on arrival and breakfast (all included) is served beside the pool. **Pros:** great location; beautiful views; homey feeling. **Cons:** no elevator in one section of the hotel; not right in city center. ⊠ *Largo Carvalho do Outeiro 4* ☎ *244/765806* ⊕ *www.casadoouteiro.com* ▨ *16 rooms* ⚲ *In-room: a/c, refrigerator (some), Wi-Fi (some). In-hotel: pool, gym, Internet terminal, Wi-Fi hotspot, laundry service* ⊘ *DC, MC, V* ¶◉ *BP.*

$ ☂ **Hotel do Mestre Afonso Domingues.** Named for the principal architect of the famous Batalha monastery, this pousada is full of modern comforts in a two-story, white-stucco building. Though the outside may look rustic, the inside has been recently remodeled, and the good-size guest rooms are furnished in a simple, modern style but come in many different bold colors with trendy lamps. Several look out to the monastery, which is literally right next door, and most have a balcony. The monastery can also be seen from the first-floor restaurant ($$$) and artsy-styled lounge. The menu includes several types of bacalhau and a lamb pie, and there's an extensive wine list. The hotel is also right behind a pretty outdoor shopping area that sells crafts and souvenirs. **Pros:** next to monastery; great service; comfortable rooms. **Cons:** can get noisy from outside traffic; restaurant is a bit pricey. ✉ *Largo Mestre Afonso Domingues 6* ☎ *244/765260* ⊕ *www.hotel.mestreafonsodomingues.pt* ➯ *22 rooms, 2 suites* ☖ *In-room: a/c, safe, Internet. In-hotel: restaurant, room service, bar, laundry service, Wi-Fi hotspot, parking (free)* ▭ *AE, DC, MC, V* ⍐⍈ *BP.*

$ ☂ **Hotel Villa Batalha.** A recent addition to Batalha, this hotel is right on the outskirts of the city, but still has a view of the monastery. It boasts a large spa and wellness center with a Jacuzzi, sauna, and steam room as well as an indoor pool that overlooks the private gardens. The spacious rooms are decorated in a stylish spa motif, with rich chocolate browns, reds, and tans, and many rooms have balconies with monastery views. Aside from visiting the historical monuments of Batalha, guests can also enjoy a round of golf on their private golf course along the river as well as a game of tennis. The restaurant, Adega dos Frades ($$$), offers traditional Portuguese cuisine and includes an outdoor patio. **Pros:** a wide variety of activities is offered; excellent spa; close to monastery. **Cons:** location has a bit of a commercial feeling; can get crowded from a lot of large group bookings and conferences. ✉ *Rua Dom Duarte I, 248, Batalha* ☎ *244/240400* ⊕ *www.hotelvillabatalha. com* ➯ *93 rooms, 44 suites* ☖ *In-room: a/c, safe (some), Wi-Fi (some). In-hotel: restaurant, room service, golf course, tennis court, pool, gym, spa, bicycles, laundry service, Internet terminal, Wi-Fi hotspot, parking (free)* ▭ *AE, D, DC, MC, V* ⍐⍈ *BP.*

OFF THE BEATEN PATH

Parque Natural das Serras de Aire e Candeeiros. This sparsely populated region straddles the border between Estremadura and the Ribatejo and is roughly midway between Lisbon and Coimbra. Within its 75,000 acres of scrublands and moors are small settlements, little changed in hundreds of years, where farmers barely eke out a living. In this rocky landscape, stones are the main building material for houses, windmills, and the miles of walls used to mark boundary lines. In the village of Minde, you can see women weaving the rough patchwork rugs for which this region is known. The park is well suited for leisurely hiking or cycling. If you're driving, the N362, which runs for approximately 45 km (28 mi) from Batalha in the north to Santarém in the south, is a good route.

LEIRIA

11 km (7 mi) north of Batalha.

Leiria is a pleasant, modern, industrial town at the confluence of the Rios Liz and Lena, overlooked by a wonderfully elegant medieval castle. The region is known for its handicrafts, particularly the fine handblown glassware from nearby Marinha Grande.

GETTING HERE AND AROUND

The best option to get here is by car, and there are two alternative highways between Lisbon and Leiria (A1 and A8) that take about an hour and 15 minutes. From Batalha it's 15 minutes. It's also possible to take a Rede Expresso Bus from Lisbon to Leiria. ⇨ *For Rede Expresso info, see Bus Travel, above.*

ESSENTIALS

Bus Station Leiria (✉ *Av. Herois de Angola* ☎ *244/811507*).

Visitor Info Leiria (✉ *Jardim Luís de Camões* ☎ *244/848770*).

EXPLORING

Castelo. Leiria's castle, built in 1135 by Prince Afonso Henriques (later Portugal's first king), was an important link in the chain of defenses along the southern border of what was at the time the Kingdom of Portugal. When the Moors were driven from the region, the castle lost its significance and lay dormant until the early 14th century, when it was restored and modified and became the favorite residence of Dom Dinis and his queen, Isabel of Aragon. With these modifications the castle became more of a palace than a fortress and remains one of the loveliest structures of its kind in Portugal. Within the perimeter walls you'll encounter the ruins of a Gothic church, the castle keep, and—built into the section of the fortifications overlooking the town—the royal palace. There's also a museum. Lined by eight arches, the balcony of the palace affords lovely views. ☎ *244/813982* ⌨ *Castle and museum €2* ☉ *Apr.–Sept., Tues.–Sun. 10–6; Oct.–Mar., Tues.–Sun. 9–5.*

Museu do Vidro. Marinha Grande, just west of Leiria, is known for its fine-quality lead crystal, which has been produced in the region since the 17th century. The former Royal Glass Factory, founded in the 18th century, is now the site of this museum, with a collection of glass and crystal from several periods and factories. A shop is in the reception area. ✉ *Praça Gulhereme Stevens, Marinha Grande* ☎ *244/573377* ⌨ *€1.50* ☉ *June–Sept., Tues.–Sun. 10–7; Oct.–May, Tues.–Fri. 10–6.*

WHERE TO EAT AND STAY

$ ✗ **Casinha Velha.** This restaurant makes its home within an old house
PORTUGUESE   with rustic Portuguese furniture, 1 km (½ mi) from downtown. The menu includes a noteworthy bacalhau *com natas* (with cream), as well as *cabrito assado* (roasted kid [baby] goat), but which isn't served on Wednesday and Friday. ✉ *Rua Professores Portelas 23, Marrazes* ☎ *244/855355* ▭ *AE, DC, MC, V* ☉ *Closed Tues.*

$ ✗ **O Casarão.** Five kilometers (3 mi) south of Leiria, in Azoia at the
PORTUGUESE   Nazaré turnoff, O Casarão occupies a large country house surrounded by gardens. The service and presentation are flawless without being

pretentious, and the extensive menu includes several ancient recipes from nearby monasteries. Try *Ensopado de Robalo com Gambas* (sea bass stew with prawns) or *Rojões à Portuguesa* (mixed pork and sausage marinated in wine). Be sure to leave room for the homemade pastries such as *nata do céu* ("cream of heaven"). The comprehensive wine list displays the labels of 120 varieties. ⊠ *Cruzamento de Azoia* ☎ *244/871080* ▤ *AE, DC, MC, V* ⊗ *Closed Mon.*

$$$$ ✕ **Tromba Rija Marrazes-Leiria.** The place to go in the region is this res-
PORTUGUESE taurant 1 km (½ mi) from Leiria on N109 in Marrazes. Arched stone
Fodor'sChoice walls lend it a medieval atmosphere. A long table displays more than
★ 35 different regional appetizers in clay pots. Main dishes include *pato bravo com molho de cogumelos* (wild duck with mushroom sauce) and *lombo de porco recheado com ameixas* (loin of pork stuffed with prunes). From Friday dinner through Sunday lunch, they offer a large tasting buffet, which is the best option if you want to indulge in a smorgasbord of Portuguese specialties. It is a very well-known restaurant, so make reservations, be prepared to wait, and be aware that the appetizers, wines, cheeses, and desserts can add up to a hefty bill. ⊠ *Rua Professores Portela 22, Leiria* ☎ *244/852277* ⊕ *www.trombarija.com* ⚐ *Reservations essential* ▤ *AE, DC, MC, V* ⊗ *Closed Mon., no dinner Sun. and holidays.*

$ ⌂ **Casa da Nora.** This pretty farmhouse turned cozy hotel is in the beautiful countryside just a short drive outside of Leiria. It sits right next to a small river with a darling little waterfall and mill whose peaceful splashing add to the tranquility of the house's green, trellised garden that's lined with stone seats; there's a little path that leads to the outdoor pool and Jacuzzi, which are open year-round. The river even has a small "beach" area for swimmers, sunbathers; fishing, canoeing, and tennis are also available. The rooms are modern and decorated with warm browns and soft tans and are available in various sizes, from double to family size with either a shower or bath. Half of the top-floor rooms have a rooftop terrace over the river with a view of the old farming village. The restaurant ($$) serves excellent Portuguese and international cuisine for lunch and dinner, and there's a cute little café with an outdoor patio across the street in case you want a snack. **Pros:** friendly staff; great riverside location; perfect getaway for couples. **Cons:** no telephone in rooms; no elevator. ⊠ *Largo José Marques da Cruz, 8, Cortes-Leiria* ☎ *244/891189* ⊕ *www.casadanora.com* ⇨ *12 rooms, 3 suites* ⚒ *In-room: a/c, no telephone, Wi-Fi (some). In-hotel: restaurant, bar, tennis court, pool, water sports, bicycles, laundry service, Wi-Fi hotspot, parking (free), some pets allowed* ▤ *AE, D, DC, MC, V* ⱺ *CP.*

$ ⌂ **Eurosol Residence.** This apartment-hotel is in front of a pretty park and is a 15-minute walk from downtown. Rooms are available as studios or one and two bedrooms and are simple but pleasantly furnished with a modern kitchenette. And in case you don't feel like cooking, breakfast is included in the booking price, and there is a bar and restaurant open for lunch and dinner during the week. The restaurant, Cozinha Nova ($$), serves a gourmet fusion of Portuguese-Italian cuisine and boasts an award-winning cappuccino, along with other delicious coffee drinks. Other amenities include a large fitness center and rooftop pool and patio, offering spectacular views of the castle and city below. **Pros:** convenient location to city center; awesome views from rooftop and pool; free garage parking. **Cons:** restaurant closed Saturday evening and Sunday; no room service. ⊠ *Comissão Da Iniciativa, 13, Leiria* ☎ *244/860460* ⊕ *www.eurosol.pt/residence* ⤶ *58 apartments* ♿ *In-room: a/c, safe (some), kitchen (some), refrigerator (some), Wi-Fi (some). In-hotel: restaurant, bar, pool, gym, laundry service, Wi-Fi hotspot, parking (free), some pets allowed.* ▤ *AE, D, DC, MC, V* |◎| *BP.*

¢ 🔛 **Hotel S. Luís.** This newly renovated hotel in a quiet neighborhood overlooking the town is a five-minute walk from the park in the town center. Rooms are large and comfortable, with simple furnishings, but the walls are painted in rich colors. Many rooms have a balcony, and the ones on the fifth and sixth floors have partial views of the nearby castle. **Pros:** great location; very clean; friendly staff. **Cons:** parking away from hotel; noisy at night from outside traffic; breakfast lacking a bit of variety. ⊠ *Rua Beatriz Machado,* ☎ *244/848370* ⤶ *54 rooms* ♿ *In-room: a/c, Internet (some). In-hotel: bar, parking (free)* ▤ *AE, DC, MC, V* |◎| *CP.*

SHOPPING

The **Santos Barrosa Vidros** (⊠ *Apartado 1, Marinha Grande* ☎ *244/570100*), a factory museum, displays all types of glass products. Call ahead of time to arrange for a tour, as hours are erratic. Admission is free.

THE RIBATEJO

To the east of Estremadura, straddling both banks of the Rio Tejo, the Ribatejo is a placid, flat, fertile region known for its vegetables and vineyards. It's also famous for its horses and bulls; you may well see campinos in red waistcoats and green stocking caps moving bulls along with long wooden poles. As a consequence of its strategic location, the Ribatejo is home to a number of imposing castles as well as such diverse sights as the bullfighting centers of Vila Franca de Xira and Santarém and the shrine at Fátima.

VILA FRANCA DE XIRA

30 km (18 mi) north of Lisbon via the A1.

Vila Franca de Xira is an excellent place to see Portuguese bullfights, known as the *tourada,* which are held from Easter through October. Although it's different from any version of this ancient spectacle in Mexico or Spain, Portuguese and Spanish bullfights have a common origin. Both forms were born in the Middle Ages in the struggle between Moors and Christians for the Iberian Peninsula, both were essentially arts of the nobility, and both were practiced by horsemen. Bullfighting remained essentially the same in Portugal and Spain until the middle of the 18th century. Its subsequent development into two separate styles, the matador on foot becoming protagonist in Spain and the horseman continuing to play the leading role in Portugal, was caused by the disapproval of Bourbon monarch Felipe V, who ascended to the Spanish throne in 1700. The king's French sensibilities were offended by the gore and violence of bullfighting, and he soon prohibited the practice. Spain's noblemen were forced to comply. Bullfighting, however, had become too popular to disappear. The horsemen noblemen's retinue of grooms and other helpers took the art over for themselves.

GETTING HERE AND AROUND

Vila Franca de Xira is served by bus (both through Ribatejana and Boa Viagem bus lines) that takes you to Lisbon, Santarém, and Almeirim. Taking the train is another option, either on the Linha da Azabuja suburban line or the Interegional line to Porto. By car it is 20 minutes away from Lisbon and another 20 minutes from Santarém. Benavente is only a 15-minute drive. ⇨ *For more information about bus and train travel, see Bus Travel and Train Travel, above.*

ESSENTIALS

Bus Info **Vila Franca de Xira-Ribatejana Bus Station** (✉ *Rua Serpa Pinto 132-A* 🕿 *263/276025*).

Visitor Info **Vila Franca de Xira** (✉ *Rua Almirante Cándido dos Reis 147* 🕿 *263/285605*).

EXPLORING

Praça de Touros. The bullring at Praça de Touros is one of Portugal's finest. It contains a small museum with a collection of bullfighting memorabilia. ✉ *Palha Blanco* 🕿 *219/273057 museum* 🎫 *Museum free* ⊗ *Museum Tues.–Sun. 10–12:30 and 2–6.*

Museu do Ar *(Air Museum).* Not all the area sights are related to bullfighting. The air museum, in nearby Alverca, has a captivating collection of old airplanes. ✉ *Largo dos Pioneiros da Aviação–Alverca 8 km (5 mi) south of Vila Franca de Xira* 🕿 *219/678984* 🎫 *€3* ⊗ *Tues.–Sun. 10–5. Closed Mon., Christmas, New Year's Day, and Easter Sun.*

WHERE TO EAT AND STAY

$ ✕ **O Forno.** This century-old wine warehouse has been converted into
PORTUGUESE a restaurant with open grill and an old wood-fire oven. Try the bacalhau assado *com batata a muro* (roasted with potatoes "a muro"—fist smashed) and *arroz de tamboril com gambas* (monkfish rice with shrimp). Wine bottles are displayed on big wooden barrels. ✉ *Rua Dr. Miguel Bombarda 143* 🕿 *263/282106* 🗀 *AE, DC, MC, V* ⊗ *Closed Tues.*

$$$ ✕ **O Redondel.** This restaurant inside the walls of the famous bullring
PORTUGUESE sees a lot of action. It's considered Vila Franca's top eatery, with a
Fodor's Choice menu full of regional dishes. There are high-vaulted brick ceilings, and
★ in keeping with the theme, the dining room is adorned with bullfight posters and memorabilia. You don't have to have attended a fight to eat here. ✉ *Estrada de Lisboa–Arcadas da Praça de Touros* 🕿 *263/272973* ⊕ *www.restauranteoredondel.com* ⌕ *Reservations essential* 🗀 *AE, DC, MC, V* ⊗ *Closed Mon. and June.*

¢ 🏨 **Lezíria Parque Hotel.** This modern, four-story hotel off the main Lisbon–Porto road is a comfortable base from which to explore the bull- and horse-breeding region across the Rio Tejo. Rooms are small but have comfortable beds decorated in reds and nice hardwood, and about 70%

Bullfighting

Bullfighting in Portugal remains true to its equestrian origins. As part of their training, medieval Portuguese and Spanish knights honed their equestrian skills and developed the dexterity of their horses in combat with the notoriously belligerent and agile Iberian fighting bulls. Long after these dangerous exercises lost their military utility, the noblemen continued to practice them. Displays of skill and courage, staged in castle courtyards and town squares, gradually evolved into today's spectacles.

In Spain, the evolution of bullfighting has produced the dramatic figure of the matador, a solitary figure who fights a deadly duel with his opponent from a proletarian position, on the ground. In Portugal, however, the aristocratic tradition of the horseman bullfighter has remained intact (though following a decree by the Marquês de Pombal in the 18th century, bulls aren't killed in Portuguese rings). The star of the Portuguese show is the elegant *cavaleiro*, costumed as an 18th-century nobleman, with plumed hat and embroidered coat. The aim of the bullfight—known as the *tourada*—is to show off the courtly skills of the horse and its rider. Even today, horseback bullfighters tend to come from the wealthy and aristocratic segments of society, whereas the greatest matadors have typically come from more humble origins.

During a bullfight the horse must make precisely timed movements to avoid being gored and to best position its rider for placing the darts. Using exceptional equestrian skills, the cavaleiro provokes the bull and, just inches away from the animal's padded horns, deftly places a colorfully festooned *bandarilha* (dart) in a designated part of the bull's back. With each pass of an ever-shorter bandarilha, the danger to horse and rider increases—in spite of the bull's blunted horns. At the proper moment, when the bull is sufficiently fatigued, the final dart is placed, and with a flourish the cavaleiro exits the arena.

The stage is now set for the *pega*, an audacious display of bravery with burlesque overtones. A group of eight men—called the *forcados*—dressed in bright-crimson vests and green stocking caps parades into the arena, and the leader, hands on hips, confronts the tired but still-enraged bull. When the bull charges, the leader meets him head on with a leap and literally seizes the bull by the horns. While he tries to hang on to the furious bull's head, suspended between its horns, the other men rush in and, with one of them hanging on to its tail, try to force the animal to a standstill. At times this can be an amusing sight, but there's an ever-present element of danger (forcados have been killed during the pega). At the end of the spectacle, a few cows are led in to lure the bull from the ring. If he has shown exceptional bravery, the bull will be spared for stud purposes; otherwise, he will be slaughtered for the meat. The best place to view bullfighting today is in Vila Franca de Xira.

have balconies. The ground-floor coffee shop is quite pleasant, with an outdoor patio and lots of natural light. The hotel arranges jeep tours of the surrounding wetlands, as well as river cruises on the Tejo. **Pros:** good value for money; convenient location for access to motorway; comfortable. **Cons:** Wi-Fi isn't free; noisy for the rooms that face the railroad; immediate area surrounding hotel isn't good for walking around. ✉ *Estrada Nacional1-Povos, Vila Franca de Xira* ☎ *263/276670* ⊕ *www.continentalhotels.eu* ⇌ *103 rooms, 4 suites* ⚲ *In-room: a/c, safe (some), Wi-Fi. In-hotel: restaurant, bar, laundry service, Wi-Fi hotspot, parking (free)* ▤ *AE, DC, MC, V* ❘⊙❘ BP, MAP.

EN ROUTE

On the Rio Tejo's east bank, between Vila Franca de Xira and Santarém, is a region of marshy plains and rich pasturelands known as the Lezíria. The area contains many stud farms, where Portugal's best bulls and horses are bred. As you drive through the town of Benavente and the surrounding countryside, look for campinos in the fields working the bulls and horses.

FUN FESTIVALS

Had Ernest Hemingway and his buddies taken a wrong train and wound up in Vila Franca de Xira some 60 years ago, perhaps Pamplona would have remained an unsung, grimy industrial town, and the world would have flocked instead to the Ribatejo each year for one of Portugal's greatest parties. The first week of July sees the **Festa do Colete Encarnado** *(Festival of the Red Waistcoat),* during which the downtown streets are cordoned off, and the bulls are let loose as folks try their luck at dodging the charging beasts. At night the streets are alive with fado music and flamenco dancing.

4

BENAVENTE

30 km (18 mi) northeast of Vila Franca de Xira.

Benavente is a small, country town in the heart of rural Ribatejo and of the *Leziria,* which is Portuguese for the rich and fertile landscape found on the shores of the Tejo River. The central location of Benavente is a great starting point for exploring the surrounding area, where there are several places for horseback riding, golf, wine tasting, and other outdoor activities. Benavenente dates back to the 12th century when Portuguese colonists settled on the southern bank of Tejo River.

GETTING HERE AND AROUND

Benavente is served by Bus 902 (through Ribatejana) that takes you to Lisbon or Vila Franca de Xira. By car it is 35 minutes away from Lisbon and another 15 minutes from Vila Franca de Xira.

ESSENTIALS

Bus Info **Ribatejana Benavente Bus Station** (✉ *Praça do Município* ☎ 263/516282).

Visitor Info **Benavente Tourism** (☎ 263/655202 ⊕ *www.benavente-digital.com*).

EXPLORING

Cruzeiro do Largo do Calvário. Check out the town center where you can find the Cruzeiro do Largo do Calvário, a large, stone cross that dates back to 1644. Also here is the **Igreja da Misericordia,** a church that dates back to the 13th century.

Reserva Natural do Estuário do Tejo. This extensive natural reserve area lies along the banks of the Tejo river and has diverse fauna and flora, great bird-watching, and hiking through the Leziria area.

WHERE TO EAT AND STAY

¢ ✕ **Tipico os Moços.** On the outskirts of the historical center, this quaint
PORTUGUESE   little restaurant is named for the gathering place for the bullfighting *forcados,* and is decorated with *azulejo* murals of these men who brace themselves to tackle the bull head on in the Portuguese style. Service is friendly and the food is a really great value for your money—there are large, inexpensive portions, which are, of course, delicious. Try the *bacalhau á lagareiro com migas de grelos* (oven-roasted salt cod with slivers of garlic served with local bread stuffing mixed with greens) or the *bife de Vitela á Moço* (veal steak with roasted shrimp and a creamy mustard sauce), and save room for one of their house-made desserts like the *bolo de bolacha com três sabore*s (cookie cake with three flavors—cookie, chocolate, and caramel). Come early if you want to avoid the crowd and occasional smokers. ⊠ *Largo Jogo Bola 6/7, Herdade da Calada, Benavente* ☎ *263/517199* ▤ *AE, DC, MC, V.*

¢ 🏨 **Benavente Vila Hotel.** Opened in June 2010, this small boutique hotel is in the plaza of Benavente's historical center. Rooms are clean with a simple yet modern style that includes white linens splashed with lime-green footers. The same style carries into the rest of the hotel with the third-floor restaurant ($), bar, and lounge being the highlight with a wrap-around corner balcony that has panoramic views of the city and Ribatejo countryside. The hotel offers some great package deals in association with its tourist shop to help you explore and thoroughly enjoy what the area has to offer. There are golf packages with lessons, gastronomy packages with visits to local wineries, and adventure packages with horseback riding and a river cruise ride. **Pros:** great views of the city and countryside; friendly staff; good value for money. **Cons:** no designated parking; rooms are a bit small. ⊠ *Praça Da República Nº 39/40, Benavente* ☎ *263/518210* ⊕ *www.benaventevilahotel.pt* ⤳ *20 rooms, 2 suites* ⚐ *In-room: a/c, safe (some), Internet (some). In-hotel: restaurant, room service, bar, bicycles, laundry service, Internet terminal, Wi-Fi hotspot.* ▤ *V* ⭐ *BP.*

SPORTS AND THE OUTDOORS

GOLF

RibaGolfe (⊠ *Vargem fresca EN 119, Km 23, Infantado-Benavente* ☎ *263/930040* ⊕ *www.ribagolfe.pt* ⚓ *Reservations essential* ⛳ *18 holes. Ribagolfe I: 6,707 m.; Ribagolfe II: 6,214 m. Par 72/73* 💳 *€50 per round weekdays, €65 per round weekends* ☞ *Facilities: driving range, putting green, bunker and chipping area, golf carts, hand-pulled carts, rental clubs, pro shop, restaurant, bar),* a 20-minute drive away has two, 18-hole courses designed by architects Peter Townsend and Michael King of European Gold Design with more than 6,000 yards each in size set in beautiful sloping terrain lined with large, cork oak trees. It also has a training center with a driving range, putting and pitching greens and a practice bunker.

HORSEBACK RIDING

The **Companhia das Lezirias** (⊠ *Largo 25 de Abril 17, Samora Correia* ☏ *263/650600 Equestrian Center Contact: André Machado Faria— 926/729180 or 961/523119* ⊕ *www.cl.pt* ⊗ *By appointment only*) is the largest agriculture, animal, and forest farmstead in Portugal, covering about 44,500 acres. The area stretches across Ribatejo's Leziria landscape, from Samora-Correia all the way down toward the town of Alcochete and includes the marshlands of Vila Franca de Xira and the Tejo Natural Esturary Reserve. The farmstead is filled with forests of cork oaks, stone pines, and eucalyptus trees, which the company harvests annually. Rice is also grown and sold under the "Belmonte" and "Bom Sucesso" labels, and the company does organic cattle farming and breeds prize-winning Lusitano stallions. For organized group activities, the company can arrange a number of radical sports, such as paintball, crossbow shooting, canoeing, and hot-air-balloon rides, as well as guided tours of the area and production facilities, wine tastings and lunches. But the best choice for tourists here is the excellent equestrian facilities, which offer lessons, guided riding excursions, and horse-drawn-carriage rides through the beautiful cork forests and Lezirian landscape. Various riding tours include a half-day ride for €40, a full-day ride with picnic for €75, and carriage rides for €100 (minimum three people). You must call or email ahead of time to arrange rides or lessons.

EN
ROUTE

If you're a fan of wine, stop by the prestigious **Casa Cadaval** (⊠ *Rua Vasco da Gama, Muge, Salvaterra de Magos* ☏ *243/588040* ⊕ *www. casacadaval.pt* ⊗ *Tastings by appointment only for at least 4 people; Shop: Mon.–Thurs. 9–12:30 and 2–5, Fri. 9–12:30 and 2–6; weekends 10–1 and 2–5*), on your way to Almeirim. This winery, on the Herdade de Muge estate, has belonged to the Alvares Pereira Melo (Cadaval) family since 1648. Along with being a stud farm, the estate has a wine store with a tasting room. The winery produces red, white, and rosé wines under the Casa Cadaval, Marquesa de Cadaval, and Padre Pedro labels using both native and international grape varieties such as Pinot Noir. The tasting room is available for scheduled visits for at least four or more people, but they also have a walk-in shop open to the public to purchase their wines.

ALMEIRIM

40 km (25 mi) northeast of Vila Franca de Xira; 4 km (2½ mi) east of Santarém.

Almeirim, a pretty country town just across the river from Santarém, is surrounded by vineyards and cork oak forests. Many people from nearby cities and all over Portugal come to this town dubbed the "capital of stone soup," which is a widely known local recipe that has cute story behind it. ⇨ *See legend below.*

GETTING HERE AND AROUND
Almeirim is served by the Ribatejana Bus 902 from Santarém and Vila Franca de Xira (via Benavente) and Rede Expressos from Lisbon. By car, it is about 50–60 minutes away from Lisbon, 40 minutes from Vila Franca de Xira, and only 10 minutes from Santarém.

ESSENTIALS
Visitor Info **Almeirim Tourism (Camara Municipal)** (✉ *R. 5 de Outubro* ☎ *243/597927 or 243/594107).*

EXPLORING
Quinta da Alorna. This 500-acre farm and winery was established in 1723 by the Marquês de Alorna, a viceroy of India. The chardonnay comes highly recommended. There's a shop right outside the entrance for tasting and purchasing the wines. ✉ *EN118 at Km 73* ☎ *243/570709* ⊕ *www.alorna.pt* ⊗ *Weekdays 10–noon and 3–5.*

Quinta do Casal Branco. For the gastronome in you, spend a day wining and dining at this 1,630-acre estate; 346 acres are vineyards. The quinta has been owned by the same family for more than 200 years and used to be one of largest royal falconry grounds in the country. The winery produces red, white, rosé, and sparkling wines as well as olive oil under numerous labels, which include Capoeira, Terra de Lobos, "Q," their falcon tribute Falcoaria, and their Casal Branco namesake. They use local native grape varietals like the reds *Castelão* and the white *Fernão Pires* as well as international grape varieties such as Syrah, Merlot, Cabernet Sauvignon, and Petit Verdot. Prescheduled guided tours of the cellar, tastings, and lunches or dinners in the small restaurant are available, or you can stop by their Cellar shop, which is open every day for purchasing their wines and olive oil, as well as homemade jams, cheeses, and traditional sausages. ✉ *EN118 at Km 69* ☎ *243/592412* ⊕ *www.casalbranco.com* ⊗ *By appointment only. Shop: Mon.–Sun. 10–6.*

WHERE TO EAT
$

PORTUGUESE

✕ **O Forno.** One of the most known restaurants in Almeirim to have *Sopa da Pedra,* this place is your typical Portuguese style with large and noisy family-style seating. Its name means "the oven" but it's actually referring to a large grill in the center of the open kitchen where all of the hot food is prepared. The Sopa da Pedra is served in a steaming metal cauldron for two or more people and is perfectly paired with a big hunk of crusty, fresh bread topped with a piece of the local cheese that is served at the beginning of the meal. Wash it all down with a big glass of the local house *tinto.* If you're still hungry after the soup, try

LOCAL LEGENDS

Almeirim is visited mostly because it has a number of restaurants that serve a local delicacy called **Sopa da Pedra** (stone soup). A local legend says there was once a friar on a pilgrimage traveling through the area who was too proud to beg for food so he knocked on the doors of the houses and asked for only a pot "to make a delicious and filling... stone soup." Then he took a *pedra* (stone) and dropped it into a boiling pot of water. A little later, he tasted it and approached a housewife, saying, "it just needs a little seasoning." So, she came back with some salt, to which he said "maybe a little bit of sausage or if you also have some potatoes left over from the previous meal then maybe that would make it just a bit better." So she came back with all three and added them to the pot. Eventually, everyone in the village came to contribute to

the soup, with carrots, beans, meat, sausage, and other vegetables until it had indeed become a very hearty soup. At the end, the friar fished the stone out of the pot, washed it off, and tucked it into his pocket to save for the next meal. Today Almeirim's sopa da pedra recipe is judged as the best around and it can easily be eaten as a meal on its own or as a starter to accompany other regional dishes if you have a healthy appetite. Some places still put a small (washed) stone at the bottom. ■TIP➔ **You can find most of the sopa da pedra restaurants across from the bullfighting ring in the Largo da Praça de Touros.** Don't forget to pay a visit to the friar himself. There's a statue of him sitting in front of his soup, located just down the street from the bullfighting plaza on Rua de Coruche.

the *costeletas de borrego* (rustic-style lamb chops) served with rice and french fries. ⊠ *Largo da Praça de Touros 23, Almeirim* ☎ *243/592916* ⊟ *AE, DC, MC, V* ⊘ *Closed Tues.*

OFF THE BEATEN PATH

Alpiarça is a pleasant little town just 7 km (4 mi) northeast of Almeirim. Here you'll have the chance to see how a wealthy country gentleman lived at the beginning of the 20th century. The **Casa dos Patudos** (⊠ *N118* ☎ *243/558321* 🎫 *€2.50* ⊘ *Oct.–Mar., daily 10–noon and 2–5; Apr.–Sept., daily 10–noon and 2–6* ⊘ *Closed holidays*), now a museum, was the estate of José Relvas, a diplomat and gentleman farmer. This unusual three-story manor house with its zebra-stripe spire is surrounded by gardens and vineyards and is filled with an impressive assemblage of ceramics, paintings, and furnishings—including Portugal's foremost collection of Arraiolos carpets.

EN ROUTE

About 32 km (19 mi) northeast of Almeirim, on the way to Torres Novas, is the town of **Golegã,** one of Portugal's most notable horse-breeding centers. During the first two weeks of November, this is the site of the colorful **Feira Nacional do Cavalo** (*National Horse Fair* ⊕ *www.horsefairlusitano.org*), the most important event of its kind in the country. It has riding displays, horse competitions, and stalls that sell handicrafts.

SANTARÉM

7 km (4½ mi) northwest of Almeirim.

Present-day Santarém, high above the Tejo, is an important farming and livestock center. It holds the largest agricultural fair in the country. Even with a tradition of bull breeding and bullfighting, Santarém curiously has what is considered the ugliest bullring on the Iberian Peninsula. Santarém also has bull farms, a working stud farm, and a winery that can be visited.

Some historians believe that Santarém's beginnings date from as early as 1200 BC and the age of Ulysses. Its strategic location led several kings to choose it as their residence, and the Cortes (Parliament) frequently met here. Thanks to its royal connections, Santarém is more richly endowed with monuments than other towns of its size. The Portuguese refer to it as their "Gothic capital."

GETTING HERE AND AROUND

Santarém is served by bus (Ribatejana via Vila Franca de Xira and Lisbon and Rede Expressos via Lisbon) and also by the intercidades, alpha-pendular, and regional trains coming from Lisbon, Vila Franca de Xira, and many other stops along the way up north. By car, it's 45 minutes away from Lisbon, 25 minutes from Vila Franca de Xira, and five minutes from Almeirim. ⇨ *For more information about bus and train travel, see Bus Travel and Train Travel, above.*

ESSENTIALS

Bus Station **Santarém** (✉ *Av. Brasil 41* ☎ *243/333200*).

Visitor Info **Santarém Tourism** (✉ *Rua Capelo e Ivens 63* ☎ *243/304437*).

EXPLORING

Igreja da Graça *(Graça Church).* The 14th-century Gothic church contains the gravestone of Pedro Álvares Cabral, the discoverer of Brazil. There's also a tomb of the explorer in Belmonte, the town of his birth, but no one is really sure just what (or who) is in which tomb. Note the delicate rose window whose setting was carved from a single slab of stone. ✉ *Largo Pedro Álvares Cabral* ☎ *No phone* ☉ *Tues., Wed., and weekends 9:30–12:30 and 2–5:30, Thurs. and Fri. 10–12:30 and 2–5:30.*

Portas do Sol. Walk up to this lovely park within the ancient walls. From this vantage point you can look down on a sweeping bend in the river and beyond to the farmlands that stretch into the neighboring Alentejo.

WHERE TO EAT AND STAY

$ ✕ **Adiafa.** Excellent grilled meats and good service are the norm at this
PORTUGUESE   large typically Ribatejo restaurant by the bullring. Non-meat eaters can try the *mangusto com bacalhau assado* (açorda with roasted codfish and fresh herbs). In winter, a fire in the fireplace may well welcome you. ✉ *Campo Emilio Infante da Câmara* ☎ *243/324086* ▭ *AE, MC, V* ☉ *Closed Tues. and 2nd half of Aug.*

¢   ✕ **Taberna da Quinzena.** Photos of patrons vie for your attention with
PORTUGUESE   bullfighting posters at this restaurant in a former house. It's run by the great-grandson of the original owner. Specialties include *toiro bravo*

CLOSE UP

Portugal's Oldest Food Festival

Starting from Mid-October until early November, Santarém hosts **Festival Nacional de Gastronomia de Santarém** (✉ *Casa do Campino-Campo Infante da Câmara, Santarém* ☎ *243/330330 or 243/325670* ⊕ *www.festivalnacionaldegastronomia.com* ✉ *€2.50* ☉ *Weekdays noon–4, weekends noon–midnight*), the oldest gastronomy festival in Portugal. It's held in the Casa do Campino, next to the bullfighting ring, where numerous restaurants from all over the country come to showcase the best gastronomy delights of their area and restaurant. Restaurants from two different regions outside of Portugal are also invited, and in 2010 they had food showcased from Galiza in Spain and the former Portuguese territory, the islands of São Tomé & Principe off the coast of Africa. On the weekends during the festival, the Casa do Campino's large banquet hall, Salão Nobre, hosts regional lunches for €30 a person starting at 1 pm, and there is the national pastry fair in the *Pavilhão do Futuro*.

4

(wild bull), *entrecosto com arroz de feijoca* (spareribs with red bean rice), and *mangusto com bacalhau assado*. ✉ *Rua Pedro de Santarém 93* ☎ *243/322804* ⊕ *www.quinzena.com* ✉ *No credit cards* ☉ *Closed Sun. and Aug. 15–31.*

¢ 🏨 **Corinthia Santarém Hotel.** Rooms at this contemporary hotel overlook the plains or the town. Some rooms have balconies, complimentary morning newspapers, bathrobes, and trouser presses; all are equipped with such gadgets as hair dryers and alarm clocks. **Pros:** right off the city center; great views of the plains and town. **Cons:** hotel a bit run-down; no Wi-Fi. ✉ *Av. Madre Andaluz* ☎ *243/309500* ⊕ *www.santaremhotel. net* ➬ *99 rooms, 6 suites* ♿ *In-room: a/c, safe, Internet. In-hotel: restaurant, room service, bar, pools, gym, laundry service, parking (free)* ✉ *AE, DC, MC, V* ❙◯❙ *BP.*

¢ 🏨 **Hotel Rural Santarém.** Built in a wine cellar more than 200 years old, this pretty little country hotel is 10 km (6 mi) outside the city in the farming town of Azóia de Baixo. Rooms are simply furnished with a rustic yet clean style, but the bathrooms are modern, and all rooms have balconies or terraces that look out to the swimming pool and rolling green hills, forests, and olive groves. This is the perfect spot for watching the sunset in rural Ribatejo. Along with a tennis court, the hotel has on-site stables and offers horseback riding from April through the end of October. **Pros:** in a pretty rural area, away from the crowds; beautiful views of the surrounding countryside; quiet and peaceful. **Cons:** double beds are small and a bit hard; a/c only in second-floor rooms; no restaurant. ✉ *Quinta dos Xendros, Azóia de Baixo* ☎ *243/467040* ⊕ *www.hotelruraldesantarem.com* ➬ *11 rooms, 1 suite* ♿ *In-room: a/c (some), Wi-Fi (some). In-hotel: bar, tennis court, pool, laundry service, Wi-Fi hotspot, parking (free), some pets allowed* ✉ *AE, MC, V* ❙◯❙ *BP.*

CONSTÂNCIA

18½ km (11 mi) southeast of Tomar; 4 km (2½ mi) east of Castelo de Almourol.

Peaceful little Constância is at the confluence of the Zêzere and the Tejo. It's best known as the town where poet Luís de Camões was exiled in 1548, the unfortunate result of his romantic involvement with Catarina de Ataíde, the "Natercia" of his poems and a lady-in-waiting to Queen Catarina. There's a bronze statue of the bard in a reflective pose at the riverbank. The town is surrounded by beautiful Ribatejan countryside and is a 10-minute drive to the famous Castelo de Almourol.

GETTING HERE AND AROUND

The best way to get to Constância is by car. Driving from Lisbon takes about 1 hour 25 minutes, from Tomar about 30 minutes, and from Santarém about 40 minutes on A23 and A1.

ESSENTIALS

Visitor Info Constância (✉ *R. Anes Oliveira, 4-A* ☎ *249/730050*).

EXPLORING

Castelo de Almourol. For a close look at this storybook edifice on a craggy island in the Rio Tejo, take the 1½-km-long (1-mi-long) dirt road leading down to the water from N3. The riverbank in this area is practically deserted, making it a wonderful picnic spot. (In summer you can take a boat to the island.) It couldn't be more romantic: an ancient castle with crenellated walls and a lofty tower sits on a greenery-covered rock in the middle of a gently flowing river. The stuff of poetry and legends, Almourol was the setting for Francisco de Morais's epic novel *Palmeirim da Inglaterra* (*Palmeirim of England*) about two knights fighting for a princess's favor. ■TIP→ **To catch the boat ride across the river to the castle during the week, prior reservations must be made, but on weekends it's not necessary, as the boat departs hourly.** ✉ *Ilhota do Tejo, Almourol* ☎ *249/720358* ⊕ *www.cm-vnbarquinha.pt* 💷 *€1.50 for boat to cross river* ۞ *Nov.–Mar., daily 10–5; Apr.–Oct, daily 10–7.*

WHERE TO STAY

¢ 🛏 **Quinta de Santa Barbara.** If you're looking for a place to immerse yourself in the Portuguese countryside, look no farther. The Quinta, a short drive from town, has several sprawling buildings—a few of which date from the 16th century—on some 45 acres of farmland and pine forests overlooking the Tejo. Each of the seven spacious rooms in the main house is individually decorated with 18th-century Portuguese reproductions and has a modern tiled bathroom. The small restaurant ($$), with a barrel-vault ceiling and stone walls, specializes in local dishes. **Pros:** unique ambience; beautiful location a short drive from town; quiet and peaceful. **Cons:** no phone or TV in rooms; no elevator. ✉ *2 km (1 mi) east of Constância on IP6; follow directions on sign at traffic circle, Refeitório Quinhentista* ☎ *249/739214* ⊕ *www.quinta-santabarbara. com* 🛏 *7 rooms, 2 suites* ⚿ *In-room: a/c, no phone (some), no TV (some), refrigerator (some). In-hotel: restaurant, bar, tennis court, pool, laundry service, Wi-Fi hotspot, parking (free)* 🖃 *MC, V* ۞ *CP.*

Fodor'sChoice
★

SPORTS AND THE OUTDOORS

The English-speaking guides at **Glaciar-Desportos Bar** (✉ *Av. das For-ças Armadas, Parque de Campismo* ☎ 249/739972 ⊕ *www.glaciar-sportsbar.com*) lead a wide variety of adventure activities on both the Tagus and the Zêzere rivers and in the surrounding forest, the Xarneca Alentejana. Half-day excursions include those by canoe, all-terrain bike (BTT), horse back, or on foot. Food is not included unless you make arrangements beforehand. You can always grab a bite at their meeting point's Bar Esplanada do Zêzere on the riverbank. They also organize multiday camping trips for children. The per-person rates range from €8 for biking, to €20 for canoeing, and €50 for horseback riding. They also offer special bike excursions from Marinha Grande to São Pedro de Moel and São Pedro de Moel to Nazaré.

4

ABRANTES

16 km (10 mi) east of Constância.

Abrantes became one of the country's most populous and prosperous towns during the 16th century, when the Rio Tejo was navigable all the way to the sea. With the coming of the railroad and the development of better roads, the town's commercial importance waned. The breathtaking views of the valley from the top of the castle remain, however, and the historical center and friendly locals have also stayed true to tradition. A stroll through the narrow cobblestone streets is a perfect way to spend a lazy afternoon.

GETTING HERE AND AROUND

If you're already in the area, Abrantes is an easy 20-minute drive from Constância or 40-minute drive to Tomar. From Lisbon, it's about a 1½-hour drive; you can take the train from the Rossio station, but it's a two- to three-hour ride and you have to change trains at least twice. By bus, the Rede Espressos and Rodotejo leave from Lisbon daily.

ESSENTIALS

Visitor Info Abrantes (✉ *Esplanada 1 de Maio* ☎ 241/362555 ⊕ *www.cm-abrantes.pt*).

EXPLORING

Castelo. Walk up through the maze of narrow, flower-lined streets to this 16th-century castle. Much of it is in disrepair, but with a bit of imagination you can envision what an impressive structure this must have been. The garden between the twin fortifications is a wonderful place to watch the sun set with its panoramic views: the play of light on the river and the lengthening shadows along the olive groves provide a stirring setting for an evening picnic.

WHERE TO EAT

$ ✕ **Cristina.** You'll have a pretty garden view from this agreeable restau-
PORTUGUESE rant. The specialties include açorda de savel and *lombinhos com migas* (loin of pork served with bread crumbs). When in season, enguias *fritas* (fried eel) is also served. ✉ *Estrada Nacional N3, Rio de Moinhos* ☎ 241/881177 ⊕ *www.restaurante-cristina.com* ⚑ *Reservations essential* ▭ MC, V ☺ *Closed Mon. No dinner Sun.*

$ ✕ **O Fumeiro.** This pleasant, little restaurant is handily situated in the
PORTUGUESE old part of town over a café. The food is simple but good, consisting
almost entirely of regional specialties. Try the cabrito assado if it's
available. ✉ *Rua do Pisco 9* ☎ *241/363893* ▭ *AE, MC, V* ⊘ *Closed
Sun. and 2nd half of August.*

**EN
ROUTE**

Castelo de Belver is a fairy-tale castle planted on top of a cone-shape hill;
the fortress of Belver was built in the last years of the 12th century by
the Knights Hospitallers under the command of King Sancho I. The castle commands a superb view of the Tejo. In 1194 this region was threatened by the Moorish forces who controlled the lands south of the river,
except for Évora. The expected attack never took place, and the present
structure is little changed from its original design. The walls of the keep,
which stands in the center of the courtyard, are some 12 feet thick, and
on the ground floor is a great cistern of unknown depth. According to
local lore, an orange dropped into the well will later appear bobbing
down the river. To get here follow N244-3 through the pine-covered
hills to Chão de Codes, then take N244 south toward Gavião.

TOMAR

24 km (15 mi) east of Fátima; 20 km (12 mi) northeast of Torres Novas.

Tomar is an attractive town laid out on both sides of the Rio Nabão,
with the new and old parts linked by a graceful, arched stone bridge.
The river flows through a lovely park with weeping willows and an
old wooden waterwheel. The town is best known for being the former
headquarters of the Order of the Knights Templar and home to their
Convento do Cristo (⇨ *See review below*), which is a UNESCO World-
Heritage Site. The town also hosts the Festival of the Tabuleiros every
four years. This ancient tradition is also the oldest festival in Portugal
and consists of parades of girls carrying large *tabuleiros*, platters piled
high with 30 loaves of bread fixed on rods, interspersed with flowers
and topped with a crown. They wear these unusual headpieces in honor
of the Holy Spirit, but the festival actually dates back to pagan times.

GETTING HERE AND AROUND

There's a train line between Lisbon and Tomar with several daily departures. Taking the bus (Rede Expressos) is another possibility. Driving to
Tomar takes 1 hour 15 minutes from Lisbon and close to 25 minutes
from Santarém or Fátima. ⇨ *For more information about Rede Expressos, or train travel, see Bus Travel and Train Travel, above.*

ESSENTIALS

Bus Station Tomar (✉ *Varzea Grande* ☎ *967/449875*).

Visitor Info Tomar Tourism (✉ *Av. Dr. Cândido Madureira* ☎ *249/329000 or
249/329823*).

EXPLORING

Aqueduct. In Pegões, some 5 km (3 mi) northwest of Tomar, is a 5-km-
long (3-mi-long) aqueduct, built in the 16th century to bring water to
Tomar. It joins the walls of the Convent of Christ.

Fodor's Choice ★ **Convento de Cristo** *(Convent of Christ)*. Atop a hill rising from the Old Town is the remarkable Convento de Cristo. You can drive to the top of the hill or hike for about 20 minutes along a path through the trees before reaching a formal garden lined with azulejo-covered benches. This was the Portuguese headquarters of the Knights Templar, from 1160 until the order was forced to disband in 1314. Identified by their white tunics emblazoned with a crimson cross, the Templars were at the forefront of the Christian armies in the Crusades and during the struggles against the Moors. King Dinis in 1334 resurrected the order in Portugal under the banner of the Knights of Christ and reestablished Tomar as its headquarters. In the early 15th century, under Prince Henry the Navigator (who for a time resided in the castle), the order flourished. The caravels of the Age of Discovery even sailed under the order's crimson cross.

The oldest parts of the complex date from the 12th century, including the towering castle keep and the fortresslike, 16-sided Charola, which, like many Templar churches, is patterned after the Church of the Holy Sepulchre in Jerusalem and has an octagonal oratory at its core. The paintings and wooden statues in its interior, however, were added in the 16th century. The complex's medieval nucleus acquired its Manueline church and cluster of magnificent cloisters during the next 500 years. To see what the Manueline style is all about, stroll through the church's nave with its many examples of the twisted ropes, seaweed, and nautical themes that typify the style, and be sure to look at the chapter house window, probably the most photographed one in Europe. Its lichen-encrusted sculpture evokes the spirit of the great Age of Discovery. ☏ *249/313481* ⊕ *www.conventocristo.pt* ✉ *€6, free Sun. and holidays until 2 pm* ☉ *June–Sept., daily 9–6:30; Oct.–May, daily 9–5:30, closed Easter Sun., May 1, Christmas Day, and New Year's Day.*

Igreja de Santa Maria do Olival. Across the Rio Nabão is the 13th-century Igreja de Santa Maria do Olival, where the bones of several Knights Templar are interred, including those of Gualdim Pais, founder of the order in Portugal. Popular belief—supported by some archaeological evidence—has it that the church was once connected with the Convent of Christ by a tunnel. ⊠ *Estrada de Marmelais de Baixo* ☏ *No phone* ✉ *Free* ☉ *Weekdays 10–5, weekends 11–5.*

Museu-Sinagoga Luso-Hebraico Abraham Zacuto Sinagoga de Tomar. In the Old Town, walk along the narrow, flower-lined streets, particularly Rua Dr. Joaquim Jacinto, which takes you to the heart of the Jewish Quarter and this modest museum. Built in the mid-15th century, this is Portugal's oldest synagogue, though it's no longer used as such. Inside is a small museum with exhibits chronicling the Jewish presence in the country. The once-sizable community was considerably reduced in 1496 when Dom Manuel issued an edict ordering the Jews either to leave the country or convert to Christianity. Many, who became known as Marranos, converted but secretly practiced Judaism. ⊠ *Rua Dr. Joaquim Jacinto 73* ☏ *249/329814* ✉ *Donations accepted* ☉ *Apr.–Sept., Tues.–Sun. 10–7; Oct.–Mar., Tues.–Sun. 10–5. Closed Mon., Christmas Day, and New Year's Day.*

Waterwheel. In the gardens by the Rio Nabão there's an enormous working wooden waterwheel. It's typical of those once used in the region for irrigation and thought to be of either Arabic or Roman origin. ⊠ *Av. Marquês Tomar.*

WHERE TO EAT AND STAY

¢ ╳ **A Bela Vista.** The date on the calçada reads "1922," which was when
PORTUGUESE the Sousa family opened this attractive little restaurant next to the old arched bridge. For summer dining there's a small, rustic terrace with views of the river and the Convent of Christ. Carrying on the family tradition, Eugenio Sousa presides over the kitchen, which turns out great quantities of hearty regional fare. Try the cabrito assado or the *secretos porco preto* (black pork cutlets) and wash it down with a robust local red wine. ⊠ *Rua Marquês Pombal 6 Ponte Velha* ☎ *249/312870* ⊟ *No credit cards* ⊘ *Closed Tues., no dinner Mon.*

$$ ╳ **Chico Elias.** This restaurant owes its fame to owner and chef Maria do
PORTUGUESE Céu's creativity. Guests are recommended to call a day ahead of time
Fodor'sChoice because the special dishes take time to prepare. What can be more creative
★ than *feijoada de caracoís* (bean stew with snails) or *coelho na abóbora* (rabbit in a pumpkin)? Her other specialty is bacalhau *com broa* (with corn bread). ⊠ *Rua Principal 70, Algarvias* ☎ *249/311067* ⚑ *Reservations essential* ⊟ *No credit cards* ⊘ *Closed Tues., no dinner Sun.*

$ ▦ **Hotel dos Templários.** A large, modern hotel in a tranquil park along
Fodor'sChoice the Rio Nabão, the Templários has many units with views of the Con-
★ vent of Christ. Standard rooms are huge with large beds and look more like a suite, with a sitting area and both a shower and bath. All rooms also have sizable balconies or terraces. The big, airy dining room in the restaurant "Grão Mestre" ($$$), has picture windows facing the park, panoramic views of the river, and serves interesting regional dishes. The hotel has both an indoor and outdoor pool and a spa that includes a "physio-therapy room for posture." With its spacious grounds, reasonable rates, and many amenities, the hotel makes a good base for exploring the whole area. It can arrange boat tours also. **Pros:** excellent rooms; lots of amenities; location and views are great. **Cons:** Wi-Fi isn't free; the spa and restaurant are a bit pricey. ⊠ *Largo Candido dos Reis 1* ☎ *249/310100* ⊕ *www.hoteldostemplarios.pt* ⚑ *177 rooms, 16 suites* ♧ *In-room: a/c, safe, Wi-Fi (some). In-hotel: restaurant, bar, tennis court, pools, gym, spa, water sports, Wi-Fi hotspot, laundry service, parking (free)* ⊟ *AE, DC, MC, V* ⎢◎⎥ *BP.*

¢ ▦ **Residencial Cavaleiros de Cristo.** The Cavaleiros de Cristo (Knights Templar) is a three-story modern pension in the historic center near the Nabão River. Rooms, in which the color yellow predominates, are pretty basic, but some have great views of the garden terrace and surrounding hills. The Convento is within walking distance if you don't mind walking up the hill. **Pros:** great location in Tomar's historic center; friendly staff. **Cons:** difficult to find parking; bathrooms are tiny. ⊠ *Rua Alexandre Herculano 7* ☎ *249/321203* ⚑ *16 rooms* ♧ *In-room: a/c, Wi-Fi (some). In-hotel: room service, bar, laundry service, Wi-Fi hotspot* ⊟ *AE, DC, MC, V* ⎢◎⎥ *CP.*

From Tomar you can take N113 northwest to Ourem and visit its walled medieval castle, including its palace, church with crypt, and Gothic fountain built by king Afonso IV in the 15th century. To reach Castelo de Bode from Tomar, take EN 110 south. Set between hills and forests with inviting sandy beaches and placid waters, the lake (Estalagem Vale Manço) offers boating, fishing, and water sports.

FÁTIMA

20 km (12 mi) northwest of Torres Vedras; 16 km (10 mi) southeast of Batalha; 20 km (12 mi) southeast of Leiria.

On the western flanks of the Serra de Aire lies Fátima, an important Roman Catholic pilgrimage site that is, ironically, named after the daughter of Mohammed, the prophet of Islam. If you visit this sleepy little Portuguese town in between pilgrimages, it will be difficult to imagine the thousands of faithful who come from all corners of the world to make this religious affirmation, cramming the roads, squares, parks, and virtually every square foot of space. Many of the pilgrims go the last miles on their knees.

GETTING HERE AND AROUND

The Rede Expressos bus lines can take you to Fátima from Lisbon or Leiria. Another option is driving, which will take close to 1 hour from Lisbon and 15 minutes from Leiria. ⇨ *For more information about Rede Expressos, see Bus Travel, above.*

ESSENTIALS

Bus Station Fátima (✉ *Av. D. José Alves Correia Silva* ☎ *249/531611*).

Visitor Info Fátima (✉ *Jardim Luís de Camões* ☎ *249/531139*).

EXPLORING

Basilica. At the head of the huge esplanade is the large neoclassical basílica (built in the late 1920s), flanked on either side by a semicircular peristyle. ✉ *Rua do Imaculado Coração de Maria* ☎ *249/539600* ⊕ *www.santuario-fatima.pt* 🎫 *Free* 🕐 *Easter–Oct., daily 7:30 am–9 pm; Nov.–Easter, daily 7:30 am–8 pm.*

Capela das Aparições (*Chapel of Apparitions*). This 20th-century chapel is built on the site where the appearances of the Virgin Mary are said to have taken place. A marble pillar and statue of the Virgin mark the exact spot. Gifts, mostly gold jewelry and wax reproductions of body parts, are burned as offerings in the hope of achieving a miraculous cure.

The **Museu das Aparições** (*Museum of Apparitions* ✉ *Rua Jacinto Marto* 🎫 *€2.50* 🕐 *Nov.–Mar., daily 9–6; Apr.–Oct., daily 9–7*) has representations of scenes depicting the appearances of the Virgin Mary to the young shepherds in 1917. Dialogues between the children and the Virgin Mary are recorded in various languages. ✉ *Rua do Imaculado Coração de Maria* ☎ *249/539600* ⊕ *www.santuario-fatima.pt* 🎫 *Free* 🕐 *Easter–Oct., daily 7:30 am–midnight; Nov.–Easter, daily 7:30 am–midnight.*

Casas dos Pastorinhos. These are the cottages, in the nearby hamlet of Aljustrel, where the three shepherd children who saw the Virgin Mary were born. To reach them, turn off Avenida Papa João XXIII at the

Catholic Stories

CLOSE UP

It all began May 13, 1917, when three young shepherds—Lucia dos Santos and her cousins Francisco and Jacinta—reported seeing the Virgin Mary in a field at Cova de Iria, near the village. The Virgin promised to return on the 13th of each month for the next five months, and amid much controversy and skepticism, each time accompanied by increasingly larger crowds, the three children reported successive apparitions. This was during a period of anticlerical sentiment in Portugal, and after the sixth reputed apparition, in October, the children were arrested and interrogated. But they insisted the Virgin had spoken to them, revealing three secrets. Two of these, revealed by Lucia in 1941, were interpreted to foretell the coming of World War II and the spread of communism and atheism. In a 1930 Pastoral Letter, the Bishop of Leiria declared the apparitions worthy of belief, thus approving the "Cult of Fátima."

In May 2000, Francisco and Jacinta were beatified in a ceremony held at Fátima by Pope John Paul II. The third secret, which was revealed after the beatification, foretold an attempt on the life of the pope. On the 13th of each month, and especially in May and October, the faithful flock here to witness the passing of the statue of the Virgin through the throngs, to participate in candlelight processions, and to take part in solemn masses.

rotunda and take the N356 to Aljustrel and then turn right at the Centro Francisco e Jacinta Marto. The house of Francisco and Jacinto Marto is up the street on the right followed by the house of Lúcia dos Santos farther up and to the right. ☉ *May–Oct., daily 9–1 and 2:30–6:30; Nov.–Apr., daily 9–1 and 2–6.*

☺ **Grutas da Moeda** (Coin Caves). The hills to the south and west of Fátima are honeycombed with limestone caves. Legend has it that many years ago, a wealthy man carrying a bag of coins was traveling through the woods when he was attacked by a gang of thieves. Struggling from the attack, the man fell into one of the cave grottoes still carrying the bag of coins. Through the cave, the lost coins were spread around, thus giving the place its name. Within about a 25-km (15-mi) radius of the town are four major caverns—São Mamede, Mira de Aire, Alvados, and Santo António—equipped with lights and elevators. On a guided tour (ask for an English-speaking guide) you can see the subterranean world of limestone formations, underground rivers and lakes, and multicolor stalagmites and stalactites. ☎ *244/70430 or 244/703838* ⊕ *www.grutasmoeda. com* ☞ *€5 to visit each cavern, €2.50 for children 6–12, under 6 free* ☉ *Oct.–Mar., daily 9–5; Apr.–June, daily 9–6; July –Sept., daily 9–7.*

Museu de Arte Sacra e Etnologia *(Museum of Sacred Art and Ethnology). This* hosts a vast collection of Portuguese religious art as well as a rare collection of ethnographic objects from the various peoples the Portuguese missionaries came in contact with around the world: in the Amazon, Angola, Guinea, Mozambique, and the Far East. ✉ *Rua Francisco Marto 52* ☎ *249/539470* ⊕ *www.consolata.pt* ☞ *€2.50* ☉ *Nov.–Mar., Tues.–Sun. 10–5; Apr.–Oct., Tues.–Sun. 10–7.*

Museu de Cera *(Wax Museum).* In the center of town, the wax museum has 30 tableaux depicting the events that took place in Fátima when the child shepherds first saw the apparitions in 1917. ✉ *Rua Jacinto Marto* ☎ *249/539300* ⊕ *www.mucefa.pt* 🎫 *€6, €3.50 for kids under 12* ⊙ *Apr.–Oct., daily 9:30–6:30; Nov.–Mar., daily 10–5.*

WHERE TO EAT

$ ✕**Retiro dos Caçadores.** A big brick fireplace, wood paneling, and stone
PORTUGUESE walls set the mood in this cozy hunter's lodge, where the food is simple, but portions are hearty and the quality is good. This is the best place in town for fresh game, especially the *codornizes* (quails) and *coelho* (rabbit), which comes in casserole style with rice or potatoes. ✉ *Rua São João Deus 44, Cova Iria (Fátima)* ☎ *249/531323* ⊕ *www. retirodoscacadores.com* ▤ *MC, V* ⊙ *Closed Wed.*

$$ ✕**Tia Alice.** Considered the area's best restaurant, Tia (Aunt) Alice is con-
PORTUGUESE cealed in an inconspicuous old house with French windows, across from the parish church near the sanctuary at Cova de Iria. A flight of wooden stairs inside leads down to an intimate dining area with a wood-beam ceiling and stone walls. The cabrito assado is worth trying, as is the *bacalhau gratinado* (salt cod with potatoes, onions, béchamel sauce, and shrimp), which serves two. It's quite pricey for what is normally standard Portuguese fare, but the quality, service and large portion sizes make up for it. After dinner, stop in at the little artisanal shop at the top of the stairs, which sells handpainted ceramics by various local artists. ✉ *Rua do Adro, Cova Iria (Fátima)* ☎ *249/531737* ⌕ *Reservations essential* ▤ *AE, DC, MC, V* ⊙ *Closed Mon. and July. No dinner Sun.*

WHERE TO STAY

¢ ⌂**Casa São Nuno.** This large pink, rectory-style inn just a few minutes' walk from the sanctuary is run by the Carmelites but is open to visitors of all faiths. There's a good-size chapel at the front of the inn and the halls are decorated with display cases of the crusader swords of São Nuno. The austere rooms are clean and comfortable with plain beds and a large crucifix adorning the wall over them. The restaurant serves inexpensive meals all day, and there's a souvenir shop where pilgrims can purchase gifts for a reasonable price. **Pros:** good value for money; private entrance to sanctuary; friendly service. **Cons:** attracts mostly older, religious clientele; not a good choice for nonreligious people or those seeking a romantic vacation. ✉ *Av. Beato Nuno 271* ☎ *249/530230* ⇥ *150 rooms* ⌕ *In-room: a/c, Internet (some). In-hotel: 2 restaurants, bar, laundry service, Wi-Fi hotspot, parking (free)* ▤ *AE, MC, V* ◉*CP, MAP, FAP.*

¢ ⌂**Hotel Dom Gonçalo & Spa.** There is a pastoral view of gardens and
⊙ pinewoods from every window of this elegant boutique hotel, which is ¼ mi from the Fátima sanctuary. The spacious rooms are decorated in spa-chic style with sea blues and chocolate browns, along with colorfully wrapped chocolate candies greeting you on the nightstand when you enter. Included in the price, guests have full access to the spa's fitness center, heated indoor pool, Jacuzzi, sauna, and steam room. The restaurant, O Convite ($$), has long been a favorite in this part of the country and serves traditional Portuguese cuisine cooked with fresh ingredients. Children can enjoy the hotel's playground, and there's a kid's club on the

weekends in high season. **Pros:** excellent service; great amenities; free Wi-Fi. **Cons:** not close to monastery; no Wi-Fi in rooms; restaurant is a bit pricey. ⊠ *Rua Jacinto Marto 100* ☎ *249/539330* ⊕ *www.hoteldg. com* 🖵 *71 rooms* ⚿ *In-room: a/c, safe, Internet (some), Wi-Fi (some). In-hotel: restaurant, bar, pool, gym, spa, laundry service, bicycles, children's programs (ages 2–12), parking (free)* ⊟ *AE, DC, MC, V* ⦿⦿ *BP.*

$ ⬚ **Hotel Fátima.** This is the closest hotel to the sanctuary and has an excellent view of it from many of the rooms, several of which have terraces. The decor of the hotel and one section of rooms and suites are quite dated but have been kept in decent condition. Other sections of the hotel have rooms that have been recently renovated with modern decor. There is a large lounge and bar area, and the Fátima restaurant ($$) serves good-quality Portuguese food. **Pros:** closest hotel to the sanctuary; many of the rooms have views of sanctuary. **Cons:** dated rooms; some rooms reek of smoke; Wi-Fi isn't free. ⊠ *Rua João Paulo II, Apartado 11* ☎ *249/533351* ⊕ *www.hotelfatima.com* 🖵 *126 rooms, 9 suites* ⚿ *In-room: a/c, safe (some), Wi-Fi (some). In-hotel: restaurant, room service, bar, laundry service, parking (free), Wi-Fi hotspot* ⊟ *AE, DC, MC, V* ⦿⦿ *EP.*

¢   ⬚ **Hotel Santa Maria Fátima.** This recently renovated hotel is right in the center of Fátima and is a five-minute walk to the sanctuary. The decor is modern, with a large lobby and lounge area dressed in heavenly whites with a hint of gold. The standard rooms are simple, but for not too much more you can reserve a superior double room with soft white bed linens and warm, fuzzy carpeting for maximum comfort. A wide variety of large triple and family rooms as well as suites are also available. The restaurant ($$) serves Portuguese and international cuisine at affordable prices, and guests have free access to park in the hotel's secure, underground garage. **Pros:** friendly staff; great value for money; secure covered parking. **Cons:** no gym or pool; not a wide variety at breakfast. ⊠ *Rua de Santo António, Fátima* ☎ *249/530110* ⊕ *www.hotelstmaria. com* 🖵 *173 rooms, 9 suites* ⚿ *In-room: a/c, safe (some), Wi-Fi (some). In-hotel: restaurant, room service, bar, laundry service, Internet terminal, Wi-Fi hotspot, parking (free)* ⊟ *AE, D, DC, MC, V* ⦿⦿ *BP.*

¢   ⬚ **Luna Fátima Hotel.** This modern six-story pink-and-white hotel rises from among a grove of trees in the center of the town, a seven-minute walk from the basilica. The pink-and-white theme of the outside facade is carried over into the interior. As you enter a room, your attention is immediately drawn to the focal point, an elegant cherrywood bed set against a pink wall. **Pros:** near monastery; satellite TV. **Cons:** Wi-Fi isn't free; staff isn't always friendly. ⊠ *Av. Beato Nuno* ☎ *249/530410* 🖵 *85 rooms* ⚿ *In-room: a/c, safe. In-hotel: restaurant, room service, bar, Internet terminal, Wi-Fi hotspot, laundry service, parking (free)* ⊟ *AE, DC, MC, V* ⦿⦿ *BP.*

Évora and
the Alentejo

WORD OF MOUTH

"We drive on through the dry, barren Alentejo. As far as we can see it's flat and very empty. Suddenly in the distance appears Castelo de Vide. It is absolutely spectacular. The houses are all shining white and lead up the slopes to a castle. It is without a doubt one of the most glorious town settings I've ever laid eyes on."

—travellingdad

"The spectacular hilltop towns in the Alentejo . . . it's hard to believe how untouristed they are. My husband and I figured that if it was in France, for example, the town would be crawling with tourists and there would be admission charges and controlled access."

—Nikki

www.fodors.com/community

Updated by
Lauren Frayer

The Alentejo, which means "the land beyond the Rio Tejo" (Tagus River) in Portuguese, is a vast, sparsely populated area of heath and rolling hills punctuated with stands of cork and olive trees. Here you'll find a wide variety of attractions—from the rugged west-coast beaches to the Roman and medieval architecture of Évora, and the green northern foothills dotted with crumbling castles that form the frontier with Spain.

Over the centuries the pastoral countryside has been the scene of innumerable battles: between Romans and Visigoths, Moors and Christians, Portuguese and Spaniards, Portuguese and French, and finally (in the 1830s) between rival Portuguese factions in a civil war. Few hilltops in the region are without at least a trace of a castle or fortress.

Portugal is the world's largest producer of cork, and much of it comes from the Alentejo. This industry is not for people in a hurry. It takes two decades before the trees can be harvested, and then their bark can be carefully stripped only once every nine years. The numbers painted on the trees indicate the year of the last harvest. Exhibits at several regional museums chronicle this delicate process and display associated tools and handicrafts.

The undulating fields of wheat and barley surrounding Beja and Évora, the rice paddies of Alcácer do Sal, and the vineyards of Borba and Reguengos de Monsaraz are representative of the region's role as Portugal's breadbasket. Traditions here are strong. Herdsmen tending sheep and goats wear the *pelico* (traditional sheepskin vest), and women in the fields wear broad-brim hats over kerchiefs and colorful patterned dresses over trousers. Dwellings are dazzling white; more elegant houses have wrought-iron balconies and grillwork. The windows and doors of modest cottages and hilltop country *montes* (farmhouses) are trimmed with blue or yellow, and colorful flowers abound. The best time to visit the Alentejo is spring, when temperatures are pleasant and the fields are carpeted with wildflowers. Summer can be brutal, with the mercury frequently topping 37°C (100°F). As the Portuguese say, "In the Alentejo there is no shade but what comes from the sky."

ORIENTATION AND PLANNING

GETTING ORIENTED

This is the country's largest province, and it's divided roughly into two parts: the more mountainous Alto, or "upper," Alentejo north of Évora, and the flatter Baixo, or "lower," Alentejo that lies to the south. The area stretches from the rugged west-coast beaches all the way east to Spain, and from the Tejo in the north to the low mountains on the bor-

TOP REASONS TO GO

Going back in time. Wander amid megaliths erected 2,000 years before Stonehenge, Roman ruins, Moorish forts, and medieval monasteries in the province where Portugal's history is best preserved.

Wide open spaces. With a third of Portugal's land area and only a 20th of its population, Alentejo offers pristine open space even in one Europe's smallest countries. Stand atop a well-preserved medieval fortress and gaze out at undulating cork and wheat fields on every horizon. Even the more densely populated coastline

has all of the Algarve's charm with none of its tourists.

Traditional rural festivals. From Portuguese-style flamenco along the border with Spain to autumn chestnut roasts in northern hill-town squares, and sardine festivals on the coast, every weekend offers another reason to celebrate in rural Alentejo.

Food and wine. Alentejano cuisine is considered Portugal's best, with centuries-old farming practices that were organic long before it was trendy. The highlight is *porco preto,* free-range black pigs that graze on acorns under Alentejo's ever-present cork trees.

der of the Algarve, Portugal's southernmost province. Its central hub, Évora, is rich with traditional Portuguese architecture.

Évora. One of Portugal's best-preserved medieval towns, Évora's imposing outer walls give way to winding cobblestone lanes dotted with architectural gems from the Romans, Visigoths, Moors, and the Middle Ages. It's also a lively university town, and a good base from which to explore Alentejo.

Side Trips from Évora. Visit some of Portugal's best-kept secrets—rustic wineries, horse farms, medieval castles, Roman ruins, and prehistoric stone sculptures—all within day-tripping distance from Évora. Tapestries and carpets from the unassuming little village of Arraiolos are famous the world over.

Alto Alentejo. Portugal's most stunning walled fortresses and cliff-top castles dot the province's northern half, along the frontier with its old archenemy, Spain. With the highest mountains in southern Portugal, this area has a more varied landscape than the flatter south, and is the country's best-kept secret for hiking and mountain-biking.

Baixo Alentejo. This is Portugal's breadbasket, with undulating wheat fields, olive groves, and cork forests that stretch to golden dunes and dramatic cliffs over the Atlantic.

PLANNING

WHEN TO GO

Spring comes early to this part of Portugal. Early April to mid-June is a wonderful time to tour, when the fields are full of colorful wildflowers. July and August are brutally hot, with temperatures in places such as Beja often reaching 37°C (100°F) or higher. By mid-September things cool off sufficiently to make touring this region a delight.

PLANNING YOUR TIME

You should allow 10 days to get a feel for the region, exploring Évora and visiting some outlying attractions such as Monsaraz, Castelo de Vide, and Mértola. This will also allow time for a day or two of sunbathing on a west-coast beach. If you skip the beach, you can cover the most interesting attractions at a comfortable pace in seven days. Three days will give you time to explore Évora and its surroundings along with one or two additional highlights.

GETTING HERE AND AROUND

AIR TRAVEL

You can fly into the Lisbon or Faro airports and then take ground transportation into the region. Évora is roughly 130 km (80 mi) from Lisbon and about 225 km (140 mi) from Faro.

Airports Faro Airport (☎ 289/800617 or 289/800801). **Lisbon Airport** (☎ 21/841–3500 or 21/841–3700 ⊕ www.ana.pt).

BUS TRAVEL

There are few places in this region that aren't served by at least one bus daily. Express coaches run by several regional lines travel regularly between Lisbon and the larger towns such as Évora, Beja, and Estremoz. Because several companies leave for the Alentejo from different terminals in Lisbon, it's best to have a travel agent do your booking. Standard buses between Lisbon and Évora run at least once every hour between 6 am and 9:30 pm, and cost €12.

Bus Contacts Belos Transportes S.A. (✉ Nova Garogem Rodoviaria, Évora ☎ 266/769410 ✉ Av. 9 de Abril 57, Estremoz ☎ 268/322282). **Eva Transportes** (✉ Praça Marechal Humberto Delgado, Estrada das Laranjeiras, Lisbon ☎ 808/224488 or 213/581466 ⊕ www.eva-bus.com). **Rede Nacional de Expressos** (✉ Rodoviaria do Alentejo, Terminal Rodoviario, Évora ☎ 266/769410 ⊕ www.rede-expressos.pt).

CAR TRAVEL

One of the best features of Alentejo is its seemingly untouched beaches and villages—for which you'll need a car to reach. Driving will give you access to many out-of-the-way spots. A good network of modern toll roads crisscrossing the country, as well as very little traffic, makes driving quick but expensive. A two-hour drive on the main A6 toll road from Lisbon to Évora costs about €10 for a standard sedan, and about €15 for an SUV. There are no confusing big cities in which to get lost, although parking can be a problem in some of the towns such as Évora.

The toll highway A6, which branches off A2 running south from Lisbon, takes you as far as the Spanish border at Caia, where it links up with the highway from Madrid. This road provides easy access to Évora and the Upper Alentejo. The A2 runs south to the Algarve, as does the nontoll IP1/E01. Farther inland and south of Évora, the IP2/E802 is the best access for Beja and southeastern Alentejo. The N521 runs 105 km (65 mi) from Cáceres, Spain, to the Portuguese border near Portalegre. To the south, the N433 runs from Seville, Spain, to Beja, 225 km (140 mi) away.

Car Rentals **121carhireportugal.com** (⊕ *www.121carhireportugal.com*). **Algarve Car Hire** (⊕ *www.carhire-algarve.com*). **Aluvia Rent-A-Car** (✉ *Rua Professor Henrique de Barros, No. 26A, Loja 10, Lisbon.* **Auriga-Crown Car Hire** (✉ *Aeroporto Internacional de Faro, Faro* ☎ 289/800670 ✎ *faro@aurigacrown.com*). **Faro Car Hire** (✉ *Apartado 488, Portimao, Algarve* ☎ 960/204709 ⊕ *www.farocar.com*). **Portugal-auto-rentals.com** (⊕ *www.portugal-auto-rentals.com*).

Traffic Info **Estradas** (⊕ *www.estradas.pt*).

TRAIN TRAVEL

The Portuguese government has approved plans for a high-speed rail network stretching across Alto Alentejo, which will eventually cut train travel time between Madrid and Lisbon from nine hours to as few as four, but the service isn't scheduled to debut until at least 2015. Until then, train travel in the vast Alentejo is not for people in a great hurry. Service to the more remote destinations is infrequent—and in some cases nonexistent. A couple of towns, including Évora and Beja, are connected with Lisbon by several trains daily. The Intercidades train leaves from Lisbon's Oriente Station in the Parque da Nações to the Alentejo. You can also catch the Intercidades train at Lisbon's Entrecampos Station.

Train Stations **Beja CP Train Station** (✉ *Largo da Estação* ☎ 284/326135). **Évora CP Train Station** (✉ *Largo da Estação* ☎ 266/742336).

RESTAURANTS

In the Alentejo, the country's granary, bread is a major part of most meals. It's the basis of a popular dish known as *açorda,* a thick, stick-to-the-ribs porridge to which various ingredients such as fish, meat, and eggs are added. Açorda *de marisco*—bread with eggs, seasonings, and assorted shellfish—is one of the more popular varieties. Another version, açorda *alentejana,* consists of a clear broth, olive oil, garlic, coriander (cilantro), slices of bread, and poached eggs. *Cação,* also called baby shark or dogfish, is a white-meat fish with a single bone down the back and is mostly served in a fish soup or as part of a porridge.

Pork from the Alentejo is the best in the country and often is combined with clams, onions, and tomatoes in the classic dish *carne de porco à alentejana.* One of Portugal's most renowned sheep's milk cheeses—tangy, but mellow when properly ripened—is made in the Serpa region. Alentejo wines—especially those from around Borba, Reguengos de Monsaraz, and Vidigueira—are regular prizewinners at national tasting contests.

Elvas, near the Spanish border, is known for its tasty sugar plums. *Ameixas D'Elvas* (Elvas plums) were exported with port wine to England and the Americas and became a popular Christmas sweet among the English. The plums are the green, very sweet Rainha Claúdia variety. The Alto Alentejo region offers the best climate for growing them and pesticides aren't used. As the supply is small and the demand is great, the plums are considered a gourmet treat. They can be eaten fresh, as prunes, dipped in a sugar syrup, candied, or as a jam.

Between mid-June and mid-September reservations are advised at upscale restaurants. Many moderate or inexpensive establishments, however, don't accept reservations and have informal dining rooms where you share a table with other diners. Dress at all but the most luxurious restaurants is casual.

HOTELS

The best accommodation in Alentejo has long been considered the chain of government-run *pousadas,* hotels housed in historic properties like medieval convents or castles. But the pousadas' reign has been challenged recently by a new crop of private luxury hotels, such as the twin Hotel M'AR De AR properties in Évora, that provide better value and luxury services. The pousadas have recently begun lowering their rates to compete—good news to travelers. Still, some of the finest pousadas in the country are in the Alentejo, including one in the old Lóios convent in Évora and another in the castle at Estremoz. Many of the pousadas are small, some with as few as six rooms, so reserving well in advance is essential. There are also a number of high-quality, government-approved private guesthouses in the region. Look for signs that say "Turismo Rural" or "Turismo de Habitação." In summer, air-conditioning is absolutely necessary in Évora, where temperatures can soar to more than 44°C (110°F).

WHAT IT COSTS IN EUROS					
	¢	$	$$	$$$	$$$$
Restaurants	under €10	€10–€15	€16–€20	€21–€25	over €25
Hotels	under €80	€80–€140	€141–€200	€201–€260	over €260

Restaurant prices are per person for a main course at dinner. Hotel prices are for a standard double room, including tax, in high season (off-season rates may be lower).

EMERGENCIES

Beja and Évora have hospitals with emergency rooms, and their approaches are marked "Hospital"; the emergency room is marked "Urgências." All sizable towns have at least one drugstore that's open weekends, holidays, and after normal store hours. Local newspapers usually keep a schedule, and notices are posted on all pharmacy doors. Across Portugal and most of Europe, dial 1-1-2 for emergencies, which is the local equivalent of 9-1-1.

Emergencies Évora Police (⊠ *Rua Francisco S. Lusitano, Évora* ☎ *266/702022*). **General emergencies** (☎ *112*). **Hospital da Misericordia** (⊠ *Av. Sanches de Miranda, Évora* ☎ *266/760630*). **Hospital Distrital** (⊠ *Rua Dr. António F. C. Lima, Beja* ☎ *284/310200*). **Hospital do Espírito Santo** (⊠ *Largo Sr. da Pobreza, Évora* ☎ *266/740100 or 266/758424*).

VISITOR INFO

The tourist office in Évora can schedule a variety of guided or unguided tours of megalithic sites, area wineries, and other attractions by bus, van, horse-drawn carriage, or foot. Many of the major sites are also covered by a wide selection of day tours from Lisbon.

Contacts Association of Tour Guides in Alentejo (*AGIA* ☎ *963/702/392* ⊕ *www.alentejoguides.com*). **Cityrama** (⊠ *Av. Praia da Vitória 12-B, Saldanha, Lisbon* ☎ *21/319–1085* ⊕ *www.cityrama.pt*). **RSI Sightseeing Tours** (⊠ *Edificio de St. Catarina 12-Lj 4, Évora* ☎ *266/747871 or 266/747872* ✐ *info.Évora@rsi-viagens.com*).

Great Itineraries

You can make convenient loops starting and finishing in Lisbon, or you can extend your travels by continuing south to the Algarve from Beja or Santiago do Cacém. You should allow 10 days to get a feel for the region, exploring Évora and visiting some outlying attractions such as Monsaraz, Castelo de Vide, and Mértola. This will also allow time for a day or two of sunbathing on a west-coast beach. If you skip the beach, you can cover the most interesting attractions at a comfortable pace in seven days. Three days will give you time to explore Évora and its surroundings along with one or two additional highlights.

Numbers in the text correspond to numbers in the margin and on the Évora, the Upper Alentejo, and the Lower Alentejo maps.

IF YOU HAVE 3 DAYS

Be sure to include **Évora**, one of Portugal's most beautiful cities, in your first day of exploring. The following morning visit the rug-producing town of **Arraiolos** and then continue on to **Estremoz** and its imposing fortress,

which doubles as a pousada. Head east past Borba and its marble quarries to **Vila Viçosa**, site of the Paço Ducal. Then continue south to the white-washed village of **Terena**. In the morning visit the fortified hilltop town of **Monsaraz** before returning to Lisbon.

IF YOU HAVE 7 DAYS

After a day and night in **Évora**, head to the **Aqueduto da Agua da Prata** and the prehistoric sites just outside town, which include the **Cromlech and the Menhir of Almendres** and the **Dolmen of Zambujeiro**. On the way to your next overnight stop in **Estremoz**, take a break in **Arraiolos**. From Estremoz head east to the fortified town of **Elvas**, stopping en route at the Paço Ducal in **Vila Viçosa**. The following day continue to **Monsaraz**, with a stop along the way at **Terena**. From Monsaraz head south to **Beja**, inspecting the Roman ruins at **São Cucufate** en route. The next day head west to **Santiago do Cacém** for more Roman ruins and a few hours at the beach. On your seventh day return to Lisbon, stopping along the way to see the castle at **Alcácer do Sal**.

ÉVORA

130 km (81 mi) southeast of Lisbon.

Dressed in traditional garb, shepherds and farmers with faces wizened by a lifetime in the baking sun stand around the fountain at Praça do Giraldo; a group of college girls dressed in jeans and T-shirts chats animatedly at a sidewalk café; a local businessman in coat and tie purposefully hurries by; and clusters of tourists, cameras in hand, capture the historic monuments on film—all this is part of a typical summer's day in Évora. The flourishing capital of the central Alentejo is also a university town with an astonishing variety of inspiring architecture. Atop a small hill in the heart of a vast cork-, olive-, and grain-producing region, Évora stands out from provincial farm towns the world over: the entire inner city is a monument and was declared a UNESCO World Heritage site in 1986.

GETTING HERE AND AROUND

Évora is, above all, a town for walking. Wherever you glance as you stroll the maze of narrow streets and alleys of the Cidade Velha (Old Town), amid arches and whitewashed houses, you'll come face to face with reminders of the town's rich architectural and cultural heritage. West of Praça do Giraldo, between Rua Serpa Pinto and Rua dos Mercadores you have the old Jewish quarter of narrow streets lined with medieval houses. A tourist bus (€1 for all-day ticket) sponsored by the city follows a blue line marked on the street through the historic center. To get on just raise your hand anywhere along the blue line; you can get off whenever you wish. The area surrounding Évora is a rich agricultural region with scattered small villages and some of Portugal's earliest inhabited sites.

Cabs within Évora's city limits and outside the city limits charge €0.55 per kilometer. Note that if you travel to another town from Évora, such as Beja, you'll have to pay for the taxi's return trip. To get a cab, head for one of the many taxi stands around town, such as the one in Praça do Giraldo (you can't hail them on the street) or call Radio Taxis Évora.

TIMING

Allow at least 2½ hours to tour Évora, or even three, depending on how long you decide to spend relaxing with a drink in the gardens.

SAFETY AND PRECAUTIONS

Wear comfortable shoes! Like all of Portugal's medieval towns, Évora's marble and limestone cobblestones are charming, but they can be treacherous underfoot, especially in rain or high heels.

VISITOR AND TOUR INFO

Walking tours of Évora are available through RSI and Mendes e Murteira, and both companies can also organize bus or van tours of the district's archaeological sites. AGIA (⇨ *see contact info above*) offers 90-minute guided tours of Évora.

The Évora tourist office is helpful and can schedule tours or make phone calls to hotels or restaurants. The Alentejo wine route office is also open daily for tastings and can help schedule visits to local wineries.

ESSENTIALS

Carriage Tours Circuitos Turisticos (✉ *Rue Miguel Bombarda 37, Évora* ☎ *266/702717 or 266/705127* ✎ *reservas@turalentejo.webside.pt*).

Taxi Radio Taxis Évora (☎ *266/734734*).

Tour Info Mendes e Murteira (✉ *Rua 31 de Janeiro 15-A, Évora* ☎ *266/739240 or 917/236025* ✎ *m.murteira@mail.telepac.pt*). **RSI Sightseeing Tours** (✉ *Edificio de St. Catarina 12-Lj 4, Évora* ☎ *266/747871 or 266/747872* ✎ *info.Évora@ rsi-viagens.com*).

Visitor Info Évora Tourist Office (✉ *Praça do Giraldo 73* ☎ *266/777071* ⊕ *www.cm-evora.pt* ☉ *Apr.–Oct., 9–7, Nov.–Mar., 9–6*). **Região de Turismo de Évora** (✉ *Rua de Aviz 90, Évora* ☎ *266/730440*). **Rotas dos Vinhos do Alentejo** (✉ *Praça Joaquim Antonio de Aguiar 20-21* ☎ *266/746498* ⊕ *www.vinhosdoalentejo.pt* ☉ *Mon. 2–7, Tues.–Fri. 11–7, Sat. 10–1*).

Évora

R. da Mouraria

Largo
dos Duques
de Cadaval

R. do Colégio

R. José Elias Garcia

R. do Menino Jesus

R. de D. Isabel

Jardim
de Diana

Largo do
Colégio

Largo
do Conde
de Vila Flor

R. da Freiria de Cima

R. Gabriel Victor do
Monte Pereira

R. João de Deus

Largo
Alexandre
Herculano

R. do Conde da Serra
da Toureja

R. de Machede

R. do Alfeirão

R. 5 de Outubro

Jardim
do Chá

R. de Serpa Pinto

Évora
Tourist
Office

R. de Diogo Cão

R. de Valdevinos

R. da Moeda

Largo da
Misericórdia

R. da
Misericórdia

Cordovil
Mansion

Largo
dos
Mercadores

R. da

Largo de
Alvaro Velho

R. das Três Senhoras

R. do Raimundo

República

Largo
da
Graça

Largo da
Dr. Alves
Branco

R. Bernardo Matos

R. Romão Ramalho

Praça
1 de
Maio

R. da Rampa

R. Romão Ramalho

Capela
dos Ossos

R. do Cicioso

R. 24 de Julho

R. do Albarim

Jardim
Municipal

R. da República

Av. da Gulbenkian

Av. Marechal Carmona

Praça de
Touros

A BIT OF HISTORY

Although the region was inhabited some 4,000 years ago—as attested to by the dolmens and menhirs in the countryside—it was during the Roman epoch that the town called Liberalitas Julia in the province of Lusitania first achieved importance. A large part of present-day Évora is built on Roman foundations, of which the Temple of Diana, with its graceful Corinthian columns, is the most conspicuous reminder.

The Moors also made a great historical impact on the area. They arrived in 715 and remained more than 450 years. They were driven out in 1166, thanks in part to a clever ruse perpetrated by Geraldo Sem Pavor (Gerald the Fearless). Geraldo tricked Évora's Moorish ruler into leaving a strategic watchtower unguarded. With a small force, Geraldo took control of the tower. To regain control of it, most of the Moorish troops left their posts at the city's main entrance, allowing the bulk of Geraldo's forces to march in unopposed.

Toward the end of the 12th century Évora's fortunes increased as the town became the favored location for the courts of the Burgundy and Avis dynasties. It attracted many of the great minds and creative talents of Renaissance Portugal. Some of the more prominent residents at this time were Gil Vicente, the founder of Portuguese theater; the sculptor Nicolas Chanterene; and Gregorio Lopes, the painter known for his renderings of court life. Such a concentration of royal wealth and creativity superimposed upon the existing Moorish town was instrumental in the development of the delicate Manueline-Mudéjar (elaborate, Moslem-influenced) architectural style. You can see fine examples of this in the graceful lines of the Palácio de Dom Manuel and the turreted Ermida de São Bras.

EXPLORING

Note that unless otherwise specified, few of the churches mentioned below have regular visiting hours. To view the interiors of the others you may have to sit in on a mass (times for services are usually posted on church doors) and look around afterward.

TOP ATTRACTIONS

Igreja de São Francisco. After the Sé, this is the grandest of Évora's churches. Its construction in the early 16th century, on the site of a former Gothic chapel, involved the greatest talents of the day, including Nicolas Chanterene, Oliver of Ghent, and the Arruda brothers, Francisco and Diogo. The magnificent architecture notwithstanding, the bizarre **Capela dos Ossos** (Chapel of Bones) is the main attraction. The translation of the chilling inscription over the entrance reads "We Bones Who Are Here Are Waiting for Yours." The bones of some 5,000 skeletons dug up from cemeteries in the area line the ceilings and supporting columns. With a flair worthy of Charles Addams, a 16th-century Franciscan monk placed skulls jaw-to-cranium so they form arches across the ceiling; arm and leg bones are neatly stacked to shape the supporting columns. ■ TIP➔ **It costs €1 to take photos anywhere in the church or chapel.** ⊠ *Praça 1 de Maio*

☎ 266/704521 🎟 €2 adults, €1.50 students and seniors ☉ Mon.–Sat. 9–12:45 and 2:30–5:10, Sun. 10–12:45.

NEED A BREAK?

Off Rua 24 de Julho, a few steps from the Igreja de São Francisco, the **Jardim Municipal** *(Municipal Gardens)* is a pleasant place to rest after the rigors of sightseeing. The extensive and verdant gardens are landscaped with plants and trees from all over the world.

Fodor's Choice
★

Igreja dos Lóios (*Lóios Church or Igreja Sao Joao*). This small church next to the former Convento dos Lóios, which is now the Pousada dos Lóios, houses one of the most impressive displays of 18th-century *azulejos* (painted and glazed ceramic tiles) anywhere in Portugal. The sanctuary, dedicated to St. John the Evangelist, was founded in the 15th century by the Venetian-based Lóios Order. Its interior walls are covered with azulejos created by Oliveira Bernardes, the foremost master of this unique Portuguese art form. The blue-and-white tiles depict scenes from the life of the church's founder, Rodrigo de Melo, who, along with members of his family, is buried here. The bas-relief marble tombstones at the foot of the high altar are the only ones of their kind in Portugal. Note the two metal hatches on either side of the main aisle: one covers an ancient cistern, which belonged to the Moorish castle that predated the church (an underground spring still supplies the cistern with potable water), and beneath the other hatch lie the neatly stacked bones of hundreds of monks. This bizarre ossuary was uncovered in 1958 during restoration work. Enhanced by the 16th-century Renaissance gallery, the cloister is now an integral part of the Pousada dos Lóios. ■ TIP→ **No photos are allowed.** ✉ *Largo do Conde de Vila Flor* ☎ 967/979763 🎟 €3 for church, €5 for combined ticket with Cadaval Palace ☉ Tues.–Sun. 9–12:30 pm and 2–6 pm.

Museu de Évora *(Évora Museum)*. Reopened in 2008 after renovations, the museum is in a stately, late-17th-century baroque building between the Sé and the Largo do Conde de Vila Flor, a plaza that's the site of several important structures. The museum, once a palace that accommodated bishops, contains a rich collection of sculpture and paintings as well as interesting archaeological and architectural artifacts. The first-floor galleries, arranged around a pleasant garden, include several excellent carved pillars and a fine Manueline doorway. Highlights of the collection are in the meantime being exhibited at the Igreja de Santa Clara on Rua Serpa Pinto. ✉ *Largo do Conde de Vila Flor* ☎ 266/702604 ⊕ *www.ipmuseus.pt* 🎟 €4 ☉ Tues. 2–6, Wed.–Sun. 10–6.

Fodor's Choice
★

Praça do Giraldo. The arcade-lined square in the center of the old walled city is named after Évora's liberator, Gerald the Fearless. During Caesar's time the square, marked by a large arch, was the Roman forum. In 1571 the arch was destroyed to make room for the fountain, a simple half sphere made of white Estremoz marble and designed by the Renaissance architect Afonso Álvares.

NEED A BREAK?

The **Café Arcada** (✉ *Praça do Giraldo, Rua do Raimundo 7* ☎ *266/741777* ☉ *Daily 8 am–10:30 pm*), opposite the fountain on Praça do Giraldo, is an Évora institution. The large hall, divided into snack bar and restaurant sections, is decorated with photos of the big bands that played here in the 1940s. Tables on the square are just the place from which to watch the city on parade.

Rua 5 de Outubro. The narrow cobblestone pedestrian thoroughfare is lined with souvenir shops and whitewashed houses with wrought-iron balconies. It's one of the town's most attractive streets and connects the Praça do Giraldo and the cathedral.

Fodor's Choice ★ **Sé.** Two massive asymmetrical towers and battlement-ringed walls give the Sé a fortresslike appearance. The transitional Gothic-style cathedral was constructed in 1186 from huge granite blocks. It has been enhanced over the centuries with an octagonal, turreted dome above the transept; a blue-tile spire atop the north tower; a number of fine Manueline windows; and several Gothic rose windows. At the entrance, Gothic arches are supported by marble columns bearing delicately sculpted statues of the apostles. With the exception of a fine baroque chapel, the granite interior is somber. The cloister, a 14th-century Gothic addition with Mudéjar vestiges, is one of the finest of its type in the country. Statues of the evangelists decorate the corners. Housed in the Sé's towers and chapter room is the **Museu de Arte Sacra da Sé** (Sacred Art Museum). Of particular interest is a 13th-century ivory *Virgin of Paradise*, whose body opens up to show exquisitely carved scenes of her life. Her head is a 16th-century wooden replacement, strangely out of proportion with her figure. ✉ *Largo Marquês de Marialva* ☎ *266/759330* ✆ *Cathedral, cloister, tower, museum €4.50; cathedral, cloister, tower €3.50; cathedral and cloister €2.50; cathedral only €1.50* ⊙ *May–Aug., daily 9–5; Sept.–April, daily 9–12:30 and 2–5 (last admission 1 hr before closing).*

NEED A BREAK? Just behind the **Sé**, Jardim do Cha's (✉ *Largo Dr. Mario Chico 7 Évora* ☎ *266/702367*) leafy terrace provides a refuge from the tourist track and a comfortable place to contemplate history over a cup of herbal tea. The café also offers yoga and vegetarian cooking classes.

Fodor's Choice ★ **Templo Romano** *(Roman Temple).* The well-preserved ruins of the Roman Temple dominate Largo do Conde de Vila Flor. The edifice, considered one of the finest of its kind on the Iberian Peninsula, was probably built in the 1st to 2nd century AD. Although it has long been referred to as the Temple of Diana, historians believe that the use of the Corinthian order of architecture in its columns and entablature indicates that it was dedicated to an emperor. The temple, largely destroyed during the invasions of the barbarian tribes in the early 5th century, was later used for various purposes, including that of municipal slaughterhouse in the 14th century. It was restored to its present state in 1871. ✉ *Largo do Conde de Vila Flor.*

WORTH NOTING

Jardim de Diana *(Diana Garden).* Opposite the Templo Romano, the restful, tree-lined park looks out over the aqueduct and the plains from the modest heights of what is sometimes grandiosely referred to as "Évora's Acropolis." You can take in nearly 2,000 years of Portuguese history from here. One sweeping glance encompasses the temple, the spires of the Gothic Sé, the Igreja dos Lóios, and the 20th-century pousada housed in the convent. A garden café at the corner of the park is a great spot to reflect on the architectural marvels before you, with a glass of port in hand. ⊠ *Largo do Conde de Vila Flor.*

Largo das Portas de Moura. One of Évora's most beautiful squares is characterized by paired stone towers that guard one of the principal entrances to the walled old city. The spires of the Sé rise above the towers, and in the center of the square is an unusual Renaissance fountain. The large white-marble sphere, supported by a single column, bears a commemorative inscription in Latin dated 1556. Overlooking the fountain is the Cordovil Mansion, on whose terrace are several particularly attractive arches decorated in the Manueline-Mudéjar style. ⊠ *Bounded by Ruas D. Augusto Eduardo Nunes, Enrique da Fonseca, Mendes Esteves, de Machede, and Miguel Bombarda, a 5-min walk southeast of the Sé.*

NEED A BREAK?

Off the Largo das Portas de Moura, the old Cordovil Mansion has reopened as **Boa Boca** (⊠ *Largo da Portas de Moura 25* ☎ *266/704632* ⊕ *www.boaboca-gourmet.com* ☯ *Weekdays 10–1 and 3–7, Sat. 10:30–1),* a gourmet emporium exhibiting homemade Portuguese products: wine, tea, chocolate, and liqueurs.

Palácio de Dom Manuel. At the entrance to the Jardim Municipal, only a part of this former royal palace remains. The existing wing was restored after a fire in 1916 and displays a row of paired, gracefully curved Manueline windows. On the building's south side there's a notable arcade of redbrick sawtooth arches. Currently used as an art gallery, the palace has witnessed a number of historic events since its construction in the late 15th century. It was here, for instance, in 1497, that Vasco da Gama received his commission to command the fleet that would discover the sea route to India.

WHERE TO EAT

¢ ✕ **Adega do Alentejano.** Dine on hearty, simple food with in-the-know
PORTUGUESE locals at this pleasantly rustic Alentejo wine cellar. Walk through the beaded curtain made of wine corks into a simple dining room with red-and-white-checkered tablecloths, blue-and-white-tiled walls, and huge Roman-style clay wine jugs. The signature dish is tomato soup, a meal in itself, with soaked bread, a poached egg, and dried sausage served on the side. Black pork steaks are also a specialty. Stick to the very reasonable local wine from the barrel, and you'll be agreeably surprised by the bill. ⊠ *Rua Gabriel Vito do Monte Pereira 21* ☎ *266/706796* ▭ *No credit cards* ☯ *Closed Sun.*

$ ✕ **Cozinha de Santo Humberto.** One of Évora's oldest restaurants was
PORTUGUESE once a wine cellar. Try the *sopa de peixe alentejana* (a mixed fish soup) or the *carne de porco com ameijoas* (small pieces of pork sautéed with clams). Game dishes such as grouse, wild boar, and partridge are particularly good in season (Santo Humberto, is, after all, the patron saint of hunters). The list of Alentejo wines is excellent. There's a cheaper café attached. ⊠ *Rua da Moeda 39* ☎ *266/704251* ▭ *AE, DC, MC, V.*

5

$ ✕ **O Fialho.** The charming elderly
PORTUGUESE   owner, Amor Fialho, is the third
Fodor'sChoice   generation of Fialhos to operate
★   this popular, traditional restaurant.
He doesn't speak English but takes
kindly to foreign visitors, and may
invite you into the kitchen to see
his delicacies prepared, or take you
on a tour of his rustic dining room,
complete with photos of the Spanish king's visit. The rustic dining
room, with a beamed ceiling and
painted plates hung on its walls, is
regularly packed on weekends, and
reservations for Saturday or Sunday
are essential. Fialho's renowned specialties are *Borrego assado* (roasted
lamb) or *perdiz de convento a car-
tuxa* (roast partridge with potatoes
and carrots), made according to a
recipe from a nearby monastery.
There's a wide selection of Alentejo
wines. ✉ *Travessa das Mascarenhas
16* ☎ *266/703079* ⌚ *Reservations essential on weekends* ▭ *AE, DC,
MC, V* ⊘ *Closed Mon.*

> **SHOPPING**
>
> The brightly colored hand-painted
> plates, bowls, and figurines from
> the Upper Alentejo are popular
> throughout Portugal. The best
> selection of this distinctive type
> of folk art is in and around
> Estremoz, where the terra-cotta
> jugs and bowls are adorned with
> chips of marble from local quar-
> ries. Saturday morning the *rossio*
> (town square) is chock-full of
> vendors displaying their wares.
> Redondo and the village of São
> Pedro do Corval, near Reguen-
> gos de Monsaraz, are also good
> sources of this type of pottery, as
> is Évora. The village of Arraiolos,
> near Évora, is famous for its hand-
> embroidered wool rugs.

$$ ✕ **Tasquinha do Oliveira.** The charming husband-and-wife duo of Manuel
PORTUGUESE   and Carolina own and operate this tiny upscale dining room with huge
taste. Intricately decorated with local ceramics and bottles of local wine
lining the walls, there are only 14 seats in the entire restaurant, creat-
ing the atmosphere of the Oliveiras' own family dining room where
you'll rub shoulders (literally) with other guests. The tiny size makes
reservations essential, and the restaurant is frequently booked solid with
birthday parties and other events on Friday and Saturday nights. Spe-
cialties are lamb, pork, and game dishes, served up by Carolina in the
open kitchen, while Manuel runs the show outside. There are excellent
Alentejo wines on offer. ✉ *Rua Cándido dos Reis 45-A* ☎ *266/744841*
⌚ *Reservations essential on weekends* ▭ *AE, MC, V* ⊘ *Closed Sun.
and Aug. 1–15.*

WHERE TO STAY

$$ ⊡ **Hotel M'AR De AR Aqueduto.** The only five-star hotel inside Évora's old
Fodor'sChoice   city walls, this new property opened in 2008 as the premier place to stay.
★   Its luxury is unmatched, with stark, modern decor that manages to echo
the city's medieval character. Just inside the lobby, you can look down
through a glass floor to see the ruins of an ancient cistern preserved
under the building, which was once a 16th-century palace and convent.
Rooms are spacious, with views over a wonderful central courtyard and
swimming pool surrounded by an orange grove. The building seamlessly
connects to the city's old walls and aqueduct, of which most rooms offer
spectacular views. With this incredible hotel, the M'AR De AR hotel

chain is challenging Portugal's pousadas, offering better amenities, more luxury, and unbeatable service for less money than the sometimes dowdy and cramped pousadas. Aqueduto offers an array of activities, from Alentejan cooking classes to horseback or bicycle tours of the countryside, and wine-tasting trips to a nearby convent. The luxurious spa is also open to the public. **Pros:** best hotel in Évora; offers supreme luxury at a competitive price. **Cons:** some visitors might find the modern style a bit stark or cold. ⊠ *Rua Cândido dos Reis 72* ☎ *266/740700* ⊕ *www.mardearhotels. com* 🛏 *64 rooms, 4 suites, 2 rooms with built-in spa facilities* 🔽 *In-room: a/c, safe, refrigerator, DVD (some), Internet, Wi-Fi. In-hotel: 2 restaurants, room service, bar, pool, gym, spa, bicycles, children's programs (ages 4–12), laundry service, Internet terminal, Wi-Fi hotspot, parking (free)* ▭ *AE, D, DC, MC, V* ⦿ *CP, MAP, FAP.*

$$$ ▣ **Pousada dos Lóios.** This luxurious pousada is in the 16th-century convent opposite the Templo Romano. Renovated in 2004, the former nuns' quarters and monks' cells have been polished off with modern conveniences, retaining their old-world style but with no trace of monastic austerity. Opulent period furnishings dot bedrooms and elegant public spaces that deserve a visit even if you don't plan to spend the night. Order a glass of tawny and perch by the fireplace in the charming, fit-for-a-king lobby. Superbly prepared Alentejo specialties are served in the restaurant ($–$$$), a marvel of Manueline details. Although a crop of newer, more affordable luxury hotels are increasingly luring travelers away from Alentejo's pousadas, the Pousada dos Lóios is an exception, with a loyal international clientele willing to pay for its extraordinary history and setting. **Pros:** arguably Portugal's most famous and stately pousada, located in the heart of Évora's historic center; free guided tours included. **Cons:** expensive for what you get; small bathrooms and narrow hallways; packed mostly with fellow foreigners. ⊠ *Largo do Conde de Vila Flor* ☎ *266/730070* ⊕ *www.pousadas.pt* 🛏 *36 rooms, 1 suite* 🔽 *In-room: a/c, safe, Wi-Fi (some). In-hotel: restaurant, room service, bar, pool, children's programs (ages 3–12), laundry service, Wi-Fi hotspot, parking (free), Internet terminal* ▭ *AE, DC, MC, V* ⦿ *CP, FAP, MAP.*

¢ ▣ **Residencial Policarpo.** This charming, family-run guesthouse offers one of the best values in Évora. Every room is unique, with high ceilings, wood beams, and hand-painted local furniture. This hotel, in a quiet section of the city behind the cathedral, is a great choice for families, with several different options for rooms of different sizes and numbers of beds, and private parking out back. A French-Portuguese couple have raised their children and grandchildren here, and are especially helpful with local tips for places off-the-beaten tourist path. Couples should ask for room 101, a special suite with tiled walls and a towering wooden bed, or room 202, with a spectacular view of the cathedral. **Pros:** family hospitality, local antiques, art gallery in breakfast room. **Cons:** only half of rooms have air-conditioning and en suite bathrooms. ⊠ *Rua da Freiria de Baixo 16, Rua Conde da Serra da Tourega, Évora* ☎ *266/702424* ⊕ *www.pensaopolicarpo.com* 🛏 *19 rooms* 🔽 *In-room: a/c (some), no TV (some), Wi-Fi. In-hotel: no restaurant, room service (breakfast only), bar, bicycles, children's programs (ages 3–12), Internet terminal, Wi-Fi hotspot, parking (free)* ▭ *No credit cards.*

$ ⊡ **Solar de Monfalim.** In a historic 16th-century nobleman's quarters with a delightful arched gallery overlooking the street, this comfortable, family-run guesthouse provides quiet, old-fashioned hospitality in the heart of the old city. Climb the winding outer stone staircase lined with blue-and-white tiles and flowers and have a cool drink on the shaded veranda or a hot chocolate in front of a roaring fire. Under new management since April 2009, the simple, spacious rooms have been updated throughout. History buffs will love the antiques and musical instruments on display. This hotel is a favorite for architecture lovers and visiting professors. ■TIP→ **Children under 8 stay free. Pros:** an architectural gem with charming, family-oriented hospitality in the heart of the old city. **Cons:** winding entry staircase means no access for handicapped or disabled; no restaurant in the guesthouse. ⊠ *Largo da Misericórdia 1* ☎ *266/750000* ⊕ *www.monfalimtur.pt* ⇄ *26 rooms* ⌂ *In-room: a/c, safe, Wi-Fi. In-hotel: room service (breakfast only), bar, bicycle rental, Internet terminal, Wi-Fi hotspot, parking (paid)* ⊟ *AE, MC, V* ⫧⊙⫧ *CP.*

NIGHTLIFE AND THE ARTS

Bar Alarga (⊠ *Praça 1° de Maio 14* ☎ *266/746257*) is a nightclub popular with students from the nearby university. Drink specials include fruity cocktails and Brazilian caipirinhas. Open from 10 pm to 3 am.

Cosa Nostra (⊠ *Pateo do Salema 9* ☎ *266/771140*) is a bistro and lounge club with a quiet bar and terrace that gets busier after midnight. Hours and admission prices vary depending on events; check with the local tourist office for current listings.

Every July the Casa Cadaval hosts the **Festival Évora Clássica** (⊠ *Jardim do Paço* ☎ *266/744300*), during which nationally and internationally renowned classical musicians perform, including the Gulbenkian Orchestra. Performances are held at the Garcia de Resende Theater and the Palácio das 5 Quinas. Tickets cost €10–€15.

The dance club **Praxis Clube** (⊠ *Rua de Valdevinos 21* ☎ *No phone*) has two dance floors, one for house music and the other for chart favorites.

SHOPPING

Rua 5 de Outubro is lined with shops selling regional handicrafts such as painted furniture, hand-painted ceramics, leather, cork, basketwork, ironwork, rugs, and quilted blankets.

At the top of Rua 5 de Outubro, **O Cesto Artesano** (⊠ *Rua 5 de Outubro 57-A/77* ☎ *266/703344* ⬠ *o.cesto@hotmail.com* ☉ *Daily 9–7*) specializes in local cork products and ceramics.

O Pierrot (⊠ *Rua 5 de Outubro 67-A* ☎ *266/703021* ⊕ *www.opierrot. net* ☉ *Closed Mon.*) sells Alentejo regional handicrafts, from cork and leather to furniture and Alentejo wines. **Mont'Sobro** (⊠ *Rua 5 de Outubro 66* ☎ *266/704609* ⊕ *www.montsobro.com* ☉ *Daily 9:30–7*) focuses solely on handmade cork products, and sells everything from cork photo frames and handbags to cork-lined umbrellas.

For local Alentejo wines, cheese, ham and port, pop into **Charcutaria Macaroca** (⊠ *Rua 5 de Outubro 61* ☉ *Daily 10–7*) for a delicious selection of Évora's finest gourmet products. Opened in July 2010, owner Maria Saragoca plans a free international shipping service for her products as well.

Outside the city gate, the workshop of Portugal's most internationally known sculptor, **João Cutileiro** (⊠ *Estrada de Viana 13* ☎ *266/703972* ✎ *jc.ml@netvisao.pt*), can be visited by appointment. He works in the finest Alentejo and imported marble. Some of his best pieces are female nudes, historical figures, and trees. His most famous sculpture is a statue of Sebastian of Portugal, inaugurated in 1973 in Lagos, in the Algarve. To arrange a visit, you must first call between noon and 1, or 4, and 8 to make an appointment, or send an email.

SPORTS AND THE OUTDOORS

FOUR-WHEEL DRIVING AND BIKE TOURS
TurAventur (⊠ *Quinta de Serrado—Sr. dos Aflitos* ☎ *266/743134* ⊕ *www.turaventur.com*) organize jeep tours to megaliths and other sights, as well as bike tours in the surrounding countryside.

HORSEBACK RIDING
The **Equeturi** (⊠ *Quinta do Bacêlo* ☎ *266/742884*) horseback-riding center is about 2 km (1 mi) from Évora on the road to Montemor-o-Novo. It gives lessons and conducts escorted rides in the countryside. Reservations are advised.

WALKING TOURS
Professor Murteira Reis of **Mendes e Murteira** (⊠ *Rua 31 de Janeiro, 15-A* ☎ *266/739240 or 917/236025* ✎ *m.murteira@mail.telepac.pt*) organizes historical walking tours for groups of two to five people. These also can include visits to prehistoric sites in the region, nature walks, bird-watching, and ballooning. A half-day walking tour costs €80, not including monument fees. Tours by car are an additional €30.

SIDE TRIPS FROM ÉVORA

A trip through the countryside surrounding Évora will take you to some of the earliest-inhabited sites in Portugal, the country's carpet and tapestry-making center, and to a stunning medieval castle in the lively town of Montemor-o-Novo. The area is also considered the capital of Iberian megaliths, with pastoral fields dotted with dolmens and menhirs (huge carved stones usually marking ancient graves or religious sites). While impressive, the megaliths are difficult to spot by car or to navigate by foot, and are better viewed as part of an organized tour (⇨ *see Tours above under Évora Essentials*). By foot or bicycle, it's rewarding to follow the path of Évora's ancient aqueduct, which crosses the city's medieval walls and juts out across rolling wheat fields and cork groves. A new system of trails along disused railways and ancient public footpaths delivers vast views of the countryside.

GUADALUPE

12.4 km (8 mi) northwest of Évora.

The village of Guadalupe has a 17th-century chapel that is dedicated to Nossa Senhora de Gaudalupe (Our Lady of Guadalupe). Henry the Navigator was known to attend mass at this chapel. However, the area is better known for its prehistoric relics.

GETTING HERE AND AROUND

Guadalupe is difficult for people to find, and is better seen as part of an organized megalithic tour rather than solo. However, if you do plan to drive, head northwest from Évora's center on the N114 for about 10 km (6 mi), and then turn left on a tiny road called Estrada do Norte, which takes you into the village of Guadalupe.

GETTING ORIENTED

Along the roughly two-hour drive from Lisbon to Évora, the first hill town you'll see is also one of the most spectacular: Montemor-o-Novo. The region's megaliths are also scattered mostly west of Évora, and northward you'll find the charming village of Arraiolos, famous for its hand-stitched carpets and impressive pousada.

EXPLORING

Unless otherwise noted, all sites below are less than a 30-minute drive from Évora, and can be visited as part of a half-day excursion from the city. Évora's tourist office can provide maps and directions.

Aqueduto da Agua da Prata. The graceful arched Silver Water Aqueduct, which once carried water to Évora from the springs at Graça do Divor, is best seen along the road to Arraiolos (EN 144-4). You can also see a section of it within Évora, along the Rua do Cano in the city's northwest corner. Constructed in 1532 under the patronage of Dom João III, the aqueduct was designed by the famous architect Francisco de Arruda. Extensive parts of the system remain intact and can be seen from the road. Stop by Évora's tourist office for a map of the aqueduct and footpaths alongside it. ⊠ *Extends 18 km (11 mi) north of Évora.*

Cromlech and the Menhir of Almendres. West of Évora in the tiny village of Guadalupe is the Menhir of Almendres, an 8-foot-tall Neolithic stone obelisk believed to have been used in fertility rites. Several hundred yards away is the cromlech, 95 granite monoliths arranged in an oval in the middle of a large field on a hill. The monoliths face the sunrise and are believed to have been the social, religious, and political center of the agro-pastoral, seminomadic population. The site is also believed to be linked to astral observations and predictions, fertility rites, and the worship of the mother goddess. ⊠ *15 km (9 mi) west of Évora, Guadalupe.*

Dolmen of Zambujeiro. The 20-foot-high Dolmen of Zambujeiro is the largest of its kind on the Iberian Peninsula. This prehistoric monument is typical of those found throughout Neolithic Europe: several great stone slabs stand upright, supporting a flat stone that serves as a roof. These structures were designed as burial chambers. ⊠ *12 km (7 mi) southwest of Évora. From N380 (the Évora–Alcáçovas road) take the turnoff to Valverde.*

ARRAIOLOS

22 km (14 mi) northwest of Évora.

Arraiolos, dominated by the ruins of a once-mighty walled fortress, is a typical hilltop Alentejo village of whitewashed houses and narrow streets. What distinguishes it is its worldwide reputation as a carpet-producing center. In the 16th century, as Portuguese trade with the East grew, an interest developed in the intricate designs of the carpets from India and Persia, and these patterns served as models for the earliest hand-embroidered Arraiolos carpets. The colorful rugs aren't mass-produced in factories but are handmade by locals in their homes and cottages. An authentic Arraiolos rug, made of locally produced wool, has some 4,000 ties per square foot. To discourage imitations, in 1992 the town council designed a blue seal of authenticity to be affixed to each carpet.

■ TIP → While Arraiolos lacks official tourist attractions, the highlight of any visit here is an afternoon spent browsing its tiny carpet shops, where you can see locals weaving and stitching the fine tapestries by hand.

GETTING HERE AND AROUND

Arraiolos is spread over two steep hills, the taller one dominated by the castle and most of the town's center—including carpet shops, restaurants and guesthouses—just below it, and one housing the impressive pousada. In a valley between the two is a festival parade ground and the bus station.

VISITOR INFO

The tourist office can supply departure information for buses (roughly every two hours) to and from Évora, with connections there to Lisbon.

ESSENTIALS

Post Office Correios (✉ *Largo Prof. Dordio Gomes* ☎ *266/490030*).

Visitor Info Arraiolos Tourist Office (✉ *Câmara Municipal, Praca do Municipio 27* ☎ *266/490254*).

WHERE TO EAT AND STAY

$ × **O Alpendre.** Next to the parish church in the center of town, this res-
PORTUGUESE   taurant decorated in typical Alentejo style serves regional dishes such as *migas* (bread fried in olive oil, garlic, and coriander and served alongside meat or fish) with asparagus and *sopa de cação* (dogfish soup). Try the *carne de porco preto* (black pork). Popular for Sunday lunch, the restaurant is a warm family setting, with terra-cotta walls and a huge stone oven in the center of the dining room. Reservations essential on Sunday, when parties of only three or more will be seated. ✉ *Bairro Serpa Pinto 22* ☎ *266/419024* ⊟ *AE, DC, MC, V* ⊗ *No dinner Mon.*

$$$ ⊡ **Pousada da Nossa Senhora da Assunção.** If you need to sleep on your decision about which carpet to buy, consider an overnight stay in this picturesque pousada. It's a little more than a kilometer (½ mi) outside of town in an old 16th-century convent that has been restored and tastefully padded with modern comforts. Although most of Portugal's other pousadas retain their old style throughout, the Arraiolos hotel seamlessly blends old and new, with stark modern decor like Japanese platform beds next to 400-year-old fireplaces. Staff are particularly

attentive here, and on request can arrange activities from horseback riding to rabbit hunting and paintball games. The decor of the restaurant ($–$$), which is open to the public, is also contemporary, but the menu favors traditional regional dishes. **Pros:** unique blend of old and new; small-town charm and service in hotel with international standards. **Cons:** modern decor can feel a bit bland; the walk to town is short but steep, with few sidewalks on a busy thoroughfare. ✉ *Val das Flores, apartado 61* ☎ *266/419340 or 266/419365* ⊕ *www.pousadas.pt* ⤴ *30 rooms, 2 suites* ♿ *In-room: a/c, safe, Internet, Wi-Fi (some). In-hotel: restaurant, room service, bar, tennis court, pool, bicycles, laundry service, Internet terminal, Wi-Fi hotspot, parking (free)* ▭ *AE, DC, MC, V* ⧒ *CP, FAP, MAP.*

SPORTS AND THE OUTDOORS
HORSEBACK TOURS
Coralie Baldrey (✉ *Moinho da Boavista, Arraiolos* ☎ *938/549489* ⊕ *www.equilusitania.com*) offers horseback tours through the Arraiolos countryside on thoroughbred Lusitanian horses.

SHOPPING
The main street of Arraiolos is lined with showrooms and workshops featuring the town's famous hand-embroidered wool rugs. One of the town's best rug selections can be found at **Casa Tiraz** (✉ *Praca da Republica 1* ☎ *266/419057*) on Arraiolos's main town square. **Isilda Vieira** (✉ *Rua Bombeiros Voluntários 7* ☎ *266/499057*) is a small rug shop in Arraiolos. The owner, Isilda, does rug restoration while she is in the shop. Also try **Fabrica de Tapetes Hortense** (✉ *Rua Alexandre Herculano 22* ☎ *266/419648*) or two more shops down the same street, **Vitorino Paulo, Tapetes de Arraiolos** (✉ *Rua Alexandre Herculano 27* ☎ *266/41906*) and **Sempre Noiva** (✉ *Rua Alexandre Herculano 33* ☎ *266/490040).*

MONTEMOR-O-NOVO

30 km (18 mi) west of Évora.

Driving east from the Portuguese capital, the first hilltop castle settlement you'll hit is also one of the most impressive. Montemor-e-Novo, or simply Montemor for short, has been a settlement from the time of the Romans, and its castle has been renovated and expanded by successive generations of Arab rulers, Christian monks, and Portuguese royals since then. Today the town is a prosperous agricultural hub with a surprisingly happening arts scene, and gastronomic festivals throughout the year. Montemor makes a pleasant half-day stop to or from Évora.

GETTING HERE AND AROUND
About 100 km (62 mi) east of Lisbon, Montemor is just past the point where the Portuguese capital's limits disappear into the countryside. It's an easy hour-and-a-half drive from Lisbon, or about 30 minutes west of Alentejo's main city, Évora. Montemor is easily identified from afar by its hilltop castle, on a steep hill towering over clusters of houses hugging its sides.

ESSENTIALS

Montemor Train Station Estacao Rodoviaria (✉ *Carreira de S. Francisco* ☎ *266/892110*).

Taxis Taxi Montemor (☎ *266/892333 or 266/892444*).

Visitor Info Montemor-o-Novo Tourist Office (✉ *Largo Calouste Gulbenkian* ☎ *266/898103* ⊕ *www.cm-montemornovo.pt*).

EXPLORING

Castelo de Montemor-o-Novo. This huge complex towers over the city. The property includes an ancient gate to the city (Porta da Vila) that could be closed during possible times of attack or revolution, a Casa da Guarda (guard station), and Torre do Relogio (clock tower). Until the mid-20th century, part of a convent inside the castle walls housed an orphanage. You can climb up onto the outer castle fortifications and walk around the complex for a 360-degree view of the town below and plains beyond. It's also a pleasant walk up to the castle through Montemor's winding, steep side streets lined with 17th-century manor houses and Manueline doorways. ✉ *Porta de Vila* ☎ *No phone* ⌨ *Free* ☉ *Open during daylight hrs.*

Convent of St. João de Deus. This former convent houses the municipal library, the town archives, and an art gallery with temporary exhibits from local artists and on Montemor's history. On March 8, the building is the hub of a citywide festival celebrating Montemor's patron saint, the 16th-century figure St. John of God. ✉ *Rua de Avis* ☎ *No phone* ⌨ *Free* ☉ *Gallery weekdays 10–12:30 and 2–6, Sat. 2–6.*

Misericordia Church. This church has a splendid Manueline doorway, 17th-century altar pieces, and an 18th-century organ crafted in Italy. Near the front of the church, there rests a beautiful 15th-century Pieta sculpture carved from local marble. ✉ *Rua Teofilo Braga* ☎ *No phone* ⌨ *Free* ☉ *Open occasionally on weekdays and all day Sun. for masses.*

WHERE TO EAT

¢ ✕ **Cafe Almansor.** Across the main square is another old-fashioned haunt
PORTUGUESE for Montemor locals. Don't be put off by the slightly dark, dated art deco style inside. Café Almansor makes one of the best cups of coffee in town, for about 60¢. This is also a popular local hangout, serving simple toasts and sandwiches. ✉ *Praca de Republica 7* ☎ *266/892209* ▭ *No credit cards* ☉ *Thurs.–Tues. 8:30 am–11:30 pm.*

¢ ✕ **Sociedade Circulo Montemorense.** The best spot to sip a coffee or glass
PORTUGUESE of wine in the sunshine is in the front garden of this social club in Mon-
Fodor'sChoice temor's main square. In pleasant weather you'll struggle to find a seat
★ at this relaxed see-and-be-seen establishment—the town's most popular. Inside are banquet and game rooms for members, but the garden and bar are open to the public, with views of a charming park across the street. Food is simple lunch fare, including thick ham and cheese toasts, a variety of sandwiches, and occasionally soup. ✉ *Praca de Republica* ☎ *266/896063* ▭ *No credit cards* ☉ *Tues.–Sun. noon–midnight.*

ALTO ALENTEJO

Alto Alentejo (the Upper Alentejo) is the hillier, rockier half of the great Alentejo plain and has the region's highest mountain ranges—the Serra de São Mamede and the Serra de Ossa. Neither is very lofty, though, and the undulating fields, heaths, and cork plantations that make up most of the landscape leave the bigger impression. Quarries scar the landscape around Borba, Estremoz, and Vila Viçosa, but they produce Portugal's finest marble. (Portugal is second to Italy in marble exports.) Modern wine-making techniques have revolutionized production in Alto Alentejo's vineyards, and some of Europe's finest wines are now produced in areas such as Borba, Reguengos de Monsaraz, and Portalegre.

MONSARAZ

50 km (31 mi) southeast of Évora.

The entire fortified hilltop town of Monsaraz is a living museum of narrow, stone-surfaced streets lined with ancient white houses. The town's 150 or so permanent residents (mostly older people) live mainly off tourism, and because they do so graciously and unobtrusively, Monsaraz has managed to retain its essential character.

Old women clad in black sit in the doorways of their cottages and chat with neighbors, their ever-present knitting in hand. At the southern end of the walls stand the well-preserved towers of a formidable 13th-century castle. The view from atop the pentagonal tower sweeps across the plain to the west and to the east over the Rio Guadiana (Guadiana River) to Spain. Within the castle perimeter is an unusual arena with makeshift slate benches at either end of an oval field. Bullfights are held here several times a year and always in the second week of September (during the festival of Senhora Jesus dos Passos, the village's patron saint).

GETTING HERE AND AROUND

Approaching from any direction, you can't miss the tiny village perched on a hilltop surrounded by steep walls. Drive halfway up to the parking lot, then enter Monsaraz on foot through one of four arched entry gates. This is also where daily buses from Évora will drop you off; check with the tourist office for bus timetables.

ESSENTIALS

Internet Espaço Internet Monsaraz (⌧ *Largo Dom Nuno Álavares Pereira 9* ☎ *266/557063*).

Visitor Info Monsaraz Tourist Office (⌧ *Praça Dom Nuno Álavares Pereira* ☎ *266/557136* ⊕ *www.monsaraz.pt* ☉ *Daily 9:30–1 and 2–5:30*).

EXPLORING

Barragem do Alqueva. Gazing out across Alentejo from atop Monsaraz, if the valleys below look flooded, that's because they are. In the late 1990s, Portugal and Spain jointly began work on a huge dam that created the 250 sq km (96 sq mi) Alqueva reservoir, Europe's largest lake. Most of the smaller lakes and flooded valleys you see from Monsaraz are part of the reservoir system. The project cost nearly €2 billion and aims to alleviate the dry Alentejo's chronic water shortages for decades to come.

Alto Alentejo

Sertã

Castelo Branco

N112 · N118 · N233 · N240

N253

N110

Rio Tejo (River Tagus)

SPAIN

Castelo de Bode

Sardoal

Belver

IP6

Abrantes

N118

IP2/E802

Almourol Castle

N2

N243

Ponte de Sor

N119

N18

Castelo de Vide

N246

Marvão

Parque Natural da Serra de São Mamede ◆

Portalegre

N359 · N246

Coudelaria de Alter ◆

N2

N369

Esperança

N251

N245

Monforte

N18/E802

N243

Campo Maior

N373

→ TO LISBON

N370 · N2 · N4

Estremoz

Borba

N4/E90

Elvas

S E R R A   D E   O S S A

Arraiolos

Na. Sta. da Graça do Divor

A6/IP7 · N18/E802

Évoramonte

N254

Vila Viçosa

Montemor-o-Novo

Cromlech and the Menhir of Almendres

N114

Aqueduto da Água da Prata ◆

N18/E802

Terena

N381

Guadalupe

Dolmen of Zambujeiro

N380

Évora
see detail map

N255

São Pedro do Corval

Rio Guadiana

N2

N254

Reguengos de Monsaraz

N252

Monsaraz

N5 · N2

Portel

N384

N386

0 — 20 miles

0 — 30 km

N18/E802 · N258

Moura

5

You can drive or walk across the dam, but one of the best ways to see the lake's expanse is by boat. Visit the **Amieira Marina** across the lake from Monsaraz in the town of Portel, where you can rent boats or book day trips on the lake. ⊠ *Albufeira de Alqueva, Amieira* ☎ *266/734448* ⊕ *www.amieiramarina.com.*

Menhir of Outeiro. The area around Monsaraz is dotted with megalithic monuments. This 18-foot-high menhir, 3 km (2 mi) north of town, is one of the tallest ever discovered.

Museu Monsaraz. This small museum, next to the parish church, displays religious artifacts and the original town charter, signed by Dom Manuel in 1512. The former tribunal contains an interesting 15th-century fresco that depicts Christ presiding over figures of Truth and Deception. ⊠ *Praça Nuno Álvares Pereira* ☎ *No phone* 🎟 *€1* ☉ *Daily 10–1 and 2–6.*

WHERE TO EAT AND STAY

¢ ✕ **Casa do Forno.** The labor of love of two ambitious women (Gloria and Mariana), Casa do Forno is a popular restaurant. At the entrance is a huge, rounded oven with an iron door, hence the name (*forno* is Portuguese for "oven"). Picture windows line the dining room and afford a spectacular view over the rolling plains. The Alentejan menu appropriately features roasts; one special dish worth trying is the *borrego assado no forno* (roast lamb prepared according to an ancient recipe of the nearby monastery). ⊠ *Travessa da Sanabrosa* ☎ *266/557190 or 962/454940* 🖃 *AE, MC, V* ☉ *Closed Tues.*

PORTUGUESE

¢ ✕ **Lumumba.** This little restaurant in one of the old village houses has a devoted clientele that hails from both sides of the Portuguese–Spanish border. The dining room is small, but there is a terrace for outside dining with views over the valley to distant mountains. The menu is classic Alentejo, with good lamb and kid roasts and casseroles. Although their main specialty is *ensopado de borrego* (lamb stew), when available, the grilled fish dishes are also excellent; try the *chocos grelhados* (grilled squid) or the *peixe espada grelhada* (charcoal-grilled blade fish). ⊠ *Rua Direita 12* ☎ *266/557121* 🖃 *AE, DC, MC, V* ☉ *Closed Mon.*

PORTUGUESE

¢ 🏠 **Casa Pinto.** This small, rustic guesthouse—a true romantic hideaway—occupies an old, restored, white home on the main street of the walled town. Inside, exquisite rooms are decorated each according to a different Portuguese explorer's destination—Macau, Goa, Mombasa, Dili, and Asilah. With antique furnishings and fantastic valley views, the sunsets alone are worth the price of a room. **Pros:** roof terrace offers best view in town; cozy and intimate; romantic setting. **Cons:** rooms are on the small side; no space for extra beds for children. ⊠ *Praça Dom Nuno Álavares Pereira 10* ☎ *266/557076* ⊕ *www.casapinto.net* 🛏 *5 rooms* 🖔 *In-room: a/c, Wi-Fi. In-hotel: room service (breakfast only), laundry service, Internet terminal, Wi-Fi hotspot, parking (free), some pets allowed* 🖃 *AE, DC, MC, V* 🍴 *CP.*

Fodor's Choice
★

$ 🏠 **Horta da Moura.** This ancient Moorish farm is now a sprawling rural hotel complex, with horses, an organic garden and plenty of space to wander the countryside on foot or mountain bike. From the swimming pool, you'll gaze out on 1,000-year-old olive groves on a terraced hillside dotted with the remnants of old wells and other ruins. The main house, whose white-stucco facade has blue trim and an arched portico,

Fodor's Choice
★

is typical of Alentejo-style architecture. The cozy interior has vaulted brick ceilings with wooden beams, fireplaces, and traditional furnishings. The outlying buildings include stables, a riding school, a crafts room, and a recreation center with a large fireplace. A small winery and second restaurant opened in 2011. The helpful staff arranges walking, horseback riding, cycling, and bird-watching trips along the river, as well as 4x4 and canoe excursions and fishing trips. The hotel is also used for corporate retreats, weddings, and family reunions. With several different size suites and rooms, it's good value for families or groups; babysitting is available. ■ TIP→ **If you plan on bringing the kids, make sure you ask about the special rates for children; babysitting is also available. Pros:** gorgeous rustic charm; lots of open space; numerous friendly staff. **Cons:** inaccessible by public transport; only four of the 25 rooms are doubles, the rest are suites. ⊠ *Horta da Moura, Monsaraz, Apartado 64, Monsaraz* ☎ *266/550100* ⊕ *www.hortadamoura. pt* ↪ *4 double/single rooms, 21 suites (various sizes)* ⚮ *In-room: a/c, refrigerator (some), DVD, Internet (some), Wi-Fi. In-hotel: 2 restaurants, room service, bar, pool, water sports, bicycles, children's programs (ages 4–12), laundry service, Wi-Fi hotspot, parking (free)* ⊟ *AE, DC, MC, V* ◎ *CP, FAP, MAP.*

SHOPPING

Reguengos de Monsaraz, 16 km (10 mi) west of Monsaraz, is a sleepy little Alentejo town often simply called Reguengos. It's the center of a large wine-producing region and is also known for its handwoven rugs. The 19th-century neo-Gothic church here was built by the same Lisbon architect who built Lisbon's bullfight arena.

NEED A BREAK?

Restaurant Central (⊠ *Praça da Liberdade 10* ☎ *266/502219* ⊙ *Daily 10 am–11 pm*) **is a great place to stop for some authentic Alentejano cuisine on your way to Monsaraz or after a wine-tasting. The restaurant has good value daily specials, with a smaller bar-café offering tapas and good local wines, too. Next door to Restaurant Central,** O Gato **(⊠ *Praça da Liberdade 11–13* ☎ *266/502353* ⊕ *www.residencialogato.com*) has a charming restaurant, bed-and-breakfast, and pastry shop.**

The tiny hamlet of **São Pedro do Corval,** 5 km (3 mi) northeast of Reguengos, is one of Portugal's major centers for inexpensive hand-painted pottery.

Herdade do Esporão, the famed wine estate that produces Esporão, one of Portugal's top labels, is a beautiful, sprawling property overlooking a lake that you won't believe is tucked away in the outskirts of this small Alentejo town. The winery's driveway cuts across miles of vineyards, up to the main house with an arched portico showcasing the vast property. The winery offers 40-minute tours of its facilities with a free glass of wine at the end. You can sample wines at the bar (you pay according to the number and type of wines tasted). Pair wines with sophisticated Portuguese cuisine in their elegant restaurant ($$; lunch only, reserve ahead). Famed chef Julia Vinagre prepares dishes with wine, olive oil, and vinegar from the estate, which, along with other products, are also on sale at the shop. Restaurant guests can take a free tour. ⊠ *Herdade do Esporão, Apartado 31; from Reguengos follow signs to Esporão/*

Zona Industrial and then signs for Turismo Rural, Reguengos de Monsaraz 🏛 *266/509280* ⊕ *www.esporao.com* ☉ *Shop Tues.–Sun. 9:30–6; tours Tues.–Sun. noon, 3:30, and 5; bar Tues.–Sun. 10–6.*

TERENA

28 km (17 mi) north of Reguengos.

Terena, with its castle on a hill, has a charter dating from 1262 and is a place where tourists are still a curiosity. Drive—or better yet, stroll—along the narrow Rua Direita past the white houses, some with Gothic doorways, others with baroque or Renaissance ones. The small, well-preserved castle was one of several built in this area to defend the border with Spain, which lies across the Rio Guadiana, 11 km (7 mi) east.

GETTING HERE AND AROUND

Terena lies about halfway between Vila Vicosa and Monsaraz. Follow signs to the castle and park on a hillside landing near the bus stop. There is no public transportation here.

ESSENTIALS

Terena's tiny tourist office has closed as of this writing, though may open again in 2012. With barely a few hundred inhabitants in this village, there are no tourist facilities except for a single small hotel (⇨ *see review below*). But the allure here is visiting a village nearly untouched by tourism. You will have the castle and surrounding lanes all to yourself.

WHERE TO STAY

$
Fodor'sChoice
★

🏨 **Casa de Terena.** A restored 18th-century house in out-of-the-way Terena has been turned into a lovely inn. It has six comfortably furnished guest quarters, with a blend of Portuguese and African decor. The South African owners are a charming couple who've lived all over the world and are eager to share travel tips and tales. Their warm hospitality includes tapas and wine in the evenings, and they can arrange a host of activities including cycling, fishing, horseback riding, and golf. This tiny hotel has none of the anonymity of larger hotels, and you'll feel like a guest in a cozy home. ■ TIP→ **Children under 10 stay free. Pros:** personal hospitality in a rural retreat. **Cons:** Terena's charm is in its remoteness, but there's not much to do here besides relax; no activities for children. ⊠ *Rua Direita 45, Terena* 🏛 *268/459132* ⊕ *www.casadeterena. com* 📞 *6 rooms* ⌂ *In-room: no phone, no a/c, Wi-Fi. In-hotel: room service (breakfast only), bar, bicycles, laundry service, Wi-Fi hotspot, no parking, some pets allowed* ⊟ *No credit cards* ⦿ *CP, FAP MAP.*

VILA VIÇOSA

18 km (11 mi) northeast of Terena.

A quiet town with a moated castle, Vila Viçosa is in the heart of the fertile Borba plain. It has been closely linked with Portuguese royalty since the 15th century, but this association hasn't always been a happy one: in 1483 King João II, seeking to strengthen his grip on the throne, moved to eliminate the second Duke of Bragança, his brother-in-law and most formidable rival, who controlled more than 50 cities, castles, and towns from Vila Viçosa. After much intrigue and counter intrigue, the unfortunate duke was beheaded in Évora's main square.

Court life in Vila Viçosa flourished in the late 16th and early 17th centuries, when the huge palace constructed by the fourth Duke of Bragança (Jaime) was the scene of great royal feasts, theater performances, and bullfights. This all came to an abrupt end in 1640, when King João IV, the eighth Duke of Bragança and the first Portuguese to occupy the throne after 60 years of Spanish domination, elected to move his court to Lisbon. Thereafter, Vila Viçosa slipped into relative oblivion. In more recent times Portugal's second-to-last king, Carlos I, and the young Prince Luís Filipe spent their last night in the palace. The following day, February 1, 1908, in response to a royal decree that mandated exile for "political" crimes, they were assassinated by members of a secret political society while riding in an open carriage.

Today Vila Viçosa is a pleasant, bustling town that remains affluent because of its ties to the region's wine industry and marble quarries. Most residents still live in the town center, and it's less touristy and untainted by shopping malls and suburban sprawl that have cropped up on the edges of other provincial towns. The huge Praça da Republica, lined with orange trees and anchored by a castle on one end and a 17th-century church on the other, is one of the finest squares in all of Alentejo.

GETTING HERE AND AROUND
Vila Viçosa lies just past Borba, south of the highway that connects Évora with the Spanish border. Praça da Republica stretches across the town center, with the Paço Ducal and pousada about 300 meters to the northwest. Bus service from Évora is infrequent and slow, and Vila Vicosa is best reached by private car.

ESSENTIALS
Bus Station Belos Transportes (✉ *Largo D. João IV* ☎ *266/769410*).

Taxi Vila Vicosa (✉ *Praça da Republica* ☎ *268/980115*).

Visitor Info Vila Viçosa Tourist Office (✉ *Praça da Republica 34* ☎ *268/881101* ⊕ *www.cm-vilavicosa.pt* ☉ *Daily 9–12:30 and 2–5:30*).

EXPLORING
Marble Museum. This museum offers an interesting look at Alentejo's local marble industry, which has sustained Vila Viçosa and made it prosperous. It's inside the old, disused train station, which is covered in intricate blue-and-white tiles and worth seeing in its own right. ✉ *Av. da Estaçao, Vila Viçosa* ☎ *268/889314* 🎫 *€1.05* ☉ *Oct.–Mar., Tues.–Sat. 9–12:30 and 2–5; Apr.–Sept., Tues.–Sat. 9–12:30 and 3–5:30. Closed Mon.*

Museu dos Coches *(Coach Museum).* After the tour of the Ducal Palace you can visit this nearby museum), with its collection of horse-drawn conveyances and antique automobiles. Note that if you've seen or plan to see Lisbon's coach museum, you can skip this one; it's interesting but isn't in the same league as the one in the capital. ✉ *Terreiro do Paço* ☎ *268/980659* 🎫 *€2* ☉ *Apr.–Sept., Tues. 2:30–5:30, Wed.–Fri. 10–1 and 2:30–5:30; weekends 9:30–1 and 2:30–6; Oct.–Mar., Tues. 2–5, Wed. 10–1 and 2–5, Thurs.–Sun. 9:30–1 and 2–5. Closed Mon.*

Paço Ducal *(Ducal Palace). The* palace and the nearby *castelo* (castle) draw a great many visitors. Built of locally quarried marble, the palace's main wing extends for some 360 feet and overlooks the expansive Palace Square and the bronze equestrian statue of Dom João IV. At the north end of the square note the Porta do Nó (Knot Gate) with its massive stone shaped like ropes—an intriguing example of the Manueline style.

The palace's interior was extensively restored in the 1950s and contains all you'd expect to find: azulejos, Arraiolos rugs, frescoed ceilings, priceless collections of silver and gold objects, Chinese vases, Gobelin tapestries, and a long dining hall adorned with antlers and other hunting trophies. The enormous kitchen's spits are large enough to accommodate several oxen, and there's enough gleaming copper to keep a small army of servants busy polishing. Dom Carlos, the nation's penultimate king, spent his last night here before being assassinated in 1908; his rooms have been maintained as they were. Carlos was quite an accomplished painter—some say a better painter than he was a monarch—and many of his works (along with private photos of Portugal's last royal family) line the walls of the apartments. The palace itself as well as its armory, its treasury, and the castle and hunting museum can each be visited in separate guided tours.

The ground floor of the castle has displays of objects ranging from Paleolithic to 18th century and mainly Roman artifacts discovered during excavations. These include pieces from ancient Mediterranean civilizations—Egypt, Rome, Carthage, and also pre-Columbian. Also on view are coaches from the 17th to the 20th century. Hunting, rather than war, is the dominant theme of the armory that holds more than 2,000 objects. The treasury displays crucifixes from Vila Viçosa and those belonging to Dona Catarina de Bragança as well as more than 200 pieces of jewelry, paintings, crystal, and ceramics. The porcelain collection is made up of blue-and-white china from the 15th to 18th century. ⊠ *Terreiro do Paço* ☎ *268/980659* ✆ *Palace €6; armory €3; treasury and porcelain collection €2.50 each; castle, archaeology museum, and game and hunting museum €3* ⊙ *Apr.–Sept., Tues. 2:30–5:30, Wed.–Fri. 10–1 and 2:30–5:30; weekends 9:30–1 and 2:30–6; Oct.–Mar., Tues. 2–5, Wed. 10–1 and 2–5, Thurs.–Sun. 9:30–1 and 2–5. Closed Mon.*

WHERE TO STAY

$ 🖵 **Aldeamento de Peixinhos.** What used to be a charming 17th-century manor house surrounded only by an orange grove is now dwarfed by a modern, low-rise hotel complex built around it, offering one-, two- and three-bedroom apartments. Rooms are still available for rent in the manor house, which is decorated in period furnishings and has a large salon with a fireplace. The complex is in a good location a little over ½ km (¼ mi) from town. The rustic manor house is preferable for couples but lacks modern amenities like a/c. The sprawling grounds and apartments are a good option for families with children or for long stays, with plenty of space and views of both Vila Viçosa's old town and the surrounding countryside. **Pros:** plenty of space for children; modern amenities; large apartments are a good option for groups. **Cons:**

CLOSE UP

The Allure of Azulejo

It's difficult to find an old building of any note in Portugal that isn't adorned somewhere or other with the predominantly blue-tone ceramic tiles called *azulejos*. The centuries-old marriage of glazed ornamental tiles to Portuguese architecture is a match made in heaven.

After the Gothic period, large buildings made entirely of undressed brick or stone became a rarity in Portuguese architecture. Most structures had extensive areas of flat plaster on their facades and interior walls that cried out for decoration. The compulsion to fill these empty architectural spaces produced the art of the fresco in Italy; in Portugal, it produced the art of the azulejo.

The medium is well suited to the deeply rooted Portuguese taste for intricate, ornate decoration. And, aesthetics aside, glazed tiling is ideally suited to the country's more practical needs. Durable, waterproof, and easily cleaned, the tile provides cool interiors during Portugal's hot summers and exterior protection from the dampness of Atlantic winters.

The term *azulejo* comes not from the word *azul* (blue in Portuguese), but from the Arabic word for tiles, *az-zulayj*. But despite the long presence of the Moors in Portugal, the Moorish influence on early Portuguese azulejos was actually introduced from Spain in the 15th century.

The very earliest tiles on Portuguese buildings were imported from Andalusia. They're usually geometric in design and were most frequently used to form panels of repeated patterns. As Portugal's prosperity increased in the 16th century, the

growing number of palaces, churches, and sumptuous mansions created a demand for more tile. Local production was small at first, and Holland and Italy were the main suppliers. The superb Dutch-made azulejos in the Paço Ducal in Vila Viçosa are famous examples from this period. The first Portuguese-made tiles had begun to appear in the last quarter of the 15th century, when a number of small factories were established, but three centuries were to pass before Portuguese tile making reached its peak.

The great figure in 18th-century Portuguese tile making is António de Oliveira Bernardes, who died in 1732. The school he established spawned the series of monumental panels depicting hunting scenes, landscapes, battles, and other historical motifs that grace many stately Portuguese homes and churches of the period. Some of the finest examples can be seen in the Alentejo—in buildings such as the university in Évora and the parish church in Alcácer do Sal—as well as at the Castelo de São Felipe in Setúbal. In Lisbon's Museu do Azulejo you can trace the development of tiles in Portugal from their beginnings to the present.

Portuguese tile making declined in quality in the 19th century, but a revival occurred in the 20th century, spearheaded by leading artists such as Almada Negreiros and Maria Keil. Today, some notable examples of tile use by contemporary artists can be seen in many of the capital's metro stations.

5

characterless comfort on what used to be a charming old estate; no Internet or Wi-Fi. ☒ *Estrada de Peixinhos, Vila Viçosa* ☎ *268/886870* ⊕ *www.peixinhos.com* ⇨ *26 apartments, 6 regular rooms, 1 superior room, 1 suite* ⚐ *In-room: a/c (some), no phone (some), safe (some), kitchen (some), refrigerator (some). In-hotel: restaurant, room service, bar, tennis court, 2 pools, bicycles, children's programs (ages 3–10), laundry facilities, laundry service, parking (free)* ▭ *No credit cards* ⦿ *CP, EP, FAP, MAP.*

$$$
Fodor's Choice
★

🏨 **Pousada de D. João IV.** If you're hooked on Vila Viçosa's history, this inn next door to the palace has all the atmosphere you'll need. It's in a restored 16th-century convent that's furnished with period reproductions. Its restaurant ($$–$$$$), open to the public, even serves dishes based on old convent recipes. The convent is owned by the Portuguese royal family's foundation and leased to the pousada, an arrangement that has resulted in a slow pace of restoration work—but there are marvelous half-restored frescos to peruse. Ask reception to let you peek into a peeling, secret chapel from the late 16th-century, where nuns in seclusion could pass into the main church undetected. Each room is unique, including one with a tiled passageway and iron bars separating a nun's living quarters from visitors, with a turnstile through which pilgrims could pass gifts. Even if you can't stay the night, it's worth a visit to tour the hotel and sip a glass of port by the salon's huge fireplace. Friendly, helpful staff can arrange walking tours, biking or hiking trips, hot-air ballooning, or visits to local wineries and marble quarries. **Pros:** a history buff's dream; period furnishings and half-restored frescos on hallway walls. **Cons:** expensive. ☒ *Convento das Chagas, Terreiro do Paço* ☎ *268/980742* ⊕ *www. pousadas.pt* ⇨ *39 rooms* ⚐ *In-room: a/c, safe, Wi-Fi. In-hotel: restaurant, room service, bar, pool, bicycles, children's programs (ages 2–12), laundry service, Internet terminal, Wi-Fi hotspot, parking (free)* ▭ *AE, DC, MC, V* ⦿ *CP, FAP, MAP.*

$
Fodor's Choice
★

🏨 **Quinta do Colmeal.** About 3 km (2 mi) outside Vila Viçosa, this ancient Roman hermitage has been a farm since the 17th century, changing hands from Portuguese royals and army generals to a Dutch couple who bought the property in 1999. They've kept the farm's historic touches— centuries-old olive, fig, almond, and orange groves—but added modern amenities as well, transforming an old water cistern into a natural swimming pool, for example. A cluster of buildings include the original country manor with two smaller cottages for rent, plus a bakery and oven hut. Rent a tiny cottage for two, surrounded by wildflowers, and you'll feel like a guest in a hidden patch of paradise. **Pros:** romantic; rustic charm for an extremely good price; warm, personal hospitality; good options for families or those who want to immerse themselves in nature. **Cons:** a bit of a walk from town. ☒ *Estrada Vila Viçoso, Apartado 227, São Romão* ☎ *919/569751 or 627/050401* ⊕ *www.quintainportugal.eu* ⇨ *3 cottages* ⚐ *In-room: a/c (some), no phone (some), kitchen, refrigerator, Internet (some). In-hotel: bar, pool, bicycles, laundry facilities, laundry service, Internet terminal, parking (free), some pets allowed* ▭ *No credit cards* ⦿ *EP, CP.*

EN
ROUTE

On the main road between Vila Viçosa and Estremoz, you'll see dirt-and-rock piles strewn about the countryside. These tailings are the residue of centuries of extracting high-quality marble from the region's many quarries. The town of Borba, about 4 km (2½ mi) northwest of Vila Viçosa, has a pleasant conglomeration of modest whitewashed houses, noble mansions, and small churches—all beautifully decorated with marble. Borba is one of the Alentejo's major wine producers, and the town's vintners have won many national prizes. With an advance reservation, you can stop by a vineyard for a tasting.

ESTREMOZ

31 km (19 mi) northwest of Vila Viçosa.

Estremoz, which lies on the ancient road that connected Lisbon with Mérida, Spain, has been a site of strategic importance since Roman times, and the castle, which overlooks the town, was a crucial one of the Alentejo's many fortresses. Estremoz is most closely associated with Isabel of Aragon, although she spent only a short time here. Married to Dom Dinis—a Portuguese king—in 1282, she arrived in 1336 and after a brief stay became ill and died. The luxurious Pousada da Rainha Santa Isabel, which occupies the castle, was named for her. It was also in Estremoz in 1367 that the queen's grandson Pedro, the lover and secret husband of Inês de Castro, died. The Portuguese people loved Queen Isabel and over the ages have handed down many tales and legends of her humility and charity. She was beatified in the 16th century, then canonized in 1625 by Pope Urban VIII. A statue in the castle square commemorates her. From atop the castle tower you'll have a magnificent view over the Alentejo plains. Today Estremoz is a bustling rural hub that's the seat of eastern Alentejo's growing arts scene, as well as a military garrison town complete with sword-wielding guards outside the cavalry regiment's headquarters across from the main park. Chock-full of history but not resting on its laurels, Estremoz is unfortunately often overlooked in favor of its more touristy sister city Évora, but it shouldn't be. Make Estremoz your base for exploring this half of the Alentejo and you won't be disappointed.

GETTING HERE AND AROUND

Estremoz lies about 45 km (30 mi) northeast of Évora along the nontoll road IP2. Most of the city lies within a low outer protective wall, with the castle, pousada, and some museums stop a central hill with another wall around it. Everything is within walking distance inside town.

TOUR INFO

Rainha Santa Isabel, Viagens e Turismo Lda can arrange historical walking tours. Paladares e Aventuras can arrange mountain biking, 4x4 tours, horseback riding, and other adventure sports.

ESSENTIALS

Car Rental Alenrent Rent a Car Lda (✉ *Rua Capitao Mouzinho de Albequerque 11* ☎ *268/333929*).

Tour Guides Paladares e Aventuras (✉ *Rua Francisco Manuel Cardoso 23 Arcos* ☎ *268/891040 or 912/322911* ⊕ *www.paladareseaventuras.com*). **Rainha**

Santa Isabel, Viagens e Turismo Lda (✉ *Lg. Combatentes de Grande Guerra 9–10* ☎ *268/333228*).

Visitor Info **Estremoz Tourist Office** (✉ *Casa de Estremoz, Rossio Marquês de Pombal* ☎ *268/333541* ⊕ *www.cm-estremoz.pt* ☼ *Daily 9–1 and 2–6*).

EXPLORING

Museu de Arte Sacra. Housed in a towering 17th-century convent next to the tourist office, it's worth a peek to see 17th- and 18th-century religious trinkets, and climb a blue-and-white tiled stairway for an impressive view from the building's bell towers. ✉ *Rossio Marquês de Pombal* ☎ *967/528298* 🎟 *€1* ☼ *Weekdays 9–12:30 and 2–5:30, weekends 2–5:30.*

NEED A BREAK? If you'd like to grab a sandwich, cup of tea, or glass of wine between museum visits, there's no place better than **Gadanha** (✉ *Largo Dragoes de Olivença 84-A, Estremoz* ☎ *268/333262 or 965/171521* ⊕ *www.merceariagadanha.com* ☼ *Mon.–Thurs. 9 am–10 pm, Fri. and Sat. 9 am–11 pm, Sun. 10–10*). You'll likely end up leaving with more than what you ate as this deli also sells gift-wrapped gourmet treats like local ham, cheese, sweets, liqueurs, and chocolates.

The lower town, a maze of narrow streets and white houses, radiates from the **Rossio,** a huge, central square. Stands lining it sell the town's famous colorful pottery. In addition to the multicolored, hand-painted plates, pitchers, and dolls, note the earthenware jugs decorated with bits of local white marble.

Royal Palace. The former Royal Palace, an impressive hilltop fortress towering over the city, is now a luxury pousada (⇨ *see listing below*). The complex is the highlight of any visit to Estremoz, and the pousada is open to the public as well as those able to afford a room inside. The palace was built in the 13th century by Portugal's king Dom Dinis. It's named after his wife, Queen Isabel of Aragon, who died here in 1336. In recent centuries it's been used as an ammunition dump, university, and military garrison. An explosion in 1698 destroyed much of the medieval structure except the **Torre das Tres Coroas** (Tower of the Three Crowns), which you can still climb today, with fantastic views of Estremoz and the surrounding countryside. The palace was restored after the ammunition blast and fire, and was converted into a hotel in 1970. The interior is like a museum, housing an impressive collection of 17th- and 18th-century artifacts and furniture. Across the street, Queen Isabel's personal chapel, **Capela de Santa Isabel,** a striking, richly decorated enclave lined with azulejos, is also open to visitors. ✉ *Largo de D. Dinis* ☎ *268/332075* 🎟 *Free admission to pousada lobby, tower, and chapel.*

NEED A BREAK? There are several refreshment stands and snack bars along the Rossio, but for more substantial fare try the **Café Alentejano** (✉ *Rossio Marquês de Pombal 13–15, Estremoz* ☎ *268/337300 or 268/337303 or 967/286311* 🍽 *MC, V* ☼ *Daily 9–11 am*). From this popular 60-year-old art deco–style café and its first-floor restaurant, you can watch the goings-on in the square. Inexpensive accommodation can be found upstairs.

WHERE TO EAT AND STAY

$ ✕ **Adega do Isaias.** Hidden away on

PORTUGUESE a narrow side street a few minutes'

Fodor's Choice walk from the square, this is the

★ best place in town for hearty, no-
nonsense roasts and grilled meats.
The front part of the former wine
cellar is a rustic brick bar with a
pork leg mounted on the counter,
and a charcoal grill nestled in the
front window alcove. Walk past the
bar area across a sloping, concrete-
floor into a cozy dining room, lined
with huge terra-cotta wine jugs. The

<table>
<tr><td>

CASTLES

In much of the Alentejo, you can't
drive far without seeing a castle
or a fortress crowning one of the
hills. Some, such as the castles at
Estremoz and Alvito, have been
restored and converted into luxuri-
ous *pousadas* (inns). Others, includ-
ing those at Castelo de Vide and
Viana do Alentejo, are open for you
to clamber about their battlements.

</td></tr>
</table>

furnishings are basic—benches at planked tables—and you can expect
the service to be casual, at best. But the food will be great, and the place
will probably be packed. Specialties include *burras* (pork chin), *migas*
with wild asparagus, and *sopa de cacao*, or dogfish soup, a hearty dish
made with a bony local fish which is sometimes also called baby shark.
There's also a long list of Alentejo wines at very reasonable prices. ⊠ *Rua
do Almeida 21* ☎ *268/322318* ✆ *adegadoisaias@sapo.pt* ☐ *No credit
cards* ☾ *Mon.–Sat. noon–3 and 7–10 and last 3 wks Aug.*

$$ ✕ **São Rosas.** The castle in the historic center of town also houses this

PORTUGUESE gastronomic landmark, serving traditional cuisine in an upscale, white
tablecloth setting that caters to pousada guests and weekenders from
Lisbon. Margarida Cabaço, owner and chef, offers traditional Alentejo
savories. When in season, wild asparagus, wild mushrooms, and truffles
appear on the menu. Specialties include *tarte de perdiz* (partridge pie)
and *sela de borrego* (baked lamb). For fish try the trout with *chou-
riço* (smoked sausage) and *poejos* (native herb) or the *sopa de cação*
(dogfish soup). The tomato soup, soaked with bread and served with
dried sausage on the side, is indeed a meal in itself. ⊠ *Largo D. Dinis
11* ☎ *268/333345* ⊕ *www.saorosas.pmeevolution.com* ⌂ *Reservations
recommended* ☐ *AE, DC, MC, V* ☾ *Tues.–Sun. 12:45–3 and 7:45–10.*

$ ✕ **Zona Verde Restaurante.** This traditional restaurant is a favorite with

PORTUGUESE locals, serving massive portions of Alentejo specialties like dogfish soup,
borrego assado (roasted lamb) and porco preto (black pork). Even half-
portions are huge, and a good value. ⊠ *Largo Dragoes de Olivença 86,
Estremoz* ☎ *268/324701 or 964/501676* ☐ *No credit cards* ☾ *Daily
noon–3 and 7–11.*

$$ ▦ **Páteo dos Solares.** This modern hotel occupies a large old house that
has been restored using traditional materials and lots of marble. It's
near the old walls in the center of town, with a huge swimming pool
and patio overlooking vineyards and farmland that slope down from
the edges of Estremoz. Ample meeting rooms and facilities make this
hotel popular with corporate retreats from Lisbon, but it's also a good
choice for families, with a huge terrace, kid's room, and games area.
Some rooms have their own fireplace and Jacuzzi. The lovely restaurant, open to the public, is decorated with intricate tile mosaics and a
roaring communal fireplace. Friendly, multi-lingual Belgian-Portuguese

manager Evangeline can help arrange wine or ceramics tours, or hiking trips into the neighboring countryside. **Pros:** sprawling property with modern facilities retains a historic feel, just steps from the town center. **Cons:** expensive; you might find yourself surrounded only by corporate conference attendees. ⊠ *Rua Brito Capelo* ☎ *268/338400* ⊕ *www.pateosolares.com* ⇴ *41 rooms, 1 suite* ⚿ *In-room: a/c, safe, refrigerator (some), Wi-Fi. In-hotel: restaurant, room service, bar, pool, laundry service, Wi-Fi hotspot, parking (free)* ⊟ *AE, DC, MC, V* |O| *CP, FAP, MAP.*

$$

Fodor's Choice

★

Pousada da Rainha Santa Isabel. If there's one pousada in all of Portugal that you splurge on, this should be it. Dubbed the "museum of all pousadas," this hotel really evokes the feeling of staying in a medieval castle—because it is one. Each room is different, some with massive four-poster canopy beds and all of them decorated in lavish 17th- and 18th-century antique furnishings that comprise a world-class collection in their own right. The ornate dining room seats 260, amid stone pillars and high arched porticos adorned with chandeliers. From the floor-to-ceiling windows behind velvet curtains in the bar area, or outside on the sprawling terrace with its swimming pool, you have a view across Estremoz below and out across what was once the king of the castle's domain. Views are even more spectacular from the adjoining tower, open during daylight hours, and also available for private lunches (enquire at reception). Another architectural highlight is the soaring, blue-and-white azulejo-bedecked stairway leading from reception to the second floor. When the building was converted into a hotel in 1970, engineers did a wonderful job of adding amenities in hidden places such as a small elevator discreetly tucked behind a stairway or modern closets masked in medieval wooden screens. The restaurant's emphasis is on traditional Alentejo dishes and old-fashioned recipes. The *perdiz caçador* (partridge in red wine) is good in autumn. ■ TIP→ **If you plan on bringing the kids, make sure you ask about the special rates for children.** **Pros:** an architectural gem; history buffs will find this their favorite hotel in Portugal. **Cons:** besides a billiards room, no activities for children. ⊠ *Largo D. Dinis 1* ☎ *268/332075* ⊕ *www.pousadas.pt* ⇴ *33 rooms* ⚿ *In-room: a/c, safe, refrigerator (some), Wi-Fi (some). In-hotel: restaurant, room service, bar, pool, bicycles, laundry service, Internet terminal, Wi-Fi hotspot, parking (free)* ⊟ *AE, DC, MC, V* |O| *CP, FAP, MAP.*

¢

Residencial Carvalho. An affordable, family-run guesthouse in the center of town, this hotel has large clean rooms with a/c and satellite TV. Decor is no frills, but you can't beat the price and location. ■ TIP→ **Children under 8 stay free.** **Pros:** good value and location. **Cons:** some of the front street-facing rooms can be a bit noisy at night. ⊠ *Largo da Republica 27* ☎ *268/339370* ✉ *joaodcpires@sapo.pt* ⇴ *17 rooms* ⚿ *In-room: a/c, Internet (some). In-hotel: room service (breakfast only), laundry service, Internet terminal* ⊟ *No credit cards* |O| *CP.*

ÉVORAMONTE

17 km (10 mi) southwest of Estremoz; 42 km (26 mi) northeast of Évora.

Évoramonte is a medieval town that sits along the western flank of the Serra de Ossa at an altitude of 1,550 feet. Drive up to the castle for a view that extends as far as the Serra da Estrela. The castle here, built in Italian Renaissance style, is distinguished by a massive round tower at each of its four corners. Also note the heavy Manueline ropes that run, like ribbons on a Christmas package, around the exterior; they're joined at the entrance with two tidy concrete knots.

The famous Alentejo soup, made with stale bread, garlic, olive oil, coriander, and water, is said to have originated in Évoramonte. The convention held here in 1834 to end the civil war between the Liberals and the Miguelists took so long that by the end only stale bread was left to eat—and thus was born the popular *sopa alentejana.*

GETTING HERE AND AROUND

You'll have to go by private car, but the short journey from Évora or Estremoz is worth making, just for the view from atop Évoramonte. The steep drive up the mountain isn't recommended in rain or heavy winds.

ESSENTIALS

Visitor Info Évoramonte Tourist Office (✉ *Rua de Santa Maria* ☎ *268/959227* 🕑 *Summer 10–1 and 2:30–6; winter 10–1 and 2–5:30. Closed Mon. and Wed.*).

EXPLORING

Castelo. The reason this tiny hilltop village exists is the impressive fortress, first founded in 1160 but rebuilt after a 1531 earthquake. Legend has it that the knotted rope sculpture molded into the castle walls is supposed to represent loyalty of the Portuguese royal family. *Rua Santa Maria* ☎ *No phone* 💶 *€2* 🕑 *Tues.–Sun. 10–1 and 2–5. Closed last weekend every month.*

Celeiro Comum. Atop this windswept hill, you'll be surprised to find Inacencia Lopes's tiny craft and antiques shop open nearly every day. The young artist lives down the hill and climbs up each day to her workshop, where she paints unique religious figurines and other collectables. *Rua Santa Maria 11* ☎ *966/759534* 🕑 *Summer daily 9–9; winter daily 10–5:30.*

WHERE TO EAT

$$
PORTUGUESE
✕ **Convençao.** Whether you choose a table inside the rustic but posh dining room or outside on the terrace, you'll find a cozy place to enjoy this restaurant's fine Alentejan specialties. Try the roasted lamb or tomato soup. Upstairs from the restaurant is a charming hotel of the same name, with antiques-filled rooms available for €40 a night. Rooms with balconies, offering spectacular views off Évoramonte's cliffside, cost €5 more. It's something of a novelty to sleep atop the castle hill, though a bit isolated. ✉ *Rua Santa Maria 26, Évoramonte* ☎ *268/959217* ⊟ *No credit cards* 🕑 *Closed Mon.*

5

ELVAS

40 km (25 mi) east of Estremoz; 15 km (9 mi) west of Spain.

Elvas, extensively fortified because of its proximity to the Spanish town of Badajoz, was from its founding an important bastion in warding off attacks from the east. Portugal's most formidable 17th-century fortifications are characterized by a series of walls, moats, and reinforced towers. The size of the complex can best be appreciated by driving around the periphery of the town. Inside you'll find a bustling, vibrant city with a stately town square, an impressive castle, an array of historic churches and museums, and almost no tourists.

GETTING HERE AND AROUND

Elvas lies on the Spanish frontier, just 15 km (9 mi) west of Badajoz. Praça da República lies at the center, with the castle at the town's northern end. The pedestrian Rua de Alcamim provides a lovely traffic-free entrance by foot from Elvas's southern walls. The bus station lies just outside the city walls, with service several times daily to Évora (check with the tourist office for updated timetable). Inside the city walls, there's a tourist bus that takes you to all the major sites: It costs €5 for adults and €2.50 for children, running 10–3 everyday but Wednesday and Sunday.

ESSENTIALS

Bus Info **Comboio Turistico** (⊠ *Praça da República* ☎ *268/622236*).

Internet **Espaço Internet** (⊠ *Praça da República* ☎ *268/623090* ✎ *loja. ja.elvas@hotmail.com* ✉ *Free Internet access* ☉ *Weekdays 9–7*).

Tour Guides **AGIA, Associacao de Guias Interpretes do Alentejo (Elvas)** (☎ *933/259036* ⊕ *www.visitelvas.com* ✉ *€12 for 2-hr tour* ☉ *Call for schedule*).

Visitor Info **Elvas Tourist Office** (⊠ *Praça da República* ☎ *268/622236* ⊕ *www. cm-elvas.pt/turismo* ☉ *Summer 9–7; winter 9–5:30. Closed Jan. 1, May 1, Easter Sun., Christmas Day*).

EXPLORING

Aqueduto da Amoreira. The 8-km (5-mi) *Amoreira Aqueduct* took more than a century to build and is still in use today. It was started in 1498 under the direction of one of the era's great architects, Francisco de Arruda—who also designed the Aqueduto da Agua da Prata north of Évora. The first drops of water didn't flow into the town fountain until 1622. Some parts of the impressive structure have five stories of arches; the total number of arches is 843. The aqueduct is best viewed from outside the city walls, on the road to/from Lisbon.

Castelo. From the Church of Our Lady of the Assumption walk up the hill past a pillory and two stone towers spanned by a graceful Moorish loggia. At the castle's battlements you'll have a sweeping view of the town and its fortifications. There's been a fortress here since Roman times, though this structure's oldest elements were built by the Moors and expanded by a handful of Portuguese monarchs. ⊠ *Parada do castelo* ☎ *No phone* ✉ *€1.50* ☉ *Weekdays 9:30–1 and 2:30–5:30. Closed weekends and holidays.*

Museu de Arte Contemporanea de Elvas. Opened in 2007, this is a rare modern art museum in otherwise traditional Alentejo, a province which often tends to look more to the past than the current era. The museum focuses on Portugal's 20th-century artists, and is definitely worth a visit if you're at all curious about modern aesthetics in these historic corridors. The well-organized exhibits feature about 300 works that rotate throughout the year. The baroque-style building itself is also exquisite, and used to be a hospital run by a religious order. Upstairs there's a chapel lined with azulejos, and a café with nice views of Elvas. ⊠ *Rua de Cadeia, Elvas* ☎ *268/637150* 🖼 *€2* ⊙ *Tues. 2:30–6, Wed.–Sun. 10–1 and 2:30–6.*

WHERE TO EAT AND STAY

$$
PORTUGUESE
✕ **A Bolota Castanha.** People drive miles to dine at this well-known restaurant 16 km (10 mi) from Elvas in the town of Terrugem. First started by famous restaurateur Júlia Vinagre, she's turned the restaurant over to new owners, but the quality hasn't changed, serving traditional Alentejan food in an elegant setting. The house takes pride in its *cozido de grão* (boiled dinner with pork, smoked sausages, cabbage, and chickpeas), but their menu also lists international dishes such as spinach with shrimp au gratin and delicious sorbets for dessert. ⊠ *Quinta Janelas Verdes, Rua Madre Teresa, Terrugem* ☎ *268/656118* ⚐ *Reservations essential on weekends* ⊟ *AE, DC, MC, V* ⊙ *Closed Mon.*

¢
PORTUGUESE
✕ **A Coluna.** This simple, local restaurant serves Alentejo classics like salted cod, grilled pork, and veal inside a welcoming white stucco dining room decorated with blue-and-white tiles. If you're brave, try the *cabrito* (baby goat), a local delicacy. The weekend tourist menu, offered all day for lunch and dinner, is a great value at €10. It includes any starter, main course and dessert off the menu. At lunch, the deal includes wine as well. ⊠ *Rua do Cabrito 11, Elvas* ☎ *268/623728* ⊟ *No credit cards* ⊙ *Closed Tues.*

¢
▦ **Antonio Mocisso e Garcia Coelho Quartos.** This simple guesthouse in the city center is great value if you just want a place to sleep within a short walk of all the sights. **Pros:** clean rooms at a cheap price. **Cons:** some rooms have small windows with little natural light; no on-site restaurant. ⊠ *Rua Aires Varela 15* ☎ *268/622126* ⟿ *20 rooms* ⌂ *In-room: a/c, no phone (some). In-hotel: room service (breakfast only), laundry service, Internet terminal* ⊟ *No credit cards* ⎮⊙⎮ *CP.*

$
Fodor's Choice
★
▦ **Hotel São João de Deus.** Housed in a 17th-century convent and military hospital just inside the city's southwest walls, this is Elvas's most luxurious hotel for the price. Each room is unique, and some have medieval wood screens, converted fireplaces, and headboards made of blue-and-white azulejos. Two pools and a terrace are tucked behind the city ramparts. **Pros:** this hotel's restoration preserves historic architecture better than the pousada's interior, and is a better value. **Cons:** some rooms are a bit small. ⊠ *Largo S. João Deus 1* ☎ *268/639220* ⊕ *www.hotelsaojoaodeus.com* ⟿ *56 rooms* ⌂ *In-room: a/c, safe, Internet (some), Wi-Fi. In-hotel: restaurant, room service, bar, 2 pools, bicycles, laundry service, Internet terminal, Wi-Fi hotspot, parking (free)* ⊟ *AE, D, DC, MC, V* ⎮⊙⎮ *CP, MAP, FAP.*

$ ⬚ **Pousada de Santa Luzia.** Portugal's first pousada, opened in 1942, is in a two-story, Moorish-style building 12 km (7 mi) from one of the major border crossings between Spain and Portugal. The cheerful, decent-size guest rooms have bright floral fabrics, hand-painted Alentejo furniture, and modern tiled bathrooms that are small but adequate. The large restaurant ($$$) has arched windows overlooking a garden and is open to the public, long a favorite with Elvas residents. One of the most popular dishes is *bacalhau dourado* (cod sautéed with eggs, potatoes, and onions). **Pros:** splendid views down into Spain; good restaurant. **Cons:** more modern, with less character than other pousadas. ✉ *Av. de Badajoz,* ☎ *268/637470* ⊕ *www.pousadas.pt* ⮐ *25 rooms* ⚮ *In-room: a/c, safe (some), Wi-Fi (some). In-hotel: restaurant, room service, bar, tennis court, pool, bicycles, laundry service, Internet terminal, Wi-Fi hotspot, parking (free)* ▭ *AE, DC, MC, V* ⦿ *CP, FAP, MAP.*

PORTALEGRE

47 km (29 mi) northwest of Campo Maior.

Portalegre is the gateway to the Alentejo's most mountainous region as well as to the Parque Natural da Serra de São Mamede. The town is at the foot of the Serra de São Mamede, where the parched plains of the south give way to a greener, more inviting landscape. Because it's a larger, more modern town, Portalegre lacks a bit of the charm of the whitewashed hamlets in the south of the province. But the city's vibrant spirit, buoyed by its large university, more than makes up for it. Unlike some of those deserted southern towns, Portalegre is alive with a diverse community and economy, and still has a gothic cathedral, castle, and walled old town to explore. It's a great base for outdoors lovers who want easy access to nearby mountains and villages. And history buffs will also enjoy exploring the remnants of Portalegre's once-thriving textile industry, for which it has a worldwide reputation for the quality of its handmade tapestries and which fetch high prices.

GETTING HERE AND AROUND

Portalegre is Alto Alentejo's largest hub, with good public transportation links. The tourist office can provide an updated bus schedule, with service several times daily to/from Évora. The city center is divided by the Jardim do Tarro, a public garden, with most historical points of interest to the south within easy walking distance, and residential areas to the north.

The tourist office also offers free guided walking tours at 9:30 on first Saturday of every month. Depending on the size and speed of the group tours last up to 3½ hours and cover all major tourist sites in Portalegre, except for museums. The walk follows a circuit inside the city limits, and isn't strenuous.

ESSENTIALS

Car Rental Alenrent Portalegre (✉ *Av. do Brasil 19* ☎ *245/203694*).

Internet Instituto Portugues da Juventude (✉ *Estrada do Bonfim* ☎ *245/301900* ⊕ *www.juventude.gov.pt* ✉ *Free Internet access* ⊙ *Weekdays 9:30–12:30 and 2–5:30*).

Tour Guides **Tempo Sem Fim** (✉ *Av. da Extremadura Espanhola 2-F* ☎ *245/366076* ⊕ *www.temposemfim.pt*).

Visitor Info **Portalegre Tourist Office** (✉ *Rua Guilherme Gomes Fernandes 22* ☎ *245/307445* ◷ *Daily 9:30–1 and 2:30–6*).

EXPLORING
TOP ATTRACTIONS

Castelo. Walk south from the central Jardim do Tarro, past rambling 17th- and 18th-century rowhouses and up the sloping cobblestone streets to Portalegre's castle, which dates from the early 14th century. In the 1930s, the castle's walls were dissembled to open streets around it to traffic. Now a wooden structure, somewhat controversial in its design, links the castle's body with an adjacent tower, where you can climb up for splendid views of the cathedral and city. ✉ *Rua Luis Barahona, Portalegre* ☎ *245/307540* ▣ *Free* ◷ *Tues.–Sun. 9:30–1 and 2:30–6.*

Fodor's Choice ★   **Coudelaria de Alter.** If you're interested in horses, you must visit the Coudelaria de Alter (Alter Stud Farm), 22 km (14 mi) southwest of Portalegre. It was founded by Dom João V in 1748 to furnish royalty with high-quality mounts. Dedicated to preserving and developing the extraordinarily beautiful Alter Real (Royal Alter) strain of the Lusitania breed, the farm has had a long, turbulent history. After years of foreign invasion and pillage, little remains of its original structures, but a huge modern equestrian complex now surrounds the older buildings. Fortunately, the equine bloodline, one of Europe's noblest, has been preserved, and you can watch these superb horses being trained and exercised on the farm. There are also three small but interesting museums here: one documents the history of the farm, one has a collection of horse-drawn carriages, and one has displays on the art of falconry. You can also watch falcons going through their daily training sessions. The town of Alter do Chão itself, with the battlements of a 14th-century castle overlooking a square, is also worth a stroll. ✉ *Coutada do Arneiro, follow signs along a dusty track 3 km (2 mi) northwest of Alter do Chão, Alter do Chão* ☎ *245/610070* ⊕ *www.alterreal.pt* ▣ *€3.80* ◷ *Daily 9:30–5; horse shows May 15–Sept. 14, daily 10:30–3, Sept. 15–May 14, daily 11–3; falconry demonstrations Tues., Thurs., weekends at 10:30 and 11:30.*

Museu de Tapeçaria Guy Fino. This wonderful museum holds a more contemporary collection of the tapestries that made Portalegre world-famous. The museum is named after Guy Fino, the founder of one of the city's textile factories. ✉ *Rua da Figueira 9* ☎ *245/307530* ⊕ *www.mtportalegre.pt* ▣ *€2* ◷ *Tues.–Sun. 9:30–1 and 2:30–6.*

Sé. About 400 meters north of the castle lies Portalegre's cathedral, a 16th-century church and the town's most prominent landmark. The 18th-century facade is highlighted with marble columns and wrought-iron balconies. Inside are early 17th-century azulejos depicting the Virgin Mary. ✉ *Praça do Município* ☎ *245/330322* ▣ *Free* ◷ *Tues. 8:15–noon, Wed.–Sun. 8:15–noon and 2:30–6. Closed the day after holidays.*

NEED A BREAK?   The bohemian **Pontofinal Paragrafo** (✉ *Rua Luiz de Camoes 43, Portalegre* ☎ *245/382041* ✍ *pontofinal.paragrafo@gmail.com* ◷ *Mon.–Sat. 9–8*) coffeeshop and bookstore opened in 2009 along the main street toward

5

Portalegre's cathedral and castle. It draws a mix of students, bookworms, and wannabe poets. It's got a lovely atmosphere and serves an array of cakes, teas, wine, and cocktails.

WORTH NOTING

Mosteiro de S. Bernardo. Founded in 1518, the Monastery of Saint Bernard is a beautiful renaissance property that includes a tiled church, cloisters with a central garden and fountain, and a mausoleum. The monastery closed after the last monk died in 1878, and since then the building has been used as a seminary, high school, municipal museum, and military barracks. It's now used by the National Guard, which opens the building to visitors during selected hours. ⊠ *Av. George Robinson, Portalegre* ☎ *245/307400* 🎫 *Free* ☉ *Daily 9–12:30 and 2–6.*

Parque Natural da Serra de São Mamede. You can enter this 80,000-acre nature park roughly 5 km (3 mi) northeast of Portalegre. It extends north to the fortified town of Marvão and the spa town of Castelo de Vide, and south to the little hamlet of Esperança on the Spanish border. The sparsely inhabited park region is made up of small family plots, and sheepherding is the major occupation. The area is rich in wildlife, including many rare species of birds, as well as wild boars, deer, and wildcats. It's a pristine, quiet place for hiking, riding, or simply communing with nature, and you'll rarely spot another tourist for miles and miles. For information about activities, contact the park office. ⊠ *Rua General Conde Jorge de Avilez 22, 1* ☎ *245/909160 or 245/203631.*

WHERE TO EAT AND STAY

¢ ✕ **O Abrigo.** On a quiet street around the corner from the cathedral

PORTUGUESE you'll find this small, husband-and-wife-run restaurant. You enter the cork-lined dining area through a snack bar. One of the best dishes on the menu is the *migas alentejanas* (a tasty fried-pork-and-bread-crumbs concoction), served on a terra-cotta platter. ⊠ *Rua de Elvas 74* ☎ *245/331658* 🔧 *Reservations essential on summer weekends* ▬ *MC, V* ☉ *Wed.–Mon. noon–3 and 7–10.*

¢ ✕ **O Escondidinho.** This restaurant is a charming local favorite. Decorated

PORTUGUESE with traditional tiles and brick archways, it serves up amazing Alen-

Fodor'sChoice tejo dishes like migas (fried breadcrumbs with coriander and garlic),

★ porco preto (black pork), and grilled fish. Half portions are huge and economical. Don't be surprised if you return twice in one weekend. ⊠ *Travessa das Cruzes 1, Portalegre* ☎ *245/202728* ▬ *No credit cards* ☉ *Daily noon–4 and 7–11.*

¢ 🏠 **Pensao Novo.** This clean, simple guesthouse has 15 rooms in each of two downtown rowhouses. Family owned and operated, this is the best of Portalegre's budget options, and a good value. ■TIP➔ **Children under 2 stay free and cribs are available. Pros:** clean rooms; good value; big breakfast buffet included. **Cons:** front rooms are vulnerable to street noise; no restaurant. ⊠ *Rua 31 Janeiro 30* ☎ *245/331212 or 245/330812* ⊕ *www.albergariadobonfim.pai.pt* ⤴ *30 rooms* ⚙ *In-room: a/c, Internet, Wi-Fi. In-hotel: room service (breakfast only), some pets allowed* ▬ *MC, V* ▮⊙▮ *CP.*

$ 🏠 **Quinta da Dourada.** This sprawling horse farm and vineyard is 7 km (4 mi) from Portalegre, but it feels like it's way out in the countryside, with 360-degree views of rolling hills, rows of grapevines and forests—all from the swimming pool. The family-run hotel is a rural oasis in the Mamede mountain foothills, with an outdoor brick oven and trellis-laden patio. The Portuguese owner, Nuno Malata Correia, and his Spanish wife breed beagle puppies and offer free bicycles for use on the property. They also make their own wine, an excellent peppery red, which is served with wine and cheese in the early evening or with dinner on request. **Pros:** rural retreat just a few minutes' drive from town; gorgeous swimming pool and gardens; kids are welcome. **Cons:** too far (and too steep a climb) to walk from town; no restaurant but meals can be prepared upon request. ⊠ *Serra de S. Mamede* ☎ *937/218654 or 245/203487* ⊕ *www.quintadadourada.com* ↪ *4 apartments, 2 double rooms* ♿ *In-room: a/c, no phone (some), refrigerator (some), Wi-Fi (some). In-hotel: room service, pool, bicycles, laundry service, Internet terminal, Wi-Fi hotspot, parking (free), some pets allowed* ⊟ *No credit cards* ⦿ *CP, FAP, MAP.*

Fodor'sChoice ★

¢ 🏠 **Solar das Avencas.** This historic manor adjacent to a park is exquisitely adorned with local tapestries and chock-full of antiques. The house has been in Antonio Manuel Manta's family for 200 years, and it feels like you're a guest in the couple's home. You'll be warmed by their hospitality, and by the complimentary glass of port they normally share on arrival. With only five rooms, the hotel fills quickly with locals on holiday weekends, and reservations are recommended well in advance. Most of the rooms have fireplaces and high ceilings, and one has an annex with extra beds for children or a group. **Pros:** historic property with warm family hospitality; staying here offers a more authentic, historic experience than even some pousadas, at a fraction of the price. **Cons:** no central heating, but cozy fireplaces in bedrooms; no restaurant. ⊠ *Parque Miguel Bombarda 11* ☎ *245/201028* ↪ *5 rooms* ♿ *In-room: a/c, no phone (some), refrigerator (some), Internet (some), Wi-Fi (some). In-hotel: room service (breakfast only), laundry service, parking (free)* ⊟ *No credit cards* ⦿ *CP.*

Fodor'sChoice ★

5

MARVÃO

25 km (15 mi) northeast of Portalegre.

The views of the mountains as you approach the medieval fortress town of Marvão are spectacular, and the town's castle, atop a sheer rock cliff, commands a 360-degree panorama. The village, with some 120 mostly older inhabitants, is perched at 860 meters (2,800 feet) on top of a mountain, and laid out in several long rows of tidy, white-stone dwellings terraced into the hill.

The biggest event of the year here is the boisterous chestnut festival in early November, when marching bands take to the tiny streets and transform Marvão into a homemade wine-swigging, chestnut-roasting party. But be forewarned: parking is impossible, and hotels book up sometimes a year beforehand.

GETTING HERE AND AROUND

Marvão lies north of Portalegre and east of Castelo de Vide, in the Serra Mamede mountains overlooking Spain. For the most scenic approach from Portalegre, take N359 18 km (11 mi) to Marvão. The narrow but well-surfaced serpentine N359 rises to an elevation of 2,800 feet, past stands of birch and chestnut trees and small vegetable gardens bordered by ancient stone walls. At Portagem take note of the well-preserved Roman bridge.

The drive up to Marvão, hugging the side of the mountain, is breathtaking but can also be hazardous in harsh weather. Although you can drive through the constricted streets, it's best to park in spaces outside the town walls and walk in as Marvão is best appreciated on foot.

ESSENTIALS

Visitor Info Marvão Tourist Office (✉ *Largo de Santa Maria* ☎ *245/909131* ⊕ *www.cm-marvao.pt* ✉ *Free Internet access inside* ☉ *Daily 9–12:30 and 2–5:30).*

EXPLORING

Castelo. You can climb the tower of the castle and trace the course of the massive Vauban-style stone walls (characterized by concentric lines of trenches and walls, a hallmark of the 17th-century French military engineer Vauban), adorned at intervals with bartizans, to enjoy breathtaking vistas from different angles. Given its strategic position, it's no surprise that Marvão has been a fortified settlement since Roman times or earlier. The present castle was built under Dom Dinis in the late 13th century and modified some four centuries later, during the reign of Dom João IV. At the time of this writing, the castle was open 24 hours, with no admission charge. The town plans some renovations in 2012, including the addition of a café and small museum, and possibly an admission fee. ✉ *Rua do Castelo, Marvão* ☎ *No phone* ✉ *Free* ☉ *24 hrs.*

Museu Municipal. At the foot of the path leading to the castle is Marvão's municipal museum, in the 13th-century Church of Saint Mary. The small gallery contains a diverse collection of religious artifacts, azulejos, costumes, ancient maps, and weapons. ✉ *Igreja de Santa Maria, Rua do Castelo, Marvão* ☎ *245/909132* ✉ *€1.25* ☉ *Daily 9–12:30 and 2–5:30.*

Santo António das Areias. Scattered among the chestnut groves, 5 km (3 mi) northeast of Marvão, are some two dozen prehistoric dolmens. They're difficult to locate on your own, however, and it's best to ask the tourist office to organize a group with a guide. Some pieces of the dolmens and photos of them can also be found in the Museu Municipal.

WHERE TO EAT AND STAY

$ ✕ **Casa do Povo.** Nestled into a corner rowhouse, this simple dining room

PORTUGUESE   serves up classic Alentejo dishes and local wines. The bar downstairs has a patio with good views for sundowners. The restaurant offers a €9 daily tourist menu that's decent value, including soup, main course, dessert, and a drink. Any of Casa do Povo's soups are worth tasting, especially the dogfish soup with coriander. ✉ *Travessa do Chabouco, Marvão* ☎ *245/993160* ✉ *casadopovo.rest@sapo.pt* ▭ *DC, MC, V* ☉ *Fri.–Wed. noon–2:30 and 7–9:30.*

¢ ✕ **Varanda do Alentejo.** This boisterous bar and restaurant is a favorite
PORTUGUESE among locals and out-of-town families who gather here on Sundays.
The cuisine is typical Alentejan, with specialties like migas with potato
(fried breadcrumbs with garlic and coriander), grilled pork, and fish.
The atmosphere is warm and friendly. Owner Fernando Rosado also has
five rooms for rent upstairs, at €45 for a standard double. ⊠ *Rua das
Protas da Vila 12, Marvão* ☎ *245/993272* ⊕ *www.varandadoalentejo.
com* ⊲ *Reservations essential on Sun.* ⊟ *No credit cards* ⊗ *Daily
noon–3 and 7–10.*

¢ 🏨 **Casa D. Dinis.** This Marvão house from the 17th century has stone
arches and thick walls. Original murals depicting scenes from the Alentejo adorn the rooms. Drinks and breakfast are served on a panoramic
terrace overlooking the valley, the ideal place to relax after a day of sightseeing. In winter, you can relax to the crackling sound of burning wood
in the fireplace in the cozy lounge. Its snack bar, Castelo Bar, is across
the street and serves small dishes and salads. That's also where owner
Cristina Andrade cooks a casual midday meal for all the local workers in
town; ask if you can join them for an authentic, nontouristy experience.
This hotel is also popular with hiking and mountain-biking groups. **Pros:**
cozy; no-frills family hospitality; terrace offers some of the best views
in town. **Cons:** the Andrade family's contract to operate the hotel may
run out in 2012, so management (and quality) may change. ⊠ *Rua Dr.
António Matos Magalhães 7* ☎ *245/993957* ⊕ *www.casadomdinis.pai.pt*
⤴ *8 rooms* ⚅ *In-room: a/c, Wi-Fi (some). In-hotel: no restaurant, room
service (breakfast only), bar, laundry service, Wi-Fi hotspot, some pets
allowed, kids under 2 stay free* ⊟ *AE, DC, MC, V* �🍽 *CP.*

$ 🏨 **Hotel El Rei Dom Manuel.** A 200-year-old house inside the castle walls was
completely renovated to create this inn. Five of its rooms have fantastic
cliff-side views, and others range in size, with good options for families
who need extra beds. All are decorated with traditional locally made
furnishings, tile floors, wood paneling, and heavy draperies. The restau-
rant inside is open to the public only for dinner, ($$) serving regional
fare. There's also a TV lounge for children. ■TIP→ **If you plan on bring-
ing the kids, make sure you ask about the special rates for children.** **Pros:** his-
toric building in quiet location; good views. **Cons:** decor is a bit dated.
⊠ *Largo da Olivença* ☎ *245/909150* ⊕ *www.turismarvao.pt* ⤴ *15 rooms*
⚅ *In-room: a/c, safe (some), refrigerator (some), Internet, Wi-Fi. In-hotel:
restaurant, room service, bar, laundry service, Internet terminal, Wi-Fi
hotspot, parking (free)* ⊟ *AE, DC, MC, V* �🍽 *CP, FAP, MAP.*

$ 🏨 **Pousada de Santa Maria.** In 1967 several old houses within the city
walls were joined to create the Pousada de Santa Maria. The rooms
are decorated with traditional Alentejo furnishings, and the restaurant,
open to the public, ($$) serves some of the best regional dishes in the
village. The back of the hotel is encased in glass, with gorgeous views
of the mountains and countryside. Because the hotel is actually a string
of rowhouses merged together, it lacks the grand expanses and open
salons of other pousadas, though its price tag is commensurately lower
as well. Still, if you have to choose one or two pousadas to visit, this
one can be missed. ■TIP→ **If you plan on bringing the kids, make sure you
ask about the special rates.** **Pros:** cozy atmosphere, especially in winter

when Marvão can be windswept and deserted. **Cons:** lacks extraordinary features and grandiose charm of other pousadas. ⊠ *Santa Maria de Marvão* ☏ *245/993201 or 245/993202* ⊕ *www.pousadas.pt* ⇆ *28 rooms, 3 suites* ♿ *In-room: a/c, safe (some), Internet, Wi-Fi. In-hotel: restaurant, room service, bar, laundry service, Internet terminal, Wi-Fi hotspot, parking (free)* ⊟ *AE, DC, MC, V* ⊚❙ *CP, MAP, FAP.*

CASTELO DE VIDE

8 km (5 mi) west of Marvão.

A quiet, hilltop town, Castelo de Vide is a picturesque place with pots of geraniums and dazzling flower beds throughout town. It's more lively than Marvão, with more options for restaurants, hotels, and sights, but still retains its rustic village feel. When Marvão holds its annual chestnut festival, drawing thousands of tourists from all over Portugal and Spain, Castelo de Vide holds a smaller, more intimate festival in its open-air market, complete with a pig roast and old men in felt hats sharing jugs of their homemade wine. You might be surprised to see a bagpiper strolling through the crowds during Castelo de Vide's festivals; the diverse town still celebrates some traditions from its ancient Gallic and Celtic ancestry.

There are steep cobbled streets that provide beautiful views of the whitewashed town against a backdrop of olive groves and hills. As you walk along, notice the many houses with Gothic doorways in various designs. (The tourist brochures proclaim that Castelo de Vide has the largest number of Gothic doorways of any town in Portugal.) Castelo de Vide's history is as a spa town, renowned for its fresh mountain springs that feed a fountain in the main square today.

GETTING HERE AND AROUND

An intriguing backcountry lane connects Marvão with Castelo de Vide. About halfway down the hill from Marvão, turn to the right toward Escusa (watch for the sign) and continue through the chestnut- and acacia-covered hills to Castelo de Vide.

If you're traveling from Portalegre, take the N246 directly. At the town's main square is the Praça Dom Pedro V, with the castle to the west and a park to the east.

The tourist office can supply maps for unguided tours of Castelo de Vide's historic houses, gothic doorways, and fountains, as well as of megalithic sites in the area.

ESSENTIALS

Taxi **Castelo de Vide Taxi Service** (⊠ *Praça Dom Pedro V* ☏ *245/901271* ⊡ *€10 to Marvão* ⊗ *24 hrs*).

Visitor Info **Castelo de Vide Tourist Office** (⊠ Praça Dom Pedro V ☏ *245/901361* ⊕ *www.cm-castelo-vide.pt* ⊡ *Free guided tours* ⊗ *Summer 9–7 daily; winter 9–12:30 and 2–5:30 daily*).

EXPLORING

Castelo. From the Judairia it's a short climb to the ruins of Castelo de Vide's castle. Go up into the tower and inside the well-preserved keep to the large Gothic hall, which has a picture window looking down on the town square and the church. ⊠ *Rua Direita do Castelo,* ☎ *No phone* 🎟 *Free* ⊙ *Daily 9–12:30 and 2–6.*

Mercado Franco. On the last Friday of every month this open-air market is held in Sitio do Canapé, next to the Municipal Market. You can find bargains in everything from T-shirts, shoes, and jewelry, to electronic equipment.

Praça Dom Pedro V. Castelo de Vide's large baroque central square is bordered by the Igreja de Santa Maria (St. Mary's Church) and the town hall. An alleyway to the right of the church leads to the town symbol, a canopied, 16th-century marble fountain. Another cobblestone lane leads from the fountain up to the Juderia (ancient Jewish quarter). The tourist office, on the north side of the square, often pipes classical music through speakers across the area, particularly around the holidays. ⊠ *Praça Dom Pedro V, Castelo de Vide* ☎ *No phone* ⊕ *www.cm-castelo-vide.pt.*

Sinagoga. A Jewish community is believed to have existed in Castelo de Vide since the 12th century, and reached its peak in the 15th century, bolstered by Jews fleeing the Inquisition in neighboring Spain. This tiny synagogue is believed to be from the late 13th century. There's a tiny sign outside, but otherwise you might miss it—it looks exactly like all the other rowhouses. The synagogue was adapted from existing buildings, with two separate prayer rooms for men and women. ⊠ *Rua da Judairia, Castelo de Vide* ☎ *No phone* 🎟 *Free* ⊙ *June–Sept., daily 10–8; Oct.–May, daily 10–5:30.*

WHERE TO EAT AND STAY

¢ ✕ **Doces & Companhia.** This modern upscale coffeeshop serves light
PORTUGUESE lunches like scones, cakes, baguettes, and sandwiches, and makes the perfect stop between sightseeing trips around town. The outdoor terrace in back offers superb views of the hillside across from Castelo de Vide. A kids' table with crayons and coloring books is downstairs. ⊠ *Praça Dom Pedro V, 6, Castelo de Vide* ☎ *245/901408* ▭ *AE, DC, MC, V* ⊙ *Mon.–Sat. 8:30–7:30, open until 11:30 in summer, closed Sun.*

$ ✕ **Restaurante D. Pedro V.** This is the best option for a traditional Alen-
PORTUGUESE tejan meal in Castelo de Vide. Walk through the entryway bar into a lovely domed dining room decorated like an old wine cellar. Specialties include goat and lamb roasts and dogfish soup with local chestnuts. The €16 tourist menu, which includes a soup or starter, main course, dessert and wine, is a good value. ⊠ *Praça Dom Pedro V, Castelo de Vide* ☎ *245/901236* ⊕ *www.dpedrov.com.pt* ⩟ *Reservations essential on weekends* ▭ *AE, DC, MC, V* ⊙ *Tues.–Sun. noon–3 and 7–10.*

$ ⛉ **Casa Amarela.** The beautifully restored 17th-century manor house on
Fodor'sChoice Castelo de Vide's main square is a luxurious and intimate place to stay.
★ Stone stairways lead to intricately decorated rooms filled with period antiques and with huge marble bathrooms. The breakfast room has a traditional clay tiled floor and a huge fireplace. The hotel is the pride and joy of Victor Guimaraes, whose family has owned the building for

generations, and who did much of the 2002 restoration work himself. ■ TIP→ **Children under 6 stay free. Pros:** luxurious, intimate settling with views over Praça Dom Pedro V. **Cons:** outside rooms overlooking the square might get some noise on summertime weekends; no restaurant; no pool, but there's free access to pool at sister hotel, Casa do Parque, across town. ⊠ *Praça Dom Pedro V, 11* 🕾 *245/901250 or 245/905878* ⊕ *www. casaamarelath.com* 🖅 *11 rooms* 🖒 *In-room: a/c, no phone, Wi-Fi (some). In-hotel: room service (breakfast only), bar, laundry service, Internet terminal, Wi-Fi hotspot, parking (free)* ═ *No credit cards* ❑❙ *CP.*

¢ 🔡 **Casa do Parque.** This charming guesthouse is a more affordable option owned by the same Castelo de Vide family as Casa Amarela. It's set about 500 meters away, overlooking the village park, and it has the closest swimming pool to the town center. With more character than Hotel Castelo de Vide, this is a good option for those who want to absorb local atmosphere close to all the sights. There's also a great restaurant of the same name, open to the public, which serves traditional Alentejo dishes and attracts crowds on Sunday. ■ TIP→ **Children under 6 stay free. Pros:** quaint and clean; gorgeous swimming pool amid flowering trees. **Cons:** not as stately as Casa Amarela, but not as costly either. ⊠ *Av. da Aramenha 37* 🕾 *245/901250* ⊕ *www.casadoparque.net* 🖅 *25 rooms* 🖒 *In-room: a/c, no phone, Wi-Fi (some). In-hotel: restaurant, bar, pool, laundry service, Wi-Fi hotspot* ═ *No credit cards* ❑❙ *CP, FAP, MAP.*

¢ 🔡 **Hotel Castelo de Vide.** Remodeled under new management in 2006, this hotel caters mostly to large groups, with facilities for family reunions or corporate retreats. The restaurant is no longer open to the public but prepares meals on request for groups of 15 or more. The golf course that the hotel used to partner with is also now closed. Still, it's a perfectly fine option for those who want to be close to the town center and still have a swimming pool. A good option for families, who will likely have the pool and sprawling terrace all to themselves. Babysitting and packed lunches available too. ■ TIP→ **Children under 5 stay free. Pros:** good value, especially for groups. **Cons:** clean but characterless; restaurant for prebooked groups only. ⊠ *Av. da Europa* 🕾 *245/908210* ⊕ *www.hotelcastelodevide.com* 🖅 *53 rooms* 🖒 *In-room: a/c, refrigerator (some), Internet, Wi-Fi. In-hotel: room service (breakfast only), bar, pool, laundry service, Internet terminal, Wi-Fi hotspot, parking (free), some pets allowed* ═ *AE, MC, V* ❑❙ *CP, FAP, MAP.*

BAIXO ALENTEJO

Extending south of Évora and from the rugged west-coast beaches east to the border with Spain, Baixo Alentejo (the Lower Alentejo) is a vast, mostly flat region of wheat fields, cork oaks, and olive trees. It rains very little here, and the summer months are particularly hot. Shepherds wearing broad-brim hats and sheepskin vests still tend their sheep in the fields. Gypsies still set up camp with makeshift tents, horse carts, and open fires. These scenes from a rapidly disappearing way of life contrast sharply with the modernization taking place in the region.

VIANA DO ALENTEJO

37 km (23 mi) southeast of Évora.

The attractive castle at Viana do Alentejo—with its rough stone walls, brick battlements, and round turrets—was constructed in 1313 to the very specific orders of Portuguese king Dom Dinis. He decreed that the pentagonal walls should be tall enough that a horseman with a lance measuring 9 *côvados* (an ancient unit of measure equal to 66 centimeters [26 inches]) couldn't injure anyone on the battlements. The fortified parish church within the walls of the castle—designed by the famous Diogo de Arruda—has a pleasing combination of battlements, spires, and ornate Manueline elements. Below the castle a delightful Renaissance fountain enhances the town square. Viana do Alentejo is also noted for a primitive-style pottery, sold in several small shops in town.

GETTING HERE AND AROUND

Viana do Alentejo is an easy drive south of Évora on the N254, and a pleasant stop along back roads en route to Beja. The village sprawls out from the castle, with the main square, a fountain, and some cafés just behind it.

ESSENTIALS

Visitor Info **Viana do Alentejo Tourist Office** (⊠ *Praça da República 1* ☎ *266/930012* ⊕ *www.cm-vianadoalentejo.pt* ☉ *Daily 10–1 and 2–5:30. Closed Sun. in winter, Mon. in summer).*

EXPLORING

Castelo. Viana do Alentejo's castle is the highlight of any visit here. The building dates from the 14th century, and about 100 years later it hosted a session of Parliament. The fortress's majestic interior merges with the stately parish church, whose vaulted ceilings also bear the king's coat of arms. There are also two beautiful stained-glass windows, and an alcove covered in 16th-century azulejos from Seville. ⊠ *Rua do Relogio, Viana do Alentejo* ☎ *No phone* 🎟 *Free* ☉ *Daily 10–1 and 2–5:30. Closed Sun. in winter, Mon. in summer.*

WHERE TO EAT

¢ ✕ **Restaurante A Cave.** This traditional restaurant is housed in an old wine
PORTUGUESE cellar, with bottles of local wines lining the walls. Specialties include grilled fish, roasted lamb, and porco preto. In summer, you can eat on the shaded terrace outside. ⊠ *Loteamento do Mauforo, Lote 17, Viana do Alentejo* ☎ *266/791094* 🍽 *No credit cards* ☉ *Tues.–Sun. 9 am–midnight.*

ALVITO

12 km (7 mi) south of Viana do Alentejo.

Alvito is a typical, sleepy Alentejo town on a low hill above the Rio Odivelas. Noted for its fortresslike 13th-century parish church, the town also has a 15th-century castle converted into a pousada and a number of modest houses with graceful Manueline doorways and windows. The castle was built in 1482 by the Baron of Alvito, the first individual permitted to have his own castle. King Manuel I was born and died here.

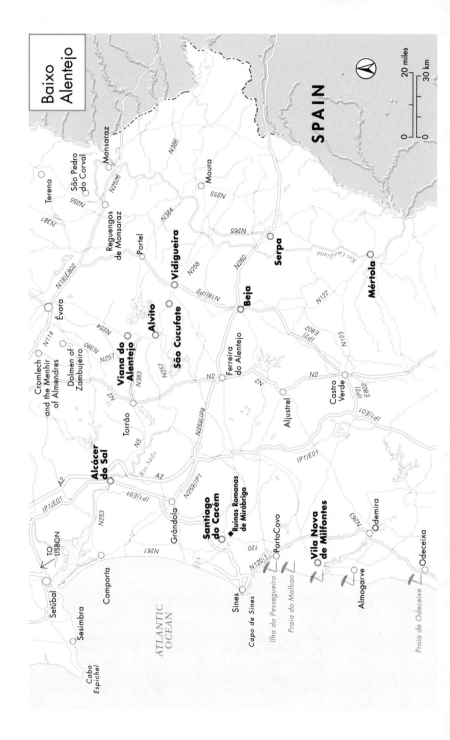

Baixo Alentejo

SPAIN

ATLANTIC OCEAN

Cabo Espichel
Sesimbra
Setúbal
TO LISBON
Comporta
Cabo de Sines
Sines
Porto Covo
Ilha do Pessegueiro
Praia do Malhao
Vila Nova de Milfontes
Almograve
Praia de Odeceixe
Odeceixa
Odemira
Grândola
Santiago do Cacém
Ruinas Romanas de Mirábriga
Alcácer do Sal
Torrão
Viana do Alentejo
Alvito
São Cucufate
Évora
Cromlech and the Menhir of Almendres
Dolmen of Zambujeiro
Reguengos de Monsaraz
Portel
Vidigueira
Monsaraz
São Pedro do Corval
Terena
Moura
Serpa
Beja
Ferreira do Alentejo
Aljustrel
Castro Verde
Mértola
Rio Guadiana
Rio Sado

N261
N253
A2
IP1/E01
N5
N2
N254
N114
N380
N257
N383
N2
N259/IP8
N259/IP1
N120-1
120
N390
IP1/E01
N2
N122
N123
IP2/E802
IP2/E802
IP1/E01
N260
N258
N255
N255
N384
N386
N2536
N381
N18/E802
N18/IP2
N363

0   20 miles
0   30 km

GETTING HERE AND AROUND

Alvito lies south of Viana do Alentejo on the way to Beja, along the N257 and N258. There is no public transport in this remote, rural part of Portugal, and having your own car is essential for exploring the area. The small village of Alvito stretches just a few blocks out from the castle in all directions.

ESSENTIALS

Visitor Info Alvito Tourist Office (✉ *Rua dos Lobos 13* ☎ *284/480808* ⊘ *Weekdays 9–12:30 and 2–5:30, Sat. 10–12:30 and 2–5:30*).

WHERE TO EAT AND STAY

¢

PORTUGUESE

✕ **O Camões.** Northwest of Alvito (7 km [4½ mi]), the main attraction of this large, popular restaurant is its wood-burning oven in which delicious legs of lamb, pork, and other meats are cooked to perfection. They're first marinated in coriander, oregano, and aromatic herbs that grow in the region. Owner Sr. Camões is also well known for his açorda dishes, the most popular being *açorda de cação* (baby shark porridge). The atmosphere is cozy and authentic, with brick domed walls, wood paneling, and a huge antique chandelier dangling overhead. ✉ *Rua 5 de Outubro 15, Vila Nova da Baronia* ☎ *284/475209* ▭ *No credit cards* ⊘ *Tues.–Sun. 9 am–2 am.*

$

Fodor's Choice

★

🏠 **Pousada do Castelo de Alvito.** This pousada is within the walls of the fortress at the edge of the village. The essential architectural elements of a castle, including crenellated battlements and massive round towers, have been retained, and there's a large garden, and a courtyard. Vaulted Gothic ceilings, red clay–tile floors, oil paintings with gold-leaf picture frames, and red-and-gold-patterned upholstery add to the medieval atmosphere. Rooms fit for a king have beautiful arched Manueline windows and stone window benches. More than any other pousada, this really feels like you're staying in a 15th-century castle, with window seats set in thick walls that look out onto rolling plains. The power is known to cut out in autumn storms, but that only adds to the atmosphere—in candlelight. The cozy restaurant, which is open to the public, ($$$) serves a variety of Alentejo specialties, including an excellent *bacalhau caldeirada* (codfish stew). Knowledgeable, friendly staff can book bread-making, wine or pottery workshops, as well as horseback-riding and architecture tours. Things to keep the kids occupied include a pool, playground, and board games lounge. ∎TIP→ **If you plan on bringing the kids, make sure you ask about the special rates. Pros:** countryside setting makes the castle even more spectacular. **Cons:** this is a cozy retreat, but if you're looking for nightlife you'll be hard pressed to find any. ✉ *Largo do Castelo, Apartado 9* ☎ *284/480700* ⊕ *www.pousadas.pt* ⇆ *20 rooms, 1 suite* ⌂ *In-room: a/c, safe, Wi-Fi (some). In-hotel: restaurant, room service, bar, pool, bicycles, children's programs (ages 4–12), laundry service, Internet terminal, Wi-Fi hotspot, parking (free)* ▭ *AE, DC, MC, V* ⦿*CP, FAP, MAP.*

SÃO CUCUFATE

11 km (7 mi) southwest of Alvito.

GETTING HERE AND AROUND

São Cucufate lies west of Vidigueira, along the N258 toward Alvito. You can spot the ruins from the road, just outside the village of Vila de Frades.

It's a rural village without a tourist office, public transportation, or any other facilities for visitors. The tourist office in Vidigueira is the closet one (⇨ *see info below*).

ESSENTIALS

Visitor Info **Vidigueira Tourist Office** (✉ *Complexo de Piscinas Municipais* ☎ *284/437410* ⊕ *www.cm-vidigueira.pt* ⊘ *Tues.–Sun. 9–1 and 2–4*).

EXPLORING

São Cucufate. It's believed that these 2,000-year-old ruins of a two-story Roman villa were part of an extensive Roman settlement that included a swimming pool, tanks for hot and cold water, and a sophisticated plumbing system made from clay bricks. Coins and other artifacts that have turned up indicate a 1st-century Roman presence. The villa's ground floor was probably used as a barn, with the living quarters above it. Remnants of the original heating and drainage systems are visible. The building was later adapted and used in the 13th century as a monastery. The frescoes in the little chapel that still stands on the site were painted in the late 15th and early 16th centuries. There's an information center and a café. ✉ *Estrada de Vila Alva (N258 from Vila Alva to Vidigueira), Vila de Frades* ☎ *284/441113* ✇ *€2* ⊘ *May–Sept. 15, Tues. 3–6, Wed.–Sun. 9:30–1 and 3–6; Sept. 16–Apr., Tues. 2–5, Wed.–Sun. 9–12:30 and 2–5.*

BEJA

23 km (14 mi) southeast of Vidigueira.

Midway between Spain and the sea is Beja, the Lower Alentejo's principal agricultural center that spreads itself across a small knoll. Much of the oldest part of town retains a significantly Arabic flavor—students of Portuguese even claim that the local dialect has Arabic characteristics—the legacy of more than 400 years of Moorish occupation.

Beja, founded by Julius Caesar and known as Pax Julia, was an important town in the Roman province of Lusitania during the 1st century. The name Pax Julia was chosen because it was here, after a long struggle, that peace was finally established between the Lusitanian chiefs and Julius Caesar. You can see Roman artifacts and other tokens of Beja's long history at the wonderful regional museum in the Convento da Conceição and at the excavations in nearby Pizões.

Beja is also the legendary spot where a Portuguese nun fell passionately and secretly in love with a French army officer—their love letters created a scandal throughout 17th-century Europe (you can visit the convent where the love affair is said to have started).

Beja is often overlooked in favor of its more popular and beautiful sister city, Évora, but that just means you'll have the town all to yourself to explore. It's also a classic example of an Alentejo town center that's been emptied of its residents, some of whom have moved to modern apartment complexes on the city's outskirts, and many others who've left altogether, seeking employment in Lisbon or Porto. Walking Beja's streets, it seems like the majority of the population is over 65—a sobering idea when it comes to the future here.

Many of the town's most interesting monuments were destroyed in the 19th century during the population's fury against the church's domination. In spite of that, Beja has an important valuable heritage, and it can all be explored on foot.

GETTING HERE AND AROUND
Beja lies in the center of Baixo Alentejo, along the IP2 about halfway between Évora and the Algarve. The city's walkable center is bisected east to west by a public garden and three grand squares: Largo Dom Nuno Alvares Pereira, Largo dos Duques de Beja, and Praça da Republica.

ESSENTIALS
Visitor Info Beja Tourist Office (✉ *Rua Capitão João Francisco de Sousa 25* ☎ *284/311913* ⏱ *Daily 10–1 and 2–6*).

EXPLORING
Castelo. Beja's castle is an extensive system of fortifications, whose crenellated walls and towers chronicle the history of the town from its Roman occupation through its 19th-century battles with the French. Once inside the central courtyard, climb up the castle's ramparts to the impressive 42-meter (140-foot) **Torre de Menagem,** a stone tower with gorgeous views of the surrounding countryside. ✉ *Largo de Santo Amaro* 🖼 *Free* ⏱ *June–Sept., Tues.–Sun. 10–1 and 2–6; Oct.–May, Tues.–Sun. 9–noon and 1–4.*

odor's Choice
★ **Convento de Nossa Senhora da Conceição.** Facing a broad plaza in the center of the oldest part of town, the Convent of Our Lady of the Conception was founded in 1459 by the parents of King Manuel I. Favored by the royal family, this Franciscan convent became one of the richest of the period. It now houses the **Museu Regional Rainha Dona Leonor** (Queen Leonor Regional Museum), whose exhibits are of interest both to scholars of local history as well as casual visitors. If there's one museum you visit in Beja, this should be it. It's tough to decide which is more impressive, the exhibits inside or the building itself. You walk into an ornate, gold-encrusted chapel with saints' relics, and then proceed through the convent's old cloisters covered in azulejos from the 16th- and 17th-centuries. Some of them comprise panels depicting scenes from the life of St. John the Baptist, and there's also a section of Moorish tiles. At the far end of the second-floor gallery is the famous Mariana Window, named for the 17th-century nun Mariana Alcoforado, whose love affair with a French officer is the stuff of local legend. ✉ *Largo da Conceição* ☎ *284/323351* ⊕ *www.museuregionaldebeja.net* 🖼 *€2 (includes admission to Museu Visigótico), free admission on Sun. morning* ⏱ *Tues.–Sun. 9:30–12:30 and 2–5:15.*

AN AFFAIR TO REMEMBER

As the story goes, Mariana Alco-forado (1640–1723), a young Beja nun, fell in love with a French count named Chamilly, who was in the Alentejo fighting the Spaniards. When he went back to France, the nun waited longingly and in vain at the window for him to return. The affair was made public when five passionate love letters attributed to Mariana to the count were published in France in 1669 (the popular collection was known as the *Portuguese Letters*). The scandal brought a measure of lasting international literary fame to this provincial Alentejo town. But it's likely that it was actually another Frenchman who penned the infamous letters, after hearing of the love story. Nevertheless, French nobles apparently began using the word "portugaise" as a synonym for a passionate love letter.

Igreja de Santa Maria. *St. Mary's Church*, across the square from the Convento de Nossa Senhora da Conceição, was once a mosque, and can be easily recognized by its massive round pillars, Mudéjar arches, and its bell tower similar in design to that of the famed Giralda Tower in Seville. ⊠ *Largo de Santa Maria* ☎ *284/328438* 🖃 *Free* ☺ *Weekdays 10–5, weekends check mass schedule.*

NEED A BREAK?

Luiz da Rocha (⊠ *Rua Capitão João Francisco de Sousa 63* ☎ *284/323179* ⊕ *www.luizdarocha.com* ☺ *Daily 9 am–11 pm.*) is a Beja institution, founded in 1893. The art deco–style main café on the ground floor serves great coffee and *conventuais,* sweets made according to recipes from local convents. In the pedestrian section of streets just outside the city walls, this is a good local spot to have a sandwich between museum visits.

Praça da República. This stately square stretches across the western part of the city center, anchored at one end by the 16th-century Igreja de Misericordia, whose sprawling stone veranda used to be an open-air market. At one end is an ornate royal pillory from the 16th-century reign of Dom Manuel, restored in the 20th-century. The square is also lined with lovely Manueline archways under residential buildings. ⊠ *Praça da República Beja.*

WHERE TO EAT

¢   ╳ **Adega Tipica 25 Abril.** This rustic restaurant with red-and-white-check
PORTUGUESE   tablecloths and cork carvings adorning the walls serves typical Alentejan dishes, and along with another similar restaurant across the street, it's the best value in town. The atmosphere is authentic, with long wooden tables for boisterous families and intimate little two-seaters tucked behind huge clay wine jugs. The house wine—literally cheaper than the bottled water—is a wonderful value and complement to any meal. ⊠ *Rua da Moeda 23, Beja* ☎ *284/325960* ⚓ *Reservations essential on summer weekends* ▭ *No credit cards* ☺ *Closed Mon.*

¢   ╳ **Casa de Pasto a Pipa.** Across the street from Adega Tipica 25 Abril,
PORTUGUESE   this narrow little locals' favorite is another popular place for traditional Alentejan cuisine. The *prato del dia*, or daily menu specials, are

a good value, with around €10 covering a starter or soup, main course, and dessert. ⊠ *Rua da Moeda 8, Beja* ☎ *284/327043 or 968/115032* ⌲ *Reservations essential on summer weekends* ▤ *MC, V* ⊘ *Closed Sun.*

$ ✕ **Enoteca Magna Casa.** This tiny but wonderful wine bar serves huge
PORTUGUESE plates of tapas along with a selection of Alentejo's best wines. The lovely
odor'sChoice green-tiled exterior looks like an old rowhouse and masks a modern
★ wine bar inside, with walls lined with local bottles. The food is simple and rustic, with a succession of innovative tapas plates paired to the wine of your choice. Sit back and let the friendly husband-and-wife owners choose for you—you won't be disappointed. ⊠ *Rua Dr. Aresta Branco 45, Beja* ☎ *284/326287* ⌲ *Reservations essential on summer weekends* ▤ *No credit cards* ⊘ *Mon.–Sat. 6 pm–midnight.*

$ ✕ **Teotónius.** Dine on traditional Alentejan fare in this agreeable restaurant
PORTUGUESE with vaulted ceilings. You can also take a seat alfresco beneath fruit trees in the inner courtyard. The *carne de porco à alentejana* (pork with clams) is recommended. Other specialties include snails and fondue. ⊠ *Rua Sousa Porto 43–45* ☎ *284/328010* ▤ *AE, DC, MC, V* ⊘ *Closed Mon.*

WHERE TO STAY

¢   ▦ **Monte Horta do Cano.** A kilometer and a half (1 mi) from Beja on the road to Ferreira do Alentejo, this rustic inn—once a farming estate—has six handsome rooms. On tap for the energetic are tennis, swimming, and clay-pigeon shooting. For those otherwise inclined there's an old wine cellar converted into a bar where you can linger over fine Alentejo wines and snacks of regional bread, cheeses, and cured sausage. **Pros:** rustic charm with good selection of outdoor activities. **Cons:** decor is a bit dated. ⊠ *Horta do Cano Apartado 1018* ☎ *284/326156* ⊕ *www.hortadocano.com* ⬐ *6 rooms* ⌂ *In-room: a/c, safe (some), Internet (some). In-hotel: restaurant, room service, bar, tennis court, pool, bicycles, children's programs (ages 4–12), laundry service, Internet terminal, Wi-Fi hotspot, parking (free), some pets allowed* ▤ *No credit cards* ⎮◎⎮ *CP, FAP, MAP.*

¢   ▦ **Pensão Residencial Santa Bárbara.** This elegant guesthouse has a cozy stone fireplace and a great location in Beja's pedestrian zone just outside the old city walls. There are several options for larger rooms with extra beds for families. **Pros:** good location, historic details inside. **Cons:** front rooms with balconies can be a bit noisy overlooking the street; no restaurant. ⊠ *Rua de Mértola 56* ☎ *284/312280* ⊕ *www. residencialsantabarbara.pt* ⬐ *26 rooms* ⌂ *In-room: a/c, Internet (some). In-hotel: room service (breakfast only), bar, laundry service, Internet terminal* ▤ *No credit cards* ⎮◎⎮ *CP.*

$$ ▦ **Pousada do Convento de São Francisco.** Surrounded by spacious gardens is an old convent that has been tastefully converted into a comfortable pousada. The former chapel has been preserved and incorporated into the complex. Alentejo dishes fill the menu in the restaurant, which is open to the public as well ($$$); the *bacalhau com natas* (salt cod cooked with a cream sauce) is delicious. **Pros:** elegant old-world style with modern swimming pool surrounded by palm trees; good option for children, with space to run around outside. **Cons:** more expensive; less historic detail than other pousadas. ⊠ *Largo Dom Nuno Álvares Pereira* ☎ *284/313580* ⊕ *www.pousadas.pt* ⬐ *34 rooms, 1 suite*

5

⟳ In-room: a/c, safe, Internet (some), Wi-Fi (some). In-hotel: restaurant, room service, bar, tennis court, pool, bicycles, children's programs (ages 4–12), laundry service, Internet terminal, Wi-Fi hotspot, parking (free) ▭ AE, DC, MC, V ⦿ CP, FAP, MAP.

$ ⊞ **Residencial Bejense.** This little inn along Beja's pedestrian shopping
Fodor'sChoice   zone was the first public hotel in town, founded in 1889. Since then it's
★   changed hands several times, undergoing renovations but still retaining its old stone doorway covered in vines and flowers. The entryway and lobby are lined with gorgeous hand-painted tile murals of country life around Beja. A common room upstairs has a long brick fireplace and wood beams, the perfect spot to sip a glass of port in the evening. Rooms are flowery and spacious, and some are decorated in azulejo tiles and wall murals. **Pros:** warm service; family-run establishment; elegant, comfortable style; good location. **Cons:** no restaurant. ⊠ Rua Capitão João Francisco de Sousa 57 ☎ 284/311570 ⊕ www.residencialbejense. com ⇥ 24 rooms ⟳ In-room: a/c, safe (some), Wi-Fi (some). In-hotel: room service (breakfast only), bar, laundry service, Internet terminal, Wi-Fi hotspot ▭ MC, V ⦿ CP.

SERPA

27 km (17 mi) southeast of Beja.

In this sleepy agricultural town, men pass the time by gathering together in the compact Praça da República under the shadow of an ancient stone clock tower. One of the most authentic towns on the Alentejan plain, Serpa's whitewashed medieval center is surrounded by rolling hills and vineyards, well off the tourist path but definitely worth a visit. In cubbyholes along narrow, cobbled streets, carpenters, shoemakers, basket weavers, and other craftsmen work in much the same manner as their forefathers.

Serpa's sleepy streets explode with life several times a year with festivals that draw visitors from across the Spanish border and around Europe, celebrating Serpa's local delicacies, including one of Portugal's most renowned sheep's milk cheeses.

GETTING HERE AND AROUND
Serpa lies along the IP8 east of Beja, and about equidistant to the Spanish border. It's best to park outside the old city walls near the impressive aqueduct, and navigate the town center by foot.

ESSENTIALS
Visitor Info Serpa Tourist Office (⊠ Largo D. Jorge de Melo 2-3 ☎ 284/544727 ⊕ www.cm-serpa.pt ⊗ Apr. 1–Sept. 30, daily 10–7; Oct. 1–Mar. 31, daily 9–6.).

EXPLORING
Aqueduto. This impressive structure from the 11th century used to ferry water to Serpa from wells in the countryside. In the 17th century, a wheel pump was added just outside the city's southern walls, and still stands there today. Follow the aqueduct's walls from the pump out across the city's west side. ⊠ Rua dos Arcos, Serpa

Castelo. Serpa's 11th-century aqueduct (⇨ *see review above*) forms an integral part of the walls of the 13th-century castle, from which there's a stunning view of town. The huge ruined sections of wall tottering precariously above the entrance are the result of explosions ordered by the Duke of Ossuna during the 18th-century War of the Spanish Succession. ⊠ *Alcacova Castelo, Serpa* ☎ *284/540100* 🎫 *Free* ☉ *Daily 9–12:30 and 2–5:30.*

TRADITIONAL MUSIC

If you're lucky, you may hear a group of Alentejo men, dressed in typical garb of sheepskin vest and trousers, singing medieval songs (*cante alentejano*), similar to Gregorian chants. These singers are famous all around Portugal.

Museu do Relógio. *The Clock Museum* displays a collection of 1,100 clocks in the domed rooms of the former Convento do Mosteirinho (Mosteirinho Convent). ⊠ *Rua do Assento* ☎ *284/543194* ⊕ *www.museudorelogio. com* 🎫 *€2* ☉ *Tues.–Fri. 2–5, weekends 10–12:30 and 2–5.*

Museu Etnográfico. *Serpa's Ethnographic Museum,* housed in the old market building, exhibits traditional crafts such as cheese, basket, and chair making, as well as ironwork and pottery. ⊠ *Largo do Corro, Serpa* ☎ *284/540120* 🎫 *Free* ☉ *Daily 9–12:30 and 2–5:30.*

WHERE TO EAT AND STAY

$
PORTUGUESE
✕ **Cervejaria Lebrinha.** At the entrance of town near the Abade Correia da Serra (public gardens), this spacious *cervejaria* (beer house) is said to have been pouring the best beer in Portugal since 1957. They don't brew the Sagres beer, but it's said the secret is in the pour. Old pictures adorning the walls take you back in time to the way Serpa used to be. Wild asparagus with eggs is a good choice for a starter, and then try the grilled carne de porco preto, which is always a tasty choice. As in most cervejarias, the atmosphere is casual, and the service is fast and good. On festival days, when tourists crowd the city center, this is the place to escape the crowds and hang with locals instead. ⊠ *Rua Calvário 6-8* ☎ *284/549311* 🍴 *No credit cards* ☉ *Wed.–Mon. 11 am–2 am; closed Sept. 1–15.*

$
PORTUGUESE
Fodor's Choice
★
✕ **Molhó Bico.** Hands down, this restaurant in a restored wine cellar near Praça da República serves the best food in Serpa, and perhaps even all of Alentejo. Huge wine barrels sit at the entrance to a traditional dining room with domed ceilings, tile floors, and antique farm implements hanging on the walls. In winter, the specialty is grilled pork; in summer try the gazpacho to start, followed by the fried fish. The Serpa cheese and the Alentejo wines are good at any time of year. Keep an ear out for some cante alentejano at this restaurant. ⊠ *Rua Quente 1* ☎ *284/549264* 🍴 *Reservations essential on weekends and festivals* 🍴 *AE, DC, MC, V* ☉ *Thurs.–Tues. noon–3:30 and 7–11.*

¢
Fodor's Choice
★
🏠 **Casa de Serpa.** Its labyrinth of passageways, whitewashed walls, vaulted ceilings, and interior open courtyard reflect the Arabic influence in this 200-year-old manor house near the Igreja do Salvador. Each charming room has a character of its own, where the Alentejo and Arabic are fused in an elegant combination. The breakfasts are special with fresh orange juice, honey from the region, and *queijadinhas* (cheese tarts). The manor is in the center of town and within walking distance of restaurants. Owner Miguel Bentes will arrange bicycle tours of the

5

town for you. He also owns several apartments on an adjacent street, which are a good choice for large families or groups who want more space and access to a kitchen. **Pros:** charming style; friendly management; good location. **Cons:** no restaurant. ⊠ *Largo do Salvador 28* ☎ *284/549238 or 963/560624* ⊕ *www.casadeserpa.com* ⇨ *6 rooms* ⚑ *In-room: a/c, no phone (some), kitchen (some), refrigerator (some), Wi-Fi (some). In-hotel: room service (breakfast only), bar, bicycles, laundry service, Internet terminal, Wi-Fi hotspot* ⊟ *No credit cards* ¶⊙¶ *CP.*

$ ▦ **Estalagem de São Gens.** On a hill above Serpa's fortifications, this modern, white-domed, Moorish-style hotel is relaxed and informal. The Arabic influence continues as you walk through the green-tile entrance to the lobby, with its many arches and vaulted ceilings. Many of the rooms have a small terrace; bright, cheery fabrics nicely offset the white walls and ceilings. From the swimming pool, you have fabulous views of the surrounding countryside. While this hotel is no longer part of the official pousadas chain, it still offers decent comfort at a much more reasonable price. **Pros:** gorgeous views; large property; good for families. **Cons:** it's a bit of a walk into town, along a busy road with no sidewalk. ⊠ *Alto de São Gens, 2 km (1 mi) south of Serpa (off N260 to Spain)* ☎ *284/540420 or 963/228275* ⊕ *www.estalagemsgens.com* ⇨ *16 rooms, 2 suites* ⚑ *In-room: a/c, safe (some), Wi-Fi. In-hotel: restaurant, room service, bar, pool, laundry service, Internet terminal, Wi-Fi hotspot, parking (free)* ⊟ *AE, DC, MC, V* ¶⊙¶ *CP, MAP, FAP.*

SHOPPING

You can buy the famous Serpa cheese in the historic town center at **Rouparia** (⊠ *Rua de Nossa Senhora* ☎ *284/549612*), a small cheese factory owned by José Bule.

You can also order Serpa cheese online from a local company, **Queijaria Guilherme** (⊠ *Monte Vale de Faia, Cruz da Cigana, Apartado 728, Serpa* ☎ *284/595422 or 968/603737* ⊕ *www.queijariaguilherme.com*).

MÉRTOLA

56 km (35 mi) south of Serpa.

The ancient walled-in town of Mértola is on a hill overlooking the Rio Guadiana and its Roman quay. Its occupiers have included the Phoenicians, Carthaginians, Romans, and Arabs. Under the Romans, it was an important copper-mining center, and it was the capital of the Moorish kingdom in Portugal until 1238, when the Christians—under the command of Santiago "Mata Mouros" (Moor Killer)—seized it.

Mértola has seen several archaeological excavations in recent years. The artifacts from these digs are all part of the Museu Arqueológico (Archaeology Museum), which has branches—each with displays from different periods—in several locations around town. At any one of them you can buy a combined ticket for €5 that covers the entrance to all the town's museums.

GETTING HERE AND AROUND

Mértola lies inside the protected Parque Natural do Vale do Guadiana, about equidistant from Spain and the Algarve. Follow the N122 road into town and park below the hilltop village, which is best explored on foot.

The natural park office can give you helpful maps and advice on how to explore one of Portugal's least-touristed—and most spectacular—national parks.

ESSENTIALS

Natural Park Info Parque Natural do Vale do Guadiana (✉ *Rua D. Sancho II, 15* ☎ *286/610090*).

Visitor Info Mértola Tourist Office (✉ *Rua da Igreja* ☎ *286/610109* ⊕ *www.cm-mertola.pt* ☉ *Daily 9–12:30 and 2–5:30*).

EXPLORING

Castelo de Mértola. Built in 1292, this castle contains carved stone from the Roman, Moorish, and Christian periods. The courtyard has a very deep cistern in the center. From the castle's **Torre de Menagem,** you can look down on archaeological digs along the sides of the fortress, and out over the river and rolling hills toward Spain. ☎ *No phone* 🎟 *€5 (ticket gains entrance to castle, several museums, and the Igreja Matrix)* ☉ *Oct.–June 10–12:30 and 2–5:30; July–Sept. 10–1 and 3–7. Closed Mon.*

Convento de São Francisco. This 400-year-old convent on a hill overlooking Mértola had fallen into ruin before a Dutch family stumbled upon it and bought it in the 1980s. The convent building is now open to the public three days a week (by prearranged appointment), and all 40 hectares of surrounding land are a biological garden of local plants and flowers maintained without pesticides. There's also a water museum displaying a complex and sophisticated irrigation system designed in Moorish times. The convent hosts environmental projects and an artist-in-residence, with rotating exhibitions. You can even rent a room in the convent or a cottage on the grounds. ✉ *Convento de São Francisco, Mértola* ☎ *286/612119* ⊕ *www.conventomertola.com* 🎟 *Free* ☉ *By appointment only.*

Largo Luis de Camoes. This charming square lies at the heart of town, lined with citrus trees. The town hall sits on the square's western end, with the **Torre do Relogio,** an impressive clock tower built in the late 16th century, on the opposite side. ✉ *Largo Luis de Camoes, Mértola* ☎ *No phone.*

Museus de Mértola. One ticket gains you admission to a handful of fine museums all within walking distance of one another on the town's hilltop, which together make a wonderful afternoon of sightseeing. The **Núcleo Islamico** has impressive displays of jewels, metal items, and a collection of ceramics from the 9th to 13th centuries, when Mértola was ruled by the Moors. The **Casa Romano** is a restored, Roman-era house in the basement of the city hall. You can walk through the house's foundations and view a small collection of pottery and kitchen tools excavated nearby. The nearby **Museu de Arte Sacra** has religious statues and carvings from the 16th through 18th centuries, borrowed from Mértola's various churches. The museum group's old-est collection is housed in the **Museu Visigótico–Basílica Paleocristã** and includes funery stones and other artifacts excavated from the site of the town's palaeo-Christian basilica and nearby cemetery. ⊠ *Praça Luís de Camões* ☎ *286/610100* ⊕ *museus.cm-mertola.pt* ⊡ *€5* ⊙ *Sept. 16–June 30, Tues.–Sun. 9–12:30 and 2–5:30; July 1–Sept. 15, Tues.–Sun. 9:30–12:30 and 2–6.*

WHERE TO STAY

¢ 🖼 **Residencial Beira Rio.** Some guest rooms in this former mill have bal-conies overlooking the Rio Guadiana; others face town. There are also two sitting rooms and a dining room. A buffet-style breakfast is served on the terrace. Friendly management can help arrange canoeing, jeep or fishing trips. **Pros:** wonderful views from terrace. **Cons:** rooms with-out balconies can be a bit cramped or noisy; no restaurant. ⊠ *Rua Dr. Afonso Costa 108* ☎ *286/611190* ⊕ *www.beirario.pt* ⤶ *24 rooms* ⌂ *In-room: a/c, no phone (some), Wi-Fi (some). In-hotel: room service (breakfast only), bar, laundry service, Internet terminal, Wi-Fi hotspot* ⊟ *AE, DC, MC, V* ⦿ *CP.*

VILA NOVA DE MILFONTES

162 km (101 mi) northwest of Mértola.

This small resort town is at the broad mouth of the Rio Mira, which is lined on both sides by sandy beaches. Overlooking the sea is an ivy-covered, late-16th-century fortress that protected Milfontes from the Algerian pirates who regularly terrorized the Portuguese coast. It was built on ancient Moorish foundations, because it was believed that the spirits there would ward off the pirates. The fortress has been restored and converted into a small guesthouse.

WHEN TO GO

Vila Nova de Milfontes is more historic and less touristy than many beach towns farther south in the Algarve, but it fills with Portuguese vacationers during the August school holidays. It's best to visit any time except then, when reservations can be difficult.

GETTING HERE AND AROUND

Vila Nova de Milfontes lies about halfway between the Setúbal Pen-insula and the Algarve, along the N390/N393, and buses make the trip daily from both Lisbon and Faro. The tourist office can provide updated bus timetables. The town center lies north of the Rio Mira, but its beaches stretch to both sides of the river.

ESSENTIALS

Visitor Info **Vila Nova de Milfontes Tourist Office** (⊠ *Rua António Mantas* ☎ *283/996599* ⊙ *Daily 10–1 and 2–6.*).

WHERE TO EAT AND STAY

$ ✕ **Restaurante Marisqueira O Pescador.** Locals fondly refer to this bus-
SEAFOOD   tling, air-conditioned *marisqueira* (seafood restaurant) as *"o Moura"* (Moura's place, a reference to the owner's name). Moura and his wife started off as fish sellers in the nearby market, so you know the seafood quality will be good. Try the monkfish with rice or seafood combo

stew. Though meals are quite affordable here, as at any seafood house, large lobsters can claim a price as high as €60. ✉ *Largo da Praça 18* ☎ *283/996338* ▭ *No credit cards* ⏲ *Daily 9 am–10:30 pm.*

$ SEAFOOD Fodor's Choice ★ ✕ **Tasca do Celso.** This wonderful spot serves up some of the best seafood and traditional Portuguese dishes on the entire coastline. The rustic dining room has old fashioned Alentejan farm tools hanging on the walls, and opens up to the airy kitchen on one side and a small shop on the other that sells gourmet treats and local wine. The restaurant's name comes from owner José Ramos Cardoso, who as a boy was nicknamed "Celso" after his father, a well-known Vila Nova de Milfontes local. Specialties include shrimp sautéed in garlic, clams with coriander, grilled fish or veal with roasted tomatoes—but you can't go wrong with anything on the menu. ✉ *Rua dos Aviadores, Vila Nova de Milfontes* ☎ *283/996753 or 968/175726* 🌐 *www.tascadocelso.com* ✍ *Reservations essential on summer weekends* ▭ *MC, V* ⏲ *Daily noon–3 and 7–midnight. Closed Mon. in winter.*

$$ Fodor's Choice ★ **Castelo de Milfontes.** In the town's castle, this inn is run along the lines of an old-fashioned guesthouse: the door closes at midnight, and dinner (included in the room rate) is served at a set time with the guests seated around a common table. Guest rooms are atmospheric and comfortable; ask for one with a sea view. **Pros:** historic charm in an old castle; intimate, romantic setting. **Cons:** a bit overpriced for rooms with hall bathroom and no TV or other modern amenities. ✉ *Largo Brito Pais, Vila Nova de Milfontes* ☎ *283/998231* *7 rooms* *In-room: a/c, no phone (some), no TV, Wi-Fi (some). In-hotel: restaurant, room service, bar, beachfront, laundry service, Internet terminal, Wi-Fi hotspot* ▭ *No credit cards* 🍽 *MAP.*

$ **Duna Parque.** This two-story apartment-hotel complex is a 10-minute walk from town and a five-minute walk from the beach. Guest quarters are in apartments and semidetached villas, all of which have living-room areas, kitchens, and open fireplaces. Some have balconies or roof terraces. The bar-restaurant, with its rustic beams and stonework, serves regional cooking. There's a three-night minimum stay in July and August, and you can write home on the broadband Internet terminal. **Pros:** plenty of space for families; good option for longer stays. **Cons:** lack of sidewalks means it's not advisable for children to walk to the beach alone. ✉ *Eira da Pedra* ☎ *283/996451* 🌐 *www.dunaparque.com* *45 units* *In-room: a/c, safe, kitchen (some), refrigerator, Internet (some), Wi-Fi. In-hotel: restaurant, room service, bar, mini-golf course, tennis court, pool, gym, spa, bicycles, children's programs (ages 4–12), laundry facilities, laundry service, Internet terminal, Wi-Fi hotspot, parking (free), some pets allowed* ⏲ *MC, V,* 🍽 *CP, FAP, MAP, AI.*

¢ **Hotel Social.** You're likely to have a water view at this hotel near the castle, be it the Rio Mira, the Atlantic, or the swimming pool (the latter is the cheapest). The restaurant, open only to hotel guests ($), has panoramic views of the sea, which is spectacular on a clear day. Good, down-to-earth Portuguese dishes include *açorda de marisco* (seafood porridge), *sopa de peixe* (fish soup), and a variety of grilled fish that the Portuguese prepare so well. For those who prefer meat, try the *borrego à casa* (lamb stew). The hotel's 1970s-style facade is a bit of an eyesore, but the interior was updated in 2005. You can't beat the location, which is right across the street from beaches and a short walk to the town center. There are double or triple rooms, as well as an apartment with a kitchen and two large dormitories—all great options for groups. **Pros:** best view in town; a more affordable price than the castle hotel across the street. **Cons:** 1970s decor clashes with beauty of surroundings. ⊠ *Av. Marginal* ☎ *283/996517 or 283/996239* ⊕ *www.scmodemira.pt/hsocial1001.html* ⤶ *28 rooms, 1 apartment, 2 dormitories* ⚹ *In-room: a/c, safe (some), kitchen (some), refrigerator (some), Internet (some), Wi-Fi. In-hotel: restaurant, room service, bar, pool, gym, beachfront, water sports, children's programs (ages 4–12), laundry facilities, laundry service, Internet terminal, Wi-Fi hotspot, parking (free), some pets allowed* ▭ *No credit cards* ¶⊘ *CP, FAP, MAP.*

BEACHES

The calm waters of the Franquia River beach, extending from the castle all the way to the Farol beach, are good for water sports and families with children. There are several scenic beaches between Porto Covo and Vila Nova de Milfontes. Rock formations stud Ilha do Pessegueiro beach, which is across from a tiny rocky island with a ruined fort, accessible by boat. The Aivados beach attracts fishermen, nudists, and surfers. The long Malhão beach is very popular and backed with dunes and fragrant scrubland. There are good access points and plenty of parking.

SANTIAGO DO CACÉM

40 km (25 mi) northeast of Vila Nova de Milfontes.

Santiago do Cacémis, a quiet regional market town that receives few tourists, is on a busy thoroughfare toward what's now an industrial port at Sines. The town's castle, built by the Knights of the Order of Santiago (St. James) on the site of Moorish ruins, dominates the community and affords sweeping views to the sea, marred only by the oil refineries at Sines. Inside the parish church, you can see a sculpture of St. James battling the Moors. The oldest part of town, just below the castle, is a maze of narrow streets with several well-preserved 17th- and 18th-century manor houses.

GETTING HERE AND AROUND

Santiago do Cacém lies about 16 km (10 mi) inland from the Atlantic at the junction of the N120 and N261. You can drive into the town center, where there's plenty of parking near the castle.

ESSENTIALS

Visitor Info **Santiago do Cacém Tourist Office** (⊠ *Praça do Mercado Municipal* ☎ *269/826696 or 269/826887*).

EXPLORING

Castelo. The town's castle was originally a Moorish structure, rebuilt by Christians in the 13th century. Alongside the main structure is a small chapel dedicated to St. Peter, which was added in the 16th century. ⊠ *Calçada do Castelo, Santiago do Cacém* ☎ *269/829400* ⤶ *Free* ⊙ *24 hrs.*

Miróbriga. Just outside town, off N121 to Ferreira do Alentejo, you can explore the excavations of the city of Miróbriga. The Celts originally settled this site in the 4th century BC; in the 1st century AD, it became a Roman town. The ruins, although not nearly as extensive or well preserved as those at Conímbriga near Coimbra, contain the interesting sanctuaries of Venus and Esculapius (god of medicine). ✉ *Cumeadas* ☎ *269/818460* 🎫 *€2* ⊘ *Tues.–Sun. 9–12:30 and 2:30–5:30.*

Museu Municipal. This museum housed in a former prison at the center of town has several exhibits on Alentejo life, including one that shows the stages of and implements used in cork production. An ethnographic section has typical living quarters decorated in 19th-century styles, one modeled after a poor family's house and another with period furnishings from a nearby count's palace. ✉ *Praça do Município* ☎ *269/827375* 🎫 *Free* ⊘ *Tues.–Fri. 10–noon and 2–5, Sat. noon–6.*

WHERE TO EAT AND STAY

$ ✕**Cerro da Inês.** A short drive outside Santiago, this traditional restaurant is in a somewhat bizarre, yet beautiful, location atop a water tower. The regional food is excellent, and so are the vistas of the historic town and the countryside. ✉ *Rua Padre Hermano Ferreira de Almeida Lima, Vila Nova de Santo Andre, Santiago do Cacém* ☎ *269/823883* 🚫 *No credit cards* ⊘ *Closed Mon.*

PORTUGUESE

$$ 🏨**Pousada da Quinta da Ortiga.** This lovely old estate, 5 km (3 mi) from Santiago do Cacém, is amid 10 acres of trees and farmland. With wood-panel ceilings and Arraiolos carpets, it evokes life in a rural villa—rustic but with touches of luxury. The intimate restaurant ($$), which serves cuisine of the region, is more like a family dining room than a commercial establishment, and is open to the public only on weekends. The property also has a lovely swimming pool set amid manicured gardens. While not part of the official pousadas chain, this property offers comparable accommodation at a similar price. **Pros:** luxury in a rural setting; plenty of space for children; water sports and bicycle rental can be arranged. **Cons:** overpriced. ✉ *Off IP8 to Sines, Apartado 67* ☎ *269/822074* 🛏 *13 rooms* ♿ *In-room: a/c, safe (some), Internet (some), Wi-Fi. In-hotel: restaurant, room service, bar, pool, children's programs (ages 4–12), laundry service, Internet terminal, Wi-Fi hotspot, parking (free)* 🚫 *AE, DC, MC, V* ❑◯❑ *CP, FAP, MAP.*

SPORTS AND THE OUTDOORS

DONKEY TOURS

Discover beautiful Alentejo scenery—coastlines, windmills, cork trees, and rolling hills that in spring are blanketed in flowers—on a donkey (safe even for grandmothers). On the road to Cercal, 14 km (8½ mi) from Santiago do Cacém, a sign on a dirt road points left to **Os Moinhos do Paneiro** (✉ *Vale Seco* ☎ *912/609566*). A half-day donkey ride for two is €35; a full day is €60 plus €10 an hour for a guide.

HORSEBACK RIDING

The sparse population and minimal automobile traffic make this region a delight for equestrian outings. Whether for a few hours or a few days, you'll get an authentic perspective of the Alentejo on horseback. Overnight tours include lodging at bed-and-breakfasts and meals both on the trail and at local restaurants. Trails provide a variety of backdrops—including castles, villages, and prehistoric sites. Sines beach is good for horseback riding.

For instruction and for riding on the beach at Sines, contact **Centro Equestre de Santo André** (✉ *Monte Velho, Santo André* ☎ *269/751235* ⊕ *www.cesa.pt*).

SAFARI TOUR

To experience the adventure of an African safari in the middle of the Alentejo, head to **Badoca Park,** home to tigers, giraffes, zebras, chimpanzees, yaks, buffalo, antelope, and other animals that roam free. For the best photo ops, join the one-hour safari tour that takes you around the park on a minitrain. There's a wooded picnic area for packed lunches, or you can eat at the restaurant, which is spectacularly decorated as an African lodge. ✉ *Herdade da Badoca, Apartado 170; exit A2 at Grandola/Sines exit onto IC33; the park entrance is at Km 34 (6 km [4 mi] southwest of Santiago do Cacém), Vila Nova de Santo André* ☎ *269/708850* ⊕ *www.badoca.com* 🎟 *€16 entrance and safari tour for adults, €14 for children.* ☉ *Daily 10–5.*

> ## BEACHES
>
> Some of Europe's finest and least crowded beaches are on the rugged stretch of Portugal's west coast that extends from the southern extreme of the Alentejo at Odeceixe north to where Sines rests on the tip of the Tróia Peninsula. Some beaches—such as Praia do Carvalhal and Praia Grande at Almograve—don't have any facilities and are uncrowded even in July and August. The beaches at Vila Nova de Milfontes and at Porto Covo have restaurants and the usual beach facilities. Exercise great care when swimming: the surf is often high, and strong undertows and riptides are common.

ALCÁCER DO SAL

52 km (32 mi) northeast of Santiago do Cacém.

Salt production here has nearly disappeared, but it was because of this mineral that Alcácer do Sal became one of Portugal's first inhabited sites. Parts of the castle foundations are around 5,000 years old. The Greeks were here, and, later, the Romans, who established the town of Salatia Urbs Imperatoria—a key intersection in their system of Lusitanian roads. During the Moorish occupation, under the name of Alcácer de Salatia, this became one of the most important Muslim strongholds in all of Iberia. In the 16th century Alcácer prospered as a major producer of salt, and a brisk trade was conducted with the northern European countries, which used it to preserve herring. The hilltop castle is the town's most prominent attraction. Red-tile-roof buildings descend from the castle to the riverbank in long horizontal rows.

GETTING HERE AND AROUND

Alcácer do Sal lies upstream from the mouth of the Sado River, a quick drive south from Lisbon on the main north-south highway, the A2. Most of the town lies on the river's northern bank, and there's ample parking in the center.

The tourist office can arrange half- or full-day boat trips or guided walks along the Sado River.

ESSENTIALS

Tours Rotas do Sal (✉ *Estação dos Caminhos de Ferro 2, Apartado 152, Ameira, Alcacer do Sal* ☎ *967/066072 or 962/375950* ⊕ *www.rotasdosal.pt*).

Visitor Info Alcácer do Sal Tourist Office (✉ *Praça Pedro Nunes 1* ☎ *265/610079* ⊕ *www.cm-alcacerdosal.pt* ☾ *Mon.–Sat. 9–5.*).

EXPLORING

Fodor's Choice
★

Cripta Arqueológica do Castelo. Opened in 2008, this stunning underground fortress displays archaeological relics from 2,600 years of settlement here. In the mid-1990s, archaeologists discovered traces of an Iron Age settlement from the 6th century BC, underneath the town's castle. Structures are believed to have existed here from Roman times, with later castles being built one on top of another through Moorish and medieval times. The current castle and adjacent church are from the 13th century. ✉ *Castelo de Alcácer do Sal (in basement of D. Alfonso II pousada), Alcácer do Sal* ☎ *265/612058* ☒ *Free* ☾ *Winter 9–12:30 and 2–5:30; summer 10–1 and 3–7. Closed Mon.*

Reserva Natural do Sado. The marshlands and the estuary of the Rio Sado that extend to the west of Alcácer form this vast nature reserve. The riverbanks are lined with salt pans and rice paddies, and the sprawling park gives shelter to wildlife such as dolphins, otters, white storks, and egrets. From the beach town of Comporta, Route N261 runs south along the coast through a mostly deserted stretch of dunes and pine trees with some undeveloped sandy beaches.

WHERE TO EAT AND STAY

$
PORTUGUESE

✕**Hortelã da Ribeira.** Beneath the castle, this restaurant is named for the wild mint (*hortelã*) that grows on riverbanks. Owner Maria Helena Fideles uses this herb and other Alentejo herbs in many delicious fish dishes—*arroz de tamboril* (rice with monkfish), *chocos* (squid), and *ameijoas* (clams). An interesting feature in the restaurant is its walls adorned with animal-motif tiles hand-painted by the local villagers. Sit in the rustic dining room, or outside on the terrace in summer. ✉ *Estrada Santa Luzia, lote 2* ☎ *265/613271* ▭ *AE, DC, MC, V* ☾ *Tues.–Sat. noon–4 and 7–10. Closed for Sun. dinner and all day Mon.*

$
PORTUGUESE

✕**Porto Santana.** You can take your lunch outside with a view of the Rio Sado. Dinner is served indoors as at night the outdoor area becomes a bar. The specialty here is sopa de cação (dogfish soup). ✉ *Rua Senhora Santana* ☎ *265/613454 or 969/020740* ▭ *AE, DC, MC, V* ☾ *Closed Mon. dinner and all day Tues.*

¢

⊡**Albergaria da Barrosinha.** This typical whitewashed, one-story Alentejo country house is set in the midst of a huge farm estate surrounded by cork and pine trees. Red-and-white striped curtains and bedcovers elegantly match the red clay–tile floors. To contrast with the red, bathrooms are decorated in blue-and-white Alcobaça tiles. The inn organizes horseback riding, hiking, and biking tours for you. Game lovers can feast in the restaurant. **Pros:** rustic farm with space for children. **Cons:** too far to walk into town. ✉ *Estrada Nacional 5, Barrosinha*

5

☎ *265/623142 or 265/613048* ⤵ *17 rooms, 2 suites* ⚅ *In-room: a/c, safe, Internet (some), Wi-Fi. In-hotel: restaurant, room service, bar, bicycles, laundry service, Internet terminal, Wi-Fi hotspot, parking (free), some pets allowed* ▭ *AE, DC, MC, V* ¶◯¶ *CP, FAP, MAP.*

$$ **Pousada de Dom Afonso II.** In the ancient castle that overlooks the Rio Sado, this very attractive pousada looks out over the rooftops of the town and the green plains across the river. Guest rooms are comfortable and tastefully appointed with elegant wooden furniture, blue sofa chairs, and Oriental rugs to match. Public areas are medieval inspired with stone and brick walls, stone floors, wooden furniture, and illumination imitating medieval torches. There is plenty of sunning space around the rectangular pool at the edge of the castle wall and turret. **Pros:** beautiful, well-preserved medieval architecture makes the lobby alone worth a visit, regardless of whether you can afford to stay here. **Cons:** a bit expensive, but the pousada has cut its rates in recent years to compete with other rural hotels. ⊠ *Castelo de Alcácer* ☎ *265/613070* ⊕ *www.pousadas.pt* ⤵ *33 rooms, 2 suites* ⚅ *In-room: a/c, safe, Wi-Fi (some). In-hotel: restaurant, room service, bar, pool, bicycles, children's programs (ages 4–12), laundry service, Internet terminal, Wi-Fi hotspot, parking (free)* ▭ *AE, DC, MC, V* ¶◯¶ *CP, FAP, MAP.*

The Algarve

WORD OF MOUTH

"If you can manage it, drive over to Sagres. That's where Henry the Navigator plotted his voyages, and one of the most spectacular sea vistas in the world, lots of good eats, and fun ceramic places to stop on the way. [It's] a wonderful day trip. Oh yes, walk along the beach and stop at a restaurant called the 'Cataplana.' It's outdoor dining and you will recognize it by the huge copper dish mounted out front. A local specialty."

—clarasong

Updated by
Brendan de
Beer and
Carrie-Marie
Bratley

Appealing, yes—perhaps too appealing for its own good. The Algarve is deservedly popular with millions of annual vacationers who throng here for sun, sandy beaches, superb golf, and all the other enticements of the seaside resorts. Along with the region's popularity has come progress, and during the past two decades, the Algarve has been heavily developed, with parts of the once pristine, 240-km (149-mi) coastline now overbuilt.

Until the construction of the airport at Faro in the 1960s, the Algarve was rarely visited by tourists, and for centuries before that it remained isolated from the rest of Europe. Phoenicians, Romans, and Visigoths established fishing and trading communities here, but it wasn't until the arrival of the Moors in the 8th century that the region became an important strategic settlement. It was the Moors who gave the province its name—Al Gharb (the Land to the West)—and who established their capital at the inland town of Silves (then called Chelb). In those days it had direct access to the sea and at its peak was a grand city with a population of more than 30,000.

The Algarve measures a mere 40 km (25 mi) north to south, bordered on the north by the Serra de Monchique (Monchique Mountains) and the Serra de Caldeirão (Caldeirão Mountains) and on the east by the Rio Guadiana (Guadiana River). Its location in the south, protected by hills, makes the Algarve much warmer than any other place in the country in winter; and in summer, the coast is cooled by sea breezes. The vegetation is far more luxuriant; the land, originally irrigated by the Moors, supports a profusion of fruits, nuts, and vegetables; and the fishing industry has always flourished.

Even where development is at its heaviest, construction takes the form of landscaped villas and apartment complexes, which are generally made of local materials and blend well with the scenery. And there are still small, undeveloped fishing villages and secluded beaches, particularly in the west. The west is also home to extraordinary rock formations and idyllic grottoes. In the east a series of isolated sandbar islands and sweeping beaches balances the crowded excesses of the middle. To see the Algarve at its best, though, you may have to abandon the shore for a drive inland. Here, rural Portugal still survives in hill villages, market towns, and agricultural landscapes, which, although only a few miles from the coast, seem a world away in attitude.

TOP REASONS TO GO

Fun in the sun. One of Europe's sunniest places, the Algarve guarantees great weather pretty much all year round, but avoid August as temperatures can hit the high 90 degrees Fahrenheit and traffic will test the steeliest of nerves.

Glitz and glamour. During peak season the Algarve becomes a destination with such sheen it rivals Europe's glitziest hot spots. Jet-setters travel from far and wide to be at what are fast becoming world-renowned events.

Green tee. With 37 acclaimed golf courses to its name, this area is becoming one of Europe's most popular golfing destinations, especially in the cooler months.

Best-kept secrets. The Algarve is home to several breathtaking spots that are largely overlooked—rock formations, hidden lagoons, salt mines—unless you know a local.

Festivals galore. From city-size *festas* to the hundreds of smaller, rural village affairs, you can be sure that somewhere, at some point, there will be something going on to suit your tastes.

Fantastic food and drink. Rapidly making a culinary name for itself on the international gastronomy scene, the Algarve is home to award-winning restaurants, Michelin-stars, and up-and-coming vineyards.

6

ORIENTATION AND PLANNING

GETTING ORIENTED

The Algarve's main roads—the EN125 and the A22/Via do Infante motorway—and its train line connect towns and villages along the entire coast, though rail travelers should beware that the train service is very slow and stations are often some way from the center of the town, resort, or village they purport to serve. If you rent a car, you can see the entire region in a week, albeit at a fairly brisk pace. Even if you plan to stay at one resort for several days, make an effort to see both the eastern and western ends of the province and an inland town or two; each has a distinct character.

For touring purposes, the province can conveniently be divided into four sections, starting with Faro—the Algarve's capital—and the nearby beaches and inland towns. The second section encompasses the region east to the border town of Vila Real de Santo António, from which you can cross into Spain. The most built-up part of the coast, and the section with the most to offer vacationers, runs from Faro west to Portimão. The fourth section covers Lagos, the principal town of the western Algarve, and extends to Sagres and Cabo São Vicente.

Faro and Environs. Known as the capital of the Algarve, Faro is a busy, cosmopolitan city home to a pretty marina, the region's only international airport and several universities that give it a trendy, vibrant feel. It is, however, surrounded by quaint villages that warrant a visit for their authenticity.

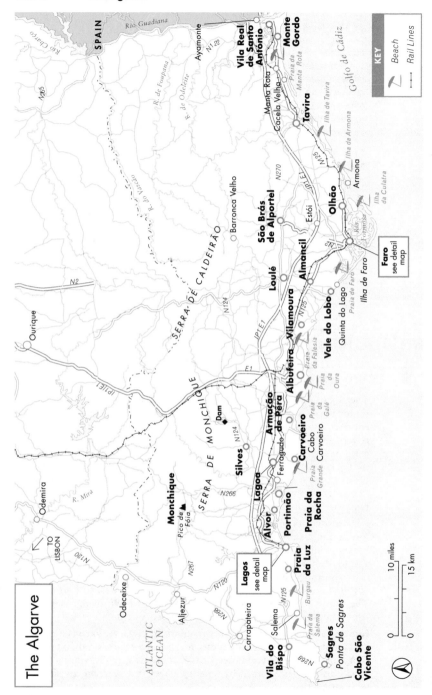

The Algarve

SPAIN

Rio Guadiana

KEY

Beach

Rail Lines

ATLANTIC OCEAN

Golfo de Cádiz

SERRA DE CALDEIRÃO

SERRA DE MONCHIQUE

Ourique

Odemira

TO LISBON

Odeceixe

Aljezur

Carrapateira

Vila do Bispo

Sagres

Cabo São Vicente

Ponta de Sagres

Salema

Praia da Salema

Burgau

Praia da Luz

Lagos see detail map

Alvor

Portimão

Praia da Rocha

Lagoa

Silves

Monchique

Pico de Fóia

Dam

Ferragudo

Carvoeiro

Praia do Carvoeiro

Praia Grande

Armação de Péra

Praia da Galé

Praia da Oura

Praia da Falésia

Albufeira

Vilamoura

Loulé

São Brás de Alportel

Barranca Velho

Almancil

Vale do Lobo

Quinta do Lago

Praia do Lago

Estói

Faro see detail map

Olhão

Ria Formosa

Ilha de Faro

Ilha da Culatra

Ilha da Armona

Armona

Ilha de Tavira

Tavira

Cacela Velha

Manta Rota

Praia da Manta Rota

Vila Real de Santo António

Monte Gordo

Ayamonte

R. do Charco

R. de Foupana

R. de Odeleite

R. Seixe

R. Mira

Pico de Fóia

10 miles

15 km

N122

N125

N120

N267

N266

N124

N2

IP1 E1

E1

N270

N2

N125

N398

N268

N268

The Eastern Algarve. Better known for being largely unaffected by mass tourism as well as its unique roofs, the Eastern Algarve remains true to its regional roots, both in terms of architecture and attitude.

The Central Algarve. The central Algarve is where it all happens: the region's wealthiest area, it's where younger crowds get their kicks and jet-setters relax. Summers entail busy beaches, bustling bars and restaurants, and lots of beautiful people.

Lagos and the Western Algarve. Famous for its waves and wilderness, the Western Algarve is laid back and cool. A surfer's paradise, its unspoiled beauty and invigorating breezes inspired Henry the Navigator's expeditions.

PLANNING

WHEN TO GO

Winter is mild: if you seek solitude and don't mind limiting your swimming to heated hotel pools, it's the perfect time to visit. There are plenty of bargains to be had as well. Algarvean springs, with their rolling carpets of wildflowers, are delightful. Late in the season, you can just about take a dip in the ocean, and there's plenty of space to lay out your beach blanket. Summer (July and August) is high season, when lodging is at a premium, prices are at their highest, and crowds are at their thickest. But summer also brings warmer seas, piercing blue skies, and warm, golden sands at the foot of glowing ocher-red cliffs.

GETTING HERE AND AROUND

AIR TRAVEL

TAP Air Portugal has regular daily service from Lisbon and Porto. Flying time from Lisbon to Faro is 45 minutes; from Porto, 90 minutes. All international and domestic airlines use Faro Airport, which is 6 km (4 mi) west of town. It's easy to find your way into Faro: after around 4 km (2½ mi), signs along the road from the airport direct you right into town.

Public Eva buses run frequently between the airport and Faro city, with tickets costing in the region of €1.65 per person. A taxi from the terminal building to the center of Faro costs around €10 (there's a small extra charge for baggage). Ask the staff at the airport tourist office for a list of prices for rides to other destinations in the region. Always make sure that you agree on a price with the taxi driver before setting off.

Airline **TAP Air Portugal** (🖀 289/818538).

Airport **Faro Airport** (🖀 289/800800, 289/800801 for flight information ⊕ www.ana-aeroportos.pt).

BUS TRAVEL

Various companies run daily express buses between Lisbon and Lagos, Portimão, Faro, Tavira, and Vila Real de Santo António. Allow for 3½–4½ hours' travel time for all these destinations. Generally this is more comfortable than traveling by train, and some of the luxury coaches have a restroom, TV, and food service. Any travel agency in Lisbon can reserve a seat for you; in summer, book at least 24 hours in advance.

The main form of public transportation in the Algarve is the bus; the main company in the region is Eva. Every town and village has its own terminal. You may have to walk from the main road to the more isolated beach areas, however. Tickets are relatively inexpensive, although a bus ride always costs more than the comparable train journey. Most ticket offices have someone who speaks at least a little English. The booklet *Guia Horário,* which costs €3 and is available at main terminals, lists every bus service, with timetables and information in English. Alternatively, purchase a three-day tourist pass for €25.80, which allows unlimited bus trips to some 16 popular tourist destinations across the Algarve, both inland and along the coast.

⚠ **Some local services are infrequent or don't run on Sunday or national holidays.**

Bus Contact **Eva Buses** (☎ *289/899760 or 289/899740).*

CAR TRAVEL

To reach the Algarve from Lisbon—an easy 240-km (150-mi) drive south—cross the Ponte 25 de Abril and take the toll road to Setúbal. Beyond here, the main A2 motorway runs directly south, via Alcácer do Sal, Grândola, Aljustrel, and Castro Verde, eventually joining the A22/ Via do Infante, the Algarve's main east–west motorway, near Guia, north of Albufeira. To reach Portimão, Lagos, and the western Algarve, turn right; go straight to reach Albufeira; and turn left for Faro and the eastern Algarve. The drive from Lisbon to Faro, Lagos, or Albufeira takes about three hours, longer in summer, on weekends, and on holidays.

In the east, a suspension bridge crosses the Rio Guadiana between Ayamonte in Spain and Vila Real de Santo António in Portugal. The secondary east–west road, the EN125, extends 165 km (102 mi) from the Spanish border all the way west to Sagres. It runs parallel to the coast and the A22/Via do Infante Motorway, but slightly inland, with clearly marked turnoffs to the beach towns. Be very careful on this route, as it's one of Portugal's most hazardous. In summer expect traffic jams in several places along it. In addition, portions of highway are under construction and roadwork and diversions add to the traffic near the busy resorts.

It's also worth bearing in mind that as of April 2011 tolls will be introduced on the A22/Via do Infante motorway. While the EN125 is toll-free and runs parallel to the A22 across the width of the Algarve, it is single lanes in both directions and in terms of condition still leaves something to be desired. Once dubbed one of the deadliest roads in Europe, the EN125 has come a long way since the 1980s, but despite ongoing work and hefty investment, locals and regional politicians remain adamant it's not yet a viable alternative to a motorway.

In inland areas, minor country roads aren't always well maintained; when driving at night in rural areas, look out for mopeds without lights. Signage throughout the region has, in recent years, been renewed and replaced, having experienced a pretty thorough (and much-needed) overhaul.

Car Rental Contacts **Auto Jardim** (✉ *Head office, Av. da Liberdade, Albufeira* ☎ *289/580500688* ✉ *Faro Airport* ☎ *289/800881, 289/889457 or 289/889458).*

TAXI TRAVEL

If you intend to take a cab from Faro Airport there will be plenty of vehicles waiting outside the arrivals area, day and night. Fares to key destinations are preestablished, and rates should be regulated by ANTRAL, a national entity. Nevertheless, always establish the price before you set off to avoid unexpected surprises. Luggage is extra. In Faro, you can call for taxis or hail them on the street, and around €4–€5 will get you across town (traffic permitting).

Taxis **ANTRAL taxis** ☎ *289/827203.*

TRAIN TRAVEL

There are regular daily departures to the Algarve from Lisbon. The route runs directly from the center of Lisbon, Portugal's capital, through Setúbal to the rail junction of Tunes (three hours from Lisbon) and continues on to Albufeira (another 10 minutes), Faro (another 40 minutes), and all stations east to Vila Real de Santo António (another two hours). For the western route to Silves (another 20 minutes) and Lagos (another hour), you must change trains at Tunes.

The railroad connects Lagos in the west with Vila Real de Santo António in the east—running close to the EN125. Several trains a day run the entire often-scenic route, which takes three to four hours; tickets are very reasonably priced, and the trip is pleasant. Most trains including the slower regional ones will have a first-class carriage that is often made up of old-fashioned, individual compartments. Some of the faster trains don't stop at every station, and some of the stations are several miles from the towns they serve, although there's usually a connecting bus. The main train stations generally have someone who speaks some English, but it's easier to get information at tourist offices. At the Faro and Lagos offices, timetables are posted. The national rail company is CP.

Train Contact **CP National Main Office** (✉ *Calçada do Duque, Lisbon* ☎ *21/1023000*).

RESTAURANTS

Unless otherwise noted, casual dress is acceptable throughout the Algarve. Reservations are not needed off-season, but in summer, you'll need them at most of the better restaurants.

Algarvean cooking makes good use of local seafood. The most unusual of regional appetizers, *espadarte fumado* (smoked swordfish), is sliced thin, served with a salad, and best when accompanied by a dry white wine. Restaurants generally serve their own version of *sopa de peixe* (fish soup) as well as a variety of succulent shellfish: *percebes* (barnacles), *santola* (crab), and *gambas* (shrimp). Main courses often depend on what has been landed that day, but there's generally a choice of *robalo* (sea bass), *pargo* (bream), *atum* (tuna), and espadarte.

At simple beach cafés and harbor stalls the unmistakable smell of *sardinhas assadas* (charcoal-grilled sardines) permeates the air—they make a tempting lunch served with fresh bread and smooth red wine. Perhaps the most famous Algarvean dish is *cataplana*—a stew of clams, pork, onions, tomatoes, and wine, which takes its name from the lidded utensil used to steam the dish. You have to wait for cataplana to be specially prepared, but once you've tasted it, you won't mind waiting again and again.

In inland rural areas, game highlights most menus, with many meat dishes served *do forno* (oven roasted). Specialties include *cabrito* (kid [baby goat]), *leitão* (suckling pig), and *codorniz* (quail), as well as *ensopado de borrego* (lamb stew).

The Algarve is known for its almonds, oranges, and figs, but these rarely appear in restaurants, where the choice of dessert is often limited to flan, ice cream, and perhaps a fresh fruit salad. Typical Algarvean sweets include rich egg, sugar, and almond custards that reflect the Moorish influence, including *doces de amendoa* (marzipan cakes in the shapes of animals and flowers), *bolos de Dom Rodrigo* (almond sweets with egg-and-sugar filling), *bolo Algarvio* (cake made of sugar, almonds, eggs, and cinnamon), and *morgado de figos do Algarve* (fig-and-almond paste). You will find these on sale in *pastelarias* (cake shops) and in some cafés.

> ### ALGARVE MARKET DAYS
>
> All the main towns and villages have regular food markets, usually open daily from 8 until around 2.
>
> **Albufeira**: first and third Tuesday of the month
>
> **Loulé**: first and fourth Sunday of the month
>
> **Lagos**: first Saturday of the month
>
> **Portimão**: first Monday of the month
>
> **Sagres**: first Friday of the month
>
> **Silves**: third Monday of the month

HOTELS

There are busy beachside hotels and secluded retreats in posh country estates. Apartment and villa complexes with luxurious amenities are often built on the most beautiful parts of the coast. They may be 5 km (3 mi) from the nearest town, but most have bars, restaurants, shops, and other facilities. Budget lodgings are also available.

In most towns and resorts, you'll be approached by people offering reasonably priced *quartos* (rooms) in private houses, which are almost always clean and cheerful, if small and with shared bathrooms. Don't expect to pay less than around €25 for a reasonable double room per night. Also don't agree to take a room without seeing it first; it may be farther from the town center than you were led to believe.

In summer, reservations at most places are essential, and rates often rise by as much as 50% above off-peak prices. Since the weather from September through May is still good, you might want to consider an off-peak trip to take advantage of the lower prices.

WHAT IT COSTS IN EUROS					
	¢	$	$$	$$$	$$$$
Restaurants	under €10	€10–€15	€16–€20	€21–€25	over €25

Restaurant prices are per person for a main course at dinner. Hotel prices are for a standard double room, including tax, in high season (off-season rates may be lower).

WHAT IT COSTS IN EUROS					
Hotels	under €80	€80–€140	€141–€200	€201–€260	over €260

Restaurant prices are per person for a main course at dinner. Hotel prices are for a standard double room, including tax, in high season (off-season rates may be lower).

EMERGENCIES

Each region has a health center for primary medical (outpatient) treatment; local tourist offices can supply addresses and phone numbers. There are public and private hospitals in Faro and Portimão. Each town has at least one pharmacy that stays open all night; consult the notice posted on every pharmacy's door for current schedules.

Emergency Contacts General Emergencies (☎ 112). **Police** (✉ Rua da Policia de segurança Pública, N° 32, Faro ☎ 289/899899 ✉ Rua General Alberto Carlos daSilveira, Lagos ☎ 282/780240).

Hospital Information Faro (✉ Rua Leão Penedo ☎ 289/891100). **Portimão** (✉ Sítio do Poço Seco ☎ 282/450300).

TOUR OPTIONS

Many companies and individual fishermen along the coast rent out boats for excursions. These range from one-hour tours of local grottoes and rock formations to full-day trips that often involve a stop at a secluded beach for a barbecue lunch. Main centers for coastal excursions are Albufeira, Vilamoura, Portimão, Tavira, Lagos, Sagres, Vila Real, and Armação de Pêra. Consult the tourist offices in these towns for details or simply wander down to the local harbor or along the riverfront, as in Portimão and Lagos, where the prices and times of the next cruise will be posted.

Jeep "safaris" are a unique way to see fascinating inland villages. Lunch is usually included in the price. Algarve operators include Megatur and Zebra Safari. Riosul Viagens arranges cruises up the Rio Guadiana, which runs between Portugal and Spain. It also has half-day overland tours by jeep and full-day cruise-jeep tours that take you off the beaten path up to the village of Foz de Odeleite. Turinfo can organize boat trips, jeep tours, and other activities around the Sagres Peninsula.

Tour Contacts Megatur (✉ Rua Conselheiro Bivar 80, Faro ☎ 289/807485/6 ⊕ www.megatur.pt). **Riosul Viagens e Turismo Lda** (✉ Rua Tristão Vaz Teixeira 15C, Monte Gordo ☎ 281/510200 or 962/012112 ⊕ www.riosul-tours.com). **Zebra Safari** (✉ Arcadas de S. João, Loja X, Areias de São João, Albufeira ☎ 289/583300).

FARO AND ENVIRONS

Many people fly in to Faro and pass straight through on their way to beaches east and west, which is unfortunate. The city's harbor and Cidade Velha (Old Town) are both worthy of a night's stay or more, and its many facilities make it a fine base for touring the region. The towns and villages that ring Faro contain their own sights worth seeing, from beaches and markets to churches and ruins.

FARO

270 km (168 mi) southeast of Lisbon.

The Algarve's prosperous provincial capital has around 100,000 residents. Founded by the Moors, the city was taken by Afonso III in 1249, at the end of the Arab domination. Much of its early architecture was lost in the late 16th century, when it was sacked by the English under the earl of Essex. It was further damaged by two 18th-century earthquakes, the latter of which, in 1755, also destroyed Lisbon. Remnants of the medieval walls and some historic buildings, however, can still be seen in the delightful Cidade Velha (Old Town). Here, quiet streets and squares, where balconies and tile work adorn even the most unappealing facade, are perfect for a stroll.

East of the harbor, in the pedestrian shopping streets around Rua de Santo António, you'll find much of what makes Faro tick as a tourist town: bars, restaurants, shops, and sidewalk hawkers touting souvenirs and snacks. During the 19th century a prosperous community of Jews from Gibraltar and Morocco settled in Rua de Santo António, boosting the growth of local trade. Around 1830, this community took the initiative of building two synagogues and a cemetery, which later, with the almost complete disappearance of the Jewish population, fell into ruins. Faro now boasts a unique Jewish Heritage Center that features a museum and the city's Jewish cemetery, which is still visible, as well as walking tours throughout the city that stop at important Jewish relics.

GETTING HERE AND AROUND

Despite being the region's largest city, most of the main attractions in Faro, as with all Algarvean cities and towns, can pretty much be covered on foot. Nonetheless, urban buses are frequent and taxis are cheap if you need to get from one end of town to the other quickly. Faro can be reached by train and bus from anywhere in the Algarve.

TIMING

Allow about two hours to tour Faro's historic quarter in leisure, stopping when a pastry display case calls your name. The distances between monuments and museums here are short and the streets are easily navigated. Avoid touring in the heat of the day in summer, as the streets have little shade and the town is virtually treeless except for orange trees, which are not exactly shade givers. Allow a good 20 minutes to tour the ethnographic museum and 40 minutes for the archaeological museum. If you are a church fan, the Sé will not disappoint. Don't miss the Igreja do Carmo's Chapel of the Bones, which takes half an hour to thoroughly digest, although the Igreja de São Pedro is far more attractive inside.

ESSENTIALS

Bus Contacts Eva (✉ *Av. da República* ☎ *289/899760*).

Taxis Taxis Antral Faro (✉ *São Pedro* ☎ *289/827203*).

Train CP (✉ *Largo da Estação* ☎ *808/208208*).

Visitor Info Faro (✉ *Airport* ☎ *289/818582* ✉ *Rua da Misericórdia 8–12* ☎ *289/803604*).

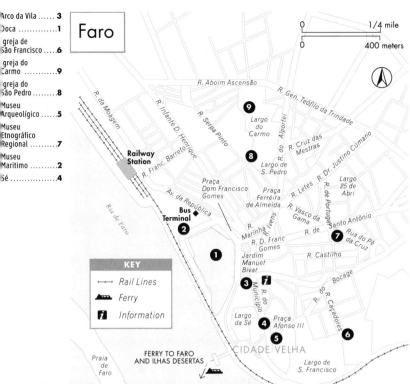

EXPLORING

Arco da Vila. The entrance to the Cidade Velha is through this 18th-century gate that stands in front of the Jardim Manuel Bivar (Manuel Bivar Garden). At the top is a niche sheltering a white-marble statue of St. Thomas Aquinas, plus storks that nest here permanently.

Doca *(dock).* The small dock—flanked by Faro's main square, the Praça Dom Francisco Gomes, and the Jardim Manuel Bivar—is filled with small pleasure craft rather than working fishing boats. A good time to come here is at dusk when the sun sets dramatically over the lagoon.

Igreja do Carmo *(Carmo Church).* Just north of the city center, this baroque church looks very out of place amid the modern buildings surrounding it. Inside, a door to the right of the altar leads to the Capela dos Ossos (Chapel of the Bones) set in an outside garden area. The tiny chapel walls are covered in more than 1,000 skulls and bones dug up from the adjacent monks' cemetery—an eerie sight, to say the least, but a fairly common custom in Portugal. ⊠ *Largo do Carmo* ☎ *289/824490* 🎟 *€0.75* ⊙ *Weekdays 10–1 and 3–5, Sat. 10–1.*

Igreja do São Pedro *(St. Peter's Church).* This 16th-century church is perhaps the prettiest of Faro's churches, and it has an unusual altar set to the left of the main altar. It's entirely carved in gilded chestnut wood and a delicate frieze depicts the Last Supper. ⊠ *Largo de S. Pedro* 🕾 *No phone* ⊗ *Daily 9–1 and 3–7.*

Sé *(Cathedral).* The squat, mostly Renaissance-style Sé, built in 1251 over a former mosque and originally belonging to the Order of Santiago, faces the Largo da Sé, a grand square bordered by orange trees and whitewashed palace buildings. The cathedral retains a Gothic tower but is mostly of interest for its interior full of 17th- and 18th-century azulejos. On one side of the nave is a red chinoiserie organ, dating from 1751. Best of all, however, is the view from the top of the church tower, looking out over Cidade Velha rooftops and across the lagoon. ⊠ *Largo da Sé* 🕾 *No phone* 🖭 *€2* ⊗ *Mon.–Sat. 10–5:30; tower 10–2.*

BEACHES

The closest beach to town is the long, sandy **Praia de Faro,** on the Ilha de Faro (Faro Island), a sandbar 5 km (3 mi) southwest of town. It's near the airport and is a 25-minute ride from town on Bus 16, which runs every hour 8 am–10 pm. You can catch it at the boat basin or opposite the bus terminal. Crowds pack in during peak season and on weekends. There's no surfing here, nor are water-sports rentals available.

WHERE TO EAT AND STAY

¢ ✕**Adega Nova.** A seating arrangement of long wooden tables lined by benches keeps things lively at this down-to-earth *adega* (wine cellar), where the Portuguese dishes are expertly prepared. You'll find more good cheer, as well as drinks, in the tile-covered bar. It's a good thing, too, as this place is close to the train station in an otherwise dreary area. ⊠ *Rua Francisco Barreto 24* 🕾 *289/813433* ▤ *No credit cards.*

PORTUGUESE

¢ ✕**Dois Irmãos.** In business since 1925, this large, central restaurant (one of several good places on this street) specializes in cataplana, as evidenced by the utensils that hang from its wood-beam ceiling. Almost any of the other seafood dishes are worth trying, too. Just save room for the flan. Choose your wine from one of the hundreds of bottles that line the upper walls. ⊠ *Largo do Terreiro do Bispo 14–15* 🕾 *289/823337* ▤ *AE, DC, MC, V.*

PORTUGUESE

¢ ✕**Mesa dos Mouros.** The Moors' Table occupies an ancient stone house right by the Sé. You can either eat indoors or dine alfresco on a raised wooden terrace looking across the cobbled square, which is fringed with orange trees. Despite the antiquity of its surroundings, this is a stylish restaurant that serves good fish dishes and Spanish tapas. ⊠ *Largo da Sé* 🕾 *289/878873* ▤ *MC, V.*

SPANISH

$ 🏨 **Hotel Eva.** From this well-appointed hotel on the main square, you have views of the boat basin and the Cidade Velha. There's a bar with occasional evening entertainment, as well as a rooftop pool and top-floor restaurant. Rooms are modern and comfortably furnished; ask for one overlooking the harbor area. There's also a courtesy bus to the town beach on nearby Ilha de Faro. **Pros:** in the very heart of Faro; within walking distance to all amenities and attractions; short taxi, car, or bus ride to airport (5–10 minutes, depending on traffic). **Cons:** can be rather noisy because a bus terminal is adjacent to the hotel; no nearby beach. ⊠ *Av. da República 1* 🕾 *289/001000* 🛏 *148 rooms* ⟡ *In-room: safe, Wi-Fi. In-hotel: restaurant, bar, pool, laundry service, refrigerator, Wi-Fi hotspot* ▤ *AE, DC, MC, V* ⦿*BP, FAP, MAP.*

¢ ⊞**Hotel S. Algarve.** Formerly known as Residencial Algarve, the original building was constructed in the 1880s for a wealthy maritime family. It was renovated to mirror the original style and is now one of Faro's nicest budget hotels. Even the bathrooms recall those in much more upscale establishments. Rooms are bright and have pine furnishings, stone floors, and simple pastel-color throw rugs. The hotel is a few steps from the center of town. **Pros:** located in downtown Faro; private underground garage; two-minute walk from railway station, five-minute walk from main bus terminal; luggage storage available. **Cons:** rooms small; hot water is inconsistent; no pool. ⊠ *Rua Infante Dom Henrique 52* ☎ *289/895700* ⊕ *www.hotelsolalgarve.com* ⤳ *40 rooms* ⌂ *In-room: a/c. In-hotel: restaurant, bar, pool, spa* ⊟ *MC, V* ⑩ *BP.*

$$$ ⊞**Monte do Casal.** This 18th-century luxury boutique hotel is slightly out of Faro, near Estoi. The British owner and chef Bill Hawkins trained in the kitchens of Claridges and the Savoy, which makes dining here a highlight well accompanied by a formidable wine list. Rooms have old brass-cornered furniture, and nearly all have private patios overlooking the pool and botanical gardens. From Faro take the N2 north toward São Bras and exit for Estoi. Follow signs for Moncarapacho for 2½ km (1½ mi), where the hotel is signposted on the left. Children under 16 are not allowed (except in July). **Pros:** an ideal destination for those looking for a tranquil retreat in which to recharge; excellent on-site dining; personalized service; spectacular views. **Cons:** no surrounding amenities; isolated location; not for young, adventure-seeking families or young couples wanting to stay in a location with pulsing nightlife. ⊠ *Cerro do Lobo, Estoi* ☎ *289/990140* ⊕ *www.montedocasal.pt* ⤳ *18 rooms* ⌂ *In-room: safe, Wi-Fi. In-hotel: restaurant, bar, pool, spa, no kids under 16* ⊟ *MC, V* ⑩ *BP, MAP.*

NIGHTLIFE

Café-goers throng Faro's central pedestrian streets at night. Rua do Prior, in particular, is known for its wide selection of late-closing bars. Friday night is the best time for barhopping. In a 500-year-old building in the heart of Faro's historic area, opposite the marina, **Columbus Lounge Bar** (⊠ *Praça D. Francisco Gomes No. 13* ⊕ *www.barcolumbus.com*) is popular with the fashion crowd and specializes in exotic cocktails. Don't be put off by the silly name: **Kingburger** (⊠ *Rua do Prior 40* ☎ *289/828085*) rocks until well into the morning. If you're after a full-fledged dance club, visit trendy **24 Julho** (⊠ *Rua do Prior 38* ☎ *289/282468*), which is patronized almost exclusively by the locals on weekends, when it stays open until 7 am.

OLHÃO

8 km (5 mi) east of Faro.

During the Napoleonic Wars, the inhabitants of this 18th-century port town on the Ria Formosa (a *ria* is a briny river) defied the French blockade on trade with Britain and profited from smuggling. With the proceeds, they built North African–style, cube-shape whitewashed houses. In 1808, local fishermen reputedly sailed to Brazil to inform the exiled Dom João VI that the French had departed from Portugal. Because of their loyalty and courage (they sailed without navigational aids), the fishermen's hometown was granted a town charter. Although modern construction has destroyed much of its charm, Olhão's port is still colorful, and its intricate Cidade Velha is appealing. To get a bird's-eye view climb the parish church's bell tower.

GETTING HERE AND AROUND

Olhão can be reached by bus or train from anywhere in the Algarve, though those coming from the western end of the region may have to change buses in Albufeira or Faro.

ESSENTIALS

Bus Contact Eva (✉ *Rua General Humberto Delgado* ☎ *289/702157*).

Visitor Info Olhão (✉ *Largo Sebastião Martins Mestre 6A* ☎ *289/713936*).

EXPLORING

Olhanense Football Club & Stadium. Seeing top teams play soccer in the Algarve used to be a rarity until Olhanense gained promotion to the Portuguese First Division. Operating on a shoe-string budget, the club has many English expat fans and a trip to the Estádio José Arcanjo is advised between September and May. ☎ *289/704112* ⊕ *www.scolhanense.com*.

Roman ruins. The ruins at Milreu, about 10 km (6 mi) northwest of Olhão, were first excavated in 1877. The settlement was once known as Roman Ossonoba, and the remains—including a temple (later converted into a Christian basilica) and mosaic fragments adorning some of the 3rd-century baths—date from the 2nd through the 6th century. A few of the more portable pieces are on display in Faro's archaeological museum. ☒ *€2* ⊙ *Apr.–Sept., Tues.–Sun. 9:30–12:30 and 2–6; Oct.–Mar., Tues.–Sun. 9:30–12:30 and 2–5*.

Shellfish Festival. The Shellfish Festival or Festival de Marisco is a must for those who are in the Algarve in mid-August. The event lasts four to six days and besides attracting top performers, the food on offer is an absolute and renowned delicacy. ✉ *Loulé riverfront* ⊕ *www.festivaldomarisco.com* ☒ *€8* ⊙ *7:30 pm–1:30 am*.

BEACHES

Adding to the allure of this area's beaches is the designation of this entire section of coastline, including islands and river inlets, as a nature reserve, thanks to the great number of migratory birds that flock here on their way south for winter. To reach beaches on the nearby islands, take a ferry from the jetty at the east end of the municipal gardens. A small kiosk there posts timetables and sells tickets. If it's closed, buy the tickets on board. From June to September, ferries run hourly each day; from October through May there are three or four trips daily. Schedules are available at the tourist office. The fare is about €1.

The **Ilha da Armona,** about 15 minutes east of Olhão, has some fine, isolated stretches of sand, as well as vacation villas and café-bars. The sandy **Ilha da Culatra,** 15 minutes by ferry from Olhão, has several ramshackle fishing communities; at the southern village of Farol, you'll find agreeable beaches.

SHOPPING

Fodor'sChoice ★ One of the Algarve's best food markets, the **Mercado dos Pescadores** (⊗ *Mon.–Sat. 7–2*) is held in the riverfront buildings in the town gardens. Feast your eyes on the shellfish for which Olhão is renowned; mussels, in particular, are a local specialty.

> **ORIGINS OF A NAME**
>
> The city's name, Olhão, originates from the Arab word *Al-Hain,* meaning natural spring. Phonetic influences over the centuries resulted in Al-Hain eventually becoming Olhão.

ÃO BRÁS DE ALPORTEL

18 km (11 mi) northwest of Olhão.

Inland, São Brás is a regional center for processing cork. It's an unremarkable place, but there are two reasons why it makes a refreshing break from the developed coastline: its museum of traditional dress and its *pousada* (inn).

GETTING HERE AND AROUND

The best way to get to this area is by taxi or bus. Alternatively, you can catch a train to Loulé or Faro, then take a bus or a taxi to São Brás. A taxi from Faro would cost approximately €20 and would take around 20 minutes. A taxi from Loulé would be slightly quicker and cheaper. A bus from Faro takes approximately 45 minutes and costs €3.75. A bus from Loulé costs €2.95 and takes 25 minutes.

ESSENTIALS

Visitor Info São Brás de Alportel (⊠ *LG de S. Debastião 23* ☎ *289/843165*).

EXPLORING

Casa da Cultura António Bentes, Museu do Traje Algarvio *(Antonio Bentes Cultural Center, Algarve Costume Museum).* The cultural center and museum are just a short walk from the center of town. Here you'll find a charmingly old-fashioned collection of local costumes—featuring black lacework, bright colors, and the rooster emblem of Portugal—and various other regional rural bygones. ⊠ *Rua Dr. José Dias Sancho 61* ☎ *289/840100* w*www.museu-sbras.com* ☞ *€2* ⊗ *Weekdays 10–1 and 2–5, weekends 2–5.*

The Cork Route. Acclaimed internationally for producing unique items made from cork, São Brás now boasts a Cork Route, a guided walking tour tailored for visitors of all ages. Different tours explore a whole new world of sensations that you might not otherwise experience. Feel the bark of the Cork Oak, smell the countryside in which it grows, learn about the numerous ways in which it can be transformed, and the purposes it serves. Walks range from the more adventurous for the younger visitor, and include extreme sports, to more gentle treks for the senior visitor. Prices vary in accordance to tour. ☎ *289/840 018* ⊕ *www.rotadacortica.pt.*

6

WHERE TO EAT AND STAY

$$ ⊞ **Pousada Palácio de Estoi.** Located 8 km (5mi) from São Brás in the charming neighboring village of Estoi, Pousada Palácio de Estoi provides a comfortable base for exploring the region. Converted from a 19th-century palace the guesthouse offers a sense of luxury and history as well as a plethora of activities, such as horseback riding, country walks, and fishing. Despite its palatial exterior, inside the decor is sleek and contemporary. All rooms have a balcony with a garden view. The restaurant ($$$$), which is open to the public, offers an ambitious menu of fine regional dishes made from fresh local produce; it's a sophisticated taste of the Eastern Algarve. **Pros:** a unique, rural Algarve experience; quality over quantity is the name of the game; bath robes provided in rooms. **Cons:** this is not the place for budget travelers; the interior design contradicts the palace's sense of history; minimum room-service charge of €10 per request. ⊠ *Rua São José, Estoi* ☎ *289/990150* ⊕ *www.pousadas.pt* ⇆ *60 rooms, 3 suites* ⚭ *In-room: a/c, no phone, Internet. In-hotel: restaurant, bar, pools (outdoor and indoor), spa* ⊟ *AE, DC, MC, V* ⚭ *BP, MAP.*

LOULÉ

13 km (8 mi) west of São Brás de Alportel.

This little town is known for its crafts and its vibrant Saturday-morning fair, held in and around the landmark central market, which is enclosed and topped by a red onion dome. The narrow cobbled streets—particularly Rua da Barbacà—around the castle and the church are lined with whitewashed houses and workshops (closed Saturday afternoons and Sunday) where a few artisans still make lace, leather, and copper items. Note the many houses with very finely sculpted (or filigreed) plasterwork on their white chimneys—a typical old Algarve sight. The rest of Loulé is overwhelmed by the main boulevard and modern buildings, but there's a pleasant municipal park at the top of town.

GETTING HERE AND AROUND

Trains run straight to Loulé from most major cities and towns in the Algarve, and buses run directly from Portimão, Albufeira and Faro, costing between €3 and €6. A bus from Portimão would take about two hours to Loulé. The good news is that exploring the city does not require a car and can be covered on foot.

ESSENTIALS

Bus Contact Eva (⊠ *Rua Nossa Senhora de Fátima* ☎ *289/416655*).

Visitor Info Loulé (⊠ *Edifício do Castelo* ☎ *289/463900*).

EXPLORING

Campina de Cima Salt Mines. Several kilometers of stunning rock-salt galleries run beneath the streets of Loulé. Sporadically open to the public for organized events, it's worth asking at the local tourist office if or when they may be open. Alternatively, more information about the mines can be requested at Loulé City Hall. ■ TIP→ **This is not an adventure for the claustrophobic.** ☎ *289/463900.*

Castelo de Loulé *(Loulé Castle)*. Once a Moorish stronghold, Loulé has preserved the ruins of the medieval castle, which was enlarged in 1268 after the site had been occupied and fortified since Neolithic times. These days, it houses the historical museum and archives as well as the tourist office. ⊠ *Largo Dom Pedro I* ☎ *No phone* 💶 *Free* ☉ *Weekdays 9–5:30, Sat. 10–2.*

> ### LOULÉ'S STREET FESTIVALS
>
> The Med World Music Festival in May and the elegant Noite Branca, or White Night (a white outfit is compulsory), event in late August are hugely popular and attract thousands of tourists each year. ⊕ www.cm-loule.pt.

Igreja Matriz *(Parish Church)*. This restored 13th-century church has handsome tiles, wood carvings, and an unusual wrought-iron pulpit. ⊠ *Largo Pr. C. da Silva* ☎ *No phone* ☉ *Mon.–Sat. 9–noon and 2–5:30.*

WHERE TO STAY

¢ 🔟 **Loulé Jardim Hotel.** Portuguese business travelers are drawn to this hotel, which is well off the main road on a small square in the old part of town, yet only a short drive (8 km [5 mi]) from the coast. Rooms are modest and clean; prices leave you with extra money to buy some of those items crafted in town. **Pros:** attractive, well-kept sunny exterior and comfortable interior; in the center of Loulé; free private garage for off-road parking. **Cons:** no tea- or coffeemaking facilities in room; the historic city of Loulé is not for those looking for neon nightlife; beaches are a 15-minute drive away. ⊠ *Praça Manuel D'Arriaga* ☎ *289/413094* ⊕ *www.loulejardimhotel.com* 📲 *52 rooms* 🛏 *In-room: no a/c, safe. In-hotel: bars, pool, laundry service, Wi-Fi* 🟰 *AE, MC, V* 🍴 *BP.*

SHOPPING

Believed to be one of the oldest municipal markets in the Algarve, if not the country, **Loulé Municipal Market** (⊠ *City Centre* ☎ *289/400600* ☉ *Mon.–Sat. 9–1*) is a hive of smells, colors, and sounds. This distinct, century-old Moorish-styled market is well worth a visit, especially on a Saturday morning.

THE EASTERN ALGARVE

The eastern portion of the province, known as the Sotavento, is a region of flat, sandy beaches that are more difficult to access than those in the western Algarve because of their locations on spits, sandbars, and islands. Mudflats between Faro and the Spanish border are protected areas for breeding birds. Although there has been some development along the coast, this is primarily a quiet, low-key area, though its principal town, Tavira, is an important fishing port.

TAVIRA

Fodor's Choice
★

30 km (18 mi) east of Loulé; 28 km (17 mi) east of Faro.

At the mouth of the quiet Rio Gilão, Tavira is immediately endearing, with its castle ruins, riverfront gardens, and old streets. Many of the town's white, 18th-century houses retain their original doorways and coats-of-arms; others have peculiar four-sided roofs that rise pyramid-like (they are known as roof screens), and still others are completely covered in tiles. The town also has more than 30 churches, most dating from the 17th and 18th centuries. One of two river crossings—the low bridge adjacent to the arcaded Praça da República—is of Roman origin, although it was rebuilt in the 17th century and again in recent times after sustaining damage from floodwaters.

TAVIRA'S UNIQUE ARCHITECTURE

Take a moment while you're exploring Tavira to look up and admire the peculiar four-sided roofs that rise pyramid-like—locals refer to them as roof screens. These unique architectural elements appeared in the late 19th and early 20th centuries. As the town's prosperity grew, so did the popularity of the screens, which are said to project the house's exterior face, which is simultaneously the regional's culture face. The screens are also deemed important elements in the characterization and individualization of the building.

GETTING HERE AND AROUND

Tavira is easily reached by any form of public transport. Once in Tavira there are several types of local transportation—boat, tourist train, carriage, walking tours—that make exploring the city entertaining and enjoyable.

ESSENTIALS

Bus Contact Eva (⊠ *Rua das Pelames* 🕾 *28281/322546*).

Tours Delgaturis Tourist Train (🕾 *212/680459*). **Séqua Boat Tours** (🕾 *960/170789* ⊕ *www.sequatours.com*). **Tavira Carriage Tours** (🕾 *960/170789* ⊕ *www.tavira-tours.com*). **Walking Tours** (🕾 *960/170789* ⊕ *www.walking-algarve.com*).

Visitor Info Tavira (⊠ *Rua da Galeria 9* 🕾 *281/322511*).

EXPLORING

Castelo. From the battlemented walls of the ruined central 13th-century castle you can look down over Tavira's many church spires and across the river delta to the sea. ⊠ *Stepped street off Rua da Liberdade* 🎟 *Free* ☉ *Daily 9–5.*

Igreja da Misericórdia *(Mercy Church).* This a Renaissance structure with a portal that dates from 1541. On Good Friday, a 10 pm candlelight procession begins here. From May through July, the church occasionally hosts musical performances during the Algarve International Classical Music Festival. ⊠ *West of Praça da República* 🕾 *No phone* ☉ *Daily 9–12:30 and 2–6.*

Pego do Inferno. Surrounded by rocks and trees that provide cool shade, this natural waterfall and deep, blue lagoon attract locals and tourists in hordes during the summer. Take a refreshing dip in hot months or admire its natural beauty any other time of year. A great picnic spot, its public infrastructures have recently been upgraded and more garbage bins allocated to better cater for visitors. Unfortunately, it's no longer a well-kept secret, but it is free. The Tavira Tourist Office (⇨ *see above*) can provide directions and information. ⊠ *Ribeira da Asseca, 7 kilometers from Tavira, en route to Santa Catarina* ☎ *281/322511.*

> ### CATCH OF THE DAY
>
> Because Tavira is a tuna-fishing port, you'll find plenty of local color and fresh fish; tuna steaks, often grilled and served with onions, are on restaurant menus all over town at remarkably low prices. In the harbor area, you can sample no-frills dining at its best, alongside the fishermen, at any of the café-restaurants across from the tangle of boats and nets.

Santa Maria do Castelo *(St. Mary of the Castle).* One of the town's two major churches, Santa Maria was built on the site of a Moorish mosque in the 13th century. Although it was almost entirely destroyed by the 1755 earthquake, the church retains its original Gothic doorway. ⊠ *Alto de Santa Maria (next to castelo)* ☎ *No phone* 🎫 *€1* ☉ *Daily 9:30–12:30 and 2–5:30.*

Torre de Tavira. This old water tower was converted into a camera obscura of the Leonardo da Vinci fashion in 1931. An oversize photographic camera here takes images of the panoramic views it commands of the town. The visit makes a fascinating exploration into the world of photography and a cool, shady afternoon retreat from the sweltering afternoon sunshine. ⊠ *Calçado da Galeria 12* ☎ *No phone* 🎫 *€3* ☉ *Daily 10–5.*

BEACHES

Fodor's Choice ★

Directly offshore and extending west for some 10 km (6 mi) is the **Ilha de Tavira,** a long sandbar with several good beaches. Ferries run to the island every half hour in July and August and every hour May through June and September through mid-October. The fare is about €1.50 round-trip. In summer a bus (marked "Quatro Águas") runs between the center of town and the jetty 2 km (1 mi) east.

About 12 km (7 mi) east of Tavira is Manta Rota, a small community with a few bars, restaurants, hotels, and the **Praia de Manta Rota.** At this exceptional beach, sandbars merge with the shore. A particularly nice strand is the offshore sandbar at the village of Cacela Velha. From Manta Rota to Faro the underwater drop-offs are often steep and you can quickly find yourself in deep water.

WHERE TO EAT AND STAY

$ ✕ **Beira Rio.** Named for its riverbank location, the Beira Rio offers the best water views in town. Locals tend to eat in the azulejo-lined dining room; visitors are often drawn to the peaceful terrace, where watching the moon rise over the Roman bridge is alone worth the price of dinner. Well-prepared Portuguese specialties such as pork with port-wine

PORTUGUESE

sauce share the menu with steaks, pizzas, and pasta. ⊠ *Rua Borda de Agua de Assêca 46–48* ☎ *281/323165* ⊟ *AE, DC, MC, V* ☺ *No lunch.*

¢ ✕ **Ponto de Encontro.** Cross the Roman bridge to this typical Portuguese

PORTUGUESE restaurant with tiled walls and tables immaculately draped with linens. You can also relax at outside tables to view the passing scene on the small square, which in summer is abloom with flowers and closed to traffic. Algarve-style swordfish grilled with garlic, tuna fried with onion, and other fresh fish dishes are specialties. ⊠ *Praça Dr. António Padinha 39* ☎ *281/323730* ⊟ *AE, DC, MC, V.*

$ ✕ **Restaurante Imperial.** This restaurant behind the riverside gardens is

SEAFOOD well known for its fish: clams, tuna, a tasty mixed fried-fish plate—you name it. In summer, there's seating on the sidewalk. Waiters are good at their job but a little aloof: after 40 years of service, the Imperial doesn't have to try hard to attract customers. Desserts are a tad disappointing. ⊠ *Rua José Pires Padinha 22–24* ☎ *281/322306* ⊟ *MC, V* ☺ *Closed Wed. Oct.–May.*

$ ▦ **Hotel Vila Galé Albacora.** This is an absolutely charming hotel in a lovely location at the confluence of two rivers, just in front of the beaches. In fact, in the summer months boats depart from here to take you to the beach. It's traditional in architectural style, modern in decor, and not far from Tavira—it has a minibus service to and from town. **Pros:** a comprehensive resort with own restaurant and transport to/from the town of Tavira; own boat transfer to and from beach. **Cons:** waterfront location attracts insects such as mosquitoes; buffet not highly recommended. ⊠ *Quatro Águas* ☎ *281/380800* ⊕ *www. vilagale.pt* ⤵ *157 rooms, 5 suites* ♿ *In-room: safe. In-hotel: 2 restaurants, room service, pools, Internet terminal, Wi-Fi hotspot* ⊟ *AE, DC, MC, V* ⦿ *BP, FAP, MAP.*

¢ ▦ **Marés Residencial e Restaurante.** Only a stone's throw from the waterfront (and the summer ferry to the Ilha de Tavira), this tiny hotel is above an excellent Portuguese restaurant ($$–$$$$) that shares the same name. Some of the rooms have balconies that offer river or town views; all provide basic comforts and have bathrooms decorated with rustic tile work. A rooftop terrace looks out over Tavira's distinctive pyramid-shaped roofs. The boat out to Tavira island leaves from directly in front of this hotel. **Pros:** traditional hotel; best location at a sensible price. **Cons:** rooms above restaurant can be noisy; breakfast buffet is disappointing. ⊠ *Rua José Pires Padinha 134/140* ☎ *281/325815* ⊕ *www.residencialmares.com* ⤵ *24 rooms* ♿ *In-room: a/c. In-hotel: restaurant, Wi-Fi* ⊟ *AE, DC, MC, V* ⦿ *BP.*

SPORTS AND THE OUTDOORS

Fodor'sChoice **Quinta de Cima.** This is the sister course to Quinta da Ria and is a stiffer

★ test. Also designed by Rocky Roquemore, water hazards abound, and length as well as accuracy are the premiums. The strength of the challenge is tempered by some wonderful views in a superb setting. Visitors are required to produce a handicap certificate. ⊠ *Apartado 161, Vila Nova de Cacela* ☎ *281/950580* ⊕ *www.quintadariagolf.com* ⚐ *18 holes. 6,586 m. Par 72. Slope 133* ▣ *€75 per round* ⚲ *Facilities: driving range, putting green, chipping area, golf carts, hand-pulled carts, electric trolleys, rental clubs, pro shop, golf lessons, restaurant, bar.*

MONTE GORDO

22 km (14 mi) east of Tavira.

Pinewoods and orchards break up the flat landscape around this large resort area, just 4 km (2½ mi) from the Spanish border. Relentlessly modern, Monte Gordo has plenty of hotels, restaurants, and nightspots but falls well short on charm and character.

GETTING HERE AND AROUND
Rent a car if you're planning to visit the resort area.

ESSENTIALS
Visitor Info **Monte Gordo** (✉ *Av. Marginal* ☎ *281/544495*).

BEACH

The flat, 12-km-long (7-mi-long) **Praia de Monte Gordo** is a popular beach. The seawater here has the highest average temperature in the country, but it, too, can go from warm to ice cold within a day.

WHERE TO EAT AND STAY

¢ ✕**Mota.** Large, lively, and unpretentious, this well-established restau-
PORTUGUESE rant is on the sands of the Praia de Monte Gordo. Seating is on a large covered terrace facing the ocean. During the day you can drop in for a snack or salad if you don't want a full meal; in the evening you're served regional dishes while live music plays in the background. ✉ *Praia de Monte Gordo* ☎ *281/512340* ▭ *No credit cards.*

$ ⌂**Alcázar.** Outside, white balconies contrast with a redbrick facade; inside, sinuous arches and low, molded ceilings recall a cave's interior—or that of an Arab tent. Rooms have their own terraces and window boxes. The staff is accommodating, and the location—two blocks from the beach—is convenient. **Pros:** food good and varied; rooms are spacious. **Cons:** high ceilings mean lighting can be dim in rooms at night; computer in hotel lobby expensive to use. ✉ *Rua de Ceuta 9* ☎ *281/510140* ⌨ *hotelalcazar@hotel-alcazar.com* 🛏 *130 rooms* ⌂ *In-room: safe, a/c, refrigerator, Wi-Fi. In-hotel: restaurant, bar, tennis court, pools, laundry service, Internet terminal* ▭ *AE, DC, MC, V* ⧖ *BP, MAP.*

$ ⌂**Casablanca Inn Hotel.** Not being on the main drag is a major advantage at this cozy, cavelike hotel with Moorish tile work in the guest rooms and restaurant. The 1970s style and layout is best captured in the outdated split-level lounge bar, dance floor, and extravagant buffet restaurant with a domed, mirrored ceiling. Guest rooms have extras such as a coffeemaker, hair dryer, and ironing board. The solarium and the heated indoor pool help ward off any out-of-season chill. **Pros:** walking distance to beach; free reserved parking spaces for hotel guests—but only four. **Cons:** slow service; pool is small. ✉ *Praceta Casablanca* ☎ *281/511444* 🛏 *42 rooms* ⌂ *In-room: safe, a/c. In-hotel: restaurant, bar, pools, laundry service, Wi-Fi* ▭ *AE, DC, MC, V* ⧖ *BP, MAP.*

NIGHTLIFE

In addition to a wealth of nightclubs and discos, Monte Gordo has a **casino** (✉ *Av. Infante* ☎ *281/530800* ⊕ *www.solverde.com*) with blackjack and roulette, among other games, as well as a slot-machine room. From July through September, you can have dinner and see a

6

cabaret show for €75; from October through June the cost is €50. You must be 18 or older to enter (bring your passport), and dressy-casual attire is best.

VILA REAL DE SANTO ANTÓNIO

4 km (2½ mi) east of Monte Gordo; 47 km (29 mi) east of Faro.

This community on the Rio Guadiana is the last stop before Spain. The original town was destroyed by a tidal wave in the 17th century and wasn't rebuilt until the late 18th century, when the Marquês de Pombal constructed a new, gridded town. Consequently, Vila Real, which took only five months to complete, is a showpiece of 18th-century planning. Like most border towns, it's a lively place, with plenty of bars and restaurants and some traffic-free central streets that encourage evening strolls. If you're interested in a short excursion across the border, visit Ayamonte, the town's Spanish counterpart, and a far livelier place to visit. Just across the Guadiana River, Ayamonte can be reached during the day and early evening on the charmingly old-fashioned ferryboat.

GETTING HERE AND AROUND

Vila Real de Santo António is on the Algarve's most eastern end. It's easiest reached by train. From Vila Real there's a ferry that carries both vehicles and passengers across the Guardiana River, to Spain. A one-way crossing to and from Ayamonte, Spain, should cost in the region of €4.50 per car and €1.35 per passenger. In summer the ferries cross every 30 minutes, the rest of the year they cross roughly every hour. Alternatively, use the suspension bridge that was inaugurated in 1986; it's free.

ESSENTIALS

Bus Contact Eva (✉ *Av. da República* ☎ *281/511807*).

Ferry Empresa de Transportes do Rio Guadiana (☎ *281/543152*).

Visitor Info Monte Gordo (✉ *Av. Marginal* ☎ *281/544495*).

EXPLORING

The company **Riosul Viagens e Turismo** (✉ *Rua Tristão Vaz Teixeira 15 C, Monte Gordo* ☎ *281/510200* ⊕ *www.riosultravel.com*) arranges daylong river cruises that include lunch, a stop for a swim, and a final stop in the timeless village of Foz de Odeleite before returning by boat to Vila Real. It also offers jeep safaris. The company has shuttle service from all eastern and central Algarve hotels to the Vila Real de Santo António dock. The cost is €38 to €49, depending on pickup location.

WHERE TO STAY

¢ **Arenilha Guest House.** Possibly the most modern B&B in Vila Real de Santo António, the Arenilha is no frills, but contemporary and clean. In the historical part of town, it offers simply furnished rooms that are comfortable. A buffet breakfast is included in the price. **Pros:** free parking; close to amenities; good value for money. **Cons:** breakfast is served in a nearby restaurant, not in the hotel itself; no pool. ✉ *Rua D.*

Pedro V 55 ☎ *281/107699 or 281/ 512565* ⬚ *60 rooms* ♿ *In-room: a/c. In-hotel: bar* ⊟ *AE, DC, MC, V* ⦁○⦁ *BP, MAP.*

$ ⬚ **Coração da Cidade.** As the name indicates, this traditional family-run B&B is in the heart of the city. It also boasts its own restaurant 100 meters from the hotel, in which patrons can enjoy wholesome, home-cooked Portuguese and Mediterranean cuisine. Breakfast is also served in this restaurant. Basic but clean, all rooms have private balconies. **Pros:** great location; kids under 3 stay free and there are free cots for kids under 2. **Cons:** no Internet; few facilities; B&B could use an update. ⊠ *Rua Sousa Martins 17* ☎ *281/530470 or 961/946116* ⬚ *20 rooms* ♿ *In-room: a/c. In-hotel: restaurant, bar* ⊟ *AE, DC, MC, V* ⦁○⦁ *BP, MAP.*

$ ⬚ **Hotel Apolo.** This hotel is in the center of Vila Real de Santo António, within walking distance of the historic part of town. It is a 3 km (1.86 mi) walk to the nearest beach. The rooms are soundproofed for extra comfort and there is a lovely garden and sun terrace. **Pros:** good range of activities available from hotel; private parking. **Cons:** breakfast needs improving; paint job could use a face-lift. *Av. Bombeiros Portugueses* ☎ *281/512448* ⊕ *www.apolo-hotel.com* ⬚ *42 rooms* ♿ *In-room: a/c. In-hotel: restaurant, bar, Wi-Fi, pool, parking (free)* ⊟ *AE, DC, MC, V* ⦁○⦁ *BP, MAP.*

THE CENTRAL ALGARVE

The central Algarve, between Faro and Portimão to the east, has the heaviest concentration of resorts, but there are also exclusive, secluded hotels and villas. In between built-up areas are quiet bays and amazing rock formations of arches, sea-stacks, caves, and blowholes. Shell-encrusted ocher-and-red cliffs contrast beautifully with the brilliant blues and greens of the sea. With a car it's easy to travel the few miles inland that make all the difference: minor roads lead into the hills and to towns that have resisted the changes wrought upon the coast.

ALMANCIL

10 km (6 mi) northwest of Faro.

Almancil, which is now easily accessed from both the A22 and the EN125, is near two of the region's biggest draws: the seaside resort areas of Quinta do Lago, roughly 5 km (3 mi) to the south, and Vale do Lobo, about 5 km (3 mi) to the southwest. Wealthy Europeans love these complexes for their superb hotels and sports facilities. Golf is the thing here, but tennis and horseback riding are also popular.

GETTING HERE AND AROUND

Almancil can be reached by bus or train from anywhere in the Algarve, though those coming from the western end of the region may have to change buses in Albufeira. Once in town, most venues can be visited on foot.

EXPLORING

Centro Cultural de São Lourenço. A pair of 200-year-old cottages downhill from the Igreja de São Lourenço have been transformed into a cultural center. The center has exhibits of contemporary Portuguese works, and it holds occasional classical music concerts.

> **DOWN DEEP**
>
> Walk along the beach heading left (facing the sea) and you will come across a string of three beach bars, all of which are well known for their fresh seafood barbecues.

Don't miss the delightful sculpture garden to the rear. ⊠ *São Lourenço* 🕾 *289/395475* 🖃 *Free* ☉ *Tues.–Sat. 10–7.*

Igreja de São Lourenço *(Church of St. Lawrence)*. Almancil's biggest draw is this church, built in 1730. Notable are the church's blue-and-white, floor-to-ceiling azulejo panels and its intricate gilt work. ⊠ *São Lourenço* 🕾 *289/395451* 🖃 *€2* ☉ *Mon. 2–5, Tues.–Sat. 10–1 and 2–5.*

WHERE TO EAT AND STAY

$ ✕ **Sr. Franco.** The finger-lickin' chicken that's grilled over charcoal pits
PORTUGUESE in this large, spotless restaurant has won awards for owner Joaquim Guerréiro (he concocts a special seasoning of local herbs). For an even better dining experience order a side salad (with tomatoes, onions, and ample fresh oregano) and top everything off with a bottle of Portuguese *vinho verde,* a fruity, faintly sparkling wine. The food is well worth the 5-km (3-mi) trip southwest from Almancil. ⊠ *Estrada de Quarteira, Escanxinas* 🕾 *289/393756* 🖃 *AE, DC, MC, V.*

$$$$ 🛏 **Hotel Quinta do Lago.** Since this once-exclusive hotel was taken over by the Ria Park hotel chain, standards in service have dropped and it has become overpriced. But the many celebrities who own villas within the complex are still a draw, and a stay here does win you substantial discounts at area golf courses. Numerous other sporting activities, from horseback riding to clay-pigeon shooting, can be arranged at a price. Set amid hundreds of acres of parkland, the hotel's extensive manicured lawns and sterile "nature trails" have displaced the natural habitat for local birds and rare species in the Ria Formosa nature reserve. The beach and sandbar are accessed via a wooden bridge—don't miss the beach massage service provided. **Pros:** good location; impeccable standard of food and service; nearby facilities include first-rate golf-courses and restaurants; direct access to the beach. **Cons:** seasoned luxury travelers may find the decor a little dated; expensive rates. ⊠ *Quinta do Lago* 🕾 *289/350350* ⊕ *www.hotelquintadolago.com* ↪ *121 rooms, 20 suites* ♨ *In-room: a/c, safe, Internet, Wi-Fi. In-hotel: 2 restaurants, room service, bars, tennis courts, pools, gym, bicycles, laundry service, Internet terminal* 🖃 *AE, DC, MC, V* ⓞ *BP, MAP.*

SPORTS AND THE OUTDOORS

WATER PARK

Just east of Vilamoura, and north of Quarteira, you'll find **Aquashow** (⊠ *E.N. 396, Quarteira* 🕾 *289/389396* ⊕ *www.aquashowpark.com* 🖃 *€18* ☉ *May–Sept.*), a large water park that also includes daily shows of birds of prey and parrots, as well as the Oasis Tropical Park with more than 60 exotic species.

VALE DO LOBO

5 km (3 mi) southwest of Almancil.

Vale do Lobo is a gated luxury villa complex that attracts the super-rich and famous from the world over (but yes, it's still open to all). Le Meridien Dona Filipa Hotel has two prestigious 18-hole golf courses, and other greens include extensive and well-tended gardens lined with palms and exotic shrubbery. A private security firm keeps a close eye on things while you make use of the helipad, health spa, indoor riding school, fitness centers, the David Lloyd Tennis Club, a yachting club, polo pitches, and a host of restaurants, bars, and cafés. The area is a second home to wealthy Europeans. The local beach is one of the cleanest in the Algarve and remains relatively quiet during peak months. You can access the beach from below the Dona Filipa Hotel, where most of the restaurants are clustered.

GETTING HERE AND AROUND

Due to the wealthy nature of this resort, public transport is hardly used, though should this be on a list of to-dos, a bus to Almancil followed by a taxi to Vale do Lobo is recommended.

ESSENTIALS

Taxi **FaroTaxis** (☎ 960/204709 wwww.farotaxi.com).

Visitor Info **Monte Gordo** (✉ Av. Marginal ☎ 281/544495).

WHERE TO STAY

$$$$ Le Meridien Dona Filipa Hotel. Rooms at this striking hotel are pleasant and have balconies, most of which overlook the sea. The service is superb, and the landscaped grounds are extensive. Although the hotel has its own tennis courts, it's also very close to the locally renowned Vale do Lobo Tennis Center. A stay here gets you reduced green fees and preferential tee times at the prestigious San Lorenzo Golf Club, which is owned by the hotel. Dining choices ($$$–$$$$) include the Dom Duarte restaurant, which has a Portuguese menu; the Primavera, which serves Italian cuisine; and the Grill, which offers local and international fare. **Pros:** not as expensive as neighboring up-market resorts; regular hotel shuttle to San Lorenzo Golf Course. **Cons:** 10-minute drive from hotel to San Lorenzo Golf Course; hotel in need of some updating. ✉ *Vale do Lobo* ☎ *289/357200* ⊕ *www.starwoodhotels.com* 🛏 *147 rooms* ⟡ *In-room: a/c, safe, Internet. In-hotel: 3 restaurants, room service, bars, golf course, tennis courts, pool, children's programs (ages 6–12), laundry service, no-smoking rooms, Internet terminal, Wi-Fi* ⊟ *AE, DC, MC, V* ⃝ *BP.*

SPORTS AND THE OUTDOORS

GOLF

Ocean Course Vale do Lobo. The Ocean Course emerged from an earlier design by Sir Henry Cotton and is a combination of the original "orange" and "green" courses of three 9-hole loops. The undulating fairways are fringed by pine, olive, orange, and eucalyptus trees. Accuracy is the key factor. The course can be challenging and correct club selection is always worth a few shots. Practice facilities include play from mats and from grass. A handicap certificate is required. ✉ *Vale do Lobo–Almancil* ☎ *289/353465* ⊕ *www.valedolobo.com* 🏌 *18 holes. 6,137 m. Par 73* 💲*€155 per round* ☞ *Facilities: driving range, putting green, chipping area, golf carts, hand-pulled carts, pro shop, restaurant, swimming pool, tennis academy, bar.*

Royal Course Vale do Lobo. A much more difficult challenge than its sister course, Ocean Course Vale do Lobo, the Royal Course is much longer and is defended by more water and bunkers. Sir Henry Cotton laid out the original course, but significant changes have been introduced by Rocky Roquemore to bring it more up-to-date. The pick of the holes is the famous 16th, which requires a carry of 200 yards over three spectacular cliffs to reach the sanctuary green. A handicap limit of 27 for men and 35 for women is enforced here. ✉ *Vale do Lobo–Almancil* ☎ *289/353535* ⊕ *valedolobo.com/golf/royal-golf-course* ⚓ *Reservations essential* 🏌 *18 holes. 6,059 m. Par 72* 💲*€165 per round* ☞ *Facilities: driving range, putting green, chipping area, golf carts, hand-pulled carts, pro shop, restaurant, swimming pool, tennis academy, bar.*

HORSEBACK RIDING

At **Horses Paradise** (✉ *Rua Cistoval Tires Norte* ☎ *289/394189*) riding rates per hour range from €19 to €40.

TENNIS

The **Vale do Lobo Tennis Academy** (✉ *Vale do Lobo* ☎ *289/357850* ⊕ *www.algarvetenis.com*) has 14 all-weather courts, a bar, a pro shop, a pool, a gym, a steam room, and a restaurant. Court fees start at €26.

VILAMOURA

10 km (6 mi) west of Almancil.

What was once a prosperous Roman settlement is today a prosperous resort community with the Algarve's biggest marina—an enormous, self-contained, 1,000-berth complex with apartments, hotels, bars, cafés, restaurants, shops, and sports facilities. The town of Vilamoura and the area surrounding it also have several luxury hotels and golf courses as well as a major tennis center and casino.

GETTING HERE AND AROUND

Besides renting a car, you can reach Vilamoura by train, though the nearest stops are Albufeira in the west and Loulé in the east. Once at these stations, a bus can be caught to Vilamoura.

ESSENTIALS

Bus EVA bus terminal (✉ *Alto dos Caliços* ☎ *289/580611*).

Visitor Info Monte Gordo (✉ *Av. Marginal* ☎ *281/544495*).

EXPLORING

Just off a corner of the marina, the excavations of Roman ruins at the site known as Cêrro da Vila, where Vilamoura was first established, have revealed an elaborate plumbing system as well as several mosaics. The small, well-laid-out **Museu de Cêrro da Vila** gives access to the site and exhibits its pieces found here. ✉ *Av. Cerro do Vila* ☎ *289/312153* 💲*€2* ⊘ *Nov.–mid-Apr., daily 9:30–12:30 and 2–6; mid-Apr.–Oct., daily 10–1 and 4–9.*

WHERE TO STAY

$ **Hotel Apartamento do Golfe.** You can opt for an affordable, self-catered holiday in these roomy studio and one-bedroom apartments neatly set around a central swimming pool. Maid service is optional. Golf players will be in their element, as the hotel is flanked on all sides by high-quality courses. A buffet barbecue (¢–$) is laid out each night in summer with unlimited food and plenty of sangria flowing. The suave hotel manager entertains guests with impromptu karaoke performances (ask him to try out his Frank Sinatra impression). The hotel is also within a 10-minute drive of a casino, riding center, local tennis club, fishing club, shooting range, cinema complex, bowling, and the Vilamoura Marina. **Pros:** spacious; clean rooms that are well-equipped (i.e., microwave oven, toaster, electric kettle); quiet location; courtesy bus to Praia da Falésia beach; good value for money. **Cons:** nightlife and shopping a short drive away. ⊠ *Quarteira* ☎ *289/303140* ⊕ *www.hotelvilamouragolf.com* ⇲ *35 apartments* ⚐ *In-room: a/c, safe, kitchen, Internet. In-hotel: restaurant, room service, pool, Wi-Fi* ⊟ *AE, DC, MC, V* ⍾◯⍾ *BP, FAP, MAP.*

$$$ **Hotel Dom Pedro Golf.** Part of a highly successful vacation complex, the Dom Pedro is close to the casino, not far from a splendid beach, and five minutes from the marina. Rooms are attractively furnished, and there's a garden in which to relax. The hotel also has a comprehensive range of facilities and a free shuttle service to local golf clubs. **Pros:** stone's-throw from the marina; courtesy bus to popular golf courses; good maid service. **Cons:** decor dated; proximity to popular bars can be a nuisance to some; some perceive the hotel's five-star rating as ambitious. ⊠ *Rua Atlântico* ☎ *289/300700* ⊕ *www.dompedro.com* ⇲ *266 rooms* ⚐ *In-room: a/c, safe, Internet. In-hotel: restaurant, room service, bar, tennis courts, pools, Internet terminal, Wi-Fi, spa, gym* ⊟ *AE, DC, MC, V* ⍾◯⍾ *BP, FAP, MAP.*

NIGHTLIFE

A big part of Vilamoura's nightlife scene is its **Casino Vilamoura** (⊠ *Set back from marina, behind Marinotel hotel* ☎ *289/310000* ⊕ *www.solverde.pt*), open nightly 4 pm–3 am. You'll find two restaurants, a dance club, and the usual selection of games on 20 tables, and more than 500 slot machines. For a set price you can see the nightly show and have a free drink; prices vary according to shows. Dress is smart-casual, and you must be 18 to enter.

SPORTS AND THE OUTDOORS

GOLF

Oceanico Millennium Course Vilamoura. Martin Hawtree extended an existing 9-hole layout to create this visitor-friendly course on the vast Vilamoura estate. It shares the umbrella pine tree backdrop common to the other two Vilamoura courses but is a little shorter in length. Tee times can be reserved online, and reservations are advised. ⊠ *Vilamoura, Quarteira* ☎ *289/310333* ⊕ *www.oceanicogolf.com* ⚑ *18 holes. 6,176 m. Par 72* ⛳ *€77 per round* ☞ *Facilities: driving range, putting green, chipping area, golf carts, hand-pulled carts, caddies on request, rental clubs, pro shop, golf academy/lessons, restaurant, bar.*

Old Course Vilamoura. One of the great golf courses of Europe, this Frank Pennink layout needed considerable refurbishment a few years ago.

Renamed the Old Course, it is the original and is widely regarded as the best of the Vilamoura layouts because of its subtle routing and challenging holes. Umbrella pines line the fairways, and the crack of ball on timber is almost a signature tune on this famous course. The maximum handicap for men is 24 and for women 28. ⊠ *Vilamoura, Quarteira* ☏ *289/310333* ⊕ *www.oceanicogolf.com* ⚓ *Reservations essential* ⚑ *. 18 holes. 6,254 m. Par 73. Slope 138* ⊡ *€119 per round* ⚲ *Facilities: driving range, putting green, chipping area, golf carts, hand-pulled carts, caddies on request, rental clubs, pro shop, golf academy/lessons, restaurant, bar.*

HORSEBACK RIDING

Horses are available for lessons and for trail rides at the **Centro Hípico da Estalagem de Cegonha** (⊠ *Estalagem de Cegonha* ☏ *289/302577*). Rates start at €18.

SAILING

To rent a sailboat, just walk around Vilamoura Marina and inquire at any of the various kiosks that deal with water sports. **Polvo Watersports** (⊠ *Vilamoura Marina* ☏ *289/301884* ⊕ *www.marina-sports.com*) offers a wide range of water activities, including Jet Ski and sailboat rentals, dolphin-watching trips, and parachute rides behind a speedboat. **Portugal Sail & Power** (⊠ *Vilamoura Marina* ☏ *289/366993 or 965392655* ⊕ *www.euro-sail.co.uk*) specializes in sailing courses and multiday trips.

If you'd like to relax and let someone else do the work, book a "Route of the Grottoes" cruise on the **Llana Cruises** (⊠ *Vilamoura Marina* ☏ *289/302318* ⊕ *www.algarve-seafaris.com*), which has 5½- and 3-hour cruises for €30 and €13, respectively. The company also offers big-game fishing at €50 for those fishing and €30 for those spectating, and reef fishing at €30 and €20, respectively.

ALBUFEIRA

12 km (7 mi) west of Vilamoura.

Taken by the Arabs in AD 716 and named Al-Buhera—Castle of the Sea—brash Albufeira has mushroomed from a fishing village into the Algarve's largest and busiest resort. The town beach attracts thousands of visitors daily, and the noisy center is full of cafés, bars, restaurants, discos, and souvenir shops. Albufeira ages a bit during the shoulder seasons when it draws older (often retired) visitors, mainly from northern Europe.

One of the last Algarve towns to hold out against the Christian army in the 13th century, Albufeira still has a distinctly Moorish flavor, most apparent in the steep, narrow streets and whitewashed houses snuggled on the hill that marks the center of the Cidade Velha. (A few words of caution: streets leading into the older parts of town may be difficult for some people to climb.)

GETTING HERE AND AROUND

Despite Faro being the capital of the Algarve, Albufeira is ideally and centrally located to visit the region. Public transportation is also rather good due to the thousands of tourists who travel in and around the city on any given day. Trains are frequent from most Algarvean towns and cities due to its central position, and stop here while passing through to other destinations. The biggest bus terminals in the Algarve are found in Albufeira.

ESSENTIALS

Bus Contacts Eva (✉ *Alto dos Caliços* ☎ *289/589055 or 289/580614*).

Visitor Info Albufeira (✉ *Rua 5 de Outubro* ☎ *289/585279*).

EXPLORING

Zoomarine. Just 6 km (4 mi) northwest of Albufeira, this popular and very pleasant marine park has low-key rides, swimming pools, performing parrots, and dolphin and sea lion shows. Those with the nerve, and willingness to part with €135, can take part in a dolphin interaction experience. The latest innovation is the new 4-D cinema that features an ecological, friendly story that can be very touching in parts. Hotel pickups are available. ✉ *N125, Km 65, Guia* ☎ *289/560300* ⊕ *www.zoomarine.com* 🎟 *€20* ☉ *Nov.–Mar., daily 10–5; Apr.–June and mid-Sept.–Oct., daily 10–6; July–mid-Sept., daily 10–7:30*.

BEACHES

On most summer days, the **town beach,** which is reached by tunnel from Rua 5 de Outubro, is so crowded that it may be hard to enjoy its interesting rock formations, caves, and grottoes, not to mention sand and sea. If you want more space, you'll have to move farther afield. **Praia da Oura,** 2 km (1 mi) east of Albufeira, is pretty but extremely crowded throughout most of the year. The beautiful **Praia da Galé,** 4 km (2½ mi) west of Albufeira, has the classic Algarve rock formations; just don't expect it to be deserted. There's free parking at all the beaches.

WHERE TO EAT AND STAY

$ ✕ **A Ruina.** For charcoal-grilled seafood, especially sardines or tuna
SEAFOOD steaks, this big, rustic restaurant is the place to go. Start with a shell-fish salad and choose your main course from the display. You can sit on the beach or in one of two simple but attractively furnished dining rooms. There's a roof terrace and a top-floor bar, too. ✉ *Cais Herculano, Praia dos Pescadores* ☎ *289/512094* ⊕ *www.restauranteruina.com* ▤ *MC, V*.

$ ✕ **Cabaz da Praia.** You'll have views of the beach from the cliff-side ter-
FRENCH race of this long-established restaurant. Its name means "beach basket," and it has been converted from an old fisherman's cottage. There's fine French-Portuguese cooking here—fish soup, grilled fish served imaginatively, and chicken with seafood. Try the soufflé, perhaps the restaurant's most popular dish. ✉ *Praça Miguel Bombarda 7* ☎ *289/512137* ▤ *MC, V* ☉ *Closed Thurs. No lunch Sat.*

$ ✕ **La Cigale.** This beachfront restaurant, 9 km (5½ mi) east of Albu-
CONTINENTAL feira, is renowned among locals for its excellent French and Portuguese cooking. The terrace is the most sought-after place to dine; reserve a table on it well in advance. The only drawback here is the parking situation—you must park up in the town and walk down the steep street to the harbor. ✉ *Praia de Olhas d'Agua* ☎ *289/501637* ⊕ *www.restaurantelacigale.net* ▤ *DC, MC, V* ☉ *Closed Dec.–Feb.*

$$$$
Fodor'sChoice
★

⊞ **Grande Real Santa Eulália.** Grande in name and grand in style and location, the Santa Eulália is in a privileged, locked-gate, beachfront position yet just a stone's throw from shops, bars, and more. It has large, modern, rooms—insist on one that faces the sea—and a whole host of facilities, not least of which is the impressive Real Spa Thalasso. The restaurant of choice here is Le Club where, surrounded by a soothing modern ambience reflecting the natural light and overlooking the bay, you can enjoy the finest of creative Italian and international cuisine. **Pros:** heated outdoor pool. **Cons:** not within walking distance of Albufeira; sketchy wireless connection; no indoor pool. ⊠ *Praia da Santa Eulália* ☏ *289/598000* ⊕ *www.hoteisreal.com* ↴ *344 rooms, 29 suites* ⚒ *In-room: a/c, safe, refrigerator, Wi-Fi. In-hotel: 5 restaurants, bars, tennis courts, pools, spa, concierge, laundry service, public Internet, parking (free)* ▭ *AE, DC, MC, V* ⦿| *BP, MAP.*

$$
⊞ **Hotel Vila Galé Cerro Alagoa.** One of Albufeira's most comfortable lodgings is a 10-minute walk from the main square. Smart, well-equipped rooms have private balconies; be sure to ask for one with a sea view, or you may end up facing the busy main road. A courtesy bus runs you to nearby beaches. Book well in advance for summer stays here, as package-tour operators tend to book whole blocks of rooms. **Pros:** central to both old and new towns. **Cons:** bar drinks expensive. ⊠ *Via Rápida* ☏ *289/583100* ⊕ *www.vilagale.pt* ↴ *279 rooms, 31 suites* ⚒ *In-room: a/c, safe. In-hotel: restaurant, 2 bars, pools, gym, Wi-Fi hotspot* ▭ *AE, DC, MC, V* ⦿| *BP, MAP.*

$$$$
Fodor'sChoice
★

▪ **Vila Joya.** This German-run exclusive jewel is set in lush, exotic gardens with no luxury spared. The highlight is definitely the cuisine ($$$–$$$$) of the finest and highest-rated restaurant in Portugal (two Michelin stars). Austrian chef Dieter Koschina buys lobster, crayfish, and turbot from the local fishermen but brings truffles, goose liver, and caviar from the best markets in Europe. Guest rooms and arabesque suites have a stylish, almost boudoir quality about them but are anything but tacky. Suites overlook the heated pool and semiprivate beach where a bar serves margaritas, caipirinhas, and a host of other exotic cocktails. **Pros:** crème da la crème of fine dining; exclusivity at its best; nice spa. **Cons:** a short drive from main town; concealed location; this is high-end luxury travel with prices to match. ⊠ *Praia da Galé* ☏ *289/591795* ⊕ *www.vilajoya.com* ↴ *12 rooms, 5 suites* ⚒ *In-room: a/c, safe, Wi-Fi. In-hotel: restaurant, bars, tennis courts, pool, laundry service, Wi-Fi hotspot* ▭ *AE, DC, MC, V* ⦿| *BP, MAP.*

NIGHTLIFE

The owner, the music, and the clientele are all mellow at the cliff-side **Bizarro's** (⊠ *Rua Latino Coelho* ☏ *289/512824*). It's the perfect bar from which to watch the sun go down.

Club 7½ (⊠ *Rua São Gonçalo de Lagos 5* ☏ *No phone*) stays open for drinking and dancing until 7 am. Its dress code is on the strict side. The long-established club **Kiss** (⊠ *Off Av. Dr. Francisco Sá Carneiro, Montechoro* ☏ *289/515639*) is crowded and glitzy and often has DJs. It's not for the prudish: scantily clad female go-gos dance on various stages.

SHOPPING

Every night in the height of summer, stalls with fairy lights wind their way through the center, selling handicrafts and tourist trinkets. It's fun to browse, and you may pick up the occasional interesting piece. A market is held on the first and third Tuesday of the month at the fairgrounds. You can buy anything from lightbulbs to cheap shoes and clothes, but it isn't a produce market. For high-quality Portuguese ceramics, crystal, and porcelain go to **La Lojas** (⊠ *Rua Candido dos Reis 20* ☎ *289/513168*).

Bookworms (⊠ *Rua Manuel Teixeira Gomes Lofa, Edifício Telhas Verdes* ☎ *289/543576 or 91/698–4030*), the best little shop of its kind, offers a wide selection of new English-language books, second-hand books, leather and personalized bookmarks, and commercial and handmade cards.

ARMAÇÃO DE PÊRA

14 km (8½ mi) west of Albufeira.

At this bustling resort, it's best to reserve your room near the sea, rather than behind the main road where apartment-hotels are crammed together. Year-round, local boats can take you on two-hour cruises to caves and grottoes west along the shore, past the Praia Nossa Senhora da Rocha (Beach of Our Lady of the Rocks)—a beach named after the Romanesque chapel above it. To arrange tours, head to Praia Armação de Pêra—a wide sandy beach with a promenade—or Praia Nossa Senhora da Rocha and speak with the fishermen directly.

GETTING HERE AND AROUND

The town can be reached either by stopping at Portimão in the west or Albufeira in the east to hop on a bus that will shuttle you to this seaside resort.

ESSENTIALS

Bus Solpraia (⊠ *Av. General Humberto Delgado, 18-r/c* ☎ *282/313, 282/334 bus ticket office*).

Visitor Info Armação de Pêra (☎ *282/312145*). **Monchique** (⊠ *Largo dos Choroes* ☎ *282/911189*).

EXPLORING

Aside from ferrying vacationers to and from adjacent cove beaches, the fishermen no longer work from the shores of Carvoeiro, 6 km (4 mi) west of Armação de Pêra. Still, it has just about maintained the character of a fishermen's settlement. The town has a harbor with shell-shape beaches, and a short walk or boat journey away—at Algar Seco—are interesting rock formations.

WHERE TO EAT AND STAY

$ ╳**Indian Bollywood.** A cult following of faithful customers returns each
INDIAN year to this culinary and architectural landmark set opposite the fish-
Fodor'sChoice ermen's beach Praia Nossa Senhora da Rocha (you can't miss the tur-
★ baned turrets). Though hot and spicy tandoori dishes are the draw, mild options are plentiful, as are vegetarian dishes. A take-out service

is available. ✉ *Rua da Praia, Edifício Vista Mar 1, Praia do Carvoeiro* ☎ *282/313755* ▭ *AE, MC, V.*

$$$ 🛏 **Holiday Inn.** This hotel, formerly Hotel Garbe, recently underwent a general overhaul following a takeover by the Holiday Inn chain. Despite now belonging to an international chain, the same standards of personalized, friendly service have been maintained. In fact the staff has remained largely unchanged, as have the hotel's main features. The bar, lounge, and restaurant—all with terraces that provide unhindered sea views—maximize the superb position of this ideally located hotel. It's atop a low cliff at the western end of the beach and is built on several levels, with steps to the sands below. It's in the town of Armação de Pêra, within walking distance of all attractions, bars, and restaurants. Public rooms are bright and appealing; guest rooms have modern furnishings. **Pros:** the beach is on your doorstep; good on-site Indian restaurant. **Cons:** ongoing changes may mean rooms vary in decor. ✉ *Av. Marginal* ☎ *282/320260* ⊕ *www.holidayinn.com* ↙ *166 rooms, 19 suites* ♿ *In-room: a/c, safe, refrigerator, Wi-Fi. In-hotel: 2 restaurants, room service, pool* ▭ *AE, MC, V* ⦿ *BP, FAP, MAP.*

$$$$ 🛏 **Vila Vita Parc.** Within walking distance of Armação de Pêra, between the Pestana Viking and the Hotel Inn, Vila Vita Parc is an award-winning resort of impeccable standards. Surrounded by lush, mature gardens, the pampering begins as soon as the wrought-iron gates open to welcome you. Gentle colors, dark-wood details, fireplaces, and Mediterranean-Moorish touches make this resort an exclusive oasis. From its cliff-top setting, landscaped gardens wind down to two sequestered beaches. All rooms, beautifully furnished and in different styles, are spacious and have either a sea or garden view or both. The Vila Vita Vital is a luxurious spa offering all kinds of relaxing treatments. Also on-site is the Michelin-star-awarded Ocean Restaurant, which has a five-course set menu (€90; excluding drinks). **Pros:** excellent on-site wine cellar. **Cons:** not for couples or singles wanting to experience the Algarve's wilder side. ✉ *Porches* ☎ *282/310100* ⊕ *www.vilavitaparc.com* ↙ *91 rooms, 74 suites* ♿ *In-room: a/c, safe, refrigerator, Wi-Fi. In-hotel: 7 restaurants, room service, 5 bars, golf course, tennis courts, pools, gym, spa, beachfront, water sports, concierge, children's programs (ages 8–16), laundry service* ▭ *AE, DC, MC, V* ⦿ *BP, FAP, MAP.*

SPORTS AND THE OUTDOORS

Aqualand. Just north of town, and close to Alcantarilha, you'll find this fun water park that has just celebrated its 20th anniversary. Considered the largest such park on the Algarve, Aqualand is home to the Banzai Boggan and the highest ride in Portugal, the Kamikaze. ✉ *E.N. 125 Alcantarilha* ☎ *282/320230* ⊕ *www.aqualand.pt* 🎟 *€16.50* ☉ *Late May–mid-Sept.*

CARVOEIRO

5 km (3 mi) west of Armação de Pêra.

This busy resort town maintains much of its fishing-village charm, which is what drew increasing numbers of foreigners to settle here in the first place. An abundance of high-quality restaurants and lodgings makes this the ideal base for access to both east and west coasts. Small beaches lie at the foot of steep, rocky cliffs. Waves have sculpted the distinctive yellow rock into intricate archways and stacks encrusted with fossilized shells.

GETTING HERE AND AROUND

The closest train station is Portimão, with bus services running regularly to this quaint fishing village.

ESSENTIALS

Train Lagoa Main Terminal (P282/341301).

Visitor Info Armação de Pêra (☎ 282/312145). **Monchique** (✉ Largo dos Choroes ☎ 282/911189).

WHERE TO EAT AND STAY

¢

CHINESE

✕ **Grande Muralha.** Tasty chopstick adventures await you on the main Estrada do Farol close to the town center. This outstanding Chinese restaurant has garnered a good reputation for its noodle, duck, and shrimp rice dishes. If you are looking for a break from the charcoaled chicken and fish routine, this is the place to break the monotony. ✉ Estrada do Farol, Praia do Carvoeiro ☎ 282/357380 ▭ AE, MC, V.

$

INDIAN

✕ **O Indiano.** There are three Indian restaurants in Carvoeiro, and this one has the best location right by Carvoeiro's beach. The sumptuous menu of kebabs, tandoori, light and spicy curries, and vegetarian dishes are also available to go. ✉ Edifício 2M, Estrada do Farol, Praia do Carvoeiro ☎ 282/356999 ▭ AE, MC, V.

$
☾

⛆ **Tivoli Almansor.** This hotel took 30 years to complete but was worth the wait. The stunning cliff scenery can be had from every room, and although it's slightly worn at the edges, the excellent service and cuisine make up for any shortfall. Kids love this hotel, and so do budding divers, who can use the on-site Dutch/German-run diving school, perhaps the best in the Algarve. A steep, stone stairwell leads down to a private beach that has amazing cave formations even by Algarve standards. The deep blue bay shines a translucent magenta in bright sunshine, and clear waters mean snorkeling is a must. **Pros:** excellent location; great onsite dive shop; good place to bring the kids. **Cons:** rooms and bathrooms need updating; comfortable downhill walk to main town square but the uphill return walk may be challenging for the less able-bodied. ✉ Vale do Covo ☎ 282/310100 ⊕ www.tivolihotels.com ⇄ 289 rooms, 4 suites ⚵ In-room: a/c, safe, Internet. In-hotel: 2 restaurants, room service, bars, golf course, tennis courts, pool, gym, spa, beachfront, diving, water sports, concierge, children's programs (ages 8–18), laundry service ▭ AE, DC, MC, V ⍾⍟⎮ BP, FAP, MAP.

SPORTS AND THE OUTDOORS

The **Carvoeiro Clube de Ténis Club** (✉ Mato Serrão ☎ 282/357847 ⊕ www.carvoeiroclubedetenis.com) has 12 courts as well as a fitness center, a swimming pool, and a restaurant.

The **Tivoli Almansor Diving Centre** (✉ Vale do Covo ☎ 282/351194 ⊕ www.tivoli-diving.com) is an excellent diving school offering many different PADI courses suited to the individual. It offers dives twice daily from a modern speedboat that takes you up to 3 nautical mi from the coastline. You can dive between 32 and 115 feet of depth. From the boat you will see a reef, underwater caves, wrecks, corals, and an amazing variety of sea life. Rates for one day are €29.50; six days €145–€205 or 10 days €239–€325. The staff all speak English.

Vale da Pinta. American course architect Ronald Fream carved the Vale da Pinta layout through an ancient olive grove where some of the trees are more than 700 years old. Fream was the perfect choice for the job, because he is highly regarded for his sensitivity to environmental issues. Five sets of tees on each hole make this an enjoyable course for all levels of ability. There is a chance for ending in style on the par-5 18th for those who can hit the ball long. Booking two weeks in advance is advised for those looking for specific tee times. The greens are large, and there is a feeling of space here near the village of Carvoeiro. Handicap limits are 27 for men and 35 for women. ⊠ *Apartado 1011, Carvoeiro, Lagoa* 🕾 *282/340900 www.pestanagolf.com* 🏌 *18 holes. 5,861 m. Par 71* 🏌 *€90 per round* ☞ *Facilities: driving range, putting green, chipping area, golf carts, hand-pulled carts, rental clubs, pro shop, golf academy/ lessons, restaurant, bar.*

LAGOA

10 km (6 mi) northwest of Armação de Pêra; 15 km (9 mi) northwest of Carvoeiro.

This market town is primarily known for its wine, *vinho Lagoa*; the red is particularly good.

GETTING HERE AND AROUND
Lagoa is home to a large bus terminal, which connects with Portimão and Albufeira.

ESSENTIALS
Bus Lagoa Bus Terminal (⊠ *Rua Jacinto Correia* 🕾 *282/341301*).

Visitor Info Armação de Pêra (🕾 *282/312145*). **Monchique** (⊠ *Largo dos Choroes* 🕾 *282/911189*).

EXPLORING
The principal winery, the **Cooperativa de Lagoa** (⊠ *EN125* 🕾 *282/342181*), is on the main road just after the Carvoeiro junction, on the left. Call if you're interested in joining a prearranged group tour. At any time during normal working hours you can pop in to the office (at the side of the building) to sample the wine and buy a bottle or two.

SHOPPING
Along the EN125 in nearby Porches, you can stop at roadside shops that sell both mass-produced and handmade pottery. **Olaria Pequena** (⊠ *EN125, between Porches and Alcantarilha* 🕾 *282/381213*), which means "the small pottery," is owned and run by a friendly young Scot, Ian Fitzpatrick, who has worked in the Algarve for years. He sells his handmade pieces at very reasonable prices. The shop is open Monday through Saturday from 10 to 1 and 3 to 6.

SPORTS AND THE OUTDOORS

The biggest of the Algarve's several water parks is **Slide & Splash,** east of Lagoa. The rides, such as the huge Black Hole and Blue Hole, are also the most exciting of their kind in the region. The park is open daily at 10 am from Easter through October; closing times vary greatly, so call ahead to confirm. ⊠ *Vale de Deus, just off N125 (signposted), Estômbar* ☎ *282/341685* ⊕ *www.slidesplash.com* ✍ *€16.50* ⊙ *Easter–Oct., daily beginning at 10.*

SILVES

Fodor's Choice *7 km (4½ mi) northeast of Lagoa.*

★

Once the Moorish capital of the Algarve, today Silves is one of the region's most intriguing inland towns. Rich and prosperous in medieval times, it remained in Arab hands until 1249, although not without attempts by Christian forces to take it. In 1189, after a siege led by Sancho I, the city was sacked by Crusaders, who subsequently put thousands of Moors to the sword. Silves finally lost its importance after its almost complete destruction by the 1755 earthquake. Today it's an enjoyable excursion from the coast; trains, buses, and a river service using traditional Portuguese gondolalike boats make the 20-km (12-mi) trip north from Portimão.

GETTING HERE AND AROUND

The easiest way to get to Silves is by bus, via Lagoa, if you're coming from the Eastern Algarve. If you're coming from the Western end, the easiest route is via Portimão. The train station is around 7 kilometers from the city center; a taxi from the station into Silves should cost no more than €10 at peak times (nights, weekends and national holidays).

ESSENTIALS

Bus Silves Bus Station (⊠ *Bilheteira Mercado Municipal, Rua Francisco Pablos, Edifício do Mercado* ☎ *282/442338*).

Taxis Taxi (☎ *282/442541*).

EXPLORING

Fortaleza. In the 12th century the Moors built a sandstone fortress with an irregular polygonal plan that survived untouched until the Christian sieges. Its impressive parapets were restored in 1835 and still dominate the upper part of town. You can walk around the fort's remaining walls or clamber about its crenellated battlements, taking in the views of Silves and the hills. (Keep an eye open: some places have no guardrails.) Its gardens are watched over by a statue of King Dom Sancho I, and its capacious water cistern is now a gallery space devoted to temporary exhibitions, some of which have nothing to do with the fort. ☎ *282/445624* ✍ *€1.25* ⊙ *June–Sept., daily 9–8 (last admission 7:30); Oct.–May, daily 9–6 (last admission 5:30).*

Museu Arqueológia. Although the labels are in Portuguese, the items on display at Silves's archaeology museum still give interesting insights into the area's history. A primary attraction is an Arab water cistern, preserved in situ, with a 30-foot-deep well. The museum is a few minutes' walk below the cathedral, off Rua da Sé. ⊠ *Rua das Portas de Loulé*

☎ *282/442325* 🎟 *€1.50* 🕙 *Daily
May–Sept., Tues.–Sun. 10–7; Oct.–
Apr., Tues.–Sun. 9–6.*

Santa Maria da Sé. The 12th- to 13th-
century Cathedral of St. Mary, built
on the site of a Moorish mosque,
saw service as the principal cathedral of the Algarve until the 16th
century. The 1755 earthquake and
indifferent restoration have left it
rather plain inside, but its tower—
complete with gargoyles—is still a
fine sight. ⊠ *Rua da Sé* ☎ *No phone*
🎟 *Free; donations accepted* 🕙 *Mon.–Sat. 9–6:30, Sun. 8:30–1.*

> **TO MARKET**
>
> Silves's **mercado** *(produce mar-
> ket)*, liveliest in the morning, is
> at the foot of town, close to the
> medieval bridge. If you arrive at
> lunchtime, have a delicious meal
> of spicy grilled chicken or fish
> from the outdoor barbecue at one
> of the simple restaurants here.
> The market is closed Sunday.

WHERE TO EAT

¢ ✕ **Churrasqueira Valdemar.** At this grill room on the riverfront behind
BARBECUE the market, whole chickens are barbecued outside over charcoal. Eat
under the stone arches and enjoy your *piri-piri* (spicy) chicken with
salad, fries, and local wine. ⊠ *Facing river, behind market* ☎ *No phone*
☐ *No credit cards.*

$ ✕ **Rui Marisqueira.** The fish and shellfish are remarkably good value,
PORTUGUESE which is the main reason why the crowds from the coast come up into
the hills to dine here. Grilled sea bream and bass are usually available,
and there's locally caught game—wild boar, rabbit, and partridge—in
season. ⊠ *Rua Comendador Vilarinho 27* ☎ *282/442682* ☐ *AE, MC,
V* 🕙 *Closed Tues.*

PORTIMÃO

15 km (9 mi) southwest of Silves.

Portimão is the Algarve's most important fishing port. Even before the
Romans arrived, there was a settlement here, at the mouth of the Rio
Arade (Arade River). Devastated in the 1755 earthquake, the town was
revived by the fish-canning industry in the 19th century. Although colorful boats now unload their catch at a modern terminal across the river,
contemporary Portimão, sprawling with concrete high-rise buildings,
remains a cheerful, busy place.

Rather than staying in Portimão, most visitors choose one of the excellent local beach resorts and visit Portimão as a day trip, especially to
shop. If you prefer to stay in town, the local tourist office can help you
find accommodations at one of the hotels or *pensões* (pensions), which
are of reasonable quality. The marina, **Marina de Portimão,** has a wealth
of boutiques, upscale restaurants, and bars. Lunch outdoors at the Doca
da Sardinha ("sardine dock") between the old bridge and the railway
bridge is a must. You sit at one of many inexpensive establishments,
eating the excellent charcoal-grilled sardines (a local specialty), chewy
fresh bread, and simple salads and drinking local wine. Around you,
the air is thick with barbecue smoke and the tang of the sea.

GETTING HERE AND AROUND

Portimão can be reached by train. The city's impressive Vai e Vem bus service is excellent and enables commuters and visitors to reach all four corners of the city at a minimal cost.

ESSENTIALS

Bus Armação de Pêra (☎ 282/312145). **EVA/MT** (✉ Av. Guanaré ☎ 282/418120). **Monchique** (✉ Largo dos Choroes ☎ 282/911189).

Visitor Info Portimão (✉ Av. Zeca Afonso ☎ 282/531800).

BEACH

Across the bridge from and 5 km (3 mi) east of Portimão is the former fishing hamlet of Ferragudo. Despite its fine beach, **Praia Grande**, Ferragudo shows no sign of going down the mass-market tourist route. Right on the beach is the restored 16th-century Castelo de São João (St. John's Castle), built to defend Portimão and now privately owned. There are plenty of restaurants and bars near the beach as well as places to rent sailboards.

WHERE TO EAT AND STAY

$$$

PORTUGUESE

✕**Dockside.** Set amid the rows of bars and eateries around Portimão's marina, Dockside is an upscale marquee restaurant specializing in generous quantities of live shellfish and *francesinhas* (toasted rye sandwiches filled with ham, fried steak, and pork sausage, covered with melted cheese and coated with a spicy seafood sauce), and a variety of cataplanas. Good local and imported draft beer is served at the table. Reservations are recommended. ✉ *Marina de Portimão* ☎ *282/417268* ▭ *AE, DC, MC, V.*

¢

SEAFOOD

✕**Flor da Sardinha.** This is one of several open-air eateries next to the bridge, by the fishing harbor, whose staff grills fresh sardines on quayside stoves and serves them to crowds seated at plastic tables. A plateful of these delicious fish, with boiled potatoes (never fries!) and a bottle of the local wine, is one of Portugal's best treats. ✉ *Cais da Lota* ☎ *282/424862* ▭ *No credit cards.*

$$

Fodor'sChoice

★

🏨**Tivoli Arade.** This hotel has a simple but stylish 1970s retro interior cleverly laid out around two large swimming pools complete with wooden deck bars and palm gardens. The spacious rooms have kitchens, all you need to prepare a meal, and private terraces. Blocks of rooms are colored ocher, burnt sienna, and beige to match the changing shades of the *falesia*, or Algarve cliffs. If you are traveling by boat, this is the perfect place to base yourself at a moderate price. The beach is a 10-minute walk to the other side of the marina below the old town. **Pros:** stunning views over river; short walk to Praia da Rocha (main beach, strip of bars and restaurants) and marina. **Cons:** marina very fashionable in summer with national and international "in" crowds; local bars host a series of summer parties until the early hours. ✉ *Marina de Portimão* ☎ *282/460200* ⊕ *www.tivolihotels.com* ⤶ *196 suites* ⌂ *In-room: safe, kitchen, refrigerator, Internet. In-hotel: restaurants, room service, bars, pools, gym, diving, Internet terminal* ▭ *AE, DC, MC, V* ❙◎❙ *BP, MAP.*

6

SHOPPING

Portimão's main shopping street is Rua do Comércio. Shops on Rua de Santa Isabel specialize in crafts, leather goods, ceramics, crystal, and fashions. The enormous **Continente Shopping Center** (⊠ *N124 at Av. Miguel Bombarda, toward Praia da Rocha*), open daily 10–10, has a plethora of shops, restaurants, and cinemas under one roof.

Gabys (⊠ *Rua Direita 5* ☏ *282/411988*) sells good-quality leather items. For ceramics, porcelain, crystal, and handmade copper items, visit **O Aquario** (⊠ *Rua Vasco da Gama 42* ☏ *282/426673*). There are high-class shoes and leather goods at **St. James** (⊠ *Rua de Santa Isabel 26* ☏ *282/424620*).

> ## SHOPPING
>
> Probably the best town in which to shop is Portimão, where you can spend at least half a day browsing. In summer, the main resorts have a lot of roadside stalls (a good area is outside the lighthouse at Cabo São Vicente), at which you can buy jewelry, handicrafts, art, and clothes. Look for reasonably priced hand-knit sweaters in stores throughout the Algarve. The best places to look for handmade copper items and other metal crafts are Portimão, Lagos, and Loulé. Small woven sisal baskets make good souvenirs and are available nearly everywhere.

SPORTS
AND THE OUTDOORS

Santa Bernarda. Take a sailing trip on the twin-masted pirate ship *Santa Bernarda* that departs from the harbor and offers either a Caves Expedition or a Sailing & Caves of Carvoeiro expedition for €25, or a full-day Robinson Tour for €50. ⊠ *Rua Júdice Fialho 11* ☏ *967/023840* ⊕ *www.santa-bernarda.com.*

Fodor'sChoice ★ **Penina.** On what was once a flat and uninteresting field, Sir Henry Cotton worked his design magic and created his most famous course 5 km (3 mi) from the old fishing town of Portimão at the western end of the Algarve. It is considered the masterpiece among his many layouts because of its difficult challenge and the beautiful setting he created by planting more than 100,000 trees. Sir Henry held court here for years, welcoming the great and good from world golf to the lavish Penina resort. The course that began the Portuguese golf boom in the 1960s has had a face-lift and remains a stern test of golf. The par-3 13th was recently considered as one of the top 500 holes in the world. Although the course is busy at most times, golfers on different seldom come into contact due to the mature trees and wide fairways. Le Meridien Penina hotel guests are entitled to special green fee rates. On the championship course, a handicap of 28 is required for men and 36 for women to play. *EN125 Portimão8501-952* ☏ *282/420224* ⊕ *www.lemeridienpenina.com* ⌦ *Reservations essential* ⚑ *18 holes. 6,273 m. Par 73* ⚐ *€120 per round* ☞ *Facilities: driving range, putting green, chipping area, golf carts, hand-pulled carts, electric trolleys, rental clubs, pro shop, golf academy/lessons, restaurant, bar.*

PRAIA DA ROCHA

3 km (2 mi) southeast of Portimão.

Praia da Rocha was one of the first resorts in the Algarve to undergo a transformation for the mass market, and it's now dominated by high-rise apartments and hotels. Its excellent beach is made all the more interesting by a series of huge colored rocks worn into strange shapes by the wind and sea. Buses run throughout the day between the town and Portimão.

GETTING HERE AND AROUND

As is the case with Portimão, Praia da Rocha is easily reached through the use of the Vai e Vem bus service; bus tickets can be purchased at Hotel Jupiter on Avenida Tomás Cabreira. Portimão station also has regular trains running to Lagos in the west and Faro in the east.

ESSENTIALS

Bus **Vai e Vem** (☎ 282/415041).

Visitor Info **Praia da Rocha** (✉ *Av. Tomás Cabreira* ☎ 282/419132).

EXPLORING

Fortaleza de Santa Catarina. The 16th-century fortress was a defensive castle and provides wonderful views out to sea and across the Rio Arade to Ferragudo. Directly below the fortress, on the river side, is one of the Algarve's growing number of marinas. On the other side a long concrete jetty extends into the Atlantic. ✉ *Av. Tomás Cabreira.*

WHERE TO EAT AND STAY

¢ ✕ **Arrais.** Formerly well-known as the Cabassa restaurant, Arrais was,
ITALIAN in 2005, established to offer good food and friendly service at middle-of-the-road prices. Daily specialties vary, but a fixture on the menu is fresh fish, perfectly complimented by the glorious sea view. Meatier specialties include steak, lamb, and *porco preto* (black pork) dishes. ✉ *Edif. Stª Catarina, Av. Tomás Cabreira* ☎ 282/498282 ▭ *AE, DC, MC, V* ☉ *Closed Sun. (dinner) and Mon. (all day).*

¢ ✕ **Dolce Vita Pizzaria.** Locals come to Dolce Vita for its fabulous home-
PIZZA made pizzas and pasta, refreshing sangria, and charming wooden decor. Meals are served on bench tables with tiled tops that add extra quirkiness to this popular eatery. In summer be sure to make a reservation. ✉ *Edif. Mar Azul, Loja 1, R/C* ☎ 282/419444 ▭ *AE, DC, MC, V.*

$ ✕ **Titanic.** Off the main strip in a quieter part of the area is one of Praia da
FRENCH Rocha's oldest and best known restaurants. Titanic offers a ship-shape dining experience that specializes in French cuisine and aims to serve up a romantic, intimate atmosphere, styled on the original Titanic's interior. ✉ *Rua Engº Francisco Bivar, Edifício Columbia* ☎ 282/422371 or 963/087860 ⊕ *www.titanic.com.pt* ▭ *AE, DC, MC, V.*

$$$ ⊡ **Hotel Algarve-Casino.** The sea vistas from this classy hotel are spectacular, so be sure to book a room with a view. The Moorish-style public rooms are bright, the spacious guest rooms have tile floors and balconies, and the casino has a restaurant as well as shows. **Pros:** great location on Praia da Rocha's main strip; plenty of spots to lounge around the pool. **Cons:** dated decor and average food (particularly the dinner buffet) mean that it does not quite justify its five-star rating—but definitely a good four star. ✉ *Av. Tomás Cabreira* ☎ 282/402000 ⊕ *www.solverde.pt* ⇗ *192*

6

rooms, 16 suites ☐ In-room: a/c, safe, Wi-Fi (some). In-hotel: 3 restaurants, room service, tennis courts, pools ☐ AE, DC, MC, V Ⓞ BP, MAP.

ALVOR

5 km (3 mi) west of Portimão.

Characterized by a maze of streets, lanes, and alleys that intersect one another, the handsome old port of Alvor is one of the Algarve's best examples of an Arab village. In summer, many vacationers are attracted to Alvor's excellent beaches.

GETTING HERE AND AROUND
Alvor is now connected by Portimão's Vai e Vem bus service, though taxis are widely used in this popular fishing village.

ESSENTIALS
Bus **Vai e Vem** (☎ 282/400800).

Taxi **Taxiarade** (☎ 282/460610).

BEACHES
If the small, covelike **Praia dos Três Irmãos** is too crowded, there's always space to spare on one of the beaches to either side.

WHERE TO EAT AND STAY

$$
PORTUGUESE
✕ **Atlântida.** This is a charming restaurant with an absolutely lovely location on the eastern part of this dramatic beach. Specialties here include live shellfish, fresh fish, cataplanas, and flambées, supported by a selection of fine wines. ✉ *Praia do Três Irmãos* ☎ *282/459647* ☐ *MC, V* ☺ *No lunch. Thurs. and Jan.*

$$$
🏨 **Le Meridien Penina Golf & Resort.** The Meridien has everything you would expect from one of the world's leading hotel chains, including well-groomed grounds. Significantly reduced green fees are offered at the adjacent 18-hole golf course designed by Henry Cotton. A bus shuttles you to and from the hotel beach, which has a restaurant (reservations essential) and water-sports facilities. A supervised children's village has its own pool and restaurant. There's a choice of six restaurants ($$$–$$$$), including the Grill Room, which serves excellent Portuguese dishes, and the Sagres Restaurant, with its lively theme evenings. **Pros:** made-to-order omelets at breakfast; good on-site à la carte restaurants; children are well catered to with kids club and menus. **Cons:** dinner buffet disappointing; drinks are expensive. ✉ *Montes de Alvor, Penina* ☎ *282/420200* ⊕ *www.starwoodhotels.com* 🛏 *196 rooms* ☐ *In-room: a/c, safe, Internet. In-hotel: 5 restaurants, room service, bars, golf courses, tennis courts, pool, gym, beachfront, water sports, concierge, children's programs (ages 8–16), laundry service, no-smoking rooms* ☐ *AE, DC, MC, V* Ⓞ *BP, FAP, MAP.*

$$
Fodor's Choice
★
🏨 **Pestana Alvor Praia.** Rooms at this split-level hotel have views of the sea or the Serra de Monchique. Decor is extra funky, with lime, red currant, and white, Italian-designed sofas and easy chairs. You won't be at a loss for home entertainment with a CD and DVD player. The hotel has opened a spa with treatments, heated indoor pool, massage, and beauty salons. Although it's an easy walk to the pleasant sands below, there's

an elevator that can take you down to the beach. The dining room has picture windows overlooking the coast, and there's a deck with a snack bar. All of the restaurants ($$–$$$) are first class: O Almofariz serves Algarvean specialties, Sale e Pepe offers Tuscan cuisine, and Harira has Moroccan fare. **Pros:** private parking with sun shades; free lounge chairs on beach for hotel guests; efficient house-keeping; short (15–20 minutes) walk to Alvor town and local amenities. **Cons:** Plastic glasses for pool drinks. ✉ *Praia dos Três Irmãos* ☎ *282/400900* ⊕ *www.pestana. com* ⤴ *178 rooms, 14 suites* ⌂ *In-room: a/c, safe, Internet, refrigerator. In-hotel: 3 restaurants, room service, bars, tennis courts, pools, beachfront, children's programs (ages 7–15), laundry service* ▭ *AE, DC, MC, V* ⦿ *BP, MAP.*

MONCHIQUE

25 km (15 mi) northeast of Alvor; 20 km (12 mi) north of Portimão.

The winding road up to Monchique from Portimão or Silves brings the surprise of lush greenery and an oasis of brightly colored villas surrounded by waterways and fruit groves.

GETTING HERE AND AROUND

Getting to Monchique can be quite tricky without a car. It's recommended that people travel by bus to either Silves or Portimão, or by train to Portimão, and from those cities catch a bus to Monchique. The best way to get to Foia, the highest peak in the Algarve, is by taxi, from Monchique town center.

ESSENTIALS

Bus Ticket Office (☎ *282/418120*).

Taxi Praia da Rocha (☎ *282/418871*).

Visitor Info Monchique (✉ *Largo dos Choroes* ☎ *282/911189*).

EXPLORING

Caldas de Monchique. The Monchique Thermal Complex is renowned for its healing spa waters that bubble out of the ground to create a paradise microclimate where "anything grows." The small chapel of Caldas is where many go for a blessing or to pray in thanks for the health of those who drink its waters. The **Thermas de Monchique** is just below the chapel and is intrinsic to the area. Visitors come not only for the water's healing properties but for pampering spa treatments. Modern spa facilities complement those for health treatments concerned with digestive, bone, kidney, and respiratory problems. ☎ *282/910910* ⊕ *www.monchiquetermas.com.*

Monchique. Follow the road north from Caldas de Monchique and within 10 minutes you will be in this tiny market town, which is known for its rich handicrafts, including leather, basketwork, woodwork, and embroidery.

Pico de Fóia. A short drive west of Monchique on N266-3 brings you to the highest point in the Serra de Monchique. At 2,959 feet, this affords panoramic views—weather permitting—over the western Algarve. There's also a café here.

WHERE TO EAT AND STAY

¢ ✕ **Teresinha.** Just west of Monchique, modest Teresinha has good coun-
PORTUGUESE try cooking, a simple interior, and an outdoor terrace that overlooks a
valley as well as the coast. The ham and the grilled chicken are particularly tasty. ⊠ *Estrada da Fóia* ☎ *282/912392* ▤ *MC, V.*

¢ ▦ **Estalagem Abrigo da Montanha.** This pleasant, rustic inn—in the heart
of the Serra de Monchique—has magnolia trees, a camellia-filled garden, and panoramic views. A leisurely lunch in the Abrigo restaurant
($$–$$$), where dependable regional dishes are prepared, makes for
an enjoyable afternoon. If you want to stay longer to take in the scenery, be sure to reserve in advance for one of the welcoming rooms (all
with views). **Pros:** wood-burning fires in suites; indoor pool. **Cons:**
half-hour drive to coastal towns and beaches; no Internet access in
the rooms. ⊠ *Corto Pereiro, Estrada da Fóia* ☎ *282/912131* ⊕ *www.
abrigodamontanha.com* ↶ *16 rooms* ⚙ *In-room: a/c. In-hotel: restaurant, bar, pool, Internet terminal* ▤ *AE, DC, MC, V* ▯◎▯ *BP.*

$ ▦ **Longevity Wellness Resort.** This mountain retreat was inaugurated in
2010 and is 20 minutes from Silves or 25 minutes from Portimão.
The resort enjoys breathtaking views of the Algarve coastline and is
becoming increasingly popular with national and international tourists who are looking for privacy and tranquility without being too
far from civilization. It's the first integrated five-star wellness resort in
the Algarve in which all elements are organized to provide a memorable experience in wellness and healthy living. **Pros:** brand new eco-
friendly resort; a vast range of services to enhance well-being. **Cons:**
car needed to explore further; may still experience teething problems
as is brand new. ⊠ *Lugar do Montinho* ☎ *282/240100, 282/240110, or
800/240110* ⊕ *www.longevitywellnessresort.com* ↶ *195 rooms* ⚙ *In-
room: a/c, safe, kitchen, Internet. In-hotel: restaurant, bar, pool, spa*
▤ *AE, DC, MC, V* ▯◎▯ *BP.*

LAGOS AND THE WESTERN ALGARVE

From the bustling town of Lagos, the rest of the western Algarve is easily accessible. This is the most unspoiled part of the region, with some
genuinely isolated beaches and bays along an often wind-buffeted route
that reaches to the southwest and the magnificent Cabo São Vicente.

LAGOS

13 km (8 mi) west of Portimão; 70 km (43 mi) northwest of Faro.

An attractive, busy fishing port with some cove beaches nearby, Lagos
draws an international crowd. And yet, the inhabitants seem to follow
a way of life that goes beyond catering to visitors.

The town has a venerable history. Its deepwater harbor and wide bay
have made it a natural choice for various groups of settlers, starting with
the Carthaginians, who founded the town around 400 bc. Under the
Moors, Lagos was a center for trade between Portugal and Africa. Even
after the town fell to the Christians in 1241, trade continued and was
greatly expanded under Prince Henry the Navigator, who used Lagos

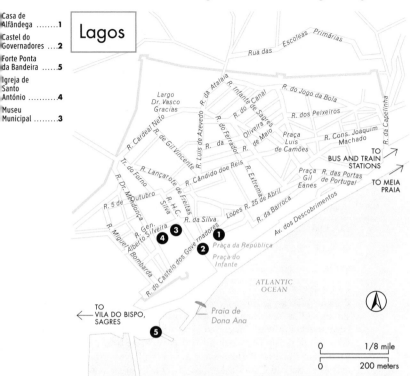

6

as his base. It later became capital of the Algarve, a role it lost after the great earthquake of 1755 reduced much of it to rubble. Nonetheless, some interesting buildings remain, as does the circuit of defensive walls, built between the 14th and 16th centuries over older Moorish bastions. Some of the best-preserved sections can be seen from near the expansive Praça da República, at the southwest end of Avenida dos Descobrimentos. The main pedestrian streets leading off the central Praça Gil Eanes are lined with stores (including several good antiques shops), restaurants, cafés, and bars—all of which do a roaring business in summer. As with many cities and towns along the Algarve, trying to find a parking place here stretches one's patience to the extreme.

GETTING HERE AND AROUND

Lagos is 80 km (50 mi) from the Faro airport. You can get to Lagos, from the airport, via bus, train, or taxi. The Lagos train and bus station are near each other and the marina, from where most of the city can be explored on foot. If you can't get around on foot, Lagos has a local bus system called Onda, which follows eight routes between 7 am and 8 pm every day. The tourist train, which departs from the marina, is another great way to see the town. It costs around €3 and runs daily starting at 10 am.

TIMING

Although the main historic sights of the old town are all in close prox-imity, allow at least two hours for a tour. Be prepared to join lines for museums and, if it is summertime, to negotiate bustling crowds of backpackers, sightseers, and shoppers who throng the many bars, cafés, restaurants, and clothing and crafts shops. The Casa da Alfândega will probably occupy you for half an hour alone. Allow plenty of time to explore the Igreja de Santo António: it is striking in appearance from the outside and is full of surprises once you get inside. The churches between Praça da Republica and Rua do Castelo dos Governadores have unusual architectural styles that make them well worth a visit, but photography is discouraged within them.

ESSENTIALS

Bus **Eva** (✉ *Largo Rossío de São João* ☎ *282/762944 or 282/422105* ⊕ *www.eva-bus.com*). **Onda** (⊕ *www.aonda.pt*).

Taxi **Taxi** (☎ *282/763587*).

Train **CP** (✉ *Largo da Estação* ☎ *282/762930*).

Visitor Info **Lagos** (✉ *Sitio de São João* ☎ *282/763031*).

EXPLORING

Casa da Alfândega. Prince Henry the Navigator brought the first African slaves to Portugal for his personal use in 1441. He later established a slave market in West Africa to cope with increasingly large and barbaric slave auctions; by 1455 around 800 slaves were transported to Portugal each year. The first African slave market in Europe was held under the arches of the old Casa da Alfândega. The building now contains an art gallery with changing exhibits and is sometimes used for concerts and theater productions. It's open only during exhibitions and shows; ask at the tourist office for details. ✉ *Praça da República* ☎ *No phone* 💲 *Free.*

Castelo dos Governadores *(Governor's Palace).* It was from the Manu-eline window of this palace that the young king Dom Sebastião is said to have addressed his troops before setting off on his crusade of 1578. The palace is long gone, though the section of wall with the famous window remains and can be seen in the northwest corner of the Praça da República. The crusade was one of Portugal's greatest-ever disasters, with the king and some 8,000 men killed in Morocco at Alcácer-Quibir. (Dom Sebastião is further remembered by a much maligned, modernis-tic statue that stands in Praça Gil Eanes.)

Forte Ponta da Bandeira. This 17th-century fort defended the entrance to the harbor in bygone days. From inside the fort you can look out at sweeping ocean views. For an interesting perspective on the rock formations and grottoes of the area's shoreline, take one of the short boat trips offered by the fishermen near the Ponta da Bandeira. Check for departure times on the quayside boards. ✉ *Av. dos Descobrimentos* ☎ *282/761410* 💲 *€3* ☉ *Tues.–Sun. 9:30–12:30 and 2–5.*

Fodor'sChoice **Igreja de Santo António.** This early-18th-century baroque building is
★ Lagos's most extraordinary structure. Its interior is a riot of gilt extrava-gance made possible by the import of gold from Brazil. Dozens of

cherubs and angels clamber over the walls, among fancifully carved woodwork and azulejos. ✉ *Entrance via Museu Regional on Rua General Alberto Silveira* ☎ *282/762301* 💶 *€3 includes entry to Museu Regional* ⏱ *Tues.–Sun. 9:30–12:30 and 2–5:30.*

Museu Municipal Dr. José Formosinho. This regional museum houses an amusing jumble of exhibits, including mosaics, archaeological and ethnological items, and a town charter from 1504—all arranged haphazardly. ✉ *Rua General Alberto Silveira* ☎ *282/762301* 💶 *€3 includes entry to Igreja de Santo António* ⏱ *Tues.–Sun. 9:30–12:30 and 2–5:30.*

BEACHES

The largest beach near town and one of the best centers for water sports is the 4-km (2½-mi) stretch of **Meia Praia,** to the northeast. You can walk to it in less than five minutes simply by crossing the footbridge. If you want to go farther along, however, you can take a bus from the riverfront Avenida dos Descobrimentos, and in summer there's a ferry service a few hundred yards from Forte Ponta da Bandeira.

You can reach the prettiest beach south of town—**Praia de Dona Ana**—by car or on an enjoyable 30-minute walk along a cliff top. If you hoof it, pass the fort, turn left at the fire station, and follow the footpaths, which go to the most southerly point. A short way beyond Praia de Dona Ana is the attractive **Praia do Camilo.** Just beyond this beach is the Ponta da Piedade, a much-photographed group of rock arches and grottoes.

WHERE TO EAT

¢ ✕ **Café do Mar.** In a great location just outside town and overlooking the
PORTUGUESE dramatic Praia da Batata and the Lagos bay, the Café do Mar serves good, modest fare. Eat inside, or at the outside tables, and you'll find a variety of fresh fish available, along with pasta and salads. What's more, there's a small public parking area just yards away—a rarity in this busy town. ✉ *Av. Descobrimentos* ☎ *282/788006* 💳 *MC, V.*

$ ✕ **No Patio.** This cheerful restaurant with an inner patio is owned and
ECLECTIC run by acclaimed chef Martyn Allen. Menus vary according to season to incorporate the best of local produce. Eating here is best described as alfresco dining at its finest. Only the freshest ingredients are used to create Portuguese food with international flair. Be sure to try No Patio's famous starter, seared scallops with a pea puree and crispy bacon. As a main, try rump of lamb with poached red-current pears, and round off with a mouthwatering, homemade lemon mascarpone cream. In winter, No Patio has a beautiful open log fire to add warmth and romance. ✉ *Rua Lançarote de Freitas 46 r/c* ☎ *282/763777 or 912/582636* 💳 *AE, MC, V* ⏱ *Closed Sun. and Mon.*

¢ ✕ **O Galeão.** Tucked away on a backstreet is this bustling, informal, local
PORTUGUESE restaurant—it's so popular that you'll wait in line unless you've made a reservation. Established in 1981, it has an extensive menu of regional, national and international dishes. The food is first-rate, particularly the steaks—for once, fish, although well cooked, isn't the main event. A reasonably priced wine list encourages you to sample regional choices. ✉ *Rua da Laranjeira 1* ☎ *282/763909* 💳 *AE, DC, MC, V* ⏱ *Closed Sun.*

¢–$ ✕ **Piri-Piri.** On one of the main streets this small, low-key restaurant—
PORTUGUESE done in understated pastels—has an inexpensive but extensive menu.
The long list of Portuguese dishes includes a variety of market-fresh
fish, but the specialty is the zesty piri-piri chicken that gives the restaurant its name. ⊠ *Rua Lima Leitão, 15* ☎ *282/763803* ⊕ *piri-pirilagos.
tripod.com* ⊟ *MC, V.*

WHERE TO STAY

$ 🛏 **Casa da Moura.** It's a little hard to find at first, and you must phone
Fodor'sChoice before you arrive because the door is locked. Once inside, it's like being
★ in your own apartment with no lobby personnel. The Moroccan interior
is superb, as is the private pool area surrounded by cacti. Rooms are
named after Moroccan towns (such as Agadir and Taza) and vary from
doubles to large suites. All are stylishly decorated in the same somber
Arab theme throughout. A highlight is the buffet breakfast served on
the rooftop terrace with charming panache. Fresh fruits, honey, and
pancakes abound, or if you prefer, an omelet will instantly be prepared
to your liking. **Pros:** deep bathtubs; personalized service; loads of character; breakfast is great. **Cons:** street-facing rooms can be noisy; reception desk unmanned on occasion; cash only. ⊠ *Rua Cardeal Neto 10*
☎ *282/770730* ⊕ *www.casadamoura.com* ⇄ *3 rooms* ⚙ *In-room: a/c,
safe, kitchen, Internet. In-hotel, pool* ⊟ *No credit cards* 🍽 *EP.*

¢ 🛏 **Surf Experience.** This spacious and central house is open to all who
have an interest in surfing, regardless of age. The owners of the house
run a surf camp and offer special packages for surfers including accommodation, breakfast, and lunch, plus facilities such as board repair and
off-road transport as well as airport pickup. The daily rates work out to
be very reasonable, considering that the large classic town house is modern, comfortable, and comes with maid service and spectacular views of
the Lagos beaches from two large terraces. **Pros:** free Wi-Fi; fully loaded
digital entertainment system; cooking facilities. **Cons:** geared for the surf
crowd. ⊠ *Rua dos Ferreiros 21* ☎ *282/761943* ⊕ *www.surf-experience.
com* ⇄ *8 rooms, 4 with bath* ⚙ *In-room: no a/c, kitchen. In-hotel: bar,
laundry facilities, Wi-Fi hotspot* ⊟ *No credit cards* 🍽 *BP, FAP, MAP.*

$$ 🛏 **Tivoli Lagos.** At the eastern edge of the old town and an easy walk
from the town center, this state-of-the-art hotel has an unusual design:
it's strung across several levels with gardens, lounges, and patios. Guest
rooms are large and elegantly appointed, with attractive tiling behind
the bed headboards and in the bathrooms, and even on some lamps
and tabletops. A bus shuttles you to Meia Praia, where the hotel has
very good beach and water-sports facilities. The hotel's terrace grill
restaurant remains one of the best choices for seafood and service in
Lagos. There's also a good Italian restaurant that bakes pizza in a wood-
burning oven. Furthermore, the Tivoli Lagos has its own beach bar,
which is open all year and specializes in a cool finger-food concept
accompanied by chill-out music. Open in winter from 10 to 6, and in
summer, afternoons, evenings, and nights. **Pros:** good value for money;
free above-ground parking; paid underground parking; near to bus
and train station. **Cons:** at far right end of Lagos—a bit of a walk to
center. ⊠ *Rua António Crisógno dos Santos* ☎ *282/790079* ⊕ *www.
tivolihotels.com* ⇄ *324 rooms, 11 suites* ⚙ *In-room: a/c, safe, Wi-Fi.*

In-hotel: 3 restaurants, pool, bar, room service, bars, tennis courts, pools, gym ⊟ *AE, DC, MC, V* ⦿ *BP, MAP.*

NIGHTLIFE

There are a number of bars at the end of Rua 25 de Abril, most playing music that's brutally loud. Perhaps the most refined of Lagos' loud-music bars is **Bon Vivant** (⊠ *Rua 25 de Abril* ☎ *282/761019*), which has four distinct bar areas and a rooftop terrace way above the din.

Fodor'sChoice   An excellent bar is **Mullens** (⊠ *Rua Cândido dos Reis 86* ☎ *282/761281*
★   *or 918480071*), whose enthusiastic staff helps keep things swinging until 2 am; full meals are served, too. For dancing or cuddling on couches by a fireplace, try **Phoenix** (⊠ *Rua 5 de Outubro 11* ☎ *282/760503*), which plays disco and pop until 5 am. The classy **Stevie Ray's** (⊠ *Rua Senhora da Graça* ☎ *914923883* ⊕ *stevie-rays.com*) features a live music lounge that's dedicated to blues, jazz, Latino, soul, and international music and serves imported beers and French champagne.

SPORTS AND THE OUTDOORS

If you want to see dolphins, and do so with a company that supports their protection, then head for **Algarve Dolphins** (⊠ *Av. Descobrimentos, 19* ☎ *282/764144* ⊕ *www.algarve-dolphins.com*), which for €35 will take you on a 90-minute ocean trip. They guarantee that you'll see dolphins because, if you don't, you go on another trip for free.

PRAIA DA LUZ

6 km (4 mi) west of Lagos.

There was once an active fishing fleet here, and a favorite pastime was to watch the boats being hauled onto the broad, sandy beach that lends the community its name. The boats are gone, but this is still an agreeable destination—despite the development that has hit it. At the western edge of town a little church faces an 18th-century fortress that once guarded against pirates and is now a restaurant. Many of the accommodations available in Luz are in private villas and apartments; the tourist office in Lagos may be able to advise about them.

GETTING HERE AND AROUND

Praia da Luz is less than an hour from the Faro airport by car, and having a car is the easiest way to get around town. There is a regular bus service that runs from Faro; it stops right outside the village's picturesque church located by the seaside. You can also take the train to Lagos, and then catch a taxi or bus to Praia da Luz.

ESSENTIALS

Transportation **Bus** (☎ *282/762944*). **Taxi** (☎ *282/763587*).

EXPLORING

**OFF THE
BEATEN
PATH**

For a break from the coast and its buzz, you can head inland to the small, quiet town of **Vila do Bispo** at the western terminus of the N125 highway. The interior of its parish church, in the Praça do Igreja at the center of town, is covered with 18th-century azulejos. To see it, come on a Sunday morning; the church is open only for services at 11:30.

BEACHES

Four kilometers (2½ mi) west of Praia da Luz is **Burgau,** a fishing village with narrow, steep streets leading to it. Although the town has partly succumbed to the wave of tourism that has swept over the Algarve, its fine beach remains unchanged. The relaxed, low-key village of **Salema,** 5 km (3 mi) west of Burgau, is blessed with a 1,970-foot-long beach at the foot of green hills.

WHERE TO EAT AND STAY

$ ✕ **Blue Wave Bar & Restaurant.** Blue Wave is a cross between a laid-back
ECLECTIC   surf joint and an upmarket, cosmopolitan eatery. It's so cool, that in 2009 it appeared in *MaxMen* (Portugal's version of *Maxim* magazine). Take the rough road west from Burgau, and then an even rougher one down to the Praia Almadena. You'll be rewarded with this delightful surprise on a deserted cove. Specialties include locally caught grilled fish as well as a creative snack menu for hungry beach-goers. ✉ *Praia Almadena* ☎ *282/697035 or 966/927059* ⊕ *www.bluewavebeachbar.com* ▭ *MC, V.*

¢   ✕ **Café Correia.** Favorites at this rustic family-run restaurant in the inland
PORTUGUESE   town of Vila do Bispo are the stuffed squid and the rabbit cooked with beer and an onion sauce, among other regional Costa Vicentina specialties. The wine list, presented in a well-worn ledger, contains 180 varieties. ✉ *Rua Primeiro de Maio, 4, Vila do Bispo* ☎ *282/639127* ▭ *No credit cards* ☾ *Closed Sat.*

$$ ⊞ **Bela Vista.** This family-owned hilltop hotel's horseshoe configuration gives all the spacious guest quarters a great sea view. Rooms and suites have terraces as well as many modern conveniences. The restaurant is excellent, and the nearby beach is fine. **Pros:** child-friendly; quiet; walking distance to Luz town. **Cons:** some feel this hotel is overpriced. ✉ *Praia da Luz* ☎ *282/788655* ⊕ *www.belavistadaluz.com* ⤿ *39 rooms, 6 suites* ♿ *In-room: a/c, safe, refrigerator, Wi-Fi. In-hotel: restaurant, bar, tennis court, pools, gym* ▭ *AE, DC, MC, V* ⦿| *BP.*

$$ ⊞ **Romantik Natur.** Set within verdant gardens complete with sculptures, this holiday village west of Praia da Luz offers an ambience of calm and peacefulness that will soothe the soul. **Pros:** lots to do including tennis courts, board games, books, pools, and so on. **Cons:** Burgau 20-minute walk; Lagos 10-minute drive. ✉ *Sítio Cama da Vaca* ☎ *282/697323* ⊕ *www.romantiknaturehotel.com* ⤿ *20 rooms, 40 apartments* ♿ *In-room: a/c. In-hotel: restaurant, bar, tennis court, 3 pools, Internet terminal* ▭ *MC, V* ⦿| *BP.*

SPORTS AND THE OUTDOORS

Lessons with certified scuba instructors, wreck dives, and night dives are available at **Blue Ocean Divers** (✉ *Center Motel Ancora, Estrada de Porto de Mós* ☎ *964/665667* ⊕ *www.blue-ocean-divers.de*). Praia da Luz's broad bay provides an excellent venue for windsurfing. Instruction and equipment rental are available directly on the beach.

SAGRES

Fodor's Choice ★ *30 km (18 mi) southwest of Praia da Luz; 3 km (2 mi) southeast of Cabo São Vicente.*

In the 19th century, this village, amid harsh, barren moorland, was rebuilt over earthquake ruins. Today there's little of note apart from a fort and a series of fine, sweeping beaches.

GETTING HERE AND AROUND

Sagres is worth a visit, but with infrequent buses, renting a car is recommended for those wishing to travel to the most western tip of the Algarve. Sagres is approximately an hour and 15 minutes at a leisurely drive from Portimão and a little over two hours from Faro.

ESSENTIALS

Visitor Info Sagres (⊠ *Rua Comandante Matoso* ☎ *282/624873*).

EXPLORING

Fortaleza de Sagres. Views from the Sagres Fortress, an enormous run of defensive walls high above the crashing waves, are spectacular. Its massive walls and battlements make it popular with kids. The importance of this area dates to as early as the 4th century BC, when Mediterranean seafarers found it to be the last sheltered port before the wild winds of the Atlantic. In the late 8th century, according to local religious tradition, the mortal remains of the 4th-century martyr of Zaragoza, St. Vincent, washed up here. This led to a Vincentine cult that attracted pilgrims until the destruction of the sanctuary in the mid-12th century. The fortress was rebuilt in the 17th century, and although some historians have claimed that it was the site for Prince Henry's house and famous navigation school, it's more likely that Henry built his school at Cabo São Vicente. But this doesn't detract from the powerful atmosphere. Certainly the **Venta da Rosa** (Wind Compass, or compass rose) dates from Prince Henry's period. Uncovered only in the 20th century, this large circular construction made of stone and packed earth is in the courtyard just inside the fortress. The simple Graça Chapel is of the same age.

A stark, modern building within the fort houses an **exhibition center** (☎ *282/620140* *€3* ☉ *May–Sept., daily 10–8:30; Oct.–Apr., daily 10–6:30*), with revolving exhibits documenting the region's history, flora, fauna, and nautical themes. The tunnel-like entrance to the fortress is about a 15-minute walk from the village; three buses a day run this way on weekdays. (☉ *Closed May 1 and Dec. 25*).

WHERE TO EAT AND STAY

¢
PORTUGUESE
✕ **O Retiro do Pescador.** This outdoor grill is incredibly good value and serves a range of meats as well as the most flavorful fresh fish in Sagres. The homemade brandy is worth a try, as are the typical regional desserts prepared by the owner's wife and family. ⊠ *Vale das Silvas* ☎ *282/624438* ☐ *No credit cards.*

$
PORTUGUESE
✕ **Vila Velha.** Traditional Portuguese cuisine is given a twist of healthy, organic flavor here, and dishes include a range of international vegetarian options. From the terrace grill you can watch the sunset over Cabo São Vicente (Cape St. Vincent). Because of the popularity of this restaurant with local expats, it's recommended that you book in advance.

Lunch can be arranged for large groups. ⊠ *On headland between fishing harbor and Praia da Mareta* ☎ *282/624788, 917128402* ⊕ *www. vilavelha-sagres.com* ⊟ *MC, V* ⊗ *Closed Mon.*

$$$$
Fodor's Choice
★

🖭 **Martinhal Beach Resort & Hotel.** Inaugurated in the spring of 2010, Martinhal offers the latest in luxury lodgings. Perched on the edge of the beautiful Martinhal beach and surrounded by natural landscapes, it embodies the natural essence of the Western Algarve, to very high standards. Located near the historic village of Sagres, this resort also boasts an accomplished gastronomy available in three restaurants: the formal O Terraço restaurant specializes in traditional Portuguese cuisine made from the best of seasonal produce; As Dunas offers light beach-lunch fare like fresh, grilled fish; Os Gambozinos is a more casual, family eatery. Menus feature the best of typical national dishes. **Pros:** family villas available as well as several types of rooms; beachside location; excellent facilities for children and babies. **Cons:** finishing touches still being applied; five-minute drive to nearest supermarket. ⊠ *Quinta do Martinhal, Apartado 54* ☎ *282/240200* ⊕ *www.martinhal.com* ⇨ *38 rooms* △ *In-room: a/c, safe, Wi-Fi. In-hotel: restaurant, bar, spa, pools* ⊟ *AE, DC, MC, V* ⊗ *BP, MAP.*

$

🖭 **Pousada do Infante.** In a two-story country house across the bay from the Fortaleza de Sagres, this pousada has a glorious view of the sea and the craggy cliffs. Guest rooms are homey, and public areas are comfortable—particularly the terrace bar, which is a perfect place to watch sunsets. Throughout the pousada are Moorish embellishments such as minarets and arches alongside the pool. The service and the Portuguese food in the well-respected restaurant ($$$$) are accomplished; expect seafood specials such as fried squid or clams with pork and, for dessert, perhaps almond cake. **Pros:** unique views to last lighthouse on mainland Europe; three-course dinner menu for about €20. **Cons:** not as small or intimate as other pousadas; make sure to ask for a room with panoramic views. ⊠ *On headland between fishing harbor and Praia da Mareta* ☎ *282/620240* ⊕ *www. pousadas.pt* ⇨ *51 rooms* △ *In-room: a/c, safe, refrigerator, Internet (some). In-hotel: restaurant, bar, tennis court, pool* ⊟ *AE, DC, MC, V* ⊗ *BP.*

NIGHTLIFE

Sagres is a well-known haunt of young travelers, and there are several music bars near the village square. **A Rosa dos Ventos** (⊠ *Praça da República* ☎ *282/624480*) is the town's most popular bar, attracting a motley crowd of European travelers. It also serves local snacks, burgers, and salads. The loud, lively **Last Chance Saloon** (⊠ *Road to Praia da Mareta* ☎ *282/624113*) is on the pub-crawl route for most young merrymakers passing through Sagres. It also claims to be the last place to get a drink before Madeira.

SPORTS AND THE OUTDOORS

The best fishing in Sagres is in winter when seas are rough; *sargo* (big bream bass) and *dourada* (mahimahi) are the main catches. Smaller bream, mullet, mackerel, and bass can be caught during the more settled summer months. **Baleeira** is a small fishing port of Sagres, which houses up to 100 fishing boats, some more than 65 feet in length. You can hire a local fisherman and his boat for a three-hour fishing trip from Salema to Sagres and back with possible swimming stops at lonely beaches along the way.

CABO SÃO VICENTE

6 km (4 mi) northwest of Sagres; 95 km (59 mi) west of Faro; 30 km (18 mi) southwest of Lagos.

At the southwest tip of Europe, where the land juts starkly into the rough Atlantic waters, is Cabo São Vicente, called *O Fim do Mundo* (The End of the World) by early Portuguese mariners. Legends attach themselves easily to this desolate place, which the Romans once considered sacred (they believed it was where the spirits of the light lived because with sunset the light disappeared). It takes its modern name from the martyr St. Vincent, whose relics were brought here in the 8th century; it's said that they were transported to Lisbon 400 years later in a boat guided by ravens.

This is not the crowded, overdeveloped Algarve of the south coast. From here you can see the spectacular cliff tops at Murração looking onto seemingly endless deserted beaches. Vast flocks of migratory birds round Cape St. Vincent and the Sagres headlands each year with the navigational precision that would have truly astounded Columbus. He learned how to navigate at Prince Henry's school of navigation after the armed convoy he was traveling with was attacked by pirates off Cape St. Vincent in 1476. Sixteen years later he set sail from here to discover the Americas.

GETTING HERE AND AROUND

Lack of adequate and regular public transportation means renting a car is the best, if not only, option.

EXPLORING

Fodor'sChoice ★ The keeper of the isolated **Faro de São Vicente** *(St. Vincent Lighthouse)* opens it to visitors at his discretion. The beacon is said to have the strongest reflectors in Europe—they cast a beam 96 km (60 mi) out to sea. The views from the lighthouse are remarkable. Turquoise water whips across the base of the rust-color cliffs below, the fortress at Sagres is visible to the east, and in the distance lies the immense Atlantic.

VILA DO BISPO

10 km (6 mi) north of Cabo São Vicente.

Though not particularly attractive itself, Vila do Bispo lies at the crossroads between west and south coastal roads and makes a good base for local beaches. What draws people to this area is the Parque Natural Sudoeste Alentejano e Costa Vincentina—a less traveled region of designated park area that contains some of the Algarve's wildest beaches and has become a mecca for surfers from all over the world. Portugal's best surfing beach is Amado, which at almost 13 km (8 mi) in length has enough room for the dozens of surfing camps and schools that have sprung up around it. Aljezur, a far prettier town, lies about 20 km (12 mi) northeast, but still lacks good hotels and restaurants, which can be found in the Vila do Bispo environs.

GETTING HERE AND AROUND

As is the case with its neighbor to the south, Cabo São Vicente, the lack of adequate and regular public transportation to and from Vila do Bispo means renting a car is the best, if not only, option.

WHERE TO EAT AND STAY

$ ✕ **A Eira do Mel.** This restaurant excels at mixing local recipes and ECLECTIC produce with sophisticated international cuisine. The flavors and artful presentation attract a youthful and vibrant crowd of faithful regulars. ⊠ *Estrada do Castelejo, Mercado Municipal* ☎ *282/639016* ⊕ *www.eiradomel.com* ⊟ *MC, V* ⊙ *Closed Mon.*

¢ ✕ **O Sitio do Forno.** This simple restaurant is run by a fishing family who PORTUGUESE catch the menu early in the morning and cook it without any frills.
Fodor'sChoice Charcoal-grilled tiger prawns, shrimp, *percebes* (goose-neck barnacles),
★ mussels, haddock, and sole are served with lemon, garlic, or coriander. Bread, local sausage *(chouriço),* and potatoes in olive oil and olives complement the fish. The waiter, apart from being the fisherman's son, also happens to be the local mayor—the youngest in Portugal. Local fishermen mingle with curious travelers, making for a good and unusual atmosphere. ⊠ *Praia do Amado, Carrapateira* ☎ *96/3558404* ⊟ *No credit cards* ⊙ *Closed Mon.*

$ ▦ **Monte Velho Nature Resort.** This converted farmhouse offers hip,
Fodor'sChoice luxurious accommodation with stunning panoramic views toward the
★ beaches of Amado and Murração. The charming owners, Henrique and Vera, are perfect hosts, and the hotel offers all kinds of activities such as a 4-km (2½-mi) donkey ride to the beach, quad motorbikes, surfing classes, and massage. Breakfasts are long, drawn-out affairs (served from 9 to 11 am) with a sumptuous spread of local delicacies. The seven individually decorated suites come with their very own hammocks for the semiprivate patios. **Pros:** eco-friendly; beaches are quiet, even in summer. **Cons:** no pool, telephone or TV in rooms; closest Internet café in nearby village; a car is essential; beaches are 4 km (2½ mi). ⊠ *Herdade do Monte Velho, Carrapateira* ☎ *282/973207/ 966/007950* ⊕ *www.wonderfulland.com/montevelho* ⇒ *5 rooms, 8 suites* ⌂ *In-room: no a/c, no TV, no phone. In-hotel: Internet terminal, bicycles* ⊟ *MC, V* ⫶◯⫶ *BP, FAP, MAP.*

Coimbra and the Beiras

WORD OF MOUTH

"Coimbra is a lively city and one of the best places to hear authentic fado, especially in one of the tiny atmospheric *tascas* where the students hang out. Another high point—literally—has to be the spectacular Serra da Estrela; the region's highest mountain range and *the* place to head for if you're into hiking or cycling in the great outdoors."

–Mary McLean

"While not on par with the Roman ruins of Rome, Conimbriga is interesting and worth a visit. A highlight is the re-creation of a villa's water garden."

–Michael

Updated by
Josephine
Quintero

This is a region that many visitors overlook and, as a result, it is undeniably one of the least spoiled areas of Portugal. Even the coastal resorts have, overall, retained their intrinsic local character and charm. The Beiras is an area of true diversity with an abundance of beaches, lagoons, and mountains. The natural beauty of the scenery also serves as a fitting gateway to the drama of the Douro and the Minho farther north.

To the east, Portugal's highest mountains, the Serra da Estrela, rise to nearly 6,600 feet and provide a playground of alpine meadows, haunting forests, wooded hills, and clear streams. High in this range's granite reaches, a tiny trickle of an icy stream begins a tortuous journey to the sea. This is the Rio Mondego, praised in song and poetry as the most Portuguese of all rivers. The longest river entirely within the country and the lifeblood of the Beiras, it provides vital irrigation to fruit orchards and farms as it flows through the region's heart.

Coimbra is one of Portugal's most fascinating and historic cities. It's also the country's first capital and home to one of Europe's earliest universities. It's a lively town with one of the country's most picturesque historic quarters. There are winding medieval streets flanked by taverns, shops, and restaurants. The university rises above the river which continues, closer to the sea, under the imposing walls of Montemor Castle. The *rio* (river) then widens to nurture rice fields before merging with the Atlantic at the popular beach resort of Figueira da Foz. Archaeology buffs will also appreciate the region's extraordinary Roman ruins—particularly at Conímbriga, the country's largest excavated site.

ORIENTATION AND PLANNING

GETTING ORIENTED

The Beiras region encompasses the provinces of the Beira Litoral (Coastal Beira), the Beira Baixa (Lower Beira), and the Beira Alta (Upper Beira). In total this area covers an impressive one-quarter of Portugal's landmass.

The onetime medieval capital and largest city in the region, Coimbra (pronounced *queembra*), is a good place to start your exploration. To the west of the city are the seaside resort of Figueira da Foz and the canals and lagoons in and around the delightful old port of Aveiro. Farther inland is the must-see city of Viseu, with its wonderful parks and historic old quarter. The mountain resort of Caramulo and the belle epoque towns of Luso and Curia are some of the country's most popular spas. The region's eastern area includes Portugal's highest mountains—

TOP REASONS TO GO

Foot-tap to the fado. Discover the delights of this university city's distinctive style of fado at one of Coimbra's atmospheric fado houses.

Get away from it all. Head for the peaceful beauty of the Buçaco forest, the country's most revered woods and a monastic retreat during the Middle Ages.

Step back in time. Explore the fascinating archeological site of Coinímbriga, Portugal's finest Roman site with mosaics, baths, an aqueduct and more.

Enjoy sand between your toes. Take a sunset walk along Figueira's wide 2-km (1.2-mi) long sandy beach or, if you are feeling really energetic, grab your surfboard and head for the surf.

Lace up those hiking boots. The vast Parque Natural da Sierra da Estrela has extensive well-marked trails and stunning natural scenery.

the Serra da Estrela—the renowned Dão wine region, and a chain of ancient fortified towns along the Spanish border.

Coimbra. Between Lisbon and Porto, the crowning glory of the Beira Litoral, Coimbra is one of Portugal's most fascinating cities exuding the vibrancy of a student town, combined with a real sense of history.

The Western Beiras. The coastal region is remarkably unspoiled with miles of golden sand, backed by sand dunes and forests of pine trees and centered round the only sizable resort: Figueira da Foz.

The Eastern Beiras. The more mountainous eastern region is home to some of the Portugal's most spectacular scenery and is the historic heart of the country with ancient towns like Viseu, Guarda, and Trancosa set among mountain peaks and verdant valleys.

PLANNING

WHEN TO GO

Although the Beiras's coastal beaches are popular in summer, the crowds are nothing like those in the Algarve. The water along this shore isn't as warm as it is farther south, and as a consequence the season is considerably shorter. Plan your beach time here between early June and mid-September.

With the exception of the eastern regions, the interior isn't subject to the blazing heat of the Alentejo or the Algarve's interior and so is well suited for summertime touring. Aside from occasional showers, the weather is comfortable between early April and mid-November. Winters, especially in the eastern mountain towns, are harsh.

PLANNING YOUR TIME

If you have just three days, you can visit Coimbra and the coast, unless you head straight inland to the mountains. Don't let the distances fool you into being overambitious: the mountain roads may not be long, but they take a lot of time to drive. A week is enough time to experience Coimbra, visit a spa and the coast, and explore the Serra da Estrela.

A BIT OF HISTORY

This region has played an important role in Portugal's development. The Romans built roads, established settlements, and in 27 BC incorporated into their vast empire the remote province known as Lusitania, which encompassed most of what is now central Portugal, including the Beiras. They left many traces of their presence, including the well-known and well-preserved ruins at Conímbriga, near Coimbra. The Moors swept through the territory in the early 8th century and played a leading role for several hundred years. Many of the region's elaborate castles and extensive fortifications show a strong Moorish influence. The towns along the Spanish frontier have been the scene of many fierce battles—from those during the Wars of Christian Reconquest to those during the fledgling Portuguese nation's struggle against invaders from neighboring Castile.

The Beiras also played a part in Portugal's golden Age of Discovery. In 1500 Pedro Álvares Cabral, a nobleman from the town of Belmonte on the eastern flank of the Serra da Estrela, led the first expedition to what is now Brazil. Much of the wealth garnered during this period, when tiny Portugal controlled so much of the world's trade, financed the great architectural and artistic achievements of the Portuguese Renaissance. Throughout the region there are fine examples of the Manueline style, the uniquely Portuguese art form that reflects the nation's nautical heritage. The cathedrals at Guarda and Viseu, the Igreja e Mosteiro de Santa Cruz (Church and Monastery of Santa Cruz) in Coimbra, and the Convento de Jesus (Convent of Jesus) in Aveiro are especially noteworthy.

During the 19th-century Peninsular War, between Napoléon's armies and Wellington's British and Portuguese forces, a decisive battle was fought in the tranquil forest of Buçaco. Later in the same century, this area witnessed a much more peaceful invasion, as people from all corners of Europe came to take the waters at such well-known spas as Luso, Curia, and Caramulo. Around the turn of the 20th century, when the now tourist-packed Algarve was merely a remote backwater, Figueira da Foz was coming into its own as an international beach resort.

GETTING HERE AND AROUND
AIR TRAVEL
Coimbra is 197 km (123 mi) north of Lisbon and 116 km (72 mi) south of Porto. Both cities are connected to Coimbra via the A1 (E80) highway. Intercontinental flights usually arrive in Lisbon, but Porto has an increasing number of European connections, including through several budget airlines.

BUS TRAVEL
Buses of various vintages can take you to almost any destination within the region, and unlike train stations, which are often some distance from the town center, bus depots are central. Although this is a great way to travel and get close to the local people, it requires a great deal of time and patience.

Regional and local bus schedules are posted at terminals, and you can also get information at local tourist offices. Rede Expressos provides comfortable bus service between Lisbon, Porto, and Coimbra, and to other parts of the Beiras. International as well as regional services are available at the Rodoviário da Beira Litoral bus station in Coimbra and at the Rodoviário da Beira Interior stations in Castelo Branco and Covilhã.

Contacts **Rede Expressos** (✉ *Av. Fernão de Magalhães 2D, Coimbra* ☎ *239/855270* ⊕ *www.rede-expressos.pt*). **Rodoviário da Beira Interior** (✉ *Rodrigo Rebelo 3, Castelo Branco* ☎ *272/340120* ⊕ *www.rbi.pt* ✉ *Central de Camionagem, Covilhã* ☎ *275/334914*). **Rodoviário da Beira Litoral** (✉ *Av. Fernão de Magalhães, Coimbra* ☎ *239/855270*).

CAR TRAVEL

The Beiras, with their many remote villages, are suited to exploration by car. Distances between major points are short; there are no intimidating cities to negotiate; and except for the coastal strip in July and August, traffic is light. Roads in general are good and destinations well marked; however, parking is a problem in the larger towns.

Although you can zip from Lisbon to Coimbra on the A1 toll highway in less than two hours or drive from Porto to Coimbra in under an hour, resist the temptation. The heart and soul of the Beiras are along the many miles of more minor roads—those squiggly little lines lacing Portugal's map.

Allow plenty of time for journeys the moment you are off the main highways. Many of the mountain roads are switchbacks that need to be treated with extreme caution. In addition, you are almost certain to get lost with appalling signposting (usually hidden around the corner or behind a tree) and nightmarish one-way mazes in every town, from the smallest hamlet to the largest city. If you get to your destination without going around the whole town three times, consider yourself lucky. Even the locals admit to getting lost on a regular basis.

Drive defensively at all times. Portugal has one of Europe's highest traffic fatality rates, and the worst road in the country for accidents is the IP5 heading inland from Aveiro to the Serra de Estrela.

TRAIN TRAVEL

Although the major destinations in the Beiras are linked by rail, service to most towns, with the exception of Coimbra, is infrequent. Using Coimbra as a hub, there are three main rail lines in the region. Line 110, the Beira Alta line, goes northeast to Luso, Viseu, Celorico da Beira, and Guarda. Line 120 extends south through the Ribatejo to intersect with Line 130, the Beira Baixa line, which runs from Lisbon northeast through Castelo Branco and Fundão to Covilhã, the gateway to the Serra da Estrela. Going north from Coimbra, Line 100 serves Curia, Aveiro, and Ovar and continues north to Porto and Braga.

Coimbra, Luso, Guarda, Ovar, and Aveiro are on the main Lisbon–Porto and Lisbon–Paris lines. Two trains arrive from and depart for Paris daily, and in summer a daily car-train operates between Paris and Lisbon. There are also regular trains linking the principal cities in the Beiras with Madrid, Lisbon, and Porto. There are three stations in

Coimbra: Coimbra A (Estação Nova), along the Mondego River, a five-minute walk from the center of town (for domestic routes); Coimbra Parque just south of Ponte de Santa Clara (also for domestic routes); and Coimbra B (Estação Velha), 5 km (3 mi) west. International trains and trains from Lisbon and Porto arrive at Coimbra B, where there's a free shuttle to Coimbra A. There are also bus links between stations. Schedules for all trains are posted at all three stations.

Contact **Train information** (☎ 808/208208 ⊕ www.cp.pt).

RESTAURANTS

With the exception of some luxury hotel dining rooms, restaurants are casual in dress and atmosphere, although a bit less casual than in the southern parts of the country. The emphasis is generally more on the food than on the trappings. Except for pizza and the occasional Chinese restaurant, foreign food is virtually nonexistent.

At almost any of the ubiquitous beach bar–restaurants, you can't go wrong by ordering the *peixe do dia* (fish of the day). In most cases it will have been caught only hours before and will be prepared outside on a charcoal grill. You'll usually be served the whole fish along with boiled potatoes and a simple salad. Wash it down with a chilled white Dão wine, and you have a tasty, healthful, relatively inexpensive meal. In Figueira da Foz and in the Aveiro region, *enguias* (eels), *lampreia* (lamprey), and *caldeirada* (a fish stew that's a distant cousin of the French bouillabaisse) are popular.

The inland Bairrada region, between Coimbra and Aveiro, and in particular the town of Mealhada are well known for *leitão assado* (roast suckling pig). In Coimbra the dish to try is *chanfana*; this is traditionally made with tender young kid braised in red wine and roasted in an earthenware casserole. In the mountains, fresh *truta* (trout) panfried with bacon and onions is often served, as is *javali* (wild boar). *Bacalhau* (salt cod) in one form or another appears on just about every menu in the region. Bacalhau *à brás* (fried in olive oil with eggs, onions, and potatoes) is one of many popular versions of this common dish.

The Beiras contain two of Portugal's most notable wine districts: Bairrada and Dão. The reds from these districts generally benefit from a fairly long stay in the bottle; 1983 and 1985 are particularly good years, and if you see a 1983 Porta dos Cavaleiros Reserva *tinto* (red) on a wine list, grab it. The full-bodied Dão goes wonderfully with chanfana or leitão assado. The flowery whites from around here should be drunk much younger.

This region is also justly famous for its contribution to the country's dessert menus, although many of these pastry delights, such as Coimbra's *arrufada* (a small cinnamon-flavor pastry), are rarely found far from home. The tangy sheep's cheese of the Serra da Estrela is popular throughout the country.

HOTELS

There are plenty of high-quality accommodations in the western reaches of the Beiras, but the options thin the farther inland you move; make reservations in advance if you plan to travel during the busy summer months. That said, the Beiras has a great variety of lodging choices, ranging from venerable old luxury hotels to gleaming, modern hostelries. Though small, the region has several *pousadas* (inns that are members of the Turismo de Habitação organization), which make the perfect bases for exploring the entire region. In addition, there are Solares de Portugal lodgings, which are family owned and run and can range from mansions to cottages. Most establishments offer substantial off-season discounts. (High season varies by hotel but generally runs July 1–September 15.)

WHAT IT COSTS IN EUROS					
	¢	$	$$	$$$	$$$$
Restaurants	under €10	€10–€15	€15–€20	€21–€25	over €25
Hotels	under €80	€80–€140	€141–€200	€201–€260	over €260

Restaurant prices are per person for a main course at dinner. Hotel prices are for a standard double room, including tax, in high season (off-season rates may be lower).

EMERGENCIES

In all sizable towns, pharmacies operate on a rotating system for staying open after normal closing hours, including weekends and holidays. Consult a local newspaper or the notice posted on the door of every pharmacy. If you require medical assistance, hospitals in Castel Branco, Coimbra, Figueira da Foz, and Guarda have *urgências* (emergency rooms).

Emergencies General (☎ *112*).

VISITOR AND TOUR INFO

There are few regularly scheduled guided tours originating in the Beiras. The Departamento Cultural (Cultural Department) in Coimbra's town hall organizes excellent one-day bus excursions to areas around Coimbra, but they take place once a month only. If you can catch one of these, the experience is worthwhile, as the tours usually include a rewarding introduction to regional home cooking. The Coimbra town hall tourist offices can supply details. There are also a couple of companies offering guided walking tours and activities in the mountains. Other than that, the only regular tours of the Beiras originate either in Lisbon or in Porto. For further information contact a travel agency, or see the town section, *below*, for more specific tourist information.

COIMBRA

197 km (123 mi) northeast of Lisbon.

Coimbra is best known for its university. Although it was first established in Lisbon by King Dinis I in 1290 and subsequently transferred back and forth between Coimbra and Lisbon, it was finally installed on its present site in 1537. Since then the university has played an important role in the life of both the city and the nation. During the 1960s, it was a center of the unrest preceding the 1974 revolution. Many current political leaders were educated here, and Dr. António Salazar, the country's dictator from 1932 until 1968, once taught economics in its lecture halls. Today, the students add much life to the city. They proudly wear the traditional black capes and adorn their briefcases with colored

GREAT ITINERARIES

If you have just three days, visit Coimbra and the coast, or head straight inland to the mountains. Don't let the distances fool you into being overambitious: the mountain roads may not be long, but they take a lot of time to drive. A week is enough time to experience Coimbra.

IF YOU HAVE 3 DAYS

Spend your first morning in **Coimbra**, with a stroll through the Cidade Velha (Old Town) and the university. In the afternoon visit the Roman ruins at **Conímbriga**. The next day, follow the Rio Mondego to the beach resorts of **Figueira da Foz** and Buarcos, head up the coast, and move inland to visit the china factory in **Vista Alegre** and the nearby Museu do Mar. Use the rest of the day and evening to explore **Aveiro**, the famous Ria de Aveiro, and the delightful little coastal villages along the sand spit, such as Costa Nova, south of Aveiro.

IF YOU HAVE 7 DAYS

Start in **Coimbra** and **Conímbriga**, as above. The next day, stop to visit the castle at **Montemor-o-Velho** on your way to another night in **Figueira da Foz**, from which you can visit the other beach resort, Buarcos, and drive out to Cape Mondego to enjoy the view and the sunset. Continue along the dune-lined coast on the third day, and after stops in Costa Nova, **Vista**

Alegre and a visit to the nearby Museu do Mar, unpack your toiletries in **Aveiro**. The following morning, take a boat trip through the narrow waterways and marshlands that make up the Ria de Aveiro, and after lunch continue on to **Viseu** by way of **Ovar** and the castle at Santa Maria da Feira.

On your fifth day, continue east from Viseu and make a loop that includes visits to the fortified towns of **Celorico da Beira**, **Trancoso**, **Castelo Rodrigo**, and **Almeida**—a pleasant drive through the sparsely settled countryside over little-traveled roads. Spend the night in the mountain bastion of **Guarda** or at one of the charming country hotels within the Serra de Estrela. The next morning, either visit the cathedral and museum in Guarda, or devote the whole day to exploring the magnificent high reaches of the Parque Natural da Serra da Estrela, with its fabulous views, great walks, exciting wildlife and birds, and beautiful flowers. Leave the park at Seia. Continue by way of **Penacova** to the forest of **Buçaco**, just north of Coimbra. Be sure to visit the opulent Palace Hotel and, if it's within your budget, spend the night; there are more modest accommodations in the nearby spa town of **Luso**. On your last day, explore the options of the local spas before returning to Coimbra.

ribbons denoting which faculty they attend (red for law and yellow for medicine, for example). After final exams in May, they burn their ribbons with great exuberance in a ceremony called Queima das Fitas (Burning of the Ribbons).

GETTING HERE AND AROUND

There are parking facilities on and around Avenidas Fernão Magalhães. Look for the blue P sign. Rede Expressos has buses going to/from Lisbon (2½ hours) and Porto (1½ hours) daily, as well as smaller towns, including Braga (2½ hours). Trains are also run frequently to/from Lisbon and Porto with similar durations. Locally, yellow municipal buses make regular stops around the city from 6 am to midnight; multi-use tickets can be purchased from the Serviços Municipais de Transportes de Coimbra (SMTUC) office or at a tobacconist (three rides €2, 11 rides €6.10), one-day ticket €3.20. The *patufinhas* (electric minibuses) travel between Baixa and Alta Coimbra, the medieval heart of the city. Bus tickets cover both.

TIMING

Allow at least two hours for the walk around the old town; double that if you are intending to visit the attractions along the way. If you want to continue across the bridge, you'll probably need a couple more hours. The hill is very steep. For this reason, the tour starts at the top of it and works itself down.

SAFETY AND PRECAUTIONS

Coimbra is a safe city, but you should be wary of bag snatchers, particularly around the main tourist sights.

ESSENTIALS

Buses Coimbra Bus Station (✉ *Av. Fernão de Magalhães, Coimbra* ☎ *239/827081*). **Serviços Municipais de Transportes de Coimbra** (✉ *Largo do Mercado, Coimbra* ☎ *239/801100* ⊕ *www.smtuc.pt*).

Hospitals Hospital da Universidade de Coimbra (✉ *Praça Prof. Mota Pinto, Celas, Coimbra* ☎ *239/400400*).

Visitor Info Coimbra tourist office (☎ *239/488120*). **Região de Turismo do Centro** (✉ *Av. Afonso Henriques 132, Coimbra* ☎ *239/488120* ⊕ *www.turismo-centro.pt*).

EXPLORING

TOP ATTRACTIONS

Convento de Santa Clara-a-Nova *(New Santa Clara Convent)*. This convent on a hill was built in the 17th century to house the Poor Clair nuns who were forced by floods from their old convent. The remains of Queen Isabel were also moved here. The barrackslike exterior protects a sumptuous baroque church and noble cloisters that shouldn't be missed. Queen Isabel's silver shrine is behind the main altar in the church, installed there by Coimbra townspeople in 1696. The queen's original tomb—she ordered it for herself in 1330—stands in the lower choir at the other end of the church. Carved out of a single block of stone, the splendid Gothic sarcophagus is decorated with sculpted polychrome figures of Franciscan friars and nuns. An effigy of the queen dressed in her Poor Clair habit lies on top. During the Peninsular War, the French General Massena used the convent as a hospital for 300 troops wounded during the battle of Buçaco. The carefully hidden convent treasures escaped the desecration inflicted on so many Portuguese monuments during this period. ✉ *Rua Santa Isabel* ☎ *239/441674* 🕮 *Church free, cloister €1.50, cloister and lower choir €2* ☉ *Mon., Tues., Thurs., weekends 8:45–6:45, Wed. and Fri. 8:45–12:30 and 2:30–6:45.*

A BIT MORE HISTORY (COIMBRA)

Since its emergence as the Roman settlement of Aeminium, this city on the banks of the Rio Mondego has played an influential and often crucial role in the country's development. In Roman times, it was an important way station, the midway point on the road connecting Lisbon with Braga to the north, and a rival of the city of Conímbriga, across the river to the south. But by the beginning of the 5th century the Roman administration was falling apart, and Aeminium fell under the dominance of Alans, Swabians, and Visigoths in turn. By the middle of the 7th century, under Visigoth rule, its importance was such that it had become the regional capital and center of the bishopric of Conímbriga. Upstart Aeminium had finally gained ascendancy over its rival Conímbriga.

The Moorish occupation of Coimbra is believed to have occurred around the year AD 714, and it heralded an era of economic development: for the next 300 years or so, Coimbra was a frontier post of Muslim culture. North of the city there are no traces of Moorish architecture, but Coimbra has retained tangible fragments of its Muslim past—remains of old walls as well as a small gate, the Arco de Almedina, once an entrance to a medina—and the surrounding country is full of place-names of Moorish origin.

After a number of bloody attempts, the reconquest of Coimbra by Christian forces was finally achieved in 1064 by Ferdinand, King of León, and Coimbra went on to become the capital of a vast territory extending north to the Rio Douro and encompassing much of what are now the Beiras. The city was the birthplace and burial place of Portugal's first king, Dom Afonso Henriques, and was the capital from which he launched the attacks against the Moors that were to end in the conquest of Lisbon and the birth of a nation. Coimbra was the capital of Portugal until the late 13th century, when the court was transferred to Lisbon.

The figure who has remained closest to the heart of the city was the Spanish-born wife of King Dinis, Isabel of Aragon. During her life, while her husband and son were away fighting wars, sometimes against each other, Isabel occupied herself with social works, battling prostitution, and fostering education and welfare schemes for Coimbra's young women. She helped found a convent, and had her own tomb placed in it. She bequeathed her jewels to the poor girls of Coimbra to provide them with wedding dowries. When she died on a peacemaking mission to Estremoz in 1336, her body was brought back to Coimbra, and almost immediately the late queen became the object of a local cult. Isabel was beatified in the 16th century, then canonized in 1625 by Pope Urban VIII after it was determined that her body had remained undecayed in its tomb.

Convento de Santa Clara-a-Velha *(Old Santa Clara Convent).* Restorers have been excavating the interior of this ruined Gothic church, which had been immersed by mud and silt for centuries, since 2000. Founded as a Poor Clair convent in the early 14th century by Queen Isabel, widow of King Dinis and patron saint of Coimbra, the building was beset by periodic flooding and was finally abandoned in 1677. Both Queen Isabel and the tragic Inês de Castro (⇨ *see Quinta das Lagrimas for the tragic tale of Inês de Castro*) were originally interred here. Today the well-preserved convent can be visited with recent excavations revealing the original chapter house, the refectory, and a small cloister. An interpretation center also opened in 2009 providing well-documented information about the convent's history. ⌂ *Rua das Parreiras* ☎ *239/801160* ⌸ *€5, free on Sun.* ⊙ *Tues.–Sun. 10–7.*

NEED A BREAK? Why not succumb to the temptation of the pastry-filled windows of the cafés along the Rua Ferreira Borges? The **Café Nicola** (⌂ *Rua Visconde da Luz 35, Baixa*) is a good choice for sampling *arrufada*, Coimbra's most notable contribution to the world's great pastries. This curved confection is said to represent the Rio Mondego's tortuous course.

Museu da Ciência. In the university's former chemistry laboratory in a neoclassical building dating from 1773, the city's latest museum constitutes the most important science collection in Portugal and one of the most important in Europe. There are some 250,000 objects on display, and categories include botany, mineralogy, geology, paleontology, astronomy, and medicine with information provided in both English and Portuguese. There are plenty of family-friendly interactive displays and exhibits. ⌂ *Largo Marquês de Pombal* ☎ *239/854350* ⊕ *www.museudaciencia.com* ⌸ *€4* ⊙ *Tues.–Sun. 10–6.*

Sé Nova *(New Cathedral).* The 17th-century Jesuit cathedral was patterned after the baroque church of Il Gesù in Rome, as were many such churches of the day. It took a century to build and shows two distinct styles as fashion changed from classical cleanliness to the florid baroque. The woodwork, from the gilded altarpiece to the blackwood choir stalls, moved across from the Sé Velha (Old Cathedral), are particularly worth a look. There are two organs, both dating to the 18th century. The church became the local cathedral in 1772, 13 years after the abolition of the Jesuit Order by the Marquis of Pombal. There's also a modest ecclesiastical museum. ⌂ *Largo da Sé Nova* ⌸ *Church free; museum €1* ⊙ *Tues.–Sat. 8:30–noon and 2–6:30, Sun. 9–12:30.*

Sé Velha *(Old Cathedral).* Made of massive granite blocks and crowned by a ring of battlements, this 12th-century cathedral looks more like a fortress than a house of worship. (Engaged in an ongoing struggle with the Moors, the Portuguese, who were building and reconstructing castles for defense purposes throughout the country, often incorporated fortifications in their churches.) The harsh exterior is softened somewhat by graceful 16th-century Renaissance doorways. The somber interior has a gilded wooden altarpiece, a late-15th-century example of the Flamboyant Gothic style, created by the Flemish masters Olivier of

Ghent and Jean d'Ypres. The walls of the Chapel of the Holy Sacrament are lined with the touching, lifelike sculptures of Jean de Rouen, whose life-size Christ figure is flanked by finely detailed representations of the apostles and evangelists. The cloisters (closed 1–2 pm), built in the 13th century, are distinguished by a well-executed series of transitional Gothic arches. ⊠ *Largo da Sé Velha* ☎ *239/825273* ✆ *Cathedral free, cloisters €1.50* ⊗ *Mon.–Thurs. and Sat. 10–6, Fri. 10–4.*

■ **NEED A BREAK?**

The cathedral square is ringed with cafés and restaurants. Café Sé Velha (⊠ *Rua da Joaquim António Aguiar 136* ☎ *239/834098*), decorated with azulejos depicting local scenes, is one of the most inviting.

Fodor'sChoice
★

Universidade Velha *(Old University).* Coimbra University is one of the oldest academic institutions in Europe, founded in Lisbon in 1290 and transferred to the Royal Palace of Coimbra in 1537. It's still one of the country's most important universities, and it dominates the city both physically (taking up most of the hill in the center of the old town) and in numbers, with some 20,000 students. Built in 1634 as a triumphal arch, the **Porta Férrea** (⊠ *Praça Porta Férrea*) marks the entrance to the principal university courtyard and is adorned with the figures of the kings Dinis and João III. The courtyard itself holds a statue of Dom João III; it was during his reign that the university moved permanently to Coimbra. Walk to the far end of the courtyard for a view of the Mondego and across it to the Convento de Santa Clara-a-Nova. The double stairway rising from the courtyard leads to the graceful colonnade framing the Via Latina (Latin Way), the scene of colorful student processions at graduation time. Amid much pomp and ceremony, doctoral degrees are presented in the Ceremonial Hall's **Sala dos Capelos,** which is capped with a fine paneled ceiling and lined with a series of portraits of the kings of Portugal.

The 18th-century **clock-and-bell tower,** rising above the courtyard, is one of Coimbra's most famous landmarks. The bell, which summons students to class and in centuries past signaled a dusk-to-dawn curfew, is derisively called the *cabra* (she-goat; an insulting term common in other parts of Europe, particularly the Mediterranean, and used here to express the students' dismay at being confined to quarters). In the courtyard's southwestern corner is a building with four huge columns framing massive wooden doors: behind them is one of the world's most beautiful libraries, the baroque **Biblioteca Joanina.** Constructed in the early 18th century, it has three dazzling book-lined halls and a large painting of the monarch responsible for its construction—Dom João V. The library is open Monday through Saturday from 10 to noon and from 2 to 5; admission is €3. Next to the Biblioteca Joanina is the **Capela de São Miguel** (⊠ *Largo da Porta Férrea* ☎ *239/859900* ✆ *Capela de São Miguel free, Biblioteca Joanina and Sala dos Capelos €3.50, €5 for both* ⊗ *Oct.–Apr. 4, daily 9:30–noon and 2–5; Apr. 5–Sept., daily 9–7:30*), with a fine 16th-century Manueline portal opening onto the courtyard. Begun in 1517, the chapel's glories are nevertheless from the 18th century. Its baroque organ, mannerist main altar, and rococo side altars are stunning. Although there are modern dormitories and apartments, many of the students, some because of tradition and some for economic reasons, prefer the old *repúblicas* (student cooperatives) scattered around the university quarter. Those who

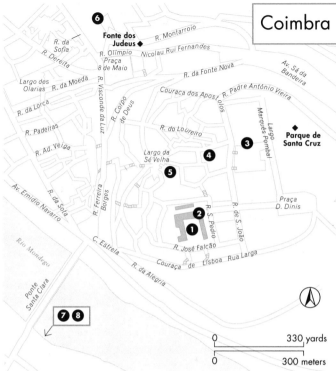

Coimbra

0 — 330 yards
0 — 300 meters

live in these ramshackle houses—with the bare minimum of creature comforts—share costs and chores, allowing themselves the one indulgence of
a cook. The dwellings were hotbeds of anti-Salazar activity during the
years of the dictatorship, and they historically attract people who lean
to the left of the political spectrum. The repúblicas aren't open to the
public, but if you can get an invitation to step inside one, don't pass up
the opportunity for a glimpse of student life. The **República Bota-Abaixo**
(⊠ *Rua São Salvador 6*), near the Museu Machado de Castro, is a typical
example of this Portuguese-style cooperative.

WORTH NOTING

Museu Machado de Castro *(Machado de Castro Museum).* Still undergoing
extensive restoration, visitors may find that the museum is only partially
open. Works should be completed by mid to late 2011 when exhibits will
include a fine collection of sculpture, including works by Jean de Rouen
and Master Pero, and an intriguing little statue of a mounted medieval
knight. The Bishop's Chapel, adorned with 18th-century *azulejos* (painted
and glazed ceramic tiles) and silks, is a highlight of the upstairs galleries,
which contain a diverse selection of Portuguese paintings and furniture.
The building, itself a work of art, was constructed in the 12th century
to house the prelates (bishops) of Coimbra; it was extensively modified
400 years later and was converted to a museum in 1912. Don't miss the

basement's well-preserved vaulted passageways—built by the Romans as storerooms for the forum that was once here—and be sure to take in the view from the terrace of the Renaissance loggia. As you exit the museum, note the large 18th-century azulejo panel depicting Jerónimo translating the Bible. ✉ *Largo Dr. José Rodrigues* 📞 *239/482469* ⊕ *mnmachadodecastro.imc-ip.pt* 🏷️ *€3, free Sun. 9:30–12:30* 🕐 *Apr.– Sept., Tues.–Sun. 10–6; Oct.–Mar., 10–12.30 and 2–6.*

Pátio da Inquisição *(Patio of the Inquisition).* Headquarters of the Portuguese Inquisition from 1548, this fine building, now part of the Coimbra Visual Arts Centre (CAV), as well as an art gallery and exhibition space, is made up of a series of houses, homes of the Inquisitors, and dungeons and torture chambers used to house the accused (mostly Jews who had actually, or only in appearance, converted to Christianity). All of these face onto a deceptively peaceful cloister and garden courtyard. ✉ *Rua Pedro da Rocha* 📞 *239/826178* 🏷️ *Free* 🕐 *Tues.–Sun. 10–7, Fri. 10–10.*

NEED A BREAK?

The **Café Santa Cruz** (✉ *Praça 8 de Maio* 📞 *239/833617* ⊕ *www.cafesantacruz.com*) is one of the most unusual watering holes north of Lisbon. Until its conversion to more pedestrian uses in 1927, this was an auxiliary chapel for the monastery. Now its high-vaulted Manueline ceiling, stained-glass windows, and wood paneling make it a great place in which to indulge a favorite Portuguese pastime: sitting in a café with a strong, murky *bica* (Portugal's answer to espresso) and a brandy, reading the day's newspaper. It's closed Sunday.

WHERE TO EAT

¢   ✕ **À Capella.** This cheap and cheerful student-run bar is in an atmo-
PORTUGUESE   spheric old chapel (Capela de Nossa Senhora da Victória) in the Jewish
Fodor's Choice   Quarter. If you want to eat dinner here, call in advance to reserve a
★   table and place a meal order. Otherwise there are drinks and bar food to
accompany the live fado music every night at 11. ✉ *Capela Nossa Senhora da Victória, Largo da Vitória–Rua Corpo de Deus* 📞 *239/833985* ⊕ *www.acapella.com.pt* ⌲ *Reservations essential* 🍽 *MC, V* 🕐 *No lunch.*

$ ✕ **O Trovador.** Seasoned travelers know that the rule of thumb is to stay
PORTUGUESE   away from restaurants near major sights. But O Trovador—just a step
away from the old cathedral—has good service and regional food as well as a manor house decor with wood paneling and traditional tile work. There is nightly fado in summer and on Friday and Saturday the rest of the year. Reservations are essential for the music. ✉ *Largo da Sé Velha 15–17* 📞 *239/825475* 🍽 *MC, V* 🕐 *Closed Sun.*

$ ✕ **Zé Carioca.** This elegant restaurant in a traditional town house has
BRAZILIAN   several dining rooms, which are slickly furnished with color coordi-
Fodor's Choice   nated decor, plus plenty of mirrors, crisp white tablecloths, and subtle
★   lighting. Best known for its traditional grilled meats, there are plenty of other options on the menu, including a tasty curry with shrimp and coconut milk. ✉ *Av. Sá da Bandeira 89* 📞 *239/835450* ⊕ *www. restaurantezecarioca.com* 🍽 *MC, V* 🕐 *Closed Sun.*

Fado

The word *fado* means "fate" in Portuguese, and like the blues, fado songs are full of the fatalism of the poor and the deprived, laments of abandoned or rejected lovers, and tales of people oppressed by circumstances they cannot change. The genre, probably an outgrowth of a popular sentimental ballad form called the *modinha,* seems to have emerged some time in the first half of the 19th century in the poor quarters of Lisbon. At first, fado was essentially a music of the streets, a bohemian art form born and practiced in the alleys and taverns of Lisbon's Mouraria and Alfama quarters. By the end of the century, though, fado had made its way into the drawing rooms of the upper classes. Portugal's last king, Dom Carlos I, was a fan of the form, and a skilled guitar player to boot.

Strictly an amateur activity in its early years, fado began to turn professional in the 1930s with the advent of radio, recording, and the cinema. The political censorship exercised at the time by Portugal's long-lasting Salazar dictatorship also influenced fado's development. Wary of the social comments *fadistas* might be tempted to make in their lyrics, the authorities leaned on them heavily. Fado became increasingly confined to fado houses, where the singers needed professional licenses and had their repertoires checked by the official censor.

Nowadays, although the tradition of fado sung in taverns and bars by amateurs (called *fado vadio* in Portuguese) is still strong, the place to hear fado—the Lisbon form of it, at least—is in a professional fado house. Called *casas de fado,* the houses are usually restaurants, too, and some of them mix the pure fado with folk dancing shows. Casas de fado are frequented by Portuguese, so don't be wary of one being a tourist trap.

There are two basic styles of fado: Coimbra and Lisbon. In both forms the singer is typically accompanied by three, or sometimes more, guitarists, at least one of whom plays the Portuguese guitar, a pear-shape 12-string descendant of the English guitar introduced into Portugal by the British port wine community in Porto in the 19th century. It is the Portuguese guitar that gives the musical accompaniment of fado its characteristically plaintive tone, as the musician plays variations on the melody. The other instruments are usually classical Spanish guitars, which the Portuguese call *violas.*

Although the greatest names of Lisbon fado have been women, and the lyrics often deal with racy, down-to-earth themes, Coimbra fado is always sung by men, and the style is more lyrical than that of the capital. The themes tend to be more elevated, too—usually serenades to lovers or plaints about the trials of love.

c
PORTUGUESE
✕ **Zé Manel dos Ossos.** This back-alley hole-in-the-wall has simple wooden tables and chairs, an open kitchen with a jumble of pots and pans, and walls plastered with an intriguing assortment of scribbled poems and cartoons. The food is great and cheap, so don't pass up the chance for a meal here—if you can get in (it's a favorite with students). For such a small place, it has an amazing choice of dishes, including a wonderful *sopa da pedra* (a rich vegetable soup served with hot stones in the pot

to keep it warm). ⊠ *Beco do Forno 12* ☎ *239/823790* ✍ *Reservations not accepted* ⊟ *No credit cards* ⊙ *Closed Sun. No dinner Sat.*

WHERE TO STAY

$ ⊞ **Astória.** The domed, triangular Astória faces the Rio Mondego and has been a Coimbra landmark since its construction in 1927. If you like your hotels with old-world charm and comforts, then you'll like this veteran. The rooms are a tad old fashioned but have plush furnishings and spacious bathrooms. Choose between a river view and the floodlighted rooftops of the old town. The two round-tower suites have the best views of all and are appropriately sumptuous. **Pros:** an iconic historic building; highly professional service. **Cons:** the hotel's former excellent restaurant has closed; no Wi-Fi in rooms. ⊠ *Av. Emídio Navarro 21* ☎ *239/853020* ⊕ *www.almeidahotels.com* ⌑ *60 rooms, 2 suites* ⌂ *In-room: a/c. In-hotel: Wi-Fi hotspot, parking (paid)* ⊟ *AE, DC, MC, V* ⦿⃒ *CP.*

¢   ⊞ **Casa Pombal.** A multilingual Dutch woman runs this charming, laid-back pension in a town house on the hill in the heart of the old town. The brightly painted rooms are simple and basic with wood floors, and the rooftop views are stunning, particularly from the two attic rooms. This is one of the friendliest places to stay, as travelers chat freely in the small courtyard. The buffet breakfast is more generous than most and includes a vegetarian option and plenty of locally sourced preserves, cold cuts, and cheeses. Book ahead. **Pros:** homey atmosphere; great views. **Cons:** rooms are on the small size; no a/c. ⊠ *Rua das Flores 18,* ☎ *239/835175* ⊕ *www.casapombal.com* ⌑ *10 rooms, 3 with bath* ⌂ *In-room: no a/c, no phone, no TV. In-hotel: Wi-Fi hotspot* ⊟ *AE, MC, V* ⦿⃒ *BP.*

¢   ⊞ **Dona Inês.** This modern glass-and-marble hotel is on the banks of the Mondego, just a few minutes' walk from the business district and not too far from the historic center. The rooms have benefited from a recent refurbishment and now sport glossy dark wood floors and attractive modern furnishings and bathrooms. An indoor pool, plus spa and Jacuzzi, opened in the spring of 2011. The hotel is one of the city's most popular venues for conferences with several meeting rooms and a business center. The restaurant is large and a little impersonal, but serves solidly reliable Portuguese cuisine, while the bar prides itself on its international head spinning cocktails. **Pros:** complimentary foreign newspapers; efficient staff. **Cons:** emphasis on business groups; not centrally located. ⊠ *Rua Abel Dias Urbano 12* ☎ *239/855800* ⊕ *www.hotel-dona-ines.pt* ⌑ *84 rooms, 12 suites* ⌂ *In-room: a/c. In-hotel: restaurant, room service, bar, tennis court, pool, spa, Internet terminal, Wi-Fi hotspot, parking (free)* ⊟ *AE, DC, MC, V* ⦿⃒ *BP, MAP.*

$$$$ ⊞ **Quinta das Lágrimas.** A former palace, this small Relais & Chateau hotel is on the grounds of the estate where Inês de Castro was supposedly killed at the order of her husband's father. The public rooms are laden with antiques, and guest rooms are furnished simply but with patrician style. The hotel has opened a modern extension (ask for rooms in the old section if possible), and a luxurious, ultramodern spa. Several rooms look over the magnificent 30 acres of garden. At the Michelin star Arcadas da Capela restaurant ($$$$), the menu sometimes offers recipes dating from the 18th century and often uses homegrown herbs, fruits, and vegetables. It has an excellent list of Portuguese and foreign wines. **Pros:** evocative historical surroundings; rates drop by half when booked online. **Cons:** expensive rates; modern wing may be too minimalist for some. ⊠ *Rua António Augusto Gonçalves* ☏ *239/802380* ⊕ *www.hotelquintadaslagrimas.com* ⤴ *35 rooms, 4 suites* ⚙ *In-room: a/c, safe, Wi-Fi. In-hotel: restaurant, room service, bar, golf course, tennis court, pool, spa, laundry service, Internet terminal, Wi-Fi hotspot, parking (free)* ▭ *AE, DC, MC, V* ⊺⊙⏐ *BP, MAP.*

OUTDOOR ACTIVITIES

O Choupal, a pleasant wooded area along the river at the city's west end, was originally a poplar grove planted as a buffer against floods. The park has a place in Coimbra's history as a setting for student serenades and poetic meditation. It's now used more by joggers than romantics. East of the old city on Praça da República, **Parque de Santa Cruz** *(Santa Cruz Park)* is a pleasant mixture of luxuriant vegetation, ornate fountains, and meandering walking paths.

BOATING

O Basófias (⊠ *Parque Dr. Manuel Braga* ☏ *969/830664* ⊕ *www.basofias. com*) offers leisurely 45-minute boat trips on the river, Tuesday–Sunday throughout the year. In winter, there are departures at 3, 4, and 5. In summer, they leave at 3, 4, 5, 6 and 7. Boats depart from the pier in Parque Dr. Manuel Braga, just upriver from the Santa Clara Bridge. The cost is €6 per person.

June through September, the student-run **O Pioneiro do Mondego** (☏ *239/ 478385* ⊕ *www.pioneirodmeng.blogspot.com*) conducts kayak trips on the Rio Mondego. You're picked up at 10 am in Coimbra and taken by minibus to Penacova, a peaceful little river town 25 km (15 mi) to the north. The descent takes about three hours, but plan on a day for the whole outing. Call the English-speaking staff for information and reservations. Trips cost €20 per person, including kayak rental.

HIKING/KAYAKING

Trans Serrano (☏ *235/778938* ⊕ *www.transserrano.com*) is an outdoor and adventure company based near Lousã Mountain, about 20 km (12 mi) southeast of Coimbra. They will provide transport and English-speaking guides for nature hikes, cultural rambles, and kayaking in the surrounding countryside.

HORSEBACK RIDING

You can arrange to horseback ride for an hour or two or take longer equestrian excursions at the **Centro Hípico de Coimbra** (⊠ *Mata do Choupal* ☏ *239/837695* ⊕ *www.centrohipicodecoimbra.blogspot.com*). It's on the right bank of the Rio Mondego, 2 km (1 mi) or so downstream from the Santa Clara Bridge.

TENNIS

At the **Clube Tenis de Coimbra** (⊠ *Av. Urbano Duarte, Quinta da Estrela* ☏ *239/403469* ⊕ *www.clubeteniscoimbra.com*), nonmembers pay a €6-per-hour court fee that covers two to four players. Rackets are available for free, but you'll have to bring your own balls or buy them from the club.

7

SHOPPING

In addition to the ubiquitous lace and cockerels, numerous stores in the city sell delicate blue-and-white Coimbra ceramics, most of them reproductions of 17th- and 18th-century patterns. This style is very distinct from the jolly earthenware associated with Portugal and can be difficult to find in other regions.

The Baixa district by the river is crowded with shops, selling everything from souvenirs to underwear and tablecloths. Major shopping streets are Rua Ferreira Borges, Praça do Comércio, Rua Eduardo Coelho, Rua Fernão de Magalhães, and Rua Visconde da Luz. The Mercado Municipal (Municipal Market) in Rua Olímpio Nicolau Rui Fernandes has a good collection of fruits and vegetables, but is not particularly charming or photogenic.

Dolce Vita (✉ *Rua General Humberto Delgado, Coimbra* ☎ *239/086302* ⊕ *www.dolcevita.pt* ☉ *Mon.–Sat. 10–10*) is a four-level glass-and-steel commercial center that has won several design awards. All the high street chains are here, as well as restaurants and cinemas. If you like mega-size commercial centers, **Forum Coimbra** (✉ *Rua da Guarda Inglesa, Coimbra* ☎ *214/136000* ⊕ *www.forumcoimbra.com* ☉ *Mon.–Sat. 10–10*) is another good bet with 146 shops, a six-screen cinema, and a large food court.

THE WESTERN BEIRAS

The western Beiras encompass shore and mountain, fishing villages and country towns, wine country and serene forest. Sights to see range from castles to cathedrals, monasteries to museums. You can also just lie in the sun by the Atlantic or sample the restorative powers of the air and mineral water in one of the inland towns.

On the gentle-faced coast, long, sandy beaches and sunbaked dunes stretch from Figueira da Foz, on the Mondego River estuary, north toward the great lagoon at Aveiro, where colorful kelp boats bob beyond fine, white-sand beaches. A bit farther inland are the vineyards of the Dão region, the Serra do Caramulo range, the lush forests of Buçaco, and the sedate spa resorts of Curia and Luso.

CONÍMBRIGA

16 km (10 mi) southwest of Coimbra.

GETTING HERE AND AROUND

There are direct buses from Coimbra to Conímbriga that leave from Rua João de Ruão 18 in the center of Coimbra at 9 am and 9:35 am, run by AVIC Joalto bus company. The bus returns at 1 and 6 pm, and the journey takes approximately 30 minutes.

ESSENTIALS

Bus AVIC Joalto (✉ *Rua João d Ruão 18, Coimbra* ☎ *239/823768* ⊕ *www.joalto.pt*).

EXPLORING

Fodor'sChoice
★

Conímbriga. One of the Iberian Peninsula's most important archaeological sites, Conímbriga began as a small settlement in Celtic or possibly pre-Celtic times. In 27 BC, during his second Iberian visit, the emperor Augustus established a Roman province that came to be called Lusitania. It was in this period that, as the Portuguese historian Jorge Alarcão wrote, "Conímbriga was transformed by the Romans from a village where people just existed into a city worth visiting." It still is.

One enters the bucolic setting via a brick reception pavilion. Pools and gardens surround the museum in which the site's Iron Age origins, heyday as a prosperous Roman town, and decline after the 5th-century barbarian conquests are chronicled. The museum also contains artifacts unearthed at the site; it's best to tour it after seeing the excavations.

At the site's entrance is a portion of the original Roman road that connected Olissipo (as Lisbon was then known) and the northern town of Braga. If you look closely, you can make out ridges worn into the stone by cart wheels. The uncovered area represents just a small portion of the Roman city, but within it are some wonderful mosaic floors. The 3rd-century House of the Fountains has a large, macabre mosaic depicting Perseus offering the head of Medusa to a monster from the deep, an example of the amazing Roman craftsmanship of the period.

Across the way is the Casa do Cantaber (House of Cantaber), named for a nobleman whose family was captured by invading barbarians in 465. A tour of the house reveals the comfortable lifestyle of Roman nobility at the time. Private baths included a *tepidarium* (hot pool) and *frigidarium* (cold pool).a Remnants of the central heating system that was beneath the floor are also visible. Fresh water was carried 3 km (2 mi) by aqueduct from Alcabideque; parts of the original aqueduct can still be seen. A bus that leaves from Rua João de Ruão 18—in the center of Coimbra and close to the river—drops you off right by the entrance to the ruins. The one-way fare is €1.50. ⊠ *Condeixa-a-Velha* ☎ *239/941177* ⊕ *www.conimbriga. pt* ⊠ *Ruins and museum Tues –Fri. €4, ruins only Mon. €2* ☉ *Ruins and Museum June–Sept., Tues.–Sun. 9–8; Oct.–May, Tues.–Sun. 10–6.*

WHERE TO EAT AND STAY

$$
PORTUGUESE

✕ **O Cabritino.** This friendly local village restaurant is strongly recommended by locals, including many people who head out from Coimbra to eat here. It has excellent traditional Portuguese food, including its signature *cabrito assado* (roast kid, as in baby goat), after which the restaurant is named. The restaurant is on the same street as the Pousada de Santa Cristina. ⊠ *Rua Francisco Lemos 9, Condeixa-a-Nova* ☎ *239/944111* ⊕ *www.ocabritino.pt* ⊟ *AE, DC, MC, V.*

$ **Pousada de Santa Cristina.** This modern pousada in the delightful town of Condeixa-a-Nova makes an ideal base for visiting the Roman ruins at Conímbriga, 1 km (½ mi) to the south, and Coimbra, 15 km (9 mi) to the northeast. The attractive inn contains spacious, comfortably furnished rooms sporting floral bedspreads and drapes and sunny yellow paintwork. The rooms have small private terraces overlooking the lawn and pool. The hotel is also home to one of the area's best traditional restaurants ($$–$$$). **Pros:** excellent facilities; tranquil location. **Cons:** car

The Beiras

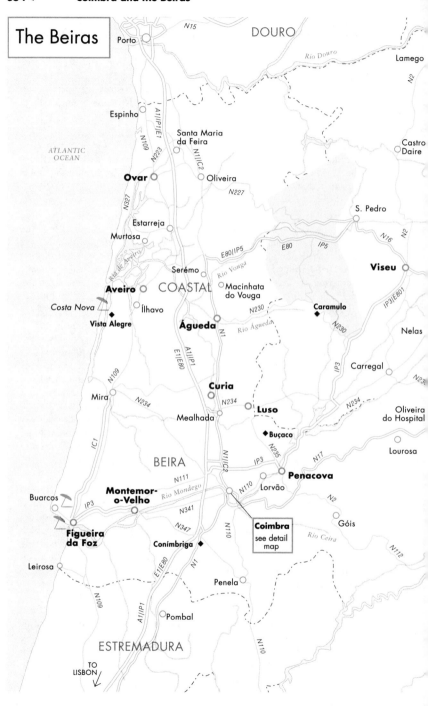

DOURO

Porto

N15

Rio Douro

Lamego

N2

Espinho

Santa Maria
da Feira

Castro
Daire

ATLANTIC
OCEAN

Ovar

Oliveira

N227

S. Pedro

Estarreja

Murtosa

E80/IP5

E80

IP5

N16

N2

Viseu

Serémo

Rio Vouga

Aveiro

COASTAL

Macinhata
do Vouga

Caramulo

IP3/E801

Costa Nova

Ílhavo

N230

Nelas

Vista Alegre

Águeda

Rio Águeda

N1

N230

Carregal

N230

Mira

N109

N234

Curia

E1/E80

A1/IP1

N234

Luso

N234

Oliveira
do Hospital

Mealhada

Buçaco

N235

IP3

N17

Lourosa

BEIRA

N111

Penacova

IP3

N1/IC2

N110

Lorvão

N2

Buarcos

Montemor-o-Velho

Rio Mondego

N341

N110

Góis

**Figueira
da Foz**

IC1

N347

N110

Coimbra
see detail
map

Rio Ceira

N112

Conímbriga

Leirosa

E1/E80

N1

Penela

N109

A1/IP1

Pombal

N110

ESTREMADURA

TO
LISBON

7

Leomil

N226

BEIRA ALTA

Aguir
da Beira

Trancoso

N102/IP2

Vila Nova
de Foz Côa

Rio Douro

Rio Agueda

Castelo
Rodrigo

N221

Pinhel

Almeida

N324

N340

N226

Freixedas

Celorico
da Beira

N221

N17

E80/IP5

E80/IP5

Mangualde

Linhares

Guarda

Castelo
Mendo

N324

N931

Gouveia

PARQUE NATURAL DA SERRA DA ESTRELA

N18-1

N18

N233-3

Aldeia
da Ponte

N339

Seia

Manteigas

Valhelhas

Centum
Cellas

Sortelha

Sabugal

N233-3

Torre

Penhas
da Saude

N339

Belmonte

Serra de Malcata

Covilhã

SPAIN

Rio Zêzere

E802/
N18

N345

N346

Penamacor

N238

Fundão

Alpedrinha

E802/N18

BEIRA BAIXA

Monsanto

Rio Erjas

ambas

N112

N233

Castelo
Branco

TO
PORTALEGRE

N240

0   20 miles

0   30 km

E802/
IP6

essential; rooms may be too flowery for some. ⊠ *Rua Francisco Lemos, Condeixa-a-Velha* ☎ *239/944025* ⊕ *www.pousadas.pt* ➽ *45 rooms* ⅏ *In-room: a/c, Wi-Fi. In-hotel: restaurant, tennis court, pool, Internet terminal, Wi-Fi hotspot, parking (free)* ⊟ *AE, DC, MC, V* ⅃◎⅃ *BP.*

MONTEMOR-O-VELHO

20 km (12 mi) west of Coimbra; 16 km (10 mi) northwest of Conímbriga.

GETTING HERE AND AROUND

The most scenic route from Coimbra to the castle, N341, runs along the Rio Mondego's south bank. The route through the village to the castle is extraordinarily complicated; park in the main square and walk up the rest of the way.

EXPLORING

Montemor-o-Velho. On a hill overlooking the fertile Mondego basin between Coimbra and Figueira da Foz, Montemor-o-Velho figures prominently in the region's history and legends. One popular story tells how the castle's besieged defenders cut the throats of their own families to spare them a cruel death at the hands of the Moorish invaders; many died before the attackers were repulsed. The following day the escaping Moors were pursued and thoroughly defeated. Legend has it that all those slaughtered at Montemor were resurrected but forever carried a red mark on their necks as a reminder of the battle.

The castle walls and tower are largely intact, though thanks to damage done during the Napoleonic invasions in 1811, little remains inside the impressive ramparts to suggest this was a noble family's home that once garrisoned 5,000 troops. Archaeological evidence indicates the hill has been fortified for more than 2,000 years. Although the castle played an important role in the long-standing conflict between the Christians and Moors, changing hands many times, the structure seen today is primarily of 14th-century origin. There are threads of the story of Inês de Castro here, for in January 1355 Dom Afonso IV, meeting in the castle with his advisers, made the decision to murder her. The two churches on the hill are also part of the castle complex; the Igreja de Santa Maria de Alcaçova dates from the 11th century and contains some well-preserved Manueline additions. ☎ *239/680380* ⊠ *Free* ☉ *July–Sept., daily 10–9; Oct.–June, daily 10–5:30.*

WHERE TO EAT

$$
PORTUGUESE
Fodor's Choice
★

✕ **Restaurante a Moagem.** Established in 1987, this restaurant is famed in these parts for its regional cuisine. Dine on specialties like *arroz de tamboril* (monkfish with rice), *bacalhau com natas* (codfish with cream), and *arroz de pata* (rice with duck). Dishes are immaculately presented (not always the case in Portugal!), with the menu changing according to what is fresh and in season. The dining room is elegant, without being stuffy and the service exemplary. ⊠ *Largo Macedo Sotto Mayor—Ponte da Alagoa, Montemor-o-Velho* ☎ *239/680225* ⊕ *www.amoagem.com* ⊟ *DC, MC, V* ☉ *Closed Mon.*

FIGUEIRA DA FOZ

14 km (8½ mi) west of Montemor-o-Velho.

There are various theories as to the origin of the name Figueira da Foz. The consensus around the busy fishing harbor at this seaside resort favors the literal translation: "the fig tree at the mouth of the river." The belief is that when this was just a small settlement, oceangoing fishermen and traders from up the river would arrange to meet at the big fig tree to conduct their business. Although today there are no fig trees to be seen, the name has stuck.

Shortly before the turn of the last century, with the improvement of road and rail access, Figueira, with its long, sandy beach and mild climate, developed into a popular resort. Today, although the beach is little changed, a broad four-lane divided boulevard runs along its length. The town side is lined with the usual mélange of apartments, hotels, and restaurants, but the beachfront has been spared from development.

GETTING HERE AND AROUND

Both bus and train services run to Figueira da Foz. Rede Expressos runs three daily buses to/from Lisbon (2¾ hours) and two daily to Leiria (one hour). Other services include hourly trips to Coimbra (1¼ hours). Trains are operated by Comboios de Portugal (CP), and there are regular services to Coimbra, Leiria, Sintra, and Lisbon. The train and bus stations are located in the same building, around a 20-minute walk east of the center.

ESSENTIALS

Bus Bus Station (✉ Av. de Saraiva de Carvalho, Figueira da Foz ☎ 233/402000 ⊕ www.rede-expressos.pt).

Hospitals Hospital Distrital da Figueira da Foz (✉ Gala, Figueira da Foz ☎ 233/402000).

Train Train Station (✉ Av. de Saraiva de Carvalho, Figueira da Foz ☎ 808/208208 ⊕ www.cp.pt).

Visitor Info Buarcos (✉ Largo Tomas de Aquino ☎ 233/433019 ✎ agueda@rotadaluz.pt). **Figueira da Foz** (✉ Av. 25 de Abril ☎ 233/422610 ⊕ www.figueiraturismo.com).

EXPLORING

Just 2 km (1 mi) north of Figueira, the town of **Buarcos** has retained some of the character of a Portuguese fishing village in spite of a heavy influx of tourists. Here colorfully painted boats are still pulled up onto the sandy beach, fishermen sit around mending nets, and many of the houses are coated in brightly colored tiles.

NEED A BREAK? There are roughly a dozen brightly painted wooden-shack restaurants on the beach. These are wonderful places for fresh grilled fish or just a cold drink. With a large sign proclaiming its name, **A Plataforma** (✉ Buarcos) is one of the best.

One of Figueira da Foz's more curious sights is the 18th-century **Casa do Paço** *(Palace House)*, the interior of which is decorated with about

7,000 Delft tiles. These Dutch tiles were salvaged from a shipwreck at the mouth of the harbor in the late 1600s. ✉ *Largo Prof. Vitor Guerra 4, around corner from main post office* ☎ *233/401320* 🎫 *Free* ⊘ *Weekdays 9:30–12:30 and 2–5.*

Centro de Artes e Espectáculos (CAE), an impressive arts center designed by Luís Marçal Grilo, sits among the open green spaces of the Parque das Abadias. Inside, the space is flexible enough to host a variety of performance events and also includes exhibition space used for arts, crafts, and photography, plus a cinema. ✉ *Rua Abade Pedro* ☎ *233/407200* ⊕ *www.cae.pt* 🎫 *Exhibits free* ⊘ *Gallery Mon.–Thurs. 10–7, Fri. 10–9.30, weekends and holidays 2–6.*

> **GREAT VIEWS**
>
> **Farol de Cabo Mondego.** Drive out to the cape where the Cape Mondego Lighthouse stands for a wonderfully uncluttered view of the coastline. The road traces a loop and returns to Buarcos.

The triangular 17th-century **Fortaleza da Santa Catarina** *(Santa Catarina Fortress)*, adjacent to the beachfront tennis courts, was occupied by the French during the early days of the Peninsular War.

Palácio Sotto Mayor, an elegantly furnished, French-style manor house, was constructed as part of the wave of development in the late 19th and early 20th century that made Figueira da Foz a world-class resort. Long in the hands of one of Portugal's leading families, the building now belongs to the owners of the casino, and local gossip has it that it was "donated" as payment for gambling debts. Its collection includes paintings and fine furnishings. ✉ *Rua Joaquim Sotto Mayor* ☎ *233/422121* 🎫 *€1* ⊘ *Tues.–Sun. 2–6.*

WHERE TO EAT

$
PORTUGUESE
Fodor'sChoice
★

✗ **O Peleiro.** In the quiet village of Paião, 10 km (6 mi) from Figueira, this restaurant—all wood and tiles—was once a tannery, and that's what the name means. Heavy on regional specialties, the menu includes *sopa da pedra* (vegetable soup)—a must. Grilled pork or veal on a spit are also excellent, and there's a good wine selection. ✉ *Largo do Alvideiro 5-7, Paião* ☎ *233/940120* ▭ *AE, MC, V* ⊘ *Closed Sun. and 1st 2 wks of May and Sept.*

$
PORTUGUESE

✗ **Quinta de Santa Catarina.** The fish dishes at this popular restaurant—in a garden on the outskirts of the town—are outstanding. The menu varies depending on the catch of the day, but ask if one of the *tambril* (monkfish) dishes is available. The house also does a really good *rojões á minhota* (Minho-style sautéed pork). ✉ *CAE, Rua Abade Pedro* ☎ *233/423468* ▭ *AE, MC, V* ⊘ *Closed Mon.*

$
SEAFOOD

✗ **Teimoso.** Although the menu choices are varied, seafood—sold by weight—is what put this seaside restaurant on the map. Parties of four can opt for the tasty *paella de marisco* (seafood paella). Locals and visitors alike gather in the dining room, which has large picture windows, to order the shellfish that comes fresh from huge saltwater tanks. Nonfish aficionados won't go hungry, however, there are several meat choices, including grilled pork, chicken curry, and roasted duck with an orange sauce. ✉ *Av. D. João 11, 70, Cabo Mondego, Buarcos* ☎ *233/402720* ▭ *AE, MC, V.*

WHERE TO STAY

¢ 🏠 **Casa da Azenha Velha.** An attractively converted flour mill on a farm
☾ a few kilometers out of town, this is a perfect place for families, with
a lovely pool, games room, and host of animals from peacocks to
ostriches and horses; horseback riding is available for guests. With
breakfast and the sitting room in the main house, the charmingly decorated bedrooms are all in converted outbuildings. There is a separate
restaurant, Azenha ($$), on the farm. **Pros:** wonderful rustic setting;
sociable. **Cons:** remote location; popular with families with children, so
can be noisy. ⊠ *Caceira de Cima* ☎ *233/425041* ⟿ *6 rooms, 1 apart-
ment* ♿ *In-room: a/c. In-hotel: restaurant, tennis court, Wi-Fi hotspot,
parking (free), some pets allowed* ⊟ *No credit cards* ⊚*I BP.*

¢ 🏠 **Hospedaria Sãozinha.** These recently refurbished and attractive three-
story hotel has a welcoming homey feel. The spotless rooms are taste-
fully furnished with comfy armchairs, shiny tiled floors, and cozy rugs.
Several rooms have small balconies overlooking the street. Aside from
satellite TV and the advantage of easy street parking, the hotel has lim-
ited facilities. Breakfast is not available, but there are plenty of cafés
nearby. **Pros:** convenient location; spotless rooms. **Cons:** no views; small
bathrooms. ⊠ *Ladeira do Monte 43, Figueira da Foz* ☎ *233/425243*
⊕ *www.hospedariasaozinha.com* ⟿ *12 rooms* ♿ *In-room: a/c, no
phone, no TV* ⊟ *MC, V* ⊚*I EP.*

¢ 🏠 **Ibis.** On a quiet street just a five-minute walk from the well known
Claridade beach, this small three-star hotel is in an attractive remod-
eled stone building built in 1914, fronted by trees. It has all the modern
appointments Ibis fans expect, and offers well-maintained, comfortable
rooms, although they are a tad bland with the predictable Ibis style pine
furniture and dark fabrics. However you can't beat the price, especially
given the excellent location. **Pros:** efficient service; clean rooms. **Cons:**
no restaurant; small rooms. ⊠ *Rua da Liberdade 20* ☎ *233/422051*
⊕ *www.ibishotel.com* ⟿ *47 rooms* ♿ *In-room: a/c, Wi-Fi. In-hotel: bar,
some pets allowed* ⊟ *AE, DC, MC, V* ⊚*I BP.*

¢ 🏠 **Mercure.** Tour groups favor this five-story, 1950s-vintage hotel, per-
haps because it overlooks a broad, sandy beach. From the glossy marble
lobby to the slick modern rooms, the decor is up to date and inviting.
Rooms are spacious and airy with sea views costing slightly more than
city views. Seafront rooms have small balconies, and the large pool
has a view of the beach. The restaurant, Astrolabeo ($$–$$$) serves
international dishes as well as regional specialties. The hotel has an
exhaustive list of facilities, including some surprising extras—like a
tanning salon. **Pros:** impeccably clean; ample sea views. **Cons:** service
can be perfunctory; gets booked up early in the summer. ⊠ *Av. 25 de
Abril 22* ☎ *233/403900* ⊕ *www.accorhotel.com* ⟿ *102 rooms, 1 suite*
♿ *In-room: a/c, safe, Wi-Fi. In-hotel: restaurant, tennis court, pool,
gym, spa, beachfront, children's programs (ages 6–12), laundry service,
Wi-Fi hotspot, parking (paid)* ⊟ *AE, DC, MC, V* ⊚*I BP, MAP.*

NIGHTLIFE

The 1886 gaming room of the **Casino da Figueira** has frescoed ceilings,
chandeliers, and a variety of table games, including blackjack and
American and Continental roulette. Banks of slot machines lie in wait

in a separate room. Within the same building there's also a belle epoque show room—site of a nightly revue at 11—as well as two cinemas, a piano bar that also has regular fado, and a restaurant. The shows are free, but drinks are expensive. Although dress is casual, jeans and T-shirts aren't permitted. The minimum age to enter is 18; bring your passport. ⊠ *Av. Bernado Lopes* ☎ *233/408400* ⊕ *www.casinofigueira. pt* 🖅 *Gaming room free* ⊙ *Table games daily 5 pm–3 am, slot machines daily 3 pm–3 am.*

SPORTS AND OUTDOOR ACTIVITIES

Activity centers on the water here. The fishing for sea bream, bass, and mullet is good at Cape Mondego and at Costa de Lavos and Gala beaches, just south of town. Carp and barbel are caught in the Quiaios Lakes, northeast of Buarcos.

You can rent sailboards and other water-sports gear from most resorts on the shore of either Figueira or Buarcos. The Quiaios Lakes are also popular for windsurfing. Board surfers often find 10- to 12-foot waves at Quiaios Beach (just north of Cape Mondego).

BOATING

Throughout the year, you can do boat and kayaking trips on the Mondego River with **Capitão Dureza** (⊠ *Rua Principal 64C, Telhado, Penacova* ☎ *918/315337* ⊕ *www.capitaodureza.com*).

EN ROUTE The most scenic route north from Buarcos is a winding road that climbs through a wooded area to the little village of Boa Viagem (Good Journey). From here you can trace the course of the Rio Mondego as it flows into the sea and then head north, following a narrow road that runs along the sand dunes to Aveiro, or turn inland to Vagos and pick up N109 to Vista Alegre.

VISTA ALEGRE

50 km (31 mi) northeast of Buarcos.

Portugal's finest china is produced here by a business that was started in 1824 as a sort of commune. Housing was furnished for workers from all parts of the country, training was provided by French master craftsmen, and the clay came from the nearby town of Ovar. Today the settlement's large, tree-filled square is bordered by the factory, a china museum and gift shop, and a small 17th-century chapel with the delicately carved tomb of the chapel's founder.

GETTING HERE AND AROUND

Unless you have your own wheels, the most convenient method of transport is by hopping on the Vista Alegre Tour, which is available from the tourist office in Aveiro 5 km (3 mi) east of Vista Alegre and includes all transportation and entrance fees.

ESSENTIALS

Visitor Info **Aveiro** (*Rua João Mendonça 8* ☎ *234/423680*). **Ílhavo** (⊠ *Praça do Municipio* ☎ *234/325911*).

EXPLORING

Through its collection of hundreds of magnificent pieces, the **Museu Histórico da Vista Alegre** *(Vista Alegre Historical Museum)* traces the development of fine porcelain at the factory from the 1850s to the present day. ✉ *Off N109* ☎ *234/320600* ⊕ *www.vistaalegreatlantis.com* 🎫 *Free* ⊙ *Tues.–Fri. 9–6, weekends 9–12:30 and 2–5.*

Two kilometers (1 mi) northeast of Vista Alegre is the small town of Ílhavo, with its brightly tiled art nouveau houses and its **Museu Marítimo de Ilhavo** *(Ilhavo Maritime Museum)*. Housed in a drab concrete building next to a fish-processing plant, the museum has an interesting collection documenting the region's close relationship with the sea and its mainstay of cod fishing. It also has some good early pieces of Vista Alegre china. ✉ *Rua Vasco da Gama, Ílhavo* ☎ *234/329608* ⊕ *www.museumaritimo. cm-ilhavo.pt* 🎫 *€2.50* ⊙ *Tues.–Fri. 10–6, weekends 2–6.*

AVEIRO

5 km (3 mi) northeast of Vista Alegre.

Aveiro's traditions are closely tied to the sea and to the Ria de Aveiro, the vast, shallow lagoon that fans out to the north and west of town. Salt is extracted from the sea here, and kelp is harvested for use as fertilizer. Swan-necked *moliceiros* (kelp boats) still glide along canals that run through Aveiro's center. In much of the older part of town, sidewalks and squares are paved with *calçada* (traditional Portuguese hand-laid pavement) in intricate nautical patterns. The town's most attractive buildings date from the latter half of the 17th century. In the last couple of years, a massive restoration project has transformed the old fishermen's quarter, just off the main canal, into a delightful little area of small bars and restaurants. A central market square hosts live entertainment in summer months.

GETTING HERE AND AROUND

There is no bus station in Aveiro, but Rede Expressos has several services including to/from Lisbon (3½ hours), Coimbra (2½ hours), Guarda (1½ hours), and Faro (6 hours). There are train services linking Aveiro to Porto, Coimbra, and Lisbon from the train station north east of the center.

ESSENTIALS

Train Station Aveiro (✉ *Av. Dr. Lourenco Peixinho, Aveiro* ☎ *808/208208* ⊕ *www.rede.expressos.pt).*

Visitor Info Aveiro (✉ *Rua João Mendonça 8, Aveiro* ☎ *234/423680* ⊕ *www.rotadaluz.pt).*

EXPLORING
TOP ATTRACTIONS

Convento de Jesus *(Convent of Jesus)*. Aveiro isn't just a fishermen's town. A royal presence is what gave impetus to the town's economic and cultural development. In 1472 Princess Joana, daughter of King Afonso V, retired against her father's wishes to the Convento de Jesus—established by papal bull in 1461—where she spent the last 18 years of her life. After four centuries, the Convento de Jesus was closed in 1874 upon the death of its last nun. It now contains the **Museu de Aveiro,** which encompasses an 18th-century church whose interior is a masterpiece of baroque art. The elaborately gilded wood carvings and ornate ceiling by António Gomes and José Correia from Porto are among Portugal's finest. Blue-and-white azulejo panels have scenes depicting the life of Princess Joana, who was beatified in 1693 and whose tomb is in the lower choir. Her multicolor inlaid-marble sarcophagus is supported at each corner by delicately carved angels. Note also the 16th-century Renaissance cloisters, the splendid refectory lined with camellia-motif tiles, and the chapel of São João Evangelista (St. John the Evangelist). Items on display, many brought from other convents, include sculpture, coaches and carriages, artifacts, and paintings—including a particularly fine 15th-century portrait of Joana by Nuno Gonçalves. ⊠ *Av. de Santa Joana Princesa* ☎ *234/423297* 🎫 *€4* 🕙 *Tues.–Sun. 10–5:30.*

Fodor's Choice
★

Ria de Aveiro. This 45-km (28-mi) hydralike delta of the Rio Vouga, was formed in 1575, when a violent storm caused shifting sand to block the river's flow into the ocean. Over the next two centuries, as more and more sand piled up, the town's prosperity and population tumbled, recovering only when a canal breached the dunes in 1808. Today the lagoon is a unique combination of fresh and salt water, narrow waterways, and tiny islands. Salt marshes and pine forests border the area, and the ocean side is lined with sandy beaches. In this tranquil setting, colorful moliceiros (low-slung, wide-bottom boats with steeply curved and brightly painted prows and sterns) glide gracefully along, their owners harvesting seaweed.

NEED A
BREAK?

Facing the canal, just down Rua João Mendonça from the tourism office, are several little **coffee houses** that specialize in regional *doces* (sweets) such as *ovos moles* (egg-yolk sweets) and biscuits and wafers of various sorts.

🕗 **Ria de Aveiro boat trips.** Although you can drive through the Ria on back roads, the best way to see the area is by boat. From mid-June to mid-September, boat trips around the lagoon depart throughout the day from the main canal, just in front of the tourism office. The fare is €8 for one hour and €22 for a two-hour ride, lunch included. During the low season, boats are available with advance booking. It may also be possible to have a one-hour tour in a moliceiro; tickets can be purchased at the tourist office, or ask at the quay. ⊠ *Canal Central* ☎ *234/838397* 🎫 *€8 or €22* 🕙 *Mid-June–mid-Sept., daily.*

WORTH NOTING

At Aveiro's northeast edge, on Rua João de Moura, the **Estação de Caminhos de Ferro** *(Railway Station)* displays some lovely azulejo panels depicting regional traditions and customs.

On the **Praça da República,** look for the graceful, three-story Câmara Municipal (Town Hall), which has a pointed bell tower. The plaza's 18th-century **Igreja da Misericórdia** *(Mercy Church* ⊠ *Praça da República* ☎ *234/426732* 🎫 *Free* 🕙 *Mon.–Sat. 9–12:30 and 2–5)* has an imposing baroque portal; the walls of the otherwise sober interior are resplendent with blue-and-white azulejos. There's a small museum here with vestments and other religious articles.

For restless youngsters, the large **Parque Municipal** *(City Park)*, south of Aveiro's center on Avenida Artur Ravara, has a well-equipped playground.

Troncalhada Ecomuseum. The museum is a salt pan where traditional methods of making salt are on display. You can see the workers extracting the salt from May until September. If you are planning on visiting, you should reserve in advance. ⊠ *Cais das Pirâmides* ☎ *234/406485* ⊕ *www.cm-aveiro.pt* ✉ *Free* ⊙ *Weekdays 10–12:30 and 2–5:30.*

TIP

The best place for viewing Aveiro's boats is along the Canal Central and Canal de São Roque, which is crossed by several attractive bridges. On the banks, to the west of these canals, are checkerboard fields of gleaming white salt pans. The industry dates back to the 10th century, when salt was used for preserving fish. The bacalhau is still a staple of the Portuguese menu.

WHERE TO EAT

$$ ✕ Mercado do Peixe. This upmarket restaurant is easy to find, just head
SEAFOOD for the city's fish market. Widely considered to be the best place for the freshest seafood in town, specialties include *caldeirada de enguias* (eel stew) and *arroz de marisco* (seafood rice). Surroundings are funky industrial chic with plenty of gleaming metal and large picture windows overlooking the canals and pretty square. ⊠ *Largo da Praça do Peixe, Aveiro* ☎ *234/383511* ✍ *Reservations essential* ▭ *MC, V* ⊙ *No dinner Sun.*

$ ✕ O Mercantel. This restaurant is the brainchild of Senhor Costa (aka
SEAFOOD Costa da Lota), who spent 13 years working at the nearby *lota* (fish market). His skill with fish is locally renowned, and people have applauded his change of career. Specialties include fresh fish, fish stew, and *arroz de marisco* (shellfish with rice). ⊠ *Rua António dos Santos Le 16* ☎ *234/428057* ▭ *AE, DC, MC, V* ⊙ *Closed Mon.*

WHERE TO STAY

¢ ▭ Arcada. At the foot of the bridge over the central canal, the location of this arched, four-story 1930s building couldn't be more convenient. It's a comfortable, family-owned classic with old-fashioned, no-frills comfort. Furnishings in the well-kept rooms have benefited from a recent update and have a glossy modern look with a steely-gray-and-black color scheme and furnishings, contrasting with scarlet cushions on the beds. The lounge and bar recall a gentlemen's club, albeit one that's slightly past its prime. **Pros:** very central; courteous, helpful staff. **Cons:** small bathrooms; rooms a little stark. ⊠ *Rua Viana do Castelo 4* ☎ *234/421885* ⊕ *www.hotelarcada.com* ⋈ *48 rooms, 5 suites* ⅗ *In-room: a/c, Wi-Fi. In-hotel: Wi-Fi hotspot, parking (paid)* ▭ *AE, DC, MC, V* ⊙ *BP.*

¢ ▭ Hotel Aveiro Center. This small, modern hotel—formerly Residential do Alboi—is in an attractive cream colored building (look for the flags) on a quiet backstreet. The rooms have shiny parquet floors, colorful area rugs, and tea- and coffee-making facilities. The staff are courteous, and the breakfast buffet is more generous than most. Located a few blocks from the main canal, there's on street parking just a few minutes walk away. **Pros:** pretty patio; free Wi-Fi. **Cons:** no restaurant; showers only, no tubs. ⊠ *Rua da Arrochela 6* ☎ *234/380390* ⊕ *www.grupoalboi.com* 🛏 *24 rooms* ⚭ *In-room: a/c, Wi-Fi. In-hotel: bar, Internet terminal* ☰ *AE, MC, V* ❑ *BP.*

\$\$

Fodor's Choice

★

Pousada da Ria. This two-story inn is about a 30-minute drive north of Aveiro, near Torreira and midway down the narrow, pine-covered peninsula that separates the Ria da Aveiro from the sea. It's filled with and surrounded by plants and flowers, and the wood-and-tile entry has a loft seating area. Through picture windows in 10 of the cheerfully furnished rooms you can watch the colorfully painted moliceiros glide along the water. The spacious restaurant (\$\$\$–\$\$\$\$), serving traditional Portuguese cuisine, has equally lovely views, a summer terrace, and a highly recommended *ensopada de cabrito* (kid stew). **Pros:** prices considerably lower if booked online; tranquil atmosphere. **Cons:** car is essential; not all rooms have views. ⊠ *Bico do Muranzel, Aveiro, Torreira* ☎ *234/860180* ⊕ *www.pousadas.pt* 🛏 *20 rooms* ⚭ *In-room: a/c, safe. In-hotel: tennis court, pool, Wi-Fi hotspot, parking (paid)* ☰ *AE, DC, MC, V* ❑ *BP.*

¢

Veneza Hotel. Formerly the Hotel Mecure, new ownership has resulted in rooms that were updated in 2009. Several are named after European cities and offer distinctive colors chemes; all are spacious with tasteful furnishings and well-equipped bathrooms. The building is a classic 1930s art deco mansion with a red-tile roof and a sunny yellow-and-white exterior with balconies. A fat palm tree sits in front, and you enter through an old wooden door. It's near the railway station, is pleasant and well run, and offers an excellent buffet breakfast, which can be enjoyed on the terrace, weather permitting. **Pros:** city-center location; recently updated. **Cons:** no restaurant; uninspired views. ⊠ *Rua Luis Gomes de Carvalho 23* ☎ *234/404400* ⊕ *www.venezahotel.pt* 🛏 *49 rooms* ⚭ *In-room: a/c, safe, Internet. In-hotel: bar, laundry service, Internet terminal, Wi-Fi hotspot, parking (paid)* ☰ *AE, MC, V* ❑ *BP.*

OUTDOOR ACTIVITIES

There's no swimming off the lagoon in town, as it's built up with ports, harbors, seafood farms, and salt pans. Within a 20-minute drive you can reach excellent beaches that stretch for miles along the massive sand spit to the north and south of town.

BICYCLING

Near the tourist office on Rua João Mendonça and at other spots around town you'll find racks with bikes that you can use to tour Aveiro and its surroundings. To free a bike, insert a €1 coin as you would a shopping cart. When you return the bike, you get your money back. In case you were wondering, there are tracker devices on the bikes to ensure their return.

HORSEBACK RIDING

Escola Equestre de Aveiro (⊠ *Quinta do Chão d'Agra, Vilarinho* ☎ *234/912108* ⊕ *www.escolaequestreaveiro.com*), about 6 km (4 mi) north of Aveiro on N109, gives classes for all levels and offers rides (reservations are necessary) into the wetlands around Aveiro. Prices range from €30 an

Beaches

There's a virtually continuous stretch of good sandy beach along the entire coastal strip known as the Beira Litoral—from Praia de Leirosa in the south to Praia de Espinho in the north. One word of caution: if your only exposure to Portuguese beaches has been the Algarve's southern coast, be careful here. West-coast beaches tend to have heavy surf and strong undertows and riptides. If you see a red or yellow flag, do *not* go swimming. The water temperature on the west coast is usually a few degrees cooler than it is on the south coast.

You have your choice of beaches. There are fully equipped resorts, such as Figueira da Foz and Buarcos, or if you prefer sand dunes and solitude, you can lay your mat down at any one of the beaches farther north. Just point your car down one of the unmarked roads between Praia de Mira and Costa Nova and head west. The beaches at Figueira da Foz, Tocha, Mira, and Furadouro (Ovar) are well suited to children; they all have lifeguards and have met the European Union standards for safety and hygiene.

hour for a group trek (up to four people) to €37 for an individual one-hour guided tour for a child or adult.

SHOPPING

The **Armazéms de Aveiro** (⊠ *Rua Conselheiro Luís de Magalhães 1* ☎ *234/422107*) sells leading Portuguese brands of high-quality ceramics and china, including Vista Alegre and Quinta Nova. The staff will ship purchases as well. The mall **Forum Aveiro** (⊠ *Rua Batalhão Caçadores 10* ☎ *234/379506* ⊕ *www.forumaveiro.com*, beside the main canal in the center of town, has dozens of little shops and restaurants.

OVAR

24 km (15 mi) north of Aveiro.

At Ria de Aveiro's northern end, Ovar is a good jumping-off point for the string of beaches and sand dunes to the north. This small town, with its many tiled houses, is a veritable showcase of azulejos.

GETTING HERE AND AROUND

Head north on N109 from Aveiro to Estarreja, then turn west and follow N109-5 through quiet farmlands, and after crossing the bridge over the Ria, continue north on N327 to Ovar.

ESSENTIALS

Visitor Info **Ovar** (⊠ *Edifício da Câmara Municipal, Rua Elias Garcia* ☎ *256/572215*).

EXPLORING

The **Câmara Municipal** *(Town Hall)*, built in the 1960s, is adorned with some unusually beautiful multicolor tile panels.

The exterior of the late-17th-century **Igreja Matriz** *(Parish Church)* is completely covered with blue-and-white azulejos. ⊠ *Av. do Bom Reitor and Rua Gomes Freire* ☎ *No phone* ☾ *Mon.–Sat. 9–12:30 and 2:30–5:30.*

The small **Museu de Ovar,** in an old house in the town center, has displays of traditional tiles, regional handicrafts, and costumes and tableaux re-creating scenes from provincial life in the past. There's also a small collection of mementos of popular 19th-century novelist Júlio Dinis, a native of Ovar and its most famous son. ⊠ *Rua Heliodoro Salgado 11* ☎ *256/572822* ⊕ *www.museuovar.wordpress.com* 🎫 *€1.50* ⊙ *Mon.– Wed. 9:30–12:30 and 2:30–5:30, Sat. 9:30–12:30.*

The fairy-tale-like **Castelo de Santa Maria da Feira** *(Castle of Santa Maria da Feira)* is 8 km (5 mi) northeast of Ovar. Its four square towers are crowned with a series of conical turrets in a display of Gothic architecture more common in Germany or Austria than in Portugal. Although the original walls date from the 11th century, the present structure is the result of modifications made 400 years later. From atop the towers you can make out the sprawling outlines of the Ria de Aveiro. ⊠ *Largo do Castelo* ☎ *256/372248* ⊕ *www.castelodafeira.com* 🎫 *€1.50* ⊙ *Tues.– Sun. 9–12:30 and 2–6.*

VISEU

82 km (51 mi) southeast of Ovar; 71 km (44 mi) southeast of Aveiro.

A thriving provincial capital in one of Portugal's prime wine-growing districts, the Dão region, Viseu has remained a country town in spite of its obvious prosperity. Its newer part is comfortably laid out, with parks and wide boulevards that radiate from a central traffic circle.

GETTING HERE AND AROUND

You can take the scenic but twisting and bone-jarring N227 across the Serra da Gralheira or the smoother, faster, but much less interesting IP1 and IP5. Alternatively there are Rede Expressos buses that run to Viseu from several surrounding towns and cities, including Vila Real (1¼ hours), Coimbra (1¼ hours), and Lisbon (3½ hours). The bus station is located just south of the center.

ESSENTIALS

Bus Viseu Bus Station (⊠ *Av. Dr António Jose de Almeida, Viseu* ☎ *232/422822* ⊕ *www.rede-expressos.pt*).

Visitor Info Viseu Tourist Office (⊠ *Av. Calousste Gulbenkian, Viseu* ☎ *232/420950* ⊕ *www.turismodocentro.pt*).

EXPLORING

Largo da Sé. One of Portugal's most impressive squares, it is bound by three imposing edifices—the cathedral, the palace housing the Museu de Grão Vasco, and the palace like Igreja da Misericórdia. The **Sé** (⊠ *Cathedral free, museum €2.50* ⊙ *Cathedral daily 9–12 and 2–5; museum Tues. 2–6, Wed.–Sun. 10–6*), a massive stone structure with twin square bell towers, lends the plaza a solemn air. Construction on this cathedral was started in the 13th century and continued off and on until the 18th century. Inside, massive Gothic pillars support a network of twisted, knotted forms that reach across the high, vaulted roof; a dazzling, gilded, baroque high altar contrasts with the otherwise somber stone. The lines of the 18th-century upper level are harsh when compared with the graceful Italianate arches of the 16th-century lower level.

The walls here are adorned with a series of excellent azulejo panels that depict various religious motifs. To the right of the mannerist main portal is a double-tier cloister, which is connected to the cathedral by a well-preserved Gothic-style doorway. The cathedral's Sacred Art Museum has reliquaries from the 12th and 13th centuries. If the Sé looks more like a fortress, the white, rococo **Igreja da Misericórdia** (*Church of Mercy* ☎*€1.50* ⊙ *Tues. 2–6, Wed.–Sun. 10–6*), across from it looks like a residential palace. The fussy ornamentation around the windows and unusual entranceway are more impressive than the interior.

Museu Grão Vasco *(Grão Vasco Museum).* Housed in a palatial former seminary beside the cathedral, this lovely museum was originally created to display the works of 16th-century local boy Grão Vasco, who became Portugal's most famous painter. In addition to a wonderful collection of altarpieces by him and his students, the museum has a wide-ranging collection of other art and objects, from Flemish masterpieces to Portuguese faience, and Oriental furniture. ⊠ *Paço dos Trê Escalões, Largo da Sé* ☎ *232/422049* ⊕ *www.ipmuseus.pt* ☎*€3, free Sun. until 2* ⊙ *Tues. 2–5:30, Wed.–Sun. 10–12:30 and 2–5:30.*

Praça da República. The tree-lined Praça da República, also known as the Rossío, is framed at one end by a massive azulejo mural depicting scenes of country life. The heroic figure in bronze, standing sword in hand, is Prince Henry the Navigator, the first duke of Viseu. The stately building across from the tile mural is the **Câmara Municipal.** Walk inside to admire the colorful Aveiro tiles and fine woodwork, and be sure to see the courtyard. Just to the south of the square, a graceful stairway leads to the 18th-century, baroque Igreja dos Terceiros de São Francisco (Church of the Brotherhood of St. Francis), behind which is a large, wooded park with paths and ponds.

Almeida Moreira, the first director of the Museu de Grão Vasco, bequeathed his Moorish-style mansion and his diverse collection of paintings, furniture, and ceramics to the city. Today it's the **Casa-Museu Almeida Moreira** *(Almeida Moreira House and Museum).* ⊠ *Rua Soar Cima* ☎ *232/423769* ☎ *Free* ⊙ *Tues.–Sat. 9–12:30 and 2–5:30.*

The square **Praça de Dom Duarte** is one of those rare places where just the right combination of rough stone pavement, splendid old houses, wrought-iron balconies, and views of an ancient cathedral (it's just below the Largo da Sé) come together to produce a magical effect. Try to be here at night, when the romance is further enhanced by the soft glow of the streetlights. There's one restaurant and one café to dip into.

WHERE TO EAT AND STAY

$
PORTUGUESE
Fodor's Choice
★

× **O Cortiço.** Viseu's most celebrated restaurant is known for the sometimes comical names of its dishes as well as for its intelligent use of old local recipes. Try the *coelho bêbedo* (drunk rabbit), which is rabbit stewed in red wine, or the bacalhau *podre* (rotten), which is actually a savory dish of salt cod braised in a tomato-and-wine sauce. ⊠ *Rua Augusto Hilário 47* ☎ *232/423853* ▭ *AE, DC, MC, V.*

¢ ▭ **Avenida.** Owned by a keen collector of African and Chinese antiques, which are liberally scattered across the public and guest rooms, this charming, small town house has the eclectic feel of a bazaar. Deep turquoises and terra-cottas are redolent of a Moroccan market. The bedrooms are small but interestingly decorated, some with antique beds and Portuguese antiques. The friendly owners can help organize activities in the region, including walks and trips in Serra da Estrela and Serra do Caramulo. The breakfast buffet is more generous than most. **Pros:** charming, homey atmosphere; individually decorated rooms. **Cons:** no restaurant; on a busy corner; can be noisy. ⊠ *Av. Alberto Sampaio 1* ☎ *232/423432* ⊕ *www.hotelavenida.com.pt* ⌁ *29 rooms, 2 suites* ⌂ *In-room: a/c, Wi-Fi. In-hotel: Wi-Fi hotspot, some pets allowed* ⊟ *AE, DC, MC, V* ⦿⫶ *BP.*

> **MORE THAN MEETS THE EYE**
>
> The history of Viseu actually goes back a lot farther than the medieval center suggests, with a thriving Iron Age settlement here before the Romans arrived. There are a number of prehistoric dolmens scattered across the surrounding countryside. A statue of a warrior stands on a rock at the edge of town, on the road to Aveiro. It's a monument to **Viriáto**, the leader of the Lusitanian resistance to the Roman invasion in the 2nd century BC. Some historians believe this was the site of his encampment.

$ ⊞ **Grão Vasco.** For many years the Grão Vasco was Viseu's leading hotel. Although it has been overtaken by newer properties, it is still a good choice and a great value. Its location in a wooded park just steps from the main square gives you the convenience of the city and the quiet of the countryside. Many of the rooms have balconies that look out on an oval pool. The restaurant serves a wide variety of principally Portuguese dishes; if it's in season, try the wild boar. **Pros:** surrounded by lovely gardens; plush rooms. **Cons:** can seem a little stuffy. ⊠ *Rua Gaspar Barreiros,* ☎ *232/423511* ⌁ *106 rooms, 3 suites* ⌂ *In-room: a/c, safe. In-hotel: restaurant, pool, Wi-Fi hotspot, parking (paid)* ⊟ *AE, DC, MC, V* ⦿⫶ *EP.*

SHOPPING

Narrow Rua Direita, in the old part of town, is lined with shops displaying locally made wood carvings, pottery, and wrought iron. The surrounding rural areas, particularly north toward Castro Daire, are well known for their strong tradition of linen, basketry, and heavy woolen goods. The lengthily named **Fundação da Câ Municipal de Viseu para a Protecção do Artesanato** (⊠ *Casa da Ribeira* ☎ *232/429761*) is the city-center sales outlet for many of these crafts.

SPORTS AND THE OUTDOORS

Montebelo. Although hardly likely to be considered as a venue for the Ryder Cup, this interesting layout near Viseu lies in a picturesque region. It's the only course for many miles and has been built in hilly countryside, almost in the shadow of Portugal's highest mountain, the Serra da Estrela. This is much more informal golf than elsewhere in the country, and a handicap certificate is not required to play here. Walkers may find the hilly terrain a little hard going, but golf carts are available. ⊠ *Farminhão, Viseu* ☎ *232/856464* ⊕ *www.golfemontebelo.pt* ⌁ *18 holes. 6,317 m. Par 72* ⛳ *9-hole course €30 weekdays, €41 weekends;*

18-hole course €44 weekdays, €54 weekends per round ☞ Facilities: driving range, putting green, chipping area, golf carts, hand-pulled carts, pro shop, restaurant, bar.

CARAMULO

24 km (15 mi) southwest of Viseu.

In the early part of the last century, when tuberculosis was rife, people came here for the beneficial effects of the fresh mountain air. Although tuberculosis is no longer the problem it once was, Caramulo hasn't lost its appeal. People still come to enjoy the heather-clad wooded slopes and to walk through the parks and gardens. Mineral water bottled at the nearby spring is popular throughout the country.

WINE ROAD

Driving to Caramulo from Viseu takes you through the heart of the Dão region. Here you'll see many vineyards, some carefully terraced. The wines pressed from these grapes are some of Portugal's finest.

The **Gabinete da Rota do Vinho Dão** (*Office of Dão Wine Routes* ☎ 232/410060) provides lists of vineyards and recommends routes to charming wine-growing villages such as Caramulo and Mangualde.

GETTING HERE AND AROUND

There are occasional buses from Coimbra but you have to change at Tondela and the connections are not always the best. In short, it's best to rent a car if you're planning on exploring this region.

ESSENTIALS

Visitor Info Caramulo (✉ Av. Dr. Jerónimo de Lacerda ☎ 232/861437).

EXPLORING

The unusual museum in the **Museu do Caramulo–Fundação Abel de Lacerda** (*Caramulo Museum–Abel de Lacerda Foundation*) was established and supported by a local doctor. Its varied collections, all from donations, include jewels, ceramics, and a fine assortment of paintings that represent such diverse artists as Salvador Dali, Pablo Picasso, and Grão Vasco. Next door to the Fundação Abel de Lacerda is the **Museu do Automóvel,** whose collection of perfectly restored antique cars includes such rare items as a 1902 Darracq. Also on exhibit are vintage bicycles and motorcycles. ✉ Av. Abel de Lacerda ☎ 232/861270 both museums ⊕ www.museu-caramulo.net ⊠ €7, valid for both museums ☉ June–Sept., daily 10–1 and 2–6; Oct.–May, weekdays 10–1 and 2–5.

OFF THE BEATEN PATH

Caramulinho. From the trailhead on N230-3 near the Hotel Caramulo, it's about a 30-minute climb to Caramulinho, at an elevation of 3,500 feet. Here at the tip of the Serra do Caramulo, you can look out across a vast panorama, taking in the coastal plain to the west and the Serra da Estrela to the southeast.

WHERE TO STAY

$$ ⬚ **Hotel do Caramulo.** This four-star hotel and spa at nearly 3,000 feet above sea level is not the world's most glamorous building, but it is designed so that 43 of the 87 rooms have panoramic views from their balconies. The contemporarily furnished rooms are a bit impersonal, but have all the usual comforts, and there is a good restaurant, Pais ($$–$$$), and bar. The real draws, however, are the excellent spa and health center and the great outdoors, with a range of energetic activities from hill-walking to rock-climbing within the Serra do Caramulo on offer. **Pros:** facilities include games and reading rooms; efficient staff. **Cons:** impersonal atmosphere; location is removed from most of the sights. ⊠ *Av. Dr. Abel Lacerda* ☎ *232/860100* ⊕ *www.hoteldocaramulo.pt* ↙ *87 rooms, 4 suites* ♤ *In-room: a/c, safe, Wi-Fi. In-hotel: restaurant, room service, bar, 2 pools, gym, spa, children's programs (ages 6–12), laundry service, Internet terminal, Wi-Fi hotspot, parking (free)* ☐ *AE, DC, MC, V.*

ÁGUEDA

25 km (15 mi) west of Caramulo, 18 km (11 mi) southeast of Aveiro.

This center for the production of paper products has an attractive parish church and several well-preserved manor houses.

GETTING HERE AND AROUND

There are occasional buses from Aveiro and Caramulo, but the only really viable form of transport is car.

ESSENTIALS

Visitor Info **Águeda** (⊠ *Largo Dr. João Elísio Sucena* ☎ *234/601412*).

EXPLORING

Águeda itself isn't particularly appealing, although it is worth visiting the richly decorated little **Igreja da Santa Eulalia,** which is dedicated to the local patron saint. There are a number of prehistoric and Roman sites in the surrounding area. What really makes a visit to this area worthwhile is the peaceful rolling fields and woodlands of the surrounding countryside.

The **Museu Ferroviário** *(Railway Museum)* is 10 km (6 mi) north of Águeda on IC2 in the village of Macinhata do Vouga. Part of the village railway station, the museum's exhibits include four steam locomotives dating from 1886. ⊠ *Estação de Caminhos de Ferro* ☎ *222/002723* ⊠ *€2* ☉ *Tues.–Sun. 9:30–1 and 2–5:30.*

WHERE TO STAY

$ ▣ **Estalagem da Pateira.** The name *pateira* comes from *pato,* the Portuguese word for "duck." This modern inn is on Portugal's largest lake, which was the private duck reserve of King Manuel I in the 16th century. If you fancy the idea of being serenaded to sleep by croaking frogs after watching a spectacular lake sunset, this place—7 km (4½ mi) west of Águeda off Route 333—is for you. The rooms are spacious and comfortable and the restaurant ($–$$) serves some excellent fare, including a very good bacalhau. **Pros:** great bicycling country; bicycles available at hotel; fabulous lakeside setting. **Cons:** car is necessary; dated furnishings in public areas. ⊠ *Rua da Pateira 84, Fermentelos* ☎ *234/721219* ⊕ *www.pateira.com* ↙ *57 rooms* ♤ *In-hotel: restaurant, room service, spa, bicycles, Wi-Fi hotspot, parking (free)* ☐ *AE, DC, MC, V* ⑩ *FAP, MAP.*

Fodor's Choice ★

CURIA

16 km (10 mi) south of Águeda; 20 km (12 mi) north of Coimbra.

This small but popular spa is in the heart of the Bairrada region, an area noted for its fine wines and roast suckling pig. The waters, with their high calcium and magnesium-sulfate content, are said to help in the treatment of kidney disorders. For the last 100 years, the spring has been contained within an elaborate treatment center that has provided rejuvenating pampering and medical treatment side by side. Curia is a quiet retreat of shaded parks—with a small lake and grand belle epoque hotels—just a half hour's drive from the clamor of the summer beach scene. Coimbra, Aveiro, Figueira da Foz, the Serra do Caramulo, and Viseu are all within an hour's drive.

GETTING HERE AND AROUND

Trains run roughly half-hourly from Coimbra and Aveiro to Curia (less on weekends). Check the CP website for more details.

ESSENTIALS

Trains Comboios de Portugal (☎ 808/208208 ⊕ www.cp.pt).

Visitor Info Curia (✉ Largo Dr. Luís Navega ☎ 231/512248 or 231/504442 ⊕ www.turismo-curia.pt).

WHERE TO EAT AND STAY

$ ✕ **Pedro dos Leitões.** Of the several restaurants specializing in suckling pig, "Suckling Pig Pete" is the most popular. Having a meal here is a near must in this area. The size of the parking lot is a dead giveaway that this is no intimate bistro, and Pedro's spitted pigs pop out of the huge ovens at an amazing rate, especially in summer. In spite of the volume, quality is maintained. The restaurant lies about 3 km (2 mi) from Curia. ✉ *Rua Alvaro Pedro 1 (N1), Mealhada* ☎ *231/209950* ⊕ *www.pedrodosleitoes.com* ⊟ *AE, MC, V* ☉ *Closed 2 wks in late June–early July.*

PORTUGUESE
Fodor'sChoice
★

$ 🛏 **Grande Hotel da Curia.** One of the fanciest hotels in the vicinity of Curia's thermal springs was built in the 1890s. Everything seems polished to perfection, from the marble floors to the mahogany furniture and paneling; fine carpets and fabrics abound. Restaurante Anadia ($$–$$$), with its wood-plank floors and soft draperies, typifies the subdued elegance throughout. The menu is primarily international, with a few regional specialties. Medical staff in the state-of-the-art health center can help you with diet and exercise programs while golfers can perfect their putting skills at the hotel's 9-hole golf course. **Pros:** tea and coffee-making facilities in the room; superb service. **Cons:** can seem impersonal; pricey. ✉ *Curia, Tamengos* ☎ *231/515720* ⊕ *www. grandehoteldacuria.com* ⤳ *84 rooms, 6 suites* ⚒ *In-room: a/c, safe, Wi-Fi. In-hotel: restaurant, bar, golf course, 2 pools, gym, spa, Wi-Fi hotspot, parking (paid)* ⊟ *AE, DC, MC, V* ⊞⃝ *BP.*

Fodor'sChoice
★

$ 🛏 **Quinta de São Lourenço.** This delightful 18th-century manor—surrounded by vineyards and pine groves—is in the tiny village of São Lourenço do Bairro. The house has six comfortable-size bedrooms with wooden floors, period furniture, and modern bathrooms. A couple of rooms have antique iron bedheads and one has a four poster bed (which is well worth requesting). Guests can make use of the small library and game room. There's also a small apartment. Meals can be arranged upon request. **Pros:** charming owners; spick-and-span rooms. **Cons:** lack of restaurants and shops nearby; decor could be a bit flowery for some. ⊠ *3 km (2 mi) from Curia on N1 to Mugofores, São Lourenço do Bairro* 🕾 *231/528168* ⊕ *www.quinta-de-s-lourenco.pt* ⟳ *6 rooms, 1 apartment* ♿ *In-room: a/c, refrigerator. In-hotel: pool, Wi-Fi hotspot, parking (free), some pets allowed* ▭ *No credit cards* ⌾ *BP.*

SPORTS AND THE OUTDOORS

Curia. Opened in 2004 as part of the Grande Da Curia Golf & Spa complex, this 9-hole course will eventually expand to 18 holes. It is located just 20 minutes from Coimbra, and the landscaping includes three artificial lakes. ⊠ *Curia* 🕾 *231/516831* ⊕ *www.curiagolfe.com* ✑ *info@curiagolfe.com* ⚑ *9 holes 2,457 m. Par 34* 🏷 *€17.50 weekdays, €25 weekends per round* ☞ *Facilities: driving range, putting green, chipping area, pro shop.*

LUSO

8 km (5 mi) southeast of Curia; 18 km (11 mi) northeast of Coimbra.

This charming town, built around the European custom of "taking the waters," is on the main Lisbon–Paris train line, in a little valley at the foot of the Buçaco Forest. Like Curia, it has an attractive park with a lake, elegant hotels, and medicinal waters. Slightly radioactive and with a low-sodium and high-silica content, the water—which emerges from the Fonte de São João, a fountain in the center of town—is said to be effective in the treatment of kidney and rheumatic disorders.

GETTING HERE AND AROUND

There are four daily buses on weekdays and two at weekends that run from Coimbra bus station to the center of Luso, near the main spa. There is also a limited number of trains from Coimbra (35 minutes); however the train station is around a 20-minute hike from the center of town.

ESSENTIALS

Bus Info Luso (⊠ *Rua Emidio Navarro 136* 🕾 *231/939133* ✑ *jtlb@oninet.pt*).

Visitor Info Luso (⊠ *Rua Emidio Navarro 136* 🕾 *231/939133* ✑ *jtlb@oninet.pt*).

WHERE TO EAT AND STAY

¢ ✕ **O Cesteiro.** At the western edge of town just past the Luso bottling
SEAFOOD   plant, this popular local restaurant serves simple fare that includes several types of salt cod, roast kid, and fresh fish. ⊠ *Rua Dr. Lúcio Abranches* 🕾 *231/939360* ▭ *MC, V* ☉ *Closed Wed.*

$ 🏨 **Grande Hotel de Luso.** This hulking, yellow-stucco complex, con-
Fodor'sChoice   structed in 1945, is a tad bombastic, but the interior is luxurious and
★   serene. Rooms are large and airy, with modern, tiled bathrooms; some bedrooms have terraces that overlook the Olympic-size pool. The hotel is adjacent to the park and renowned Luso Spa, with its many therapeutic programs. Cruz Alta ($–$$), the on-site restaurant, serves

a good selection of creatively prepared international and regional foods in a pleasant environment with a view of the pool. The management has bikes to rent and there's also a squash court and snooker table available for guests. **Pros:** stunning public areas; exquisite gardens. **Cons:** staff can seem offhand; color schemes in the rooms rather dull. ⊠ *Rua Dr. Cid de Oliveira* ☎ *231/937937* ⊕ *www.hoteluso.com* 🛏 *144 rooms, 2 suites* ♿ *In-room: a/c, Wi-Fi. In-hotel: restaurant, room service, bar, 2 pools, spa, children's programs (ages 6–12), laundry service, Internet terminal, Wi-Fi hotspot, parking (free)* ☐ *AE, DC, MC, V* �‖ *BP.*

¢ ▥ **Residencial Imperial.** One of the latest additions to the Luso accommodation scene, this neat little hotel has spick-and-span rooms with parquet floors, dark wood furniture, and colorful bedding. All the rooms have small balconies overlooking the street, where there's easy parking. It's a short walk to the center of town and spa, as well as shops and restaurants, although you may not need the latter as the Imperial's downstairs restaurant dishes up solid traditional cuisine attracting a loyal local clientele. **Pros:** excellent value; pleasantly furnished. **Cons:** the management speaks little English; small rooms. ⊠ *Rua Emídio Navarro, Luso* ☎ *231/937570* ⊕ *www. residencialimperial.com* 🛏 *14 rooms* ♿ *In-room: a/c. In-hotel: restaurant, Wi-Fi hotspot* ☐ *MC, V* �‖ *CP.*

BUÇACO

3 km (2 mi) southeast of Luso; 16 km (10 mi) northeast of Coimbra.

In the early 17th century, the head of the Order of Barefoot Carmelites, searching for a suitable location for a monastery, came upon an area of dense virgin forest. Having rejected an offer to settle in Sintra because there were too many distractions, he chose instead the tranquil forest of Buçaco. A site was selected halfway up the slope of the greenest hill, and by 1630 the simple stone structure was occupied. To preserve their world of isolation and silence, the monks built a wall enclosing the forest. Their only link with the outside world was through one door facing toward Coimbra, which one of them watched over. The Coimbra Gate, still in use today, is the most decorative of the eight gates constructed since that time.

So concerned were the Carmelites for the well-being of their forest that they obtained a papal bull in 1643 calling for the excommunication of anyone caught cutting down even a single tree. They planted a number of exotic varieties, and the forest flourished. Attracted by the calm and tranquility of the forest, individual monks left the monastery to be alone with God and nature. They built simple hermitages, where they would stay, without human companionship, for several months at a time. You can still see vestiges of these hermitages as you walk through the forest.

In 1810 this serenity was shattered by a fierce battle in which the Napoleonic armies under Massena were repulsed by Wellington's British and Portuguese troops. An obelisk marks the site of the Battle of Buçaco, a turning point in the French invasion of the Iberian Peninsula. In 1834, owing to the rise in anticlerical sentiment and the country's need for money to rebuild the economy after the war of succession between the two sons of King John VI, the government issued a decree ordering the confiscation of all monasteries and convents. The monastery was virtually abandoned.

In the early years of the 20th century, much of the original structure was torn down to construct—under the supervision of Italian architect Luigi Manini—an opulent, multiturreted, pseudo-Manueline extravaganza that was to be a royal hunting lodge. With the exception of one brief vacation and a dubious romantic fling, this "simple hunting lodge" was never used by the royal family. It became a prosperous hotel—now the Palace Hotel do Buçaco—and in the years between the two world wars it was one of Europe's most fashionable vacation addresses. Tales told in local villages have it that during World War II, when neutral Portugal was a hotbed of espionage, Nazi agents ensconced in the tower rooms beamed radio signals to submarines off the coast. Today many come to Buçaco just to view this unusual structure, to stroll the shaded paths that wind through the forest, and to climb the hill past the Stations of the Cross to the Alta Cruz (High Cross), their efforts rewarded by a view that extends all the way to the sea.

GETTING HERE AND AROUND

Most (but not all) of the buses that head for Luso, have Buçaco as their final destination. However, overall, visitors will find a car invaluable for exploring the national forest.

EXPLORING

The small **Museu Militar de Buçaco** *(Buçaco Military Museum)* houses uniforms, weapons, and various memorabilia from the Battle of Buçaco. ⊠ *On left of N234, just outside forest grounds* ☎ *231/939310* 🏷 *€1* 🕙 *Tues.–Sun. 10–12:30 and 2–5.*

WHERE TO STAY

$$

Fodor's Choice

★

Palace Hotel Buçaco. A former royal hunting lodge in a 250-acre forest, the Palace is an architectural hodgepodge that includes everything from Gothic to neo-Manueline to early Walt Disney. There's an elevator, but who can resist walking up the grand, red-carpeted stairway, its walls lined with azulejo panels, and past the suit of armor? It's worth the steep price for the restaurant's prix-fixe meals just to sit at a finely laid table and take in the carved-wood ceiling, inlaid hardwood floors, and Manueline windows. An elegantly prepared *leitão* (suckling pig) perfectly complements the Buçaco wines stored in the hotel's immense cellars. These wines are available in the restaurants at all Almeida hotels, and also to all guests. **Pros:** fairy-tale setting; superb restaurant. **Cons:** blatantly ostentatious; often booked by groups. ⊠ *Buçaco* 🚇 *Luso* ☎ *231/937970* ⊕ *www.almeidahotels.com* 🛏 *64 rooms, 4 suites* 🕭 *In-room: a/c, Wi-Fi. In-hotel: restaurant, room service, bar, laundry service, Internet terminal, Wi-Fi hotspot, parking (free)* 🚭 *AE, DC, MC, V* 🍴 *FAP, MAP.*

PENACOVA

12 km (7 mi) southeast of Buçaco; 12 km (7 mi) northeast of Coimbra.

A little town on a hill at the junction of three low mountain ranges, Penacova affords panoramic views wherever you look and wonderful hikes. The parish church in the town square was built in 1620.

GETTING HERE AND AROUND

It's advisable to have your own wheels, as public transportation is sparse in this region. From Buçaco, the most scenic route is N235, through wooded countryside along the foot of the Serra do Buçaco. If you're coming from Coimbra, take N110 along the Rio Mondego.

ESSENTIALS

Visitor Info Penacova (⌧ *Câmara Municipal, Largo Alberto Leitão 5* ☎ *239/470300*).

EXPLORING

Mosteiro de Lorvão. Just outside Penacova, in a small wooded valley, is the village of Lorvão and the Mosteiro de Lorvão. This monastery is worth visiting not just to see what's still standing, but also to feel the vibes of a departed epoch. Its origins are obscure, but there's archaeological evidence of monastic life here dating as far back as the 6th century. In the 13th century Lorvão became a convent for Cistercian nuns and was the custodian of a famed library of 12th-century illuminated manuscripts. The convent was closed down by government order in the 19th century. By that time, the impoverished nuns were partly supporting themselves by making the forerunners of the exquisitely carved willow toothpicks that you can buy in Penacova and in handicrafts shops around the country. (The nuns originally used them to decorate the little cakes they made for sale.) Still standing is a baroque church that dates primarily from the 18th century and has beautifully carved choir stalls and an ornate wrought-iron choir grille. The adjacent museum contains archaeological pieces recovered from the site as well as several illuminated manuscripts. ⌧ *Turnoff on N110, 2 km (1 mi) south of Penacova, Lorvão* ☎ *239/474430* ⌧ *Free* ☉ *June–Sept., daily 9–12:30 and 2–6:30; Oct.–May, daily 9–12:30 and 2–5.*

WHERE TO EAT AND STAY

$
PORTUGUESE
✕ **O Panorâmico.** It's easy to see how this small, family-run restaurant got its name: there's a wonderful panoramic view of the Rio Mondego as it snakes its way along to Coimbra. Be sure to try the house specialty, *lampreia à mode de Penacova* (lamprey cooked with rice). ⌧ *Largo Alberto Leitão* ☎ *239/477333* ▭ *DC, MC, V.*

¢
⌂ **Hotel Penacova.** The pink-and-yellow paint job and art nouveau–style architecture may seem out of place given the bucolic, hilltop setting. But this hotel has a lot going for it and makes a good base for exploring the countryside. It's on a site where a castle is believed to have stood when the Moors and the Christians were facing off in these territories during the 11th and 12th centuries. The all-round views command both the Mondego and Alva rivers, giving some credence to the castle theory. With a new name (formerly Palacete do Mondego) and new ownership, the guest rooms are attractively furnished and comfortable. Most of the

bathrooms have tubs as well as showers. **Pros:** spacious rooms; lovely views. **Cons:** no restaurant; Web site is in Portuguese only. ⊠ *Av. Dr. Vissaya de Barreto 3* ☎ *239/470700* ⊕ *hotelpenacova.blogspot.com* ⤴ *38 rooms, 4 suites* 🔔 *In-room: a/c. In-hotel: bar, pool, Internet terminal* ⊟ *AE, MC, V* 🍴*BP.*

OUTDOOR ACTIVITIES

HIKING

Several paths lead over the hills to the monastery in Lorvão or through the vineyards and fields down to the Rio Mondego. **Trans Serrano** (☎ *235/778938* ⊕ *www.transserrano.com*) will provide transport and English-speaking guides for nature hikes and kayaking in the surrounding countryside.

KAYAKING

Between June and September, there are kayak trips down the Rio Mondego from Penacova to Coimbra. For more information contact the student-run **O Pioneiro do Mondego** (☎ *239/478385* ⊕ *www.pioneirodmeng. blogspot.com*) or the local tourist office.

THE EASTERN BEIRAS

Life is difficult in the mountains and along the frontier with Spain. Winters are cold and harsh, and summers are broiling hot. The rugged mountains of the Serra da Estrela and the sparse vegetation of the stone-strewn high plateau present a sharp contrast to the sandy beaches, lush valleys, and densely forested peaks along the coast. As you drive east, the red-tile roofs and brightly trimmed white-stucco houses are replaced by stone-and-slate structures, reflecting the more somber environment.

Because crops don't flourish here, many inhabitants have supplemented their meager farming incomes by smuggling contraband across the Spanish border. Between 1950 and 1970, many of the villages lost their ablest workers to the factories of northern Europe; a half million Portuguese went to France alone. As a consequence, many towns are populated primarily by senior citizens.

Still, it's worth visiting this region to stand atop a centuries-old castle wall and look out on the landscape's rugged beauty. And in this part of the country, where visitors are still something of a curiosity, you'll find perhaps the warmest welcome. With many mellow old buildings uninhabited, this beautiful area is one of Europe's last great undiscovered gems for those wishing to buy a second home away from the madding crowd.

CASTELO BRANCO

150 km (93 mi) southeast of Coimbra.

The provincial capital of Beira Baixa is a modern town of wide boulevards, parks, and gardens. Lying just off the main north–south IP2 highway, it's easily accessible from all parts of the country.

GETTING HERE AND AROUND

There are regular buses to Castelo Branco from several major travel hubs in Portugal, including Coimbra, Lisbon, Guarda, Portalegre, and Faro. The town is also on the Lisbon-Guardia line with six daily trains from Lisbon. Check the Comboios de Portugal's Web site for more information.

If you are driving from Buçaco, the most scenic route is N235, through wooded countryside along the foot of the Serra do Buçaco. If you're coming from Coimbra, take N110 along the Rio Mondego.

ESSENTIALS

Bus **Castelo Branco Bus Station** (⊠ *Rua do Saibreiro, Castelo Branco* ☎ *272/340120* ⊕ *www.rede-expressos.pt*).

Hospitals **Hospital Amato Lusitano** (⊠ *Av. Pedro A. Cabral, Castelo Branco* ☎ *272/322133*).

Train **Comboios de Portugal** (⊕ *www.cp.pt*).

Visitor Info **Castelo Branco** (⊠ *Câmara Municipal, Alameda da Liberdade* ☎ *272/330339*).

EXPLORING

At the top of the town's hill are the ruins of the 12th-century **Castelo Templario** *(Templar's Castle)*. Not much remains of the series of walls and towers that once surrounded the entire community.

Fodor'sChoice
★ **Jardim do Antigo Paço Episcopal** *(Garden of the Old Episcopal Palace)*. These 18th-century gardens are planted with rows of hedges cut in all sorts of bizarre shapes and contain an unusual assemblage of sculpture. Bordering one of the park's five small lakes are a path and stairway lined on both sides with granite statues of the apostles, the evangelists, and the kings of Portugal. The long-standing Portuguese disdain for the Spanish is graphically demonstrated here; the kings who ruled when Portugal was under Spanish domination are carved to a noticeably smaller scale than the "true" Portuguese rulers. Unfortunately, many statues were damaged by Napoléon's troops when the city was ransacked in 1807. ⊠ *Rua Bartolomeu da Costa* ☎ *No phone* 🎫 *€1.50* ☉ *May–Sept., daily 9–7; Oct.–Apr., daily 9–5.*

Adjoining the Castelo Templario is the flower-covered **Miradouro de São Gens** *(St. Gens Terrace)*, which provides a fine view of the town and surrounding countryside.

Museu Francisco Tavares Proença Junior. This small, regional museum is housed in the old Paço Episcopal (Episcopal Palace). In addition to the usual Roman artifacts and odd pieces of furniture, the collection contains some fine examples of the traditional *bordado* (embroidery) for which Castelo Branco is well known. Adjacent to the museum is a workshop where embroidered bedspreads in traditional patterns are made and sold. ⊠ *Largo da Misericórdia* ☎ *272/344277* ⊕ *www.ipmuseus. pt* 🎫 *€2* ☉ *Tues.–Sun. 10–12:30 and 2–5:30.*

There's an older section of town, where you'll find the **Praça Luís de Camões,** the town's best-preserved medieval square.

WHERE TO EAT AND STAY

$ ✕ **Praça Velha.** In a stone building on a lovely square (the plaque outside reads 1685), this is by far the best restaurant in town. Of the two dining rooms, the older section with the beamed ceiling and stone floors is best. One intriguing specialty is *bife na pedra* (steak served still cooking on a hot stone slab). ✉ *Largo Luís de Camões 17* ☎ *272/328640* ⊕ *www.pracavelha.com* ▭ *AE, DC, MC, V* ⊘ *Closed Mon. No dinner Sun.*

PORTUGUESE

$ ⊡ **Rainha Dona Amélia.** The Dona Amélia is a graceful, modern, five-story hotel in the center of the town, run as part of the Best Western chain. The good-size rooms are decorated with warm earth tones and are pleasant, functional, and airy. The public areas are inviting, including Veranda Real ($$$), a small restaurant with its crisp white tablecloths and subtle lighting. Because of its proximity to the Serra da Estrela, this hotel is busiest during the ski season between November and May. **Pros:** handsome building; good location. **Cons:** the hotel's size can make it feel impersonal; some rooms lack decent view. ✉ *Rua de Santiago 15* ☎ *272/348800* ⊕ *www.bestwesternrainhadamelia.com* ⟿ *64 rooms* ⟨ *In-room: a/c, safe, Wi-Fi. In-hotel: restaurant, room service, bar, laundry service, Wi-Fi hotspot, parking (paid)* ▭ *AE, MC, V* ⦿⦿ *BP, MAP.*

¢ ⊡ **Tryp Colina do Castelo.** From its perch atop the hill, what this low-rise business-style hotel lacks in individuality, it makes up for it with its friendly, attentive staff. The public areas are spacious and modern with lots of black leather, chrome, and glass while picture windows in the restaurant afford sweeping panoramic views. The rooms are fairly standard with pine furniture, carpets and small, albeit well-equipped, ensuite bathrooms. In short, all the conveniences you could wish for are here, plus the luxury of a spa, indoor pool, and exceptionally good views. **Pros:** efficiently run; squash court. **Cons:** it's about a 20-minute walk to and from town; anonymous decor. ✉ *Rua da Piscina* ☎ *272/349280* ⊕ *www.solmelia.com* ⟿ *103 rooms, 6 suites* ⟨ *In-room: a/c, Wi-Fi. In-hotel: restaurant, room service, bar, 3 tennis courts, pool, spa, laundry service, Internet terminal, Wi-Fi hotspot, parking (free)* ▭ *AE, DC, MC, V* ⦿⦿ *BP.*

SHOPPING

Tradition in Castelo Branco dictates that a new bride makes an embroidered bedspread for her wedding night. This custom is still followed, and these delicately patterned, hand-embroidered linen-and-silk spreads are among the finest examples of Portuguese craftsmanship. There's a display-and-sales room next to the **Museu Francisco Tavares Proença Junior** (✉ *Rua Bartolomeu da Costa*); expect to empty your purse.

EN
ROUTE

As you travel north on IP2, you cross a landscape of broad plains dotted with olive trees and with the peaks of the Serra da Estrela as a distant backdrop. Thirty kilometers (18 mi) north of Castelo Branco you'll come to the village of Alpedrinha, known for its fine fountains and well-preserved remnants of the Roman road that connected this fertile agricultural region with the Spanish town of Mérida.

FUNDÃO

36 km (22 mi) north of Castelo Branco; 16 km (10 mi) south of Covilhã.

The pears and cherries grown in this region are the best in Portugal, and Fundão is the principal market town for the area's many orchards. It's also a convenient gateway to the fortified towns along the Spanish border.

GETTING HERE AND AROUND

There are six Rede Expressos buses daily running from Castelo Branco to Fundão (30 minutes), four from Lisbon (three hours) and Porto (four hours) as well as good connections from smaller towns, including Viseu (1½ hours), also with four buses daily.

ESSENTIALS

Bus **Rede Expressos** (⊕ *www.rede-expressos.pt*).

Visitor Info **Fundão** (✉ *Av. da Liberdade* ☎ *275/752770*).

EXPLORING

The 18th-century **Igreja Matriz** *(Parish Church)* is noted for its azulejos and decorative ceiling. ✉ *Largo da Igreja* ☎ *No phone* ☉ *Daily 9–7.*

WHERE TO STAY

$ ⊟ **Alambique Ouro.** This sprawling resort hotel is particularly geared toward families, so if you're seeking a tranquil stay in bucolic surroundings, go elsewhere. The leisure activities are superb and extensive, ranging from archery to paint ball, while the outside lagoon-style pool has a real "fun-in-the-sun" feel with its ideal shallow end for children and outside bar for those grown-up piña coladas. Rooms are unexceptional but comfortable with terraces and, during the high season, there is regular entertainment and children's programs. **Pros:** good deals when you book online; superb facilities. **Cons:** can be noisy with all the families; dining room has an institutional feel. ✉ *Estrado Nacional 18, Fundão* ☎ *275/774145* ⊕ *www.hotelalambique.com* ⊷ *114 rooms, 29 suites* ⟋ *In-room: a/c, Wi-Fi. In-hotel: restaurant, room service, bar, 2 tennis courts, 3 pools, gym, spa, children's programs (ages 6–12), laundry service, Internet terminal, Wi-Fi hotspot, parking (free)* ⊟ *AE, D, DC, MC, V* ⦿⊙ *BP, MAP.*

$ ⊟ **Hotel Samasa.** This comfortable if unexciting modern hotel in the town center has redecorated many of its rooms with colors that may leave you feeling as if you are living in a pot of mustard. The facilities include the surprise of a games room, complete with pool table. The hotel's Hermínia Restaurant ($$–$$$) has rustic touches, such as fieldstone on the walls, yet still feels a bit stiff. However, it offers fine food, and if you close your eyes, the facilities are fine. **Pros:** excellent location; good local cuisine. **Cons:** dreary decor; small bathrooms. ✉ *Rua Vasco da Gama* ☎ *275/751299* ⊕ *www.hotelsamasafundao.com* ⊷ *50 rooms* ⟋ *In-room: a/c, Wi-Fi. In-hotel: restaurant, room service, bar, laundry service, Internet terminal, Wi-Fi hotspot, parking (paid)* ⊟ *AE, DC, MC, V* ⦿⊙ *EP.*

7

PENAMACOR

28 km (17 mi) east of Fundão: 28 km (17 mi) southeast of Covilhã.

Like many of the towns in this region, Penamacor is a mix of old and new. Dominated by the ruins of an ancient castle, it was a key link in the chain of strategically placed fortified communities. On its outskirts are newer stucco houses, many built by Portuguese emigrants with money earned working in France and Germany.

GETTING HERE AND AROUND

Penamacor has a weekday bus service that links the town with the rest of Portugal via the larger transport hub of Covilhã. The tourist office can provide you with an up-to-date timetable.

ESSENTIALS

Visitor Info Penamacor (✉ *Av. 25 de Abril* ☎ *277/394316*).

EXPLORING

Castelo de Penamacor *(Penamacor Castle)*. This castle once guarded the northern approaches to the Rio Tejo. In the wake of the 11th- and 12th-century campaigns to reconquer this region from the Moors, Penamacor lay in ruins. In 1180 Dom Sancho I ordered the reconstruction of the fortifications. Although you can still find traces from that period, much of what you now see, including the solitary watchtower, dates from the early 16th century. If the castle is closed, ask for the key at the tourist office.

Museu Municipal *(Town Museum)*. The small but interesting museum is in a building that was a political prison until the 1974 revolution. One of the original cells has been kept intact, and among the other exhibits is the only complete Roman crematorium on the Iberian Peninsula. ✉ *Largo ex Quartel* ☎ *No phone* 🍴 *Free* 🕑 *Daily 9–12:30 and 2–5:30.*

SABUGAL

20 km (12 mi) northeast of Penamacor; 36 km (22 mi) northeast of Covilhã.

GETTING HERE AND AROUND

If you're traveling from Penamacor, follow N233 north across the high plateau. If you have to rely on public transport, there's sporadic bus service to and from Belmonte, Guarda, Penamacor, and Castelo Branco on weekdays, plus a limited service to Sortelha. The bus station is next to the market at the bottom of the town.

ESSENTIALS

Bus Station Sabugal Bus Station (✉ *Largo do Cinema* ☎ *213/581472* ⊕ *www.rede-expressos.pt*).

Visitor Info Sabugal (✉ *Praça da Republica* ☎ *271/751046* ⊕ *www.cm-sabugal.pt*).

EXPLORING

Castelo de Sabugal *(Sabugal Castle)*. The main attraction here is the 13th-century castle, which sits majestically atop a grassy knoll and is noted for its unusual pentagonal tower. Some historians maintain that the five sides represent the five shields of the Portuguese national coat of arms. Climb the stone stairs in the courtyard and walk around the battlements. The castle overlooks the Rio Côa, an important tributary of the Douro. ✉ *Câmara Municipal, Praça da Republica* ☎ *271/751040* ⊕ *www.cm-sabugal.pt* 🖅 *Free* ☉ *Tues.–Fri. 9–12:30 and 2–5:30, weekends 10–12:30 and 2:30–5:30.*

OFF THE
BEATEN
PATH
Parque Natural da Serra da Malcata. The 50,000-acre park along the Spanish border between Penamacor and Sabugal was created to protect the natural habitat of the Iberian lynx, which was threatened with extinction. Although this isn't a place of rugged beauty and spectacular vistas, it's nevertheless an attractive, quiet region of heavily wooded, low mountains with few traces of human habitation. In addition to the lynxes, the park shelters wildcats, wild boars, wolves, and foxes. The northern boundary begins about 10 km (6 mi) southeast of Sabugal.

SORTELHA

Fodor'sChoice
★
10 km (6 mi) southwest of Sabugal; 26 km (16 mi) east of Covilhã.

If you have time to visit only one fortified town, this should be it. From the moment you walk through its massive ancient stone walls, you feel as if you're experiencing a time warp. Except for a few TV antennas, there's little to evoke the 21st century. The streets aren't littered with souvenir stands, nor is there a fast-food outlet in sight. Stone houses are built into the rocky terrain and arranged within the walls roughly in the shape of an amphitheater.

GETTING HERE AND AROUND
If you're traveling from Penamacor, follow N233 north across the high plateau.

Regional trains stop at Belmonte-Manteigas station, located around 12 km (7.4 mi) away, from where visitors can catch a taxi. There is no regular bus service.

ESSENTIALS
Taxi **Sortelha Taxi** (☎ *271/388183*).

EXPLORING
♺ Above the village are the ruins of a small but imposing **castelo** *(castle)*. The present configuration dates back mainly to a late-12th-century reconstruction, done on Moorish foundations; further alterations were made in the 16th century. Note the Manueline coat of arms at the entrance. Wear sturdy shoes so that you can walk along the walls (you can circle the entire village this way). Children of all ages can let their fantasies run wild while taking in views of Spain to the east and the Serra da Estrela to the west. The three holes in the balcony projecting over the main entrance were used to pour boiling pitch on intruders. Just to the right of the north gate are two linear indentations in the stone wall. One is exactly a meter (roughly a yard) long, and the shorter of the two is a *côvado* (66 centimeters [26 inches]). In the Middle Ages, traveling cloth merchants used these markings to ensure an honest measure.

WHERE TO EAT AND STAY

There aren't any hotels or pousadas in this medieval town, but several ancient stone houses offer comfortable, although not luxurious, accommodations at very low rates.

$ ✕ **Restaurante Dom Sancho.** This pleasant little restaurant in a restored
PORTUGUESE   stone house just inside the gates within the main square began life as a bar that was the pet project of a local engineer. Since then it has become one of the area's more presentable restaurants. It specializes in game dishes such as roast wild boar and venison and provides diners with a rustic, yet elegant dining space, plus a downstairs bar. ⊠ *Largo do Corro* ☎ *271/388267* ▭ *No credit cards* ⊘ *Closed Mon. No dinner Sun.*

¢   ⌂ **Casa da Cerca.** This is a delightful place to stay up in the walled town. A charming stone faced 16th-century manor house, there are six atmospheric rooms with wooden floors, traditional decor and furnishings, and granite seats carved into the window sills. The friendly owners serve breakfast in a lovely garden, weather permitting of course. The couple also owns a couple of apartments in town for those interested in longer stays or a self-catering option. **Pros:** real sense of history; quiet location. **Cons:** rooms can seem a little austere; difficult to reach via public transport. ⊠ *Largo do Santo António* ☎ *271/388113* ⤶ *6 rooms* ⚭ *In-room: a/c. In-hotel: Wi-Fi hotspot, parking (free)* ▭ *V.*

¢   ⌂ **Casas do Campanário.** Next to the church, just inside the village walls, Casas do Campanário consists of two apartments; one can accommodate two people, the other six people. Rooms have a real homey charm with antiques, low ceilings, and a warm color scheme. The owners run nearby Bar Campanario, which has one of the most dramatic settings in town, its terrace located on a giant boulder. There's a kitchen including a refrigerator in the larger house. **Pros:** quiet surroundings; central location. **Cons:** no credit cards; advance reservations essential. ⊠ *Rua da Mesquita* ☎ *271/388198* ⤶ *2 apartments* ⚭ *In-room: a/c, kitchen (some), refrigerator (some)* ▭ *No credit cards.*

BELMONTE

14 km (8½ mi) northwest of Sortelha; 20 km (12 mi) southwest of Guarda.

Three things catch your eye on the approach to Belmonte. The first two, the ancient castle and the church, represent the historic past; the third structure, an ugly water tower, symbolizes the new industry of the town, now a major clothing-manufacturing center. Belmonte's importance can be traced back to Roman times, when it was a key outpost on the road between Mérida, the Lusitanian capital, and Guarda. You can still see elements of this road.

GETTING HERE AND AROUND

If you're driving from Penamacor, follow N233 north across the high plateau. There are daily bus services from Guarda (30 minutes); however the bus stop in Belmonte is around a 500m (0.310 mi) walk from the town center.

ESSENTIALS

Visitor Info Belmonte (✉ *Largo do Brasil, Castelo do Belmonte* ☎ *275/911488* ⊕ *www.cm-belmonte.pt*).

EXPLORING

Castelo de Belmonte *(Belmonte Castle)*. Of the mighty complex of fortifications and dwellings that once made up the castle, only the tower and battlements remain. As you enter, note the scale-model replica of the caravel that carried Cabral to Brazil. On one of the side walls is a coat of arms with two goats, the emblem of the Cabral family (in Portuguese, *cabra* means "goat"). Don't miss the graceful but oddly incongruous Manueline window incorporated into the heavy fortifications. The castle ruins are on a rocky hill to the north overlooking town. ⊠ *Free* ⊙ *Daily 10–12:30 and 2–5.*

Eco-Museu do Zêzere. The town's eco-museum describes the surrounding geology and countryside. ⊠ *Rua Pedro Álvares Cabral* ☎ *275/910010 town hall* ⊕ *www.cm-belmonte.pt/build/paginas/ecomuseu/index.html* ⊠ *€1.50* ⊙ *Daily 9.30–12:30 and 2–7:30.*

Igreja de São Tiago *(Church of St. James)*. The 12th-century stone church contains fragments of original frescoes and a fine pietà carved from a single block of granite. The tomb of Pedro Cabral is also in this church. Actually there are two Pedro Cabral tombs in Portugal, the result of a bizarre dispute with Santarém, where Cabral died. Both towns claim ownership of the explorer's mortal remains, and no one seems to know just who or what is in either tomb. If the church is closed, see if someone at the tourist office can help you gain entrance. ⊠ *Adjacent to Castelo de Belmonte* ☎ *275/911488* ⊠ *Free* ⊙ *Weekdays 9:30–12:30 and 2–6, weekends by arrangement.*

Juderia *(Jewish Quarter)*. Adjacent to the Castelo de Belmonte, a cluster of old houses makes up the Juderia. Belmonte had (and, in fact, still has) one of Portugal's largest Jewish communities. Many present-day residents are descendants of the Marranos, the Jews who were forced to convert to Christianity during the Inquisition. For centuries, many kept their faith in secret, pretending to be Christians while practicing their true religion behind closed doors. Such was their fear of repression, that Belmonte's secret Jews didn't emerge fully into the open until the end of the 1970s. The community remained without a synagogue until 1995. It is possible to do group tours that cover the history of the community and the **synagogue** by phoning ahead. ☎ *275/087766*

Monument to Cabral. Ask a Portuguese, or better yet a Brazilian, what Belmonte is best known for, and the answer will undoubtedly be Pedro Álvares Cabral. In 1500 this native son "discovered" Brazil and in doing so helped make Portugal one of the richest and most powerful nations of that era. The monument, in the town center, is an important stop for Brazilians visiting Portugal.

OFF THE BEATEN PATH

Centum Cellas. A short way outside Belmonte, on a dirt track signposted off N18, is a strange archaeological sight that has kept people guessing for years: a massive, solitary, three-story framework of granite blocks. The building is thought to be of Roman origin, but experts are unable to explain its original function convincingly or provide many clues about its original appearance. Some archaeologists believe it was part of a much larger complex, possibly part of a Roman villa which was subsequently used as a watchtower.

WHERE TO STAY

¢ 🏨 **Belsol.** Owner João Pinheiro is an enterprising hotelier who has opted for quality and good service over ostentation. In the guest rooms, rosy wood furniture and floors make a nice counterpoint to the white walls and striped, contemporary fabrics and area rugs in white, taupe, and lavender; several rooms have balconies with views of the Rio Zêzere. Stone terraces lead to swimming pools and landscaped areas. Local businesspeople favor the restaurant ($–$$) for its excellent Portuguese food. Try the trout fresh from local waters. Note that you will need wheels if you stay here—the hotel is around 8 km (5 mi) from town on the main N18 road. **Pros:** family-friendly; superb service. **Cons:** cut off from town; could be too quiet for some. ✉ *Quinta do Rio off IP2/N18, Belmonte* ☎ *275/912206* ⊕ *www. hotelbelsol.com* ⇨ *53 rooms, 1 suite* ⌂ *In-room: a/c, safe, Wi-Fi. In-hotel: restaurant, room service, bar, tennis court, pool, Internet terminal, Wi-Fi hotspot, parking (paid)* ▭ *AE, MC, V* ¶◎¶ *BP.*

$$ 🏨 **Convento de Belmonte.** Just over a kilometer (½ mi) from Belmonte on the slopes of the Serra da Esperança, this attractive pousada is in a restored Franciscan monastery founded in 1563 by a descendant of Pedro Álvares Cabral, the first European to reach Brazil. The blend of ancient and modern has been accomplished with finesse. Rooms are well equipped, handsome, and have balconies with views of the surrounding hills, and the interior cloisters are a delight. As ever in pousadas, the food ($$–$$$) is excellent, with a seasonal menu and regional variations such as stuffed partridge with spinach. **Pros:** impeccable service; gorgeous architectural detail. **Cons:** small plunge pool; can seem formal. ✉ *Serra da Esperança* ⊕ *Apartado 35, Belmonte 6250* ☎ *275/910300* ⊕ *www.pousadas.pt* ⇨ *24 rooms, 1 suite* ⌂ *In-room: a/c, safe, Wi-Fi. In-hotel: restaurant, room service, bar, pool, Wi-Fi hotspot, parking (free)* ▭ *AE, DC, MC, V* ¶◎¶ *BP.*

COVILHÃ

16 km (10 mi) southwest of Belmonte; 48 km (30 mi) north of Castelo Branco.

Although its origins go back to Roman times, there's little in present-day Covilhã of historic significance. Nevertheless, it is an attractive town that is the main business center of and southern gateway to the Serra da Estrela. It's within easy access of the main ski area.

GETTING HERE AND AROUND

There is a reasonable Rede Expressos bus service to/from Guarda (45 minutes), Lisbon (3½ hours), and Porto (5 hours). There are also daily trains that run from Lisbon via Castelo Branco and a twice-daily service to/from Guarda. The main train and bus stations are located 2 km (1.6 mi) south of the center, which is connected to the local bus terminal in the center of town by a shuttle bus.

ESSENTIALS
Bus Covilhã Local Bus Terminal (✉ *Rua Antonio Augusto D'Aguiar* ☎ *808/208208*). **Rede Expressos** (⊕ *www.rede-expressos.pt*).

Visitor Info Covilhã (✉ *Av. Frei Heitor Pinto* ☎ *275/319560*).

EXPLORING
Museu de Lanifícios *(Museum of Wool Manufacturing)*. The town is closely linked to sheep raising and is Portugal's most important wool-producing center. This museum stands within the university grounds, in a restored dye-works founded by the Marquis of Pombal in 1764. You'll learn about local wool production, its technology, and the lives of the wool workers. ✉ *Rua Marquês D'Ávila e Bolama* ☎ *275/319700* 🎟 *€2* ☉ *Tues.–Sun. 9:30–noon and 2–6.*

WHERE TO EAT AND STAY

$ ✕ **Ovelhita Restaurante.** This pleasant restaurant is in a town house just
PORTUGUESE down the road from the tourist office and has recently reopened after extensive reformations. The food is excellent, with a modern twist on the local Portuguese specialties and includes an extensive dinner buffet with plenty of choices, including vegetarian options. In the summer you can dine al fresco on the cobbled terrace where soothing classical guitar music is often accompanying diners. The restaurant is popular with local businessmen and the ladies-who-lunch brigade at lunchtime. ✉ *Largo da Infantaria XXI 19* ☎ *912/509659* 🖃 *MC, V* ☉ *Closed Sun.*

$ 🛏 **Hotel Turismo.** This hotel may be modern and functional, but it's the most lavish accommodation in town, with a luxurious spa, tennis and squash courts, and even a dance club. Guest rooms are well equipped, if a little dated with their light pine furnishings, white walls, and unimaginative artwork. The public areas could also benefit from a revamp, aside from the superb spa. There are also pretty gardens and the restaurant, Peornos ($$–$$$), is well respected among locals, and serves specialties like fresh trout from nearby mountain streams. **Pros:** superb leisure facilities; excellent service. **Cons:** small rooms and bathrooms, dated interior. ✉ *Acesso a Variante, Quinta da Olivosa* ⌂ *Covilhã* ☎ *275/330400* ⊕ *www.hotelturismocovilha.com.pt* ⤢ *104 rooms* ♿ *In-room: a/c, safe, Wi-Fi. In-hotel: restaurant, room service, bar, 2 tennis courts, 2 pools, gym, spa, children's programs (ages 6–12), laundry service, Internet terminal, Wi-Fi hotspot, parking (paid)* 🖃 *AE, DC, MC, V* ❧ *BP.*

¢ 🛏 **Tryp Dona María.** This modern three-star hotel makes up for somewhat boring, boxlike architecture with comfort amenities and great views. The carpeted rooms are a reasonable size, with simple, clean lines, wooden fittings, and white walls, but they do feel rather institutional. The public areas are all glossy marble and clean lines and the leisure activities are good, including a games rooms with card tables and a couple of pool tables and an appealing indoor swimming pool surrounded with lounge beds for a little self-pampering relaxation. **Pros:** quiet rooms; part of respected Tryp chain. **Cons:** popular for conventions; uninspired furnishings. ✉ *Alameda Pêro da Covilhã, about 1 km (½ mi) southeast of the town center* ☎ *275/310000* ⊕ *www.*

pt.solmelia.com ✈ *87 rooms, 6 suites* ⟳ *In-room: a/c, safe, Wi-Fi. In-hotel: restaurant, room service, bar, pool, gym, spa, children's programs (ages 6–12), laundry service, Internet terminal, Wi-Fi hotspot, parking (paid)* ⊟ *AE, DC, MC, V* ⊙|*BP.*

PARQUE NATURAL DA SERRA DA ESTRELA

123 km (76 mi) northeast of Coimbra.

GETTING HERE AND AROUND

There are regular buses to/from Coimbra, Aveiro, Porto, and Guarda to Covilhã and Guarda, as well as daily trains from Lisbon and Coimbra to Guarda. There are no buses that cross the natural park, although there are some limited services that travel the perimeter. Car travel is the most convenient option, although drivers should take special care, particularly at high elevations, which can be foggy or icy during the winter months.

ESSENTIALS

Visitor Info **Parque Natural de Serra da Estrela** (⊠ *Praça da República 28, Seia* ☎ *238/310440* ✎ *turismo.estrela@mail.telepac.pt*). **Região de Turismo da Serra da Estrela** (⊠ *Av. Frei Heitor Pinto, Covilhã* ☎ *275/319560* ✎ *turismo.estrela@mail.telepac.pt*).

EXPLORING

Fodor'sChoice **Parque Natural da Serra da Estrela.** Until the end of the 19th century, this
★ mountainous region was little known except by shepherds and hunters. The first scientific expedition to the Serra da Estrela was in 1881, and since then it has become one of the country's most popular recreation areas. In summer the high, craggy peaks, alpine meadows, and rushing streams become the domain of hikers, climbers, and trout fishermen. The lower and middle elevations are heavily wooded with deciduous oak, sweet chestnut, and pine. Above the tree line, at about 4,900 feet, is a rocky, subalpine world of scrub vegetation, lakes, and boggy meadows that are transformed in late spring into a vivid, multicolored carpet of wildflowers. The Serra da Estrela Natural Park is home to many species of animals, the largest of which include wild boar, badger, and, in the more remote areas, the occasional wolf.

WHERE TO EAT AND STAY

$ ✕**Cabana do Pastor.** A cozy mountain restaurant with a fireplace and
PORTUGUESE panoramas, this is a good place to try some Serra cheese. If you're lucky, the restaurant may have some at its optimum stage of maturity. The fine, locally cured *presunto* (cured ham) is also good here, and the place is famed for its *cabrito no forno,* a succulent dish of roast kid. The restaurant is 12 km (7 mi) southwest of Gouveia. ⊠ *Behind souvenir shop on N339, Seia* ☎ *238/313010* ⊟ *V.*

$$$ ▥ **Pousada de Convento do Desagravo.** In a delightful village with just
Fodor'sChoice 400 inhabitants, this gracious pousada began life as a convent in the
★ late 18th century. Today its cool white rooms and shady arched corridors are simply but elegantly furnished to maintain a sense of peace and well-being, and the restaurant ($$–$$$) serves local specialties such as duck, game, and trout. Families are also well catered to with

a children's playground and baby-sitting by request. It's also worth nothing that prices drop considerably if you reserve online. **Pros:** exudes a tangible sense of history; spacious rooms. **Cons:** expensive rates; village may be too quiet for some. ⊠ *Vila Pouca da Beira* ☎ *238/670080* ⊕ *www.pousadas.pt* ⇆*29 rooms, 8 suites* &*In-room: a/c, safe. In-hotel: restaurant, bar, tennis court, pool, Wi-Fi hotspot, parking (free)* ▤ *AE, DC, MC, V* ⊧⊚⊧ *BP.*

$$ ⊞ **Pousada de São Lourenço.** At an
Fodor'sChoice elevation of 4,231 feet, this granite
★ mountain lodge is in the heart of the Serra da Estrela, 13 km (8 mi) from the spa town of Manteigas; the views are stunning, stretching all the way to Spain on a clear day. The cozy lounge has plush seating by a fireplace, and rooms are both elegant and rustic with dark-wood furniture, fabrics in deep colors, and cozy throws on the beds. Ask for Room 207; it has a loft for sleeping and one of the best views. If you're just driving through, stop for lunch at the restaurant and try the unusual but delicious bacalhau *à lagareiro* (with corn bread, olive oil, and potatoes)—and enjoy the fabulous panoramic views. Note that there are considerable price reductions if you book online. **Pros:** fabulous retreat; stunning views. **Cons:** approached via tortuous windy road, lack of leisure facilities. ⊠ *On E232 to Gouveia* ⌂ *Manteigas* ☎ *275/980050* ⊕ *www.pousadas.pt* ⇆*21 rooms, 1 suite* &*In-room: a/c, Wi-Fi. In-hotel: restaurant, bar, Wi-Fi hotspot, parking (free)* ▤ *AE, DC, MC, V* ⊧⊚⊧ *BP.*

GREAT DRIVES

If you prefer to take in the scenery by car, the roads through the Serra da Estrela, although hair-raising at times, are well maintained. The drive between Covilhã and Seia on N339, the country's highest road, affords a breathtaking view of the Zêzere Valley. Along the way you'll pass a small fountain marking the source of the Rio Mondego. It's in this region that Portugal's noblest cheese, the tangy *queijo da Serra*, is made from the milk of ewes pastured on the rugged mountain slopes.

OUTDOOR ACTIVITIES

CAMPING

There are several official campsites within the park (ask at the tourist office for details) with basic toilet and shower facilities. There are also a number of good commercial campsites in the area. The Web directory **Virtual Portugal** (⊕ *www.portugalvirtual.pt/accommod/mountains*) has a list of campsites, such as in Guarda and Belmonte, with details of their facilities and phone numbers.

HIKING

This is a hiker's paradise, and there are plenty of well-marked trails. A comprehensive trail guide is available at tourist offices in the region, and although it's in Portuguese, the maps, elevation charts, and pictures are useful. There are also plenty of other adventure sports on offer, from hang gliding to climbing.

SKIING

With the coming of winter and the first snows, the area becomes a winter playground, offering many Portuguese their only exposure to winter sports. The highest point in continental Portugal is **Torre** (☎ 275/314727), with an elevation of 6,539 feet, within the south part of Parque Natural da Serra da Estrela. Although it has five ski lifts and the facilities have been upgraded, it can't compete with other European ski resorts. Still you'll find a restaurant and sports-equipment shops, and you can rent gear. The weekday rates for lift passes run from €12 for a half day to €24 for a full day; rates are slightly higher on weekends and at night. Equipment hire ranges from €18 for snowboards to €30 for skis. For information, contact the **Ski Station.** In Manteigas, on the far side of the mountains, you can ski and snowboard year-round thanks to the synthetic run at the **Ski Parque** (☎ 275/982870) complex. It takes about three hours to drive between Torre and Ski Parque, both of which have accommodations. The direct route between them is the highest road in Portugal and a thrilling ride above the snow line and in the clouds.

FISHING

There's excellent trout fishing in the Rio Vouga (Vouga River) and in the rivers and lakes of the Serra da Estrela—particularly in the Rio Zêzere, which cuts through one of Europe's deepest glacial valleys—and in the Comprida and Loriga lakes. The Beira Litoral is full of beaches and rocky outcroppings where you can try your luck with a variety of fish, including bass, bream, and sole. Check with the local tourist offices for information about obtaining permits. No permit is required for ocean fishing.

GOUVEIA

28 km (17 mi) northwest of Covilhã.

Nestled into the western side of the Mondego Valley, this quiet town of parks and gardens is a popular base from which to explore the Serra da Estrela.

GETTING HERE AND AROUND

At least two daily buses operated by Rede Expressos run to/from Coimbra and Lisbon. The train is less convenient as the town's train station is located 14 km (8.6 mi) from the center.

ESSENTIALS

Bus Bus Station (✉ Largo Dr Alípio de Melo ☎ 238/490180). **Rede Expressos** (⊕ www.rede-expressos.pt).

Visitor Info Gouveia (✉ Av. 25 de Abril ☎ 238/490243).

EXPLORING

The exterior of the baroque **Igreja Matriz** *(Parish Church)* is covered with blue-and-white tiles, and well-executed azulejos depicting the Stations of the Cross line the inside walls of the small, dimly lighted chapel across the street. ✉ *Praça de São Pedro* ☎ *No phone* ☉ *Daily 9–6.*

The **Museu Municipal de Arte Moderna Abel Manta,** in an 18th-century manor house, displays a good collection of the paintings by this artist, one of the country's most distinguished. He was born in Gouveia in 1888 and died in Lisbon in 1982. Today the exhibition has been expanded with the superb modern paintings by Manta's son João Abel Manta. ⊠ *Rua Direita* ☎ *238/490219* ✉ *Free* ☉ *Tues.–Sun. 9:30–12:30 and 2–6.*

OFF THE
BEATEN
PATH

Canil Montes Hermínios. Gouveia is the principal center for the Serra da Estrela sheepdogs, which are famous for their loyalty and courage. In earlier days, when marauding wolf packs were an ever-present menace, the dogs wore metal collars with long spikes to protect their throats. To learn more about the dogs, you can visit the Montes Hermínios Kennels, one of the major breeding kennels in the Vale do Rossim. ⊠ *N232 between Gouveia and Manteigas, Solar do Cão da Serra, Estrada da Serra* ☎ *238/492426* ⊕ *www.canilmontesherminios. com* ☉ *Visits by appointment.*

WHERE TO EAT AND STAY

$
PORTUGUESE
Fodor'sChoice
★

✕ **O Júlio.** Thanks to the talents of its chef, owner, and namesake, Júlio, those who love good food travel to this unassuming restaurant from miles around. Try the *truta frita do Mondego* (fried trout from the Rio Mondego) or one of the roast meat dishes, like *javali no forno* (roast wild boar) or *cabrito à serrana* (mountain kid [baby goat]). ⊠ *Travessa do Loureiro 11* ☎ *238/498016* ▭ *MC, V* ☉ *Closed Tues.*

$

🏨 **Hotel Gouveia.** This small, modern hotel on one of the main approaches to the Serra da Estrela has comfortable rooms furnished in traditional style. Several have small balconies. The ground-floor O Foural restaurant is popular with local businesspeople; service is attentive, and although the menu (and the prices) changes daily, a good bet is the roast kid. If you like tennis, there are two courts you can use for free in the nearby city park. **Pros:** convenient location; good sized rooms. **Cons:** bland furnishings; perfunctory service. ⊠ *Av. 1 de Maio* ☎ *238/491010* ⤸ *48 rooms, 3 suites* ♿ *In-room: a/c, safe, Wi-Fi. In-hotel: restaurant, room service, bar, laundry service, Wi-Fi hotspot, parking (paid)* ▭ *AE, DC, MC, V* ⦿ *BP.*

CELORICO DA BEIRA

23 km (14 mi) northeast of Gouveia; 16 km (10 mi) northwest of Guarda.

Celorico da Beira is a major producer of Serra cheese, which is made from the best-quality ewe's milk, using traditional methods. Production takes place between December and March.

GETTING HERE AND AROUND

The most convenient way to travel here is via car. The nearest train stop is at Guarda station 16 km (10 mi) away. There are sporadic local and national bus services. Contact the tourist office for times and prices.

ESSENTIALS

Visitor Info Celorico da Beira (⊠ *Rua Sacadura Cabral*).

EXPLORING

One of Europe's largest cheese markets is held on the Praça Municipal every Friday from December to May, with a cheese fair in February. If you miss the market, you can always visit the tiny **Solar de Queijo Serra** (*Serra Cheese Museum* ⊠ *Largo 5 de Outubro* ☎ *271/ 742105*).

Celorico has the requisite **castelo** watching over it from a hilltop. A large portion of the walls and an impressive tower are intact. Before visiting the castle, be sure to stop by the town hall on Rua Sacadura Cabral for the key. ⊠ *Follow Rua Fernão Pacheco from main road up through remnants of old town* 🎫 *Free* ☉ *Mon.–Sat. 10–12:30 and 2–5.*

WHERE TO STAY

¢ 🏨 **Mira Serra.** Owner Fernando Batista was the manager of a luxury hotel in the Algarve before striking out on his own with this modern, four-story establishment. The rooms are comfortable and furnished in traditional style; some have small balconies. The restaurant ($$) prepares a delicious bacalhau à brás. **Pros:** good central location for exploring the region; cozy guest rooms. **Cons:** Web site is in Portuguese only; bland building. ⊠ *Just off IP5, Bairro de Santa Eufemia* 🏠 *Celorico da Beira* ☎ *271/742604* ⊕ *www.hmiraserra.com.pt* 🛏 *42 rooms, 2 suites* ⚐ *In-room: a/c. In-hotel: restaurant, room service, bar, laundry service Wi-Fi hotspot, parking (free)* ⊟ *AE, DC, MC, V* ⏹ *EP.*

TRANCOSO

18 km (11 mi) northeast of Celorico da Beira; 26 km (16 mi) northwest of Guarda.

This town reached its pinnacle in 1282, when King Dinis chose it as the site for his marriage to Isabel of Aragon. Portions of its well-preserved castle walls and towers date from the 9th century.

GETTING HERE AND AROUND

There are daily buses to/from Guarda and twice daily buses to/from Viseu. The most central bus stop is at the Portas d'El Rei gate. Drivers take note: there is plenty of free parking here, as well.

ESSENTIALS

Bus Rede Expressos (⊕ *www.rede-expressos.pt*).

Visitor Info Trancoso (⊠ *Av. Herois de São Marcos* ☎ *271/811147*).

EXPLORING

Above one of the gates, the **Porta do Carvalho,** you can make out the figure of a knight. This was a local lad who, during one of the many battles with the Spanish, left the safety of the castle walls to capture the Spanish flag. He was caught, but before being spirited away, he defiantly hurled the flag over the wall.

EN ROUTE The most scenic route to take from Trancoso is the tortuous N226 to Friexedas followed by the N221 to Pinhel, 38 km (24 mi) to the east. Atop a hill in the Marofa range, Pinhel was a key bastion during the wars of restoration. Its most striking 17th-century remnants are two solitary towers. On one of them, below the balcony facing the town, you can make out the graceful form of a Manueline window. Taking N221 north to Castelo Rodrigo, you'll cross the Serra da Marofa and a desolate, rocky moonscape. Now much improved, this stretch was once known as the Accursed Road, because of its many bends.

CASTELO RODRIGO

60 km (37 mi) northeast of Trancoso.

This old fortified town is now mostly deserted, many of its former residents having emigrated to France and Germany.

GETTING HERE AND AROUND

You need a car to reach Castelo Rodrigo, the public transport availability is abysmal, consisting of just one daily bus to/from Guarda.

ESSENTIALS

Visitor Info **Castelo Rodrigo** (✉ *Adjacent to castle* ☎ *271/311277*).

EXPLORING

The ruins of the **fortaleza** *(fortress)* afford a panoramic view of the surrounding countryside. You pay the €1 entry at the adjacent small tourist office.

In neighboring Figueira de Castelo Rodrigo, the 18th-century **Igreja Matriz** contains several gilded wooden altars. It's open daily 9–6.

ALMEIDA

18 km (11 mi) southeast of Castelo Rodrigo.

Enclosed within a star-shape perimeter of massive stone walls, moats, and earthen bulwarks lies the quiet little town of Almeida. Less than 10 km (6 mi) from the Spanish border, it has been the scene of much fighting over the centuries. This is a place for walking, clambering along the walls and bulwarks, and giving your imagination free rein—perhaps to conjure up ghosts of battles past. The drive from Castelo Rodrigo to Almeida is winding, mountainous, and dramatic.

GETTING HERE AND AROUND

Bus transport is limited, aside from a weekday only service running between Celerico Beira with connections to Lisbon.

ESSENTIALS

Visitor Info **Almeida** (✉ *Portas de São Francisco* ☎ *271/574204*).

7

WHERE TO STAY

¢ ⊡ **A Muralha.** This modern residencial, just outside the fortifications, is the creation of former English teacher Manuel Dias, who manages the hotel, and his wife, Eliza, who runs the restaurant ($). Cork-paneled hallways lead to homey, simply furnished rooms with cork floors. Some of the rooms have balconies with views of the town and surrounding countryside. The restaurant's specialties include *cabrito no forno* and an excellent bacalhau. **Pros:** restaurant usually filled with locals, which is always a good sign; central location. **Cons:** bland decor; no Internet or Wi-Fi access. ⊠ *Bairro de São Pedro* ☎ *271/574357* ⊕ *www. amuralha.pt* ⌂ *24 rooms* ♿ *In-room: a/c. In-hotel: restaurant* ⊟ *AE, MC, V* ⊙ *BP.*

$ ⊡ **Hotel Parador de Almeida.** Portuguese architect Cristiano Moreira eloquently integrated a modern hotel into historic fortress walls. Public areas and guest rooms are spacious and light, but would benefit from an update. They have large terraces that look out across the high tablelands into Spain. You can sip your afternoon glass of chilled white port and imagine Wellington's troops facing Napoléon's armies on this very spot. The restaurant ($$–$$$), divided into two plank-floor dining rooms, serves regional dishes, including *sopa de peixe do Rio Côa* (a rich tomato-based soup made with fish from the nearby Côa River). The wine list has more than 60 selections. At the time of research, new management had just taken over the hotel so there may be some changes underfoot. **Pros:** superb location; panoramic views. **Cons:** unattractive modern building; expensive rates. ⊠ *Rua das Muralhas* ☎ *271/574283* ⊕ *www.pousadas.pt* ⌂ *21 rooms* ♿ *In-room: a/c. In-hotel: restaurant, room service, bar, Wi-Fi hotspot, parking (paid)* ⊟ *AE, DC, MC, V* ⊙ *BP.*

GUARDA

38 km (24 mi) southwest of Almeida; 36 km (22 mi) northeast of Covilhã; 60 km (37 mi) east of Viseu.

At an elevation of about 3,300 feet, Guarda is Portugal's highest city and is aptly referred to by the four Fs: *forte, feia, fria, e farta* (strong, ugly, cold, and wealthy). A somber conglomeration of austere granite buildings in a harsh, uncompromising environment, Guarda is no charming mountain hamlet, but it is interesting historically and a good base from which to explore the mountains and the fortified villages along the Spanish border. Winters are cold and gloomy, often cutting into the short springtime.

From pre-Roman times, Guarda has been a strategic bastion on the northeastern flank of the Serra da Estrela, protecting the approaches from Castile. The town is thought to have been a military base for Julius Caesar. After the fall of the Roman Empire, the Visigoths and later the Moors gained control. Guarda was liberated in the late 12th century by Christian forces and, along with a number of towns in the region, enlarged and fortified by Dom Sancho I. The dukes of Bragança were closely related to the kings of Portugal, and with rank came the privilege and aforementioned wealth. For the rather dour and purposeful local mountain residents, Guarda is still a main trading and business center.

GETTING HERE AND AROUND

Around three buses run daily to various destinations including to/from Castelo Branco, via Covilhã, (1 ¾ hours), Lisbon (5 ½ hours) and Porto (3 hours). There are direct fast IC trains from Lisbon (4 hours) and Coimbra (2 ¾ hours). However, the train station is an inconvenient 5 km (3 mi) northeast of town.

ESSENTIALS

Bus Guarda Bus Station (⊠ *Rua Dom Nuno Álvares Periera, Guarda* ☎ *271/222515*).

Hospitals Hospital Sousa Martins (⊠ *Av. Reinha Dona Amalia, Guarda* ☎ *271/222133*).

Visitor Info Guarda (⊠ *Praça Luís de Camões* ☎ *271/205530*).

EXPLORING

The **Torre de Menagem** *(Castle Keep)*, on a small knoll above the cathedral, and a few segments of wall are all that remain of Guarda's once extensive fortifications. From atop the ruins is an impressive view across the rock-strewn countryside toward the Castilian plains.

Construction on the fortresslike **Sé** *(Cathedral)* started in 1390 but wasn't completed until 1540. As a consequence, the imposing Gothic building also shows Renaissance and Manueline influences. Although built on a smaller and less majestic scale, the cathedral shows similarities to the great monastery at Batalha. Inside, a magnificent four-tier relief contains more than 100 carved figures. The work is attributed to the 16th-century sculptor Jean de Rouen. ⊠ *Praça Luís de Camões* ☎ *No phone* ☉ *Tues.–Sun. 10–1 and 3–6:30.*

The Sé occupies the north side of the **Praça Luís de Camões,** which is also the site of some fine 16th- and 18th-century houses and arcades. The statue standing in the center of the square is of Dom Sancho I.

The **Museu da Guarda** *(Guarda Museum)*, in a stately early-17th-century palace adjacent to the 18th-century **Igreja da Misericórdia** *(Church of Mercy)*, is worth a visit. It documents the region's history with a collection of prehistoric and Roman objects, old paintings, documents, arms, and ecclesiastical art. ⊠ *Rua Frei Pedro Roçadas 30* ☎ *271/213460* ⊕ *museudaguarda.imc-ip.pt* 💶*€2* ☉ *Tues.–Sun. 10–12:30 and 2–5:30.*

WHERE TO EAT AND STAY

¢ ✕ **Belo Horizonte.** Guarda isn't noted for its good restaurants, but this
PORTUGUESE modest granite-fronted establishment in the old quarter is one of the few exceptions. It serves hearty regional fare and a different dish of bacalhau daily, as well as traditional specialties like *cabrito grelhada* (grilled kid [baby goat]). ⊠ *Largo de São Vicente 1* ☎ *271/211454* ▭ *AE, MC, V* ☉ *Closed Sat.*

¢ 🏠 **Quinta da Ponte.** In the little village of Faia, 12 km (7 mi) from Guarda, in the foothills of the Serra da Estrela, this charming 17th-century manor house has been beautifully restored. Choose between apartments for four people, including kitchenettes in the modern extension, or comfortably furnished double rooms in the original historic house. Both options are light and airy and breakfast is served in the former stable block. The property is surrounded by pretty gardens. **Pros:** ideal for a relaxing vacation; good for families. **Cons:** no restaurant; could be too quiet for some. ⊠ *Faia* ☎ *271/926126* ⊕ *www.quintadaponte.com* ⤶ *2 rooms, 5 apartments* ♨ *In-room: a/c. In-hotel: pool, Wi-Fi hotspot, parking (free)* ⊟ *AE, DC, MC, V* ⫢ *EP.*

¢ ▦ **Solar de Alarcão.** To absorb Guarda's history, book a room in this

beautiful 17th-century granite house just around the corner from the Sé. Accommodations are comfortable and furnished with plush drapes and antiques; the only concessions to modernity are TVs and well-fitted bathrooms. There's also a pretty courtyard, gardens and even a small family chapel. **Pros:** atmospheric, timeless quality. **Cons:** no restaurant or bar. ⊠ *Rua Dom Miguel de Alarcão 25* ☎ *271/214392* ⤶ *3 rooms* ♨ *In-room: a/c. In-hotel: bar, some pets allowed, parking (free)* ⊟ *No credit cards* ⫢ *EP.*

Fodor'sChoice ★

Porto and
the North

WORD OF MOUTH

"We were reluctant to go to Porto but friends convinced us to include it on our trip to Portugal. It is one of the most under rated cities in Europe . . . the history, architecture and art, the riverfront areas and port houses."

—HappyTrvlr

"Northern Portugal is beautiful. The Douro Valley is a 'must see' . . . I would spend at least one full day in the area. Taking the train from either Régua or Pinhão east to the end of the line and back is a great way to spend a half a day – the scenery is incredible."

—lreynold1

Updated by
Alison Roberts
and Alexandre
Bezerra

Porto, spectacularly situated on the steep banks of the River Douro, is the undisputed capital of Portugal's northern industrial heartland. A center for finance and fashion, it is experiencing something of a tourist boom, with new restaurants and bars popping up all the time. The coast north of Porto is lined with pine forests; inland, the Minho region is equally verdant, and harbors Portugal's only national park, Peneda-Gerês. Upriver from Porto, in the Douro valley, grapes are grown that are used in Portugal's top export, port wine. This is the start of Trás-os-Montes (Beyond the Mountains), a province with harsh but striking landscapes, which harbor fascinating folk traditions.

Lining the river that made it a trading center ever since pre-Roman times, vibrant and cosmopolitan Porto centers itself some 5 km (3 mi) inland from the Atlantic Ocean. The Moors never had the same strong foothold here that they did farther south, and the city remained largely unaffected by the great earthquake of 1755; as a result, Porto's architecture shows off a baroque finery lacking in Lisbon. Its grandiose granite buildings were financed by the trade that made the city wealthy: wine from the upper valley of the Rio Douro (Douro River, or River of Gold) was transported to Porto, from where it was then exported. You can follow that trail today by boat or on the beautiful Douro rail line. There are now many wine *quintas* (estates) in the valley, some where you can stay overnight.

The remote north can be beautiful, as it is in the valley of the Rio Douro and the deep, rural heartland of the Minho, a coastal province north of Porto. The Minho is surrounded by water. It takes its name from the river forming Portugal's northern border with Spain, meets the Atlantic in the west, and is cut by the long, peaceful and parallel rivers Lima and Cávado. The Minho coast, a sweeping stretch of beaches and fishing villages, has a lush, green landscape. Some locations have been appropriated by resorts, but there are still plenty of places where you can find solitary dunes or splash in the brisk Atlantic away from crowds. Inland you can lose yourself in villages with country markets and fairs that have hardly changed for hundreds of years. It's worth planning ahead to make sure your visit coincides with a weekly market day, or one of the many summer festivals that draw expats back home.

To the northeast there's adventure at hand, in the winding mountain roads and remote towns and villages of the Trás-os-Montes (Beyond the Mountains) region. After centuries of isolation, the area is being accessed by ever more and ever better roads, but there's still great excitement in getting off the beaten track and taking rattling bus rides into the far northeastern corners. The imposing castle towers and fortress walls of this frontier region are a great attraction, but—unusual in such a small country—it's often the journey itself that's the greatest prize: traveling past voluminous man-made lakes, through forested valleys rich in wildlife, across bare crags and moorlands, and finally down to coarse, stone villages where TV aerials sit oddly in almost medieval surroundings.

The rugged uplands of the northern Trás-os-Montes are called the *Terra Fria* (Cold Land), where you may spot some unusual forms: Iron Age sculptures of boars with phallic attributes. It's believed these were worshipped as fertility symbols. There are traces of even more ancient civilizations, in the form of what is believed to be the world's largest open-air museum of paleolithic rock art.

> **FERTILE FIELDS**
>
> Little of the green countryside in the Minho is wasted. Vines are trained on poles and in trees high above cultivated fields, forming a natural canopy, for this is *vinho verde* country. This refreshing young "green wine"—light on alcohol but with fine digestive properties—is crisp. There are two types of vinho verde: red and white. Portuguese drink the red more often and export more of the white. Whatever the color, vinho verde is a true taste of the north. The best *aguardente* (Portuguese brandy) is made from distilled vinho verde; when aged, it can rival fine cognacs.

ORIENTATION AND PLANNING

8

GETTING ORIENTED

The north of Portugal can be divided into four basic regions—Porto and its immediate environs, the Douro Valley, the evergreen Minho, and the somewhat remote and untamed Trás-os-Montes area to the east, a region still slightly short on amenities yet long on spectacular scenery, ancient customs, and superb country cooking. While any trip to the north should include Porto, to get a sense of the variety of landscapes and monuments it's worth getting out of town to see at least one of these other regions.

Porto. An ancient trading city, Porto is also now a sophisticated modern metropolis. Its center is a World Heritage Site, best seen from across the River Douro, where the famous port wine cellars are located. Elsewhere, myriad art galleries and vibrant nightlife are among today's attractions.

The Coast and Douro. The coast around Porto is dotted with dunes and resorts, including two casinos within easy reach of town. Meanwhile, on the River Douro, cruise boats glide through one of Europe's most stunning landscapes, where the grapes used in the world-famous port wine are grown.

The Minho and Costa Verde. The string of beaches between Porto and the Spanish border are not called the "Green Coast" for nothing, with pine forests often providing the backdrop to dunes. Inland, the intensively

TOP REASONS TO GO

Experiencing the old and the new.
Porto might be steeped in history, but
it's a country leader in design. Major
regional centers such as Guimarães
and Braga, too, have both historical
monuments and some of the most
youthful populations in the country.

Enjoying the outdoors. No trip
to the north is complete without a
boat trip on the Douro, whose curve
after curve of terraced vineyards
together form a World Heritage Site.
The region also harbors the country's
only national park, Peneda-Gerês,
with its many marked trails, as well

as coastal bird sanctuaries and the
remote uplands of Trás-os-Montes.

Shopping for handicrafts. The Minho
is famous even in Portugal for its pottery, embroidery, and other handicrafts.
They're best viewed at local markets,
but are also available at shops in Porto
and other major centers.

Celebrating at festivals. The biggest party is on the night of June
23, when Porto residents come onto
the streets to celebrate the city's
patron saint, Saint John. Countless
village festivals across the region are
attended by large numbers of emigrants who head home each summer.

cultivated Minho region is densely populated yet equally green, with
vineyards alternating with fruit trees and forest.

Trás-os-Montes. The uplands of this remote province, whose name means
"Beyond the Mountains," are among the most difficult landscapes from
which to scrape a living, yet they have a certain wild beauty. The hardy
natives are fiercely proud of their local traditions, which often date
back to pagan times.

PLANNING

WHEN TO GO

It's best to visit the north in summer, when Porto and the Minho region
are generally warm, but be prepared for drizzling rain at any time.
Coastal temperatures are a few degrees cooler than in the south. Inland,
and especially in the northeastern mountains, it can be very hot in summer and cold in winter.

PLANNING YOUR TIME

Porto is three hours north of Lisbon by highway or express train, so
even a short trip to Portugal can include a night or two here. From
Porto, it's only another two hours through the Minho coastline up to
the Spanish border, or another three to four hours east to the less visited
Trás-os-Montes and the eastern border with Spain.

It takes only a day or two to experience the more urban pleasures of
Porto and its wine lodges and the nearby coastal resorts. Several more
days would permit a visit to the history-rich towns of Braga or Guimarães
or a trip through the lovely Douro Valley. A full week would allow you
to cover all of this and the peaceful inland towns and villages along the
rivers Lima and Minho, or you could set off for the remote northeastern
Trás-os-Montes and its fascinating towns of Bragança and Chaves.

GETTING HERE AND AROUND

AIR TRAVEL

Porto's Aeroporto Francisco Sá Carneiro, 13 km (8 mi) north of the city, is the gateway to northern Portugal. There's direct service from many European cities and TAP Portugal runs regular flights from Newark, New Jersey, to Lisbon. The airport is now served by the metro system (a 30-minute trip downtown, €2). Taxis are also available outside the terminal; the metered fare into town should run €18 to €20, including €1.60 for baggage. Outside the city limits, tariffs are based on kilometers traveled.

Weekday flights from Lisbon to Bragança via Vila Real run twice a day in both directions by Aero Vip, in twin-engine turboprop planes for 18 or 36 passengers.

Airlines Aero Vip (☎ *21/156–0369, 92/751–9895 in Bragança, 92/751–9893 in Vila Real ⊕ www.aerovip.pt*). **TAP** (☎ *707/205700 ⊕ www.flytap.com*).

Airports Aeroporto Francisco Sá Carneiro (Porto) (☎ *22/943–2400 ⊕ www.ana.pt*). **Aeródromo Municipal de Bragança** (☎ *273/381175*). **Aeródromo Municipal de Vila Real** (☎ *259/336620*).

BUS TRAVEL

Rede Expressos operates frequent bus service to and from Lisbon to major towns in the region, with the ride from the capital to Porto, the main regional hub, taking at least three and a half hours and costing €18 one way. The journey from Lisbon to Bragança, the most remote city, takes seven and a half hours (including breaks) and costs €19. Rodonorte links major towns within the northern region, with the trip from Porto to Amarante taking 50 minutes and costing €6.40 and that from Porto to Bragança taking from three hours and costing €12.20. Other local operators fill in the gaps. Major terminals are in Porto, Braga, Guimarães, Vila Real, and Chaves; the staff might not speak English, but timetables are easily decipherable with the aid of a dictionary. Within towns, local buses are generally the way to get around; Porto also has a limited metro system, a funicular, and a few antique trams aimed mainly at the tourist market.

Bus Rede Expressos (✉ *Rua Alexandre Herculano 366, Porto* ☎ *22/200–6954 ⊕ www.rede-expressos.pt*). **Rodonorte** (✉ *Travessa Passos Manuel, Porto* ☎ *22/200–5637 ⊕ www.rodonorte.pt*).

CAR TRAVEL

Porto is three hours north of Lisbon by highway (via the A1 toll highway) or by express train, so even a short trip to Portugal can include a night or two here.

The densely populated coast around Porto and the Minho region are well served with roads. A half-hour drive on the A3/IP1 toll highway will take you from Porto to Braga (for Guimarães, peel off just beyond halfway on the A7/IC5) before continuing on to Ponte de Lima and Valença on the Spanish border. The IC1 hugs the coast from Porto almost directly north to Viana de Castelo—a drive of just over an hour.

Inland, the A4/E82 toll road connects Porto to Amarante—again, a drive of about an hour. From here the three-lane IP4/E82 passes through

Vila Real, Mirandela, and Bragança en route to the Spanish border at Quintanilha—in all, about four hours from Porto. The IP3 comes up from Viseu in the Beiras through Lamego to Peso da Régua and then Vila Real. You can continue north to Chaves on the N2.

Given the nature of the terrain in this hilly region crisscrossed by river valleys, some journeys will never be anything but slow. Examples are the routes Bragança–Chaves–Braga (N103), Vila Real–Chaves (N2), and Bragança–Mirando do Douro (N218). It's best simply to accept the roads' limitations, slow down, and appreciate the scenery. Off the beaten track, always check with local tourist offices to make sure the routes you wish to follow are navigable. Roadwork and winter landslides can cause detours and delays. In isolated regions, take special care at night, because many roads are unlighted and unpaved.

In city centers, streets are often congested or out of bounds, and local drivers manic, so leave your car at your hotel. In towns in this chapter, you can cover most sights on foot (though be prepared for steep hills in Porto); visit outlying attractions by bus, taxi, or in Porto's case, metro.

TRAIN TRAVEL

Long-distance trains arrive at Porto Campanhã station, east of the center. Note that not all services from Lisbon terminate here; some continue on to Braga. From Campanhã you can take a five-minute connection to the central São Bento station. From Spain, the Vigo–Porto train crosses at Tuy/Valença do Minho and then heads south to Porto, usually stopping at both Campanhã and São Bento. From Porto some of the most scenic lines in the country stretch out into the river valleys and mountain ranges to the northeast. Even if you rent a car, try to take a day trip on one. For reservations and schedules, visit São Bento station or the tourist office.

When leaving Porto, be sure to budget plenty of time from São Bento station to make your connection—or take a taxi straight to Campanhã. For the express service to and from Lisbon, reserve your seat at least a few hours in advance.

The picturesque Douro Line is served by trains from Campanhã (some with a change at Ermesinde) and pass through Livração, Peso da Régua (Régua), and Tua on the four-hour journey to Pocinho, at the far end of the Alto Douro demarcated grape-growing region. For reservations and current schedules contact Estação de São Bento or the tourist office in Porto. On summer Saturdays (June through October), a special historic train runs between the Régua and Tua stations, with a stop at Pinhão.

Trains on the main route north along the Costa Verde depart approximately hourly from Campanhã stations and run through Barcelos and Viana do Castelo, as far as Valença do Minho.

Braga and Guimarães are served by Porto suburban services from both São Bento and Campanhã stations. Braga is also served by some long-distance trains through Campanhã.

Train Info **Estação de Campanhã** (✉ *Largo da Estação de Campanhã, Porto* ☎ *22/105–2700 or 808/208208.* **Estação de São Bento** (✉ *Praça Almeida Garrett, Porto* ☎ *22/201–9517, 808/208208 call center between 7 am and 11 pm*).

RESTAURANTS

On the whole, restaurants in Porto and the north offer extremely good value, although the smaller ones often don't accept credit cards. Dress throughout the region is informal, and reservations are usually unnecessary.

The cooking in Porto is rich and heavy. It's typified by the city's favorite dish, *tripas á moda do Porto* (Porto tripe), a concoction of beans, chicken, sausage, vegetables, and spices. Elsewhere in Portugal residents of Porto are known as *tripeiros* (tripe eaters)—a nickname earned when the city was under siege during the Napoleonic Wars and tripe was the only meat available. However, tripe doesn't dominate the menu in Porto, and dishes tend to resemble those served in the Minho region. *Caldo verde* (literally "green soup") is ubiquitous; it's made of potato and shredded kale in a broth and is usually served with a slice or two of *chouriço* sausage. Fresh fish is found all the way up the coast, and every town has a local recipe for *bacalhau* (dried salt cod); in the Minho it's often *à Gomes de Sá* (cooked with potatoes, onions, and eggs). *Lampreias* (lampreys)—eel-like fish—are found in Minho rivers from February through April and are a specialty of Viana do Castelo and Monção. In the mountains wonderful *truta* (trout) is available at any town or village close to a river.

As elsewhere in Portugal, pork is the meat most often seen on menus, but nearer the border with Spain wonderfully tender veal and steak can be found in the form of *posta mirandesa* and *barrosã*. For adventurous palates a typically *minhoto* dish is *papas de sarrabulho,* a hearty stew of shredded pork in a flour-thickened, cumin-scented, pig's-blood soup. Roast *cabrito* (kid) is popular, too. Trás-os-Montes menus are enlivened by hearty meat stews, which include parts of the pig you may wish had been left out (an ear or a trotter, for example). Sausages are a better bet, particularly *alheira* (a legacy of the Sephardic Jews, who devised this mock sausage of chicken and spices to fool religious authorities) or *chouriço*, the spicy, smoked variety. The other smoked specialty of the region is *presunto de Chaves*, a delicious cured ham from the town of Chaves. Most dishes will be served with *batatas* (potatoes) or *arroz* (rice), both fine examples of staples being raised to an art form. Potatoes here, whether roasted, boiled, or fried, have an irresistibly nutty and sweet flavor. Rice is lightly sautéed with chopped garlic in olive oil before adding water, resulting in a side dish that could easily be devoured as a main course.

The wine available throughout the north is of high quality. The Minho region's vinho verde is a light, young, slightly sparkling red or white wine. The taste is refreshing, both fruity and acid—qualities that also make it an excellent starting point for distilling *aguardente* (Portuguese brandy). Both reds and whites are served chilled (most people prefer the white), and vinho verde goes exceptionally well with fish and shellfish. The light wines made from the *Alvarinho* grape in the region of Monção are prized throughout the country. Port enjoys the most renown of the local wines (ask for *vinho do Porto*), but the Douro region, where the grapes are grown for port, also produces some of Portugal's finest table wines. Other good regions for wine include the area around Chaves, particularly at Valpaços, which produces some excellent, full-bodied, and almost creamy reds. Many Douro estates also produce fine *moscatel* dessert wines.

8

HOTELS

In Porto hotel rates rival those in Lisbon, and you should reserve rooms well in advance to avoid disappointment. Lodgings in the Minho and Trás-os-Montes regions are reasonably priced compared with their counterparts elsewhere in the country. The Turismo no Espaço Rural (Rural Tourism) network allows you to spend time at a variety of historic manor houses, country farms, and little village cottages scattered throughout the north. Many of these converted 17th- and 18th-century buildings are found in the lovely rural areas around Ponte de Lima, in the Minho region. *Pousadas* (inns) offer a variety of settings in the north, from a 12th-century monastery in Guimarães to more rustic, hunting-lodge digs in such places as the Marão mountain ridges near Amarante or a hilltop in Bragança.

WHAT IT COSTS IN EUROS					
	¢	$	$$	$$$	$$$$
Restaurants	under €10	€10–€15	€16–€20	€21–€25	over €25
Hotels	under €80	€80–€140	€141–€200	€201–€260	over €260

Restaurant prices are per person for a main course at dinner, including value-added sales tax. Hotel prices are for a standard double room, including tax, in high season (off-season rates may be lower).

EMERGENCIES

Pharmacies take turns staying open late. Schedules and addresses are posted on the door of each establishment, and listings of late-night services are carried in the local press.

Contacts **General** (☎ *112*).

PORTO

Portugal's second-largest city, with a population of roughly 250,000, considers itself the north's capital and, more contentiously, the country's economic center. Locals support this claim with the maxim: "Coimbra sings, Braga prays, Lisbon shows off, and Porto works." There's poverty here, primarily in the Ribeira neighborhood, parts of which are positively medieval. But in the shopping centers, the Boavista business district, and the port-wine trade, Porto oozes confidence.

Largely unaffected by the great earthquake of 1755, Porto has some fine baroque architecture but its public buildings are generally sober. Its location on a steep hillside above the Rio Douro, though, affords exhilarating perspectives.

The river has influenced the city's development since pre-Roman times, when the town of Cale on the left bank prospered sufficiently to support a trading port, called Portus, on the site of today's city. The 1703 Methuen agreement with England, giving commercial preference to Portuguese wines, provided Douro Valley vineyards with a new market. It was in Porto that Douro wine was first mixed with brandy to preserve it during the journey and improve it over time. The trade is still big business, based across the river in Vila Nova de Gaia.

GREAT ITINERARIES

Devote the first morning to **Porto**, followed by an afternoon tour of the port-wine lodges in Vila Nova de Gaia, across the Rio Douro. Before turning in, spend time enjoying the riverside cafés and restaurants. In the morning, drive north through the sandy coastal towns of **Vila do Conde, Póvoa de Varzim**, and **Ofir and Esposende**. After the bracing air, shopping to the sound of the waves, and a seafood lunch, head inland to the ancient city of **Braga**, with its profusion of churches. Overnight here or in the delightfully medieval **Guimarães**, which you should explore on Day 3. Worth a side trip from either town is the fascinating Citânia de Briteiros, the hilltop site of an ancient Iron Age settlement.

Alternatively, you could spend your second two days savoring the pastoral Douro Valley. Follow the winding N108 east from Porto along the river's north bank. Don't miss the view at Entre-os-Rios, where the Douro and Tâmega rivers converge. Head back up toward **Amarante**, one of the north's most picturesque towns, its halves joined by a narrow 18th-century bridge. It's worth overnighting here. On Day 3, wind your way southeast along the N101, passing through Mesão Frio, to the Douro, where you can follow the river east to **Pêso da Régua**, heart of the port-wine country, and tour a wine cellar or two. Across the river and a bit farther south is **Lamego**, with its impressive 18th-century pilgrimage shrine of Nossa Senhora dos Remédios. From either of these towns, it's not far to **Vila Real**, gateway to the remote and beautiful region of Trás-os-Montes.

You could spend the night here and head east the next day, or return to Porto.

Spend a day and night in **Porto**, then head inland and north. Take two days to explore **Braga**, including the Citânia de Briteiros, and **Guimarães**. On Day 4 go west to **Barcelos**, folk-art center of the country; try to arrive on a Thursday, when the large weekly market is filled with purveyors of everything from live pigs to hand-painted pottery. Continue north to graceful **Viana do Castelo**, along the Rio Lima. Wander its narrow stone streets and stay the night in the art deco pousada on a hill overlooking town, or drive up along the Costa Verde to **Caminha** or one of the other partially walled castle towns along the Spanish border: **Vila Nova de Cerveira, Valença do Minho**, and **Monção**.

On Day 5, head to quaint Arcos de Valdevez and rent a rowboat for a couple of hours on the river, then continue on to two nearby towns with beautiful bridges, **Ponte da Barca**, with its 15th-century arched passageway, and **Ponte de Lima**, graced with a long, low Roman footbridge. If you're in Ponte de Lima on the second Monday of the month, you can visit the country's oldest market. From here, return to Porto or Lisbon.

8

Porto is also a cultural hub, thanks to the Serralves Contemporary Art Museum and commercial galleries, many clustered along Rua Miguel Bombarda, and now to the stunning Casa da Música, or House of Music, designed by Dutch architect Rem Koolhaas. Foz do Douro, where the river flows into the Atlantic, is another fashionable spot.

GETTING HERE AND AROUND

The city is congested, so leave your car at your hotel. Central parking is difficult to find, and parts of downtown (in particular, the riverside and the winding streets of the Old Town below the cathedral) isn't accessible to cars at all. You can walk around most of central Porto, but be prepared for the steep hills, which can prove tiring in the summer heat. To reach the few outlying attractions, you can use the city's good network of buses, trams, and funicular—all run by Sociedade dos Transportes Colectivos do Porto (STCP)—or the metro. Its five lines run from 6 am to 1 am, mostly over ground as a light rail service outside the center but converging underground at the Trindade stop. Bus services are reduced after 9 pm.

Maps for all routes are available on the STCP Web site. The tourist office can provide information; they'll also sell you a Porto Card, which is valid for public transportation and entrance to 21 city sights, and discounts for others, during 24 hours (€8.50), 48 hours (€13.50), or 72 hours (€17.50). There's also a transport-only Andante Tour card valid for 24 hours (€5) or 72 hours (€11) from the first time it is used, when you must validate it at the yellow box at the entry point.

On buses, you can buy an individual ticket on board, for €1.50 one-way, but if you're going to use public transport more than once, then save money by first buying a €0.50 rechargeable Andante card from a metro station, STCP kiosk, or tobacconist's, then load it up with cash or trips. For bus journeys, the cost depends on whether trips are within the city's limits (€1 one-way) or beyond (up to €2.70). Two bus or tram trips in town cost €1.85, while 10 trips cost €7.50. There's also a €5 day bus pass, and a €11 three-day pass. Metro trips cost between €1 and €3.60, a one-day pass between €3.60 and €12.55. On each trip, tickets and Andante cards must be validated.

In downtown Porto you're never far from a taxi stand, but you can also phone for a cab. Make sure the driver turns on the meter; if you have phoned for the cab, you pay €0.80 extra. Within the city limits travelers are charged through a meter, which starts at €2 or €2.50 between 9 pm and 6 am, the weekend, or a holiday. Luggage is €1.60 extra per piece. Outside the city's perimeter (including over the river in Vila Nova de Gaia, where the port wine cellars are) the rate is €1 per kilometer (plus 20% between 9 pm and 6 am, the weekend, or a holiday). Taxis that run outside the city's perimeter have a letter "A" on the door. It's customary, but not obligatory, to tip up to 10% of the fare.

SAFETY AND PRECAUTIONS

Porto is safe compared with many major European cities, even late at night. However, there are parts of the old town below the Sé and in the riverside Ribeira, where even locals tend to avoid wandering about after dark. In general, though, the greatest danger is the odd pickpocket on public transport—do keep an eye (and preferably a hand) on your belongings. There's a special police station for tourists downtown.

TIMING
You'll need a couple of days to experience Porto and its wine lodges, and the nearby coastal resorts. Make sure you visit the port-wine lodges, and leave yourself an afternoon or evening free to relax at a riverside bar or restaurant. Art lovers may end up spending hours at the Serralves Contemporary Art Museum, whose extensive gardens will also charm visitors. And to really appreciate the Casa da Música, you should take in a concert.

Several more days here would permit a trip out to one of the region's beautiful beaches; up the lovely Douro Valley—rail or boat are options, or rental car, if you want to visit a *quinta* (wine estate); or an excursion to the history-rich towns of Braga, Guimarães, or Amarante.

VISITOR AND TOUR INFO
The main municipal tourist office is next to the city hall at the top of Avenida dos Aliados, but there are branches next to the Sé Cathedral (weekdays only) and down in the Ribeira district. They are all good for information on tours of all kinds, as is the office and Web site of Porto Tours, which acts as an efficient clearinghouse for local companies. The national tourist office has branches downtown and at the airport. The Vila Nova de Gaia municipality has its own tourist offices (closed Sunday) with information on the local port wine lodges. The organization Rota do Vinho do Porto (Port Wine Route), based upriver in Peso da Régua, can make reservations for Douro boat and train tours, hotels, and wine tastings at many of the valley's lovely *quintas* (estates). There's a similar Rota dos Vinhos Verdes promoting visits and stays associated with *vinho verde,* the young wine produced across the Minho; its office is in Porto. The regional tourism board for the whole of the north (including Porto) is based in Viana do Castelo.

In town, among companies organizing walking tours is Blue Dragon (twice-daily Tuesday–Sunday, €13 for three hours), which also offers bicycle and Segway tours (€10 and €25 respectively; booking required for all tours) and bike rental (€2.50 per hour to €12.50 for a full day). Vieguini, at the bottom of Rua do Infante D. Henrique, rents out mountain bikes (€4 per hour to €13.50 a full day) but some might see their motorized scooters (€18.50 a day to €85 for fuve days) as a better way to tackle the city's hills.

Several local companies (and some Lisbon-based ones such as Diana Tours and Cityrama) run bus tours of Porto; these usually last a half day and take in all the main sights, including the port-wine lodges in Vila Nova de Gaia. The two City Sightseeing routes run by Doura Acima (one covering downtown and Vila Nova de Gaia, including museums; the other downtown, Foz, and Boavista) depart every half hour and you may hop on and off as often as you wish. Rival bus operator Living Tours also has a minitrain that can be picked up outside the Sé Cathedral. A number of companies also operate half- and full-day coach tours to Douro Valley, the Minho, and Parque Nacional da Peneda-Gerês.

Several of the same Porto-based companies offer cruises on the Rio Douro, often with free hotel pick-up. These range from short trips

8

taking in Porto's bridges and the local fishing villages to one- and two-day cruises that include meals and accommodations. Most of the short cruises depart several times daily from the Cais da Ribeira, at the foot of Porto's Old Town.

Douro Acima specializes in rides on *rabelos,* sailboats traditionally used to transport port wine downriver. Its six vessels leave from quays in both Porto's Ribeira district and across the river in Vila Nova de Gaia.

Douro Azul has the widest range of cruises, including trips upriver of up to a week, on air-conditioned hotel boats: the *Alto Douro* (23 double cabins and one suite, restaurant, and sundecks), the *Invicta* (40 double cabins) and the newer *Douro Cruiser* and *Douro Queen* (65 double cabins each, most with private balcony, plus rooftop pool and Jacuzzis). The company's main Porto office is open weekdays only; the branch in São Bento station is also open Saturday mornings.

If you want to get above it all, Helitours offers 10-minute flights over Porto (from €45 per person) and 20-minute flights that take you farther upriver. The three-hour tour (from €325 per person) includes a trip to Mesão Frio, with a stop for lunch. The heliport is in the Massarelos area overlooking the Douro River and next to the Helitours office. Flights are for a minimum of four people.

ESSENTIALS

Hospitals **Hospital Escolar de São João** (⊠ *Alameda Professor Hernâni Monteiro* ☎ *22/551–2100*). **Hospital Geral de Santo António** (⊠ *Largo Professor Abel Salazar* ☎ *22/207–7500*). **Hospital Joaquim Urbano** (⊠ *Rua Câmara Pestana 348* ☎ *22/589–9550*). **Hospital Magalhães Lemos** (⊠ *Rua Prof. Álvaro Rodrigues* ☎ *22/619–2400*).

Public Transit **Metro do Porto** (☎ *22/508–1000 or 808/205060* ⊕ *www.metrodoporto.pt*). **STCP** (☎ *22/507–1000 or 808/200166* ⊕ *www.stcp.pt*).

Taxis **Rádio Táxis** (☎ *22/507–3900*). **Táxis Invicta** (☎ *22/507–6400* ⊕ *www.taxisporto.com*).

Tours **Blue Dragon** (⊠ *Avenida Gustavo Eiffel 280,* ☎ *22/202–2375 or 91/256–2190* ⊕ *www.bluedragon.pt*). **Cityrama** (☎ *21/319–1090* ⊕ *www.cityrama.pt*). **Diana Tours** (☎ *21/799–8540* ⊕ *www.dianatours.pt*). **Douro Acima** (⊠ *Rua dos Canastreiros 40-42, Porto* ☎ *22/200–6418* ⊕ *www.douroacima.pt*). **Douro Azul** (⊠ *Rua de S. Francisco 4, 2D, Porto* ☎ *22/340–2500* ⊕ *www.douroazul.pt* ⊠ *Estação São Bento, Praça Almeida GarrettPorto* ☎ *22/201–4292*). **Helitours** (⊠ *Alameda Basílio Teles, Massarelos Porto* ☎ *22/543–2464* ⊕ *www.helitours. pt*). **Living Tours** (⊠ *Rua de Mouzinho da Silveira 352-354, Porto* ☎ *22/832–0992* ⊕ *www.livingtours.pt*). **Porto Tours** (⊠ *Torre Medieval–Calçada D. Pedro Pitões 15, Porto* ☎ *22/200–0073 or 22/200–0045* ⊕ *www.portotours.com*). **Rota do Vinho do Porto** (⊠ *Largo da Estação, Apartado 113, Peso da Régua* ☎ *254/324774* ⊕ *www.rvp.pt*). **Rota do Vinhos Verdes** (⊠ *Rua da Restauração 318* ☎ *22/607–7300* ⊕ *www.vinhoverde.pt*). **Vieguini Scooters** (☎ *91/430–6838* ⊕ *www.vieguini.com*).

Tourist Police **Esquadra de Turismo da Polícia de Segurança Pública** (⊠ *Rua Clube dos Fenianos 11* ☎ *22/208–1833* ✉ *prtetur@psp.pt*).

Visitor Info Porto e Norte (Regional Tourism Office ✉ *Rua do Hospital Velho, Viana do Castelo* ☎ *258/820620 or 808/202202* ⊕ *www.portoenorte.pt)*. **Turismo de Portugal** (National Tourism Office ✉ *Praça Dom João I, 43, east of Av. dos Aliados* ☎ *92/741–1817, 808/781212 National Contact Center* ⊕ *www.portoturismo.pt* ✉ *Aeroporto Francisco Sá Carneiro Maia* ☎ *22/943–2400*). **Turismo Municipal (Porto)** (✉ *Rua Clube dos Fenianos 25* ☎ *22/339–3472* ⊕ *www.visitporto.travel* ✉ *Rua do Infante Dom Henrique 63, south of Praça da Liberdade* ☎ *22/206–0412 or 22/206–0413* ✉ *Terreiro da Sé* ☎ *22/332–5174* ⊙ *Closed weekends)*.

WHAT'S IN A NAME?

The importance of the river trade to the city is reflected in its current name, whose use began in early medieval times. *Porto* means simply "port," and over the centuries the city has traded widely in fish, salt, and wine. English and Spanish speakers' name for Porto—Oporto—is a result of a misunderstanding. When the Portuguese said "o Porto" (the port), traders assumed the "o" was part of the city's name.

Turismo Municipal (Vila Nova de Gaia) (✉ *Av. Diogo Leite 242, Vila Nova de Gaia* ☎ *22/370–3735* ⊕ *www.cm-gaia.pt* ✉ *Cais de Gaia, Av. Ramos Pinto, Vila Nova de Gaia* ☎ *22/375–6216)*.

EXPLORING

Fodor'sChoice ★ **Cais da Ribeira** *(Ribeira Pier).* A string of fish restaurants and *tascas* (taverns) are built into the street-level arcade of timeworn buildings along this pier. In the Praça da Ribeira, people sit and chat around an odd, modern, cubelike sculpture; farther on, steps lead to a walkway above the river that's backed by tall houses. The pier also provides the easiest access to the lower level of the middle bridge across the Douro, the Ponte Dom Luis I. Boats docked at Cais da Ribeira and across the river in Vila Nova da Gaia offer various cruises around the bridges and up the river to Peso da Régua and Pinhão.

Fodor'sChoice ★ **Estação de São Bento.** This train station was built in the early 20th century (King D. Carlos I laid the first brick himself in 1900) and inaugurated in 1915. It sits precisely where the Convent of S. Bento de Avé-Maria was located, and therefore inherited the convent's name—Saint Bento. The atrium is covered with 20,000 azulejos painted by Jorge Colaço (1916) depicting scenes of Portugal's history as well as ethnographic images. It is one of the most magnificent artistic undertakings of the early 20th century. The building was designed by architect Marques da Silva. ✉ *Praça Almeida Garret* ☎ *22/205–1714, 808/208208 national call center* ⊕ *www.cp.pt.*

Igreja de São Francisco *(Church of St. Francis).* During the last days of Porto's siege by the absolutist army (the *miguelistas*) in July 1842, there was gunfire by the nearby São Francisco Convent. These shootings caused a fire that destroyed most parts of the convent, sparing only this church. The church is an undistinguished, late 14th-century Gothic building on the outside, but inside is an astounding interior: gilded carving—added in the mid-18th century—runs up the pillars, over the altar, and across the ceiling. An adjacent museum (Museu de

8

Arte Sacra) houses furnishings from the Franciscan convent. A guided tour (call the day before) includes a visit to the church, museum, and catacombs. Note that the riverside tram ride to Foz starts here. ⊠ *Rua do Infante Dom Henrique 93* ☎ *22/206–2100* 🖃 *€3.50* 🕙 *Nov.–Feb., daily 9–5:30; Mar., Apr., and Oct., daily 9–6; May–Sept., daily 9–7.*

Fodor'sChoice ★ **Museu de Arte Contemporânea.** Designed by Álvaro Siza Vieira, a winner of the Pritzker Prize and Portugal's best-known architect, the Contemporary Art Museum is part of the Serralves Foundation and is surrounded by lovely gardens. It has changing international exhibitions, as well as work from Portuguese painters, sculptors, and designers. Check with the tourist office for the latest information. The original art deco house and its small formal garden is also worth visiting; as well as housing the foundation, it hosts small exhibitions. Various joint tickets are available, including one to the museum and to the Sea Life aquarium in Foz. To get here, take a taxi or catch the metro to Casa da Música and then Bus 201, 203, 502, or 504 from the Rotunda da Boavista; or from downtown take Bus 201 from Avenida dos Aliados—about a 30-minute ride. ⊠ *Rua D. João de Castro 210* ☎ *22/615–6500 or 808/200–543* ⊕ *www.serralves.pt* 🖃 *Museum and garden Tues.–Sat. €7, garden €3; Sun. free to 1 pm* 🕙 *Oct.–Mar. museum and house Tues.–Fri. 10–5, weekends 10–8; park Tues.–Sun. 10–7. Apr.–Sept. museum Tues.–Fri. 10–5, weekends 10–8; house Tues.–Fri. 10-5, weekends 10–7; park Tues.–Fri. 10–7, weekends 10–8.*

Palácio da Bolsa. Porto's neoclassical former stock exchange takes up much of the site of the former Franciscan convent at the Igreja de São Francisco. Guided tours (every half hour) are the only way to see the interior of this masterpiece of 19th-century Portuguese architecture. The Arab-style ballroom, in particular, is one of the most admired chambers and was designed by civil engineer Gustavo Adolfo Gonçalves e Sousa. ⊠ *Rua Ferreira Borges* ☎ *22/339–9013* ⊕ *www.palaciodabolsa.pt* 🖃 *Tours €6* 🕙 *Apr.–Sept., daily 9–6:30; Oct.–Mar., daily 9–12:30 and 2–5:30.*

Torre dos Clérigos. Designed by Italian architect Nicolau Nasoni and begun in 1754, the tower of the church Igreja dos Clérigos reaches an impressive height of 249 feet. There are 225 steep stone steps to the belfry, and the considerable effort required to climb them is rewarded by stunning views of the Old Town, the river, and beyond to the mouth of the Douro. The church itself, also built by Nasoni, predates the tower and is an elaborate example of Italianate Baroque architecture. ⊠ *Rua S. Filipe Nery* ☎ *22/200–1729* 🖃 *Tower €1.50, church free* 🕙 *Tower Sept.–May, daily 10–noon and 2–5; June and July, daily 9:30–1 and 2:30–7; Aug., daily 10–7. Church 8:45–12:30 and 3:30–7.*

OUTSIDE DOWNTOWN

Boa Nova Tea House. Architecture buffs intrigued by Álvaro Siza Vieira's work after visiting the Serralves Contemporary Art Museum might consider a trip to Matosinhos, north of Foz, to see the spectacularly sited, modernist teahouse. One of Siza's earliest projects, completed in 1963, it was designed after careful analysis of the surrounding rock formations, tides, and flora. The approach—a series of platforms and steps—provides a sense of anticipation and views of the structure and the ocean beyond it. In summer, the enormous windows slide down, creating the impression you can step right out into the sea. You can eat here, or order drinks from noon to midnight. ⊠ *Rua Boa Nova, Leça da PalmeiraMatosinhos* ☎ *22/995–1785* ⊘ *Closed Sun.*

Foz do Douro. Literally "Mouth of the Douro," this prosperous suburb is invariably known here simply as "Foz." You haven't got under the skin of Porto if you haven't come out here: it's a place where city-dwellers flock to lounge on its endless beaches or go for brisk walks on its magnificent promenades. There are some spectacularly sited beach restaurants and cafés, such as **Praia dos Ingleses** (☎ *22/617–0419*), perched above a rock-framed beach of the same name, which draws youngsters year-round with well-priced snacks and free Wi-Fi. The area is also one of the city's main nightlife hubs. A fun if slow way to get to Foz is to catch Tram 1; its route hugs the riverbank, starting next to the church of São Francisco in the Ribeira.

☺ **Sea Life.** Arguably Porto's top kids' attraction since it opened in 2009, this aquarium is at the western end of Avenida da Boavista (next to the Castelo do Queijo, a 17th-century coastal fort that's also worth a look). Sharks, jellyfish, and seahorses are among the 5,600 or so animals on display, representing more than 100 species. Joint tickets are available for Sea Life and the Serralves Contemporary Art Museum, but if you only plan to visit the aquarium, note that tickets bought online are cheaper. The nearby Parque da Cidade, a large landscaped park dotted with trees and lakes, is a lovely place for a picnic. ⊠ *1ª Rua Particular do Castelo do Queijo, Foz* ☎ *22/619–0400* ⊕ *www.sealife-porto.pt* 🎫 *€11.50* ⊘ *Weekdays 10–6, weekends 10–7 (last entry 45 min before closing).*

8

WHERE TO EAT

$
PORTUGUESE
Fodor's Choice
★

✕ **Abadia do Porto.** The cavernous interior, thick tablecloths, and well-heeled clientele tell you this is not just another *tasca*, but the food at this backstreet abbey downtown is ultratraditional. Although the decor has a monastic theme, meals here are far from austere, so come hungry to make the most of the huge servings of *cabrito assado* (roast kid), *rancho* (mixed grill), *bacalhau à Gomes Sá* (codfish with onions, potato, egg, and olives) and Porto *tripas*—tripe with beans, chouriço, and vegetables. It's all great value if you share a dish between two or even three people. The chocolate-flavor *pão-de-ló* spongecake is divine, too. ⊠ *Rua Ateneu Comercial do Porto 22–24* ☎ *22/200–8757* ⊕ *www.abadiadoporto.com* ▤ *AE, DC, MC, V* ⊘ *Closed Sun.*

$$
FUSION
Fodor's Choice
★

✕ **Buhle.** A restaurant and teahouse but also a sushi, tapas, and mixology bar, Buhle is one of Porto's "it" places, garlanded with international prizes for design and service. In a series of artfully lit glass-and-wood modules, diners choose from an eclectic selection of Portuguese comfort food and Asian cuisine: foie gras with banana mash and balsamic reduction, black cod with puree of edamame (sweet Japanese green beans) and shiitake mushrooms, or *costela mendinha* (short ribs) with saffron risotto. The wine list is among the city's most

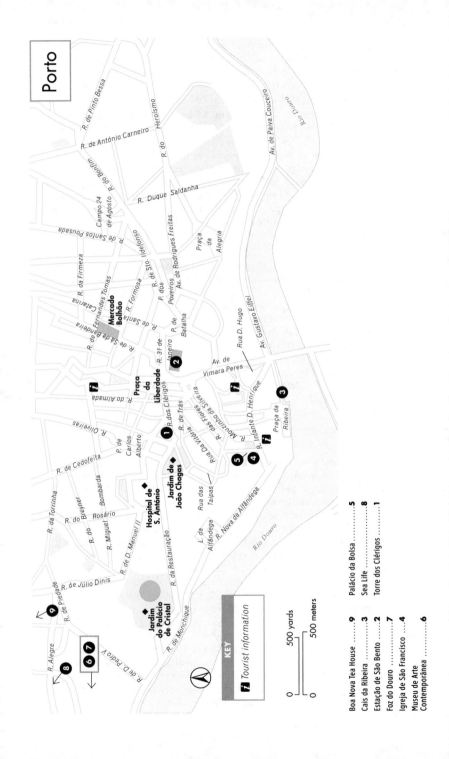

Porto

KEY

ⓘ *Tourist information*

0   500 yards

0   500 meters

Boa Nova Tea House **9**

Cais da Ribeira **3**

Estação de São Bento **2**

Foz do Douro **7**

Igreja de São Francisco **4**

Museu de Arte
Contemporânea **6**

Palácio da Bolsa **5**

Sea Life **8**

Torre dos Clérigos **1**

CLOSE UP

Port Wine

Many of the more than 16 companies with caves in Vila Nova de Gaia are still foreign owned. They include such well-known names as Sandeman, Osborne, Cockburn, Kopke, Ferreira, Calém, Taylor's, Barros, Ramos-Pinto, Real Companhia Velha, Fonseca, Rozès, Burmester, Offley, Noval, and Graham's. All are signposted and within a few minutes' walk of the bridge and each other; their names are also displayed in huge white letters across their roofs. Each company offers free guided tours of its facility, which always end with a tasting of one or two wines and an opportunity to buy bottles from the company store. Children are usually welcome and are often fascinated by the huge warehouses and all sorts of interesting machinery. From April through September, the major lodges are generally open daily 9:30–12:30 and 2–6, although some close on weekends; the rest of the year, tours start a little later and end a little earlier. Tours begin regularly, usually when enough visitors are assembled. The tourist office at Vila Nova de Gaia offers a small map of the main lodges and can advise you on hours of the smaller operations. Some lodges also have restaurants with quite sophisticated menus; a prime example is Taylor's **Barão Fladgate** (*Rua do Choupelo 250* ☎ *22/374-2800* ⊕ *www.tresseculos.pt*), whose location uphill means its garden and terrace afford magnificent views of Porto.

---

extensive, although the Douro definitely takes pride of place. In summer, a wall slides away to reveal a stylish garden. ⊠ *Av. Montevido 810, Foz* ☎ *22/010–9929* ⊕ *www.buhle.pt* ⌲ *Reservations essential* ▭ *AE, DC, MC, V* ⊘ *No lunch Mon.–Thurs.*

$$
PORTUGUESE
✕ **Chez Lapin.** At this Cais da Ribeira restaurant overlooking the river, the service may be slow and the folksy decor may be overdone, but the food is excellent. Grab a table on the attractive outdoor terrace and order generous portions of such traditional Portuguese dishes as bacalhau *à lagareiro* (baked salt cod with potatoes), sardines with rice and beans, and beef medallions with port wine. The restaurant is mainly patronized by foreign visitors, so if you're after authentic Porto cuisine in a less touristy setting, look elsewhere. The family-owned company that owns the restaurant (Douro Acima) offers river excursions on its six traditional boats docked at the quay. ⊠ *Rua dos Canastreiros 40–42* ☎ *22/200–6418* ⊕ *www.issimo.pt* ⌲ *Reservations essential* ▭ *AE, DC, MC, V.*

$$
PORTUGUESE
✕ **Dom Tonho.** Seafood is the specialty of this riverfront restaurant owned by veteran musician and Porto native Rui Veloso, which occupies a beautiful and historic building that dates back to the 16th century. Try grilled fish, one of the codfish dishes, *lombo de veado* (loin of venison) or real local specialty *tripas à moda do Porto* (tripe stew with beans and vegetables). Both smokers and nonsmokers are catered for here. There's now another Dom Tonho serving similar food just across the Dom Luís bridge in Gaia—affording amazing views of Porto itself. ⊠ *Cais da Ribeira 13–15* ☎ *22/200–4307* ⊕ *www.dtonho.com* ▭ *AE, DC, MC, V.*

8

LITTLE FRENCHIE

If you thought *tripas à moda do Porto* (tripe and bean stew) was the city's most bizarre culinary invention, then sample a *francesinha* (literally "little Frenchie"). This multilayer sandwich features cheese, cured ham, sausage, and steak, all drenched in a spicy beer-based sauce. The dish is served at diners across town in myriad variations; many locals have to have their regular fix, and there is fierce debate about who does the best. Many locals now swear by **Bufete Fase** (✉ *Rua Santa Catarina 1147* ☎ *22/205–2118* ✆ *Closed Sun.*), a tiny snack bar near the top of one of Porto's main shopping streets. **Capa Negra II** (✉ *Rua Campo Alegre 191* ☎ *22/607–8383* ⊕ *www.capanegra.com*), near the Rotunda da Boavista, has long been the most famous opponent.

$$$
PORTUGUESE
Fodor's Choice
★
✕ **DOP.** Chef Rui Paula won national fame with reinventions of traditional dishes at his restaurant DOC, upriver on the Douro. Now he's thrilling Porto foodies in this elegant refitted palace. There's a mezzanine for smokers, or watch starters being prepared downstairs. Mains include new takes on *bacalhau com broa* (codfish with cornbread) and *tripas* (tripe)—if you've tried this Porto dish elsewhere, you'll be amazed by Paula's ultralight version. There are vegetarian dishes, a wide selection of wines by the bottle (from €17) or glass, and desserts featuring rural flavors such as quince and chestnuts. There are two tasting menus: Douro (€65 for five courses) and seafood (€75 for six). ✉ *Palácio das Artes, Largo de São Domingos 18* ☎ *22/201–4313* ⊕ *www.ruipaula.com* ▭ *AE, DC, MC, V.*

$$
ECLECTIC
✕ **Shis.** On Ourigo beach out at Foz, Shis lures in diners with its waterfront views. The sushi menu is one of the city's most extensive and other dishes show clear Asian influences, for example in fish and seaweed soup, and miso with clams and tofu. Popular main dishes include Châteaubriand with eggplant tempura and ginger sauce, tournedos, and confit of bacalhau with spring greens and a rich *serra* cheese sauce. There are also various pastas and risottos. ✉ *Praia do Ourigo, Esplanada do Castelo* ☎ *22/618–9593* ⊕ *www.shisrestaurante.com* ▭ *AE, DC, MC, V.*

WHERE TO STAY

$
Fodor's Choice
★
⊡ **Boa-Vista.** The name means "nice view" and this hotel does indeed overlook the Douro estuary and the Atlantic Ocean. It's in Foz, a 10- to 15-minute taxi ride or 20-minute bus ride ticket (€1.50) west of the town center, making it handy for the area's swish restaurants and nightclubs. The handsome mid-19th-century former convent has small, simply decorated guest rooms that are well equipped. Ask for one of the pricier rooms with sea views (and Jacuzzi in the bathroom), or settle for the view from the rooftop pool and terrace. There's a spacious gym but no sauna. **Pros:** pool and terrace have fantastic views and Wi-Fi; quiet area; planning restrictions tight so this is the only hotel here. **Cons:** a ways out of town; rooms a little small. ✉ *Esplanada do Castelo 58, Foz* ☎ *22/532–0020* ⊕ *www.hotelboavista.com* ↝ *71 rooms,*

4 suites ⅃ In-room: a/c, safe, Wi-Fi. In-hotel: restaurant, room service, bar, pool, gym, laundry service, Internet terminal, Wi-Fi hotspot, parking (paid) ▭ *AE, DC, MC, V* ❍▮ *BP, MAP, FAP.*

¢ ▦ **Estoril.** The Estoril offers functional but comfortable rooms at reasonable rates. It's in a quiet location near the galleries and shops of Rua Miguel Bombarda, and has a terrace, a bar, and paid parking in a nearby garage. There's a real family feel, thanks to a comfy sitting room with fireplace. Rooms include twins, doubles, triples and one quadruple, with no a/c but heating throughout. Ask for a room with a balcony at the back; with the hens and vegetable patches you might be in rural Minho. If you want a continental breakfast (€2) you must let staff know the night before, although there is also a café next door. **Pros:** friendly atmosphere; range of room types. **Cons:** rooms a little shabby though clean; some problems with Wi-Fi. ✉ *Rua de Cedofeita 193* ☎ *22/200–2751* ⊕ *www.pensaoestoril.com* ⟿ *17 rooms ⅃ In-room: no a/c, no phone, Wi-Fi. In-hotel: bar, Internet terminal, Wi-Fi hotspot, some pets allowed* ▭ *AE, DC, MC, V* ❍▮ *EP, CP.*

$ ▦ **Grande Hotel do Porto.** If you enjoy shopping, you can't do better than the stately Grande Hotel do Porto, as it sits on the city's best shopping street. The hotel has just the right mix of old-fashioned charm and newfangled amenities. Public areas such as the lounge and library, with its daily newspapers in English, and the Windsor Bar are full of turn-of-the-last-century details; streamlined guest rooms are loaded with modern amenities. Some are rather small and rates can vary; it's worth checking for bargains. The D. Pedro II restaurant, which serves Portuguese cuisine, was recently given a modern makeover. **Pros:** good location; efficient staff; near public transportation. **Cons:** most rooms rather small; room safe costs €3 a day; restaurant kitchen closes at 10 pm. ✉ *Rua de Santa Catarina 197* ☎ *22/207–6690* ⊕ *www.grandehotelporto.com* ⟿ *86 rooms, 8 suites ⅃ In-room: a/c, safe, refrigerator, Wi-Fi. In-hotel: restaurant, room service, bar, laundry service, Internet terminal, Wi-Fi hotspot, parking (paid)* ▭ *AE, DC, MC, V* ❍▮ *BP, MAP, FAP* Ⓜ *Bolhão.*

$$$ ▦ **Infante Sagres.** Intricately carved wood details, rare area rugs and
Fodor's Choice tapestries, stained-glass windows, and antiques decorate public areas
★ in what on its inauguration in 1951 was Porto's first luxury hotel. It remains an icon, its interior now enlivened by striking contemporary furniture from local company Boca do Lobo. In guest rooms, shades of beige, cream, and white complement dark-wood furnishings and lend a contemporary character; bathrooms are all marble or sheer black, and have sophisticated lighting. Suites harbor unique antiques and dreamy Hästens beds—no wonder the place is favored by European aristos, who can also take advantage of a private treatment room. Despite the glamour, staff couldn't be nicer. **Pros:** oodles of style; central location; fine views from upper floors. **Cons:** no pool or gym; few in-room amenities; bathroom lighting more stylish than effective. ✉ *Praça D. Filipa de Lencastre 62* ☎ *22/339–8500* ⊕ *www.hotelinfantesagres.pt* ⟿ *62 rooms, 8 suites ⅃ In-room: a/c, safe, refrigerator, DVD (some), Wi-Fi. In-hotel: restaurant, room service, bar, laundry service, Internet terminal, Wi-Fi hotspot* ▭ *AE, DC, MC, V* ❍▮ *BP, EP, MAP, FAP.*

8

$ ⊡ **Pão de Açúcar.** Just off Avenida dos Aliados, this simply but elegantly decorated art nouveau pensão offers a lot of amenities for relatively modest rates. You can choose from among dark and simple rooms, suites, or six top-floor rooms with private terrace. Other guests at least may take breakfast on the top-floor terrace, with its view of the towering city hall. Windows are double-glazed throughout, keeping out downtown traffic noise. The owner also runs the Vera Cruz, a slightly smaller pensão in a modern building down the street that is equally good value, and whose breakfast room has even better views. **Pros:** recently refurbished; free Wi-Fi; prime location. **Cons:** parking a block away; TV/Internet lounge a little small. ⊠ *Rua do Almada 262* ☎ *22/200–2425* ⊕ *www.residencialpaodeacucar.com* ⟿ *50 rooms, 8 suites* ⟳ *In-room: a/c, Wi-Fi. In-hotel: room service, bar, laundry service, Internet terminal, Wi-Fi hotspot* ⊟ *AE, MC, V* ⏴⊙⏵ *BP* Ⓜ *Trindade.*

$$$ ⊡ **Pestana Porto.** Right in Porto's historic heart, the Pestana Porto is in a restored former warehouse abutted by a medieval wall, linked to several neighboring former houses. As a result, every room is different; some are unusually shaped. They have river views or overlook an alley in the Ribeira; all are contemporary, cozy, and almost cluttered with vibrant fabrics, plush carpets, throw pillows, and upholstered chairs, offsetting the restored stone window jambs and lintels. Above the reception a mezzanine comprises a business center and a small lounge with a river view. Parking is in a nearby garage with which the hotel has an accord. **Pros:** charming historic building; well located for sightseeing in Ribeira and Gaia. **Cons:** few facilities; not a good choice for families; bus stop is up a steep hill. ⊠ *Praça da Ribeira 1* ☎ *22/340–2300* ⊕ *www.pestana.com* ⟿ *45 rooms, 3 suites* ⟳ *In-room: a/c, DVD (on request), safe, refrigerator, Wi-Fi. In-hotel: room service, bar, laundry service, Internet terminal, Wi-Fi hotspot* ⊟ *AE, DC, MC, V* ⏴⊙⏵ *BP.*

$$$ ⊡ **Sheraton Porto Hotel & Spa.** Seen by many as the city's top hotel, the Sheraton Porto's declared aim is to blend design and comfort. From the towering white lobby with its velvety black sofas to the darkly handsome guest rooms, it does so empathically. The breakfast buffet is amazing, and includes a separate section for dieters. At Sunday brunch there's even a clown on hand for the kids. The luxury spa is a big draw, with its unisex sauna and steambath, and a pool and winter garden bathed in natural light. In the excellent restaurant, the glass-walled wine "cellar" organizes tastings accompanied by fine hams and cheeses for groups of up to eight. **Pros:** stunningly stylish; 24-hour luxury spa accessible via VIP lift; smoking areas in bar and restaurant. **Cons:** a little far from center; only pricier rooms have terraces; spa and Wi-Fi/Internet not included with standard room rate. ⊠ *Rua Tenente Valadim 146, Boavista* ☎ *22/040–4000* ⊕ *www.sheratonporto.com* ⟿ *241 rooms, 25 suites* ⟳ *In-room: a/c, safe, refrigerator, Internet, Wi-Fi. In-hotel: restaurant, room service, bar, 2 pools, gym, spa, laundry service, Internet terminal, Wi-Fi hotspot, parking (paid)* ⊟ *AE, DC, MC, V* ⏴⊙⏵ *EP, BP, MAP, FAP* Ⓜ *Francos.*

Fodor's Choice
★

NIGHTLIFE AND THE ARTS

Noted as a center for modern art, Porto enjoys regular and changing exhibitions at the Museu de Arte Contemporânea, as well as at a variety of galleries, many of which are on Rua Miguel Bombarda. Check local newspapers or with the tourist board for listings of current exhibitions as well as concerts. If you read Portuguese, the monthly magazine *Time Out Porto* and the pocket booklet *Guia da Noite do Porto* (available in cafés, bars, and cultural institutions) are good ways to find out what's on, and what's in.

NIGHTLIFE

BARS

A number of old-style cafés such as the **Guarany** or **Majestic** (*see Need a Break box*) are good places for an early-evening drink but don't represent what locals would term nightlife. And while the waterfront Ribeira district was once popular with bohemian bar-hoppers, it's now been left almost exclusively to tourists. But there's been a nightlife renaissance in central Porto, in the area just to the north of the Torre dos Clérigos. Fashionable bars in this area are open from mid-afternoon until 3 am (or 4 am on Friday and Saturday).

Café Candelabro (⊠ *Rua da Conceição 3* ☎ *96/698–4250* ⊕ *www. cafecandelabro.com* ☾ *Closed Sun.*) is a bohemian option where drinks run cheaper than most other bars in the area. It is supposed to close at 2 am, but hours are elastic on weekends. **Três C** (⊠ *Rua Cândido dos Reis 18* ☎ *22/201–8247* ⊕ *www.clube3c.pt* ☾ *Closed Sun.*) is one of a number of local bars housed in former shops (this one once sold cloth). Its decoration blends the antique and the contemporary, and it is a popular meeting place for fashionable thirtysomethings. **Twin's Baixa** (⊠ *Rua Cândido dos Reis 12* ☎ *91/701–2264* ⊕ *www.twins.pt*), a spinoff of a long-established nightclub in Foz, attracts well-heeled youngsters.

Fodor's Choice
★

For a glass of port, the best place is the **Solar do Vinho do Porto** (⊠ *Rua de Entre-Quintas 220* ☎ *22/609–4749*), a former manor house open from 4 pm until midnight every day but Sunday. There are lovely views of the river from the small formal garden, where chairs are often set out. As well as 120 ports by the glass (and more by the bottle), table wines from the Douro are on sale, accompanied if you like by fine cheeses and hams. You can also buy wine-related products such as glasses and glossy books on local vineyards. The best time to visit is in the late afternoon.

DANCE AND MUSIC CLUBS

For live music, go to the **Hard Club** (⊠ *Mercado Ferreira Borges,* ☎ *707/ 101–021*), in a magnificent former market hall with cast-iron pillars opposite the Palácio da Bolsa. Friday and Saturday (and some Thursdays) you might catch folk, heavy metal, or a nationally known pop group; on other nights there are cinema screenings, theater, and the odd DJ session. There's an airy café-restaurant upstairs with free Wi-Fi.

Music from the 1960s and '70s continues to draw an older upper-class crowd at **Twin's** (⊠ *Rua do Passeio Alegre 1000, Foz* ☎ *22/616–5000*).

8

THE ARTS

THEATERS AND CONCERT HALLS

Fodor's Choice ★ Porto's newest cultural jewel, **Casa da Música** (✉ *Av. da Boavista 604–610* ☎ *22/012–0220* ⊕ *www.casadamusica.com*) is a work of art by Dutch architect Rem Koolhaas, with fabulous acoustics to boot. Its construction unleashed something of the "Guggenheim effect" seen in formerly little-visited Bilbao, with architecture enthusiasts traveling to Porto primarily to see its "house of music." Three esteemed Portuguese groups are in residency here: the Remix Ensemble, Remix Orchestra, and Opera Studio. **Coliseu do Porto** (✉ *Rua de Passos Manuel 137* ☎ *22/339–4940* ⊕ *www.coliseudoporto.pt*) is one of the biggest showrooms in Portugal, with 3,000 seats. Show biz greats who have appeared here include Marcel Marceau, Pat Metheny, Diana Krall, Bob Dylan, BB King, Michael Nyman, Al Di Meola, Paco de Lucía, and Amália Rodrigues.

Designed in 1978, **Teatro Nacional de S. João** (✉ *Praça da Batalha* ☎ *22/340–1900 or 800/108675* ⊕ *www.tnsj.pt*) hosts and produces a good range of classical and contemporary concerts and plays all year-round. Tickets range from €7.50 to €16.

OUTDOOR ACTIVITIES

The main sporting obsession in Porto is *futebol* (soccer), and the city has one of the country's best teams, FC Porto, which rivals Lisbon's Benfica for domestic fame and fortune. Futebol matches are played September through May at the 52,000-seat **Estádio do Dragão** (*Dragon Stadium* ✉ *Alameda das Antas, off Av. de Fernão de Magalhães* ☎ *22/508–3300* ⊕ *www.fcporto.pt*) in the eastern part of the city by the ring road; it is served by four metro lines.

SHOPPING

The best shopping streets are those off the Praça da Liberdade, particularly Rua 31 de Janeiro, Rua dos Clérigos, Rua de Santa Catarina, Rua Sá da Bandeira, Rua Cedofeita, and Rua das Flores. Traditionally, Rua das Flores has been the street for silversmiths. Gold-plated filigree is also a regional specialty, found along the same street and along Rua de Santa Catarina. Rua 31 de Janeiro and nearby streets are the center of the shoe trade, and many shops create made-to-measure shoes on request.

You'll see port on sale throughout the city. But first taste the wine at either the Solar do Vinho do Porto or the caves at Vila Nova de Gaia. You may want to buy a bottle of the more unusual white port, drunk as an aperitif, as it's not commonly sold in North America or Britain. Try a Portonic, half-tonic water and half-white port served in a special glass that you'll see sold in most shops.

CLOTHING AND FOOTWEAR

With Portugal's large textile and apparel industries concentrated in the north, Porto unsurprisingly has more than its share of the country's leading fashion designers. Luís Buchinho was the first one to move

NEED A BREAK?

Many of Porto's old-style coffeehouses—which once rivaled Lisbon's in opulence and literary legend—have disappeared. A few have survived and are perfect places to sit and imbibe both a *cimbalino* (espresso) and the city.

The ornate **Majestic Café** (✉ *Rua de Santa Catarina 112* ☎ *22/200–3887* ⊕ *www.cafemajestic.com* ⊘ *Daily 9 am–midnight*) has piano music and temporary art exhibitions. It's on a busy pedestrian shopping street, a short walk from Avenida dos Aliados. At the attractively restored **Confeitaria do Bolhão** (✉ *Rua*

Formosa 339 ☎ *22/339–5220* ⊕ *www.confeitariadobolhao.com*) choose from an impressive range of delicious bread, cakes, and pastries. Try a feather-light *pão-de-ló* sponge cake, served fresh from the oven with the baking paper still round it.

Founded in 1933, the **Guarany Café** (✉ *Av. dos Aliados 89/85* ☎ *22/332–1272* ⊕ *www.cafeguarany.com*) is a superb place combining the early-20th-century coffeehouse atmosphere with live concerts on Friday and Saturday (fado and Cuban music) or literature presentations and discussions.

his store downtown to the Baixa, which has since become the city's most happening district.

The practical, comfortable designs on sale at **Buchinho** (✉ *Rua José Falcão 122* ☎ *22/201–0184*) have a strong urban feel to them.

At **Maria Gambina** (✉ *Rua Fonte da Luz 197, Foz* ☎ *22/610–7083*), the designer's street wear for men and women is sometimes subdued, sometimes splashed with bright red, blue, or green. It is often inspired by vintage styles.

Amid the art galleries on Miguel Bombarda are suitably funky fashion stores such as **Miau Frou Frou** (✉ *Rua Miguel Bombarda 416* ☎ *96/642–2103*), which also has unusual costume jewelery.

A former cinema now houses several fashion showcases, including veteran designer Ana Salazar and imaginative Lisbon duo **Storytailors** (✉ *Galerias Lumière Loja 14, Rua José Falcão 157* ☎ *22/201–7409* ⊕ *www. storytailors.pt*), whose frocks are often inspired in part by fairy tales.

Vogue (✉ *Rua Júlio Dinis 821* ☎ *22/600–0342*) is a good place to check out footwear from the manufacturing heartland of northern Portugal, the quality of whose design has improved hugely in recent years. It has another branch at Rua 31 de Janeiro 80.

CRAFT AND STATIONERY

For a general handicrafts emporium, try **Artesanato dos Clérigos** (✉ *Rua da Assunção 33–34* ☎ *22/200–0257*), next to Torre dos Clérigos.

One of Portugal's most talked-about retailers is **A Vida Portuguesa** (✉ *Rua da Galeria de Paris 20, 1st fl.* ☎ *22/202–2105* ⊘ *Closed Sun.*), whose Porto branch is upstairs in a magnificent former clothing store. Like the original shop in Lisbon, it carries old Portuguese brands—many with delightful packaging—of products that include soap and other toiletries, stationery, costume jewelry, handicrafts and period toys.

For luxury toiletries and perfumed paper by a local firm whose products are hard to find abroad, visit **Castelbel** (✉ *Hotel Infante Sagres, Praça D. Filipa de Lencastre 62,* ☎ *22/982–6430* ⊕ *www.castelbel.com*) on the corner of the Hotel Infante Sagres.

Fodor'sChoice ★ **Livraria Lello e Irmão** (✉ *Rua das Carmelitas 144* ☎ *22/200–2880*) is one of the most special and important bookshops in Portugal. It opened in 1906, and shelters more than 60,000 books. But it's most famous for its neo-Gothic design and two-story interior with intricate wood-carved details—locals maintain that all this helped inspire J.K. Rowling, who dreamed up Harry Potter while living in Porto.

Pedro A. Baptista (✉ *Rua das Flores 237* ☎ *22/200–2880*) deals in antique and modern silver. Downtown, the stylish **Prometeu** (✉ *Rua da Alfândega 7* ☎ *22/201–9295*) has ceramics, tiles, and other handicrafts from all over the country. It has two other shops at Rua Mouzinho da Silveira 136 and at Muro dos Bacalhoeiros 125.

FOOD AND WINE

A limited selection of port wines can be had at any supermarket, but for a wider range—and expert advice from a French expat—stop by **Vinologia** (✉ *Rua Anibal Cunha 269* ☎ *22/201–0184* ☽ *Dec.–Feb. 4–10 pm; Mar.–Nov. 2 pm–midnight*), in the Ribeira district. It organizes tastings of an astonishing selection of 200 ports, accompanied by cheeses and sweets.

MARKETS AND MALLS

If you like contemporary design, head for the **Centro Comercial Bombarda** (✉ *Rua Miguel Bombarda 285* ☎ *934337703* ⊕ *ccbombarda. blogspot.com* ☽ *Closed Sun.*) in Porto's art district. As well as fashion stores (including a showroom for grande dame Ana Salazar and playful newcomer Amilod Zareg), there's fine jewelry at **Adorna Corações** (☎ *96/466–6863* ⊕ *www.estefaniardealmeida.com*). Make sure to walk through to the back of the mall, where in the Bidonville collective young craftspeople work away in little nooks.

For a good general food market, visit the lively **Mercado Bolhão** (✉ *Rua Fernandes Tomás, Edifício Mercado do Bolhão* ☎ *22/332–6024 or 22/209–7200* ☽ *Weekdays 8–5, Sat. 8–1*), within an enclosed building. Female stallholders here are friendly but notorious nationwide for their picturesquely crude language. After working up an appetite at the Mercado Bolhão, stop in at the **Confeitaria do Bolhão** (✉ *Rua Formosa 339* ☎ *22/339–5220* ☽ *Mon.–Sat. 7–7:30*), a delicious-smelling pastry shop.

Shopping Cidade do Porto (✉ *Rua do Bom Sucesso 161* ☎ *22/600–6584* ⊕ *www.shoppingcidadedoporto.com*) is a contemporary mall. More than 13 bus lines, including numbers 3 and 56, reach the Bom Sucesso area and the center.

One of the best shopping centers is **Via Catarina Shopping** (✉ *Rua de Santa Catarina 312–350* ☎ *22/207–5600* ⊕ *www.viacatarina.pt*). Unlike most, this mall is in an old restored building. The top floor is occupied by little restaurants that re-create the Ribeira's architecture with small, medieval-style houses.

THE COAST AND THE DOURO

Espinho, south of Porto, and the main resorts to the north—Vila do Conde, Póvoa de Varzim, Ofir, and Esposende—are the best places for water-sports enthusiasts, with equipment-rental establishments often right on the beaches. Inland, the beautiful Douro Valley awaits, with its carefully terraced vineyards dotted with farmhouses stepping down to the river's edge. Drives along the river lead to romantic ancient towns. This is also the heart of prizewinning wine country, and every town has charming bars where you can pull up a chair, order a bottle and a plate of *petiscos* (mixed appetizers), and watch small-town life go by.

VILA DO CONDE

27 km (17 mi) north of Porto.

Vila do Conde has a long sweep of fine sand, a fishing port, a lace-making school, and a struggling shipbuilding industry that has been making wooden boats since the 15th century. The yards are probably Europe's oldest, and the traditional boat-making skills used in them have changed surprisingly little over the centuries. It was here that the replica of Bartolomeu Dias's caravel was made in 1987 to commemorate his historic voyage around the Cape of Good Hope 500 years earlier. Urban and industrial sprawl mars the outer parts of town, but the center has winding streets and centuries-old buildings.

Vila do Conde has been known for its lace since the 17th century, and it remains the center of a flourishing lace industry. The tourist office can give you information about the Escola de Rendas (Lace-Making School), where you can see how the famed *rendas de bilros* (bone lace) is made. Local artisans also produce excellent sweaters.

GETTING HERE AND AROUND

Though there is no regular over-ground train, Porto's metro (red line) service stops at Vila do Conde on their way to Póvoa, about every 20 minutes. The trip from the Trindade stop in central Porto normally takes over an hour but there's a once-hourly express train that takes 40 minutes. There are also frequent daily buses from Porto and from Viana do Castelo, run by local companies AVIC and Autoviação Minho. The tourist office can provide schedules.

ESSENTIALS

Visitor Info **Vila do Conde** (⊠ *Rua 25 de Abril 103* ☎ *252/248473*).

EXPLORING

The **Convento de Santa Clara** *(Convent of St. Claire)*, now a center for children with disabilities, sprawls along the north bank of the Rio Ave (Ave River), on which Vila do Conde is situated. Dom Afonso Sanches and his wife, Dona Teresa Martins, established the convent in the 14th century, and it retains its original cloister and the beautiful tombs of its founders.

Igreja Matriz. In the center of town near the market, construction on this church was begun at the end of the 15th century and completed in the early 16th. It has a superb late-Gothic portal. ⊠ *Av. Doutor Artur Cunha Araújo 46* ☎ *252/640810.*

8

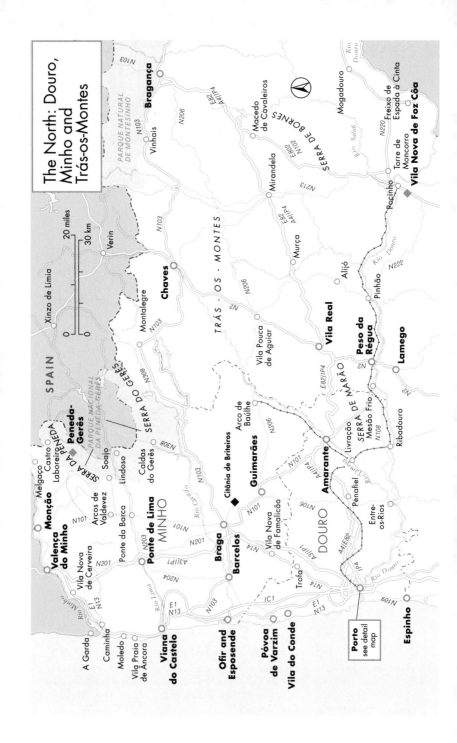

The North: Douro, Minho and Trás-os-Montes

Created in 1919 by António Maria Pereira Júnior, the Escola de Rendas Lace-Making School is attached to the **Museu das Rendas de Bilros de Vila do Conde** *(Museum of Lace Making)*. ⊠ *Rua de S. Bento 70* ☎ *252/248470* ⧉ *€1* ☼ *Tues.– Sun. 10–noon and 2–6.*

Colorful tents on the clean and coarse sand of the craggy beach **Praia de Mindelo** create a shield from inconvenient winds. From Vila do Conde, take the EN13 7½ km (4 mi) south to reach the beach's access at the small fishing village of Mindelo. The drive should take about 10 minutes.

WHERE TO STAY

$ ⛁ **Santana.** This hotel has a lovely landscaped setting on a hill above the River Ave. All rooms face the river and have their own balconies. The decor is modern and streamlined, and rooms are well equipped with amenities that include hair dryer and towel dryer. Some suites also have whirlpool baths. A wide range of massages and other treatments are available in the well-equipped spa, while you can book outdoor activities such as kayaking and diving through reception. The restaurant offers a good selection of national dishes and views of the river and the Mosteiro de Santa Clara (Santa Clara Monastery). **Pros:** lovely riverside setting; five minutes on foot to center of Vila do Conde; free facilities include Wi-Fi and use tennis courts. **Cons:** little nightlife nearby; spa can get noisy in summer. ⊠ *Monte Santana–Azurara* ☎ *252/640460* ⊕ *www. santanahotel.net* ⇆ *65 rooms, 10 suites* ⚐ *In-room: a/c, refrigerator, Wi-Fi (some). In-hotel: restaurant, room service, bar, 2 tennis courts, pool, gym, spa, bicycles, laundry service, Internet terminal, Wi-Fi hotspot, parking (free)* ▭ *AE, DC, MC, V* ⊠❯ *BP, MAP, FAP.*

PÓVOA DE VARZIM

4 km (2½ mi) north of Vila do Conde; 31 km (19 mi) north of Porto.

Póvoa de Varzim has a long beach, but the town has little of Vila do Conde's charm—except, perhaps, for the many shops and roadside stalls that sell similarly beautiful and reasonably priced hand-knit sweaters. It is, instead, a major resort, with high-rise hotels used mostly by vacationing Portuguese. The sandy beach is pleasant, but can become quite crowded in summer—possibly because not many people stay long in the water, where the summer temperature is usually about 16°C (60°F).

GETTING HERE AND AROUND

Póvoa de Varzim is linked with many northern towns, including Porto, by buses run by regional operators Rodonorte and Transdev. The Viana route is plied by Autoviação do Minho (the tourist office can provide schedules). The national Rede Expressos also serves the town, with fast buses from Lisbon. Like Rodornote, it has a local agent at the bus station. One of Porto's metro lines terminates at Póvoa, with trains as frequent as every

20 minutes; the trip from central Porto normally takes well over an hour, but once an hour there's a express train that takes 45 minutes.

ESSENTIALS

Bus **Rede Expressos** (☎ *252/611799* ⊕ *www.rede-expressos.pt*). **Rodonorte** (☎ *252/611799* ⊕ *www.rodonorte.pt*). **Transdev** (☎ *252/298300* ⊕ *www.transdev.pt*).

Visitor Info **Póvoa de Varzim** (✉ *Praça Marquês de Pombal* ☎ *252/298120*).

EXPLORING

The 1930 waterfront **Casino da Póvoa** is a main attraction. It has an outstanding restaurant called Varandas do Mar, a disco, and nightly floor shows; you must be 18 to enter (take along your passport), and smart-casual dress is your best bet. The casino offers one gambling room where you can choose a range of activities from French or American roulette to blackjack or poker, and a room with 665 slot machines. There's also an entertainment area with special events and nightly shows that begin at 10:30 pm. International stars from crooners to jazz interpreters are regular guests. ✉ *Edifício do Casino da Póvoa do Varzim* ☎ *252/690888* ⊕ *www.casino-povoa.com* ☾ *Sun.–Thurs. 3–3, Fri. and Sat. 4–4.*

WHERE TO EAT AND STAY

$$$
PORTUGUESE
Fodor's Choice
★

✕ **Egoísta.** This restaurant in the Casino has a unique view over the coastline and a very refined style. It's a worthy choice, although it tends to be a bit pricey. Chef Hermínio Costa oversees changing menus dominated by locally caught seafood. You might start with a salad of bacalhau with roast peppers, or fish and lobster soup, and then tuck into fresh fish, roasted, grilled, or sautéed. There are also delicious lamb, pork, and beef dishes. Or have it all with the tasting menu (€45, or €65 with wines). To finish, there's a selection of Portuguese cheeses and fruit compotes. A jacket is not required, but you should dress smartly. ✉ *Edifício Casino da Póvoa do Varzim* ☎ *252/690888* 🖃 *AE, DC, MC, V* ☾ *Closed Sun. and Mon. No lunch. Closed Aug.*

$
☾

🛏 **Grande Hotel da Póvoa.** This affordable beach hotel is a few paces from the sea and casino. Its restaurant and bar have stunning ocean views, as do half the guest rooms. If you want a bargain, settle for one with a view of town; these are always somewhat cheaper. The rooms, which include both smoking and nonsmoking, have modern decor and radio, plus the usual amenities. Children up to 10 get breakfast for free; lunch and dinner in the reliable Steakhouse restaurant is free for under-fives and half price for 5- to 10-year olds. The hotel has no parking but does have cheap deals with nearby facilities. **Pros:** well sited for beach, good value for families. **Cons:** no Wi-Fi in rooms; taxis can't get nearer than 20 meters (65 feet) except early in morning; hotel and car parks fill up in August. ✉ *Largo do Passeio Alegre 20* ☎ *252/290400* ⊕ *www.grandehoteldapovoa.com* 🛏 *84 rooms, 2 suites* ⌂ *In-room: a/c, refrigerator, Internet (some), Wi-Fi (some). In-hotel: restaurant, room service, bar, beachfront, laundry service, Wi-Fi hotspot* 🖃 *AE, DC, MC, V* ☉*BP, MAP, FAP.*

OFIR AND ESPOSENDE

17 km (10 mi) north of Póvoa de Varzim; 46 km (29 mi) north of Porto.

Ofir, on the south bank of the Rio Cávado, has a lovely beach with sweeping white sands, dunes, pinewoods, and water sports—a combination that has made it a popular resort. On the opposite bank of the river, Esposende, which also has a beach, retains elements of the small fishing village it once was. You'll have to drive here to appreciate these twin towns: the train line runs inland at this point, passing through Barcelos.

GETTING HERE AND AROUND

Esposende is on the national express bus network of Rede Expressos, which has a local agent in the market square. Bus services to Esposende from Porto and Viana, meanwhile, are run by Autoviação do Minho. Buses between Esposende and Braga are run by Transdev. The Esposende tourist office can provide more details; it has been in temporary premises on Largo Rodrigues Sampaio for a couple of years now but at some point soon will be returning to its permanent home on Avenida Marginal, while retaining the same phone number.

ESSENTIALS

Bus Rede Expressos (✉ *Marina Bar [local agent], Largo do Mercado, Loja 8* ☎ *253/966813*).

Visitor Info Esposende (✉ *Largo Rodrigues Sampaio 47* ☎ *253/961354*).

EXPLORING

Extending along 16 km (10 mi) of coast north and south of Esposende is the **Parque Natural do Litoral Norte**, an important haven for birds and plant life. As well as dune habitats through which you can wander on boardwalks, it includes the river beaches of the River Cávado estuary and pine and oak forest. Guided visits of up to 10 people can be arranged. (✉ *Office address: 1° de Dezembro 65, Esposende* ☎ *253/965830* ⊕ *www.icnb.pt* ⊙ *Weekdays 9–12:30 and 2–5:30*).

ESPINHO

18 km (11 mi) south of Porto.

Frequent trains and the N109 run past a string of quiet family beaches to Espinho, which has become an increasingly fashionable resort over the years. It has plenty of leisure facilities, including a casino, and a good selection of shops. The long, sandy beach is popular in summer, but you can find some space by walking through the pinewoods to less developed areas to the south.

GETTING HERE AND AROUND

Espinho is served by frequently stopping trains from Porto Campanhã to points south; some fast trains from Lisbon also stop here. The N109 highway runs nearby, and the town is also served by a four-lane spur off the A1 toll motorway. There are frequent local services from Porto's main bus station.

ESSENTIALS

Visitor Info Espinho (✉ *Rua 23, 271* ☎ *22/733–5872*).

EXPLORING

The **Casino Espinho** is by the beach. If the 500 slot machines, horse-racing machines, virtual roulette and blackjack, Portuguese dice, French and American roulette, or blackjack don't do it for you, come for the dining, dancing, and cabaret shows; foreign visitors must present their passports (18 is the minimum age), and although there's no formal dress code, smart and casual is most appropriate. ⊠ *Rua 19, 85* ☎ *22/733–5500* ⊕ *www.solverde.pt* ☉ *Sun.–Thurs. 3–3, Fri. and Sat. 4–4.*

EN ROUTE

At Freixo, 10 km (6 mi) south of Marco de Canaveses on the N211, you can visit the ruins of the Roman town of **Tungobriga,** which harbor the earliest known evidence of a Christian presence in Portugal. As well as traces of a forum, baths, and necropolis, there are colorful mosaics from a paleo-Christian church whose extent shows the place flourished even in late Roman times. The site and **museum** (⊠ *Rua António Correia de Vasconcelos 51* ☎ *255/532099* ⊕ *www.tongobriga.net*) are open for visits every day except Monday, but only in the afternoon on weekends, and from October through March you must book ahead to visit on a Sunday.

WHERE TO EAT AND STAY

$ ✕ **Aquário Marisqueira de Espinho.** This oceanfront restaurant by the
SEAFOOD   casino is one of the most traditional in Espinho. There's an enormous
Fodor's Choice   variety of fresh seafood ready to be grilled, boiled, or roasted in the
★   oven, as well as bacalhau and various fishy stews and rice dishes. Many are best split between two diners. Customers who want meat can choose between dishes such as roast veal or kid—or there's tripe and bean stew, in case you didn't get enough of that in Porto. There are also weekend specials. The wine list is well varied. ⊠ *Rua 4, 540* ☎ *22/733–1000* ⊟ *AE, DC, MC, V.*

$$$ ⊡ **Solverde Spa.** This five-star resort hotel in extensive grounds is on a hill, and most rooms have ocean views. A sandy beach lies some 110 yards away, reached by foot by using a small tunnel under the train line that runs parallel to the coast. For warmer waters, just dive into the hotel's heated saltwater pools. There's also now a swish spa with thalassotherapy (seawater) and other treaments. Of the hotel's two restaurants, one offers alfresco dining; you can also schedule a shuttle for the Solverde group's Casino Espinho, 2 km (1 mi) away on the beach. Convenient for late-night gamblers is the 24-hour room service. Deals are available for two local golf courses. Solverde also owns an aparthotel nearby. **Pros:** use of myriad facilities included in room rate; free bicycles available. **Cons:** out of town; far from train and other transport links; may feel crowded in high season. ⊠ *Av. da Liberdade 212, Praia da Granja, S. Felix da Marinha–Espinho* ☎ *22/7338030* ⊕ *www.solverde.pt* ⤳ *166 rooms, 8 suites* ⌂ *In-room: a/c, safe, refrigerator, Wi-Fi. In-hotel: 2 restaurants, room service, 2 bars, tennis court, 2 pools, gym, spa, bicycles, children's programs (ages 3–12, August only), laundry service, Internet terminal, Wi-Fi hotspot, parking (free)* ⊟ *AE, DC, MC, V* ⦿ *BP, MAP, FAP.*

OUTDOOR ACTIVITIES

The **Clube de Golfe de Miramar** has 9 holes and is 5 km (3 mi) north of Espinho. Nonmembers can play here for €35 (9 holes) or €50 (18 holes) on weekdays, or for €75 (9 holes) or €100 on weekends/holidays.

✉ *Av. Sacadura Cabral-Praia de Miramar, Arcozelo–Vila Nova de Gaia* ☎ *22/762–2067* ⊕ *www.cgm.pt).* The 18-hole **Oporto Golf Club**, founded in 1890 by members of the Port Wine Shippers' Association, is 2 km (1 mi) south of Espinho. Greens fees are €60 on weekdays and €75 weekends, when nonmembers can tee off only from 11 am to 1 pm. ✉ *Paramos–Espinho* ☎ *22/734–2008* ⊕ *www.oportogolfclub.com.*

AMARANTE

Fodor'sChoice ★ *78 km (48 mi) northeast of Espinho; 60 km (37 mi) northeast of Porto.*

Small, agreeable Amarante is the one place in Porto's environs that really demands an overnight stop. Straddling the Rio Tâmega, its halves are joined by a narrow 18th-century bridge that stretches above tree-shaded banks. Although the river is polluted (which precludes swimming), it's beautiful to look at. Rowboats and pedal boats are for hire at several points along the riverside paths. The riverbank is also the site of the local market, held every Wednesday and Saturday morning; at these times, the usually peaceful town is disturbed by manic traffic racing along the main street and over the bridge.

GETTING HERE AND AROUND

Regional bus company Rodornorte serves Lamego from Porto and other regional centers such as Guimarães. You can also take the train a good part of the way from Porto Campanhã, alighting at Livração and then catching a local bus to Amarante (about 25 minutes).

ESSENTIALS

Bus Rodonorte (✉ *Terminal Rodovíario* ☎ *255/422194*).

Visitor Info Amarante (✉ *Alameda Teixeira de Pascoaes* ☎ *255/420246*).

EXPLORING

The imposing **Convento de São Gonçalo** *(St. Gonçalo Convent),* built between the 16th and 20th centuries, is on the north side of the Rio Tâmega. The effigy of the saint, in a room to the left of the altar, is reputed to guarantee marriage to anyone who touches it. His features have almost been worn away over the years, as desperate suitors try and, perhaps, try again. ✉ *Praça da República* ☎ *255/437425* 🎫 *Free* 🕐 *Daily 8–6.*

Fodor'sChoice ★ The cloisters and associated buildings of a convent now house the tourist office and the **Museu Amadeo de Souza-Cardoso.** The museum has an excellent collection of modern Portuguese art, including important works by modernist painter Souza-Cardoso, who pursued variations of fauvism, cubism, futurism, and other avant-garde tendencies. He was born in the area and in 1906 shared an apartment with Amadeo Modigliani in Paris. He returned to Portugal in 1914, and died four years later at the age of 31. The museum also hosts temporary exhibitions and has some interesting archaeological pieces. The star attractions are the *diabos* (devils), a pair of 19th-century carved wooden figures connected with ancient fertility rites. They were venerated on St. Bartholomew's Day (August 24), when the devil was thought to run loose. The originals were destroyed by the French in the Peninsular War. In 1870, the Archbishop of Braga ordered the present two burned because

8

of their pagan function. The São Gonçalo friars didn't go that far, but they did emasculate the male diabo. ✉ *Alameda Teixeira de Pascoaes* ☎ *255/420272* 🎫 *€1* ⊘ *Tues.–Sun. 10–12:30 and 2–5:30. Last entry 12:30 and 5. Closed holidays.*

WHERE TO EAT AND STAY

$
ECLECTIC

✕ **Amaranto.** This spacious, well-appointed restaurant next to the Amaranto Hotel is on the river and near the center of town. The views from here are spectacular, and the menu has excellent regional fare. Try the *cabrito assado* (roast kid), *arroz de marisco* (seafood rice) or *bacalhau à lagareiro* (codfish baked with olive oil and garlic, and served with tiny baked potates. Wash it down with some robust local wine. The place also has a snack bar if you want something lighter and cheaper. ✉ *Edifício Amaranto, Travessa das Murtas* ☎ *255/422006* 🟰 *AE, DC, MC, V.*

$$$
PORTUGUESE
Fodor's Choice
★

✕ **Largo do Paço.** This internationally renowned restaurant in the Casa da Calçada hotel serves innovative Portuguese cuisine, and is now overseen by talented chef Vítor Matos. Carefully constructed tasting menus are on offer (including one for children and, unusually for Portugal, another for vegetarians), but you may also order à la carte. Note that portions are quite small, though, so the full menu is the best value. Dishes available might include bacalhau cooked at an ultra-low temperature to retain the maximum flavor, or *bísaro* regional pork in a blood and cumin sauce, served with chestnut gnocchi. Staff can offer expert help in choosing wine from the lengthy list (which includes the hotel's own *vinho verde*). ✉ *Largo do Paço 6* ☎ *255/410830* ⊕ *www. casadacalcada.com* ⌖ *Reservations essential.* 🟰 *AE, DC, MC, V.*

$
PORTUGUESE
Fodor's Choice
★

✕ **A Quelha.** The restaurants along or near Rua 31 de Janeiro may have river views, but they don't necessarily serve the best food. This friendly, ham-and-garlic-bedecked place—behind a service station off a square at the end of the main street—has no views, but the regional fare served on its wooden tables is fantastic. Regular dishes include *cozido à portuguesa* (a meat, bean, sausage, and vegetable stew), *cabrito assado* (roast kid) and *tripas* (tripe and beans). On weekends there's *arroz de cabidela*: chicken and rice in a rich gravy made from the animal's blood. If you're planning on having dinner, come around 7 pm, because it gets packed. ✉ *Rua da Olivença* ☎ *255/425786* 🟰 *No credit cards.*

¢

🏨 **Amaranto.** You'll have a good view over the old part of Amarante from the south bank of Rio Tâmega. This comfortable hotel is a good option if you are looking for a smart place for a fair value. The simple rooms, recently refurbished, have a standard, international look and include radio and hair dryer. The one suite and several other rooms have balconies with fine views of the city. There are seven triples. Free on-street parking and an underground car park are available nearby. The well-appointed restaurant has spectacular views, and its menu has excellent regional fare with French touches. **Pros:** nice views; free Wi-Fi hotspot; close to local shops. **Cons:** hotel lacks own parking; no exercise facilities; room service not 24 hours. ✉ *Rua Acácio Lino 333* ☎ *255/410840* ⊕ *www.hotelamaranto.com* 🛏 *34 rooms, 1 suite* ⌂ *In-room: a/c, refrigerator, Internet, Wi-Fi (some). In-hotel: room service, bar, laundry service, Internet terminal, Wi-Fi hotspot, some pets allowed* 🟰 *AE, DC, MC, V* ⑩ *BP.*

$$ Casa da Calçada. Next to the old bridge and overlooking the river,
Fodor's Choice this carefully restored former nobleman's manor is one of Portugal's
★ finest hotels. Its ground-floor lounges are comfortable, and its guest
rooms are elegant and individually furnished. The Largo do Paço res-
taurant serves inventive Portuguese cuisine, its reputation now assured
by talented chef Vítor Matos. The gardens contain a swimming pool
and a tennis court; a stay here also gets you a 20% discount at a golf
course a 10-minute drive away. **Pros:** charming setting and building;
one of Portugal's best restaurants; intimate size and ample facilities give
it the feel of a luxury resort. **Cons:** no gym; Wi-Fi not free to guests;
hotel often hosts private events that may be noisy. ⊠ *Largo do Paço 6*
☎ *255/410830* ⊕ *www.casadacalcada.com* ⤸ *26 rooms, 4 suites* ⚲ *In-
room: a/c, refrigerator, Wi-Fi. In-hotel: restaurant, room service, bar,
pool, spa, bicycles, laundry service, Internet terminal, Wi-Fi hotspot,
parking (free)* ⊟ *AE, DC, MC, V* ⦿❙ *BP.*

$$ Pousada de São Gonçalo. This modern pousada—20 km (12 mi) east of
Amarante—is in the dramatic Serra do Marão at an altitude of nearly
3,000 feet. The rugged terrain and stone exterior are matched by a rustic
interior, with wood furniture, a large fireplace, and tile floors. Despite
its size it has a pool and a spa with Jacuzzi, sauna and steambath. Staff
organize sightseeing tours and other activities: hiking and biking, golf and
shooting. The restaurant serves such satisfying regional fare as *cabrito da
montanha* (mountain goat stew). A bottle of red wine from the carefully
chosen list and a serving of regional sweets to finish and you'll feel that
all's right with the north of Portugal. Half-board and other packages are
available. **Pros:** remote yet plenty to do; nice little spa; free Wi-Fi. **Cons:**
only reachable by car or taxi; area cold in winter; no Internet terminal.
⊠ *Curva do Lancete, Serra do Marão, Ansiães* ☎ *255/460030* ⊕ *www.
pousadas.pt* ⤸ *14 rooms, 1 suite* ⚲ *In-room: a/c, Wi-Fi. In-hotel: restaurant, room service, bar, pool, spa, laundry service, Wi-Fi hotspot, parking
(free), some pets allowed* ⊟ *AE, DC, MC, V* ⦿❙ *BP, MAP.*

OUTDOOR ACTIVITIES

Golfe de Amarante, at the property of Quinta da Devesa, 5 km (3 mi)
southwest of Amarante, is an 18-hole golf course with superb mountain views. The facilities include a bar, a restaurant, a golf shop, and a
driving range. Greens fees are €50 on weekdays and €75 on weekends/
holidays. A handicap certificate is required. ⊠ *Quinta da DevezaFregim*
☎ *255/446060* ⊕ *www.golfedeamarante.com.*

PESO DA RÉGUA

35 km (22 mi) southeast of Amarante; 108 km (67 mi) east of Porto.

This small river port is in the heart of port-wine country, and all the
wine from the vineyards of the Upper Douro Valley passes through
it on its way to Porto. Local wine lodges offer tours of their cellars,
which make a nice contrast to the large-scale operations in Vila Nova
de Gaia. The new Museu do Douro now provides a long-awaited showcase for the wine-making industry. Many boat tours from Porto end in
Régua (the town's shortened name); others pause here before continuing
upriver to Pinhão, whose train station is lined with beautiful tile panels.

8

For restaurant accommodations in the wider area, check entries in the Trás-os-Montes section of this chapter for Vila Real, which is 23 km (15 mi) from Régua up the N2.

GETTING HERE AND AROUND

Régua is served by bus company Rodonorte, whose routes cover most of the region. There are also local buses from Vila Real. But most visitors using public transport prefer to take the picturesque Douro line, with regular departures from Porto Campanhã (about two hours). The quickest way by car from Porto is to take the A4 motorway toward Vila Real, turning south on the N2 just outside of town. A prettier route is the N103 along the north bank of the Douro.

TOURS

Porto-based Douro Azul does day trips to Régua as well as cruises of up to a week. Land and river trips are also organized by the Rota do Vinho do Porto (Port Wine Route), which also works with local *quintas* (estates) to help wine enthusiasts map out their own tours of the region and book cellar visits and wine tastings. In summer, there's an afternoon historic train tour (with steam or diesel engines) along the Douro from Régua via Pinhão to Tua; national train company CP or tourist offices can provide details.

ESSENTIALS

Boat Cruises **Douro Azul** (✉ *Rua de S. Francisco 4, 2D, Porto* ☎ *22/340–2500* ⊕ *www.douroazul.pt* ✉ *Estação São Bento, Praça Almeida Garrett, Porto* ☎ *22/201–4292*).

Bus **Rodonorte** (✉ *Restaurante Cantinho da Cidade (local agent), Vale das Vinhas* ☎ *254/321087* ⊕ *www.rodonorte.pt*).

Historic Train **CP** (☎ *22/105–2524* ⊕ *www.cp.pt*).

Visitor Info **Douro** (✉ *Caldas do Moledo* ☎ *254/313846* ⊕ *www.visit-douro.com*). **Rota do Vinho do Porto** (✉ *Largo da Estação, Apartado 113* ☎ *254/324774* ⊕ *www.rvp.pt*).

EXPLORING

Fodor's Choice
★
Museu do Douro. The region finally has its own museum, inaugurated in 2008 after the Douro valley was named a World Heritage Site—underscoring its importance in terms of cultural history and tourism. Housed in the imposing former headquarters of a port wine company, the institution also has a striking contemporary wing that hosts major exhibitions about the wine-making region, its history, and leading figures connected with it. Around the corner in Rua da Ferreirinha is a separate exhibit in a former warehouse that still smells faintly of wine, where you can learn about the wine-making process. The museum is also building up a network of branches around this large and very varied region. The first was opened in 2009, in Tabuaço. ✉ *Rua Marquês de Pombal, Peso da Régua* ☎ *254/310190* ⊕ *www.museudodouro.pt* ✉ *€5* ◷ *Tues.–Sun. 10–1 and 2–6.*

Quinta do Crasto. Dating to 1616, this large wine estate on the north bank of Rio Douro, between Régua and Pinhão, was already marked on the first Douro Demarcated Region Map by Baron Forrester. Wines produced here include vintage Porto. This designates wine of exceptional quality made in a single year. It must be bottled between the second and third year after the harvest; it is deep purple in color and full-bodied. It also offers L.B.V. (Late Bottled Vintage), wines of a superior quality from a single year that are bottled between the fourth and sixth year after they were made, and others. Reservations must be made to visit this property. ✉ *Gouvinhas–Ferrão, Sabrosa* ☎ *254/920020* ⊕ *www.quintadocrasto.pt.*

One of the oldest quintas in the region, **Quinta do Valado** is on the right bank of Rio Corgo near Rio Douro. This wine estate has been in the Ferreira family since 1818. It has 158 acres and vines more than 70 years old. Make reservations for a visit, which includes a wine tasting. This property holds a museum and a wine store. It is one of many quintas that also have rooms for guests, in its case five doubles costing between €95 and €150 a night. ✉ *Vilarinho dos Freires, Peso da Régua* ☎ *254/323147 or 254/324326.*

EN ROUTE Boats from Porto on Douro cruises of more than a day invariably stop at Pinhão, whose train station is plastered with 25 large *azulejo* panels depicting scenes from Douro rural life. Part of the building houses **Wine House** (☎ *254/730030* ⊕ *www.quintanova.com* ☾ *Closed Sun. mid-Oct.–mid-Apr.*) whose shop carries books about the region as well as a good selection of wines to buy or taste. It also oversees a small museum in the former railwaymen's quarters, which has interesting displays of traditional equipment used in grape harvesting, wine making, bottling, and coopering. A nearby hotel, the **CS Vintage House** (⇨ *see Where to Eat and Stay*) has a fine restaurant, a well-stocked shop, and a Wine Academy that organizes courses and sessions at which port is matched with gourmet foods such as chocolate.

WHERE TO EAT AND STAY

$$ ✗ **DOC.** This striking modern restaurant 9 km (6 mi) from Régua, on the south bank of the Douro, draws gourmets from far and wide with chef Rui Paula's take on traditional northern cuisine. Only the best ingredients are used in dishes in which bacalhau, *polvo* (octopus) and seafood often feature, as well as tender *bísaro* pork and *barrosã* veal. Tasting menus include one showcasing gourmet olive oils—among the region's most delicious products. The restaurant's wine list and its adept matching of port with food have won it awards. The riverside setting contributes to an unforgettable experience, especially if it's warm enough to dine on the wooden deck that juts out over the river. ✉ *Cais da Folgosa, EN222, Armamar* ☎ *254/858123* ⊕ *www.ruipaula.com* ⌨ *Reservations essential* ☾ *AE, DC, MC, V.*

PORTUGUESE
Fodor's Choice
★

$$$ 🏨 **CS Vintage House.** This hotel on the northern bank of the Douro, 32 km (18 mi) east of Régua in a beautifully restyled former wine warehouse, has unrivaled views. Guest rooms, picked out in soft mauves and browns, all have balconies looking out over the garden and river. Inside is a lounge-cum-games room with pool table and a cozy Library Bar; outside, a pool and tennis court. The breakfast room also has a river view, as does the sophisticated Rabelo restaurant, with its huge terrace. It's good for regional dishes or try something lighter such as *salmão fumado com salada de ovo e caviar* (smoked salmon with egg salad and caviar). **Pros:** lovely riverside setting; plenty for wine enthusiasts. **Cons:** remote spot far from larger shops and nightlife; no gym. ⊠ *Lugar da Ponte, Pinhão* ☎ *254/730230 or 800/206991* ⊕ *www.csvintagehouse. com* ➪ *37 rooms, 6 suites* ♿ *In-room: a/c, safe, refrigerator, Internet. In-hotel: restaurant, room service, bar, tennis court, pool, laundry service, Wi-Fi hotspot, parking (free)* ⊟ *AE, DC, MC, V* ⍾ *BP, MAP, FAP.*

$$ 🅱 **Quinta Nova de Nossa Senhora do Carmo.** This hillside estate on the north bank of the Douro is owned by the Amorim family, which dominates Portugal's cork industry, but its "wine hotel" is on an intimate scale. The elegant guest rooms, lounge, and restaurant—where home cooking is served also to nonguests—are in the 18th-century house. There's a winter garden, playroom, and outdoor pool with views of the terraced vineyards. Tour the winery, take a jeep trip, or walk a marked trail past a walled orchard and stones that in 1756 demarcated the Douro region. From Régua it's a 20-minute drive, but if you come by train, staff will pick you up at the Ferrão whistlestop. **Pros:** a comfortable place to get away from it all; inside view of wine making. **Cons:** few in-room amenities; no Wi-Fi; isolated unless you have a car. ⊠ *Covas do Douro, Pinhão* ☎ *254/730430 or 96/986–0056* ⊕ *www. quintanova.com* ➪ *11 rooms* ♿ *In-room: a/c, no phone, no TV. In-hotel: restaurant, bar, pool, bicycles, laundry service, Internet, parking (free)* ⊟ *AE, DC, MC, V* ⍾ *BP, MAP, FAP.*

LAMEGO

13 km (8 mi) south of Peso da Régua; 121 km (75 mi) southeast of Porto.

A prosperous town set amid a fertile landscape carpeted with vineyards and orchards, Lamego is also rich in baroque churches and mansions. It straddles the River Balsemão, a small tributary of the Douro, and is close to the great river itself. The town is flanked by two hills, one topped by a castle, the other by the Nossa Senhora dos Remédios, a major pilgrimage site. A monumental staircase leads straight up from the town's central avenue to the church steps. The surrounding region has more *quintas* (wine estates) to visit or stay—plus one of Europe's top spa hotels.

GETTING HERE AND AROUND

Lamego is served by Rodonorte regional buses and fast Rede Expresso buses from Lisbon. Tickets for the latter can be bought at local agent Totolamego. The town is not on the rail network, but it's a short ride on a Transdev bus from Peso da Régua, which is on the picturesque Douro line from Porto.

ESSENTIALS

Bus Rede Expressos (⊠ *Totolamego, Av. Visconde Guedes Teixeira* ☎ *254/656064*).

Visitor Info **Douro** (⌧ *Rua dos Bancos, Apartado 36* ☎ *254/615770*
⊕ *www.visit-douro.com*). **Lamego** (⌧ *Av. Visconde Guedes Teixeira*
☎ *254/612005*).

EXPLORING

In the heart of the Douro Valley, the wine estate **Quinta da Pacheca** has existed since 1551. A 17th-century stone marker bears a Feitoria inscription that indicates that the best-quality wine was made here, the only one that could be exported. The estate mansion has a chapel and a beautiful garden with trees that are hundreds of years old. Wine production is still done the old-fashioned way, with grapes crushed by men in a stone tank, and aging taking place in oak barrels. Reservations must be made if you want to visit this property; tours of the cellars followed by a wine tasting cost between €7 and €20. If you want to dally in this lovely setting, the Quinta also has 14 guest rooms. ⌧ *Cambes* ☎ *254/313228* ⊕ *www.quintadapacheca.com*.

Fodor's Choice
★ The town's most famous monument is the 18th-century **Santuário de Nossa Senhora dos Remédios** *(Our Lady of Cures Church and Shrine)*, which is on a hill west of the center of town and in a park of the same name. Leading to the shrine is a marvelous granite staircase of 686 steps decorated with azulejos. Landings along the way have statues and chapels. At the top, you can rest under chestnut trees and enjoy the views. During the Festas de Nossa Senhora dos Remédios, the annual pilgrimage to the shrine, many penitents climb the steps on their knees, just as they do at the shrine of Bom Jesus, near Braga. The main procession is September 8, but the festivities start at the end of August and include concerts, dancing, parades, a fair, and torchlight processions. Pilgrims use the stairs, but you can always drive up the road here to reach the shrine. ⌧ *Monte de Santo Estevão* ☎ *254/614392* ⌧ *Free* ☉ *Nov.–May, daily 7:30–6; June–Oct., daily 7:30–8.*

WHERE TO STAY

$$$$ 🏨 **Aquapura Douro Valley.** This luxurious resort 3km (2 mi) from Lamego has with its cutting-edge style helped the region brush up its image as a fashionable, not fusty destination. The contemporary architecture is offset with traditional decorative motifs. Public areas are in deep pinks and browns while guest quarters, which are bursting with amenities, are more often in cream and white. Outside, wooden decking around the pool enables you to revel in the spectacular hillside setting. Inside, the huge spa has a heated pool with water jets, two saunas, steambath, and laconium; treatment rooms all have river views, as does the 24-hour gym. Wine tastings, cookery classes (for up to four people) and cycling or bus tours can be arranged—check the Web site for deals. **Pros:** stylish and comfortable; stunning setting; spa included in room rate. **Cons:** not reachable by public transport; some find guest rooms a little dark. ⌧ *Quinta do Vale Abrão, Lamego* ☎ *254/660600* ⊕ *www. aquapurahotels.com* 🛏 *41 rooms, 9 suites, 21 villas* ⚒ *In-room: a/c, safe, kitchen (some), refrigerator, DVD, Wi-Fi. In-hotel: restaurant, room service, bar, tennis court, 2 pools, gym, spa, water sports, bicycles, laundry service, Internet terminal, Wi-Fi hotspot, parking (free)* ▤ *AE, DC, MC, V* ⎟◎⎟ *BP.*

VILA NOVA DE FOZ CÔA

90 km (56 mi) east of Peso da Régua; 235 km (75 mi) east of Porto.

The higher reaches of the Douro are known for their harsh terrain, with baking hot summers and cold winters. Yet this apparently inhospitable region was home to a prehistoric people whose rock engravings, fully mapped only in the 1990s, may now be visited with a guide. This region is also known for the delicate oil made from olives grown here, and for almonds, which in the town of Torre de Moncorvo are traditionally toasted with sugar.

GETTING HERE AND AROUND

By car, the largest town at the head of the Douro demarcated wine-making area is most easily approached from the south, from Guarda and Celorica da Beira via the N102. But it can be reached as a day trip from major Douro towns such as Peso da Régua and Lamego via the N222—a route one Fodorite described as "jaw-droppingly beautiful." National bus company Rede Expressos (see Lisbon chapter) has at least one direct bus a day to Foz Côa from Lisbon.

As for rail, the Douro line from Porto takes you as far as Pocinho, 5 km (3 mi) from Foz Côa, from where you may catch a local bus. Rodonorte also runs long-distance buses from Porto as well as Lamego, changing in Torre de Moncorvo.

ESSENTIALS

Visitor Info Vila Nova de Foz Côa (✉ *Av. Cidade Nova* ☎ *279/760329* ⊕ *www.cm-fozcoa.pt*).

EXPLORING

Parque Arqueológico do Vale do Côa. The Côa Valley Archaeological Park contains what experts say is the world's largest open-air museum of paleolithic petroglyphs, comprising engravings of big game and hunters scattered along 17 km (11 mi) of the valley. Its protection and status as a Unesco World Heritage Site came only after a lengthy national and international campaign to persuade the national government to suspend work on a hydroelectric dam on the River Côa, a tributary of the Douro that would have left the rock art underwater (and indeed had already submerged some). There's a small museum attached to the park head-quarters in Foz Côa, but note that guided visits (by jeep) to the engravings, departing from reception centers in Castelo Melhor and Muxagata, must be booked in advance. ✉ *Rua do Museu, Vila Nova de Foz Côa* ☎ *279/768260 or 279/768261* ⊕ *www.igespar.pt/en/monuments/53* 🎫 *€5 museum, €8 park visit, €12 museum and park visit* ⊗ *Museum Tues.–Sun. 9–noon and 2–5:30, park office weekdays 9–12:30 and 2–5:30.*

THE MINHO AND THE COSTA VERDE

The coastline of Minho Province, north of Porto, is a largely unspoiled stretch of small towns and sandy beaches that runs all the way to the border with Spain. The weather in this region is more inclement than else-where, a fact hinted at in the coast's name: the Minho is green because it sees a disproportionate amount of rain. It's a land of emerald valleys, endless pine-scented forests, and secluded beaches that are beautiful but not for fainthearted swimmers. Summers can be cool, and swimming in the Atlantic is bracing at best. "These are real beaches for real people," is the reply when visitors complain about the water temperature.

You can break up your time on the coast with trips inland to medieval towns along the Rio Lima or through the border settlements along the Rio Minho. The remains of ancient civilizations are everywhere; you'll encounter dolmens, Iron Age dwellings, and Celtic and Roman towns. Old traditions are carefully incorporated into modern-day hustle and bustle. Up here, you'll see more than the occasional oxcart loaded with some sort of crop, being led by a long-skirted, wooden-shod woman on both highway and country lane.

GUIMARÃES

51 km (32 mi) northeast of Porto.

Afonso Henriques was born in 1110 in Guimarães, and Portuguese schoolchildren are taught that *"aqui nasceu Portugal"* ("Portugal was born here") with him. Within 20 years he was referred to as king of *Portucale* (the united Portuguese lands between the Minho and Douro rivers) and had made Guimarães the seat of his power. From this first "Portuguese" capital, Afonso Henriques drove south, taking Lisbon back from the Moors in 1147. Today Guimarães is a town proud of its past, and this is evident in a series of delightful medieval buildings and streets. The Old Town's narrow, cobbled thoroughfares pass small bars that open onto sidewalks and pastel houses that overhang little squares and have flowers in their windowsills. In 2001 the historic center of Guimarães was classified as a World Heritage site by UNESCO, and more recently has been prettifying itself for its 2012 stint as European Cultural Capital.

GETTING HERE AND AROUND

Guimarães is served by suburban trains from Porto's São Bento and Campanhã stations, taking about 1 hour 20 minutes and costing €2.30 (or less if you have a €0.50 Andante rechargeable card). Traveling by rail from Braga is not such a good idea, because you'll have to change and buses are both quicker and cheaper. The company is Arriva, which also serves Guimarães from Porto. Fast Rede Expresso buses also serve Guimarães from Porto, Lisbon, and beyond.

ESSENTIALS

Bus Rede Expressos (✉ *Rodoviária Entre Douro e Minho, Central de Camionagem* ☎ *253/516229* ⊕ *www.rede-expressos.pt*). **Rodonorte** (✉ *Central de Camionagem* ☎ *253/423500* ⊕ *www.rodonorte.pt*).

Visitor Info Guimarães (✉ *Praça São Tiago* ☎ *253/518790*).

EXPLORING

The **Castelo de Guimarães** *(castle)* was built (or at least reconstructed from earlier remains) by Henry of Burgundy; his son, Afonso Henriques, was born within its great battlements and flanking towers. Standing high on a solid rock base above the town, the castle has been superbly preserved. A path leads down from its walls to the tiny

Romanesque Capela de São Miguel, the plain chapel traditionally said to be where Afonso Henriques was baptized but in fact built well after his death—although the baptismal font may be older. ⊠ *Rua D. Teresa de Noronha* ☎ *253/412273* ⬦ *Free* ☉ *Tues.–Sun. 10–6.*

The **Citânia de Briteiros,** 9 km (5½ mi) northwest of Guimarães, is the fascinating remains of a Celtic *citânia* (hill settlement). It dates from around 300 BC and was probably not abandoned until AD 300, making it one of the last Celtic strongholds against the Romans in Portugal, although its residents are now thought to have become gradually romanized. The walls and foundations of 150 huts and a meetinghouse have been excavated (two of the huts have been reconstructed to show their original size), and paths are clearly marked between them. Parts of a channeled water system also survive. The site was excavated in the late 19th century by Dr. Martins Sarmento, who gave his name to the museum in Guimarães, where most of the finds from Briteiros were transferred. If you intend to visit the site, don't miss that museum; you might also visit the smaller Museu da Cultura Castreja, housed in Sarmento's 19th-century family home, in the village of São Salvador de Briteiros, down below the Citânia. It contains finds from several local hill settlements and is open every day except Monday; entry is included in the Citânia ticket. ⊠ *EN (Estrada Nacional) 153, Km 55* ☎ *253/478 952* ⊕ *www.csarmento. uminho.pt* ⬦ *€3* ☉ *Daily Nov.–Mar., 9–5, Apr.–Oct. daily 9–6.*

The **Igreja de Nossa Senhora da Oliveira** *(Church of Our Lady of the Olive Branch)* is in the delightful square Largo da Oliveira. The church was founded in the 10th century to commemorate one of Guimarães's most enduring legends. Wamba, elected king of the Visigoths in the 7th century, refused the honor and thrust his olive-branch stick into the earth, declaring that only if his stick were to blossom would he accept the crown—whereupon the stick promptly sprouted foliage. In the square in front of the church, an odd 14th-century Gothic canopy sheltering a cross marks the supposed spot. ⊠ *Largo da Oliveira* ☎ *253/423919* ⬦ *Free* ☉ *Daily 8:30–noon and 3:30–7:30.*

The **Paço dos Duques de Bragança** *(Palace of the Dukes of Bragança),* below the castle, is a much-maligned 15th-century palace that once belonged to the dukes of Bragança but which is now the official regional seat of Portugal's president. Critics claim that the restoration during the Salazar regime (1936–59), which turned the building into a state residence, damaged it irrevocably. Certainly the palace's brick chimneys and turrets bear little relation to the original structure, which was an atmospheric ruin for many years. You can judge for yourself on an independent or guided tour of the interior, where you'll find much of interest—from tapestries and furniture to porcelain and paintings. You can book guided tours at the main desk. ⊠ *Rua Conde D. Henrique* ☎ *253/412273* ⬦ *€5 (€7 with guided tour), free Sun. until 12:30* ☉ *Tues.–Sun. 10–6.*

NEED A BREAK?   Guimarães is an excellent place to sample regional cakes and pastries. One of the most popular downtown is **Clarinhas** (⊠ *Largo do Toural 86/88* ☎ *253/516513*), which has a range of delicious sweets including traditional *tortas de Guimarães,* pastry rolls with an eggy pumpkin filling.

WHERE TO EAT AND STAY

$
PORTUGUESE

✕ **Café Oriental.** This venerable café on one of the city's iconic squares has an excellent restaurant attached that serves tasty regional dishes at equally mouthwatering prices. There's a €7 lunch buffet, but if you opt to go à la carte, you might try the house bacalhau (baked au gratin, with potato slices) or the breaded octopus. Or, if on this trip you're not going to make it as far as Miranda do Douro on the Spanish frontier, take the chance to sample *posta à mirandesa*, Portugal's ten-

derest steak. And don't forget to try the excellent house wine. ✉ *Largo do Toural 11* ☎ *253/414048* ⊕ *www.restaurantecafeoriental.com* 🖃 *AE, DC, MC, V* ⊘ *Closed Sun.*

> ### CASTLES
>
> There are towers, castles, and forts galore to explore in this part of the country, some of them so complete they provide a virtual medieval playground. The best include those at Guimarães, Monção, Bragança, and Chaves. Don't miss the region's two vast ornamental staircases at the pilgrimage sights of Lamego and Bom Jesus do Monte.

$
PORTUGUESE
Fodor'sChoice
★

✕ **Quinta de Castelães.** On the road to the Citânia de Briteiros *(⇨ see below En Route)*, this charmingly rustic but very professionally run restaurant is a good place to sample regional dishes. Among the best are *assado misto de cabrito e vitela* (roast kid and veal), *rolinhos de pescada* (whiting rolls, served with a seafood sauce), and bacalhau dishes such as *à broa* (with cornbread) and *com natas* (with cream)—all reasonably priced. Don't forget to try the range of finger-licking starters. The complex includes a small museum with an interesting display of agricultural implements. ✉ *EN (Estrada Nacional) 102, São João de Ponte, Guimarães* ☎ *253/557002* ⊕ *www.quintadecastelaes.com* 🖃 *DC, MC, V* ⊘ *Closed Mon. No dinner Sun.*

$
Fodor'sChoice
★

🛏 **Pousada da Nossa Senhora da Oliveira.** Town houses that date from the 16th and 17th centuries were remodeled and filled with antique reproductions to create this pousada in the historic city center. Service is courteous and efficient, and guest rooms are elegant, though not large; those facing the street can be noisy. Free parking is 100 meters away; the pousada is accessible for baggage drop-off only 7–10:30 am and 6–8 pm. There's a family games room, while outdoor activities such as golf, shooting, and horse riding can be arranged. The restaurant has been undergoing refurbishments, but if you want to sample regional cuisine at the Pousada de Santa Marinha, there's a free shuttle. **Pros:** charming historical building; picturesque central location; first half-hour Wi-Fi free. **Cons:** some rooms catch street noise; no exercise facilities. ✉ *Rua de Santa Maria* ☎ *253/514157* ⊕ *www.pousadas.pt* ⤵ *10 rooms, 6 suites* ⚒ *In-room: a/c, refrigerator, Wi-Fi. In-hotel: restaurant, room service, bar, laundry service, Wi-Fi hotspot* 🖃 *AE, DC, MC, V* ⭘ *BP, EP, MAP, FAP.*

$$$

🛏 **Pousada de Santa Marinha.** This pousada is in a 12th-century monastery that was founded by the wife of Dom Afonso Henriques to honor the patron saint of pregnant women. Antiques and extraordinary azulejo panels fill the public areas, and some guest rooms used to be monks' cells. These are complemented by a prize-winning modern wing. The stone dining room serves regional dishes; the *rojões á Minhota* (pork simmered and served with pickled vegetables) is delicious; sop up the sauce with *broa* (corn bread). A fitting dessert is *toucinho do céu*: literally "bacon from heaven" but actually an egg-and-almond pudding. There's a children's playground and games room and a range of outdoor activities. **Pros:** successful blend of historical setting and modern comfort; stunning tile panels alone worth a visit. **Cons:** out of town; limited facilities. ⊠ *Largo Domingos Leite de Castro, Lugar da Costa* ☎ *253/511249* ⊕ *www.pousadas.pt* ⤴ *49 rooms, 2 suites* ⚭ *In-room: a/c, safe, refrigerator, Wi-Fi. In-hotel: restaurant, room service, bar, pool, laundry service, Internet terminal, Wi-Fi hotspot, parking (free)* ⊟ *AE, DC, MC, V* ⦿ *BP.*

SHOPPING

Guimarães is a center for the local linen industry. The fabric is hand-spun and handwoven, then embroidered, all to impressive effect; it's available in local shops or at the weekly Friday market. Shops owned by artisans themselves offer the best linen buys. Try **A Oficina** (⊠ *Rua Paio Galvão, Loja 11* ☎ *253/515250*).

BRAGA

25 km (15 mi) northwest of Guimarães; 53 km (33 mi) northeast of Porto.

Braga is one of northern Portugal's outstanding surprises. Founded by the Romans as Bracara Augusta, it prospered in earnest in the 6th century—under the Visigoths—when it became an important bishopric. Braga's later archbishops often wielded greater power than the Portuguese kings themselves. In the 16th century, the city was beautified with churches, palaces, and fountains, many of which were altered in the 18th century.

Today Braga feels like the religious capital it is. Shops that sell religious items line the pedestrian streets around the cathedral. The Semana Santa (Holy Week) festivities here, including eerie torchlight processions of hooded participants, are impressive. There are also several interesting historical sights—most of them religious in nature—a short distance from the city. You can visit all of them by bus from the center of town; inquire at the tourist office for timetables.

GETTING HERE AND AROUND

Some long-distance trains from Lisbon terminate not in Porto but farther north in Braga, and rail is perhaps the least complicated way to make the trip from the capital. From Porto, suburban trains take between 50 minutes and 1 hour 10 minutes from downtown São Bento station, with the trip costing €2.30, or less if you have a €0.50 Andante charge card. As for buses, Transdev serves Braga from Viana do Castelo, while regional bus company Rodornorte plies routes from Porto and other regional towns, and Rede Expressos services come from as far afield as Lisbon.

ESSENTIALS

Bus Rede Expressos (☎ *253/209400* ⊕ *www.rede-expressos.pt*). **Rodonorte** (☎ *253/264693* ⊕ *www.rodonorte.pt*). **Transdev** (☎ *253/209400 or 253/209401* ⊕ *www.transdev*).

Visitor Info **Braga** (✉ *Av. da Liberdade 1* ☎ *253/262550*).

EXPLORING

The **Capela de São Frutuoso de Montélios,** about 4 km (2½ mi) north of town on the EN201, is one of Portugal's oldest buildings. The original chapel is believed to have been constructed in the 7th century in the form of a Greek cross. It was partially destroyed by the Moors and rebuilt in the 11th century.

The pedestrian Rua Diogo de Sousa leads down from the cathedral and palace to one of the city's former gateways, the 18th-century Arco do Porta Nova. Beyond it and to the right is the Museu dos Biscainhos, within a baroque mansion known as **Palácio dos Biscaínhos.** The elegant rooms are furnished in 18th-century style and display silver and porcelain collections. The ground floor of the palace is flagstone, which allowed carriages to run through the interior to the stables beyond. At the back of the palace is a formal garden with decorative tiles. ✉ *Rua dos Biscaínhos* ☎ *253/204650* ⊕ *www.ipmuseus.pt* 🎫 *€2* ☉ *Tues.–Sun. 10–12:15 and 2–5:30.*

NEED A BREAK? There are two inexpensive cafés in the arcade at the Praça da República. The **Café Astória** (✉ *Praça da República 4* ☎ *253/213438*) has mahogany-paneled walls, mirrors, marble tables, and a molded ceiling. It's a good place to enjoy a coffee and to try some of the local pastries (best in morning). Upstairs operates as a nightclub. **Café Vianna** (✉ *Praça da República–Arcada* ☎ *253/262336*) has been in business since 1871 and serves a wide variety of snacks. It's also a good place for breakfast and offers views of the fountain and gardens.

On a hilltop 5 km (3 mi) west of Braga on the N309 is the **Santuário Nossa Senhora do Sameiro,** after Fátima the most important Marian shrine (a shrine honoring the Virgin Mary, mother of Christ) in Portugal. Hundreds of thousands of pilgrims visit here annually. The church itself is of little architectural interest.

The huge **Sé Catedral** was originally Romanesque but is now an impressive blend of styles. The delicate Renaissance stone tracery on the roof is particularly eye-catching. Enter from Rua do Souto through the 18th-century cloister; the cathedral interior is on your left, and there are various interesting chapels. Steps by the entrance to the cathedral lead to the **Museu de Arte Sacra** (Museum of Religious Art), which has a fascinating collection of religious art and artifacts, including a 14th-century crystal cross set in bronze. From the magnificent *coro alto* (upper choir), which you cross as part of the tour, there are views of the great baroque double organ. Across the cloister, you'll see the Capela dos Reis (Kings' Chapel), a 14th-century chapel containing the tombs of Afonso Henriques's parents, Henry of Burgundy and his wife, Teresa. ✉ *Rua do Souto 38* ☎ *253/263317* 🎫 *Cathedral free, museum €3 (includes tour)* ☉ *Cathedral Nov.–May, daily 8–6:30; June–Oct., daily 8–7. Museum Nov.–May, daily 9–12:30 and 2–5:30; June–Oct., daily 9–12:30 and 2–6:30.*

Past the garden gateway of the Palácio dos Biscainhos is the **Zona Arqueológica** *(Archaeological Zone)*, which usually isn't open to the public. It contains the excavations of an old Roman city known as Bracara Augusta, from which Braga derives its name. To the east, the Roman city stretched as far as the large Largo de São Tiago.

WHERE TO EAT AND STAY

$ PORTUGUESE ✕ **Restaurante Inácio.** Just outside the 18th-century town gate, in a building with a lovely traditional facade, this well-known restaurant serves solid regional fare. Bacalhau is a good bet, as is the roast kid. The place also specializes in *lampreia* (lamprey) and *sável* (shad or river herring) when these are in season. The house wine is on the raw side, but the wine list is decent so you have plenty of other options. Service in the stone-clad interior is brisk and efficient. Reservations are essential on weekends. ✉ *Campo das Hortas 4* ☎ *253/613235* ▭ *AE, DC, MC, V* ⊙ *Closed Tues.*

$ PORTUGUESE Fodor's Choice ★ ✕ **Sameiro.** A meal in this long-established restaurant is worth a climb (or drive) to the top of the hill that's home to the Santuário Nossa Senhora do Sameiro. The air-conditioned dining room is spacious and pleasantly furnished, and the views are superb. The menu is unadulterated northern Portuguese cuisine. If you're brave, start with the *papas de sarrabulho* (a meaty porridge thickened with blood) before moving on to *arroz de vitela com pastelinhos de marisco* (a veal and rice concoction with little seafood pastries) or one of the various bacalhau dishes. The place is renowned for its efficient service. Lunch is served from noon to 3 pm and dinner from 7 pm to 10 pm. ✉ *Sameiro, Espinho* ☎ *253/675114* ▭ *AE, DC, MC, V* ⊙ *Closed Mon. Closed 2 wks mid-May and 1st half of Oct.*

¢ **Dona Sofia.** Right downtown, a stone's throw from the cathedral, this pleasant, well-appointed hotel is one of Braga's best bargains. The only meal served is breakfast, and the decoration throughout is simple rather than stylish, but there's nothing lacking in terms of basic comforts, and the staff is friendly. Guest rooms are reasonably sized, and have comfortable modern furnishings with plain pink or blue bedspreads; all have their own bathrooms. The breakfast room is bright and airy. There's also a large and welcoming bar. **Pros:** very central; free Wi-Fi. **Cons:** no gym; Internet terminal not free; cathedral bell sounds from 6:30 am. ✉ *Largo São João do Souto 131* ☎ *253/263160* ⊕ *www.hoteldonasofia.com* *31 rooms, 3 suites* *In-room: a/c, refrigerator, Wi-Fi. In-hotel: room service, bar, pool, laundry service, Internet terminal, Wi-Fi hotspot, parking (free)* ▭ *AE, DC, MC, V* *CP.*

$ Fodor's Choice ★ **Hotel do Elevador.** Many seasoned travelers to the north have made this charming hotel their top choice. In a 19th-century building on a wooded hill 3 km (2 mi) outside Braga, it's named after the water-operated funicular that hoists the foot-weary up to the Bom Jesus do Monte sanctuary. The high-ceilinged guest rooms are decorated in warm colors and have period furniture; most have panoramic views. The restaurant, Panorâmico do Elevador, scores highly for its food and has similar gorgeous views. There is no car park but on-street parking is free. And guests have free access to the indoor pool, gym, and spa of the upscale Hotel do Templo a few steps away. **Pros:** fabulous views;

free Wi-Fi throughout. **Cons:** no hotel parking; no exercise facilities; no Internet terminal. ⊠ *Bom Jesus do Monte* ☎ *253/603400* ⊕ *www. hoteisbomjesus.pt* ⇄ *22 rooms* ⚒ *In-room: a/c, refrigerator, Wi-Fi. In-hotel: restaurant, room service, bar, laundry service, Internet terminal, Wi-Fi hotspot, some pets allowed* ⊟ *AE, DC, MC, V* ◉ *CP, MAP, FAP.*

$ 🏨 **Mélia Braga.** This large hotel and spa inaugurated in mid-2010 has swiftly established itself as the city's most stylish and luxurious. It attracts business and leisure travelers, who all appreciate its contemporary style, ample facilities, and professionalism of its staff. White and black with dashes of lime green prevail in public areas, while guest rooms are beige and brown. The Bracara restaurant serves mainly Portuguese cuisine; it also has themed buffets. In the bar you can listen to live music as you munch tapas or sip a cocktail. Light meals are served in the pool bar. The well-equipped spa offers various treatments; there are several exercise classes and also a children's pool. **Pros:** wide range of facilities; Wi-Fi free. **Cons:** attracts many tour groups; half an hour's walk from the center. ⊠ *Av. General Carrilho de Silva Porto 8* ☎ *253/144000* ⊕ *www.meliabraga.com* ⇄ *161 rooms, 21 suites* ⚒ *In-room: a/c, safe, refrigerator, Internet (some), Wi-Fi. In-hotel: restaurant, room service, bar, 2 pools, gym, spa, laundry service, Internet terminal, Wi-Fi hotspot, parking (outdoor free/indoor paid), some pets allowed* ⊟ *AE, D, DC, MC, V* ◉ *BP, MAP, FAP.*

Fodor's Choice ★

NIGHTLIFE

Braga has an active nightlife, not least because it is one of Portugal's most important university towns. The café-bars in the arcaded Praça da República are good places for a drink and are lively at any time of the day or night. On the road between the Bom Jesus and Sameiro, the **Classic Jazz Bar** (⊠ *Estrada de Bom Jesus, Sameiro* ☎ *253/676282* ⊕ *www.classicjazzbar.com*) is an old stone house transformed into one of the region's top jazz venues. You can listen to live music as you dine on international cuisine, or go along around midnight just to sip a drink and catch the tail end of the concert. **Populum Bar** (⊠ *Campo da Vinha 115* ☎ *253/610966* ⊘ *Closed Sun.–Tues.*) is a dance club in which care has been taken to maintain traces of the building's original architecture. It has two rooms, and anything from Latin dance sessions to karaoke can be taking place at the same time. On weekends it might stay open until after 4 am.

8

BARCELOS

12 km (7 mi) west of Braga; 27 km (17 mi) northeast of Guimarães.

Barcelos, a bustling market town on the banks of the Rio Cávado with a population of some 18,000, is the center of a flourishing handicrafts industry, particularly ceramics (above all in the form of the famous Barcelos cockerel) and wooden toys and models. It's worth coming here if you plan to carry home a host of souvenirs, so if you're traveling the region by public transport, you might make the town your last stop. The best time to visit is during the famous weekly market—Barcelos is an easy day trip from Braga or Viana do Castelo, and there's not so much to do or see on other days, although the Pottery Museum is always worth visiting.

GETTING HERE AND AROUND

Barcelos is on the main rail line between Porto to Viana, but there are no direct trains from Braga. Rede Expressos buses serve the town from Lisbon as well as Porto; there is no bus station but the company has a local agent in Avenida Dr. Sidónio País. Regional operator Transdev also runs buses from Braga; but to get from Viana to Barcelos you have to change in Forjães.

ESSENTIALS

Bus **Rede Expressos** (⊠ *Av. Dr. Sidónio Pais 445* ☎ *253/814310* ⊕ *www.rede-expressos.pt*). **Transdev** (☎ *253/894-193* ⊕ *www.transdev.pt*).

Visitor Info **Barcelos** (⊠ *Largo Dr. José Novaes 8* ☎ *253/811882*).

EXPLORING

From the Campo da República, Rua Dom António Barroso leads down through the Old Town toward the river. On the left, the former medieval town tower now houses the tourist office; the **Centro de Artesanato** *(Handicrafts Center)*, which has some of the best local crafts, is nearby. Ceramic dishes and bowls, often signed by the artist, are a good buy. Figurines, too, are popular, although none approach the individuality of those made by the late Rosa Ramalho and Mistério, local potters whose work first made Barcelos ceramics famous. ⊠ *Rua D. Diogo Pinheiro 25* ☎ *253/812135* ☉ *Weekdays 9–12:30 and 1:30–5:30.*

The **Feira de Barcelos** *(Barcelos Market)*, held every Thursday in the central Campo da República, is one of the country's largest and arguably its most famous. It starts early in the morning when the mist is still rising off the ground. Vendors cry out their wares, which include almost anything you can think of: traditional Barcelos ceramics (brown pottery with yellow-and-white decoration), workaday earthenware, baskets, rugs, glazed figurines (including the famous Barcelos cock), decorative copper lanterns, and wooden toys. There are also mounds of vegetables, fruits, cheese, fresh bread and cakes, clothes, shoes, leather, and kitchen equipment. In fall and winter, the scent of roasting chestnuts wafts across the square, promising a snack to tide you over as you browse.

The Rio Cávado, crossed by a medieval bridge, is shaded by overhanging trees and bordered by municipal gardens. High above the river stands the ruin of the medieval Paço dos Condes (Palace of the Counts), where you'll find the **Museu Arqueológico** *(Archaeological Museum)*. Among the empty sarcophagi and stone crosses is the 14th-century crucifix known as the Cruzeiro do Senhor do Galo (Cross of the Lord of the Rooster). According to local legend, after sentencing an innocent man to death, a judge prepared to dine on a roast fowl. When the condemned man said, "I'll be hanged if that cock doesn't crow," the rooster flew from the table and the man's life was spared. The Barcelos cock is on sale in pottery form throughout the town; indeed, it's become something of a national symbol. ⊠ *Largo do Município* ☎ *253/821252* ☞ *Free* ☉ *Daily Nov.–Mar. 9–5:30, Apr.–Oct. 9–7.*

The **Museu de Olaria** *(Pottery Museum)*, a five-minute walk from the medieval bridge, has more than 7,000 pieces, displayed over three floors. Look for selections from current and now-extinct Portuguese workshops, private donations, and excavation finds from Portugal and all over the world, particularly from Portuguese-speaking countries. It all makes for a fascinating showcase for traditional pottery techniques and styles. There is a nice shop: if you're not in town on the right day for the weekly market, it's a good place to pick up souvenirs or presents. ⊠ *Rua Cónego Joaquim Gaiolas* ☎ *253/824741* ⊕ *www.museuolaria. org* ⊠ *€2.20, free Oct.–June, Sun. to 12:30 and July–Sept., Sun. after 2* ⊙ *Tues.–Fri. 10–5:30, weekends 10–12:30 and 2–5:30.*

There are several attractive cafés in the center of town. From the market in the Campo da República, head for the **Avenida da Liberdade** and to the front of the tourist office building on the Largo Dr. José Novais for clean, well-lighted places to sit, have a cup of coffee and a pastry, and think about heading back to the market to get an extra suitcase for all the great stuff you just bought.

WHERE TO EAT AND STAY

$ ✕ **Bagoeira.** Vendors from the town's Thursday market favor this rustic
PORTUGUESE restaurant, with its wooden ceiling, black-metal chandeliers, and vases of fresh flowers. *Grelhados* (grilled meats and fish) are prepared in full view of hungry customers on a huge old range that splutters and hisses. Other regional dishes served up here include *rojões* (tender fried pork) and *papas de sarrabhulho,* a stew thickened with pig's blood. The restaurant seats several hundred diners—and often has to on market days. If you overdo things with the cheap house wine, there is a newly built hotel attached (the Web site serves for both). ⊠ *Av. Dr. Sidonio Pais 495* ☎ *253/811236* ⊕ *www.bagoeira.com* ⊟ *AE, DC, MC, V.*

¢ ⊞ **Quinta de Santa Comba.** Just 5 km (3 mi) from Barcelos on the road to Famalicão, this fine 18th-century manor house—full of wood beams and granite—offers bed and breakfast. It's a good deal for the money. The building has been upgraded to offer modern conveniences but retains appealing features such as open fireplaces. Although there's no air-conditioning, this region is generally cool even in summer, and the hotel has heating to ward off the cold and damp in winter. While meal service is limited to the breakfast buffet, there are several restaurants nearby. In the large garden are a pool and a pretty baroque chapel. The estate also has two horses that guests may take out for rides. **Pros:** lovely garden; hotel has a real family feel. **Cons:** limited in-room amenities; no credit cards accepted. ⊠ *São Bento da Várzea, Barcelos* ☎ *253/832101* ⊕ *www.stacomba.com* ⊅ *10 rooms* ☖ *In-room: no phone, Internet. In-hotel: bar, pool, laundry service, Internet terminal, some pets allowed* ⊟ *No credit cards* ⦿ *BP.*

8

VIANA DO CASTELO

Fodor'sChoice   *45 km (28 mi) northwest of Barcelos; 71 km (44 mi) north of Porto.*
★
At the mouth of the Rio Lima, Viana do Castelo has been a prosperous trading center since it received its town charter in 1258. Many of Viana's finest buildings date from the 16th and 17th centuries, the period of its greatest prosperity. Viana is regarded as the region's folk capital and specializes in producing traditional embroidered costumes. Although these make colorful souvenirs, you'll also find less elaborate crafts such as ceramics, lace, and jewelry. The large Friday market is a good place to shop. Like many Portuguese towns, it also has its very own sweet, the *torta de Viana,* a cake roll with a yolk-and-sugar filling that can be found in local cafés. Before or after strolling through town, don't miss the excellent local beach, Praia do Cabedelo (reached by ferry from the riverside at the end of the main street).

GETTING HERE AND AROUND

Regional trains from Porto Campanhã are fast and regular; if coming from Braga, you must change at Nine. There are fast Rede Expresso buses from Lisbon, while Autoviação do Minho plies the route from Porto and Transdev regional buses serve Viana from Braga. Viana is a real hub for transport to smaller Minho towns, with frequent services by local companies such as AVIC and Salvador crisscrossing this densely populated area; for schedules, ask at the bus station or tourist office.

ESSENTIALS

Bus **Autoviação do Minho** (☎ 258/825047 ⊕ www.transdev.pt). **Central de Camionagem** (bus station) (✉ Rua Cap. Gaspar Castro, Viana do Castelo ☎ 258/825043 ⊕ www.transdev.pt). **Rede Expressos** (✉ REDM—Central de Camoinagem ☎ 258/825047 ⊕ www.rede-expressos.pt). **Transdev** (☎ 258/ 825047 ⊕ www.transdev.pt).

Visitor Info **Porto e Norte** (Regional Tourism Authority✉ Rua do Hospital Velho, Viana do Castelo ☎ 258/820620 or 808/202202 ⊕ www.portoenorte.pt). **Viana do Castelo** (✉ Rotunda da Liberdade ☎ 258/098415 ⊕ www.vivexperiencia.pt).

EXPLORING

The **Basílica de Santa Luzia** is a white, domed basilica that overlooks the town from wooded heights. A funicular railway (€3 return, open October–May, daily 10–5; June–September, 8–8) will carry you up there, or walk up a narrow footpath, about 2 km (1 mi). The views from the basilica steps are magnificent, and a staircase to the side allows access to the very top of the dome for some extraordinary coastal vistas. This steep climb, up a very narrow staircase to a little platform, is for the agile only. ✉ *Av. 25 de Abril.*

A little ways beyond the Museu Municipal are the great ramparts of the **Castelo de Santiago da Barra,** the 16th-century fortification that added the words "do castelo" to the town's name and protected Viana against attack from pirates eager to share in its wealth. The castle has since been renovated and given a new function and name: Centro de Congressos Castelo de Santiago da Barra. The congress and meeting center has an auditorium, a translation center, and all the necessary equipment to hold conferences. Outside the castle walls, Viana holds a large market every Friday. ⊠ *Castelo Santiago da Barra* ☎ *258/820270.*

A 10-minute walk west from the Praça da República across the town's main avenue, the Avenida dos Combatentes da Grande Guerra, takes you to the impressive mansion that houses the **Museu Municipal de Viana do Castelo.** The early-18th-century interior has been carefully preserved, including some lovely tile panels. The collection of 17th-century ceramics and ornate period furniture shows how wealthy many of Viana's merchants were. ⊠ *Largo de São Domingos* ☎ *258/820377* 🎫 *€2* ⊙ *Tues.–Sun. 9:30–12:30 and 2–5. Closed holidays.*

The town's best face is presented in the old streets that radiate from the **Praça da República.** The most striking building here is the **Casa da Misericórdia,** an 18th-century almshouse, whose two upper stories are supported, unusually, by tall caryatids (carved, draped female figures). The square's stone fountain, also Renaissance in style, harmonizes perfectly with the surrounding buildings, which include the restored town hall and its lofty arcades.

NEED A BREAK? **Natário (**⊠ *Rua Manuel Espregueira 37* ☎ *258/822376***),** a small café right off the main drag of Avenida dos Combatentes da Grande Guerra, is a perfect place to soak up the Minho atmosphere. The proprietor makes his own pastries, cakes, and croquettes. Brazilian writer Jorge Amado is rumored to have frequented this place when he was in town.

WHERE TO EAT AND STAY

$$
SEAFOOD ✕ **Casa d'Armas.** This cozy, romantic restaurant is in a renovated mansion near the fishing docks. Seafood is the main reason to come here, starting with fish soup and going on with main dishes such as *sapateira recheada* (stuffed crab), *polvo com azeite e alho* (octopus with olive oil and garlic) and *arroz de tamboril* (monkfish rice). But the menu also has several grilled meat dishes as well as *picanha* (tender salted and grilled Brazilian beef) and *arroz de pato* (duck rice). The house bacalhau is rather unusual: it's fried and stuff with bacon. There's also a comprehensive list of regional wines. ⊠ *Largo 5 de Outubro 30* ☎ *258/824999* ⊟ *DC, MC, V* ⊙ *Closed Wed. and 1 wk in Nov.*

$
PORTUGUESE ✕ **Os Três Potes.** The cellarlike dining room, converted from a 16th-century communal bakery and dotted with traditional rural implements, gets busy on summer weekends, when people crowd in for the folk-singing and dancing sessions. There's fado every other Friday. Sitting at tables under stone arches or on the open-air terrace, you can choose from a fine range of regional dishes: start with the *aperitivos regionais* (a selection of cod pastries and cheeses); move on to the house bacalhau, the exceedingly tender *polvo na brasa* (charcoal-grilled octopus), or the *cabrito à Serra d'Arga* (roast kid). There's a good wine list and live music on weekends. ⊠ *Beco dos Fornos 7–9, off Praça da República* ☎ *258/829928* ⌸ *Reservations essential* ⊟ *AE, DC, MC, V.*

$ ⊞ **Hotel Viana Sol.** Although this hotel has few frills, its comfortable, functional, modern rooms are reasonably priced. There is no in-house restaurant, but it's in the center of town, so there are plenty of dining options nearby. It's also just a few steps away from the River Lima, so ask for a river view (room number 222 has the pick of the bunch). As of writing, work is going on to reopen the health club, with its heated pool, gym, squash court and sauna. **Pros:** free Wi Fi. **Cons:** no a/c; no restaurant; few parking spots. ⊠ *Largo Vasco da Gama* 🕾 *258/828995* ⊕ *www.hotelvianasol.com* 🔖 *64 rooms, 1 suite* 🛆 *In-room: no a/c, safe, Wi-Fi. In-hotel: room service, bar, laundry service, Wi-Fi hotspot, parking (free)* ▭ *AE, DC, MC, V* †⊙| *BP.*

$$ \quad 🛏 **Pousada Santa Luzia do Monte.** A 1920s mansion, on a wooded out-
★ \quad crop behind the basilica, houses this pousada. The gardens and ter-
race are a delight, as are the grand public rooms—especially in winter, when the fireplaces add crackling, romantic warmth to the sometimes chilly lounges. Guest rooms are spacious and have glamorous marble baths. The restaurant serves regional and Continental cuisine and has sweeping views of both the countryside and the Atlantic. **Pros:** lovely gardens; fine views; nice sports facilities. **Cons:** a little isolated; no free Internet access. ⊠ *Monte de Santa Luzia* 🕾 *258/800370* ⊕ *www. pousadas.pt* 🔖 *50 rooms, 1 suite* 🛆 *In-room: a/c, safe, refrigerator, Wi-Fi. In-hotel: restaurant, room service, bar, tennis court, pool, laun-dry service, Internet terminal, Wi-Fi hotspot, parking (free)* ▭ *AE, DC, MC, V* †⊙| *BP.*

NIGHTLIFE

The motifs at the **Casting Bar** (⊠ *Rua Nova de São Bento 120–124* 🕾 *258/827396*) come from the world of fashion. It's popular with local students, who come to chat upstairs and dance downstairs. A young crowd flocks to **Foz Caffé** (⊠ *Av. do Cabedelo, Darque* 🕾 *258/325107*), a night-spot near the beach. The **Glamour** (⊠ *Rua da Bandeira 177* 🕾 *258/822963*) bar and restaurant is popular with twenty- and thirtysomethings. It has an open-air esplanade, theme nights, and live music regularly.

VALENÇA DO MINHO

15 km (9 mi) northeast of Caminha; 123 km (76 mi) northeast of Porto.

Valença do Minho is the major border-crossing point in this area, with roads as well as rail service into Spain. Valença's Old Town is enclosed by perfectly preserved walls, which face the similarly defended Span-ish town of Tuy. Strolling along the river and ramparts is very pleas-ant, especially in the evening, when the day-trippers from Spain—who come primarily to patronize the many shops selling Portuguese-made linen—have retreated to their own side of the river.

GETTING HERE AND AROUND

Valença is a terminus for trains from Porto via Viana do Castelo; it's a very scenic route, along the coast and then along the south bank of the Minho. Autominho buses ply a parallel route from Viana. For details, inquire at the tourist office.

ESSENTIALS

Visitor Info **Valença do Minho** (⊠ *Paiol do Campo de Marte* 🕾 *251/823374*).

WHERE TO STAY

$ **Pousada São Teotónio.** This pousada is on the highest point of Valen-
Fodor's Choice ça's old fortification. The view is superb, with the Rio Minho beneath
★ you and Spain before you on the horizon. Guest rooms are comfortable and many have balconies overlooking the river. The restaurant's
core menu is based on Minho's dishes, and *rojões à moda do Minho*
(roasted pork) is one of the specialties. Free parking is available but
outside the grounds. Note that the fort is very crowded on weekends
when Spanish day-trippers pack the narrow streets, hunting for bargains in the local linen shops. **Pros:** stunning views; excellent restaurant.
Cons: no exercise facilities; no free Wi Fi and none at all in some guest
rooms; neighborhood crowded on weekends. ⊠ *Baluarte de Socorro*
🕾 *251/800260* ⊕ *www.pousadas.pt* 🛏 *18 rooms* ♿ *In-room: a/c, safe,
refrigerator, Wi-Fi (some). In-hotel: restaurant, room service, bar, laundry service, Internet terminal, Wi-Fi hotspot* ⊟ *AE, DC, MC, V* ⦿ *BP.*

MONÇÃO

*18 km (11 mi) northeast of Valença do Minho; 144 km (89 mi) north-
east of Porto.*

The riverside town of Monção is another fortified border settlement
with a long history of skirmishes with the Spanish. In town there are
the remains of a 14th-century castle that withstood a desperate siege
in 1368. When the Portuguese supplies ran low, a local woman baked
some cakes with the last of the flour and sent them to the Spaniards
with the message that there was plenty more where that came from.
The bluff worked, the Spanish retreated, and the little cakes are still on
sale in town. Try a glass of the local vinho verde, a noteworthy wine
available in several bars. Monção has a spa but it's aimed at sickly
locals; for a modern "river spa," head 25 km (15 mi) east to Melgaço,
a usually sleepy town with another 14th-century castle that livens up
considerably on Friday, market day.

GETTING HERE AND AROUND

Monção is no longer served by trains from Porto, which now have
their terminus in Valença. From there, AVIC and Salvador buses
serve the town on their way from Viana do Castelo, with at least
three services a day. The local tourist office can provide information
on schedules.

ESSENTIALS

Visitor Info Monção (⊠ *Praça Deuladeu* 🕾 *251/652757*).

South of Monção the N101 traverses glorious rural countryside before
EN descending to the valley of the Rio Vez, a tributary of the Lima. **Arcos**
ROUTE **de Valdevez,** 35 km (22 mi) from Monção, makes a nice stop (there are
several buses a day from Viana and Braga, and less frequent ones from
Porto). It's a typically serene little river town, where you can rent rowboats. Five kilometers (3 mi) farther south you arrive at the Lima, one of
the country's most beautiful rivers. It was known to the Romans as the
River of Oblivion, because its blissful beauty was said to make travelers forget their homes. Ask at the local **Turismo** (⊠ *Rua Prof. Mário Júio*

Almeida Costa ☎ *258/51001* ⊕ *www.cmav.pt* ⊘ *Closed Sun.*) about walks along the ancient Roman roads.

WHERE TO EAT AND STAY

$ ✕ **Panorama.** Housed in the market hall in Melgaço, upriver from Mon-

PORTUGUESE ção, this restaurant is renowned for the wonderful views through its picture windows and for its starters, of which there are dozens. Among the best are *pataniscas de lampreia* (lamprey fritters), *iscas de porco preto* (liver from acorn-fed black pigs), *ovas* (fish roe in vinaigrette) and *bola de carne* (meat roll). Main dishes range from arroz de tamboril (monkfish rice) to *perdiz estufada* (stewed partridge), while the comprehensive wine list is particularly strong on reds. Finish with creamy *queijo da serra* cheese served with homemade compote. The place packs out on weekends, when it's best to book ahead. ⊠ *Rua Carvalhiças Edifício do Mercado Municipal, Melgaço* ☎ *251/410400* ⊕ *www.restaurantepanorama.eu* ⊘ *DC, MC, V* ⊘ *Closed Mon. Closed 2 wks in Oct.*

$ 🏨 **Monte Prado.** This stylish river spa on a hilltop above the River Minho at Melgaço, 25 km (15 mi) east of Monção, offers panoramic views and great value. Contemporary art dots public areas, while guest rooms are smart and comfortable, with many amenities. Suites have Mies van der Rohe chairs and whirlpool baths. Unusual spa treatments feature Alvarinho wine or white chocolate, while outdoor activities include rafting and mountain biking. In the restaurant, contemporary design meets regional cuisine (bacalhau with lamprey is a seasonal specialty) and a cellar strong in local wines. The esplanade is a lovely place to luxuriate in the views. The hotel is a good base for the Parque Nacional Peneda-Gerês. **Pros:** fantastic views; great spa; excellent value. **Cons:** no in-room Internet access; a little out of town. ⊠ *Monte Prado, Melgaço* ☎ *251/400130* ⊕ *www.hotelmonteprado.pt* ⇥ *43 rooms, 7 suites* ⌂ *In-room: a/c, safe, refrigerator. In-hotel: restaurant, room service, bar, 2 pools, gym, spa, water sports, bicycles, laundry service, Internet terminal, parking (free)* ⊟ *AE, DC, MC, V* ⊙⎮ *BP, MAP.*

PONTE DE LIMA

★ *18 km (11 mi) west of Ponte da Barca on N203; 57 km (35 mi) southwest of Monção.*

Ponte de Lima's long, low, graceful bridge is of Roman origin. It's also open only to foot traffic; drivers cross a concrete bridge at the edge of town. The main square by the old bridge has a central fountain and benches and is ringed by little cafés—the perfect places to stop for a leisurely drink. The nearby square tower still stands guard over the town, and beyond, in the narrow streets, there are several fine 16th-century mansions and a busy market. Walking around town, you'll return again and again to the river, which is the real highlight of a visit. A wide beach usually displays lines of drying laundry, and a riverside avenue lined with plane trees leads down to the Renaissance Igreja de Santo António dos Capuchos. The twice-monthly Monday market, held on the riverbank, is the oldest in Portugal, dating from 1125. On market

days and during the mid-September Feiras Novas (New Fairs) you'll see the town at its effervescent best.

GETTING HERE AND AROUND

Local bus companies such as Cura and Autoviação do Minho serve Ponte de Lima from Viana do Castelo, with buses every half hour at peak times. From Braga the firm that provides fairly frequent services is Esteves e Andreia. For schedules for all these, check with the local tourist office. Regional bus company Transdev also serves Ponte de Lima, as do fast buses from Lisbon run by Rede Expressos; they share a local agent on Rua Vasco da Gama.

ESSENTIALS

Bus Rede Expressos/Transdev (⊠ *D. Cristina, Rua Vasco da Gama* ☎ *258/942870*).

Visitor Info Ponte de Lima (⊠ *Torre da Cadeia, Praça da República* ☎ *258/942335*).

WHERE TO EAT

$ ✕**Cozinha Velha.** If you're staying in Ponte de Lima, or on your way
PORTUGUESE to or from Braga, consider making the small detour to dine at this smart showcase for Minho cuisine in Queijada. Come hungry, because you really should try one or more of the delicious starters, which include *orelha de porco* (pig's ear) and *favas com fumados* (broad beans with smoked sausage), before moving on to the hearty main dishes. The cabrito assado (kid roasted in a wood oven) and the various bacalhau dishes are particularly renowned. Then, if you can't manage one of the eggier desserts, go for the *pêra borrachona* (drunken pear, cooked in wine). ⊠ *Cangostas, Queijada* ☎ *258/749664* ⊕ *www. restaurantecozinhavelha.com* ⩍ *Reservations essential* ▤ *DC, MC, V* ☾ *Closed Tues.*

$ ✕**Encanada.** The Encanada is adjacent to the tree-lined avenue along
PORTUGUESE the riverfront. A terrace provides river views. The menu is limited, but you can count on good local cooking, with dishes that depend on what's available at the market. You might start with the *bolinhos de bacalhau*, fried potato cakes with plenty of cod in them, and then try one of the regional dishes such as *rojões* (fried pork) accompanied by a vinho verde. Braver souls might go for the *arroz de sarrabulho*, a dish made of rice and pig's blood for which this restaurant is particularly renowned. ⊠ *Passeio 25 de Abril, Mercado Municipal* ☎ *258/941189* ▤ *AE, DC, MC, V* ☾ *Closed Mon.*

PENEDA-GERÊS

The northeastern corner of the Minho is quite unlike most of this densely populated, heavily cultivated region. Here a series of forested *serras* (mountain ranges) rise up, cut through with deep valleys. A significant part of this area is protected, forming Portugal's only national park, the Parque Nacional de Peneda-Gerês. But there are striking landscapes even outside the park's borders, such as the valley of the River Cavado, which harbors Portugal's first five-star rural resort, and the River Homem, with its Vilarinho das Furnas reservoir. In 1972, the dam here—a precursor to the more actively contested projects of the present day—submerged a village whose traditional way of life is recalled in a small **Museu Etnográfico** (☎ *253/351888* ✉ *museudevilarinhodafurna@gmail.com* ☼ *Closed Mon.*) in São João do Campo (Campo do Gerês) in the southern section of the national park. The nearby town of Caldas de Gerês has a popular spa and a cluster of lodging options.

GETTING HERE AND AROUND

In terms of access, the national park itself divides into three main sections. The southern, most easily accessible part, is a two-hour drive from Braga: turn off the N103 just after Cerdeirinhas, along the N304. There are up to six buses a day from Braga to Cerdeirinhas and Caldas do Gerês, run by local hotel company Empresa Hoteleira do Gerês and by Transdev, both of which have offices in the bus station on Largo de São Francisco in Braga. Buses from Braga also stop in Terras de Bouro, just outside the national park, where there are several restaurants and pensões, but gourmets with wheels should cross the River Homem for Brufe, home to a spectacularly sited restaurant. The Vilarinho das Furnas reservoir is a little farther upstream. The N308 road skirting the national park to the south links up with Montalegre in Trás-os Montes.

The park's central region is accessible by car or bus from Ponte da Barca, from which the N203 leads 30 km (18 mi) east to Lindoso, or from Arcos de Valdevez, from which the minor N202 leads to the village of Soajo. Both towns offer basic accommodations and superb hiking. You can reach Lindoso by Salvador bus from Braga, changing in Ponte da Barca or Arcos de Valdevez.

To see the park's northern reaches, which encompass the Serra da Peneda (Peneda Mountains), it's best to approach from Melgaço, a small town on the Rio Minho, 25 km (15 mi) east of Monção. From Melgaço, it's 27 km (17 mi) on the N202 to the village of Castro Laboreiro, at the park's northernmost point. Salvador buses cover this part.

ESSENTIALS

As well as tourist bureaus and the national park offices in Braga and at the various park gates, an excellent nonofficial source of information on lodgings and organized activities in the region is the not-for-profit group Adere-PG in Ponte da Barca. The Termas do Gerês (spa) has its own visitors' bureau.

Bus **Empresa Hoteleira do Gerês** (☎ *253/615896 or 253/615897*). **Salvador** (☎ *253/263453*). **Transdev** (☎ *253/209400 or 253/209401*).

BEACHES

The Atlantic is cold, even at the height of summer, and beaches along the Minho are notoriously windswept. More pleasant is a dip in the Rio Lima or Rio Minho, although you should heed local advice about currents and pollution before plunging in. Ponte de Lima has a particularly nice wide, sandy beach. Espinho, south of Porto, and the main resorts to the north (Póvoa de Varzim and Ofir) are the best places for watersports enthusiasts.

RURAL TOURISM

The Minho region is well known for its Turismo no Espaço Rural (Rural Tourism). There are some 100 properties in the area, with a particular cluster along the Rio Lima's north bank, each no more than several miles from a town. Facilities are usually minimal; houses may have a communal lounge, tennis, a pool or access to local swimming facilities, fishing, and gardens. Rates include bed and breakfast, and some places will arrange other meals on request. The **Central Nacional de Turismo no Espaço Rural** (✉ *Praça da República, Ponte de Lima* ☎ *258/931750* ⊕ *www.center.pt*) is the central booking agency associated with the rural tourism program; its Web site includes links to the sites of Solares de Portugal (generally grander old houses), Aldeias de Portugal (village lodgings) and Casas no Campo (more remote rural digs) plus suggestions for themed tour routes.

Visitor Info Adere-PG (✉ *Largo da Misericórdia 10, Ponte da Barca* (☎ *258/452250* ⊕ *www.adere-pg.pt*). **Parque Nacional Peneda-Gerês** (✉ *Av. António Macedo, Braga* ☎ *253/203480* ⊕ *www.icnb.pt* ☉ *Closed weekends.*

EXPLORING

Fodor'sChoice
★

Parque Nacional Peneda-Gerês. The 172,900-acre park, bordered to the north by the frontier with Spain, was created in 1970 to preserve the region's diverse flora and fauna. It remains Portugal's only national park. Even a short trip to the main towns and villages contained within the park shows you wild stretches of land framed by mountains, woods, and lakes. There are some 30 marked trails. Access is free, and general information is available online, at the park's headquarters in Braga and at its half-dozen entrance gates, all of which keep office hours, at Adere-PG in Ponte da Barca (which can also arrange walking guides) and at tourist offices in Braga Viana do Castelo and Caldas do Gerês (often just labeled on maps as Gerês), where you can get a walking map. ✉ *Sede do Parque Nacional (headquarters), Avenida António Macedo, Braga* ☎ *253/203480* ⊕ *www.icnb.pt* ☉ *Open weekdays 9–12:30 and 2–5:30.*

WHERE TO EAT AND STAY

$
PORTUGUESE

✕ **O Abocanhado.** Worth a trip for its stunning situation and prize-winning design alone, this restaurant is also renowned for its regional cuisine. Perched in the Serra Amarela hills, 12 km (7.5 mi) from Terras de Bouro, the long building slots into the surrounding slate, its terrace affording panoramic views of the River Homem. Outstanding mains include tender *barrosã* steak and locally raised kid. The dessert menu has family recipes as well as standards such as *pudim abade de priscos* (egg-and-almond pudding) and ricotta with pumpkin jam. Check the Web site for opening days, which vary (daily only in August). From Braga, head north to Vila Verde and then upriver toward the Vilarinho das Furnas reservoir. ✉ *Lugar de Brufe, Brufe, Terras de Bouro* ☎ *253/352944* ⊕ *www.abocanhado.com* ⌖ *Reservations essential* ▭ *No credit cards.*

$$$ 🖭 **Aquafalls.** Blending into the landscape just off the N103 from Braga to Gerês, this five-star rural spa hotel is the first of its kind in Portugal. Its wood-and-stone construction is an elegant compromise between contemporary style and tradition. The well-appointed guest quarters—all with terraces and stunning views over the River Cávado and the Caniçada reservoir—are in the main building or in 11 bungalows that are set in extensive grounds traversed by a waterfall. The luxurious spa facilities include an ice fountain and Vichy shower; the restaurant, which is known for its outstanding regional and international cuisine, has special spa menus. There's also a minigolf course and children's playroom. **Pros:** restful setting; stunning views; many organized outdoor activities available. **Cons:** accessible only by own transport; no nightlife in the area. ⊠ *São Miguel, Caniçada, Apartado 28, Vieira do Minho* 🕾 *253/649000* ⊕ *www.aquafalls.pt* ◿ *2 rooms, 22 suites* ⌂ *In-room: a/c, safe, refrigerator, Internet (some). In-hotel: restaurant, room service, bar, tennis court, 2 pools, gym, spa, water sports, bicycles, laundry service, Internet terminal, Wi-Fi hotspot, parking (free)* ⊟ *AE, DC, MC, V* ❏◎ *BP.*

¢ 🖭 **Residencial Carvalho Araújo.** This family-run pensão in the heart of the national park is one of the best-value lodging options in the area, with doubles at €45 most of the year. All rooms have views of the town and surrounding hills, central heating (for the damp winters) and radio and TV. Open fireplaces contribute to a cozy atmosphere in the lounge, the bar (where a range of games are available) and the restaurant, whose wood-fired oven is used to prepare home-cooked dishes. Staff can arrange guided hikes in the national park and around local villages, or boat trips on the Caniçada reservoir. The place doesn't have a spa, but offers special deals on the one in town. **Pros:** friendly atmosphere; lots of activities on offer. **Cons:** limited facilities; no Internet. ⊠ *Rua de Arnaçó 6, Caldas do Gerês* 🕾 *253/391185* ⊕ *www. residencialcarvalhoaraujo.com* ◿ *26 rooms* ⌂ *In-room: no a/c. In-hotel: restaurant, bar, spa, bicycles, laundry service, Wi-Fi hotspot, parking (free)* ⊟ *AE, D, DC, MC, V* ❏◎ *CP, FAP.*

TRÁS-OS-MONTES

The name means "Beyond the Mountains," and though roads built in the 1980s have made it easier to get here than in the past, exploring this beautiful region in the extreme northeast still requires a sense of adventure. Great distances separate towns, and twisting roads can test your patience. Medieval villages exist in a landscape that alternates between splendor and harshness, and the population, thinned by emigration, retains rural customs that have all but disappeared elsewhere. Many still believe in the evil eye, witches, wolf men, golden-haired spirits living down wells, and even the cult of the dead. During winter festivals, masked men in colorful costumes roam village streets, and the region's Celtic roots are evident in the bagpipes traditionally played here.

GETTING HERE AND AROUND

Having a car is the easiest way to tour the region, but making the trip by car would mean missing out on some of the finest train journeys in the country. The trip from Porto to Mirandela provides an excellent opportunity to see the changing landscape, and you can take a bus on to Bragança. But it is slow going. Both trains and buses stop at every village, and the journey could take more than nine hours.

The main bus company operating in Trás-os-Montes is Rodonorte, whose terminal in Porto is at Rua da Ateneu Comercial. Bus trips in this region are slow and, on some of the minor routes, uncomfortable. One useful tip is to take the bus rather than the train between the neighboring towns of Guimarães and Braga. It's only 22 km (14 mi) on the road, but the circuitous train ride involves two changes.

ESSENTIALS

Bus Rodonorte (✉ *Travessa Passos Manuel, Porto* ☎ *22/200–5637* ⊕ *www.rodonorte.pt*).

VILA REAL

116 km (72 mi) northeast of Porto. By train from Porto, change at Peso da Régua to the Corgo line.

The capital of Trás-os-Montes is superbly situated between two mountain ranges, and much of the city retains a small-town air. Although there's no great wealth of sights, it's worth stopping here to stroll down the central avenue, which ends at a rocky promontory over the gushing Rio Corgo. A path around the church at the head of the promontory provides views of stepped terraces and green slopes. At the avenue's southern end, a few narrow streets are filled with 17th- and 18th-century houses, their entrances decorated with coats of arms.

For restaurants and accommodations in the southern reaches of the Vila Real district, see also entries under Peso da Régua and Lamego in the Douro section of this chapter. *Quintas* (wine estates) listed there that are in the valley of the River Corgo are just a short drive from Vila Real.

GETTING HERE AND AROUND

The Corgo valley line that runs from the banks of the Douro to Vila Real is no longer operational, but the city is served by a plethora of local and regional bus companies, including Rodonorte and Auto Viação do Tâmega. Rede Expressos long-distance buses also come here from Lisbon, Porto, and other cities across Portugal. Aero Vip also runs near-daily turbo-prop flights from Lisbon to Vila Real's municipal aerodrome.

ESSENTIALS

Aerodrome Aeródromo Municipal de Vila Real (☎ *259/336620*).

Airline Aero Vip (☎ *21/156–0369, 92/751–9895 in Bragança, 92/751–9893 in Vila Real* ⊕ *www.aerovip.pt*).

Bus **Auto Viação do Tâmega** (✉ *Quinta do Seixo* ☎ *259/322674*
⊕ *www.avtamega.pt*). **Rodonorte** (✉ *Rua D. Pedro Castro* ☎ *259340710*
⊕ *www.rodonorte.pt*).

Visitor Info **Douro** (✉ *Praça Luís de Camões 2* ☎ *259/323560*
⊕ *www.visit-douro.com*). **Vila Real** (✉ *Av. Carvalho Araújo 94* ☎ *259/322819*).

EXPLORING

The finest baroque work in Vila Real is the **Igreja dos Clérigos** *(Church of the Clergy)*, also called the Capela Nova (New Chapel), a curious fan-shape building whose facade is dominated by two heavy columns. It is believed by some to have been designed by Nicolau Nasoni, architect of Porto's emblematic Torre dos Clérigos. ✉ *Rua dos Combatentes da Grande Guerra* ☎ *No phone* 🎟 *Free* ☉ *Daily 10–noon and 2–6.*

Fodor's Choice ★ An exceptional baroque mansion believed to have been designed by Nicolau Nasoni (architect of Porto's Clérigos Tower), the **Solar de Mateus** is 4 km (2½ mi) east of Vila Real. Its U-shape facade—with high, decorated finials at each corner—is pictured on the Mateus Rosé wine label (though that is the full extent of the association, as the wine-maker is not based here). Set back to one side is the chapel, with an even more extravagant facade. The elegant interior is open to the public, as are the formal gardens, which are enhanced by a "tunnel" of cypress trees that shade the path. ✉ *N322 (road to Sabrosa), Mateus* ☎ *259/323121* ⊕ *www.casademateus.com* 🎟 *House, gardens, and tour €8.50; gardens only €5* ☉ *Nov.–Feb., daily 10–1 and 2–5; Mar.–May and Oct., daily 9–1 and 2–6; June–Sept., daily 9–7:30.*

■ **EN ROUTE** The main road northeast of Vila Real (the N15) is straight for much of its length. You can drive through exceptionally fine, high countryside; rolling, arable land continues as far as the small town of Murça, 40 km (25 mi) away. Unlike the Iron Age boar figures you'll see elsewhere in the region, Murça has its own unique boar legend. According to a tale written down in 1875, a female wild boar of great ferocity and size menaced the region's inhabitants. The Lord of Murça succeeded in hunting her down, and in honor of his deed, a monolith in the shape of a wild boar was built in the center of town, known today as the *Porca de Murça*. This unlikely monument gives its name to Murça's fine wine and extraordinary olive oil.

WHERE TO EAT AND STAY

$ ✕ **Cêpa Torta.** The Twisted Vine, next to the cooperative winery in Alijó,
PORTUGUESE is run by local youngsters who are striving to maintain its long-established tradition of adding a dash of sophistication to regional cuisine. Starters include bacalhau *línguas* (tongue—the tenderest part of the fish) and a range of cured and smoked sausages. Meat predominates among the main dishes, among them *perdiz com queneles de batata* (partridge with potato dumplings) and cabrito assado. It's all excellent value, as are the wines on a long list that encompasses the Douro, Trás-os-Montes, and beyond. ✉ *Rua Doutor José Bulas da Cruz, Alijó* ☎ *259/950177* 🖃 *DC, MC, V.*

$ ✕ **Terra de Montanha.** Not only is this an excellent restaurant, but it has
PORTUGUESE a unique design as well. Tables and seating in the two spacious dining
Fodor'sChoice rooms are within huge wine barrels. Most of the upper portions are
★ cut away, giving you a view of the room, but some barrels are more
enclosed for a sense of privacy. There's a wide range of dishes drawing on top-quality meats and other local ingredients, and an excellent
bacalhau *com presunto e broa no forno* (baked with smoked ham and
corn bread). Or you might go for something rather more unusual such
as *orelheira estufada* (stewed pig's ear). Service is friendly, and prices
are quite reasonable. They serve dinner until late here—almost midnight
on weekends. ⊠ *Rua 31 de Janeiro 16–18* ☎ *259/372075* ▭ *AE, DC,
MC, V* ☾ *No dinner Sun.*

¢ ⊡ **Miracorgo.** The reception area is handsome, the guest rooms are
bright, and the service is good—all of which more than make up for
the unattractive, modern exterior. Request a room facing the valley,
with views of the dramatic stepped terraces. The restaurant also has
panoramic views, and there's a comfortable bar and games room. The
outdoor pool is heated—with solar power. On Friday and Saturday
nights the hotel draws locals for its Disco Club. The partying can go on
into the early hours, but rooms are protected by double-glazing. **Pros:**
great views; free Wi-Fi hotspot. **Cons:** inelegant building; no gym. ⊠ *Av.
1 de Maio 76–78* ☎ *259/325001* ⊕ *www.hotelmiracorgo.com* ⇲ *144
rooms, 22 suites* ♿ *In-room: a/c, refrigerator, Wi-Fi. In-hotel: restaurant, room service, bar, pool, laundry service, Internet terminal, Wi-Fi
hotspot, parking (free)* ▭ *AE, DC, MC, V* ⧦ *BP.*

$$ ⊡ **Pousada do Barão de Forrester.** This pousada in Alijó, some 30 km
(18 mi) southeast of Vila Real, is named for Baron Forrester, a 19th-
century Scotsman whose family members were successful port vintners
and whose remarkable map of the Rio Douro helped open the river
to navigation. Time fades away as you sit reading by the fire in the
lounge, glass of port at your side. The restaurant has two terraces for
sunlit lunches and star-filled suppers—it's open to both hotel guests
and nonguests who reserve in advance. Try the river mackerel in mari-
nade or the bacalhau *à Barão de Forrester* (fried with onion and baked
potatoes). **Pros:** peaceful setting; excellent restaurant and terrace. **Cons:**
no gym; no Wi-Fi; Internet access not free. ⊠ *Rua José Rufino, Alijó*
☎ *259/959467* ⊕ *www.pousadas.pt* ⇲ *21 rooms* ♿ *In-room: a/c, refrig-
erator, Internet. In-hotel: restaurant, room service, bar, tennis court,
pool, laundry service, parking (free)* ▭ *AE, DC, MC, V* ⧦ *BP.*

BRAGANÇA

60 km (37 mi) northeast of Mirandela; 255 km (158 mi) northeast of Porto.

This ancient town in the very northeastern corner of Portugal has
been inhabited since Celtic times (from about 600 BC). The town lent
its name to the noble family of Bragança (or Braganza), whose most
famous member, Catherine, married Charles II of England; the New
York City borough of Queens is named for her. Descendants of the
family ruled Portugal until 1910; their tombs are contained within the
church of São Vicente de Fora in Lisbon. Unfortunately, since improved

roads have encouraged development, the approaches to Bragança have been spoiled by many ugly new buildings.

Above the modern town rises the magnificent 15th-century Castelo (Castle), found within the ring of battlemented walls that surround the Cidadela (Citadel), the country's best-preserved medieval village and one of the most thrilling sights in Trás-os-Montes. Bragança has locally made ceramics, and there's also a good crafts shop within the walls of the Citadel. Baskets, copper objects, pottery, woven fabrics, and leather goods are all well made here.

The central cathedral is small and disappointing, but the modern town center is attractive in its way, with a wide central avenue and several cafés that open onto the sidewalk in summer. You'll easily exhaust all the sights in less than a day, but it's worth staying overnight for the views of the castle from the pousada on the outskirts of town.

GETTING HERE AND AROUND

Trains to Bragança were discontinued some years ago, much to locals' frustration, but bus company Rodonorte serves the town from major regional centers. There are also Rede Expresso fast services from Lisbon; the company's local agent is in Avenida João da Cruz. Aero Vip also runs near-daily turbo-prop flights from Lisbon to Bragança's municipal aerodrome.

ESSENTIALS

Aerodrome Aeródromo Municipal de Bragança (☎ 273/381175).

Airlines Aero Vip (☎ 21/156–0369, 92/751–9895 in Bragança, 92/751–9893 in Vila Real ⊕ www.aerovip.pt).

Bus Rede Expressos (⊠ Sanvitur, Avenida João da Cruz 38 ☎ 273/3331826). **Rodonorte** (⊠ Rua Vale d'Alvaro ☎ 273/300180 or 273/326552).

Visitor Info Bragança (⊠ Av. Cidade de Zamora ☎ 273/381273).

EXPLORING

Fodor's Choice ★

Within the walls of the **Cidadela** *(Citadel)*, you'll find the Castelo and the **Domus Municipalis** (City Hall), a rare Romanesque civic building dating from the 12th century. It's always open, but you may need to get a key from one of the local cottages for the Igreja de Santa Maria (Church of St. Mary), a building with Romanesque origins that has a superb 18th-century painted ceiling. A prehistoric granite boar stands below the castle keep, this one with a tall medieval stone pillory sprouting from its back. The keep, the Torre de Menagem, now contains the **Museu Militar,** which displays armament from the 12th century through to World War I. The most exciting aspect of the museum is the 108-foot-high Gothic tower, with its dungeons, drawbridge, turrets, battlements, and vertiginous outside staircase. ☎ 273/322378 ☑ Citadel free; museum €2, Fri. free to noon ☼ Citadel daily sunrise–sunset, museum Sept.–July, Mon.–Wed. and Fri.–Sun. 9–noon and 2–5; Aug., daily 9–6:30.

Outside the walls of the Citadel is the Renaissance **Igreja de São Bento**, with its fine Mudèjar (Moorish-style) vaulted ceiling and a gilded retable. Founded in the 16th century to serve the attached monastery, it also has some 18th-century additions. The church does not have regular opening hours but is usually open from about 5 pm, for. ⊠ *Rua de São Francisco* ☎ *273/331595* 🔖 *Free.*

Museu Ibérico da Máscara e Traje. If you can't make your visit to the region coincide with one of the winter festivals in which local lads wearing wooden masks roam the streets, scaring children and young women, the Iberian Mask and Costume Museum is definitely worth a visit. A joint Portuguese-Spanish initiative, it has displays on midwinter celebrations in villages across Trás-os-Montes, on similar events over the border in Zamora, and on Carnival traditions in both. The many costumes on show are riotously colorful and the masks strikingly carved. Information in English is available but for guided visits you must book a week in advance. The museum's Web site has a handy festival schedule. ⊠ *Rua D. Fernando O Bravo 24–26* ☎ *273/381008* ⊕ *museudamascara. cm-braganca.pt* 🔖 *€1* 🕙 *Tues.–Sun. 10–12:30 and 2–6.*

Parque Natural de Montesinho. A swathe of hilly land north of Bragança forms as 185,000-acre protected area where some fine walks are marked out. Information can be had online, at the park headquarters in Bragança—where you can also book visits to ethnographic museums in the villages of Babe, Caravela, and Palácios—or at the Vinhais park entrance. Local wildlife includes a few wolves, which shun contact with humans. In the villages that dot the park, some ancient traditions survive. **Rio de Onor,** right on the Spanish border in Portugal's far northeastern corner, is officially a separate village from its Spanish twin, but some land is still used communally by residents from both. There are protected natural parks on the Spanish side of the frontier, too. ⊠ *Rua Conégo Albino Falcão, Lote 5* ☎ *273/300400* ⊕ *www.icnb. pt* ⊠ *Casa da Vila* ☎ *273/771416.*

OFF THE
BEATEN
PATH
Miranda do Douro, some 80 km (50 mi) southeast of Bragança, is a curiosity: the only city in Portugal to have its own officially recognized language. More closely related to Latin than is Portuguese, Mirandês was always spoken by older people and is now taught in local schools. The old traditions are just as vibrant, with spectacular folk dances taking place during the Festas de Santa Bárbara, in mid-August. The town has a hulking ruin of a castle, a museum showcasing local customs, a 16th-century cathedral with lovely decorative elements, and several imposing palaces. The **Turismo** (⊠ *Largo do Menino Jesus da Cartolina* ☎ *273/431132*) has information on daily boat trips on the Douro, where eagles may be spotted nesting on the river cliffs. The valley here forms part of **Parque Natural do Douro Internacional** (⊕ *www.icnb.pt*); its headquarters is further south in Mogadouro, but it has a branch in Miranda (☎ *273/431457 or 273/432833*).

WHERE TO EAT AND STAY

$ ✕ **Lá Em Casa.** This low-key but attractive restaurant, with its slate walls
PORTUGUESE and fireplace, is midway between the castle and the cathedral. It serves regional Portuguese food with a decent menu of fish and shellfish. As you might expect this far inland, however, such dishes are considerably more expensive than the excellent meat dishes, which include veal and lamb. They also have an unusual recipe for *arroz de pato* (baked duck

rice) that features beer. For a snack or starter, there are excellent ham and cheese platters, grilled *chouriço* and *alheira* (smoked and cured garlic sausage respectively) and a wine list whose quality matches that of the food. Chestnuts feature not only in several meaty main dishes but in desserts, too. ⊠ *Rua Marquês de Pombal 7* ☎ *273/322111* ⚐ *Reservations essential* ▤ *AE, DC, MC, V.*

$ ✕ **Restaurante Típico Dom Roberto.** The wooden balcony and signage out-
PORTUGUESE   side may remind Americans of the old American West, but this delight-
Fodor'sChoice   fully rustic house in Gimonde, 8 km (5 mi) east of Bragança, is rich in
★   regional dishes. There's pork from native *bísaro* pigs, game specialties (hare, wild boar, pheasants) and smoked sausages. For dessert, try the creamy traditional rice pudding or local cheese with homemade compote. The stone-walled, red-tiled dining room is cozy and service helpful and gracious. The owners also have six rural houses to let to tourists in the Parque Natural de Montesinho, a protected area. ⊠ *Rua Coronel Álvaro Cepeda 2, Gimonde* ☎ *273/302510* ⊕ *www.amontesinho. pt* ⚐ *Reservations essential* ▤ *AE, DC, MC, V.*

$$ ☷ **Pousada de São Bartolomeu.** On a hill just west of the town center,
Fodor'sChoice   Bragança's modern pousada offers comfort and terrific views. The bar-
★   lounge has an open fireplace and wood furnishings, and the rustic guest rooms have balconies with dreamy views of the Citadel. Note that there is nonsmoking throughout the building. It doesn't really matter that the pousada is a few miles from all the in-town restaurants: the on-site dining room serves the area's best stews and game dishes to hotel guests and nonguests alike. There's no gym but there's an outdoor pool and a smaller one for kids, too. **Pros:** all rooms have citadel views; pools for both adults and children. **Cons:** no free Internet access; no gym. ⊠ *Estrada do Turismo* ☎ *273/331493* ⊕ *www.pousadas.pt* ⚐ *27 rooms, 1 suite* ⚐ *In-room: a/c, refrigerator, Wi-Fi. In-hotel: restaurant, room service, bar, pool, laundry service, Internet terminal, Wi-Fi hotspot, parking (free)* ▤ *AE, DC, MC, V* ⎢◎⎢ *BP.*

CHAVES

55 km (34 mi) west of Vinhais; 96 km (60 mi) west of Bragança.

Chaves was known to the Romans as Aquae Flaviae (Flavian's Waters), in honor of the emperor Flavian. They established a military base here and popularized the town's thermal springs. The impressive 16-arch Roman bridge across the Rio Tâmega, at the southern end of town, dates from the 1st century AD and displays two original Roman milestones. Today Chaves is characterized most by a series of fortifications built during the late Middle Ages, when the city was prone to attack from all quarters. The town lies only 12 km (7 mi) from the Spanish border. Its name means "keys"—whoever controlled Chaves held the keys to the north of the country.

GETTING HERE AND AROUND

Chaves is served by bus company Rodonorte, which has routes to major towns in the region. Rede Expressos also serves the town from Lisbon and other towns around Portugal, and has a local ticket agent.

ESSENTIALS

Bus Rede Expressos (✉ *Auto Viação do Tâmega, Largo da Estação* ☎ *276/332361* ⊕ *www.rede-expressos.pt*). **Rodornote** (✉ *Socitransa, Av. Santo Amaro Urb. Caramanchão B1, Loja 2* ☎ *276/328123* ⊕ *www.rodonorte.pt*).

Visitor Info Chaves (✉ *Terreiro de Cavalaria* ☎ *276/348180*).

EXPLORING

The late-17th-century **Igreja da Misericórdia** *(Mercy Church)* next door to the Torre de Menagem is lined with huge panels of blue-and-white azulejos that depict scenes from the New Testament. ✉ *Praça de Camões* ☎ *276/321384* ⊗ *Daily 9–12:30 and 2–5:30.*

The most obvious landmark is the great, blunt fortress overlooking the river, the 14th-century **Torre de Menagem** *(castle keep).* This houses the **Museu da Região Flaviense** *(Flaviense Regional Museum),* which is made up of the **Museu Militar** (Military Museum), the **Museu Arqueológico**, a hodgepodge of local archaeological finds and relics that tell the town's history, and the **Museu de Arte Sacra** (Sacred Art Museum). Its grounds offer grand views of the town. The tower is surrounded by narrow, winding streets filled with elegant houses, most of which have carved wood balconies on their top floors. ✉ *Praça de Camões* ☎ *276/340500* 🔲 *Museum €1* ⊗ *Daily 9–12:30 and 2–5:30.*

WHERE TO EAT AND STAY

$ 🔲 **Forte de São Francisco.** The ruins of a 17th-century Franciscan mon-
Fodor's Choice astery have been transformed to create this remarkable hotel. Outside,
★ massive walls surround extensive gardens and courtyards. The interior is a sober blend of ancient stone and modern simplicity. Public areas are dotted with antiques and sacred art. The Franciscan monks would no doubt have frowned on the contemporary comforts of the elegant, well-equipped guest rooms and the sumptuous regional delicacies served in the Restaurante Cozinha do Convento, which include smoked sausages, *polvo à galega* (spicy octopus), wild boar, and lobster with mayonnaise salad. They might, however, have winked at the hotel's well-stocked wine cellar installed in their old water cistern. **Pros:** delightfully renovated historic building; well-stocked games room. **Cons:** no Wi-Fi in guest rooms; no gym. ✉ *Alto da Pedisqueira* ☎ *276/333700* ⊕ *www. forte-s-francisco-hoteis.pt* 🛏 *53 rooms, 5 suites* ⊗ *In-room: a/c, safe, refrigerator, Internet. In-hotel: 2 restaurants, room service, 2 bars, tennis court, pool, spa, laundry service, Internet terminal, Wi-Fi hotspot, parking (free)* ⊟ *AE, DC, MC, V* ⊗ *BP.*

¢ 🔲 **Hotel Aquae Flaviae.** Although it bears the ancient Roman name for
☉ Chaves, and it's a cannon shot away from the town's fortified tower, this is a gleaming, modern hotel. The facade has an art deco touch—it looks more like an enormous movie house than a hotel—and the interior impresses with its smooth lines and polished surfaces. The rooms are as spacious as they are attractive. If you want a break from local cuisine, the restaurant also does a Brazilian grill. As well as the children's pool, there's a games room with billiards and table tennis, indoor football, minigolf and children's playroom—plus an outdoor play area nearby. The hotel even has its own underground access to the town's Termas (thermal baths). **Pros:** wide range of indoor

8

and outdoor activities; exclusive access to thermal baths. **Cons:** game room. ⊠ *Praça do Brasil* ☏ *276/309000* ⊕ *www.hotelaquaeflaviae. com* ⇆ *159 rooms, 6 suites* ⟳ *In-room: a/c, safe, refrigerator, Internet, Wi-Fi (some). In-hotel: restaurant, room service, bar, tennis court, 2 pools, gym, spa, laundry service, Internet terminal, parking (free)* ⊟ *AE, DC, MC, V* ⍾ *BP.*

EN ROUTE

If you continue west along the N103 for 35 km (22 mi), you'll come to an enormous system of lakes and hydroelectric dams along the Cávado. At this point you can make a short side trip to see the ruined castle at Montalegre, which is visible from miles around. Take a right turn onto the N308 and drive for 12 km (7 mi). The views are worth the detour. Back on the N103, you'll follow along the edge of the great lake system, skirting drowned valleys in an endless series of long loops. Allow plenty of time, because you're sure to want to stop often to take in the incredible views. To the north is the Parque Nacional da Peneda-Gerês; there are occasional access points along the road. Finally, after passing the village of Cerdeirinhas, the road runs for 30 km (18 mi) through rocky heights and down tree-clad slopes to reach Braga, where you are firmly in the center of the Minho province.

Madeira

WORD OF MOUTH

"Be prepared for lots of uphill walking. It's amazing how people all over Madeira cultivate flowers, banana trees, and everything on such steep terraces. We planned extra time there to go hiking. Several walking tours are available, and the hotel staff recommended one for prompt pickup and excellent guides. We chose an easy 10K walk downhill, following the levado irrigation system, in the laurel forest. We were above the clouds, which made for excellent photos. Take the Blandy's Madeira cellar tour; ride the teleferico cable cars, and walk over to see the sleighs going downhill. If you are in Funchal on a summer Saturday, don't miss the fireworks over the harbor."

—Kathryn Day

Updated by
Matthew
Hancock

Floral scents fill Madeira's sea-washed air. Bird-of-paradise flowers grow wild; pink and purple fuchsia weave lacy patterns up pastel walls; and jacaranda trees create purple canopies over roads and avenues. The natural beauty of this island is like no other, from the cliffs that plummet seaward to mountain summits cloaked in silent fog. The magic has captivated travelers for centuries.

Wine connoisseurs have always savored Madeira's eponymous export, but a sip of this heady elixir provides only a taste of the island's many delights. Made up of a series of dramatic volanic peaks rising from the sea around 600 km (373 mi) off the west coast of Africa, the island has an alluring, balmy year-round temperature, ensured by warm Atlantic currents. Other draws include the promise of clear skies, the carpets of flowers, the waterfalls that cascade down green canyons, and the great hiking along the island's famous network of *levadas*. These irrigation canals have been adapted into superb walking trails, many of them passing along the dramatic coast or through an Alpine-like interior of lush woodlands.

Thanks to its position on shipping routes between Europe, Africa, and the Americas, Madeira grew up as an important trading post. The British have had strong ties to the the island thanks to a 16th-century royal marriage. Today they still flock to Madeira, mainly over winter, as do other northern Europeans, especially Germans and Scandinavians. In summer, the island is also popular with visitors from mainland Portugal, when an adventurous crowd puts Madeira's magnificent blend of sun and seascapes to good use. The island also has some excellent museums, tranquil gardens, and a range of decent restaurants.

There are a couple of beaches on Madeira and several swimming complexes, but the island has never really appealed to those wanting a beach holiday. Travelers whose priority is cosmopolitan action until dawn may also be unimpressed by Madeira. Others—of almost any age, nationality, and fitness level—are likely to be caught in its spell. However, if you do want beach time, look no further than Porto Santo, the neighboring island, which has a superb 9 km (5.6 mi) long stretch of soft sands.

This popularity has wrought change: its airport is large enough to take jumbo jets, and its numerous new roads (construction projects continue) have halved many journey times. Modern, designer hotels have the very latest facilities, and visitors can expect to find some of the best hotels anywhere in Europe. But such developments don't seem to overwhelm Madeira. Rather, it's the island's amazingly rugged interior that overwhelms all who experience it. Multiple microclimates, exotic topography and vegetation, and designated nature reserves create an amazing ecodestination. The Laurissilva forest that occupies a lofty coastal strip above the sea has been classified as part of the Madeira

TOP REASONS TO GO

Experiencing the old and the new. Madeira retains a traditional Portuguese feel, but has one foot firmly in the 21st century, with cutting edge museums, an excellent road system, and some fine modern bars and restaurants.

Experiencing the levadas. There are around 2,000 km (1,242 mi) of levadas, or drainage canals that allow easy walking access to the island's jagged mountain peaks and dramatic coastline.

Celebrating at festivals. With one of the world's biggest New Year's Day fireworks displays, a spectacular Carnival and countless local festivities, there is always reason to celebrate somewhere on the island.

Enjoying the flora. Madeira's semitropical climate and rich volcanic soil promote an astonishingly verdant array of flowers, plants, and trees, both in the wild and in some beautifully cultivated gardens.

Taking to the Atlantic. If you aren't tempted to swim in the cool Atlantic waters, head off on a boat for the chance to spot dolphins or whales or for some of the best game fishing anywhere.

Nature and UNESCO World Natural Heritage. The island is one of the few regions in the world where ancient forest dating back before the Ice Age can be found. Flora and fauna in the four nature reserves are still being discovered to this day. With this awesome heritage, Madeira has the power to keep its core a sanctuary for centuries to come.

ORIENTATION AND PLANNING

GETTING ORIENTED

9

Madeira is a subtropical island 900 km (558 mi) southwest of Lisbon—at roughly the same latitude as Casablanca. In the middle of the isle is a backbone of high, rocky peaks. Steep ravines fan out from the center like spokes of a wheel. Although Madeira is only 57 km (35 mi) long and 22 km (14 mi) wide, distances seem much greater, as the roads climb and descend precipitously from one ravine to the next. In the same island group are tiny Porto Santo, about 50 km (31 mi) northeast, which has a sandy beach popular with vacationers and its 5,000 inhabitants; the Ilhas Desertas, a chain of waterless, unpopulated islands 20 km (12 mi) southeast of Madeira; and the also-uninhabited Ilhas Selvagens, much farther south, near Spain's Canary Islands.

Funchal. Known as Little Lisbon, this is the island's only real town, a charming Atlantic port set in a natural amphitheatre, where you'll find the island's best hotels, restaurants, and nightlife.

Side Trips from Funchal. There are some sumptuous gardens a short bus ride from Funchal, while historic Monte, with its holy church and famous toboggan run, can be reached via cable car. Accessible by ferry or plane, the island of Porto Santo is a must for beachgoers.

Western Madeira. Madeira's west coast is dotted with quaint fishing villages such as Câmara de Lobos—sitting below some of the highest sea cliffs in Europe—and small resorts such as Ribeira Brava, Porto Moniz, and Calheta, which boasts its own sandy beach and the excellent Casa das Mudas museum.

Central Peaks and Santana. The Central Peaks show another face of the island, an exhilarating mountain-scape of jagged rocks often above the cloud line. Santana is home to the distinctive triangular houses, close to a craggy north coastline gauged by waterfalls.

PLANNING

WHEN TO GO

The island's lower elevations are blessed by constant soft, warm breezes, and subtropical vegetation that perfumes the air year-round. Every day seems like spring. Historically Madeira has been a winter resort, but that—like much on the island—is changing. Christmas week, when every tree in Funchal is decorated with lights and the main boulevard becomes an open-air folk museum, is still the most popular time to visit, along with New Year's Eve, when cruise ships from everywhere pull into the harbor for an incomparable fireworks display from the hills surrounding Funchal. Book far in advance if you're coming at this time. Summer can also be crowded, especially during August, when the Portuguese take vacations. Festivals—celebrating flowers in April, the island's patron saint in August, and wine in September—are popular, too.

PLANNING YOUR TIME

For ease of planning you can split Madeira into four regions: Funchal, the capital; its environs and the neighboring islands of Porto Santo; the western side of Madeira; and the peaks, gorges, and plateaus of the interior, including the the rocky northeast coast.

GETTING HERE AND AROUND

AIR TRAVEL

Madeira is served by TAP Air Portugal, which has frequent flights daily from Lisbon (1.5 hours) and London (3.5 hours). EasyJet flies to Madeira from Bristol, London Gatwick, and Stansted. Numerous flights link Funchal with other European capitals. The Aeroporto da Madeira is a 35-minute drive east of Funchal, near Santa Cruz. A public SAM bus (⇨ *See contact info under Bus Travel, below*) serves the airport roughly hourly (6:05 am–10:55 pm, less frequent on weekends) to and from Funchal.

Airlines EasyJet (🌐 *www.easyJet.co.uk*). **TAP Air Portugal** (🌐 *www.flytap.com*).

Airports Aeroporto da Madeira (☎ *291/520700* 🌐 *www.anam.pt*). **Aeroporto Porto Santo** (☎ *291/980120*).

BUS TRAVEL

Madeira has four separate bus companies. Yellow Horários do Funchal buses serve Funchal and its surrounding neighborhoods. SAM buses run to the airport and the town of Machico, while Rodoeste buses run to the north and west of the island. The small company EACL serves towns east of Funchal.

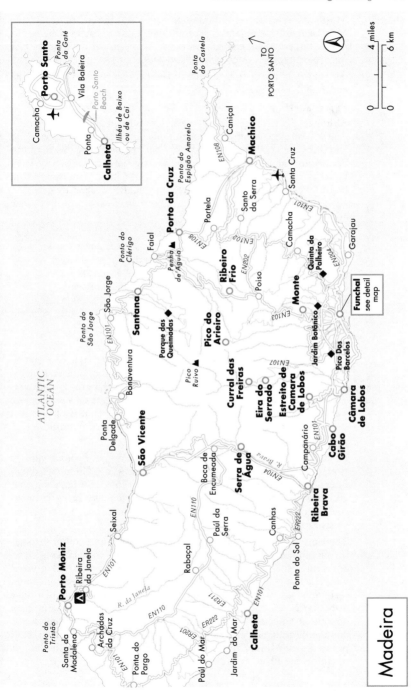

Madeira

Most services leave from an outdoor terminal at the end of Avenida do Mar. Generally, buses travel several times a day to each village on the island, but schedules change constantly, so inquire at the tourist office for departure times or check the Web sites.

Buses EACL (⌨ www.eacl.pt). **Horários do Funchal** (⊕ www.horariosdofunchal.pt). **Rodoeste** (⊕ www.rodoeste.pt). **SAM** (⌨ www.SAM.pt).

CAR TRAVEL

Although the best way to explore Madeira is by car, the terrain is steep. A new road system, mostly through tunnels, circles much of the island and links the north and south coasts, but anywhere off this road can be tortuous and slow. For example, the twisting, turning drive from Funchal to Porto Moniz in the west is only 156 km (97 mi) round-trip, but it takes all day if you go the scenic route. Road signs are generally adequate, but get an up-to-date map, particularly if you want to take advantage of Madeira's fast new highways.

Car Rental Auto-Jardim (✉ Rua Ivens 12, Funchal ☎ 291/213100, 291/524023 airport ⊕ www.autocarhire.net). **Bravacar** (✉ Caminho do Amparo 2, Funchal ☎ 291/708900, 291/524016 airport ⊕ www.bravacar.com.pt). **Lidorent** (✉ Edifício Alto Lido, Estrada Monumental, Funchal ☎ 963/108800 ⊕ www.lidorent.com). **Moinho** (✉ Porto Santo Airport, Porto Santo ☎ 291/983260 ⊕ www.moinhorentacar.com). **Rodavante** (✉ Edifício Baía, Estrada Monumental 187 2, Funchal ☎ 291/291/758506, 291/524718 airport, 291/982925 Porto Santo airport ⊕ www.rodavante.com).

TAXI TRAVEL

Taxis that are licensed to carry passengers within Funchal have a light on top, which is turned on if they are for hire. Taxis from outside Funchal won't pick up in the city limits. They're all metered, but if, for any reason, the meter is off or "not working," be sure to agree on a price before starting the journey. Rates are relatively inexpensive; a ride across town shouldn't cost much more than €8–€12, depending upon traffic.

TOURS

Boat excursions around Funchal's coast take place year-round. Choose from a range of two- to four-hour charters to Cabo Girão or Ribeira Brava; whale-watching trips on a catamaran with Sea Born; sailing boat cruises with Ventura and glass-bottom boat tours with Beluga Submarine, or cruises on a replica 15th-century sailing boat, Santa Maria. Costs range from €20 to €40 per person.

There are several companies that offer a different hiking tour through the mountains or along the levadas every day. Levels of difficulty vary, and some excursions include something extra, such as a peek at local weavers or a wine tasting in a hidden cave. Recommended companies include Madeira Explorers, Mountain Expedition (which also offer jeep safaris), and MB Tours. Travel agencies specializing in island tours abound in Funchal. Visits in buses or minivans usually include lunch and multilingual guides. Trips generally take in Cabo Girão, the inland peaks, Porto Moniz, and the village of Santana. Among the largest operators are Blandy's and Strawberry World.

Boat Tours **Beluga Submarine** (✉ *Marina do Funchal* ☎ *9670442177*
⊕ *www.belugasubmarine.net*). **Maria de Colombo** (✉ *Marina do Funchal*
☎ *291/220327* ⊕ *www.madeirapirateboat.com*). **Born** (✉ *Marina do Funchal*
☎ *291/23312* ⊕ *www.catamaran-seaborn.com*). **Ventura** (✉ *Marina do Funchal*
☎ *291/280033* ⊕ *www.venturadomar.com*).

Hiking Tours **Madeira Explorers** (✉ *C.C.Monumental Lido, 1st fl.,
Shop 23, Funchal* ☎ *291/763701* ⊕ *www.madeira-levada-walks.com*).
MB Travel (✉ *Largo dos Lavradores 7* ☎ *291/203950* ⊕ *www.mb-travel.com*).
Mountain Expedition (✉ *Estrada Ponta da Oliveira 48, Caniço* ☎ *969/677679*
⊕ *www.madeiraexpedition.com*).

Island Tours **Blandy's** (✉ *Av. Zarco 2, Funchal* ☎ *291/200660*
⊕ *www.blandytravel.com*). **Strawberry World** (✉ *Rua do Gorgulho*
⊕ *www.strawberry-world.com*).

RESTAURANTS

Madeira's cuisine is essentially Portuguese, and you'll find many similar
dishes to those on the mainland. Seafood fans should try the Portuguese
version of bouillabaisse, *caldeirada de peixes variados,* a slowly sim-
mered combination of fish, shellfish, potatoes, tomatoes, onions,
and olive oil. Also popular is *bife de atum,* a hearty tuna steak. Another
Portuguese specialty is *carne de vinhos e alhos* (pork marinated in
wine, oil, garlic, and spices, then gently boiled and quickly browned
over a high flame).

Madeira has also developed its own distinctive flavors that rely on
local ingredients. Foremost of these is the famous *espetada,* a beef shish
kebab seasoned with bay leaves and butter, traditionally a party dish
prepared in the country over open fires. The meat was once skewered
on bay twigs, but nowadays it's served on iron skewers hung vertically
from special stands placed in the center of a table so that all diners can
share. Espetada is usually accompanied by *milho frito* (fried cubes of
savory corn pudding), a side dish native to Madeira. Also on the table
of many Madeiran restaurants is *bolo de caco,* a round, flat bread
smeared with garlic butter.

The soft, white, deep-sea fish known as *espada* (often called "scabbard
fish" because of its long, swordlike shape) is served everywhere and
prepared dozens of ways—from poached à la Provençal to fried with
bananas. Espada are fished commercially only in the deep, offshore
waters of Madeira and Japan. The fishermen set out in the early evening in small boats, lower lines baited with specially prepared squid,
and laboriously pull up the catch. Sunday is a day of rest, however, so
don't look for fresh espada on Monday.

Be sure to try *lapas* (limpets), which are often served with rice. Typical desserts are bananas (small, sweet, silvery ones), mango, *paw paw*
(papaya), *anonas* (custard apples), and *maracujá* (passion fruit). Don't
leave without sampling the *bolo de mel* (a spicy honey cake made with
molasses), which is traditionally served with a glass of Madeira, the
unique wine that has become synonymous with the island. Most restaurants serve this wine; many offer diners a complimentary glass. Look
also for *vinho da casa,* a local table wine, as it's much cheaper than

imported ones and generally of high quality. Coral, a light lager, is the local *cerveja* (beer). For a tasty nonalcoholic drink, try *brisa* maracujá, a sparkling passion-fruit soda.

Many of Funchal's restaurants have long catered to northern European tastes, and several still serve bland meat dishes with boiled vegetables. A new generation, however, serves a more interesting mixture of local and international cuisine. The best places to head are Funchal Marina and around the Old Town. Top international restaurants can be found in the hotels, such as Les Faunces (top international food at Reid's Palace), Il Gallo D'Oro at the Cliff Bay, which boasts a Michelin Star, Uva at the Vine hotel and Casa da Quinta at Quinta da Casa Branca.

Less expensive regional specialties can be found in Câmara de Lobos and villages around the island.

HOTELS

Madeira is famed for the quality of its hotels. The majority are four stars and above, with facilities that are second to none. Most famous of these is Reids, the island's first hotel, which has entertained royalty and some of the most famous names of the last century. In Funchal, your options range from majestic old hotels on lavish estates to ultramodern high-rises with terraces that lap the sea. Simpler options also abound, including quiet *pensões* (pensions) and little *albergarias* (inns). Elsewhere on the island, hotels are similarly of a good standard. Consider also staying on a farm or rural bed-and-breakfast, usually in a remote part of the island. Known as Casas Rural (⊕ *www.madeira-rural.com*), you will need a car to reach these. Several low-key inns and bed-and-breakfasts also dot the island.

Some of the larger Madeiran hotels cater to package-tour operators, who offer relatively low prices and reserve huge blocks of rooms during peak holiday-travel periods. This may be one place where do-it-yourself travelers are better off going through an agency.

WHAT IT COSTS IN EUROS				
	¢	$	$$	$$$	$$$$
Restaurants	under €10	€10–€15	€16–€20	€21–€25	over €25
Hotels	under €80	€80–€140	€141–€200	€201–€260	over €260

Restaurant prices are per person for a main course at dinner. Hotel prices are for a standard double room, including tax, in high season (off-season rates may be lower).

EMERGENCIES

A 24-hour emergency service is provided by Hospital Dr. Nélio Mendonça. Pharmacies are open at night and on Sunday according to a rotating schedule. Dial 166 for information.

Contacts Funchal fire department (☎ *291/222122*). **Funchal police** (☎ *291/208400*). **General emergencies** (☎ *112*). **Hospital Dr Nélio Mendonça** (✉ *Av. Luís de Camões 57* ☎ *291/705600*).

VISITOR INFORMATION

In Funchal, Madeira's busy tourist office is open weekdays 9–5 and weekends 9–3. It dispenses maps, brochures, and up-to-date information on the constantly changing bus schedules. There are also tourist offices at the airport and in other towns as well as on Porto Santo; their hours are generally weekdays 9–5, and Saturday 9 to 1.

Visitor Info **Regional Tourism Office** (✉ Av. Arriaga 16 ☎ 291/211902 ⊕ www.madeiratourism.org). **Madeira Office in Lisbon** (✉ Av. 5 de Outubro 137a ☎ 217/817 258).

FUNCHAL

When colonists arrived in Madeira in July 1419, the valley they settled was a mass of bright yellow fennel, or *funchal* in Portuguese. Today the bucolic fields are gone, and the community that replaced them is the self-governing island's bustling business and political center. Funchal is the only town of any size on the island and the base for the the bulk of its tourism thanks to the plethora of hotels, restaurants, bars, and cafes serving delicious Portuguese pastries. And despite the tropical vegetation, Funchal's center feels decidedly Portuguese, though there's a heavy British influence, which is a holdover from the mid-16th-century marriage of the Portuguese princess Catherine of Bragança to England's King Charles II. The marriage contract gave the English the right to live on Madeira, plus valuable trade concessions. Charles in turn gave Madeirans an exclusive franchise to sell wine to England and its colonies. The island's wine boom lured many British families to Funchal, and many blue-blooded Europeans and famous vacationers such as George Bernard Shaw and Winston Churchill followed the pack to enjoy the mild winters.

GETTING HERE AND AROUND

Yellow Horários do Funchal buses serve Funchal and its surrounding neighborhoods: lines 01 and 48 run west from the city and make stops along the Estrada Monumental, where most of the hotels are. Pre-bought tickets are €1 each; consider a day pass for €3.50. You can also walk from one end of town to the other in around 30 minutes, although heading anywhere inland requires a steep uphill walk. A taxi ride across town will cost €8–€12.

TIMING

Three days are the minimum for exploring Funchal and its environs, along with some of the interior or the western coast; five days allows for a less hurried and more complete exploration of the island, including the northeast. You should use the old scenic roads as much as possible, and allow plenty of time for driving around. If, however, you're on a tight schedule or must travel at night, take advantage of the fast new roads.

SAFETY AND PRECAUTIONS

Funchal has a very low crime rate, but it pays to be careful with valuables as there are isolated cases of bag-snatchers and pickpocketing. Remember to wear high-factor sun blocks, as the sun is extremely powerful, even on cloudy days.

GREAT ITINERARIES

Three days are the minimum for exploring Funchal and its environs, along with some of the interior or the western coast; five days allows for a less hurried and more complete exploration of the island, including the northeast. You should use the old scenic roads as much as possible, and allow plenty of time for driving around. If, however, you're on a tight schedule or must travel at night, take advantage of the fast new roads.

IF YOU HAVE 3 DAYS

Devote your first day to the flower-bedecked capital city of **Funchal**. Start Day 2 early, heading for the hills just outside the city. In the morning, visit the nearby Jardim Botânico, and head up the cable car to the village of **Monte**, home of the unusual snowless sled ride. Next, go west to the coast and have a late lunch in or near the fishing village of **Câmara de Lobos**. Continue to the sea cliffs of **Cabo Girão**, with its spectacular views across the island. The terrain changes to forests as you continue along the coast to **Ribeira Brava**, another lovely seaside town. Turn inland through a rugged canyon and into a vivid green forest. You'll soon come to the mystical, cloud-shrouded peaks of the **Serra de Água**. Plan well ahead to overnight at the charming pousada here. On your last day, wake up very early and walk in the mountains or head back to the coast at **Calheta**, with its sandy beach and fantastic art museum. Drive back to Funchal, where you can spend another night or catch a flight to Lisbon or home.

IF YOU HAVE 5 DAYS

Spend your first day getting into the island rhythm by touring **Funchal**. In the morning of your second day, explore its environs, and visit the Jardim Botânico and the Quinta do Palheiro (Blandy Gardens), a former aristocratic estate. Next, head toward the village of **Monte** for a quick look around its holy church and exotic gardens. On the third day, using a good road map, follow the road to Poiso. Here, turn left and follow the signs to **Pico do Arieiro** and head out for an exhilarating hike. If you're up to the challenge, try to reach Pico Ruivo. Later, backtrack to Poiso and head north to **Ribeiro Frio**. Walk along a levada and take a break at Restaurante Ribeiro Frio, near the town's trout hatchery. Next head for **Santana** to see the thatch-roof houses for which the village is famous, then west along the stunning coastal road toward **São Vicente**. You can either overnight in São Vicente or push on to **Porto Moniz**.

In Porto Moniz pick up picnic fare, then turn inland—past Santa Madalena—toward Rabaçal, full of waterfalls and quiet pools. Follow the road to Paúl da Serra, where you'll see sheep grazing across the moors. Next, follow the signs to the flower-filled town of Canhas and on to the coastal road back into Funchal. Spend your fourth night and the next day enjoying the capital; if you have time, take a day trip to the neighboring island of **Porto Santo** for its superb beaches—then bid the island a fond *até a próxima* (until next time).

ESSENTIALS

There are plenty of banks and ATMs for cash withdrawals around the city center. The most central post office is on Avenida Zarco (*Weekdays 8:30 am–8 pm and Sat. 9–1*).

Buses Horários do Funchal
(☎ *291/705555*
⊕ *www.horariosdofunchal.pt*).

Visitor Info Tourism Office
(✉ *Av. Arriaga 16* ☎ *291/211902*
⊕ *www.madeiratourism.org*).
Tourism Office (hotel zone)
(✉ *Monumental Lido, Estrada Monumental 284* ☎ *291/775254*
⊕ *www.madeiratourism.org*).

> ### MADEIRA WINE
>
> Madeira's wine has been enjoyed for more than 500 years. It has graced the tables of Napoléon, the Russian czars, and even George Washington. In fact, the glasses raised to toast the signing of America's Declaration of Independence were filled with it.
>
> The fortified wine is served as an aperitif or with dessert, depending on its sweetness. Unlike other wines, Madeira is heated to produce its distinctive mellow flavor. The four varieties, from driest to sweetest, are Sercial, Verdelho, Boal, and Malmsey.

EXPLORING

To get to know Funchal best, spend time at the waterfront (especially the marina), in the old town, the market, and the central city squares—daily haunts of the islanders.

TOP ATTRACTIONS

Adegas de São Francisco. The St. Francis Wine Lodge takes its original name from the convent that once stood on this site. Today the operation is owned by the island's famous wine-making Blandy family and is also known as the Old Blandy Wine Lodge. Here you can see how the wine and wine barrels are made, visit cellars where the wine is stored, and hear tales about Madeira wine. One legend has it that when the Duke of Clarence was sentenced to death in 1478 for plotting against his brother, King Edward IV, he was given his choice of execution methods. He decided to be drowned in a "vat of Malmsey," a barrel of the drink. There's plenty of time for tasting at the end of the visit and a shop for purchasing the wine. ✉ *Av. Arriaga 28* ☎ *291/740110* ⊕ *www.madeirawinecompany.com* 🎫 *€5* ⊙ *Tours weekdays at 10:30, 2:30, 3:30, and 4:30, Sat. at 11. Wine shop weekdays 10–6:30, Sat. 10–1*.

Fortaleza de São Tiago. This robust construction was started by 1614, if not earlier, when French corsairs began to threaten Funchal's coveted deepwater harbor. Thanks to continuous use—by British troops when their nation was allied with Portugal against Napoléon, and during the visit of the Portuguese king Dom Carlos in 1901—much of the military stronghold has been preserved. You can wander around the ramparts which offer interesting views over the old town and sea below. A former governor's house inside it is now the **Museu de Arte Contemporânea,** which has changing exhibitions of works from the 1960s and later, most by local artists. ✉ *Rua do Portão de São Tiago* ☎ *291/213340* 🎫 *€2.50 for exhibitions, free at other times* ⊙ *Mon.–Sat. 10–12:30 and 2:30–5:30*.

9

A BIT OF HISTORY

Madeira island was discovered entirely by accident in the early 15th century at the height of Portugal's "Golden Age of Discovery" as Henry the Navigator was putting together teams of explorers. In 1418 João Gonçalves Zarco and Tristão Vaz Teixeira were blown off course during a particularly savage storm on their way to Guinea. By the time the storm subsided, they had drifted hundreds of miles off course and were lucky enough to hit upon an uninhabited island that they christened Porto Santo (Holy Port). Based on the sea captains' reports, Henry the Navigator gave the order to colonize. When Zarco and Teixeira returned to the area in 1419, they disembarked on a larger island, then covered with a nearly impenetrable forest. Zarco named it Madeira, which means "wood" in Portuguese. The name of the first settlement, Funchal, was inspired by the word *funcho* (fennel). In the 15th and 16th centuries the colony grew rich from its sugar plantations. Later, Madeira's wine industry sustained the island's growth, and in recent decades, tourism has become big business, making the island one of Portugal's top travel destinations. A statue of João Gonçalves Zarco stands at the main intersection of Avenida Arriaga and Avenida Gonçalves Zarco in Funchal, the island's capital.

Fodor's Choice
★
Jardim Botânico. The Botanical Garden is on the grounds of an old plantation 3 km (2 mi) northeast of Funchal. Its well-labeled plants—including anthuriums, bird-of-paradise flowers, and a large cactus collection—come from four continents. Savor wonderful views of Funchal, and check out the petrified trunk of a 10-million-year-old heather tree. There's also a natural-history museum, and a small exotic-birds garden. You can get here on bus 29, 30, or 31, which stop across the street from the market in front of Madeira's Electric Company. You can also take another cable car from the top of the gardens to Monte (☉ *Daily 9:30–6* 🚠*€8.25 single, €12.75 return*). ✉ *Caminho do Meio* ☎*291/211200 www.madeirabotanicalgarden.com* 🎫*€3* ☉ *Gardens daily 9–6.*

Fodor's Choice
★
Mercado dos Lavradores *(Farmers' Market).* In the center patio of the Farmers' Market, women—sometimes in Madeira's native costume of a full, homespun skirt with yellow, red, and black vertical stripes and an embroidered white blouse—sell orchids, bird-of-paradise flowers (the emblem of Madeira), anthuriums, and other blooms. The lower-level seafood market displays the day's catch. Note the rows of fierce-looking espada. Their huge, bulging eyes are caused by the fatal change in pressure between their deepwater habitat and sea level. ✉ *Largo dos Lavradores* ☉ *Weekdays 7 am– 8 pm, Sat. 7 am–2 pm.*

Museu de Arte Sacra. Funchal's Museum of Sacred Art has Flemish paintings, polychrome wood statues, and other treasures displayed in a former bishop's palace. Most of the pricelss paintings were

FESTIVAL

The **Festival de Flores** in the last week of April, brightens downtown Funchal with a carpet of *flores* (flowers), a parade, and a lot of music.

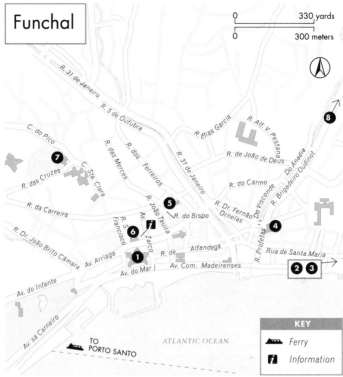

Funchal

commissioned by the first merchants of Madeira, who traded sugar for Flemish art so they could decorate their private chapels. The *Adoration of the Magi* was painted in 1518 for a wealthy trader from Machico and was paid for not in gold, but in sugar. You can tell how important this commodity was to the island by examining Funchal's coat of arms: it depicts five loaves of sugar in the shape of a cross. ⊠ *Rua do Bispo 21* ☎ *291/228900* ⊕ *www.museuartesacrafunchal.org* ⊠ *€3* ⊙ *Tues.–Sun. 10–12:30 and 2:30–6, Sun. 10–1.*

**NEED A
BREAK?**

A good place to stop for a light lunch or afternoon tea (weekdays only) is **O Patio** (⊠ *Rua da Carreira 43* ☎ *291/227376*), which entirely lives up to its name—it's a tiled open-air patio. At the same address, you can visit the Vicentes Photography museum, with some evocative black-and-white prints of the island (€2.50 entry).

Museu da Quinta das Cruzes *(Crosses Manor Museum)*. Once the home of a Genoese wine-shipping family, the 17th-century building and grounds of this museum are as impressive as its collection of antique furniture. Of special interest are the palanquins—lounge chairs once used to carry the grand ladies of colonial Madeira around town. Don't miss the small garden filled with ancient stone columns, window frames, arches, and tombstone fragments rescued from buildings that have been demolished

9

around the island. It also has an alluring café. ⊠ *Calçada do Pico 1* 🕾 *291/740670* 🎫 *€2.50* 🕙 *Tues.– Sun. 10–12:30 and 2–5:30.*

Palácio de São Lourenço. Built in the 17th century as Madeira's first fortress, the St. Lawrence Palace is still used as a military headquarters. At certain times its grand rooms are open to visitors and you can see the grand Ballroom and other state rooms filled with sumptuous works of art and antique furniture. ⊠ *Entrance on Av. Zarco* 🕾 *291/202530* 🎫 *Free* 🕙 *Wed. 10 am, Fri. 3 pm, Sat. 11 am.*

NEED A BREAK?

A classic spot to sit back and relax is the **Loja do Chá** (⊠ *Rua do Sabão 33–35, at Praça Colombo* 🕾 *916/500418*). This quaint tea shop specializes in various herbal and fruit teas, as well as coffees and cakes, which you can enjoy at outdoor tables facing a pretty square.

Fodor'sChoice ★

Teleférico da Madeira. The sleek, Austrian-engineered cable-car service has more than 40 cars that travel from Funchal's old town waterfront up to Monte at 1,804 feet above sea level. The trip takes 15 minutes one way, and there are great views to enjoy as you float silently up and over the city. ⊠ *Caminho das Barbosas 8* 🕾 *291/780280* ⊕ *www.madeiracablecar.com* 🎫 *€10 one-way, €15 round-trip* 🕙 *Daily 9:30–6 (last round-trip 5:30, last uphill trip 5:45).*

WHERE TO EAT

Don't hesitate to join the locals in the small restaurants and snack bars spread all over the narrow backstreets (such as Rua da Carreira, Rua das Murças, Rua do Bispo, Rua Queimada de Cimão, Rua Queimada de Baixo), where you will often find freshly prepared daily specials at extremely reasonable prices.

$
MEDITERRANEAN

✕ **Armazem do Sal.** Set inside a former salt warehouse, this dark space with bare brick walls and a few outdoor tables is a fashionable outlet for Italian and Madeiran-fusion cuisine. Well-presented dishes include salmon stuffed with chard; octopus with baby squids and olive mash; and spaghetti with shrimp mousse. ⊠ *Rua da Alfandega 135* 🕾 *291/241285* ⊕ *www.armazemdosal.com* 🖃 *AE, MC, V* 🕙 *Closed Sun.*

$$
MEDITERRANEAN

✕ **Casa da Quinta.** In the small and intimate original quinta on the Quinta Casa Branca's delightful grounds, the Casa da Quinta serves up some of the city's best cuisine. Delicious dishes include roasted parrot fish with garlic cream; rabbit with onion chutney; or wild sea bass in limpet broth.

The Azores: Portugal's Volcanic Isles

Looking for a vacation from your vacation, or a unique destination that's far off the beaten path—by 1,410 km (875 mi)? The remote Portuguese archipelago collectively known as the Azores could be your place. With a total population of 237,000, these nine islands are a tranquil, pastoral escape from mainland Portugal and Europe.

Geologically, the Azores are relatively young volcanic isles. They were formed less than 6 million years ago, and eruptions are still possible. The most recent volcanic activity vented in 1958, creating a fascinating moonscape of lava rock and sand that is now the western tip of Faial island. The archipelago is quite spread out, requiring short flights between most islands. São Miguel is the largest and most populated of the group, and home to the political and economic capital, Ponta Delgada. Corvo is the smallest at 17 square km (6½ square mi) with around 400 inhabitants.

The mere existence of civilization on the Azores is impressive; volcanic rock terrain and a forbidding distance from the Portuguese mainland must have made the islands inhospitable to early inhabitants. Despite these natural obstacles, the first settlers arrived in the 1430s and became a successful Portuguese colony through perseverance and hard work. They imported livestock and cleared grazing fields to create a robust meat and dairy industry, grew grape vineyards in rock beds, and built a strong fishing industry. Then, for much of the 19th century, the Azores became the European hub of whaling—two museums on Pico island document its history, which concluded with the birth of petroleum production.

Today the islands are nurturing a budding tourism industry. Nature lovers come to witness the stunning beauty of the isles, with their dormant volcanoes, natural swimming holes, and—in spring—millions of wild, blooming hydrangeas. More adventurous travelers take advantage of the hiking, world-class fishing, and excellent whale-watching available. Still others come for a brief glimpse into a simpler life that is rarely seen today in mainland Europe—small, pretty port towns of cobblestone streets, simple churches, and red-tile-roofed homes that thrive on cottage industries like fishing, cheese making, and ceramics.

Locals will explain that all nine islands are unique and each equally special, but if you're making a side trip from Lisbon and have limited time, you can get a good overview by sampling the four main islands: São Miguel with its two outstanding volcanic craters, Terceira with its many festivals and natural swimming coves, Faial and its legendary seafarers' port of Horta, and Pico, which is dominated by a massive volcanic cone rising 7,715 feet into the clouds.

For more information and details, contact the Azores Tourist Board (✉ *Rua Ernesto Rebelo 14-P, Horta, Faial* ☎ *292/200–500* ⊕ *www. visitazores.org*). Azores Express, part of SATA airlines (⊕ *www.azores-express.com*), is the main carrier to the islands and runs direct flights from Boston, and in high season, Oakland, California.

9

Each dish comes with a recommended Portuguese wine to pair with your dish. ⊠ *Rua da Casa Branca 7,* ☎ *291/700770* ⊕ *www.quintacasabranca. pt* ⌂ *Reservations essential* ⊟ *AE, DC, MC, V* ⊙ *No lunch.*

$$
ECLECTIC

✕ **Casa Velha.** In the tiled dining room, exuberant floral arrangements, white-lace curtains, and green tablecloths rustle gently in the breeze of ceiling fans. The food is prepared with great care, and menus change every few months. Start with the cream of seafood soup or the salmon rillettes with shrimp, then move on to the seafood fricassee or lobster Thermidor. Dessert might be apple with kirsch flambé. ⊠ *Rua Imperatriz D. Amelia 69* ☎ *291/2056009* ⊕ *www.casavelharestaurant.com* ⊟ *AE, MC, V.*

$
PORTUGUESE

✕ **Gavião Novo.** It's best to make reservations or to arrive early to bag a table at this cozy, traditional restaurant in the heart of the old town. The family-run restaurant offers simple local food such as grilled limpets, tuna with fried cornmeal, fish stews, and delicious kebabs. ⊠ *Rua de Santa Maria 131* ☎ *291/229238* ⊟ *AE, MC, V.*

$
CAFÉ

✕ **Golden Gate Grand Café.** Just across from the tourist office in the heart of Funchal, this restaurant-café has been open for business off and on since 1814. Sit in the airy interior, capture one of the tables that flank the sidewalk, or—even better—bag a seat on the balcony. You can pop in for coffee, light local dishes, or British-style afternoon tea, or you can settle in for a feast of creative Portuguese and international dishes. Don't miss the delicious desserts such as *sorvete de banana e maracujá* (banana and passion-fruit sorbet). ⊠ *Av. Arriaga 29* ☎ *291/234383* ⊟ *AE, DC, MC, V.*

$$$$
ECLECTIC

✕ **Il Gallo d'Oro.** The Cliff Bay Hotel should be proud of its internationally recognized gourmet restaurant, because even though this dining area is nothing special, you will find the cuisine is unforgettable. Some of the sublime dishes are bouillabaisse with scallops, pigeon with coconut and curry sauce, or *cep* (porcini) mushroom risotto, plus desserts such as Madeiran cake (made with dried fruits, spices, and molasses) with passion fruit jelly. ⊠ *The Cliff Bay Hotel, Estrada Monumental 147* ☎ *291/707700* ⊕ *www.portobay.com* ⋔ *Jacket and tie* ⊟ *AE, DC, MC, V* ⊙ *No lunch.*

$$
ECLECTIC

✕ **Riso.** This bright, modern restaurant is the place to go for rice dishes, and its location—on a ledge overlooking the sea by the Barreirinha swimming complex—makes it really special. All dishes, from starters to desserts, are based around rice. Portuguese dishes include a sublime coriander rice with prawns and fish of the day, or go for chicken curry with basmati rice or an array of risottos. Deserts include rice pudding and a devine Thai rice with coconut milk and mango. You can also pop in for a drink at the terrace before 5:30. ⊠ *Rua de Santa Maria 274* ☎ *291/280360* ⊕ *www.riso-fx.com* ⊟ *AE, DC, MC, V.*

$$$$
MEDITERRANEAN
Fodor'sChoice
★

✕ **Uva.** You'll find this restaurant at the designer hotel, the Vine, and the menu is as impressive as the locale's city views—at night the city looks like a fairy-lit oasis sparkling below. Divine dishes include wild sole with green asparagus, lamb with goat cheese and thyme, and desserts that include an unmissable Azorean pineapple carpaccio. Don't miss the homemade breads or the fine wines, which include excellent Madeiran table wines. ⊠ *The Vine, 27 Rua dos Aranhas* ☎ *963/058570* ⊕ *www. hotelthevine.com* ⊟ *AE, DC, MC, V* ⊙ *No lunch.*

WHERE TO STAY

$ ⚏ **Albergaria Dias.** Set near the historic part of the Old Town of Funchal, this friendly inn is a five-minute walk from the city center and handy for Barreirinha beach and some good bars and restaurants on the way. Each of the guest rooms has a marble bathroom, large balcony, high-quality modern furniture, and simple decor; top-floor rooms have sea views. There's a small pool, gym, library, and a back path to the Old Town. The generous breakfast includes fresh breads. **Pros:** a great location very near the old town; very friendly staff. **Cons:** there are no grounds to speak of; some rooms lack much of a view; the main entrance is on a busy through road. ⌧ *Rua Bela de São Tiago 44 B* ☎ *291/206680* ⊕ *www.albergariadias.com* ⇱ *35 rooms* ♿ *In-room: a/c, safe, refrigerator. In-hotel: pool, gym, Internet terminal, Wi-Fi hotspot, parking (free)* ▭ *AE, DC, MC, V* ⧆ *BP.*

$ ⚏ **CS Madeira.** On a spectacular oceanfront, the extremely modern, **Fodor's Choice** glass-fronted CS Madeira overlooks a stunning sea-level platform featuring a bar and swimming pools, accessed by two panoramic elevators that take you down to the sea. Once there, you can swim, arrange to go diving, or enjoy the island's biggest thellasotherapy (uses the benefits of seawater) spa. The hotel offers summer programs for children and teenagers (with computer games and Playstations), while the extremely spacious and well-equipped rooms (some interconnecting) are ideal for families. Most of the stylish rooms have balconies with ocean views and the communal areas have furniture designed by Philippe Starck. **Pros:** the sea terrace is the largest on the island; the views from upper rooms are hard to beat; hotel is able to book guests into local golf courses at a discounted rate. **Cons:** it's about a 15-minute walk from the town center. It can be confusing to find your way around the hotel. ⌧ *Estrada Monumental 175–177* ☎ *291/724214* ⊕ *www. csmadeiraatlanticresort.com* ⇱ *274 rooms, 23 suites* ♿ *In-room: a/c, safe, refrigerator. In-hotel: 4 restaurants, room service, 3 bars, tennis court, 4 pools, gym, spa, diving, water sports, children's programs (ages 4–12), laundry service, Internet terminal, Wi-Fi hotspot, parking (free)* ▭ *AE, MC, V* ⧆ *BP, MAP.*

$$ ⚏ **Quinta Casa Branca.** This boutique hotel artfully combines tradition **Fodor's Choice** with designer flare, facing a delightful 3-acre semi-tropical garden in a quiet part of town. The stylishly modern, low-rise accommodation block was designed by highly rated local architect João Favila. Most of the bright, minimalist rooms are on the ground floor and open out onto lawnside terraces; rooms in a modern annex have neat sliding shutters that open onto large balconies. The excellent restaurant is in the original 19th-century quinta across the gardens. **Pros:** gardens are a tranquil haven; it's only a short walk from the facilities of the Hotel Zone and town center; hotel is able to book guests into local golf courses at a discounted rate. **Cons:** beds could be more comfortable. ⌧ *Rua da Casa Branca 7* ☎ *291/700770* ⊕ *www.quintacasabranca.pt* ⇱ *41 rooms, 2 suites* ♿ *In-room: a/c, safe, refrigerator, DVD (some), Wi-Fi. In-hotel: restaurant, room service, bar, pool, gym, spa, laundry service, Wi-Fi hotspot, parking (free)* ▭ *AE, MC, V.*

9

¢   ⊡ **Quinta Mãe dos Homens.** On a former working farm still dotted with
☺   banana trees, this family-run quinta sits in a stunning location high
above the old town of Funchal, a short (if steep) walk from the botanical
gardens. The varied accommodations—studios and family apartments
sleep two to four; family studios and a villa sleep three to five—is simple
but spotless and great for those with children; there are kitchenettes and
sofa beds in the studios. The upper-floor studios have breathtaking views
over Funchal, while lower-floor ones open onto the gardens. The solar-
heated pool is a particular draw and shares the same views. **Pros:** in a
quiet, residential part of town away from the tourist bustle; good for
self-catering; excellent value for families. **Cons:** it is a steep 20-minute
walk into town (longer on the way back); there are few shops or restaurants nearby; reception is not always staffed. ⊠ *Rua Mãe dos Homens
39* ☎ *291/204410* ⊕ *www.qmdh.com* ⮣ *14 studios, 6 family studios, 2
family apartments, 1 villa* ⚐ *In-room: a/c (some), kitchen, refrigerator.
In-hotel: pool, laundry service, parking (free)* ▭ *AE, MC, V.*

$$$$ ⊡ **Reid's Palace.** In 1836 William Reid arrived in Madeira as a cabin
boy with £5 in his pocket. He made his wealth on the island, but died
a few years before his dream hotel was finished in 1891. On its rocky
point surrounded by 10 acres of gardens, Reid's is a destination as much
as Madeira itself. Past residents include artists John dos Passos, Pablo
Picasso, Rainer Maria Rilke, Gregory Peck (*Moby Dick* was filmed
here), and an ailing Winston Churchill, who in 1950 occupied a suite on
the ground floor. Reopened in April 2006 after refurbishment, the large
rooms are dangerously comfortable, with wide balconies and sea views.
Baths have power showerheads, towel warmers, and Molton Brown
toiletries. There's hardly a whim that can't be catered to here. **Pros:**
hotel seems tranquil even when busy; service is discreet and charming;
hotel is able to book guests into local golf courses at a discounted rate.
Cons: some rooms are on the small side; it can be confusing to find
your way around. ⊠ *Estrada Monumental 139* ☎ *291/717717* ⊕ *www.
reidspalace.com* ⮣ *128 rooms, 35 suites* ⚐ *In-room: a/c, safe, refrigerator, DVD (some), Wi-Fi (some). In-hotel: 5 restaurants, room service, 3
bars, 2 tennis courts, 3 pools, gym, spa, diving, water sports, children's
programs (ages 4–12), laundry service, Internet terminal, Wi-Fi hotspot,
parking (free)* ▭ *AE, MC, V* ⎮⊙⎮ *BP, FAP, MAP.*

$$$ ⊡ **The Vine.** Funchal's first designer hotel hits the spot if you want chic
decor right in the center of town. The ultramodern decor, by influential
local designer Nini Andrade Silva, takes its inspiration from Madeira's
landscapes and vineyards: black cobbles, frosted glass, and dark stones
set the tone. Rooms are compact and minimalist, with cascade show-
ers. The spa specializes in vine therapy (grapes, grape seeds, and grape
skins are used in treatments), while the top-floor bar and restaurant,
Uva have views to die for. **Pros:** most design-conscious hotel in Madeira,
with a fantastic restaurant and spa. **Cons:** not for those into space and
light, the rooms are quite small and many lack an outlook. ⊠ *Rua dos
Aranhas 27* ☎ *963/058570* ⊕ *www.hotelthevine.com* ⮣ *57 rooms, 27
suites* ⚐ *In-room: a/c, safe (some), refrigerator (some), Wi-Fi. In-hotel:
2 restaurants, room service, bar, pool, gym, spa, laundry service, park-
ing (free)* ▭ *AE, MC, V.*

NIGHTLIFE AND THE ARTS

NIGHTLIFE

BARS

A popular bar is the quasi-English pub, the **Prince Albert Rua da Imperatriz Dona Amélia** (☎ 291/235793), which also shows big-screen sports and has imported beers and a buzzy atmosphere. On the waterfront, **Yacht Bar** (✉ *Marina do Funchal* ☎ 926/437636 ☯ *Daily 9 am–midnight*) is the perfect spot to down a poncha—a local cocktail of distilled sugar cane, honey, and orange or lemon juice—as the sun sets, overlooking Funchal's black sand beach; the music gets going as it gets dark.

Café do Museu (✉ *Praça Municipio* ☎ 291/281121) is one of Funchal's coolest café-bars. Nestled behind the Museu de Arte Sacra, there's outdoor seating facing the delightful main square. This is a great spot to hole up for a coffee, cocktail, or even a full meal. Attached to the city's main theater, **Café do Teatro** (✉ *Teatro Municipal Baltazar Dias, Av. Arriaga* ☎ 291/226371 ⊕ *www. cm-funchal.pt* ☯ *Weekdays 9 am–midnight, weekends 9 am–4 am*) attracts an appropriately gregarious and arty crowd who enjoy sipping cocktails until the wee hours, either inside or at the outside tables.

Settle into the comfy sofas at **Chega de Saudade** (✉ *Rua dos Aranhas 20, Praça da Acif* ☎ 291/242289), which is modern bar-restaurant on two levels, for a cocktail or beer. Tucked away in a modern square in the town center, Chega de Saudade also has a raised outdoor terrace, and there's occasional live music.

CASINO

Gamblers can try their luck in the **Casino da Madeira** (✉ *Av. do Infante* ☎ 291/209100 ⊕ *www.casino-madeira.com*), which is open Sunday–Thursday 3 pm–3 am, and Friday and Saturday 4 pm–4 am. Its unusual building was designed by architect Oscar Niemeyer. You must be at least 18 years old; dress is smart casual (no sandals or sports shoes allowed).

DANCE CLUBS

Copacabana (✉ *Av. do Infante* ☎ 291/233111), beneath the Casino da Madeira, often has live Brazilian music. There's nightly dance music starting at 11 pm, which attracts a lively over-thirty crowd.

O Molhe (✉ *Estrada da Pontinha, Porto do Funchal* ☎ 925/492962 ⊕ *www.molhe.com*), an unusual but extremely stylish restaurant-bar-club, sits in a stunning position on top of a fort on the edge of Funchal harbor. There are DJ sessions with dance music most weekends, though the dazzling views back over Funchal are an equal attraction.

FOLKLORIC TRADITIONS

Madeira proudly makes the most of its folkloric traditions for visitors. No matter when you visit, there's a good chance you'll see folk dances performed at a restaurant or hotel. It may look as though the dancer has dropped a contact lens and is doing his or her level best to find it. One such dance, the Ponto do Sol, recalls the island's involvement with slavery, as the dancers move with bowed heads, their feet shuffling as though chained. Costumed dancers whirl to the music of a small guitarlike instrument called a *machête*.

9

Drum, bass, hip-hop, trance—or whichever type of music is currently in vogue—is on tap at **Vespas** (✉ *Av. Sá Carneiro 60* ☎ *291/231202* ⊕ *www.discotecavespas.com*), Madeira's largest club, in a cavernous former warehouse next to the docks. Things don't get going until after midnight.

FADO

You'll find good food as well as tear-jerking fado at **Arsénios** (✉ *Rua de Santa Maria 169* ☎ *291/224007*), with nightly performances at around 8 pm.

THE ARTS

The **Teatro Municipal Baltazar Diaz** (✉ *Av. Arriaga* ☎ *291/226371* ⊕ *www. cm-funchal.pt*) offers occasional concerts and plays. The local newspaper carries listings, but the easiest way to find out the schedule is to check at the tourist office or check out the posters outside the theater.

OUTDOOR ACTIVITIES

FISHING

Madeira is famous for its big-game fishing. You can arrange fishing excursions at the Funchal Harbor through **Turipesca** (☎ *291/231063* ⊕ *www. madeirafishingcentre.com*), which departs from the Marina do Funchal.

GOLF

Memorable views over the capital, Funchal, and the southern coast of the island are the hallmarks of **Balancal Palheiro Golf** (✉ *Sitio do Balançal, São Gonçalo* ☎ *291/790120* ⊕ *www.palheirogolf.com* ⌃ *Reservations essential* ⚐ *18 holes. 6,022 m. Par 71* ⚐ *€100 per round* ☞ *Facilities: driving range (limited), putting green, chipping area, golf carts, hand-pulled carts, rental clubs, pro shop, restaurant, bar*), a delightful Cabell Robinson–designed course built high on the mountainside. Inevitably there are great changes in elevation, and although it is possible to walk this course, the sensible option is to take to a cart, particularly in the hot summer months. It was a tight fit to contain 18 holes in this site, but there are a few great ones among them, and it's a pleasure to play all of them. A handicap certificate is required here.

SCUBA DIVING

Madeira is too far north for colorful tropical fish, but divers enjoy the clear, still seas of summer and report lots of interesting marine life and coral formations. **Manta Diving Centre** (✉ *Galomar, Rua Robert Baden Powell, Canico de Baixo* ☎ *291/935588* ⊕ *www.mantadiving.com*) can arrange dives and lessons in the clear waters of a marine reserve just east of Funchal. Prices range from €25 for a single dive tour to €375 for a full PADI dive course.

SHOPPING

For the best selection of Madeira wine, check out the **Madeira Wine Company** (✉ *Av. Arriaga 28* ☎ *291/740100* ⊕ *www.madeirawinecompany. com* ⊙ *Weekdays 10–6, Sat. 10–1*), which sells an exhaustive selection of the local tipple, covering virtually every vintage produced on the island for the past 35-odd years. Otherwise you can find Madeira wine sold in most of the island's delicatessens and better supermarkets. Despite its unpromising name, the **Casa do Turista** (⊠ *Rua Conselheiro José S. Ribeiro 2, Funchal* ☎ *291/224907*) sells museum-quality Madeiran crafts of all types, including embroidery, wicker, ceramics, wine, and liqueurs, in the 19th-century former home to the German consul. **Universal Store** (⊠ *Rua de João de Deus* ☎ *291/222142* ۞ *Mon.–Sat. 9:30–7:30, Sun. 9:30–1:20* serves a similar range of crafts as well as toys and clothes in a former Protestant church.

Madeira Shopping (⊠ *Caminho de Santa Quitéria, Santo António, Funchal* ☎ *291/100800* ⊕ *www.madeirasshopping.pt* ۞ *Daily 10 am–11 pm*) just off the main Funchal bypass north of the Hotel Zone, caters to pretty much any shopping need. The giant shopping mall has more than 100 shops selling international and national clothes and produce, and also has restaurants, cafés, and cinema screens. **Dolce Vita** (⊠ *Rua Dr Brito Câmara 9* ☎ *291/235103* ⊕ *www.dolcevita.pt* ۞ *Daily 9 am–11 pm* is another giant shopping mall in central Funchal, with a wide range of shops selling clothes, sports goods, kids' clothes, and accessories.

BASKETS
In the village of Camacha, about 10 km (6 mi) northeast of Funchal, there's a large cooperative shop on the main square, **O Relógio** (⊠ *Largo Conselheiro Aires de Ornelas 12, Camacha* ☎ *291/922777*) that sells every imaginable type of basket as well as some wicker furniture. Most of the work is done at home; on rural roads it's common to see men carrying large bundles of willow branches to be used for basketry.

FLOWERS
Tropical flowers are available boxed from any florist for shipping home. (It's legal to bring flowers into the United States from Madeira as long as they're inspected at the U.S. airport upon arrival.) Flower stands in the market and behind the church in Funchal are good value and, like most island shops that deal with visitors, pack their bouquets in special boxes to withstand trips in luggage holds. The **Quinta da Boa Visita** (⊠ *Rua Lombo da Boa Vista* ☎ *291/220468*) ۞ *Mon.–Sat. 9–5:30*, on the outskirts of town, sells orchid seedlings, orchids, and other exotic flowers.

NEEDLEWORK
Bordal (⊠ *Rua Doutor Fernão Ornelas 77* ☎ *291/222965* ⊕ *www. bordal.pt* ۞ *Weekdays 9–1 and 2–7, Sat. 9:30–1*) specializes in traditional Madeiran embroidery and produces beautifully hand-crafted linen, pillow cases, table cloths, towels, and baby clothes.

SIDE TRIPS FROM FUNCHAL

The steep mountains that rise up around Funchal are easily accessible from the capital and shelter some of Madeira's most interesting villages. Virtually a suburb of Funchal, Monte is famed for its church, exotic gardens, and hair-raising toboggan run. To see Madeira at its wildest, however, head further into the mountains to the remote village of Curral das Freiras via the dazzling viewpoint of Eira do Serrado. In contrast, a day or two on the neighbouring island of Porto Santo provides a very different landscape fringed by one of Europe's finest sandy beaches.

MONTE

☾ *6 km (4 mi) northeast of Funchal.*

Fodor's Choice
★

The village of Monte sits above Funchal at a height of 550 meters (1,804 feet). Its cool mountain air and dramatic views made it a healthy retreat for the island's wealthy in the mid-19th century, and today it still contains a number of upmarket quintas and luxuriant gardens.

GETTING HERE AND AROUND

To drive to Monte from Funchal, take Rua 31 de Janeiro. You can also hop a taxi or take Bus 20 or 21 from Praça da Autonomia or Bus 48 from the Hotel Zone. But the most enjoyable approach is on the cable car that departs from Funchal's old town. A second cable car departs from Monte down to the Jardim Botânico (same hours, €8.25 one-way, €12.75 round-trip).

ESSENTIALS

Cable Car Madeira Cable Car ⊠ *Caminho das Barbosas 8* ☎ *291/780280* ⊕ *www.madeiracablecar.com* ⊠ *€10 one-way, €15 round-trip* ☉ *Daily 9:30–6 (last round-trip 5:30, last uphill trip 5:45).*

EXPLORING

Monte Palace Tropical Gardens. The gardens have indigenous flora as well as plants from all over the world. The Monte Palace was a grand hotel from 1897 until 1943, but with the death of the last owner, it went out of business and the building and grounds were neglected for more than 40 years. In 1987 millionaire entrepreneur José Manuel Rodrigues Berardo bought the property and transformed it into this garden. Antique statues, windows, niches, and other architectural artifacts dot the grounds, tiled panels recall the adventures of the Portuguese explorers, Asian pagodas and gateways lend touches of the exotic, and cannons pour their salvos of water from a stone galleon in a lake. There is also a small museum packed with precious stones and African carvings. All this and wonderful views down to Funchal, too. ⊠ *Caminho do Monte 174* ☎ *291/742650* ⊕ *www.montepalace.com* ⊠ *€10* ☉ *Gardens 9:30–6, museum 10–4:30.*

Nossa Senhora do Monte *(Our Lady of the Mountain)*. Standing tall at the highest point in Monte is this white-stucco church, the island's most holy church. The tiny statue above the altar was found by a shepherdess in the nearby town of Terreira da Luta in the 15th century and has become the patron saint of Madeira. The church also contains the tomb of Emperor Charles I of Austria, the last Hapsburg monarch. He came to Madeira hoping that its more temperate climate would help him recover from tuberculosis, but he succumbed to the disease and died on the island in 1922. ⊠ *Largo da Fonte* ☉ *Daily 8–6.*

Tábuas de Madeira. The village of Monte is home to one of Madeira's oddest attractions: *tábuas de Madeira* or *carrinhos do Monte* (the snowless sled ride). The sleds were first created to carry supplies from Monte to Funchal; later, passenger sleighs hauled as many as 10 people at a time and required six drivers. Nowadays the rides are just for fun, and no one in Madeira should miss this experience that will take 10 years off your life and stay with you forever.

Dressed in white and wearing goatskin boots with soles made of rubber tires, drivers line up on the street below the Nossa Senhora do Monte church. The sleds, which have cushioned seats, look like big wicker baskets; their wooden runners are greased with lard. Two drivers run alongside the sled, controlling it with ropes as it races downhill on a 10-minute trip nearly back to Funchal (you will have to walk about 1 km (½ mi) to reach Funchal or take one of the many taxis that line up at the end of the ride). If the sled starts going too fast, the drivers jump on the back to slow it down. ⊠ *Serra do Monte* 🚠 *€20 for 1 person, €25 for 2, €37.50 for 3 people* ⊗ *Mon.–Sat. 9–6, Sun. 9–1.*

NEED A BREAK?

If you need refreshment before sledding back to Funchal, stop at **Alto Monte** (⊠ *Estrada dos Marmeieros* ⊗ *Mon.–Sat. 9–6, Sun. 9–1*), just above the main square, Largo da Fonte. The cosy interior is lined with soccer scarves and hats, and the terrace has fine views. The café serves good salads, sandwiches, and omelets at sensible prices.

EN ROUTE

If you're heading to Curral das Freiras, keep a lookout for the *miradouro* (viewpoint) at **Eira do Serrado,** just 16 km (10 mi) northwest of Funchal, which overlooks the Grande Curral—once thought to be the crater of a long-extinct volcano in the center of the island, sometimes referred to as Madeira's belly button. From here, Pico Ruivo and the craggy central summits look like a granite city. Island legend says the peaks are the castle fortress of a virgin princess, who can be seen sleeping peacefully in the *rocha da cara* (rock face). It's said that she wanted to live in the sky like the clouds and the moon, and was so unhappy at being earthbound that her father—the volcano god—caused an earthquake that pushed the rocky cliffs high into the sky so she could live near the heavens. Today the views are breathtaking in all directions. If you are driving to Eiro do Serrado from Funchal take Rua Dr. João Brito Câmara west, which turns into N101, and head for the miradouro at Pico dos Barcelos. Follow signs to Curral das Freiras, but take the old road rather than the new tunnel, which bypasses the viewpoint. There are also occasional Horários do Funchal buses here from Funchal.

CURRAL DAS FREIRAS

6 km (4 mi) north of Eira do Serrado.

GETTING HERE AND AROUND

The best way to get here is to drive on the old road via Eira do Serrado, or you could take Horários do Funchal bus 81 from Funchal's old town (departures roughly hourly). A new tunnel bypasses this stretch of road, so keep alert for the sign to Eira do Serrado so you won't miss the turn.

ESSENTIALS
Visitor Info **Curral das Freiras**
(✉ *Estrada Cánego Camacho*,
☎ *291/721180*).

EXPLORING
Curral das Freiras (Nuns' Shelter). An old road runs through a series of switchbacks and two tunnels that lead down to this village. The sisters of the Convent of Santa Clara took refuge in this remote valley from bands of lonely, marauding pirates. Nearly the geographic center of Madeira, the valley sits in the middle of a circle of extinct volcanoes that long ago pushed the island up from the bottom of the sea. It's a beautiful location, with village life carrying on as it has done for centuries—apart from the tourist buses that rumble in daily. There's not much to do apart from soak up the atmosphere and sample the local produce in several roadside cafés, which sell liqueurs distilled from the local chestnuts and passion fruits.

> **FAMOUS HEADWEAR**
>
> Look out for the island's famous traditional headwear for the men of Porto Santo—hats made of palm leaves. On Palm Sunday you will also see the *palmitos borda-dos* (palm leaves woven into the form of a crucifix).

PORTO SANTO

50 km (31 mi) northeast of Madeira.

Beachcombers have long loved the tiny, parched, and barren island whose golden beach is famous for its therapeutic properties. By packing themselves in the sand, which runs over 10 km (6 mi) along the entire south coast, locals cure their rheumatic pains and speed the healing of skin complaints or minor injuries.

The island's simple salâo houses are centuries old. Their unique roofs are made of salâo, a sandy clay noted for its strong adherent properties. This amazing roofing material fits extraordinarily well into the Porto Santo rural landscape. The houses are cool in summer because when the weather is very dry, cracks open up in the salâo, letting the air circulate. In winter, this material absorbs the rain. The price one pays for this natural convenience is labor: the roof needs to be replaced every year.

A huddle of tidy, whitewashed cottages and town houses with terra-cotta tile roofs, Vila Baleira—the island's main town—has a park containing an idealized statue of Christopher Columbus. Before gaining fame and his place in history, he married Isabela Moniz, daughter of Bartolomeu Perestrelo, the first governor of the island, in 1479. She died not long after, at the time of the birth of their son.

WHEN TO GO
Madeirans pack themselves onto the sands in July and August when the island becomes their summer playground. You'll find the beaches less crowded between March and June.

GETTING HERE AND AROUND

The Campo de Cima Airport is in the center of the island with regular 15-minute flights from Madeira with SATA Air Acores. Round-trip fares are around €50. Reservations should be made in advance, especially for July and August. The tiny Aeroporto Campo de Cima is a 10-minute drive north of Vila Baleira. A taxi transfer costs around €6.

The 2½-hour ferry ride from Funchal ends in Porto de Abrigo, a five-minute connecting bus ride from the main town of Vila Baleira. The *Lobo Marinho* ferry sails from Madeira to Porto Santo every day (except Tuesday from January to March and October to December). Boats leave Funchal Harbor at 8 am and return at 6 pm on most days, though check the Web site for details. The sometimes choppy one-way passage takes 2½ hours. Tickets cost €52 round-trip, and you can buy them on board or through the Porto Santo Line office, which is open weekdays 9–12:30 and 2:30–6. For sailings on summer weekends, buy tickets in advance.

Porto Santo roads are easy to handle by car, but most visitors cover the 10-km-long (6-mi-long) island on foot or by taxi. It's fairly easy to hail cabs, or you can phone for one. Buses also run up and down the main coastal highway.

ESSENTIALS

Airline **SATA Air Acores** (☎ 707227282 ⊕ www.sata.pt).

Airport **Aeroporto Campo de Cima** (☎ 291/980120 ⊕ www.anam.pt).

Ferry **Porto Santo Line** (⊠ Rua da Praia 6 ☎ 291/210300 ⊕ www.portosantoline.pt).

Taxi **Porto Santo Taxis** (☎ 291/982334).

Visitor Info **Porto Santo tourist office** (⊠ Av. Henrique Vieira de Castro, Vila Baleira ☎ 291/982361).

EXPLORING

Calheta Point. Just below Pico das Flores lies Calheta Point, where the café-restaurant, O Calhetas (⇨ *see review below*), marks the western extremity of the beach. There is probably no better way to enjoy the whole island than to stop for a drink or bite to eat, and than walk back along the beach during the sunset and admire the astonishing landscape.

Casa de Cristóvão Colombo (*Columbus Museum and Home*). This museum is housed in the old governor's house, where Columbus himself once lived. Inside, lithographs illustrate the life of Columbus. Copies of 15 portraits of the discoverer made between the 16th and 20th century prove there was little agreement on what he looked like. You can also see the restored kitchen and bedroom, maps of Colombus's journeys, and treasures from a Dutch boat that sank off Porto Santo in 1724. ⊠ *Travessa da Sacristia 2–4* ☎ 291/983405 ⊕ *www.museucolombo-portosanto.com* 🎟€1.50 ⊗ *Tues.–Sat. 10–12:30 and 2–5:30 (until 7 pm from July–Sept.), Sun. 10–1.*

Pico do Castelo. The island's series of 656- to 1,552-foot peaks make for great exploring. The summit Pico do Castelo has a small 16th-century fort that provided defense against the frequent attacks of French and Algerian pirates. Only four cannons remain. Below you to the west is Porto Santo beach, and to the east is the conical shape of Pico de Baixo and the Ilhéu de Cima. From here it's an easy walk to **Pico do Facho** (1,552 feet), the island's highest point.

Pico das Flores. Pico das Flores—a lookout at the end of a bumpy ride off the far western end of the beach—offers fine views of Madeira and the rocky, uninhabited islet called Ilhéu de Baixo.

> ### FISHING
>
> Madeira and Porto Santo are meccas for those hoping to reel in huge blue marlin, yellowfin tuna, albacore, swordfish, and dorado. The list of gilled gentry inhabiting the surrounding waters also includes bigeye tuna, barracuda, dolphin fish, wahoo, and shark.

Portela. One of your first stops on Porto Santo should be at the Portela viewpoint, which overlooks the harbor, the town, and the long ribbon of beach. Nearby is the hilltop Capela de Nossa Senhora da Graça, one of the oldest churches on the island, dating back to the 15th century.

Vila Baleira. The island's main town is little more than an attractive village clustered round the palm-lined main square, Largo do Pelourinho. From here, it's a short walk to a fantastic swath of beach and the town's elongated jetty, a popular spot for evening walks and young lovers to gaze out to sea.

WHERE TO EAT

$ ✕ **Baiana.** This attractive, wood-ceiling restaurant is a great place for
PORTUGUESE   a full meal. Tasty starters include local cheeses and garlic bread, while mains include *bife na pedra* (steak grilled on a hot stone), delicious prawns with garlic, and *feijoada* (bean stew). ✉ *Rua Dr. Nuno S. Teixeira, Vila Baleira* ☎ 291/984649 ▭ *AE, MC, V.*

$$ ✕ **O Calhetas.** This fantastic fish restaurant is at the far end of the beach
PORTUGUESE   at Ponta da Calheta. There's a smart, minimalist interior, or you can
Fodor'sChoice   dine on a sun terrace. The fresh fish of the day is always good, or try
★   the giant spicy prawns, *amêijoas* (cockles), seafood spaghetti, or *caldeirada* (fish stew). There's a free shuttle to and from town, or you can walk back in a couple of hours straight down the beach; it's safe at night. ✉ *Estrada Regional 111, Ponta da Calheta* ☎ 291/984380 ▭ *AE, DC, MC, V.*

$ ✕ **O Forno.** Near the campsite on the main coast road, this is a bus-
PORTUGUESE   tling local spot that packs people in for its excellent grilled chicken, served with salad and fries. It also serves kebabs and other meat dishes, omelets, and fresh home-baked bread. ✉ *Rampa da Fontinha, Vila Baleira* ☎ 291/985141 ▭ *AE, DC, MC, V.*

$ ✕ **Solar do Infante.** Opposite the jetty in Vila Baleira, this sleek glass-
MEDITERRANEAN   fronted restaurant with a front terrace serves interesting dishes such as salmon with shrimp, fried octopus, fresh lobster, and seafood spaghetti. Slick service and fantastic views add to the experience. ✉ *Praça do Barqueiro, Av. Manuel Gregório Pestana Junior, Vila Baleira* ☎ 291/985270 ▭ *AE, DC, MC, V.*

WHERE TO STAY

$$ 🏨 **ApartHotel Luamar.** On one of the nicest stretches of beach, 4 km (2½ mi)
☾ away from Vila Baleira, the Luamar has apartments with a lounge and
kitchenette facing its own beachside grounds and pool. Make sure you
get an apartment facing the sea rather than the coast road. Upper floors
have balconies, though the best ones are those on the ground floor with
their own terraces. It's great for families, with its own children's pool. **Pros:**
delightfully quiet for those who want to get away from it all; right on the
beach. **Cons:** there is no restaurant; some of the rooms are showing their
age. ⊠ *Cabeça da Ponta* ☎ *291/984121* ⊕ *www.torrepraia.pt* ↘ *75 apart-
ments* ⅋ *In-room: a/c, kitchen, refrigerator. In-hotel: bar, pool, beachfront,
laundry service, Internet terminal, parking (free)* ▭ *AE, DC, MC, V* ⏐◯⏐ *BP.*

$ 🏨 **Hotel Porto Santo.** On the beach about a 15-minute walk from town,
this hotel is a beachcomber's dream. Like a country club, there are
sports activities, a library-lounge, and plush rooms surrounded by palm-
studded grounds a stone's throw from the beach. A new annex includes
self-catering villas, some with their own grounds, which are great for
families. The hotel is often heavily booked throughout August, but
in spring and fall you may have the place to yourself, and the prices
drop considerably. **Pros:** recently installed spa facilities are second
to none; service is exemplary. **Cons:** some of the rooms are quite
small with dated decor; food can be disappointing. ⊠ *Campo de Baixo*
☎ *291/980140* ⊕ *www.hotelportosanto.com* ↘ *97 rooms, 5 2-bedroom
villas* ⅋ *In-room: a/c, kitchen (some), refrigerator (some). In-hotel: res-
taurant, room service, 2 bars, pool, gym, spa, beachfront, laundry ser-
vice, parking (free)* ▭ *AE, DC, MC, V* ⏐◯⏐ *BP, FAP, MAP.*

$$$$ 🏨 **Pestana Porto Santo.** The island's newest hotel is almost a resort in its
☾ own right. On a wonderfully quiet stretch of beach around 3 km (2 mi)
from Vila Baleira, the deluxe hotel and series of apartments and villas are
spread around substantial, landscaped grounds dotted with exotic plants
and dazzling flowers. Modern rooms are a little boxy, but the best ones
have sumptuous sea views, while the villas and family apartments are ideal
for families of any size. The pool complex is superb, though with the beach
right next door, it is often superfluous. **Pros:** everything you need for a
family holiday, from beach to pool to spa for the parents. **Cons:** can get
busy in high summer; guests without children may feel out of place; food
can be disappointing. ⊠ *Estrada Regional 111* ☎ *291/724241* ⊕ *www.
pestana-porto-santo.com* ↘ *135 rooms, 76 suites, 57 apartments, 6 villas*
⅋ *In-room: a/c, safe, kitchen (some), refrigerator, Wi-Fi. In-hotel: 4 restau-
rants, room service, 3 bars, tennis court, 2 pools, gym, spa, beachfront,
children's programs (ages 4–12), laundry service, Wi-Fi hotspot, parking
(free)* ▭ *AE, DC, MC, V* ⏐◯⏐ *BP, FAP, MAP* ☾ *Closed Nov.–March.*

¢ 🏨 **Residencial Central.** At the top end of town, with fine views from the
top-floor rooms, this low-rise modern building is the best budget option
in Vila Baleira. Rooms are of a decent size with tiled floors, and the best
ones have little balconies. There's also a leafy front terrace. **Pros:** good
value; stone's throw from the center of town. **Cons:** steep walk to get
to the hotel; rooms at the back of the hotel are a little gloomy. ⊠ *Rua
A. Magno Vasconcelos, Vila Baleira* ☎ *291/982226* ↘ *20 rooms* ⅋ *In-
room: a/c. In-hotel: bar, parking (free)* ▭ *No credit cards.*

9

OUTDOOR ACTIVITIES

Not just for walking tours on Porto Santo, the adventure travel company **Terras de Aventura** (⊠ *Caminho do Amparo 25* ☎ *291/708990* ⊕ *www.terrasdeaventura.com*) organizes canoeing, paragliding, mountain biking, horseback riding, and water sports. The qualified guides have plenty of local knowledge and speak English well.

CAMPING

Just west of Vila Baleira, **Parque de Campismo Porto Santo** (⊠ *Rua Gularte Medeiros Ponta* ☎ *291/982160*) is a stretch of beach just waiting for you to pitch a tent and unroll your sleeping bag.

GOLF

Designed by Spanish golfing legend Severiano Ballesteros, the **Porto Santo Golf Club and Course** (⊠ *Sítio da Lapeira*, ☎ *291/983778* ⊕ *www.portosantogolf.com* ⚑ *Reservations essential* 🏌 *18 holes. 6,434 m. Par 72* ⛳ *€70 per round* ☞ *Facilities: driving range, putting green, chipping area, golf carts, hand-pulled carts, rental clubs, pro shop, restaurant, bar*) is considered even more challenging than those on Madeira. The course bends around water features and is full of bends and slopes. Its lush fairways stand out in vivid contrast to the parched landscape around it. The plush clubhouse is a modern medley of stone, glass, and potted cacti.

SCUBA DIVING

For diving excursions off Porto Santo contact the **Porto Santo Sub Dive Center** (⊠ *Clube Naval de Porto Santo, Vila Baleira* ☎ *291/983259* ⊕ *www.portosantosub.com*).

WESTERN MADEIRA

The western stretches of Madeira see the island at its greenest and lushest, but also its most dramatic: on the high central plateau, you can see a dozen waterfalls spilling into a cool pine forest, while on the coast sea cliffs fall sheer to the Atlantic and banana plantations cling to steep, sunny slopes. On the dramatic north coast, a narrow highway clings to the cliff face between little fishing villages that seem a world away from the bustle of Funchal.

CÂMARA DE LOBOS

20 km (12 mi) west of Funchal.

On coastal route N101, you'll pass many banana plantations on the way to Câmara de Lobos—a fishing village made famous by Winston Churchill, who came here (in a borrowed Rolls-Royce equipped with a bar) to paint pictures of the multicolor boats and the fishermen's tiny homes. A plaque marks the spot where he set up his easel. Although the coast here is changing as more and more people commute to jobs in Funchal, the boats are still pulled up onto the rocky beach during the day, while children run and play in the narrow streets and grizzled old fishermen stand around chatting. The promenade that protrudes from the main plaza offers magnificent views west to Cabo Girão.

GETTING HERE AND AROUND

By car, Câmara de Lobos is an easy 20-minute drive up the coast from Funchal—you can park at pay-and-display bays around the harbor. Regular Rodoeste Bus 4 also makes the journey from Funchal, dropping passengers off at the main Largo da Repeublica.

ESSENTIALS

Visitor Info Tourist Office (⊠ *Rua Padre Eduardo Clemente Nunes Pereira* ☎ *291/943470*).

EXPLORING

Cabo Girão. At 1,900 feet, Cabo Girão is on one of the highest sea cliffs in the world. Totally uninhabited, from here you can see ribbons of terraces carved out of even the steepest slopes and farmers daringly cultivating grapes or garden vegetables. Through centuries, thousands upon thousands of *poios* (terraces) have been built in Madeira. The poios rise from sea level up the mountainsides, and the mind boggles at the dangers involved and sheer labor that went into constructing the retaining walls that hold the terraces together. In the past, neither machines nor animals were used on Madeiran farms because the plots are so small and difficult to reach. Not long ago, farmers blew into conch shells as a means of communication with neighbors across the deep ravines.

Cabo Girão is an easy drive off the main west coast highway, and there's plenty of parking close to the clifftop. Rodoeste Bus 154 also stops here, but there are only four buses daily (fewer on weekends). It's 16 km (10 mi) west of Câmara de Lobos.

> ### WINE TASTING
>
> If you're interested in sampling Madeira wine, visit the **Henriques & Henriques Vinhos,** a winery very close to Câmara de Lobos's promenade, at the western end of town. You'll be made to feel right at home during a tour of a facility that combines state-of-the-art technology with down-home hospitality. And, yes, the bottles are for sale. ⊠ *Sitio de Belém* ☎ *291/941551* ⊕ *www.henriquesehenriques. pt* ☒ *Free* ⊗ *Weekdays 9–1 and 2:30–5:30.*

WHERE TO EAT AND STAY

$$
PORTUGUESE
✕ **Vila do Peixe.** Perched on a street overlooking the sea and harbor, this is a fantastic spot to see the sunset and dine on fresh fish. The daily catch is chalked on a board and grilled at an open kitchen—local produce usually includes scabbard (both black and white), bream, parrot fish, monkfish, bass, and *lapas* (limpets), all grilled to perfection and served with fine wines. The desserts and starters are also excellent. ⊠ *Rua Dr João de Freitas* ☎ *291/099999* ⊟ *AE, DC, MC, V.*

$$
Estalagem Quinta do Estreito. Around 10 kms (6 mi) inland, this one-time estate house is the perfect base from which to explore the Levada do Norte, one of Madeira's most popular walking trails. Set in its own grounds, complete with its own lavendar field, the views from here—across fields and down to the sea—are superb. Oak is lavishly used throughout the inn. Rooms have balconies and marble baths as well as such thoughtful touches as heated towel racks and a welcoming bottle of wine and a Madeira cake. Stairs lead up to a tower library that invites you to linger. The Bacchus Restaurant ($$), which serves

nouvelle Madeira cuisine, may be reason enough for a visit, and there's a free shuttle bus to Funchal. **Pros:** great food at the restaurant; close to the facilities of the village of Estreito de Câmara de Lobos; hotel is able to book guests into local golf courses at a discounted rate. **Cons:** some rooms are quite small; you may need to make a reservation at the restaurant at busy times. ✉ *Rua José Joaquim da Costa, Estreito de Câmara de Lobos* ☎ *291/910530* ⊕ *www.quintadoestreitomadeira. com* ⤶ *53 rooms, 2 suites* ⚿ *In-room: a/c, safe, refrigerator. In-hotel: 2 restaurants, room service, 2 bars, pool, laundry service, Internet terminal, parking (free)* ⊟ *AE, DC, MC, V* ⫿⦾⫿ *BP, MAP.*

CALHETA

40 km (25 mi) west of Funchal.

Although Calheta is a historic village with a 17th-century church, it has only really developed over the last decade or so thanks to having the island's only white-sand beach—artificially created with sand imported from the Sahara. In summer, the sheltered beach gets packed, and it's a great place to relax for a day or two.

GETTING HERE AND AROUND

Calheta is just off the west-coast highway. There's usually plenty of parking along the seafront, though parking can be tricky in the village itself. It's also served by Rodoeste buses 80, 107 or 142 from Funchal (which takes around two hours).

EXPLORING

Casa das Mudas. Dramatically situated on a clifftop just outside Calheta, Casa das Mudas is the unlikely setting for one of Madeira's leading art galleries. Partly set in the 16th-century former home of Zarco's granddaughter and partly in a dramatic modern building of gray interlocking cubes, the gallery has hosted exhibitions featuring the works of artists including Picasso, Dalí, and Francis Bacon over recent years. ■**TIP**→ **Check the Web site for the latest details, and don't miss the café-restaurant for its dazzling views.** ✉ *Estrada Simão Gonçalves de Câmara 37* ☎ *291/820900* ⊕ *www.centrodasartes.com* 🎟 *Charges for some exhibits* ☉ *Tues.–Sun. 10–1 and 2–6.*

Engenhos da Calheta. This working rum distillery dates back to the 19th century. You can visit to see how the local rums and *poncha* liqueurs are made, and there is a tasting room. ✉ *Av. Dom Manuel I 29* ☎ *291/822264* ⊕ *www.engenhosdacalheta.com* 🎟 *Tasting free* ☉ *Weekdays 8 am–6 pm, Sat. 9 am–6 pm.*

WHERE TO STAY

$ ⛱ **Calheta Beach.** Right on the seafront with its own palm-studded grounds between the beach and Calheta's marina, this modern four-star hotel is popular in high season but delightfully quiet at other times and is a good value. Rooms are not huge, but the best ones peer out over the Atlantic. Families may prefer the apartments, which have self-catering facilities. **Pros:** best spot in Madeira for a beach holiday with a highly rated spa. **Cons:** gets frantic in high season while you may find yourself rattling around in a near empty hotel the rest of the year. ✉ *Vila* *da Calheta* ☎ *291/820300* ⊕ *www.calheta-beach.com* ⟿ *98 rooms, 5 suites, 36 apartments* ⊛ *In-room: a/c, refrigerator (some), Wi-Fi, kitchens (some). In-hotel: 2 restaurants, room service, 3 bars, water sports, pool, gym, laundry service, Internet terminal, parking (free)* ⊟ *AE, DC, MC, V* ⧍ *BP, MAP.*

RIBEIRA BRAVA

14 km (8½ mi) west of Cabo Girão.

This pleasant village, with a pebbly beach and bustling seafront fruit market, was founded in 1440 at the mouth of the Ribeira Brava (meaning "wide river"), hence the name. It's one of the island's sunniest spots and makes a popular destination for boat trips from Funchal. Head up the main Rua Visconde da Ribeira Brava for some quirky local shops—it also passes the back of the town's handsome church.

GETTING HERE AND AROUND

Ribeira Brava is an easy drive from Funchal and is also served by regular Rodoeste buses 7 or 142 from, from Funchal (around one hour). The bank, post office, and shops all lie on or around the main Rua Visconde da Ribeira Brava.

ESSENTIALS

Visitor Info Ribeira Brava (✉ *Forte de São Bento, Vila de Ribeira Brava* ☎ *291/951675*).

EXPLORING

Forte de São Bento. On the seafront, only a single tower remains of the 17th-century Forte de São Bento, built to protect the Ribeira Brava's citizens from pirates. It now houses the local tourist office.

SERRA DE ÁGUA

7 km (4½ mi) north of Ribeira Brava.

North from Ribeira Brava the N104 snakes through a sheer-sided canyon. In every direction you can see high waterfalls tumbling down canyon walls and into a pine forest. Avoid the new road tunnel and keep to the old road that heads up via the village of Serra de Água, an ideal starting point for a trek into Madeira's interior. Even if you don't plan to hike, consider spending the night here at the stone pousada, surrounded by moss-green rocks, ferns, and more waterfalls.

GETTING HERE AND AROUND

Rodoeste Bus 100 runs the half-hour route to Serra de Água. There are no direct links with Funchal, although it's an easy 30-minute drive.

WHERE TO STAY

¢ ⛰ **Pousada dos Vinháticos.** Guest rooms at this cozy mountain lodge on the edge of a pine forest are mostly in the original 1930s building; some quarters are in a modern pine annex. Do bring a good book in case fog weaves its otherworldly spell, forcing you to forgo your hike. Madeira specialties are featured in the restaurant ($–$$), which has an outdoor terrace where you might feel truly part of the mountain scenery. ■ TIP➜ Check the Web site for excellent deals on longer stays. Pros:

mountain setting is superb; interior is extremely cozy. **Cons:** not much to do here when the weather turns bad. ⊠ *Serra de Água* ☎ *291/724287* ⊕ *www.pousadadosvinhaticos.com* ⌁ *21 rooms* ☝ *In-room: no a/c. In-hotel: restaurant, room service, bar, parking (free)* ▭ *AE, MC, V* ¶◎¶ *BP.*

From Serra de Água the road climbs north for 6 km (4 mi) to **Boca de Encumeada** (Mouth of the Heights). There are several trailheads here, as well as good views of both the north and south coasts.

SÃO VICENTE

16 km (10 mi) northwest of Serra de Água.

The little town of São Vicente is one of the prettiest on the island, nestled in a narrow gulley just inland from the dramatic north coast. The central streets are pedestrianized and it is delightful to walk the cobbled alleys around the town's 17th-century church.

Just north of São Vicente, the road joins the north-coast highway. When it was first built, the road had to be chiseled out of the cliff face and is said to have been one of the most expensive road projects, per mile, ever undertaken. In the early 19th century, workers in baskets were suspended by rope so they could carve out ledges and tunnels along the planned route. These days tunnels bypass the trickiest sections, but it's still a dazzling drive.

GETTING HERE AND AROUND

Rodoeste buses 6 and 139 run the 2½-hour route to São Vicence from Funchal roughly three times daily. Drivers cannot enter the old town, so you should park in the large car park on the right by the main road as you head toward the coast.

ESSENTIALS

Though it is small, São Vicente has its own banks, post office, and several cafés and bars.

EXPLORING

Grutas e Centro do Vulcanismo. Just outside the village you'll find the Grutas e Centro do Vulcanismo, a series of underground caves formed during Madeira's last volcanic eruption around 890,000 years ago. Discovered in 1855, you can now pass around 1 km into the chocolate-color rock caverns before exiting into an exhibition space detailing Madeira's volcanic past. ⊠ *Sitio do Pé do Passo, São Vicente* ☎ *291/824404* ⊕ *www.grutasecentrodovulcanismo.com* ⌁ *€8* ⊗ *Daily 10–7.*

HIKING IN MADEIRA

The island is covered with footpaths that run among peaks and alongside levadas, canals that crisscross the island and often flow through tunnels, bringing valuable water from the mountains to the tiny terraced farms. The footpaths were made so the *levadeiro*, the person tending the levadas, could clear anything that blocked the flow of water. Some date from as far back as the 15th century.

One of the most breathtaking views is from Madeira's highest peak (6,102 feet) Pico Ruivo. On a clear day you can nearly see from one end of the island to the other.

WHERE TO STAY

¢ ⚏ **Estalagem do Mar.** All the rooms in this large inn on the seafront have sparkling white-tile bathrooms and most have balconies with great views over the Atlantic. Ground-floor rooms open up onto lawns and attractive landscaped grounds that surround the pool. In high season there is occasional live music in the restaurant. ■ TIP➜ **Book from the Web site for serious savings. Pros:** wonderful quiet location; facilities are excellent. **Cons:** some of the rooms are dated, and those without a sea view are less appealing; 10- to 15-minute walk into town. ✉ *Juncos, Fajã da Areia* ☎ *291/724337* ⊕ *www.hotelestalagemdomar.com* ⌨ *91 rooms, 8 suites* ⚒ *In-room: a/c, safe. In-hotel: restaurant, room service, bar, tennis court, 2 pools, gym, beachfront, bicycles, laundry service, Wi-Fi hotspot, parking (free)* ▤ *AE, DC, MC, V* ⎢◉⎢ *BP, MAP.*

EN ROUTE As you wind west along the coast, there are a number of waterfalls ahead: at Véu da Noiva (bride's veil), the road passes behind a falls. Stop at one of the viewpoints and notice the windbreaks—made of thick mats of purple heather—that protect the terraced vineyards such as those around the pretty village of Seixal.

PORTO MONIZ

16 km (10 mi) west of São Vicente.

The island's northernmost village, Porto Moniz, was a whaling station in the 19th century, but these days, its natural seapools, formed by ancient lava, make it one of the island's best day trips. There's not much to do here except splash around the pools (there are changing facilities), eat, and sunbathe, though its position below towering mountains is part of its appeal. The old houses and twisting cobblestone streets can be found uphill—most of the seafront is made up of a new town of little hotels, cafés, and restaurants.

GETTING HERE AND AROUND

Rodoeste buses 80 and 139 serve Porto Moniz from Funchal roughly two to three times daily, though the full run takes more than three hours so you may prefer to drive, which takes around 1½ hours. There's usually plenty of car parking along the seafront roads.

ESSENTIALS

Although there are plenty of restaurants and cafés along the seafront, you'll need to head up to the old town if you need the bank, post office, or shops.

Visitor Info Tourist Office (☎ *291/852555*).

EXPLORING

Aquário da Madeira. Here, you'll find a small and somewhat uninspiring aquarium built into a mock fort that displays the fish and sea creatures native to the local waters. ✉ *Rua Forte São João Batista* ☎ *291/850340* ⌨ €7 ⊘ *Daily 10–6.*

Centro de Ciência Viva (Centre for Live Science). The center holds science-related temporary exhibits. Primarily aimed at locals, so not always with English labeling, the exhibits can be first-rate, some having moved on from London's Science Museum. It also has a cybercafé and shop. ⊠ *Rotunda do Ilhéu Mole* ☎ *291/0850300* ⊠ *Fee varies per exhibition* ⊙ *Tues.–Sun. 10–7.*

WHERE TO STAY

¢ 🏨 **Euro Moniz.** This modern, high-rise hotel offers the best facilities in town. Rooms are not huge but all have contemporary decor and most face the Atlantic. Top-floor rooms in particular have great views, and low-season rates are excellent value considering the wide range of facilities. **Pros:** modern facilities; a welcoming staff. **Cons:** rooms are on the small side. ⊠ *Vila do Porto Moniz* ☎ *291/850050* ⇱ *38 rooms, 2 suites* ⌂ *In-room: a/c, safe. In-hotel: restaurant, room service, bar, pool, gym, parking (free)* ⊟ *AE, MC, V* ⏐⦿⏐ *BP, MAP.*

CAMPING

Madeira's only campsite, **Parque de Campismo do Porto Moniz** (⊠ *Ribeira da Janela* ☎ *291/853872* ⊕ *www.cm-portomoniz.pt)* is around 1½ mi east of the village in a narrow river valley, with its own small café, kids' play area, and neat lawns to camp on beneath palm trees.

EN ROUTE As you drive along the winding uphill road out of Porto Moniz to the viewpoint near Santa Madalena, look back and see the patterns made by the scrub windbreaks. At the fork, turn left on N110, a road that crosses through Madeira's wildest area, providing a unique perspective of both sides of the island. If you have time, take the road to **Rabaçal,** a remote trailhead 22 km (14 mi) southeast of Porto Moniz. From here signed trails fan out in all directions. Madeirans love to come here to picnic alongside the cascades (bring food with you) or to walk along the levadas.

Past Rabaçal, the road heads across a moorland called **Paúl da Serra** (Mountain Plain), where sheep and cattle graze and seagulls spiral overhead. This is the closest thing to flatland in Madeira, and its scrubby landscape looks out of place. From Paúl da Serra, you can turn right on N209 and follow signs south to the village of **Canhas.** The twisting road passes more terraced farms and, in 20 km (12 mi), joins the southern coastal road N101, which runs to Funchal. Or you can take the route to Boca de Encumeada and rejoin the main road (N104).

CENTRAL PEAKS AND SANTANA

The lofty peaks of central Madeira come as a surprise after the lush greenery of the coast. Mountains rise up to more than 6,000 feet, their craggy summits are often above the cloud line. Most are easily accessible to walkers, while you can drive almost to the top of one of the most awesome, Pico do Arieiro, from where there are spectacular views and great hikes. To the north and east lie the much-photographed village of Santana, with its thatch-roof A-frame houses, and a varied coastline that reaches round to Madeira's second town, Machico.

PICO DO ARIEIRO

7 km (4½ mi) northwest of Poiso; 30 km (18 mi) northeast of Funchal.

GETTING HERE AND AROUND

There is no public transport to Pico do Areiro although it's an easy drive. There are also frequent tours here from Funchal.

ESSENTIALS

There are no facilities here apart from a souvenir shop and café-restaurant.

Hiking Tours **Madeira Explorers** (✉ *C.C. Monumental Lido, 1st fl., Shop 23, Funchal* ☎ *291/763701* ⊕ *www.madeira-levada-walks.com).* **MB Travel** (✉ *Largo dos Lavradores 7* ☎ *291/203950* ⊕ *www.mb-travel.com).* **Mountain Expedition** (✉ *Estrada Ponta da Oliveira 48, Caniço* ☎ *969/677679* ⊕ *www.madeiraexpedition.com).*

EXPLORING

Pico do Arieiro. At 5,963 feet, this is Madeira's second-highest mountain. On your way here, you'll travel over a barren plain above the tree line: watch for errant sheep and goats wandering across the pavement on their way to graze on stubbly gorse and bilberry. Stop in the parking lot near the top and make the short climb to the lookout (next to a giant NATO radar), where you can scan the rocky central peaks. There are often views of the clouds below (unless you're in them), but on a clear day you can see to the southeast the Curral das Freiras valley (Corral of the Sisters), so named after the nuns of the Santa Clara convent who fled Funchal in 1565 to escape pirate raids. It's also known as the Grande Curral (Great Corral). Look in the other direction and try to spot the huge Penha de Águia (Eagle Rock), a giant monolith on the north coast. The trail from the lookout that crosses the narrow ridge leads to Pico Ruivo (6,102 feet), the island's highest point—one of the best walks on the island, though as it is a tough 8 mi return walk and sections are sometimes closed due to landslides, you are best off taking one of the many guided tours here from Funchal.

9

RIBEIRO FRIO

11 km (7 mi) north of Poiso; 17 km (10 mi) from Funchal.

The landscape grows more lush on the northern side of the island, and the road is full of waterfalls. Ribeiro Frio (Cold River) is known for its beautiful gardens—native species and nonindigenous flowers and plants grow prolifically around a government-run trout farm, the village's main sight. Ribeira Frio is also the starting point for two popular levada walks. The first is one of the island's easiest and prettiest, taking around 30 minutes round-trip. At the lookout of Balcões (meaning "balconies") jagged peaks tower behind you, and there are views over densely wooded valleys. A longer, 12-km (7-mi) hike leads along a levada to Portela. If you attempt this, it should take three to four hours. Arrange for a taxi back.

GETTING HERE AND AROUND

Ribeiro Frio is served by Horários do Funchal buses 56, 103, or 138, taking around an hour from Funchal.

WHERE TO EAT

$ ✕ **Restaurante Ribeiro Frio.** After your hike, stop at this family-owned
PORTUGUESE   mountain restaurant, aka Victor's Bar. Full meals, including trout from
the local fish farm and fine, hearty soups, are served here, as are teas
and coffees. Inside the rustic wood-and-glass building are a couple of
welcoming fireplaces. ⊠ *N103* ☎ *291/575898* 🖃 *AE, DC, MC, V.*

**EN
ROUTE**
Continue north from Ribeiro Frio on N101 and follow signs to **Faial,**
with the road descending in a series of steep curves into a deep ravine.
The tiny A-frame huts that dot the terraces along the steep sides are
barns for cows, which are prohibited from grazing. There's no horizontal pastureland, and they could easily fall off a ledge.

SANTANA

*18 km (11 mi) northwest of Ribeiro Frio; 39 km (24 mi) north of
Funchal.*

The village of Santana is famous for its A-frame, thatch-roof *palhei-
ros* (haylofts), which are unique to the island. Traditionally painted in
bright colors, they look as if they've come straight from the pages of a
fairy tale. Although few islanders still live in these dwellings, you can
look around several of the houses just off the main through road, one
of which is Santana's tourist office and the others are little craft and
souvenir shops. You'll see that the upper floor was used for sleeping,
while the lower floor was used as a living area or for storage. Cooking—and toilet facilities—was traditionally done outside, clear of the
dwelling space. Otherwise Santana is a modest, agricultural village.

GETTING HERE AND AROUND
Santana is served by Horários do Funchal Bus 56, 103, or 108, which
take around 1 hour 40 mins from Funchal.

ESSENTIALS
There are a supermarket, banks, and plenty of restaurants in the village center.

Visitor Info Santana Tourist Office (⊠ *Sítio do Serrado* ☎ *291/572992*).

EXPLORING
Parque Temático do Madeira. Familes will enjoy the "Madeira theme
park" set in 17 acres of landscaped grounds. There's a boating lake,
playground, toy train that kids can ride on, and plenty of exhibits on
aspects of the island such as a recreated watermill, models of Santana's houses, and a craft village demonstrating carving and weaving. ⊠ *Estrada Regional 101, Fonte da Pedra, Santana* ☎ *291/570410*
⊕ *www.parquetematicodamadeira.pt* 🎟 *€10, children under 14 €8*
☉ *June–Sept., daily 10–7; Oct.–May, Tues.–Sun. 10–7.*

**OFF THE
BEATEN
PATH**
Parque das Queimadas. Five kilometers (3 mi) west of Santana is a detour
where the road quickly turns into a rough mountain track. Along a trail
that passes by gorse bushes, hydrangeas, and wildflowers, the route
leads right into a wonderful forest. There are picnic tables and toilet
facilities at the Casa das Queimadas, which is used by forest rangers.
This marks the start of a great levada walk to Caldeirão Verde, a three-
to four-hour return walk to a dramatic waterfall.

PORTO DA CRUZ

20 km (12 mi) southeast of Santana.

The little fishing village of Porto da Cruz is one of the liveliest and prettiest villages on this stretch of coast. Plenty of bustling cafés and restaurants gather round an attractive little harbor. At its western end there's a great seawater swimming pool right on the seafront, which is popular in summer. Take the seafront promenade past here for an attractive walk to the Companhia does Engenhos do Norte, a working rum distillery—you can peer inside to look at its giant wooden barrels used to store the *aguardente* liqueur. This firewater, a sugarcane brandy, can be tasted at any bar in the village. It's far more palatable when tasted as part of the island's famous cocktail, poncha, mixed with honey and lemon juice.

GETTING HERE AND AROUND

Porto da Cruz is served by SAM buses (⇨ *see Bus Travel, under Funchal Getting Here and Around, above, for contact info*) 53, 78, or 208. The journey from Funchal takes around 1 hour 20 minutes.

EXPLORING

Penha de Águia *(Eagle Rock)*. Porto da Cruz also overlooks the landmark Penha de Águia, a 590-meter-high rocky crag whose sheer cliffs tower over the neighboring village of São Roque do Faial. The fertile valley setting is filled with tiny farms and gardens.

EN ROUTE Start your climb again on N101 and continue to **Portela,** where the view looks south over the gentler valley of Machico. From here it's an easy drive through pinewoods and sugarcane fields and into the town of Machico.

MACHICO

15 km (9 mi) southeast of Porto da Cruz; 26 km (16 mi) northeast of Funchal.

Local folklore says the bay of Machico was discovered in 1346 by two English lovers, Robert Machin and Anne d'Arfet, who set sail from Bristol to escape Anne's disapproving parents. The couple's ship was thrown off course by a storm and wrecked in this bay. Anne died a few days after becoming ill, and Robert then died of a broken heart. But their crew, according to legend, escaped on a raft, and news of the island made its way back to Portugal. (Legend also has it that Shakespeare heard the tale before he wrote *The Tempest.*) When the explorer Zarco arrived in 1420, he found a wooden cross with the lovers' story and the church—the island's first—where they were buried. He named the place in memory of Machin. You can visit the replica church and wander through the old quarter of the second-largest town on the island after Funchal, attractively sited in a crescent bay—a popular swimming spot in summer. The tourist office sits in the squat Forte do Amparo, built in 1706 to defend the town from pirate attacks.

GETTING HERE AND AROUND

There are several buses every hour between Funchal and Machico. The fastest service is the express SAM bus (⇨ *see Bus Travel, under Funchal Getting Here and Around, above, for contact info*), which departs roughly hourly and takes about 35 minutes.

ESSENTIALS

Central Machico has banks, a post office, and plenty of shops, cafés, and restaurants.

Visitor Info **Machico Tourist Office** (✉ *Forte do Amparo, Praça José António Almada* ☎ *291/962289*).

WHERE TO EAT

$ ✕ **Mercado de Velho.** Among the handful of atmospheric restaurants is
CAFÉ the Mercado de Velho, in a former market. You can sit at the little outside terrace that has its own fountain and enjoy omelets, salads, grills, and pasta dishes. Or, just have a coffee or drink. ✉ *Rua do Mercado, Machico* ☎ *291/965926* ▭ *AE, DC, MC, V.*

OUTDOOR ACTIVITIES

GOLF

Golf at **Santo da Serra** (✉ *N102, Casais Proximos, Santa Antonio da Serra* ☎ *291/550100* ⊕ *www.santodaserragolf.com* ↑ *18 holes. 6,039 m. Par 72* ⛳ *€90 per round* ☞ *Facilities: driving range, putting green, chipping area, golf carts, hand-pulled carts, pro shop, restaurant, bar*) often gives the impression of playing on top of the world. A setting high above the Atlantic Ocean means that the views at the end of the long climb are quite breathtaking. Occasionally the views are lost in the mist and low clouds that sometimes envelop the course, but when it's clear there are few courses that command such a spectacular outlook. Use a golf cart to tackle the huge changes in elevation. Also, bring a handicap certificate.

If you have reading knowledge of Spanish and/or French, you will find Portuguese easy to read. Portuguese pronunciation, however, can be somewhat tricky. Despite obvious similarities in Spanish and Portuguese spelling and syntax, the Portuguese sounds are a far cry—almost literally so—from their ostensible Spanish equivalents. Some of the main peculiarities of Portuguese phonetics are the following.

Nasalized vowels: If you have some idea of French pronunciation, these shouldn't give you too much trouble. The closest approach is that of the French *accent du Midi,* as spoken by people in Marseille and Provence, or perhaps an American Midwest twang will help. Try pronouncing *an, am, en, em, in, om, un,* etc., with a sustained *ng* sound (e.g., *bom = bong,* etc.).

Another aspect of Portuguese phonetics is the vowels and diphthongs written with the tilde: *ã, ão, ães.* The Portuguese word for wool, *lã,* sounds roughly like the French word *lin,* with the *-in* resembling the *an* in the English word "any," but nasalized. The suffix "-tion" on such English words as "information" becomes in Portuguese spelling *-ção,* pronounced *-sa-on,* with the *-on* nasalized: *Informação,* for example. These words form their plurals by changing the suffix to *-ções,* which sounds like "*-son-ech*" (the *ch* here resembling a cross between the English *sh* and the German *ch:* hence *informações*).

The cedilla occurring under the "c" serves exactly the same purpose as in French: It transforms the "c" into a *ss* sound in front of the three so-called "hard" vowels ("a," "o," and "u"): e.g., *graça, Açores, açúcar.* The letter "c" occurring without a cedilla in front of these three vowels automatically has the sound of "k": *pico, mercado, curto.* The letter "c" followed by "e" or "i" is always *ss,* and hence needs no cedilla: *nacional, Graciosa, Terceira.*

The letter "j" sounds like the "s" in the English word "pleasure." So does "g" except when the latter is followed by one of the "hard" vowels: hence, *generoso, gigantesco, Jerónimo, azulejos, Jorge,* etc.

The spelling *nh* is rendered like the *ny* in "canyon": e.g., *senhora.*

The spelling *lh* is somewhere in between the *l* and the *y* sounds in "million": e.g., *Batalha.*

In the matter of syllabic stress, Portuguese obeys the two basic Spanish principles: (1) in words ending in a vowel, or in "n" or "s," the tonic accent falls on the next-to-the-last syllable: *fado, mercado, azulejos;* (2) in words ending in consonants other than "n" or "s," the stress falls on the last syllable: *favor, nacional.* Words in which the syllabic stress does not conform to the two above rules must be written with an acute accent to indicate the proper pronunciation: *sábado, república, politécnico.*

Numbers

1	um, uma
2	dois, duas
3	três
4	quatro
5	cinco
6	seis
7	sete
8	oito
9	nove
10	dez
11	onze
12	doze
13	treze
14	catorze
15	quinze
16	dezaseis
17	dezasete
18	dezoito
19	dezanove
20	vinte
21	vinte e um
22	vinte e dois
30	trinta
40	quarenta
50	cinquenta
60	sessenta
70	setenta
80	oitenta
90	noventa
100	cem
110	cento e dez
200	duzentos
1,000	mil
1,500	mil e quinhentos

Days of the Week

Monday	Segunda-feira
Tuesday	Terça-feira
Wednesday	Quarta-feira

Thursday	Quinta-feira
Friday	Sexta-feira
Saturday	Sábado
Sunday	Domingo

Months

January	Janeiro
February	Fevereiro
March	Março
April	Abril
May	Maio
June	Junho
July	Julho
August	Agosto
September	Setembro
October	Outubro
November	Novembro
December	Dezembro

Useful Phrases

Do you speak English?	Fala Inglês?
Yes	Sim
No	Não
Please	Por favor
Thank you	Obrigado/a
Thank you very much	Muito obrigado/a
Excuse me, sorry	Desculpe, Com licença
I'm sorry	Desculpe-me
Good morning or good day	Bom dia
Good afternoon	Boa tarde
Good evening or good night	Boa noite
Goodbye	Adeus
How are you?	Como está?
How do you say in Portuguese?	Como se diz em Português?
Tourist Office	Turismo
Fine	Optimo
Very good	Muito bem (muito bom)
It's all right	Está bem
Good luck	Felicidades (boa sorte)
Hello	Olá
Come back soon	Até breve

Where is the hotel?	Onde é o hotel?
How much does this cost?	Quanto custa?
How do you feel?	Como se sente?
How goes it?	Que tal?
Pleased to meet you	Muito prazer em o (a) conhecer
The pleasure is mine	O prazer é meu
I have the pleasure of introducing Mr., Miss, Mrs., or Ms. . . .	Tenho o prazer de lhe apresentar o senhor, a senhora . . .
I like it very much	Gosto muito
I don't like it	Não gosto
Don't mention it	De nada
Pardon me	Perdão
Are you ready?	Está pronto?
I am ready	Estou pronto
Welcome	Seja benvindo
What time is it?	Que horas são?
I am glad to see you	Muito prazer em o (a) ver
I don't understand	Não entendo
Please speak slowly	Fale lentamente por favor
I understand (or) It is clear	Compreendo (or) Está claro
Whenever you please	Quando quizer
Please wait	Faça favor de esperar
Toilet	Casa de banho
I will be a little late	Chegarei um pouco atrasado
I don't know	Não sei
Is this seat free?	Está vago este lugar?
Would you please direct me to . . . ?	Por favor indique-me . . . ?
Where is the station, museum . . . ?	Onde fica a estação, museu . . . ?
I am American, British	Eu sou Americano, Inglês
It's very kind of you	É muito amavel
Please sit down	Por favor sente-se

Sundries

cigar, cigarette	charuto, cigarro
matches	fosforos
dictionary	dicionário
key	chave
razor blades	laminas de barbear
shaving cream	creme de barbear

soap	sobonete
map	mapa
tampons	tampões
sanitary pads	pensos higiénicos
newspaper	jornal
magazine	revista
telephone	telefone
envelopes	envelopes
writing paper	papel de carta
airmail writing paper	papel de carta de avião
postcard	postal
stamps	selos

Merchants

bakery	padaria
bookshop	livraria
butcher's	talho
delicatessen	charutaria
dry cleaner's	limpeza a seco
grocery	mercearia
hairdresser, barber	cabeleireiro, barbeiro
laundry	lavandaria
shoemaker	sapateiro
supermarket	supermercado

Emergencies/Medical

ill, sick	doente
I am ill	Estou doente
I have a fever	Tenho febre
My wife/husband/ child is ill	Minha mulher/marido/ criança está doente
doctor	doutor/médico
nurse	enfermeira/o
prescription	receita
pharmacist/chemist	farmacia
Please fetch/call a doctor	Por favor, chame o doutor/medico
accident	acidente
road accident	acidente na estrada
Where is the nearest hospital?	Onde é o hospital mais proximo?
Where is the American/ British Hospital?	Onde é o hospital Americano/ Britanico?

dentist	dentista
X-ray	Raios-X
aspirin	aspirina
painkiller	analgésico
bandage	ligadura
ointment for bites/stings	pomada para picadas
cough mixture	xarope para a tosse
laxative	laxativo
thermometer	termómetro

On the Move

plane	avião
train	comboio
boat	barco
taxi	taxi
car	carro/automovel
bus	autocarro
seat	assento/lugar
reservation	reserva
smoking/no-smoking compartment	compartimento para fumadores/não fumadores
rail station	estação caminho de ferro
subway station	estação do Metropolitano
airport	aeroporto
harbor	estação mártima
town terminal	estação/terminal
shuttle bus/train	autocarro/comboio com ligação constante
sleeper	cama
couchette	beliche
porter	bagageiro
baggage/luggage	bagagem
baggage trolley	carrinho de bagagem
single ticket	bilhete de ida
return ticket	bilhete de ida e volta
first class	primeira classe
second class	segunda classe
When does the train leave?	A que horas sai o comboio?
What time does the train arrive at . . . ?	A que horas chega o comboio a . . . ?

Travel Smart Portugal

WORD OF MOUTH

"There are lots of places only about an hour drive or so from Lisbon, but driving in the city and dealing with keeping a car is not easy so trains or buses may be best if based in Lisbon a while."

—lowcountrycarol

GETTING HERE AND AROUND

▮ AIR TRAVEL

The flying time to Lisbon is 6½ hours from New York, 9 hours from Chicago, and 15 hours from Los Angeles. The flight from London to Lisbon is just under 3 hours.

Note that several budget airlines, such as U.K.-based easyJet and Irish low-cost airline Ryanair don't allocate seats. Seating is taken on a first-come, first-served basis. Also, they generally don't serve meals but do sell (overpriced) sandwiches, drinks, and other items. If you're on a special diet, pack appropriate snacks in your carry-on bag.

When traveling with most European low-cost airlines you'll have to pay to check-in a suitcase (15 kgs max), but one carry-on case per person is free as long as it complies with the airline's specific cabin measurements and weight.

TRAVEL TIMES FROM LISBON TO:	BY AIR	BY BUS
Faro (Algarve)	50 mins	3 hours
Porto	55 mins	3 hours 30 mins
Funchal (Madeira)	1 hour 50 mins	N/A
Ponta Delgada Island, Azores	2 hours 15 mins	N/A
Coímbra	N/A	3 hours 35 mins
Fátima	N/A	1 hour 30 mins

AIRPORTS

The major gateway to Portugal is Lisbon's Aeroporto Portela (LIS), approximately 8 km (5 mi) northeast of the center of the city. A convenient AeroBus departs from outside Arrivals and goes to the city center (45 minutes, €3.50) roughly every 20 minutes from 7 am to 11 pm. A new inter-

national airport is due to open at Ota, 48 km (77 mi) north of the city, in 2017.

Oporto's Aeroporto Francisco Sá Carneiro (OPO) also handles international flights and, like Lisbon, operates an AeroBus to the city center (25 minutes, €4) from 7 am to 7:30 pm. The Aeroporto de Faro (FAO) handles the largest number of charter flights because of its location in the popular tourist destination of the Algarve. Several buses run into town (15 minutes, €1.75), while a taxi will cost approximately €12.

The organization that oversees Portugal's airports, Aeroportos de Portugal (ANA), has a handy Web site with information in English.

Airport Information Aeroporto de Faro (✉ Faro ☎ 289/800801 for flight information). **Aeroporto Francisco Sá Carneiro** (✉ Oporto ☎ 229/412141). **Aeroporto Portela** (✉ Lisbon ☎ 21/841–3500 or 21/841–3700). **ANA** (⊕ www.ana.pt).

FLIGHTS

Domestic air travel is limited and expensive. You're better off renting a car or taking the train or bus, unless time is an issue.

TAP Air Portugal has daily nonstop flights from New York (Newark Liberty International Airport) to Lisbon with connections to Faro and Oporto. Continental's daily nonstop flights between Newark Liberty International Airport and Lisbon are scheduled to provide convenient connections from destinations elsewhere in the eastern and southern United States.

British Airways and TAP have regular nonstop flights from the United Kingdom to several destinations in Portugal. From Spain, TAP, Iberia, and Spanair have daily Madrid-Lisbon flights.

Consider flying to London first and picking up an onward no-frills budget airline or charter flight: you might save money *and* have a wider choice of destinations in Portugal. There are often good deals to

Faro, in particular, because the Algarve is popular with British vacationers. In summer, last-minute, round-trip flights have cost as little as $150.

Airline Contacts British Airways (⊕ www.ba.com). **Continental Airlines** (⊕ www.continental.com). **easyJet** (Lisbon-Madeira; ⊕ www.easyjet.com). **Iberia** (⊕ www.iberia.com). **Spanair** (⊕ www.spanair.com). **TAP Air Portugal** (⊕ www.flytap.pt).

▋ BUS TRAVEL

Bus service within Portugal is comprehensive, punctual, and comfortable. Some luxury coaches even have TVs and food service, and all have a strict no-smoking policy. All that said, bus travel can be slow, and it's difficult to arrange on your own, especially given the country's baffling number of privatized bus companies. In Oporto alone there are at least 18 of them, most based at different terminals.

▋TIP→ Bus routes and companies change frequently, and bus company personnel rarely speak English. Inquire at tourist offices for bus schedules.

If you plan to buy a ticket directly from a specific bus company's office, give yourself plenty of time to purchase before you depart. Most travel agents can sell you a bus ticket in advance; it's always wise to reserve a ticket at least a day ahead, particularly in summer for destinations in the Algarve.

An under-30 card (⊕ www.cartaojovem.pt) for young adults and students should get you a discount of between 10% and 20% on the long-distance services. You can buy a card for €10 at post offices with a photo ID.

BUS CLASSES
There are three classes of bus service: *expressos* are comfortable, fast, direct buses between major cities; *rápidas* are fast regional buses; and *carreiras* stop at every crossroad. Expressos are generally the best cheap way to get around (particularly for long trips, where per-kilometer costs are lowest).

BUS LINES
Three of the largest bus companies are Rede Expressos, which serves much of the country; Rodo Norte, which serves the north; and Eva Transportes, which covers the Algarve and also has service to and from major cities, like Évora.

Buses Rede Expressos (⊕ www.rede-expressos.pt). **Rodo Norte** (⊕ www.rodonorte.pt).

▋ CAR TRAVEL

In general, Portugal's roads are in good condition. On the downside, the tolls here can add up, and the drivers are among the worst in Europe, although a crackdown on drunk driving has resulted in a 10% decrease in road death rates in recent years. ⚠ **The local driving may be faster and less forgiving than you're used to: drive carefully.**

Red tape–wise, your driver's license from home is recognized in Portugal. However, you should learn the international road-sign system (charts are available to members of most automobile associations).

GASOLINE
Gas stations are plentiful, and many are self-service. Fuel tends to cost more on motorways. At this writing gasoline costs €1.50 a liter (approximately ¼ gallon) for 98 and 95 octane *sem chumbo* (unleaded) and €1.33 for diesel. Credit cards are frequently accepted at gas stations. If you require a receipt, request *um recibo*.

ROUTES
Commercially operated *autoestradas* (toll roads with two or more lanes in either direction identified with an "A" and a number) link the principal cities, including Oporto, with Lisbon, circumventing congested urban centers. The autoestrada from Lisbon to Faro and a toll road (E90) links Lisbon with Portugal's eastern border with Spain at Badajoz (from which the highway leads to Madrid).

Many main national highways (labeled with "N" and a number) have been upgraded to toll-free, two-lane roads identified with "IP" (Itinerario Principal) and a number. Highways of mainly regional importance have been upgraded to IC (Itinerario Complementar). Roads labeled with "E" and a number are routes that connect with the Spanish network.

■ TIP→ Because of all the road upgrading, one road might have several designations—A, N, IP, E, etc.—on maps and signs.

Autoestrada tolls are steep, costing, for example, €17.60 between Lisbon and Porto, but time saved by traveling these roads usually makes them worthwhile. Minor roads are often poor and winding with unpredictable surfaces.

In the north the IP5 shortens the drive from Aveiro to the border with Spain, near Guarda. Take extra care on this route, however. It's popular with trucks (you may get stuck behind a convoy), *and* it has curves and hills.

The IP4 connects Porto through Vila Real to Bragança. Pick up the IP2 just southwest of Bragança and continue to Ourique in the Alentejo, where it connects to the IP1 down to Albufeira on the southern coast. This same IP1 is an autoestrada from Albufeira and runs east across the Algarve to the Spanish border near Ayamonte, 1½ hours east of Seville.

Heading out of Lisbon, there's good, fast access to Setúbal and to Évora and other Alentejo towns, although rush-hour traffic on the bridge Ponte 25 de Abril across the Rio Tejo (Tagus River) can be frustrating. An alternative is taking the 17-km-long (11-mi-long) Ponte Vasco da Gama (Europe's second-longest water crossing after the Channel Tunnel and Europe's longest bridge) across the Tejo estuary to Montijo; you can then link up with southbound and eastbound roads.

Signposting on these fast roads isn't always adequate, so keep your eyes peeled for exits and turnoffs.

ROADSIDE EMERGENCIES

If you are unfortunate enough to be involved in a mild accident, you will be required to fill out *Declaração amigável* (European Accident Statement), which will be used by the respective insurance companies (including those relating to rental cars) to exchange information.

All large garages in and around towns have breakdown services, and you'll see orange emergency (SOS) phones along turnpikes and highways. The national automobile organization, Automóvel Clube de Portugal, provides reciprocal membership with AAA and other European automobile associations.

Car theft is common with rental cars. Never leave anything visible in an unattended car, and contact the rental agency immediately, as well as the local police, if your car is stolen.

Emergency Services The 24-hour emergency help number is ☎ 707/509510. **Automóvel Clube de Portugal** (☎ 21/942–9103 for breakdowns south of Pombal, 22/834–0001 for breakdowns north of Pombal ⊕ www.acp.pt).

RULES OF THE ROAD

Driving is on the right. The speed limit on the autoestrada is 120 kph (74 mph); on other roads it's 90 kph (56 mph), and in built-up areas, 50 kph–60 kph (30 mph–36 mph).

At the junction of two roads of equal size, traffic coming from the right has priority. Vehicles already in a traffic circle have priority over those entering it from any point. The use of seat belts is obligatory. Horns shouldn't be used in built-up areas, and you should always carry your driver's license, proof of car insurance, a reflective red warning triangle and EU-approved reflective jacket for use in a breakdown.

Children under 12 years old *must* ride in the back seat in age-appropriate restraining devices and facing backwards for children under 18 months. Motorcyclists and their passengers must wear helmets, and motorcycles must have their headlights on day and night.

Billboards warning you not to drink and drive dot the countryside, and punishable alcohol levels are just 0.5g/L—equivalent to approximately three small glasses of beer.

CAR RENTALS

To rent a car in Portugal you must be a minimum of 21 years old (with at least one year's driving experience) and a maximum of 75 years old and have held your driving license for over a year. You may not be able to rent a car without an International Driving Permit (IDP), which can be used only in conjunction with a valid driver's license and which translates your license into 10 languages. Check the AAA Web site for more info as well as for IDPs ($10) themselves.

In general, it's a good idea to reserve your car two weeks in advance, and a month in advance if possible, for car rentals in the Algarve between May and September. Among the most common car makes are Citroën, Opel, Nissan, Fiat, and Ford. Four-wheel drive vehicles are only available from the larger international agencies, such as Avis and Hertz.

CAR RENTAL RATES

Rates in Lisbon begin at around $75 a day, with three-day rates starting at around $135 and weeklong rates starting at about $230 for a standard economy car with unlimited mileage. The Value-Added Tax (V.A.T.) on car rentals is 23% and is included in the rate. Algarve rates can be considerably higher due to the increase in demand.

Automatic cars are more expensive and harder to find than standard ones. The good news is that most rental cars have air-conditioning and, increasingly, use diesel gas, which equals a lot more mileage. There's generally a surcharge of around $75 for each additional driver, and most agencies charge a small surcharge of around $6 per day for children's car seats, which must be reserved at the time of booking.

CAR-RENTAL INSURANCE

If you own a car, your personal auto insurance may cover a rental to some degree, though not all policies protect you abroad; always read your policy's fine print. If you don't have auto insurance, then seriously consider buying the collision- or loss-damage waiver (CDW or LDW) from the car-rental company, which eliminates your liability for damage to the car.

Some credit cards offer CDW coverage, but it's usually supplemental to your own insurance and rarely covers SUVs, minivans, luxury models, and the like. If your coverage is secondary, you may still be liable for loss-of-use costs from the car-rental company. But no credit-card insurance is valid unless you use that card for *all* transactions, from reserving to paying the final bill. All companies exclude car rental in some countries, so be sure to find out about the destination to which you are traveling.

In Portugal CDW will cost around $25 a day depending on the type of car and will reduce your liability to a few hundred euros. For an additional fee, you can take out a Super CDW where you will be completely covered.

▌ TRAIN TRAVEL

Portugal's train network, Caminhos de Ferro Portugueses (CP), covers most of the country, though it's thin in the Alentejo region. The cities of Lisbon, Coimbra, Aveiro, and Porto are linked by the fast, extremely comfortable Alfa and Alfa Pendular services.

Most other major towns and cities are connected by InterCidade trains, which are reliable, though slower and less luxurious than the Alfa trains. The regional services that connect smaller towns and villages tend to be infrequent and slow, with stops at every station along the line.

▌TIP→ **Ask the local tourist board about hotel and local transportation packages that** include tickets to major museum exhibits or other special events.

TRAIN CLASSES

There are three main classes of long-distance train travel: *regional* trains, which stop at every town and village; reasonably fast *interregional* trains; and express trains appropriately known as *rápido*. Currently only operating between Lisbon and Porto (via Coimbra) is the *alfa pendular*, a deluxe, marginally faster train. There's also a network of suburban *(suburbano)* train lines.

The standards of comfort vary from *alfa pendular* train luxury—with air-conditioning, food service, and airline-type seats at which you can use a telefax and plug in your laptop—to the often spartan conditions on regional lines.

Most InterCidade trains have bar and restaurant facilities, but the food is famously unappealing. Smoking is restricted to special carriages on all Portuguese trains.

A first-class ticket will cost you 40% more than a second-class one and will buy you extra leg- and elbow room but not a great deal more on the Alfa and InterCidade trains. The extra cost is definitely worth it on most regional services, however.

BOOKING

Advance booking is mandatory on long-distance trains and is recommended in the case of popular services such as the Alfa trains. Reservations are also advisable for other trains if you want to avoid long lines in front of the ticket window on the day the train leaves. You can avoid a trip to the station to make the reservation by asking a travel agent to take care of it for you.

SPAIN–PORTUGAL ROUTE

A direct, nightly train connects Spain and Portugal. The train departs from Madrid's Chamartin station at 10:45 pm and arrives at Lisbon's Santa Apolónia station at 8:15 the following morning; for the reverse trip, the train leaves Lisbon at 10 pm, arriving in Madrid at 8:25 am the next day.

RAIL PASSES

Eurail passes provide unlimited first-class rail travel in all participating countries for the duration of the pass. If you plan to rack up the miles, get a standard pass. These are available in units from three days to three months. In addition to a standard Eurail pass, ask about special rail-pass plans. Among these are the Eurail Youthpass (in second class for those under age 26), the Eurail Saverpass (which gives a discount for two or more people traveling together), a Eurail Flexipass (which allows 10 or 15 travel days within a two-month period), the Eurail-drive Pass and the Europass Drive (which combine travel by train and rental car). It's best to purchase your pass before you leave for Europe.

■TIP➔ Be aware that if you don't plan to cover many miles, you may come out ahead by buying individual tickets instead of rail passes.

There are also special tourist tickets (bilhetes turísticos) valid for unlimited travel during 7/14/21 consecutive days, cost €112/€189/€277 (half price for those aged under 12 and over 65). Toddlers who need a seat of their own cost half the price.

Many travelers assume that rail passes guarantee them seats on the trains. Not so. Seat reservations are required on some European trains, particularly high-speed trains, and are a good idea on trains that may be crowded—particularly in summer on popular routes. You will definitely need a reservation if you purchase sleeping accommodations.

Information **CP** (☎ *707/201280, 808/208208, or 21/102-3000* ⊕ *www.cp.pt).* **Rail Europe** (☎ *800/622-8600, 0870/584-8848 U.K. credit-card bookings* ⊕ *www.raileurope.com).*

ESSENTIALS

▌ ACCOMMODATIONS

There are many different types of lodging options in Portugal. Many who travel to the Algarve region book themselves into luxurious resorts and never step outside them, thanks to amenities such as a golf course, tennis courts, and entertainment. Though there are international chain hotels in Portugal, *residências* and *pensões* (simple accommodations with private bathroom and breakfast as the only meal served) in former private homes are just as popular and very affordable. They can be found in cities and rural towns as well.

Pousadas (inns) are within historic structures, often former castles or palaces, and are usually decorated with local crafts or antique reproductions. They still offer modern amenities, such as television.

APARTMENT AND HOUSE RENTALS

The rental properties in the Algarve are in high demand. Most apartments and villas are privately owned, with a local management company overseeing the advertising, maintenance, and rent collection. Two reliable Algarve-based agencies are Villas & Vacations and Jordan & Nunn.

For lists of rental properties and reputable agents elsewhere in Portugal, contact tourist offices. Avoid time-share touts on the street; they'll try to lure you in to view a property with the promise of free vacations and cash. These are often sophisticated (and costly) scams.

Rental Agencies Jordan & Nunn (☎ 289/399943 ⊕ www.jordannunn.com). **Villas & Vacations** (☎ 289/390501 ⊕ www.villas-vacations.com).

COUNTRY HOUSES

Throughout the country, though particularly in the north, many *solares* (manors) and *casas de campo* (farm- or country houses) have been remodeled to receive small numbers of guests in a venture called Turismo de Habitação (TURIHAB). These guesthouses are in bucolic settings, near parks or monuments or in historic *aldeias* (villages). If they are larger properties, such as farmhouses, guests stay in self-contained cottages on the grounds. Breakfast is always included in the price.

The Central Nacional de Turismo no Espaço Rural (National Center for Rural Tourism) serves as a clearinghouse for information from several organizations involved in this endeavor.

Information Central Nacional de Turismo no Espaço Rural (☎ 258/931750 ⊕ www.center.pt). **TURIHAB** (⊕ www.turihab.pt).

HOME EXCHANGES

With a direct home exchange you stay in someone else's home while they stay in yours. Some outfits also deal with vacation homes, so you're not actually staying in someone's full-time residence, just their vacant weekend place. In Portugal most home-exchange properties are in Lisbon, though there are a few elsewhere, and a handful in the Algarve.

Although home-exchange is not common practice in Portugal (in fact it is practically unheard of) it could be a viable option for experienced home-swappers, particularly in summer, when peak rates apply in hotels, and especially in key regions like Lisbon and the Algarve.

Exchange Clubs Home Exchange.com (☎ 800/877–8723 ⊕ www.homeexchange.com). **HomeLink International** (☎ 800/638–3841 ⊕ www.homelink.org). **Intervac U.S** (☎ 800/756–4663 ⊕ www.intervacus.com).

HOTELS

Portugal has many excellent and reasonably priced hotels, though good properties can be hard to come by in remote inland areas. The government officially grades accommodations with one to five stars or with a category rating. Ratings, which are assigned based on the level of comfort and the number of facilities offered, can be misleading, because quality is difficult to grade. In general, though, the system works.

Most hotel rooms have such basic amenities as a private bathroom and a telephone; those with two or more stars may also have air-conditioning, cable or satellite TV, a minibar, and room service. (Note that all hotels listed in this guide have private bath unless otherwise indicated, although most hotels up to three stars will have a shower, rather than bathtub.) Note that you will also generally have a choice of twin or double (queen-size) bed. There are no king-size beds in Portugal.

High season means not only the summer months, but also the Christmas and New Year's holiday period on Madeira, Easter week throughout the country, and any time a town is holding a festival. In the off-season (generally November through March), however, many hotels reduce their rates by as much as 20%.

The Web sites of the Portuguese National Tourist Office and Mais Turismo have search engines for accommodations throughout the country.

Information Mais Turismo (⊕ *www. hotelguide.pt*). **Portuguese National Tourist Office** (✉ *590 5th Ave., New York, NY* ☎ *211/205 050* ⊕ *www.visitportugal.com*).

POUSADAS

The term *pousada* is derived from the Portuguese verb *pousar* (to rest). Portugal has a network of more than 45 of these state-run hotels, which are in restored castles, palaces, monasteries, convents, and other charming buildings. Each pousada is in a particularly scenic and tranquil part of the country and is tastefully furnished with regional crafts, antiques, and artwork. All have restaurants that serve local specialties; you can stop for a meal or a drink without spending the night.

Rates are reasonable, considering that most pousadas are four- or five-star hotels

and a stay in one can be the highlight of a visit. They're extremely popular with foreigners and Portuguese alike, and some have 10 or fewer rooms; make reservations well in advance, especially for stays in summer. Also check for seasonal and senior-citizen discounts, which can be as high as 40%.

Information Pousadas de Portugal (☎ *218/442000 or 218/4420001* ⊕ *www. pousadas.pt*).

SPAS

Concentrated mostly in the northern half of the country is a profusion of *termas* (thermal springs), whose waters reputedly can cure whatever ails you. In the smaller spas, hotels are rather simple; in the more famous ones, they're first-class. Most are open from May through October.

Information Associação das Termas de Portugal (☎ *21/794–0574* ⊕ *www. termasdeportugal.pt*).

▍COMMUNICATIONS

PHONES

The country code for Portugal is 351. When dialing a Portuguese number from abroad, dial the nine-digit number after the country code.

CALLING WITHIN PORTUGAL

All phone numbers have nine digits. Numbers in the area in and around Lisbon and Porto begin with a two-digit area code; phone numbers anywhere else in the country begin with a three-digit area code. All fixed-phone area codes begin with 2; mobile numbers, which also have nine digits, begin with 9.

For general information, dial 118 or 1820 (operators often speak English). Dial 120 from a landline phone and follow instructions to make collect calls.

Information Portugal Telecom (⊕ *www. telecom.pt*). **Yellow Pages** (⊕ *www. paginasamarelas.pt*).

CALLING OUTSIDE PORTUGAL

Calling abroad is expensive from hotels, which often add a considerable surcharge. The best way to make an international call is to go to the local telephone office or post office and have someone place it for you. Every town has such an establishment, and big cities have several. When the call is connected, you'll be directed to a quiet cubicle and charged according to the meter. If the price is €10 or more, you can pay with Visa or MasterCard.

CALLING CARDS

Purchasing a *cartão telefônico* (calling card) from a post office, newsagent, or tobacconist can save you money and the aggravation of finding enough change for a pay phone. Cards come in denominations of €5 and €10, sometimes more, and can be used from both private and public phones for national and international calls.

■ EATING OUT

The explosion of fast-food restaurants in recent years hasn't dented the Portuguese affection for old-fashioned, white-tablecloth dining—even though the tablecloth and napkins may now be made of paper. Hamburger places do a roaring lunchtime trade all over the country, but so do the traditional little restaurants that offer office workers home cooking at a modest price.

Although Portugal's plush, luxury restaurants can be good, they seldom measure up to their counterparts in other European countries. The best food by far tends be found in the moderately priced and less-expensive spots. Don't expect much in the way of decor, and if you have trouble squeezing in, remember the rule of thumb: if it's packed, it's probably good.

Restaurants featuring charcoal-grilled meats and fish, called *churrasqueiras,* are also popular (and often economical) options, and the Brazilian *rodízio*-type restaurant, where you are regaled with an endless offering of spit-roasted meats,

is entrenched in Lisbon, Porto, and the Algarve.

Shellfish restaurants, called *marisqueiras,* are numerous along the coast; note that lobsters, mollusks, and the like are fresh and good but pricey. Restaurant prices fall appreciably when you leave the Lisbon, Porto, and Algarve areas, and portion sizes increase the farther north you go.

■TIP→ **While you ponder the menu, you may be served an impressive array of appetizers. If you eat any of these, you'll probably be charged a small amount called a coberto or couvert. If you don't want these appetizers, you're perfectly within your rights to send them back. However, you should do this right away.**

Portuguese restaurants serve an *ementa* (or *prato*) *do dia,* or set menu of three courses. This can be a real bargain—usually 80% of the cost of three courses ordered separately.

Vegetarians can have a tough time in Portugal, although *sopa de legumes* (vegetable soup) is often included as a starter, together with the inevitable *salada* (salad). In general, the only other option (for vegetarians) are omelets. The larger cities and the Algarve have a few vegetarian restaurants, and Chinese and Italian restaurants are increasingly common and always have plenty of vegetarian (and vegan) options.

MEALS AND MEALTIMES

Breakfast (*pequeno almoço*) is the lightest meal, usually consisting of nothing more than a croissant or pastry washed down with coffee; lunch (*almoço*), the main meal of the day, is served between noon and 2:30, although nowadays, office workers in cities often grab a quick sandwich in a bar instead of stopping for a big meal. Some cafés and snack bars serve light meals throughout the afternoon.

About 5 pm there's a break for coffee or tea and a pastry; dinner (*jantar*) is eaten around 8 pm, and restaurants generally serve from 7 pm to 10 pm. Monday is a common day for restaurants to close, although this does vary and is noted in the restaurant listings in this guide.

Unless otherwise noted, the restaurants listed in this guide are open daily for lunch and dinner.

PAYING

Major credit cards are accepted in better restaurants and those geared to tourists, particularly on the Algarve. Humbler establishments generally only accept cash. Always check first, or you may end the evening washing dishes.

For guidelines on tipping see Tipping below.

RESERVATIONS AND DRESS

Regardless of where you are, it's a good idea to make a reservation if you can. In some places (Lisbon, for example), it's expected. We only mention them specifically when reservations are essential (there's no other way you'll ever get a table) or when they are not accepted.

For popular restaurants, book as far ahead as you can (often 30 days), and reconfirm as soon as you arrive. (Large parties should always call ahead to check the reservations policy.) We mention dress only when men are required to wear a jacket or a jacket and tie.

WINES, BEER, AND SPIRITS

Portuguese wines are inexpensive and, in general, good. Even the *vinho da casa* (house wine) is perfectly drinkable in most restaurants. Among the most popular are Bairrada from the Coimbra/Aveiro region, Ribatejo and Liziria from the Ribatejo region, and the reds from the Dão region. The light, sparkling *vinhos verdes* (green wines, named not for their color but for the fact that they're drunk early and don't improve with age) are also popular.

Both the Instituto de Vinho de Porto (Port Wine Institute) and the Comissão de Viticultura da Região dos Vinhos Verdes (Vinho Verde Region Viticulture Commission) have fascinating Web sites—with information in several languages, including English—that will help you learn more about Portuguese wines.

The leading brands of Portuguese beer—including Super Bock, Cristal, Sagres, and Imperial—are available on tap and in bottles or cans. They're made with fewer chemicals than the average American beers, and are on the strong side with a good, clean flavor. Local brandy—namely Macieira and Constantino—is cheap, as is domestic gin, although it's marginally weaker than its international counterparts.

Portugal has the world's highest alcohol consumption after Russia, so licensing laws are lax. Amazingly there is no minimum age for drinking alcohol here, although you still have to be over 16 to buy alcohol at shops, supermarkets, bars, and restaurants. Note that having brandy with your morning coffee will mark you as a local.

Wine Information **Comissão de Viticultura da Região dos Vinhos Verdes** (⊕ *www.vinhoverde.pt*). **Instituto de Vinho de Porto** (⊕ *www.ivp.pt*).

■ ELECTRICITY

The electrical current in Portugal is 220 volts, 50 cycles alternating current (AC); wall outlets take plugs with two round prongs.

Consider making a small investment in a universal adapter, which has several types of plugs in one lightweight, compact unit. Most laptops and mobile phone chargers are dual voltage (i.e., they operate equally well on 110 and 220 volts), so require only an adapter. These days the same is true of small appliances such as hair dryers. Always check labels and manufacturer instructions to be sure. Don't use 110-volt outlets marked "for shavers only" for high-wattage appliances such as hair-dryers.

■ EMERGENCIES

The national number for emergencies is 112, which is the universal emergency number within the European Union. The ambulance service in Portugal is run by volunteers and free. Contact details of English-speaking doctors can by obtained from American consular offices. Pharmacies (farmácias) will have a notice posted on the door with directions to the nearest 24-hour pharmacy.

■ HEALTH

Sunburn and sunstroke are common problems in summer in mainland Portugal and virtually year-round on Madeira. On a hot, sunny day, even people not normally bothered by strong rays should cover up. Sunscreen can be found in pharmacies and supermarkets, and some U.S. brands are available. The sun protection factor (SPF) is always noted.

Carry sunscreen for nose, ears, and other sensitive areas; be sure to drink enough liquids; and above all, limit your sun exposure for the first few days until you become accustomed to the heat. Mosquitoes are found throughout Portugal and, while they don't carry malaria, they can cause irritation so pack or buy a local insect repellent.

SHOTS AND MEDICATIONS

No special shots are required before visiting Portugal, Madeira, or the Azores, unless you have come from or recently traveled through an infected area. You might consider a tetanus-diphtheria booster if you haven't had one recently.

■ HOURS OF OPERATION

Lunchtime is taken very seriously throughout Portugal. Many businesses, particularly outside urban areas, close between 1 and 3 and then reopen for business until 6 or 7. Government offices are typically open from 9 to noon and 2 to 5. It's worth noting religious and public holidays, as most businesses grind to a halt, and even the local transport service may be reduced. Also, if the holiday falls at a weekend, then typically a Friday or Monday will also be a holiday.

Banks are open weekdays 8:30–3. Money exchange booths at airports and train stations are usually open all day (24 hours at Portela Airport in Lisbon).

Most gas stations on main highways are open 24 hours. In more rural areas, stations are open 7 am to 10 pm. Note that gas stations can seem few and far between away from the towns and cities, so if you are planning to explore in the hinterland, always start out with a full tank of gas.

Museums and palaces generally open at 10, close for lunch from 12:30 to 2, and then reopen until 5; a few, however, remain open at midday. The 29 sites of the nationwide Portuguese Institute of Museums (IPM) are closed Monday, as well as Easter Sunday, May 1, Christmas, and January 1. Some IPM museums don't open until 2 pm on Tuesday.

Pharmacies are usually open weekdays 9 to 1 and 3 to 7, and Saturday 9 to 1; 24-hour pharmacies operate in shifts; timetables of 24-hour pharmacies will be posted on the door.

Most shops are open weekdays 9 to 1 and 3 to 7, and Saturday 9 to 1. In December, Saturday hours are the same as weekdays. Shops often close Sunday. *Hipermercados* (giant supermarkets), *supermercados* (regular supermarkets), and shopping centers are typically open seven days a week from 10 am to midnight. In the seaside resorts of the Algarve, many shops, including souvenir shops and supermarkets, open all day between May and September.

HOLIDAYS

New Year's Day (January 1); Mardi Gras (better known as Carnaval, held during the last few days before Lent); Good Friday; Easter Sunday; Liberty Day (April 25); Labor Day (May 1); Corpo de Deus (May 30); Camões Day (June 10); Assumption (August 15); Republic Day (October 5); All Saints' Day (November 1); Independence Day (December 1); Immaculate Conception (December 8); Christmas Day (December 25).

If a national holiday falls on a Tuesday or Thursday, many businesses also close on the Monday or Friday in between, for a long weekend called a *ponte* (bridge). There are also local holidays when entire towns, cities, and regions grind to a standstill. Check the nearest tourist office for dates.

▌ MAIL

Expect a letter or postcard to take 7–10 days to reach the United States. Postcards mailed internationally cost €1.85; letters the same for up to 20 grams. All post is sent airmail unless otherwise specified.

The Portuguese postal service—the CTT—has a Web site in English and Portuguese with information such as how to trace mail and the location and hours of countrywide post offices.

You can buy *selos* (stamps) at *correios* (post offices) or at kiosks and shops displaying a red "correios–selos" sign. Stamp-vending machines are scattered about Lisbon.

Information CTT (⊕ *www.ctt.pt*).

▌ MONEY

Lisbon isn't as expensive as most other international capitals, but it's not the extraordinary bargain it used to be. The coastal resort areas from Cascais and Estoril down to the Algarve can be expensive, though there are lower-price hotels and restaurants catering mainly to the package-tour trade. If you head off the beaten track, you'll find substantially cheaper food and lodging.

Transportation is still cheap in Portugal when compared with the rest of Europe. Gas prices are controlled by the government, and train and bus travel are inexpensive. Highway tolls are steep but may be worth the cost if you want to bypass the small towns and villages. Flights within the country are costly.

Here are some sample prices. Coffee in a bar: €0.60 (standing), €0.80 (seated). Draft beer in a bar: €0.80 (standing), €1 (seated). Bottle of beer: €0.80. Port: €1.50–€10, depending on brand and vintage. Table wine: €5.50 (bottle), €3.50 (half bottle), €1 (small glass). Coca-Cola: €1. Ham-and-cheese sandwich: €1.50. One-kilometer (½-mi) taxi ride: €3. Local bus ride: €1. Subway ride: €0.65. Ferry ride in Lisbon: €1–€2 one-way. Opera or theater seat: €25–€50. Nightclub cover charge: €10–€25. Fado performance: €16 for the show plus a drink or €25–€40 for dinner and a show. Movie ticket: €5.50–€6 (most cinemas offer cheaper tickets on Monday). Foreign newspaper: €2.50–€5.

Museums that are part of the Portuguese Institute of Museums (IPM) are free on Sunday until 2 pm. The IPM also sells "season tickets" for two, five, and seven days that grant you entrance to all permanent and temporary exhibits during that time period. Lisbon and Oporto sell cost-saving passes that cover city transport and entry to museums and other sights. The respective tourist office can fill you in. You can often also save as much as 50% on accommodations if you visit Portugal out of season.

If you're undeterred by potentially wet weather, consider traveling November to March, when many hotels discount their rates by up to 20%. In Lisbon and Oporto, check with the tourist office about discount cards offering travel deals on public transport, reduced or free entrance to certain museums, and discounts in some shops and restaurants.

Prices throughout this guide are given for adults. Substantially reduced fees are almost always available for children, students, and senior citizens.

■TIP→ Banks never have every foreign currency on hand, and it may take as long as a week to order. If you're planning to exchange funds before leaving home, don't wait until the last minute.

ATMS AND BANKS

ATMs are ubiquitous. The Multibanco, or MB, system is state-of-the-art and reliable. The cards most frequently accepted are Visa, MasterCard, American Express, Eurocheque, Eurocard, Cirrus, and Electron. You need a four-digit PIN to use ATMs in Portugal.

Always be wary when using an ATM machine that nobody is looking over your shoulder. Similarly, if the machine appears tampered with, stay away. There is a scam throughout Europe whereupon a dummy cover is placed over the machine and/or a tiny camera notes your PIN number. There is usually a limit of €400 a day withdrawal.

ATM Locations Cirrus (☎ 800/424–7787 ⊕ www.mastercard.com). **Plus** (☎ 800/843–7587 ⊕ www.visa.com).

CREDIT CARDS

Throughout this guide, the following abbreviations are used: **AE**, American Express; **D**, Discover; **MC**, MasterCard; and **V**, Visa.

It's a good idea to inform your credit-card company before you travel, especially if you're going abroad and don't travel internationally very often. Otherwise, the credit-card company might put a hold on your card owing to unusual activity—not a good thing halfway through your trip.

Although it's usually cheaper (and safer) to use a credit card abroad for large purchases (so you can cancel payments or be reimbursed if there's a problem), note that some credit-card companies *and* the banks that issue them add substantial percentages to all foreign transactions, whether they're in a foreign currency or not. Check on these fees before leaving home, so there won't be any surprises when you get the bill.

■TIP→ Before you charge something, ask the merchant whether he or she plans to do a dynamic currency conversion (DCC). In such a transaction the credit-card *processor* (shop, restaurant, or hotel, not Visa or MasterCard) converts the currency and charges you in dollars. In most cases you'll pay the merchant a 3% fee for this service in addition to any credit-card company and issuing-bank foreign-transaction surcharges.

Merchants who participate in dynamic currency conversion programs are supposed to ask whether you want to be charged in dollars or the local currency, but they don't always do so. And even if they do offer you a choice, they may well avoid mentioning the additional surcharges. The good news is that you *do* have a choice. And if this practice really gets your goat, you can avoid it entirely thanks to American Express; with its cards, DCC simply isn't an option.

CURRENCY AND EXCHANGE

Portugal is one of the 27 European Union countries to use a single currency—the euro (€). In total, 17 EU countries use the euro. Coins are issued in denominations of 1, 2, 5, 10, 20, and 50 euro cents, as well in denominations of €1 and €2. Notes are issued in denominations of €5, 10, 20, 50, 100, 200, and 500. At this writing, the exchange rate was US$1 to €0.75.

■TIP→ Even if a currency-exchange booth has a sign promising no commission, rest assured that there's some kind of huge, hidden fee. (Oh . . . that's right. The sign didn't say no *fee*.) And as for rates, you're almost always better off getting foreign currency at an ATM or exchanging money at a bank.

PACKING

Older generations of Portuguese citizens tend to dress up more than their counterparts in the United States or the United Kingdom. That said, attitudes toward clothes have become more relaxed in recent years among the younger generations.

Jeans, however, are generally still paired with a collared shirt and, if necessary, a sweater or jacket. Dressier outfits are needed for more expensive restaurants, nightclubs, and fado houses, though, and people still frown on shorts in churches.

Sightseeing calls for casual, comfortable clothing (well-broken-in low-heel shoes, for example). Away from the beaches, wearing bathing suits on the street or in restaurants and shops is not considered good taste.

Summer can be brutally hot; spring and fall, mild to chilly; and winter, cold and rainy. Sunscreen and sunglasses are a good idea any time of the year, since the sun in Portugal is very bright.

PASSPORTS AND VISAS

Citizens of the United States need a valid passport to enter Portugal for stays of up to 90 days; passports must be valid for three months beyond the period of stay. Visas are required for longer stays and, in some instances, for visits to other countries in addition to Portugal.

RESTROOMS

Restaurants, cinemas, theaters, libraries, and service stations are required to have public toilets. Restrooms can range from marble-clad opulence to little better than primitive, but in most cases they're reasonably clean and have toilet paper, although it's always useful to carry a small packet of tissues just in case! Few are adapted for travelers with disabilities. Restrooms are occasionally looked after by an attendant who customarily receives a tip of €0.30. Train stations are likely to have pay toilets.

Find a Loo The Bathroom Diaries (⊕ *www. thebathroomdiaries.com*) is flush with unsanitized info on restrooms the world over—each one located, reviewed, and rated.

SAFETY

Be particularly cautious in crowded areas and in the poorer areas of large cities. Be wary of anyone stopping you on the street and even in car parks to ask for directions, the time, or where you're from—particularly if there's more than one person and if you have recently visited the bank or an ATM.

There's enough of a police presence in Portugal that women traveling solo are relatively safe. Take normal precautions, though, and avoid dark, empty streets at night. Ask your hotel staff to recommend a reliable cab company, and whenever possible, call for a taxi instead of hailing one on the street at night. Avoid eye contact with unsavory individuals. If such a person approaches you, discourage him politely but firmly by saying, "*Por favor, me dê licença*" ("Excuse me, please") and then walk away with resolve.

Shopkeepers, restaurateurs, and other business owners are generally honest, and credit card receipts are rarely subject to copying. There have been occasional incidents of highway robbery, where the thief slashes the victim's tires during a stop at a gas station and then follows the victim, offering to "help" when the tire goes completely flat. In other cases, the thief takes advantage of an unwary traveler who has left car keys in the ignition or money or a handbag on the seat while stopped at a gas station by telling the driver(s) that they have a puncture in a back tire and urging them to get out of the car to inspect.

▌ TAXES

Value-added tax (IVA, pronounced *ee-vah*) is 13% for hotels. By law prices must be posted at the reception desk and should indicate whether tax is included. Restaurants are also required to charge 12% IVA. Menus generally state at the bottom whether tax is included (*IVA incluido*) or not (*mais 12% IVA*). When in doubt about whether tax is included in a price, ask: *Está incluido o IVA?*

The sales tax is 23% on shop goods. A number of Portuguese stores, particularly large ones and those in resorts, will refund this amount on single items worth more than €60. Sometimes the store will subtract the tax when you make your purchase, particularly if they are arranging the shipment of goods to your home.

When making a purchase, ask for a V.A.T. refund form and find out whether the merchant gives refunds—not all stores do, nor are they required to. Have the form stamped like any customs form by customs officials when you leave the country or, if you're visiting several European Union countries, when you leave the EU.

After you're through passport control, take the form to a refund-service counter for an on-the-spot refund (which is usually the quickest and easiest option), or mail it to the address on the form (or the envelope with it) after you arrive home. You receive the total refund stated on the form, but the processing time can be long, especially if you request a credit-card adjustment.

Global Refund is a Europe-wide service with 225,000 affiliated stores and more than 700 refund counters at major airports and border crossings. Its refund form, called a Tax Free Check, is the most common across the European continent. The service issues refunds in the form of cash, check, or credit-card adjustment.

V.A.T. Refunds Global Blue (☎ *21/846–3025* ⊕ *www.global-blue.com*).

▌ TIME

Portugal sets its clocks according to Greenwich Mean Time, five hours ahead of the U.S. East Coast. Portuguese summer time (GMT plus one hour) requires an additional adjustment from late March to late October.

TIPPING GUIDELINES FOR PORTUGAL	
Bartender	$1 to $5 per round of drinks, depending on the number of drinks
Bellhop	$1 to $5 per bag, depending on the level of the hotel
Hotel Concierge	$5 or more, if he or she performs a service for you
Hotel Doorman	$1–$2 if he helps you get a cab
Hotel Maid	$1–$3 a day (either daily or at the end of your stay, in cash)
Hotel Room-Service Waiter	$1 to $2 per delivery, even if a service charge has been added
Porter at Airport or Train Station	$1 per bag
Skycap at Airport	$1 to $3 per bag checked
Taxi Driver	15%–20%, but round up the fare to the next dollar amount
Tour Guide	10% of the cost of the tour
Valet Parking Attendant	$1–$2, but only when you get your car
Waiter	10%–20%, with 20% being the norm at high-end restaurants; nothing additional if a service charge is added to the bill

▌ TIPPING

Service is included in café, restaurant, and hotel bills, but waiters and other service people are poorly paid, and you can be sure your contribution will be appreciated. If, however, you received bad service, never feel obligated (or intimidated) to leave a tip. Also if you have something small, a sandwich or *petiscos* (appetizers) at a bar you can leave just enough to round out the bill to the nearest €0.50.

CRUISES

Portugal is a port of call for many cruise liners, including those listed below. Most stop at Lisbon, while a few include Madeira in their itinerary. There are also companies which offer more localized cruising opportunities, including River Cruise Tours which offer luxury boat trips along the Douro River from Porto to the Spanish border.

Local Cruise Line **River Cruise Tours** (☎ 888/942–3301 ⊕ www.rivercruisetours.com) in the U.S.

▍TRIP INSURANCE

Comprehensive trip insurance is valuable if you're booking a very expensive or complicated trip (particularly to an isolated region) or if you're booking far in advance. Comprehensive policies typically cover trip-cancellation and interruption, letting you cancel or cut your trip short because of illness, or, in some cases, acts of terrorism in your destination. Such policies might also cover evacuation and medical care. Some also cover you for trip delays because of bad weather or mechanical problems as well as for lost or delayed luggage.

Another type of coverage to consider is financial default—that is, when your trip is disrupted because a tour operator, airline, or cruise line goes out of business. Generally you must buy this when you book your trip or shortly thereafter, and it's available to you only if your operator isn't on a list of excluded companies.

Always read the fine print of your policy to make sure that you're covered for the risks that most concern you. Compare several policies to be sure you're getting the best price and range of coverage available.

Insurance Comparison Info **Insure My Trip** (☎ 800/487–4722 ⊕ www.insuremytrip.com).

Square Mouth (☎ 800/240–0369 ⊕ www. squaremouth.com).

Comprehensive Insurers **Access America** (☎ 800/284–8300 ⊕ www.accessamerica.com). **AIG Travel Guard** (☎ 800/826–4919 ⊕ www. travelguard.com). **CSA Travel Protection** (☎ 800/873–9855 ⊕ www.csatravelprotection. com). **Travelex Insurance** (☎ 888/228–9792 ⊕ www.travelex-insurance.com). **Travel Insured International** (☎ 800/243–3174 ⊕ www.travelinsured.com).

▍VISITOR INFORMATION

Portuguese National Tourist Offices **Portuguese National Tourist Office Web site** (⊕ www.visitportugal.com). **United States** (✉ 590 5th Ave., 4th fl., New York, NY ☎ 212/354–4403).

INDEX

PHOTO CREDITS

ABOUT OUR WRITERS

Brendan de Beer was born in Johannesburg, South Africa and has lived in Portugal since 1997. He works as a journalist and radio commentator and is a keen golfer. Brendan updated the Algarve and Travel Smart chapters, and wrote the golf feature in Experience Portugal.

Lauren Frayer is a former correspondent for The Associated Press in Washington D.C., Israel and the Palestinian Territories, Egypt, Iraq, and Pakistan. She recently spent a year driving a Land Rover across Africa, from Cairo to Cape Town. Since then she has lived in Portugal and Spain, and writes for several publications. Lauren updated the Evora and the Alentejo chapter.

Matthew Hancock has worked in Portugal as a teacher, journalist, and writer. Now living in England, he has written several guides about Madeira and Portugal and contributes to various magazines, newspapers, and on-line travel publications. Matthew updated the Madeira chapter.

Journalist and travel writer **Josephine Quintero** is from England and has worked in California, the Middle East, and since 1990, in southern Spain, from where she makes frequent trips into neighboring Portugal. Josephine writes for many magazines and travel publication mainly covering the Iberian peninsula. Josephine updated the Coimbra and the Beiras chapter.

Alison Roberts is a freelance journalist, writer, and translator who has lived in Lisbon since 1997. Born in Barnet, UK, she has also lived in Canada, India, and Germany. After a spell in local newspapers she spent several years in financial journalism before branching out into a broader range of subjects. In Portugal, she has worked as a correspondent for international broadcasters as well as writing and editing guides to Lisbon and other parts of the country. Her interest include travel, languages, and culture. Alison updated the Experience Portugal, Lisbon, and Porto and the North chapters.

Andrea Smith grew up in Alexandria, Virginia, just outside of Washington, D.C., and graduated from The Culinary Institute of America with degrees in Culinary Arts and Hospitality Management. She has been active in the food and beverage industry for almost 10 years in New York, Washington, D.C., and Miami before moving to Lisbon in early 2008. Since then, she has written about Portuguese food and wine for Catavino.net and worked as the database administrator for wineblogger.info. Andrea updated the Lisbon Environs and Estremaudra and the Ribatejo chapters, and wrote the food and wine features in Experience Portugal.